WordPerfect® 6.0

For Windows™

Covers Version 6.0a

Katie Layman
Gavilan College, Gilroy, California

and

LaVaughn Hart
Chabot College, Hayward, California

PRENTICE HALL
Englewood Cliffs, New Jersey 07632

Library of Congress Cataloging-in-Publication Data

Layman, Katie.
WordPerfect 6.0 for Windows / Katie Layman and LaVaughn Hart.
p. cm.
Includes index.
ISBN 0-13-034653-5 :
1. WordPerfect for Windows (Computer file) 2. Word processing. I. Hart, LaVaughn.
Z52.5.W655L385 1994 94-127511
652.5'536--dc20 CIP

Acquisition editor: *Carolyn Henderson*
Editorial/production supervision: *Cathleen Profitko*
Cover design: *Maureen Eide*
Buyer: *Paul Smolenski*
Editorial assistant: *Jane Avery*

Printed in the United States of America

10 9 8 7 6 5 4 3 2

ISBN 0-13-034653-5

Prentice-Hall International (UK) Limited, *London*
Prentice-Hall of Australia Pty. Limited, *Sydney*
Prentice-Hall of Canada Inc., *Toronto*
Prentice-Hall Hispanoamericana, S.A., *Mexico*
Prentice-Hall of India Private Limited, *New Delhi*
Prentice-Hall of Japan, Inc., *Tokyo*
Simon & Schuster Asia Pte. Ltd., *Singapore*
Editora Prentice-Hall do Brasil, Ltda., *Rio de Janeiro*

CONTENTS

Part 4—A Step in the Right Direction: Advanced Documents and Features

Part 5—A Giant Step: Use Desktop Publishing

Part 6—Step Right Up Create Special Documents

Part 7—The Final Step: Advanced Techniques

Appendices

Introduction

The purpose of this textbook is to provide students with simple step-by-step instructions to quickly master WordPerfect 6.0 for Windows. Numerous hands-on activities and easy-to-follow instruction lists within the text's chapters allow students to learn by doing. All of these carefully guided walk-thoroughs are accompanied by thorough, precise explanations of each WordPerfect function being introduced, making ***WordPerfect® 6.0 for Windows*** appropriate for use in individualized instruction programs as well as for use in traditional classrooms.

By focusing on the *tasks* students need to perform along with the help from WordPerfect functions, ***WordPerfect® 6.0 for Windows*** aids instructors in their efforts to assist students in acquiring the work-ready skills needed to succeed in today's job market. But the book's commitment to students' acquisition of these skills does not stop here.

As students work through the text's activities, they are introduced to the proper format for various business documents (e.g., memorandums, letters, reports, résumés, and newsletters). What's more, all of the text's activities are based on authentic, real-world documents—"just what students will encounter in everyday life on the job," according to one reviewer. And because students can never have too much training in or reinforcement of their basic English and grammar skills, each chapter includes an *Enriching Language Arts Skills* section and activity.

Finally, the end-of-chapter and end-of-part sections—*The Next Step* and *Checking Your Step* sections, respectively—are designed to fulfill the competencies and basic skill requirements that have been identified by Tech Prep and the Secretary's Commission on Achieving Necessary Skills (SCANS), U. S. Department of Labor. *The Next Step* and *Checking Your Step* activities reinforce students' reading, writing, thinking, and decision-making skills. SCANS icons are placed within the text so that instructors and students can quickly identify the activities that build SCANS/Tech Prep competencies.

Content Highlights

Above all else, ***WordPerfect® 6.0 for Windows*** is committed to providing students with the work-ready skills they need to excel. The book's pedagogical system and the features described in the following section have been carefully crafted to achieve this end. Some of the key components of this performance-based system are as follows:

The chapter opening *Features Covered* sections identify the WordPerfect features introduced in the chapter and provide students with a clear road map of precisely what is to come.

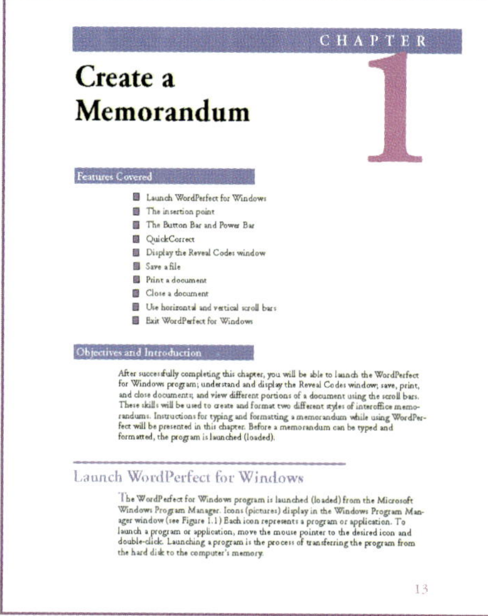

CHAPTER 1

Create a Memorandum

Features Covered

- Launch WordPerfect for Windows
- The insertion point
- The Button Bar and Power Bar
- QuickCorrect
- Display the Reveal Codes window
- Save a file
- Print a document
- Close a document
- Use horizontal and vertical scroll bars
- Exit WordPerfect for Windows

Objectives and Introduction

After successfully completing this chapter, you will be able to launch the WordPerfect for Windows program; understand and display the Reveal Codes window; save, print, and close documents; and view different portions of a document using the scroll bars. These skills will be used to create and format two different styles of interoffice memorandums. Instructions for typing and formatting a memorandum while using WordPerfect will be presented in this chapter. Before a memorandum can be typed and formatted, the program is launched (loaded).

Launch WordPerfect for Windows

The WordPerfect for Windows program is launched (loaded) from the Microsoft Windows Program Manager. Icons (pictures) display in the Windows Program Manager window (see Figure 1.1) Each icon represents a program or application. To launch a program or application, move the mouse pointer to the desired icon and double-click. Launching a program is the process of transferring the program from the hard disk to the computer's memory.

13

Objectives and Introduction preview chapter material in terms of the actual tasks students will perform as they work through the chapter and provide a narrative overview of the chapter material.

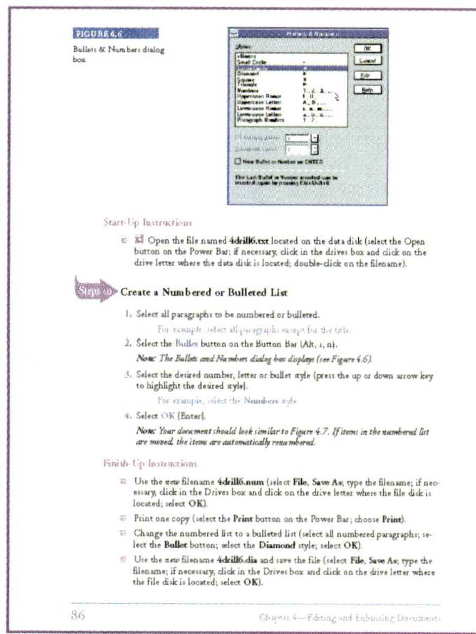

FIGURE 4.6

Bullets & Numbers dialog box

Start-Up Instructions

- Open the file named **4drill6.txt** located on the data disk (select the Open button on the Power Bar; if necessary, click in the drives box and click on the drive letter where the data disk is located; double-click on the filename).

Steps to **Create a Numbered or Bulleted List**

1. Select all paragraphs to be numbered or bulleted.

   For example, select all paragraphs except for the title.
2. Select the Bullet button on the Button Bar (Alt, i, n).

   Note: The Bullets and Numbers dialog box displays (see Figure 4.6).
3. Select the desired number, letter or bullet style (press the up or down arrow key to highlight the desired style).

   For example, select the Numbers style
4. Select OK (Enter).

   Note: Your document should look similar to Figure 4.7. If items in the numbered list are moved, the items are automatically renumbered.

Finish-Up Instructions

- Use the *new* filename **4drill6.num** (select **File**, **Save As**; type the filename; if necessary, click in the Drives box and click on the drive letter where the file disk is located; select **OK**).
- Print one copy (select the **Print** button on the Power Bar; choose **Print**).
- Change the numbered list to a bulleted list (select all numbered paragraphs; select the **Bullet** button; select the **Diamond** style; select **OK**).
- Use the *new* filename **4drill6.dia** and save the file (select **File**, **Save As**; type the filename; if necessary, click in the Drives box and click on the drive letter where the file disk is located; select **OK**).

86 Chapter 4—Editing and Enhancing Documents

Numerous screen captures clarify concepts and instructions for students as they proceed through each chapter.

Careful step-by-step instruction lists are provided in the body of the chapter and are accompanied by a *Steps to* icon in the margin to make them easy for students to find when referring back to the text later.

In addition to the step-by-step instruction lists, activity-specific *Start-Up Instructions* and *Finish-Up Instructions* are clearly identified and provide information necessary to the completion of in-chapter activities. These, coupled with the *Steps to* icon, give students the best of both worlds—detailed, enumerated step-by-step tutorials now and easy-to-locate generic instruction lists later, when the text needs to function as a reference manual.

Each end-of-chapter *Self-Check Quiz* includes true/false, multiple choice, and short answer questions, enabling students to check their understanding of key chapter concepts and procedures. (Answers are provided at the back of the book.)

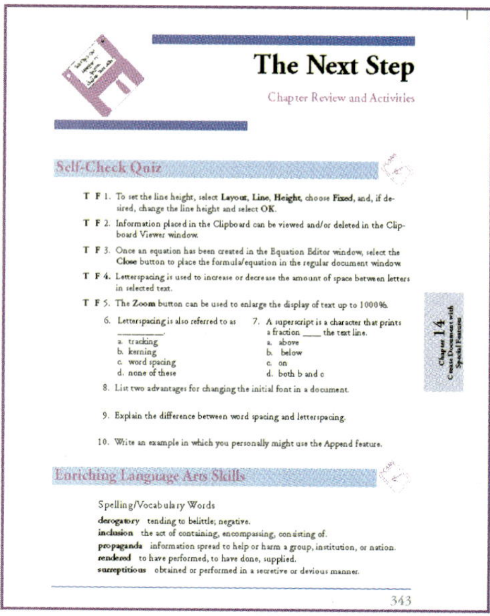

The Next Step

Chapter Review and Activities

Self-Check Quiz

T F 1. To set the line height, select **Layout**, **Line**, **Height**, choose **Fixed**, and, if desired, change the line height and select **OK**.

T F 2. Information placed in the Clipboard can be viewed and/or deleted in the Clipboard Viewer window.

T F 3. Once an equation has been created in the Equation Editor window, select the **Close** button to place the formula/equation in the regular document window.

T F 4. Letterspacing is used to increase or decrease the amount of space between letters in selected text.

T F 5. The **Zoom** button can be used to enlarge the display of text up to 1000%.

6. Letterspacing is also referred to as __________.
   a. tracking
   b. kerning
   c. word spacing
   d. none of these
7. A superscript is a character that prints a fraction ____ the text line.
   a. above
   b. below
   c. on
   d. both b and c
8. List two advantages for changing the initial font in a document.
9. Explain the difference between word spacing and letterspacing.
10. Write an example in which you personally might use the Append feature.

Chapter 14 Create Documents with Special Features

Enriching Language Arts Skills

Spelling/Vocabulary Words

derogatory tending to belittle; negative.
inclusion the act of containing, encompassing, consisting of.
propaganda information spread to help or harm a group, institution, or nation.
rendered to have performed, to have done, supplied.
surreptitious obtained or performed in a secretive or devious manner.

343

A unique *Enriching Language Arts Skills* section at the end of each chapter reinforces students' spelling and grammar skills—skills the student is called on to use in the chapter's final hands-on activity.

Many guided, hands-on *Activities* at the close of each chapter let students practice—in a structured, unintimidating environment—what they've learned in the chapter.

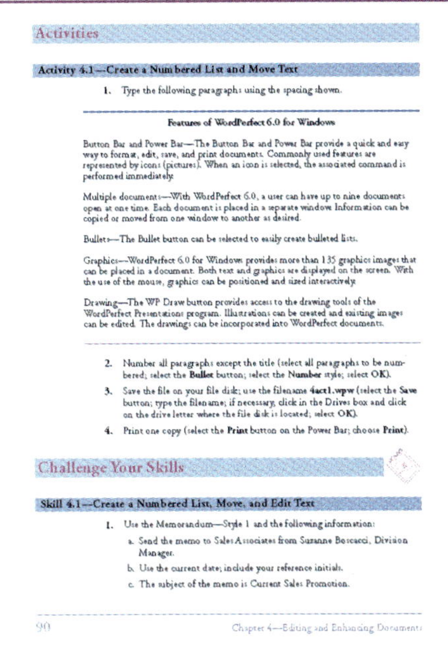

Activities

Activity 4.1—Create a Numbered List and Move Text

1. Type the following paragraphs using the spacing shown.

Features of WordPerfect 6.0 for Windows

Button Bar and Power Bar—The Button Bar and Power Bar provide a quick and easy way to format, edit, save, and print documents. Commonly used features are represented by icons (pictures). When an icon is selected, the associated command is performed immediately.

Multiple documents—With WordPerfect 6.0, a user can have up to nine documents open at one time. Each document is placed in a separate window. Information can be copied or moved from one window to another as desired.

Bullets—The Bullet button can be selected to easily create bulleted lists.

Graphics—WordPerfect 6.0 for Windows provides more than 135 graphics images that can be placed in a document. Both text and graphics are displayed on the screen. With the use of the mouse, graphics can be positioned and sized interactively.

Drawing—The WP Draw button provides access to the drawing tools of the WordPerfect Presentations program. Illustrations can be created and existing images can be edited. The drawings can be incorporated into WordPerfect documents.

2. Number all paragraphs except the title (select all paragraphs to be numbered; select the **Bullet** button; select the **Number** style; select **OK**).
3. Save the file on your file disk; use the filename **4act1.wpw** (select the **Save** button; type the filename; if necessary, click in the Drives box and click on the drive letter where the file disk is located; select **OK**).
4. Print one copy (select the **Print** button on the Power Bar; choose **Print**).

Challenge Your Skills

Skill 4.1—Create a Numbered List, Move, and Edit Text

1. Use the Memorandum—Style 1 and the following information:
   a. Send the memo to Sales Associates from Suzanne Boscacci, Division Manager.
   b. Use the current date; include your reference initials.
   c. The subject of the memo is Current Sales Promotion.

90 Chapter 4—Editing and Enhancing Documents

Independent *Challenge Your Skills* activities at the close of each chapter give students ample practice to apply what they have learned without the help of guided instructions.

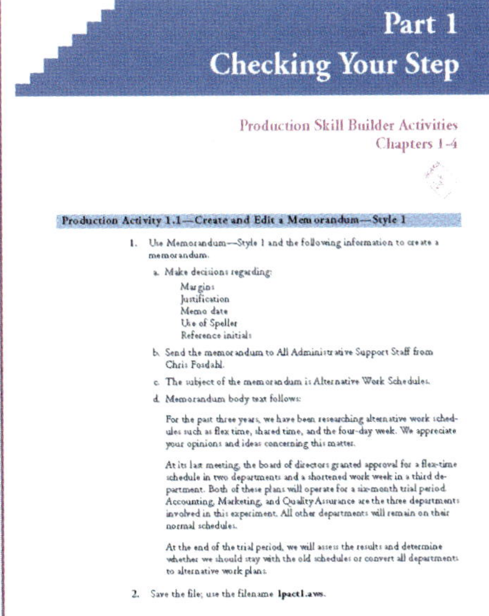

Part 1
Checking Your Step

Production Skill Builder Activities
Chapters 1-4

Production Activity 1.1—Create and Edit a Memorandum—Style 1

1. Use Memorandum—Style 1 and the following information to create a memorandum.
   a. Make decisions regarding:
      Margins
      Justification
      Memo date
      Use of Speller
      Reference initials
   b. Send the memorandum to All Administrative Support Staff from Chris Fosdahl.
   c. The subject of the memorandum is Alternative Work Schedules.
   d. Memorandum body text follows:

      For the past three years, we have been researching alternative work schedules such as flex time, shared time, and the four-day week. We appreciate your opinions and ideas concerning this matter.

      At its last meeting, the board of directors granted approval for a flex-time schedule in two departments and a shortened work week in a third department. Both of these plans will operate for a six-month trial period. Accounting, Marketing, and Quality Assurance are the three departments involved in this experiment. All other departments will remain on their normal schedules.

      At the end of the trial period, we will assess the results and determine whether we should stay with the old schedules or convert all departments to alternative work plans.
2. Save the file; use the filename **1pact1.aws**.

97

End-of-part *Checking Your Step* production skill-builder activities allow students to stretch their mastery of the program and to develop their decision-making and critical-thinking skills. The production skill-builder activities can be used for testing, hands-on projects, or as brief office simulation exercises.

An excellent reference source is the *QuickClicks* booklet provided with each copy of the text. The *QuickClicks* booklet lists all the WordPerfect features presented and includes page references should the student want to go back to a chapter for additional information.

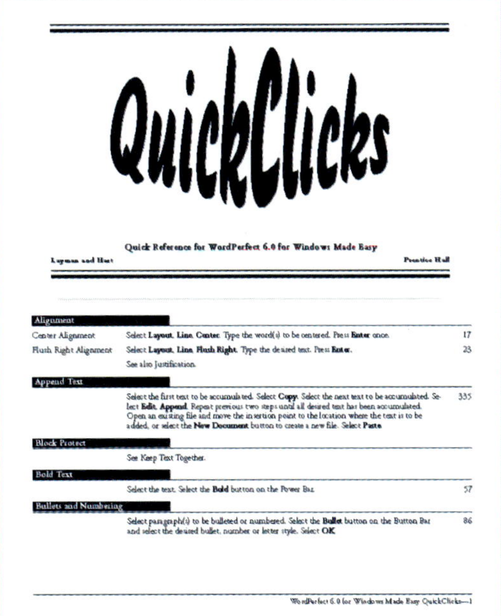

QuickClicks

Quick Reference for WordPerfect 6.0 for Windows Made Easy

Layman and Hunt — Prentice Hall

Alignment

Center Alignment	Select **Layout**, **Line**, **Center**. Type the word(s) to be centered. Press **Enter** once.	17
Flush Right Alignment	Select **Layout**, **Line**, **Flush Right**. Type the desired text. Press **Enter**.	23
	See also Justification.	

Append Text

Select the first text to be accumulated. Select **Copy**. Select the next text to be accumulated. Select **Edit**, **Append**. Repeat previous two steps until all desired text has been accumulated. Open an existing file and move the insertion point to the location where the text is to be added, or select the **New Document** button to create a new file. Select **Paste**. 335

Block Protect

See Keep Text Together.

Bold Text

Select the text. Select the **Bold** button on the Power Bar. 57

Bullets and Numbering

Select paragraph(s) to be bulleted or numbered. Select the **Bullet** button on the Button Bar and select the desired bullet, number or letter style. Select **OK**. 86

WordPerfect 6.0 for Windows Made Easy QuickClicks—1

Instructor Support Materials

A comprehensive ***Instructor's Resource Manual*** is available which contains solutions for the end-of-chapter short-answer questions and *all* practice activities, end-of-chapter activities, challenge activities, and skill-builder production activities. The manual includes a chapter overview, student objectives, lecture notes, teaching suggestions, and one or more additional activities for each chapter. Also provided are production and theory tests. Included with the ***Instructor's Resource Manual*** are a student data disk and instructor's disks. The student data disk includes unformatted files for practice activities, end-of-chapter activities, challenge activities, and production activities. The instructor's disks contain formatted files for the practice activities, end-of-chapter activities, challenge activities, and production and theory tests.

To the Student

Every chapter is divided into several sections with each section explaining a different Word function. An overview of each function is provided followed by Start-Up Instructions which present information or actions to be taken in order to prepare you for a hands-on practice activity. Following the Start-Up Instructions are numbered step-by-step instructions which guide you through each action necessary to perform the feature being learned. These are identified by the Steps to icon. Finish-Up Instructions follow each set of step-by-step instructions and indicate what should be performed in order to complete the practice activity.

The text for many chapter activities is provided on the data disk supplied to your instructor. You will see this icon in the text to indicate that the data (text) is available on disk. This saved text is necessary in order to perform the activity identified by the disk icon.

Answer the Self-Check Quiz questions and check your answers with the answer key provided at the back of the book. If desired, study the vocabulary words, punctuation, capitalization, or typing rule provided in the Enriching Language Arts section. Many of these vocabulary words and punctuation rules are used in the last activity of the Challenge Your Skills section at the end of each chapter and in the final Production Skill Builder Activity that is provided in each Part.

ACKNOWLEDGMENTS

A sincere thank you to our editor, Carolyn Henderson, for her avid support and constant attention to our business *and* personal needs. Using your superb editorial skills, you guided us through every detail needed to improve our book(s). Thank you!

Thank you, Jeanette Hart, for your assistance in writing the *WordPerfect 6.0 for Windows* manuscript. Your presentation of material and explanations were most valuable. Many thanks too, for writing a comprehensive ***Instructor's Resource Manual*** and for creating the student and instructor disks.

Kathy Ponti, College of San Mateo, thank you is too small of a word to express how much we appreciated your keystroke testing skills. You certainly provided us with questions and suggestions that assisted in creating accurate instructions.

Cathleen Profitko, thank you for your production assistance. We appreciate you keeping us on schedule! Paul Smolenski, we are most grateful to you for always "going to bat" for our projects! Your support is always appreciated.

A huge thank you to the sales representatives and support staff at Prentice Hall, Inc. who have contributed and continue to contribute outstanding support for the success of the ***Made Easy*** series.

To Nancy Evans, our marketing manager, we very much appreciate your interest in marketing our books. Thank you for personally meeting with us and for responding promptly to our requests. We are happy to welcome you as a new member of our team! Natacha St. Hill, marketing assistant, thank you for **all** your excellent assistance. We always know we can count on you to promptly process our book requests!

Again we send a special salute to Jane Avery for assisting with our many phone calls, swiftly processing contract agreements, and promptly responding to our numerous requests. Your expert clerical skills and amiable service are highly praised.

Deborah Leighton at Maine Proofreading service, you are the best! We appreciate your superb copyediting skills and your quick turn-around time. Your queries and comments assisted us in making many improvements to our manuscript.

Helen LeFevre, Courier Epic, your constant assistance with the many challenges of printing this book is tremendously appreciated! Thank you for your support.

We are most grateful to our reviewers, who shared pertinent suggestions for the organization of material and specific ideas for improving the book. Your confirmation(s) of the activities, step-by-step procedures, and text content were appreciated. Thank you, Quinthia Foster, Microcomputer Technology Institute; Dianne Pannell, Harrisburg Area Community College; Kaye Peterson, Yavapai College; and Deborah Wareing, Scottsdale Community College.

To the participants at the Focus Group in Boston, Massachusetts, we extend our biggest thank you for sharing your teaching ideas and specific suggestions for enhancing the appearance and content of the book. Thank you, Susan McGowan, Caroleann Bready-Lyons, and Marilyn Sherry of Massasoit Community College; Eileen Zisk of the Community College of Rhode Island–Lincoln; Mary Belluardo and Jack Szeredy of Quinsigamond Community College; Barbara Cotoia and Roberta Neuschatz of Mt. Wachusett Community College; and Hannah Darling of the Computer Learning Center, Somerville, Massachusetts.

Layout Ruler

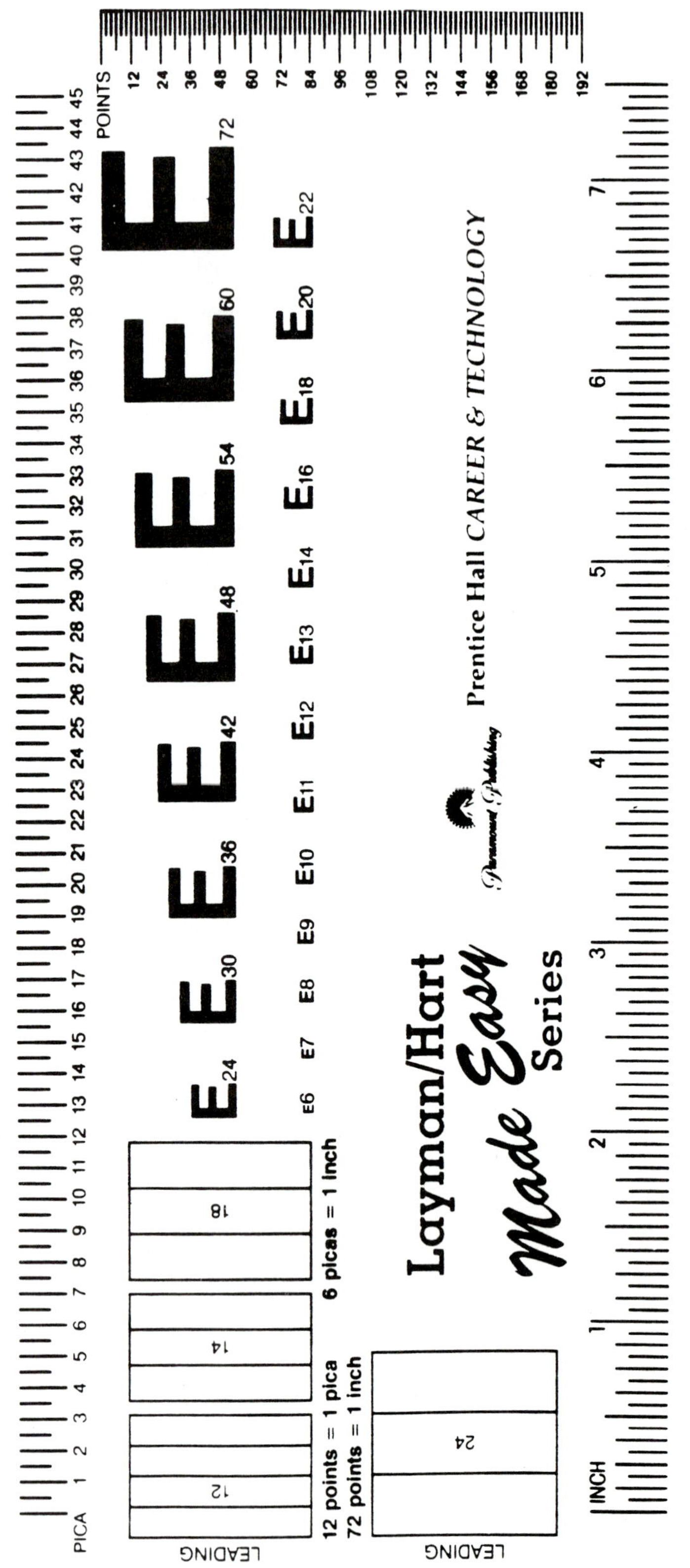

WordPerfect 6.0 for Windows Power Bar and Button Bars

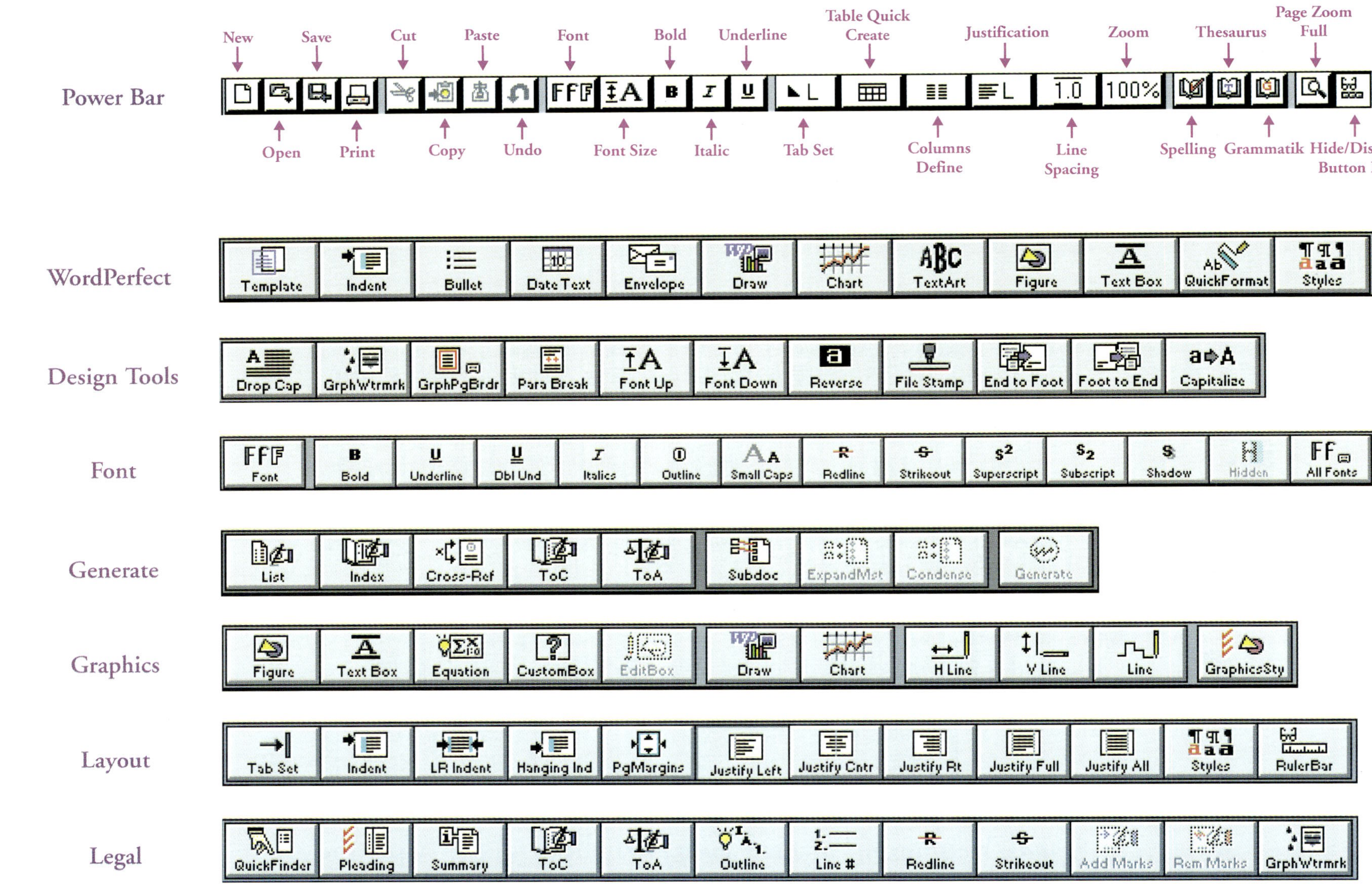

WordPerfect 6.0 for Windows Power Bar and Button Bars *(cont'd.)*

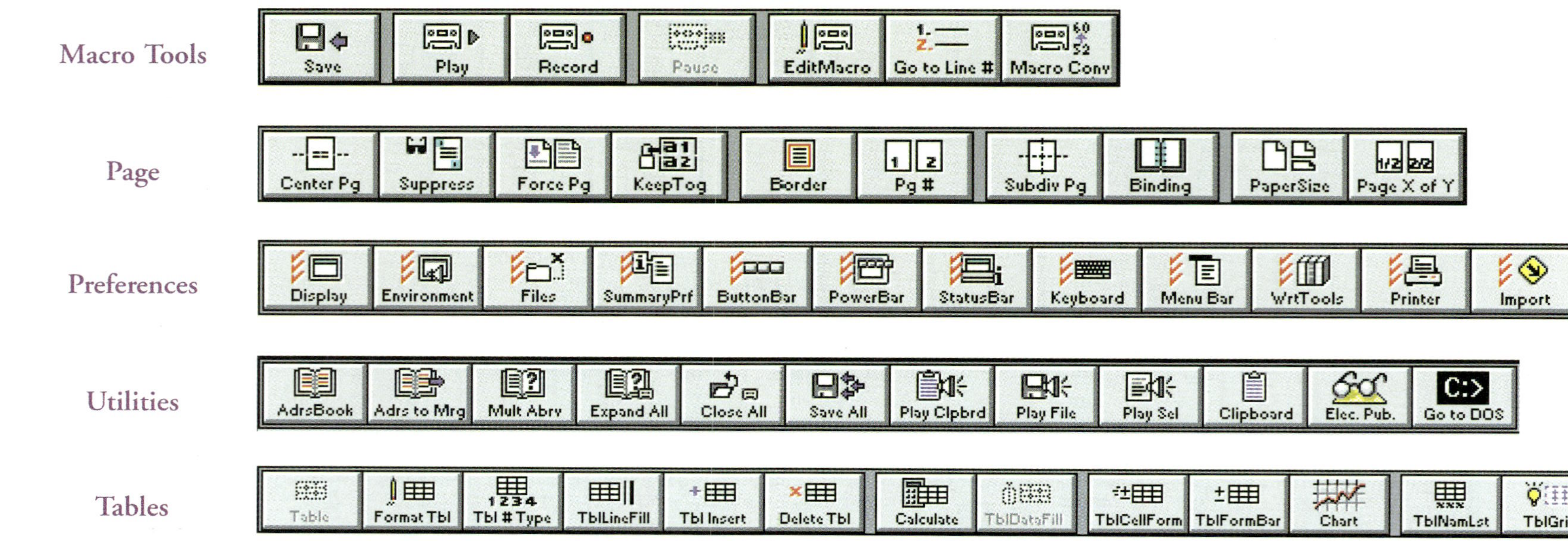

What Is a Microcomputer System?

A *microcomputer system* is a small computer system designed to provide methods for creating, processing, storing, and printing data. A small computer system normally includes the computer, keyboard, mouse, monitor, printer, and software programs. Many microcomputer systems today, however, include internal fax modems, sound boards, CD ROM players, and stereo speakers, and are referred to as *multimedia* systems.

The microcomputer system consists of two basic elements: hardware and software. The physical components of the microcomputer system are called hardware; the programs that instruct the computer to perform functions are called software.

Hardware

The microcomputer hardware includes the monitor (TV-like screen), keyboard, mouse, computer unit, disk drives, and printer. The hardware can be seen, felt, and touched. The IBM PC and compatible computers enclose the disk drive(s) with the computer. The monitor, keyboard, mouse, and printer are attached to the computer via cables (see Figure I.1). The computer unit and the attached hardware make up a microcomputer system.

The computer unit holds the electronic circuitry where the main memory and central processing unit (CPU) reside. The CPU processes and controls information by storing data, performing operations, and transferring information from one location to another. The CPU is often referred to as the "brains" of the computer.

Software

Software programs are lists of instructions that tell the computer what to do. The master program is the disk operating system (DOS). DOS directs the basic operation of the microcomputer system and carries out procedures within application programs. Application programs are more advanced software designed to perform specific tasks. Common applications are word processing, spreadsheet, database, communications, graphics, drawing, and desktop publishing programs.

DOS and application programs are stored on master disks. A copy of DOS and an application program can be transferred to the computer's memory when the computer is turned on. Transferring a copy of a program to the computer's memory is called "loading the program." The disk is being "read" when a copy of a program or other information is transferred from the disk into the computer's memory.

FIGURE I.1

The PC hardware

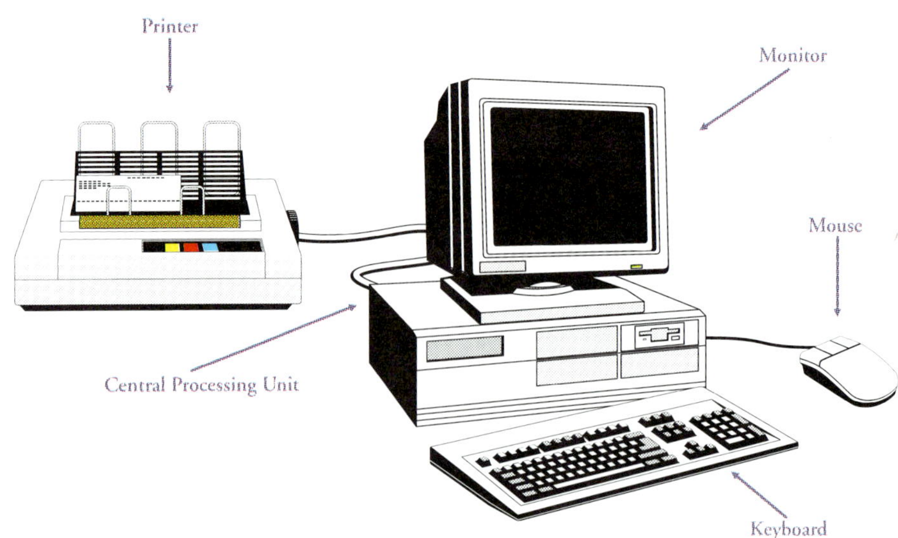

System Requirements and Recommendations for WordPerfect for Windows 6.0 and 6.0a

Minimum System Requirements*	Recommended System Requirements
386 IBM PC or compatible	386 (or higher) IBM PC or compatible
6M RAM	8M (or more) RAM
32M hard disk space, Version 6.0; 28M hard disk space, Version 6.0a	30–32M hard disk space free
Windows 3.1 running in enhanced mode	Windows 3.1 running in enhanced mode
VGA graphics adapter and monitor	SVGA graphics adapter and monitor
Mouse or other pointer device	Mouse or other pointer device

*WordPerfect features may not perform in an acceptable way when using the minimum system requirements.

What Are Disks?

Disks are storage devices. Information that is processed and used by a computer must be stored on either a hard or floppy disk. Because the computer's memory is temporary, all programs and data are erased when the computer is turned off. Therefore, disks are used to store programs and data.

The rigid hard disk usually resides inside the computer and is not removed by the user. Programs are normally stored on a hard disk. However, removable hard disks, contained in plastic cartridges, are also available. A floppy disk, contained in a plastic

FIGURE I.2

Hard disk and floppy disks

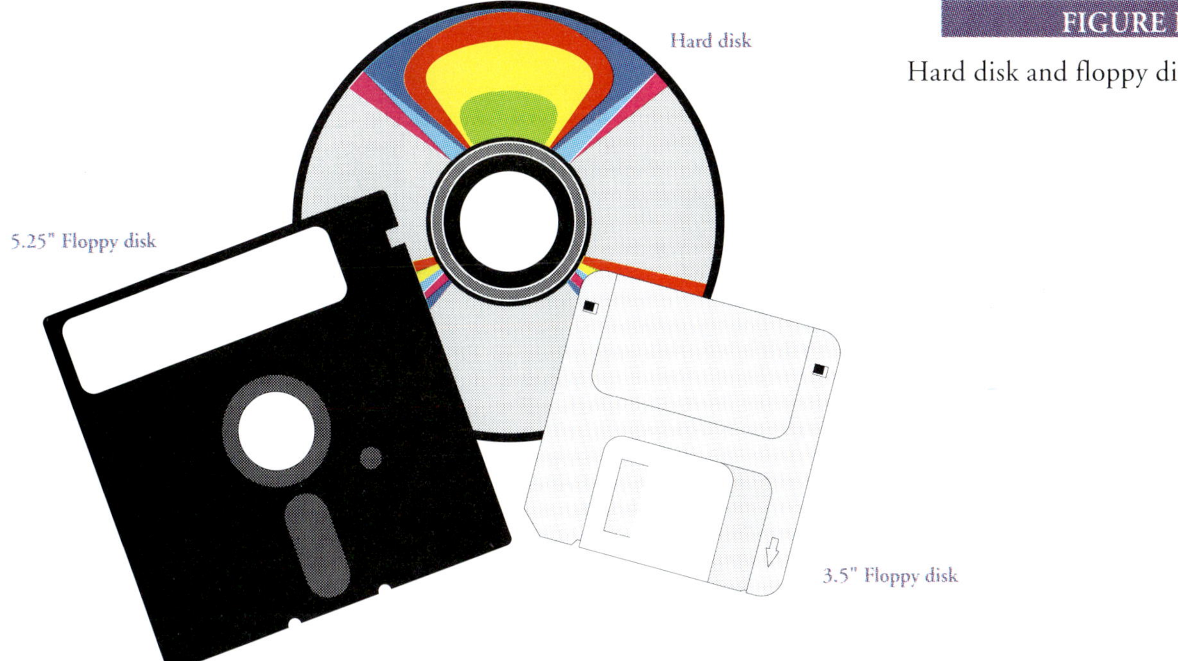

cartridge or paper jacket, is flexible and can be handled by the user. Floppy disks are generally used to store data or files. The most commonly used disk sizes are 5.25" and 3.5" (see Figure I.2).

Information that has been created is saved on either a floppy disk or a hard disk. A floppy disk is referred to as a *file disk* or *data disk*. If information, such as a letter, memorandum, or statistical data, is not saved on a disk, the information will be lost from the computer's temporary memory when the computer is turned off. When a copy of the information is transferred from the computer's memory to a disk, the process is called *saving*. Saving information to a disk is also called "writing" to a disk.

Care for Floppy Disks

Floppy disks should be labeled using a felt-tip pen. Store disks in a dry, protected location. Avoid dust, smoke, bending, and extreme temperatures. (Keep disks out of the sun and away from beverage containers!) Any magnet or magnetized object can damage the data on a disk; therefore, avoid using a paper clip on a disk, especially a paper clip that has been stored in a holder with a magnetized ring at the top.

Formatting a Floppy Disk

Before information can be saved on a disk, the disk must be formatted (prepared) with electronic instructions to partition the disk into storage areas, to create a directory, to check for disk defects, etc.

The formatting process is usually performed only once. If a disk is formatted a second time, all information previously saved on the disk is erased.

Format a File Disk Using Windows' File Manager

1. If necessary, turn on the computer and load Windows.

2. Double-click on the File Manager icon usually located in the Window's Main group.
3. Select Disk, Format Disk.
4. Select the down arrow button in the Disk In option box; select the disk drive letter where the disk to be formatted is located (e.g., select Drive A: or Drive B:).
5. Generally, the Capacity option box displays the appropriate disk capacity. If necessary, however, select the down arrow button in the Capacity option box and select the correct disk capacity.
6. Select OK.

   Note: The message, "Formatting will erase ALL data from your disk...," displays.
7. Select Yes.

   Note: A "Formatting disk" message displays with various messages indicating the formatting progress.
8. When the Format Complete dialog box displays, select Yes or No to indicate whether you want to format another disk (e.g., select No).
9. Select **File, Exit**.

What Is DOS?

DOS is the disk operating system for IBM PC and compatible microcomputers. DOS is a collection of related programs that controls and manages the computer's operations. DOS is necessary to handle the temporary storage and processing of information and to direct the orderly transfer or sharing of information between the computer unit and the disk, monitor, keyboard, printer, etc. In order for the computer to operate, the DOS programs must be accessible when the computer is turned on. Generally, DOS programs are stored on the hard disk.

What is Windows?

W*indows* is a program that works in conjunction with DOS to enable a user to perform computer tasks more easily. Windows provides a structure within which many programs can operate. Windows programs have a common way of accomplishing tasks. For example, the procedure for saving a file is the same when working with most Windows programs. In addition, data can be easily transferred from one Windows program to another. For example, a graph created in a Windows spreadsheet program can be easily transferred to a Windows word processing program.

The Windows program allows the user to complete tasks such as launching (loading) programs, copying files, formatting disks, and deleting files. When performing traditional DOS tasks such as copying files, formatting a disk, etc., using a mouse and the Window's drop down menus is usually much easier than remembering and typing DOS commands.

When Windows is loaded, the Program Manager window displays on the screen (see Figure 1.1 on page 12). The Windows program is often referred to as a graphical user interface because icons (pictures) display on the screen to represent each program. The user can launch a program simply by placing the mouse pointer on the program icon and pressing the left mouse button twice rapidly. This is called double-clicking (see page 6).

Windows allows multiple programs to run at the same time. Each program is placed in a separate *window*. The windows for each application program share common elements. For example, the Title bar, Menu bar, scroll bars, and control boxes are elements common to each application program. These common elements provide a standard method for accomplishing tasks. For example, the File, Print option is used in any Windows application to print a document. As more and more application programs are written to operate in Windows, the more common the elements will become to simplify the learning of additional Windows programs.

Windows programs are also compatible with each other (i.e., the information in each program can be transferred and shared easily between programs). For example, a spreadsheet file can be transferred to a WordPerfect document window. A *link* is established between the spreadsheet and WordPerfect files so that any changes made in the spreadsheet file are automatically changed in the linked file.

What are Directories and Paths?

A *directory* is a named location on a disk where a group of files is stored. A directory is used to keep files organized in separate areas on the disk under different directory names. Application programs such as word processing, spreadsheet, and database programs are usually stored on the computer's hard disk. The files for each application program can be kept together in one directory location. For example, all the WordPerfect program files are stored in a directory named *wpwin60.*

Other directories can be created and grouped together in the *wpwin60* directory. Any directories created in the *wpwin60* directory are called subdirectories. For example, if the subdirectory named *memos* was created, *memos* would be a subdirectory of the *wpwin60* directory.

A path is a route from a disk drive letter (root directory) to the location of a file or subdirectory. For example, the path for a file named *mem3* that is located in the subdirectory named *memos* that is in the *wpwin60* directory is: *c:\wpwin60\memos\mem3.* When using WordPerfect 6.0 for Windows, the various directories and subdirectories can be chosen in the Directories boxes that are available in the Open and Save As dialog boxes.

Filenames

Every file to be saved is assigned a filename. Filenames can contain one to eight characters and, if desired, a filename extension of one to three characters. The filename extension is separated from the first 1–8 characters by a period. For example, *morris.ltr* or *martin.ltr* are valid filenames. However, *morganstern.ltr* is not a valid filename because there are more than eight characters before the filename extension.

Any letter (a to z) or number (0–9) and most symbols can be used in a filename. A filename cannot contain spaces, commas, backslashes, asterisks, or a second period.

A filename should represent the information and/or person's name contained in the file. For example, a letter written to Gerry Anderson concerning a tax assessment could be assigned the name *g-andsn.tax* or *anderson.ltr*.

What Is WordPerfect 6.0 for Windows?

The WordPerfect word processing program is one of the most popular programs in the world. WordPerfect 6.0 for Windows is the most current version of WordPerfect for the Windows environment. In addition to the WordPerfect 6.0 for Windows program, a WordPerfect 6.0 for DOS program is available. WordPerfect 6.0 for DOS and WordPerfect 6.0 for Windows contain many common elements such as a Menu bar, Button Bar, Ribbon, Ruler, and dialog boxes which enable the user to perform editing, saving, text formatting, etc. more quickly and efficiently.

The Mouse (Pointer Device)

There are various types of pointer devices. The mouse pointer device and the track-ball are presently the most popular. The mouse is a hand-held device used to move an arrow or rectangular symbol (pointer symbol) on the screen. The mouse pointer is moved over the screen area until the pointer symbol touches the item or items to be selected. The left button on the mouse device is pressed to initiate the desired action, such as selecting options, sizing windows, formatting text, or creating objects.

Generally, the mouse is held between the thumb and little or ring finger. The index finger or middle finger is used to press the mouse buttons. To maintain consistent control of the mouse, hold the mouse motionless when pressing the mouse buttons.

When the mouse is moved over a flat surface, the pointer symbol moves in the same direction on the screen. When the mouse reaches the edge of the flat surface, hold the mouse firmly, lift, and relocate. Also, alternating between a short rubbing stroke and lifting the mouse slightly using wrist movement can be very helpful when the mouse reaches the flat surface edge.

The track-ball pointer device is stationary; the "ball" is moved by a finger or the palm of the hand. The track-ball can be built into the keyboard, or it can be connected to the computer via a cable.

The pointer symbol changes shape depending on the location on the screen where the pointer is positioned. For example, the pointer symbol changes to a two-headed arrow when sizing graphic boxes or windows and to a four-headed arrow when moving graphic boxes or windows (see chapters 13 and 16). The mouse pointer shapes are shown in Figure I.3.

Different techniques are used to initiate an action with the pointer device. The following list shows the basic actions:

FIGURE I.3

Mouse pointer shapes

	Used to select buttons, menu commands, and graphic boxes.		An up selection arrow is used in a table to select cells.
	Insertion point		A left selection arrow is used in a table to select rows and/or columns.
	I-beam mouse pointer. Used to locate the insertion point in text.		Indicates that a graphics box or window can be moved.
	Displays when the Help keys, Shift and F1, are pressed.	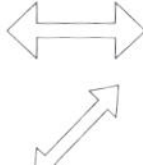	Indicates that a graphics box or window can be sized.

Click	Press the left button once and release.
Double-click	Press the left button twice rapidly.
Drag	Press and hold down the left button while moving the mouse or trackball.
Point	Move the pointer to a specific position on the screen.

The WordPerfect Document Window

The WordPerfect document window displays after the program is launched (loaded). The window is displayed in full size (maximized). (See Chapter 16 for changing the window size.) Each part of the window is shown in Figure I.4.

The Title bar displays at the top of the window and contains the application name and document title. The Control box displays on the left side of the Title bar and when selected provides keyboard users the capability to size, move, close, or switch to another program. The Minimize and Restore buttons are displayed on the right side of the title bar and are used to change the size of the application window. When the *Minimize* button is selected, the application is reduced to a small icon and the Program Manager or another application window is displayed. To return the program to the screen, double-click on the WPWIN 6.0 icon. If the WPWIN 6.0 icon cannot be seen on the screen, press **Ctrl** and **Esc** to display the Task List and double-click on WordPerfect. (See Chapter 16 for additional information on managing document windows.)

The Menu bar displays directly below the Title bar. Each menu in the Menu bar contains commands that are used to instruct WordPerfect to perform specific functions. To view the menu commands, click to select the Menu. The menu "drops down" and a list of the menu commands displays with the first item highlighted. When a menu command is highlighted, a brief description of that command displays at the top of the screen.

Each drop-down menu has a list of additional menu commands that are accessed easily by pointing and clicking the mouse or by pressing a designated letter from the

FIGURE I.4

WordPerfect 6.0 for Windows document window

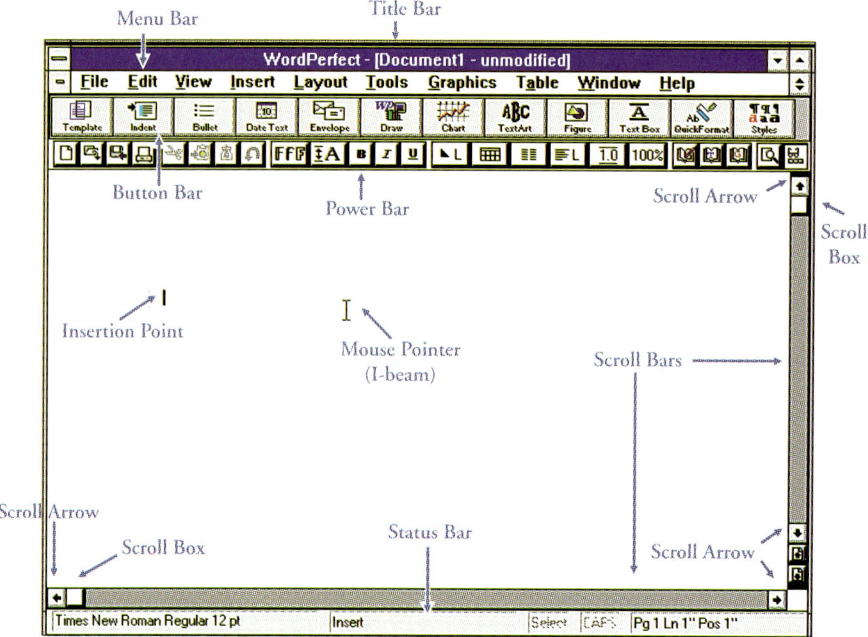

keyboard. The first item listed in a drop-down menu is highlighted. An underline displays beneath one letter in each menu command that can be typed to select the desired option. Listed beside some of the commands are keystrokes that can be used to activate a command. For example, in the File menu F3 displays next to the Save As command and Ctrl + S displays next to the Save command. Some menu commands are followed by three periods (**Save As...**) or a right arrow to indicate that, if selected, a dialog box or list of additional commands will display.

A *Button Bar* or *Power Bar* can be displayed and used to quickly activate frequently used functions. Once a button is selected, a dialog box displays or the function is performed immediately. (The Button Bar contains text and pictures whereas the Power Bar contains only pictures.)

The Button Bar and Power Bar are defaulted (preset) to display on the screen. By selecting the **View** menu, however, the user can choose to display only the Button Bar or the Power Bar. A checkmark beside the bar name in the **View** menu indicates that the bar is displayed. If desired, the Button Bar and/or Power Bar can be removed from the screen in order to see more of a document on the screen. The Button Bar and/or Power Bar can be chosen to display when the program is launched.

The Power Bar is used to quickly format text such as fonts, point sizes, columns, and justification. The Power Bar contains other buttons that are used to create tables, set decimal tab alignment and/or cut and paste text.

A Ruler contains a measurement scale that shows the placement of tabs, column margins, and left and right margins. The Ruler is used to change tabs and margin settings without accessing a menu.

Dialog Boxes

Dialog boxes provide additional WordPerfect commands. The dialog boxes display after menu commands or Button Bar buttons are selected. For example, when the **Print** button or the **File**, **Print** comand is selected, the Print dialog box displays (see Figure I.5).

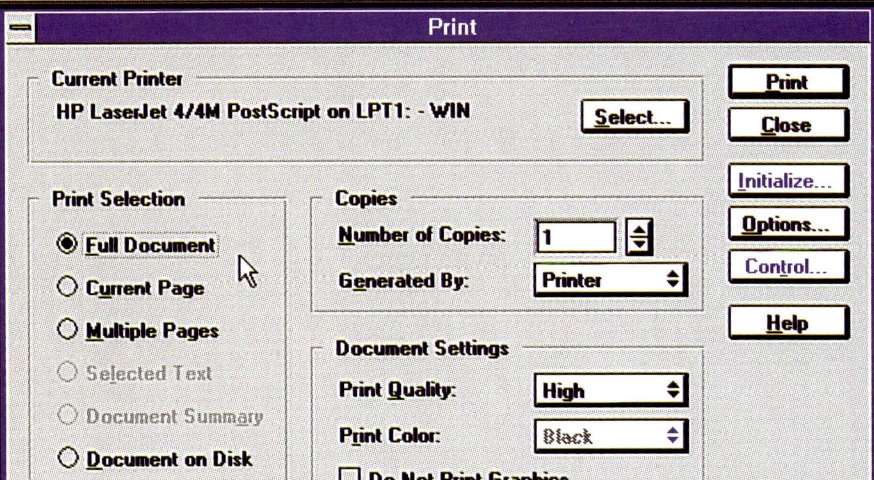

FIGURE I.5

Print dialog box

In a dialog box, instructions are supplied to the program by selecting from a list of options and/or by typing information. Often a dialog box contains commands followed by three periods (...). When these commands are selected, a second dialog box with additional options displays. The second dialog box allows the user to provide more specific information on how the chosen command is to be accomplished.

Part 1
The Beginning Step

Create and Edit Business Documents

Chapters 1-4

- Launch WordPerfect
- The Button Bar and Power Bar
- Center text
- Reveal Codes
- Scroll bars
- Print a document
- Save a document
- Close a document
- Exit WordPerfect
- Open a document
- Select text
- Delete and insert text
- Undo and Undelete
- View a document
- Use the Help feature
- Use the automatic date feature
- Change justification
- Bold, underline, and italic text attributes
- Change margins
- Font changes
- Speller
- Page Zoom Full view
- Move and copy text
- Find and replace text
- Indent and double-indent
- Numbered and bulleted lists
- Print selected text

CHAPTER

Create a Memorandum

Features Covered

- Launch WordPerfect for Windows
- The insertion point
- The Button Bar and Power Bar
- QuickCorrect
- Display the Reveal Codes window
- Save a file
- Print a document
- Close a document
- Use horizontal and vertical scroll bars
- Exit WordPerfect for Windows

Objectives and Introduction

After successfully completing this chapter, you will be able to launch the WordPerfect for Windows program; understand and display the Reveal Codes window; save, print, and close documents; and view different portions of a document using the scroll bars. These skills will be used to create and format two different styles of interoffice memorandums. Instructions for typing and formatting a memorandum while using WordPerfect will be presented in this chapter. Before a memorandum can be typed and formatted, the program is launched (loaded).

Launch WordPerfect for Windows

The WordPerfect for Windows program is launched (loaded) from the Microsoft Windows Program Manager. Icons (pictures) display in the Windows Program Manager window (see Figure 1.1) Each icon represents a program or application. To launch a program or application, move the mouse pointer to the desired icon and double-click. Launching a program is the process of transferring the program from the hard disk to the computer's memory.

FIGURE 1.1

Sample of the Windows Program Manager screen. (Icons may be arranged differently on each computer screen, because icons can easily be rearranged in the Program Manager.)

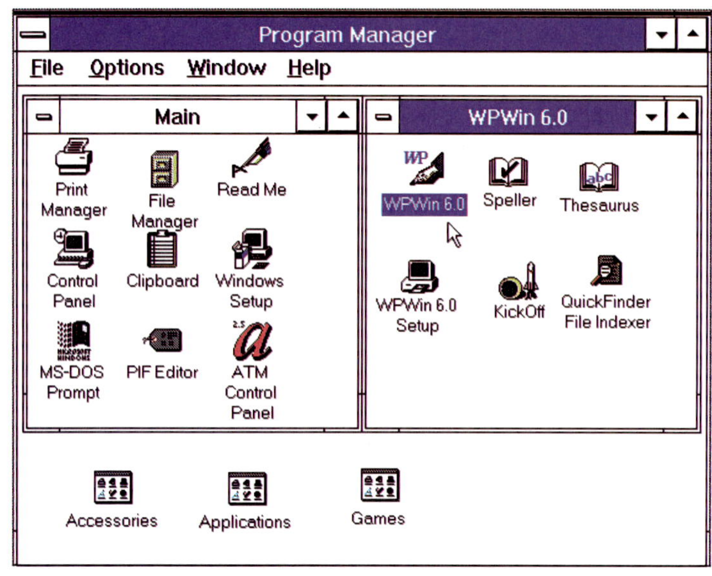

When the WordPerfect for Windows program is launched, the WordPerfect document window displays with a Title bar, Menu bar, Button Bar, and Power Bar at the top of the screen and a Status bar at the bottom of the screen (see Figure 1.2).

Note: *The first set of instructions in each step-by-step instruction in this textbook uses the mouse/trackball device. Place the mouse pointer on the option desired; press the left mouse button (click once) to select. The instructions for using the keyboard keys immediately follow the instructions for using the mouse and are indicated in braces { }, e.g., {Alt, f, c* **or** *Ctrl and F4}.*

Start-Up Instructions

- The computer and monitor should be turned on and the Windows Program Manager displayed on the screen. If necessary, see your instructor and write down the steps needed to display the Program Manager on your screen.

  ____

  ____

- Place a formatted file disk in drive A or B.

Steps to Launch (Load) the WordPerfect for Windows Program

1. Move the mouse pointer to the WPWin6.0 icon; quickly press the left mouse button twice (double-click).

   Note: *An hourglass displays on the screen to indicate that the program is being launched. Keys pressed while the hourglass is present are ignored by the program. The copyright screen displays briefly, then the WordPerfect document window displays (see Figure 1.2).*

   If a different method is used to launch (load) WordPerfect for Windows on your computer, see your instructor or instructional assistant and write the steps needed on the following lines.

   ____

   ____

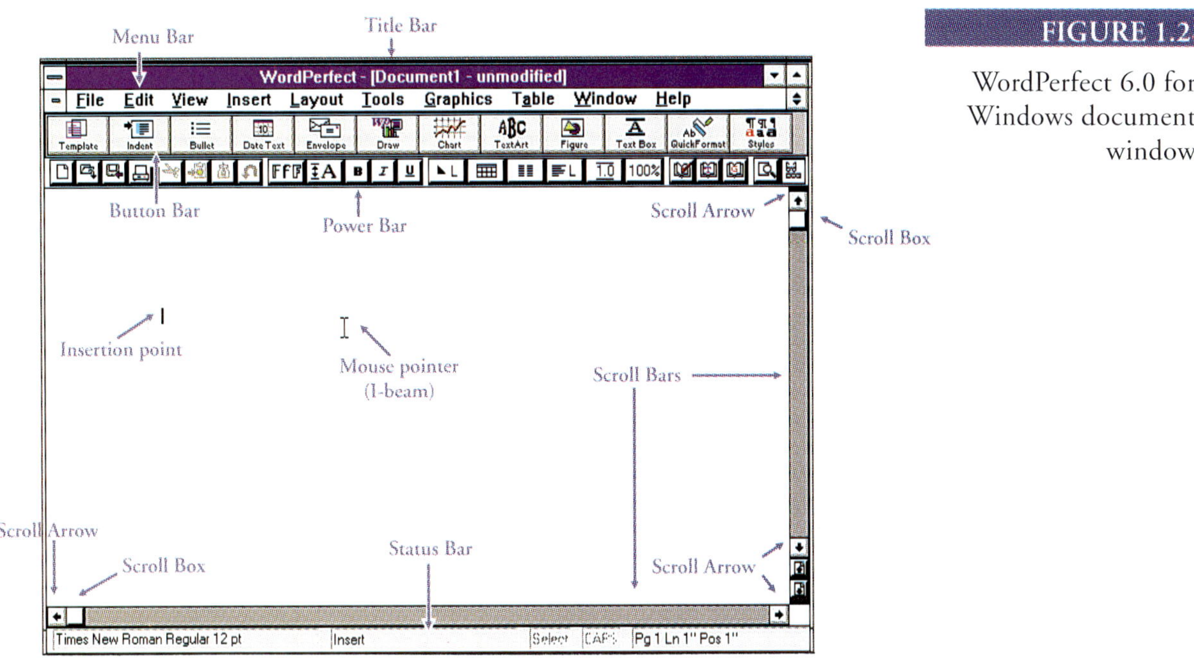

FIGURE 1.2

WordPerfect 6.0 for Windows document window

Insertion Point

The traditional cursor has been separated into two parts—an insertion point and a mouse pointer. The insertion point indicates the location where the next action takes place and displays as a bold, blinking vertical line. The insertion point will move to characters and lines that have been typed. However, the insertion point will not move into blank space unless the **Enter** key or **Spacebar** is pressed. As the **Enter** key or **Spacebar** is pressed or text is typed, the insertion point moves. See also Steps to Move the Insertion Point Quickly, page 25.

The second part of the traditional cursor is the mouse pointer. The mouse pointer symbol moves around the screen as the mouse is moved on the desktop. The shape of the mouse pointer changes depending on the location of the mouse pointer on the screen. For example, the mouse pointer is an I-beam when located in the text area, but usually changes to an arrow when the mouse pointer is out of the text area. See the Introduction, Figure I.3, for a list of the various mouse pointer shapes.

The mouse device can be used to move the insertion point by placing the pointer at the desired location and pressing (clicking) the left mouse button once. When *Num Lock* is turned off, the direction (arrow) keys on the 10-key numeric keypad can be used to move the insertion point up, down, left, or right one character or line at a time. On many keyboards, a duplicate set of arrow keys is provided on separate keys.

The Button Bar and Power Bar

WordPerfect provides an easy way to access frequently used commands via the *Button Bar* and *Power Bar* (see Figure 1.3). The Button Bar and Power Bar are two rows of buttons that display below the Menu bar. A mouse must be used to select a button on the Button Bar and Power Bar. When the mouse pointer is placed on a button on the Button Bar or Power Bar, the name of the button and a brief description of the purpose of the button displays in the Title bar.

FIGURE 1.3

The Button Bar and Power Bar

WordPerfect Button Bar

Power Bar

The WordPerfect Button Bar is the preset (default) Button Bar and is usually displayed because it contains options for working more quickly with commonly-used WordPerfect features. Other Button Bars can be accessed by moving the mouse pointer to any button in the Button Bar and clicking the *right* mouse button once to display a list of available Button Bars. For example, the Graphics Button Bar could be selected when working with graphic images.

If the Button Bar is not displayed on the screen, select **View**, **Button Bar**. If a Button Bar is displayed, selecting **View**, **Button Bar** will remove the Button Bar from the screen.

The Power Bar option buttons represent other commonly used features such as New Document, Open, Save, Print, Font Face, Justification, and Columns. If the Power Bar is not displayed on the screen, select **View**, **Power Bar**. If the Power Bar is displayed, selecting **View**, **Power Bar** will remove the Power Bar from the screen.

In addition to the Button Bar and Power Bar, a Ruler Bar and feature-specific Feature Bars can be displayed on the screen. The use of the Ruler Bar and Feature Bars will be discussed in later chapters.

QuickCorrect

The QuickCorrect feature automatically corrects common typing and spelling errors. For example, if the characters "teh" are typed followed by a space, WordPerfect will automatically display the correct word "the." Also, if two uppercase letters are typed followed by other lowercase letters and a space, WordPerfect will change the second uppercase letter to a lowercase letter. Customizing the QuickCorrect feature is covered in Appendix A.

Formatting

Formatting is the process of determining the placement and arrangement of a document when it is printed on a page. The arrangement of a document includes the amount of blank space in the left, right, top, and bottom margins. Formatting also includes alignment, underline/bold text, capitalization, and the number of vertical and horizontal spaces used between words and lines.

The purpose of formatting is to arrange text in a manner that is attractive and easy to read. This textbook includes information on formatting memorandums, letters, tables, reports, mailing labels, newsletters, reports, etc.

In this chapter, formatting using different justification options will be introduced to create memorandum styles. The Center and Flush Right alignment options will be discussed as well as the format for the main text of a memorandum called *body text.* The justification options and body text format will be used throughout this book.

Wordwrap

One automatic formatting feature of word processing programs is wordwrap. As you type text, the **Enter** key is pressed only at the end of a paragraph or short line. When text reaches the right margin, the insertion point automatically returns to the beginning of the next line. This automatic return feature is called *wordwrap.*

When wordwrap is used, a hidden code, *SRt* (soft return), is inserted at the end of each line. The hidden code can be viewed by using the Reveal Codes features (see the section on Reveal Codes beginning on page 18). Wordwrap automatically formats the document paragraph to adjust to the left and right margins. If words are inserted or deleted from the paragraph, text automatically readjusts to the margins.

Memorandum—Style 1

There are many acceptable formats for memorandums. In a traditional memorandum, a heading, such as *Memorandum, Memo,* or *Interoffice Correspondence,* is typed or preprinted at the top of the page. The memorandum heading is followed by the recipient's name, author's name, date, and subject. The words, *To:, From:, Date:,* and *Subject:* usually precede the recipient's name, author's name, the date and subject and are called "lead words." The lead words can be typed in the memorandum or preprinted.

The main text of the memorandum (body text) is typed using wordwrap within each paragraph to automatically begin new lines. The **Enter** key is pressed twice after each paragraph. Each paragraph begins at the left margin. After the final paragraph, the **Enter** key is pressed twice followed by the initials of the person typing the memorandum.

Start-Up Instructions

- Use the following information to begin creating the memorandum shown in Figure 1.4.

Use Center Alignment (Horizontal Centering)

1. The insertion point should be located on the left side of the screen.
2. Select Layout, Line, Center {Alt, L, L, c *or* Shift and F7}.

   Note: *The insertion point moves to the middle of the document window.*
3. Type the word(s) to be centered.

   For example, type Memorandum.
4. Press Enter once.

   Note: *The word(s) are now horizontally centered on the screen and a hidden center code is placed in the document. (See Reveal Codes on page 19.) The insertion point is now located at the left margin one line below the heading.*

FIGURE 1.4

Memorandum—Style 1

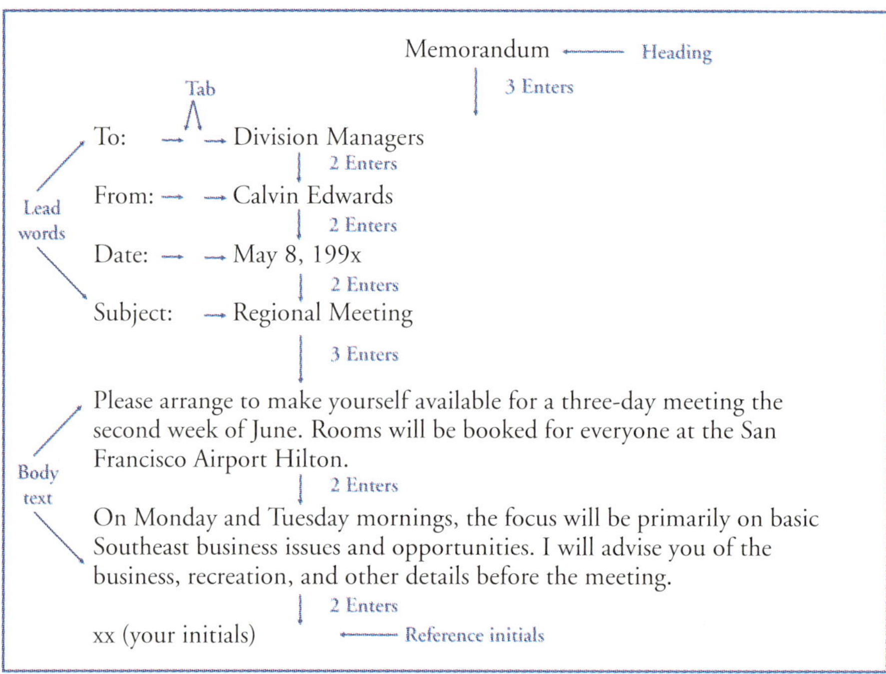

Start-Up Instructions

- Press the **Enter** key two more times to create two blank lines after the heading.
- Backspace to correct errors made while typing. For now, ignore any errors noticed after the memorandum is typed.
- Use wordwrap when typing the body text paragraphs.

  Note: The paragraph lines may not end with the same words as shown in Figure 1.4.

Steps to Create a Memorandum

1. Press the Tab key once or twice after the lead words as shown in Figure 1.4.

   *Note: The **Tab** key is pressed once or twice after the lead words in order to align the heading information. Visually check that the information following the lead words is aligned.*

2. Press the Enter key three times after the subject line and two times after each paragraph, including the last paragraph.
3. With the insertion point at the left margin, begin typing the text of the first paragraph. When the insertion point reaches the right margin, continue typing. Wordwrap will automatically return the insertion point to the left margin.
4. Press Enter twice after the last paragraph, then type your initials in lowercase letters.

Reveal Codes

When formatting options such as Center alignment are selected, WordPerfect places *hidden* codes in the document. To view these codes on the screen, the Reveal Codes feature is used. When Reveal Codes is activated, the screen is divided into two sections. The regular document window with the typed document displays at the top of the screen. The document text and formatting (hidden) codes display at the bottom of the

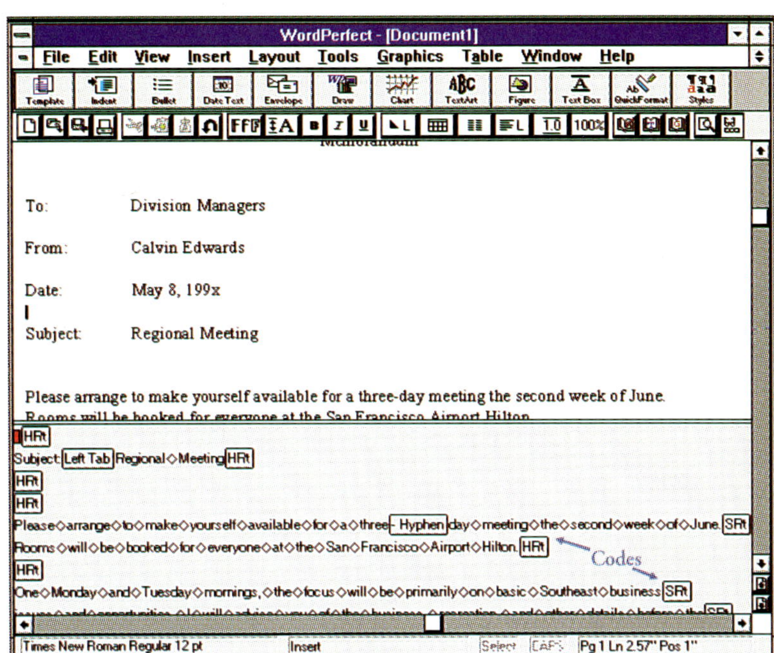

FIGURE 1.5

Reveal Codes window

screen. This section is known as the Reveal Codes window. The first code displayed in the Reveal Codes window is *Open Style: InitialStyle* (explained in Chapter 15).

The Reveal Codes window is routinely used to identify codes. The exact position of the insertion point is indicated by a red or shaded block. The movement of the red or shaded block in the Reveal Codes window corresponds to the movement of the insertion point in the document window.

A diamond (◊) is placed in the Reveal Codes window when the **Spacebar** is pressed. Two of the most frequently inserted codes are *SRt* and *HRt.* A soft return, *SRt,* occurs automatically each time wordwrap returns the insertion point to the left margin. A hard return, *HRt,* occurs each time the **Enter** key is pressed.

Start-Up Instructions

- Press and hold the **Ctrl** key and tap the **Home** key once to move the insertion point to the top of the document.

Steps to Turn on Reveal Codes

1. Select View, Reveal Codes {Alt, v, c *or* Alt and F3}.

   Note: The screen is divided into two sections: the document window at the top and the Reveal Codes window at the bottom (see Figure 1.5). Notice that the insertion point in the document window and the red or shaded block in the Reveal Codes window are located at the exact same position in the document. Press the down arrow key repeatedly to move simultaneously the insertion point in the document and the red or shaded block in the Reveal Codes window.

Steps to Turn Off Reveal Codes

1. When the Reveal Codes window is displayed on the screen, selecting View, Reveal Codes removes the Reveal Codes window {Alt, v, c *or* Alt and F3}.

Save a File

After a document is created, save the document to the computer's hard disk or to a floppy disk. Saving is the process of transferring the document from the computer's temporary memory to permanent memory on a hard disk or floppy disk. A saved document is referred to as a *file*.

When a document is saved, a filename is assigned. A filename can be one to eight characters with no spaces. If desired, a period and a one- to three-letter filename extension can be added (see Filenames on page 5). If a filename extension is not typed, WordPerfect automatically adds the extension *.wpd* (WordPerfect document) to the filename when a document is saved.

Before a named document is saved, the location of the disk where the file is to be saved must be selected. For example, if a file is to be saved to a disk that is located in the A drive, WordPerfect must be instructed to access the A drive.

Files can also be saved to different directories on the computer's hard disk or floppy disks. For example, a memo file could be saved to a directory named c:\memos (see What Are Directories and Paths? on page 5.)

Once a document has been saved, the filename and location display in the Title bar (as long as the mouse pointer is below the Power Bar). If a saved document is changed, selecting the **Save** button on the Power Bar or choosing **File**, **Save** will save the edited file immediately using the filename displayed in the Title bar. To save the edited file with a new filename, see Steps to Use Save As to Rename a File on page 38.

Start-Up Instructions

- A file disk should be placed in the A or B disk drive.

Save a New File

1. Select the Save button on the Power Bar {Alt, f, s *or* Ctrl and s}.

   Note: The Save As dialog box displays. The current drive and directory display below the words "Save As" at the top center of the dialog box, e.g., a:\ or c:\wpwin60\wpdocs. The insertion point is located in the Filename box.

2. In the Filename box, type a filename with eight characters or less (no spaces).

   For example, type **1drill1**. (Do not type the period.)

   Note: Check the accuracy of the filename before continuing. If necessary, use the Backspace key to erase an incorrect filename and type the corrected filename.

To Select a Different Drive

3. Move the mouse pointer to the box below the word "Drives" and click the left mouse button once {Alt and v, press the down arrow key}.

   Note: A list of available drives displays.

4. Move the mouse pointer to the desired drive letter and click once {press the up or down arrow key to highlight the desired drive letter, press Enter}.

   For example, move the mouse pointer to the drive letter containing your file disk, i.e., a: or b:, and click once.

Note: The newly selected drive displays below the words "Save As" at the top center of the dialog box.

To Complete the Save Process

5. Select OK {press Enter}.

   Note: *The document is saved on the file disk that is located in the selected disk drive. If the mouse pointer is located below the Power Bar, the document name is displayed in the Title bar of the WordPerfect document window, e.g., a:\1drill1.wpd–unmodified. The three letter extension .wpd is added automatically to the filename when the file is saved.*

   Note: *If the message displays, "File: a:\1drill1.wpd already exists. Do you want to replace it?," select* ***Yes*** *to replace, select* ***No*** *to return to the Save As dialog box and type a new filename, or select* ***Cancel*** *to return to the WordPerfect document window without saving the document.*

Select a Different Directory

Note: *The following steps are provided for your information.*

1. In the Directories box, click on the root directory symbol, e.g., c:\.

   Note: *A list of available directories displays in the Directories box.*

2. Move the mouse pointer to the desired directory name and click once.

   Note: *A list of available subdirectories displays in the Directories box.*

Print a Document

A document can be printed by using the **File**, **Print** command or by selecting the **Print** button on the Power Bar. After **Print** is selected in the Print dialog box, the entire document will be printed. Individual pages or sections of a document can be printed if desired. Additional information concerning printing is discussed in Chapters 5 and 10.

Start-Up Instructions

- The printer should be turned on. If you are sharing a printer, check that the switch box or local area network printer is selected for your printer.
- The document to be printed should be displayed in the document window.

Steps to Print a Document

1. Select the Print button on the Power Bar {Alt, f, p *or* F5}.
2. Select Print to print the document {press Enter}.

Close a Document

Once a document has been typed, saved, and printed, the document is usually cleared from the document window before a new document is begun. However, more than one document window can be displayed on the screen at one time. (See Chapter 16, The Windows in WordPerfect.) Closing a document is often referred to as *clearing a document* from the screen. After a document is closed, a blank WordPerfect document window displays and a new document can be typed or an existing document can be opened. If more than one document has been opened, you may need to close another document window or select **File**, **New** to obtain a clear document window.

Close a Document

1. Select **File**, **Close** {press Alt, f, c *or* Ctrl and F4}. The document will be removed from the document screen.

   Note: If a message displays, "Save changes to...?", select **No** *{press n} to close without saving changes. Repeat Step 1 if more than one window is open.*

Memorandum—Style 2

Memorandum—Style 2 illustrates a second acceptable memo format. The lead words and body text format are the same as Memorandum—Style 1. However, the heading "Interoffice Correspondence" is used, and the lead words are arranged on only two lines. See Figure 1.6.

In Memorandum—Style 2, the date and subject are typed at the right margin. The Flush Right alignment feature is used to move the insertion point to the right margin. As text is typed, the insertion point moves back towards the left margin. The final character in the line is located at the right margin. When **Enter** is pressed, the insertion point returns to the left margin.

When using Memorandum—Style 1 or Style 2, the lead word "To:" is followed by the recipient's name or a name that identifies a group of individuals, e.g., sales representatives, district managers, etc. Also, a distribution list can be typed after the body text, identifying the individuals who are part of the group. If copies of the memo are to be sent to other individuals, the notation "c:" is typed below the distribution list and followed by a list of people to whom copies are to be sent.

Start-Up Instructions

- Use the following steps to type the memorandum shown in Figure 1.6.
- Use Center alignment (**Shift** and **F7**) before typing the memorandum heading, **Interoffice Correspondence**. Press the **Enter** key three times.
- Type the lead word **To:** and press the **Tab** key once. Type **Sales Representatives**.

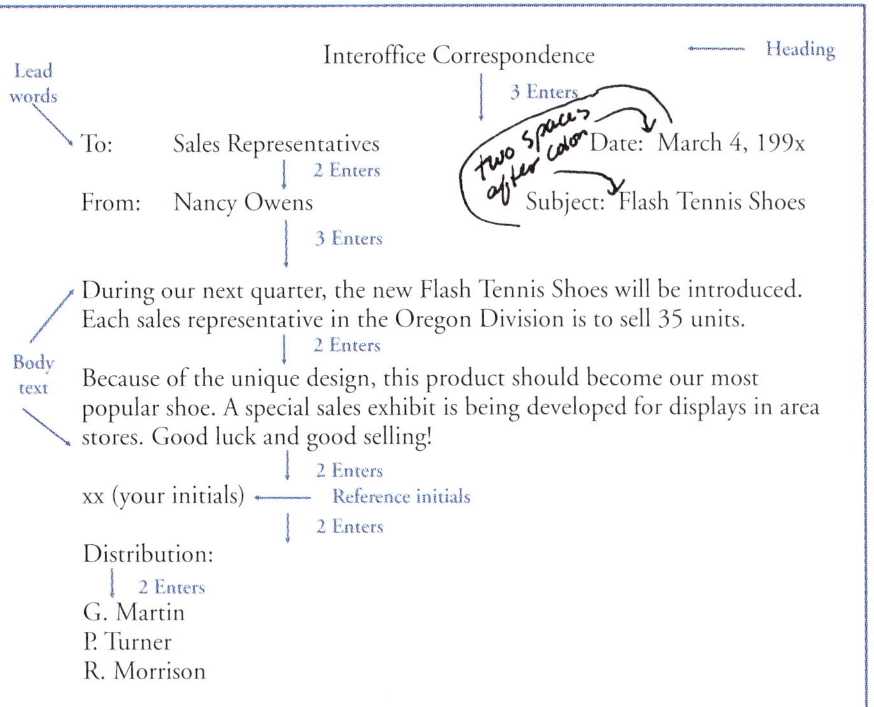

Interoffice Correspondence

To: Sales Representatives   Date: March 4, 199x

From: Nancy Owens   Subject: Flash Tennis Shoes

During our next quarter, the new Flash Tennis Shoes will be introduced. Each sales representative in the Oregon Division is to sell 35 units.

Because of the unique design, this product should become our most popular shoe. A special sales exhibit is being developed for displays in area stores. Good luck and good selling!

xx (your initials)

Distribution:

G. Martin
P. Turner
R. Morrison

FIGURE 1.6

Memorandum—Style 2

Steps to Use Flush Right Alignment

1. Select **Layout, Line, Flush Right** {Alt and F7}.

   Note: The insertion point moves to the right margin. As text is typed, the insertion point remains at the right margin and the text moves back towards the left margin.

2. Type the desired text.

   For example, type the lead word **Date** followed by a colon, two spaces, and the current date. Press the **Enter** key twice.

Finish-Up Instructions

- Continue to type the memorandum with the spacing indicated in Figure 1.6.
- Save the memorandum on your file disk; use the filename **1drill2**—Chapter 1, drill 2. (Select the **Save** button on the Power Bar; type the filename in the Filename box; if necessary, click in the Drives box and click on the drive letter where the file disk is located; select **OK**.)
- Print one copy (select the **Print** button on the Power Bar; choose **Print**).

Scrolling Horizontally and Vertically

Scrolling is the process of moving text quickly up, down, left, or right in order to view parts of the document not displayed in the document window. A vertical scroll bar displays at the right of the screen and a horizontal scroll bar displays at the bottom of the screen. Each scroll bar contains a scroll box and scroll arrows (controlled by the mouse) that can be used to view various parts of a document. To scroll quickly from page to page in a multiple-page document, the Previous Page and Next

FIGURE 1.7

WordPerfect for Windows document window with scroll bars

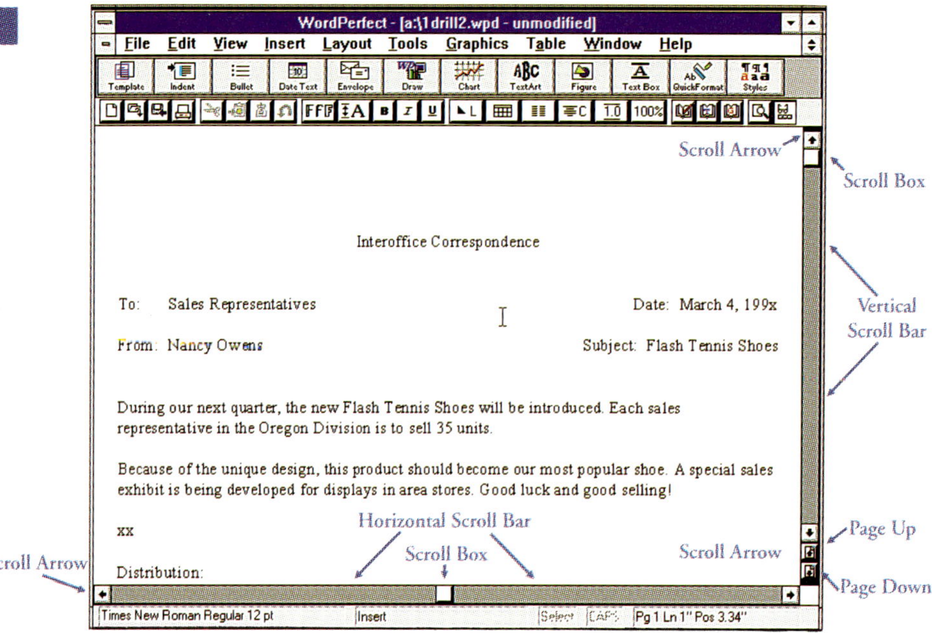

Page buttons located at the bottom of the vertical scroll bar can be used. See Figure 1.7.

Start-Up Instructions

- With the file named **1drill2.wpd** displayed in the document window, use the following steps to practice vertical and horizontal scrolling.
- Press and hold the **Ctrl** key and tap the **Home** key once to move the insertion point to the top of the document.

Use the Mouse for Vertical or Horizontal Scrolling

1. Place the mouse pointer on the scroll box in the vertical scroll bar on the right side of the document window; press and hold the left mouse button, then drag the scroll box up or down to scroll. Release the mouse button.

   For example, move the mouse pointer to the vertical scroll box; press and hold the left mouse button while dragging the box down; release the mouse button.

   Note: The text on the screen scrolls. However, the insertion point does not change location in the text. To change the location of the insertion point, see the Steps to Move the Insertion Point Quickly on page 25.

2. Place the mouse pointer on the up scroll arrow located at the top of the vertical scroll bar or the down scroll arrow located at the bottom of the vertical scroll bar and click the left mouse button once to scroll the text down or up a single line.

   For example, place the mouse pointer on the down scroll arrow located at the bottom of the scroll bar and click once or twice.

   Note: Holding down the left mouse button while pointing to the up or down scroll arrows will cause the text to move continuously up or down.

3. Place the mouse pointer on the scroll box in the horizontal scroll bar at the bottom of the document window; press and hold the left mouse button and drag the scroll box to the left or right. Release the mouse button.

   For example, move the mouse pointer to the scroll box in the horizontal scroll bar; press and hold the left mouse button while dragging the box to the right. Release the mouse button.

Move the Insertion Point

To relocate the insertion point to various parts of the document, use the arrow keys or move the mouse pointer and click on the desired location. For example, the mouse can be used to relocate the insertion point to any position in the document by pointing on the desired position and clicking once. The up, down, left, and right arrow keys as well as the **Page Up** (PgUp), **Page Down** (PgDn), **Home**, and **End** keys can also be used to relocate the insertion point.

Move the Insertion Point Quickly

Using the Mouse

1. Move the mouse pointer to any location in the document and click. The insertion point moves to that location.

   Note: If the desired location is not visible in the document window, scroll the text to display the desired location. (See Steps to Use the Mouse for Vertical or Horizontal Scrolling on page 24.)

Using the Keyboard

1. To move the insertion point to the left side of a line, press the **Home** key.
2. To move the insertion point to the right side (end) of a line, press the **End** key.
3. To move the insertion point to the beginning of the document, press and hold the **Ctrl** key and tap the **Home** key once.

   *Note: Press **Ctrl** and **Home**, **Ctrl** and **Home** to move the insertion point to the right of the "Open Style: InitialStyle" code and in front of any other codes that could be at the top of the document.*
4. To move the insertion point to the last character in the document, press and hold the **Ctrl** key and tap the **End** key once.
5. To move the insertion point to the top of the document window, press the **Page Up** key once.
6. To move the insertion point to the bottom of the document window, press the **Page Down** key once.
7. To move the insertion point to the left one word, press the **Ctrl** and **left arrow** keys.
8. To move the insertion point to the right one word, press the **Ctrl** and **right arrow** keys.

9. To move the insertion point to the top of the previous page, press the Alt key and then press the Page Up key once.

10. To move the insertion point to the top of the next page, press the Alt key and then press the Page Down key once.

11. To move the insertion point to a different page, press Ctrl and g (Go To), type the page number desired, press Enter.

Exit WordPerfect

After completing your work, the WordPerfect for Windows program is exited and the Windows Program Manager screen displays. If desired, Windows can be closed and the cursor returned to the system prompt, e.g., C:\. Remember to always save your files before exiting the WordPerfect program.

Exit WordPerfect

Note: If necessary, save your file before exiting the WordPerfect program using the Steps to Save a New File on page 20.

1. Select File, Exit {Alt, f, x *or* Alt and F4}.

   *Note: If a message displays, "Do you want to save changes to...?", select **Yes** to save changes or select **No** to abandon changes.*

The Next Step

Chapter Review and Activities

Self-Check Quiz

T F 1. Launching is the process of transferring the WordPerfect program from a hard disk to the computer's memory.

T F 2. Formatting is the process of determining the placement and arrangement of a document when it is printed on a page.

T F 3. To center a line of text, select **Layout**, **Line**, **Center**.

T F 4. To print all the text in a file, select **File**, **Print**, **Close**.

T F 5. A document can be saved only to a floppy disk.

6. The Reveal Codes window displays
   a. hidden codes.
   b. in the document window at all times.
   c. by selecting **View**, **Page**.

7. The Button Bar
   a. is referred to as the Power Bar.
   b. can be removed from the screen by selecting View, **Button Bar**.
   c. can be accessed by using keystrokes.

8. Press the **Enter** key to
   a. begin a new paragraph.
   b. end a short line.
   c. both a and b.

9. What is the difference between the insertion point and the mouse pointer?

10. List the two steps to use Flush Right alignment.

Enriching Language Arts Skills

Each chapter contains vocabulary/spelling words and basic rules for punctuation, capitalization, or grammar. The last *Challenge Your Skills* activity in each chapter is identified by the ➾ symbol and has mistakes in spelling, punctuation, capitalization, and/or grammar that are to be corrected. These activities should be proofread and corrected to produce a document that is grammatically accurate and ready for distribution.

Spelling/Vocabulary Words

acquisition the act of purchasing or obtaining an item.

spiraling increasing upward or downward in a circular motion.

enormous huge, big.

liquidation to close a business in order to receive cash for the assets.

Introductory Adverbs and Phrases

A comma often follows an introductory adverb or phrase, because the word or phrase provides a transition from the previous sentence. Some common introductory adverbs/phrases are: *however, for example, also, consequently, in other words.*

Examples:

A decision was made yesterday to postpone the approval of the budget. Consequently, the purchase order for the new desks will be delayed.

The post office requested that we use the new extended zip code. In other words, use the current 5-digit zip code followed by the new 4-digit extension.

Activities

Activity 1.1—Create a Memorandum—Style 1

1. If necessary, launch (load) the WordPerfect program (see page 14).
2. If errors are made while typing, use the **Backspace** key to delete. For this chapter, ignore any errors noticed *after* the memo is typed.
3. Use Memorandum—Style 1 (see page 17) and type the following memorandum.

Memorandum

To: Al Lindsay

From: Virginia Ashlan

Date: (Use current date)

Subject: Action Plan Version 5.0

The newest version of the Action Plan program is currently available.

An information bulletin is being sent to all consultants informing them that the instructional materials are now available at all our regional offices. Old versions of Action Plan diskettes and manual contents can be destroyed. The binders can be reused with the new material, and the diskettes can be recycled.

xx (your initials)

---

4. Save the file on your file disk; use the filename **1act1** (Chapter 1, activity 1). (Select the **Save** button on the Power Bar; type the filename; if necessary, click in the Drives box and click on the drive letter where the file disk is located; select **OK**.)
5. Print one copy (select the **Print** button on the Power Bar; choose **Print**).
6. Close the document to clear the document window (select **File**, **Close**).

Activity 1.2—Create a Memorandum—Style 1

1. If necessary, launch (load) the WordPerfect program (see page 14).
2. If errors are made while typing, use the **Backspace** key to delete. For this chapter, ignore any errors noticed *after* the memo is typed.
3. Use Memorandum—Style 1(refer to page 17) and type the following memorandum.

Memorandum

To: All Sales Agents

From: Peter Roth, Division Manager

Date: (Use current date)

Subject: Application Procedures for Multiple Contracts

The purpose of this memorandum is to clarify the procedure for processing exchanges when more than one contract is involved.

The correct procedure is to list each company name along with the policy number for each policy that will be relinquished for the purpose of exchange.

At policy delivery, the policyowner will sign both of the contract forms. Return the forms and policies to the Policy Change Department. If you have questions, please feel free to contact us in Marketing Services.

xx (your initials)

4. Save the file on your file disk; use the filename **1act2** (Chapter 1, activity 2). (Select the **Save** button on the Power Bar; type the filename; if necessary, click in the Drives box and click on the drive letter where the file disk is located; select **OK**.)
5. Print one copy (select the **Print** button on the Power Bar; choose **Print**).
6. Close the document to clear the document window (select **File**, **Close**).

Activity 1.3—Create a Memorandum—Style 2

1. If necessary, launch (load) the WordPerfect program (see page 14).
2. If errors are made while typing, use the **Backspace** key to delete. For this chapter, ignore any errors noticed *after* the memo is typed.
3. Use Memorandum—Style 2 (refer to page 23) and type the following memorandum.

Interoffice Correspondence

To: See Distribution Below　　Date: (Use current date)

From: Gene Hunter　　Subject: Reimbursement Rates

All offices have been provided with the new fuel reimbursement rates that should be placed into effect immediately. Each office will photocopy a set of the rates and forward the rate sheets to all area representatives.

You will notice that an additional amount for the seasonal adjustment has been added to each rate. If gasoline prices decline this fall, revised rates will be published to reflect any changes at that time.

xx (your initials)

Distribution:

S. Bentley
L. Jardine
W. Moyer

4. Save the file on your file disk; use the filename **1act3** (Chapter 1, activity 3). (Select the **Save** button on the Power Bar; type the filename; if necessary, click in the Drives box and click on the drive letter where the file disk is located; select **OK**.)
5. Print one copy (select the **Print** button on the Power Bar, choose **Print**).
6. Close the document to clear the document window (select **File**, **Close**).

Challenge Your Skills

The *Challenge Your Skills* section at the end of each chapter contains a group of activities that reinforce understanding of the chapter's concepts. The activities require decision-making skills. The *Challenge Your Skills* activities should be completed only after completing appropriate chapter drills and activities.

Skill 1.1—Create a Memorandum—Style 1

1. If necessary, launch the WordPerfect program.
2. If errors are made while typing, use the **Backspace** key to delete. For this chapter, ignore any errors noticed *after* the memo is typed.
3. Use Memorandum—Style 1 and the following information.

a. Send the memorandum to the MIS Staff from Veronica Pearson. The subject of the memorandum is Network Access Problems.

b. Use the current date; include your reference initials.

The network has caused loss of productivity in recent weeks. Explanations of known problems are summarized below.

The recent Broadway virus that attacked the entire network caused a productivity loss of two days. MIS took effective action in returning us to operation quickly.

On Monday and Tuesday the network could not be accessed from the IBM PS/2. An unreliable connection was found between the network and the PS/2. Printing could not be accomplished from the Compaq AT. The printer cable had been disconnected from the switch box.

Angelo's computer receives a high number of "Error on Network Server ONEA Abort, Retry?" messages. Jayne Gurry has been notified. This is a recoverable error.

Thanks to all MIS users for your interest in resolving network problems rapidly.

---

4. Save the file on your file disk; use the filename **1skill1** (Chapter 1, skill 1).
5. Print one copy and close the document to clear the document window.

Skill 1.2—Create a Memorandum—Style 2

1. If necessary, launch the WordPerfect program.
2. If errors are made while typing, use the **Backspace** key to delete. For this chapter, ignore any errors noticed *after* the memo is typed.
3. Use Memorandum—Style 2 and the following information.

   a. Send the memorandum to USL Agents from Joyce Bixler. The subject of the memorandum is Purchase of Policies.

   b. Use the current date; include your reference initials.

   c. The memo is to be distributed to the following persons: Russell Crimmins, Catherine Goldfarb, Marilyn Scutro, and Edith Zehr.

United Security Life will soon acquire the life and annuity policies of Hampton Insurance Company. Hampton Insurance Company (HIC) is a small-stock life insurer that has experienced financial difficulty and is being liquidated.

As a part of the liquidation process, USL has agreed to purchase HIC's life and annuity policies. This will ensure that all the life and most of the annuity policies continue without loss to the policyholders.

We think that the acquisition of HIC will help us control our unit expenses, which is certainly in everyone's best interest. If you have any questions regarding the acquisition, please contact my assistant, Lois Schloneger.

4. Save the file on your file disk; use the filename **1skill2** (Chapter 1, skill 2).
5. Print one copy and close the document to clear the document window.

Skill 1.3—Create a Memorandum—Style 2; Language Arts

1. If necessary, launch the WordPerfect program.
2. If errors are made while typing, use the **Backspace** key to delete. For this chapter, ignore any typing errors noticed *after* the memo is typed.
3. Use Memorandum—Style 2 and the following information.
   a. Send the memorandum to GLI Representatives from I. Arigone, Field Manager. The subject of the memo is Blood Test Limit.
   b. Use the current date; include your reference initials.
   c. The memo is to be distributed to the following persons: T. Deyo; B. Hurwicz; R. Juarez; E. Tang; L. Tolleson; and M. Warrick.
   d. While typing, correct two spelling errors and one punctuation error.

This is a reminder that effective with new business written next month, Global Life Insurance's new blood test rules call for a blood test at $100,000. GLI participated in a recent study involving a large number of the better known insurance companies and a solid majority are requiring blood tests for any policies amounting to $100,000 or greater. Our research combined with the spireling increase in medical costs, makes this adjustment necessary.

We need your full cooperation involving applications for amounts between $95,000 to $99,999, which occur on persons opposed to a blood test. Most people who object to obtaining a blood test are not trying to hide a prior condition. Unfortunately, there is a small segment of people who already know they have a pre-existing condition, and we cannot discern which type of person is objecting. Consequently you are to arrange a blood test on those individuals whose policy amounts barely slide in under the actual rule limits.

It is widely believed that many companies will eventually be forced to increase premiums in order to avoid the consequence of liquidtion. It is our hope that by seeking your cooperation on the above measures, GLI can forestall or avoid sterner remedies later.

---

4. Save the file on your file disk; use the filename **1skill3** (Chapter 1, skill 3).
5. Print one copy.
6. If you have completed your work, exit WordPerfect (select **File**, **Exit**).

CHAPTER 2

Edit a Memorandum

Features Covered

- Open a document
- Select text
- Delete text
- Insert text
- Replace text using the Typeover mode
- Save and rename a document file
- Undo and Undelete
- View a document
- Use the Help feature

Objectives and Introduction

After successfully completing this chapter, you will be able to open a previously created document; delete, insert and replace text; and save a document with a new filename. You will also be able to use the Viewer and Help features. Once a memorandum has been created, the author can make revisions to the document. Revisions can include information to be deleted, inserted, or replaced.

Open a Document

Before a file is edited, the saved document is opened and displayed in the document window. Opening a document is the process of transferring a document file from a disk to the computer's memory. When a file is opened, the document displays in a new document window. As many as nine files can be opened (in memory) at the same time (see Chapters 9 and 16). To open a file, select the **Open** button on the Power Bar, choose the desired drive/directory, and double-click on the filename.

The last four files that have been opened are listed at the bottom of the File menu. To open one of the four listed files, move the mouse pointer to the filename and click once. If WordPerfect cannot locate the selected file, a message displays ". . . File not found."

FIGURE 2.1

Open File dialog box

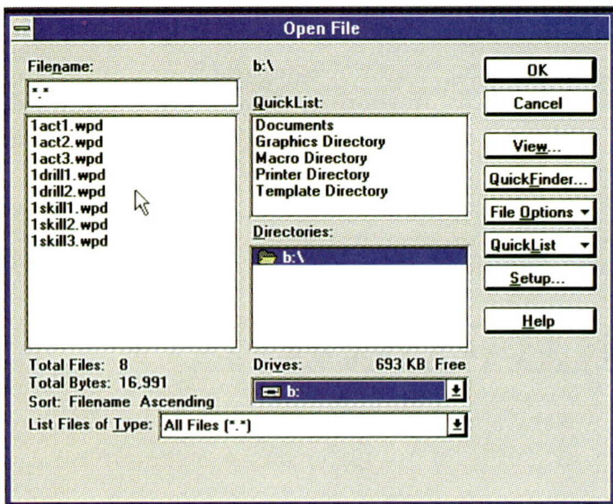

Steps to Open a File

1. Select the Open button on the Power Bar {Alt, f, o *or* Ctrl and o}.

   Note: The Open File dialog box displays (see Figure 2.1).

2. *To display the files stored on a different drive,* move the mouse pointer to the Drives box and and click once. Move the mouse pointer to the desired drive letter and click once {Alt and v, press the down arrow key, press the up or down arrow key to highlight desired drive letter, press Enter}.

3. Move the mouse pointer to the desired filename and double-click {Alt and n, press the Tab key once, press the down arrow key to highlight the desired filename, press Enter}.

   For example, double-click on the file named **1drill1.wpd**.

   Note: Wait a moment and the selected file displays in the document window.

Delete and Insert Text

Text can be deleted by using the Backspace key or the Delete (Del) key. When the Backspace key is pressed, the character or space to the left of the insertion point is erased. When the Delete key is pressed, the character or space to the right of the insertion point is erased. Text deleted by using the Backspace or Delete keys can be returned to the screen by using the Edit, Undo or Edit, Undelete commands (see Undo Erased Text, page 38.

Selected text can be erased and replaced without using either the Delete or Backspace key. The text to be deleted is selected. When the first character of the new text is typed, the selected text is deleted.

Text can be selected and deleted. A character, word, sentence, line, paragraph, or entire document can be selected and deleted. After text is selected and the Delete or Backspace key is pressed, the deleted text is placed in the Clipboard. The Clipboard is temporary memory that holds the deleted text. When additional text is selected and deleted, the original text held in the Clipboard is erased and replaced with the last deleted text.

Text is inserted by placing the insertion point at the location where the new characters are to be typed and typing the characters. As the inserted text is typed, the characters to the right of the insertion point move over and provide space for the new text.

Select Text

Using the Mouse

a. *Drag method:* To select any quantity of text, move the mouse pointer (I-beam) to the beginning of the text to be selected; press and hold the left mouse button while dragging the mouse to highlight the desired text. Release the mouse button.

b. *Shift and Click method:* To select any quantity of text, move the mouse pointer (I-beam) to the left of the first character to be selected and click the left mouse button once. Move the mouse pointer (I-beam) to the right of the last character to be selected. Press and hold the **Shift** key and click the left mouse button once. Release the **Shift** key.

c. *To select a word,* move the mouse pointer to any character in the desired word and double-click.

d. *To select a sentence,* move the mouse pointer to any word in the desired sentence and triple-click, or move the mouse pointer into the left margin next to the desired sentence and click once.

e. *To select a paragraph,* move the mouse pointer to any location within the paragraph and click four times, or move the mouse pointer into the left margin beside the desired paragraph and double-click.

Using the Edit, Select Command

a. To select a sentence, place the insertion point in the desired sentence and choose **Edit, Select, Sentence** {Alt, e, e, s}.

b. To select a paragraph, place the insertion point in the desired paragraph and choose **Edit, Select, Paragraph** {Alt, e, e, a}.

c. To select a page, place the insertion point anywhere in the desired page and choose **Edit, Select, Page** {Alt, e, e, p}.

d. To select the entire document, choose **Edit, Select, All** {Alt, e, e, L}.

Using Keystrokes

1. Place the insertion point to the left of the character at the beginning of the text to be selected.

2. Press **F8**.

Note: *The word **Select** displays in bold in the Status bar.*

3. Use any of the following keystrokes.

a. To select one character to the right or left, press the **right arrow** or **left arrow** key.

b. To select one line up or down, press the up or down arrow key.

c. To select to the end of the line, press the End key.

d. To select to the beginning of the line, press the Home key.

e. To select to the beginning of the document, press the Ctrl and Home keys.

f. To select to the end of the document, press the Ctrl and End keys.

g. To select to the top of the screen, press Page Up (PgUp).

h. To select to the bottom of the screen, press Page Down (PgDn).

i. To select one word to the right or left, press Ctrl and the left or right arrow key.

j. To select one paragraph up or down, press Ctrl and the up or down arrow key.

Steps to Turn Off Select

1. To turn off select and remove the highlight from text, click once {F8}.

Steps to Delete Text

1. Once the desired text has been selected, press the Delete (Del) key.

Shortcuts for Deleting Text Without Selecting Text

a. To delete an entire word, position the insertion point to the left of any character in the word to be deleted and press Ctrl and Backspace.

Steps to Delete an Enter/Blank Line or Tab Code

1. Turn on Reveal Codes (Alt and F3).
2. Move the insertion point to left of the *HRt* or *Left Tab* code.
3. Press the Delete key.
4. Turn off Reveal Codes (Alt and F3).

Steps to Insert Text or Spaces

1. Place the insertion point to the left of the character or space that will follow the inserted text or space.
2. Type the text or space to be inserted.

   Note: *If text is erased as new text is typed, press the Insert (Ins) key once to turn off the Typeover mode. See also the Replace Text Using the Typeover Mode section which follows.*

Replace Text Using the Typeover Mode

When text is replaced using the Typeover mode, the original character(s) are deleted and new characters are substituted. For example, if the insertion point is located to the left of the character "b" in the word "band" and the character "s" is typed, the "b" is deleted and the character "s" displays on the screen, changing the word to "sand." Replacing text using the Typeover mode is accomplished by first pressing the **Insert** (Ins) key, then typing the new character(s). When the Insert key is pressed, the word *Typeover* displays in the Status bar. When the **Insert** key is pressed again, the word *Insert* displays in the Status bar.

Steps to Replace Text

1. Place the insertion point to the left of the first character of the text to be replaced.
2. Press the Insert (Ins) key.

   Note: The word "Typeover " displays in the Status bar.
3. Type the new character(s).
4. When you have finished replacing the text, press Insert again to turn Typeover off.

   Note: If desired, select ***Edit, Undo*** *to restore the replaced text.*

Start-Up Instructions

- The file named **1drill1.wpd** typed in Chapter 1 (Figure 1.4) should be opened and displayed in the document window. (If necessary, select the **Open** button on the Power Bar; if necessary, click in the Drives box and click on the drive letter where the file disk is located; double-click on the desired filename.)
- Review the steps to select and/or delete text and the steps to replace text using the Typeover mode.
- Make the changes shown in Figure 2.2.
- Continue with the Steps to Use Save As to Rename a File.

Save and Rename a File

Once a document (file) has been edited, the changed file can be saved using a new filename. Using a different filename keeps a copy of the original file and saves the changed file under a new filename. If the changed file is saved with the original file-name, the original file is erased and replaced by the corrected file.

Start-Up Instructions

- The file named **1drill1.wpd** should be displayed in the document window.

FIGURE 2.2

Changes for Memorandum—Style 1

Memorandum

To: Division Managers

From: Calvin Edwards, Regional Manager

Date: May 8, 199x

Subject: Western Regional Meeting

Please arrange to make yourself available for a three-day meeting the second week of June. Rooms will be booked for everyone at the San Francisco Airport Hilton for three days and two nights.

On ~~Monday~~ Tuesday and ~~Tuesday~~ Wednesday mornings, the focus will be primarily on basic South~~east~~west business issues and opportunities. I will advise you of the business, recreation, and other details before the meeting. On Thursday we will join with Jan Hasimi's group to discuss the new marketing promotion.

¶ Casual attire will be appropriate for Tuesday and Wednesday. Thursday's attire will be announced pending the determination of the meeting location.

xx

Steps to Use Save As to Rename a File

1. With the document displayed in the document window, select **File, Save As** button {Alt, f, a *or* F3}.
2. Type the new filename. (If necessary, select the drive where the file disk is located by clicking the Drives box and clicking on the desired drive letter).

   For example, type **a:2drill1r**. (Do not type the period.)
3. Select **OK** {press Enter}.

Finish-Up Instructions

- Print one copy (select the **Print** button on the Power Bar; choose **Print**).
- If additional changes are made to the document, select the **Save** button on the Power Bar to save but to not rename the document. If no changes are made to the document after printing, clear the screen (select **File, Close**).

Undo Erased Text

Text that has been selected and deleted with the Delete or Backspace keys can be reinserted (or put back) into the document. When text is reinserted, the deleted text is retrieved to the screen. Reinserting text is referred to as "undo" or "undelete."

> The Association rules have been updated. The updated rules will be placed in your mailboxes over the weekend. The revised rules are easy to read and comprehend.

FIGURE 2.3

Practice paragraph to use for Undoing and Undeleting erased text

There are two methods for reinserting text: Undo and Undelete. When the **Undo** command is selected, the deleted text is restored to the original location. If **Undelete** is selected, the text will be restored at the location of the insertion point.

The **Undo** command must be selected immediately before another action is attempted. Text that has been reinserted using Undo can be deleted again by selecting the **Undo** command a second time.

Start-Up Instructions

- Type the paragraph shown in Figure 2.3.
- Select and delete the first sentence.

Steps to Undo Deleted Text

1. After the text has been selected and deleted, select the Undo button on the Power Bar {Alt, e, u *or* Ctrl and z}.

   Note: *The text returns to the screen and displays in its original location.*

Start-Up Instructions

- The paragraph typed previously from Figure 2.3 should be displaying in the document window.
- Select the second sentence including the space following; press **Delete**.

Steps to Undelete Deleted Text

1. After text has been selected and deleted, move the insertion point to the location where the deleted text is to be restored.

   For example, move the insertion point to the left of the first character in the first sentence.

2. Select Edit, Undelete {Alt, e, n *or* Ctrl and Shift and z}.

   Note: *The deleted text displays highlighted in the document window where the insertion point is located.*

3. Select Restore {Enter}.

   Note: *To stop the undelete process, select* ***Cancel*** *{Esc}.*

Finish-Up Instructions

- Close the document without saving (select **File**, **Close**).

The Viewer

The contents of a file can be displayed in the Viewer window before a file is opened by selecting the **View** button in the Open File or Save As dialog box. By displaying a document in the Viewer window, you can quickly scan the document's contents to determine whether or not you want to open the file. The Viewer window may not display all of the document's formatting.

Steps to Use the Viewer to View a Document

1. Select the Open button on the Power Bar {Alt, f, o *or* Ctrl and o}.
2. If necessary, select a different drive by clicking in the Drives box and then clicking on the desired drive letter.

   For example, check that the drive where your file disk is located displays at the top center of the dialog box. If necessary, select the a: or b: drive.

3. Move the mouse pointer to the desired filename and click once {press the Tab key once, press the up or down arrow key to highlight the desired filename}.

   For example, move the mouse pointer to the file named **1drill1.wpd** and click once.

4. Select the View button in the Open File dialog box.

   Note: *The Viewer window displays the text for the selected file. The displayed text cannot be edited in the Viewer window. Also note that formatting, such as centering, does not display in the Viewer.*

5. To view another file, move the mouse pointer to another filename and click once {press the up or down arrow key to highlight the desired filename}.

   For example, move the mouse pointer to the file named **2drill1r.wpd** and click once.

6. Select OK to open the file displayed in the Viewer window {Enter} or select Cancel to close the Open File dialog box without opening a file {Esc}.

   For example, select **OK** to open the file named **2drill1r.wpd**.

Finish-Up Instructions

- Close the document (select **File**, **Close**).

Using Help

WordPerfect has an online Help feature that provides detailed information about program topics and specific instructions for performing commands. The Help feature can be accessed at any time through the Help menu or from any dialog box or menu.

The Help feature can be accessed in several ways. One method is to select the **Help** menu and choose the **How Do I** option. A list of of topics displays (see Figure 2.4). The

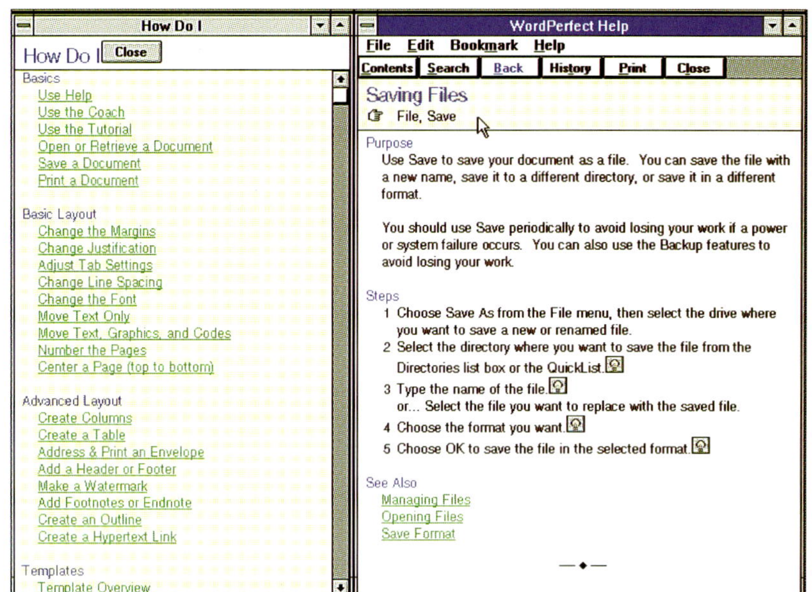

FIGURE 2.4

How Do I and WordPerfect Help windows

desired topic is selected in order to display the WordPerfect Help information for the chosen topic. A list of topics can also be displayed by selecting **Help**, **Contents**.

When a topic is selected, additional information can be viewed by selecting "jump terms," "pop-up terms," or a "lightbulb hint" icon. Words that display with an underline are referred to as *jump terms*. When a jump term is selected, a new WordPerfect Help window displays with information on a related topic. Words that display with a dotted underline are referred to as *pop-up terms*. When a pop-up term is selected, additional information displays on the screen. The *lightbulb hint* icon can be selected to obtain information on how to use a feature. To remove pop-up or lightbulb hint information from the screen, click the mouse button once.

Another method of accessing the Help feature is to select a menu command or display a dialog box and press **F1**. Help information displays for the menu command or for each option shown in the dialog box. To display help information about buttons on the Button Bar or Power Bar or other areas of the document window, the Help: What Is? feature is accessed by pressing the **Shift** and **F1** keys, moving the mouse pointer to the item, and clicking the mouse button once.

WordPerfect also provides a Coach option that walks you through the steps necessary to complete a task. With the Coach option, WordPerfect will prompt each step and if desired, hints can be viewed to assist you in completing a task. A tutorial covering basic WordPerfect features such as creating, saving, and printing files can be accessed by selecting the **Help**, **Tutorial** option.

Access Help Using the How Do I Command

1. Select the Help menu {Alt, h}.
2. Select How Do I {h}.
3. Move the mouse pointer to the desired topic and click once {press the Tab key repeatedly until the desired topic is highlighted, press Enter}.

   For example, select **Save a Document**.

   Note: The WordPerfect Help window containing information on the selected topic displays (see Figure 2.4). Continue with Steps to Print a Help Topic.

Steps to Print a Help Topic

1. Display the desired help topic in the WordPerfect Help window.

    For example, the Directory Dialog Box (Save As) help topic should be displaying in the WordPerfect Help window.

2. Select the **Print** button in the WordPerfect Help window {Alt and p}.

Steps to Exit the Help Feature

1. Select the **Close** button in the WordPerfect Help and/or in the How Do I windows {Al and L *or* Alt and F4}.

Steps to Access Help Using the Contents Command

1. Select **Help, Contents** {Alt, h, c}.
2. Move the mouse pointer to the desired topic and click once {press the Tab key repeatedly to highlight the desired topic, press Enter}.

    For example, select **Keystrokes.**

3. Select **Close** to exit the WordPerfect Help window {Alt and L *or* Alt and F4}.

Steps to Access the Help Feature for a Menu Command or Dialog Box

1. Highlight the menu command desired or display the desired dialog box.

    For example, select the Open button on the Power Bar {Alt, f, o}.

    Note: The Open File dialog box displays on the screen.

2. Press **F1**.

    Note: The WordPerfect Help window explaining the Open command displays. Additional information can be obtained by selecting words that have a dotted underline or by selecting a lightbulb hint icon. Also, in some WordPerfect Help windows, a list of related topics displays at the bottom of the help information. The additional help information can be accessed by selecting words that are underlined.

3. Select **Close** {Alt and L *or* Alt and F4}.

    Note: The dialog box for the option selected displays again on the screen.

4. If desired, complete any actions necessary using the options in the dialog box or select **Cancel** {Esc} to return to the WordPerfect document window.

Steps to Access the Help: What Is? Feature

1. Press the **Shift** and **F1** keys.

    Note: A question mark is added to the mouse pointer.

2. Move the mouse pointer to the item where information is desired and click once.

For example, move the mouse pointer to the **Undo** button on the Power Bar and click once.

Note: A WordPerfect Help window displays containing information on the Undo feature.

3. Select **Close** to exit the WordPerfect Help window {Alt and L *or* Alt and F4}.

The Next Step

Chapter Review and Activities

Self-Check Quiz

T F 1. Once text has been selected and deleted, it is not possible to undo the deleted text.

T F 2. A file can be opened by selecting the **Open** button on the Power Bar, clicking in the Drives box and selecting the drive letter where the file disk is located, and then double-clicking on the desired filename.

T F 3. Place the insertion point to the left of a character and press the **Delete** key once to delete the character.

T F 4. The **Backspace** key is used to delete characters to the left of the insertion point.

T F 5. When text is replaced, the original characters are deleted and new characters are substituted.

6. Typeover is turned on and off by pressing the _______ key.
   a. **Home**
   b. **Up arrow**
   c. **F1**
   d. **Insert**

7. Before a document can be viewed in the Viewer window, the _____ button is selected.
   a. **Save**
   b. **Open**
   c. **Close**

8. The Help feature can be used by
   a. selecting **Help**, **Contents**.
   b. pressing **F1**.
   c. selecting **Help**, **How Do I**.
   d. all of the above.

9. State the difference between the Undo and Undelete features.

10. List the steps to save and rename a file.

Enriching Language Arts Skills

Spelling/Vocabulary Words

commendable being of high quality; approved of.
nominated suggested appointment to some position.
negotiations the process of reaching an agreement.

Introductory (Dependent) Clauses

A comma should follow a dependent clause. (A dependent clause has both a subject and verb but cannot stand alone as a sentence.) An introductory dependent clause often begins with *if, in, when, since,* or *as.*

Example:

As you prepare your expense report, remember to use the updated gasoline rate schedule.

Activities

Activity 2.1—Open a File and Edit a Memorandum

1. If necessary, launch the WordPerfect program.
2. Open the file named **1act1.wpd** that was typed in Chapter 1, page 28. (Select the **Open** button on the Power Bar; if necessary, click in the Drives box and click on the drive letter where the file disk is located; double-click on the desired filename.)
3. Make the revisions shown.

Memorandum

To: Al Lindsay
From: Virginia ~~Ashlan~~ Paragon, CSS Director
Date: (Use current date)
Subject: Action Plan Version 5.0

The newest version of the Action Plan (Version 6.1) program is currently available.

An information bulletin is being sent to all consultants informing them that the instructional materials are now available at all our regional offices or from CSS. Old versions of

---

Action Plan diskettes and manual contents can be destroyed. The binders can be reused with the new material, and the diskettes can be recycled. If you have binders, please either send them to CSS or let us know the number of binders you have and we will send you the newest contents.

To install Action Plan on a PC, insert Disk 1 in drive A and type A:APINSTAL at the DOS prompt.

xx

---

4. Proofread and correct any errors.
5. Use the *new* filename **2act1r** (Chapter 2, activity 1, revised) and save the revised file. (Select **File**, **Save As**; type the new filename; if necessary, click in the Drives box; select **OK**.)
6. Print one copy (select the **Print** button on the Power Bar; choose **Print**).
7. Close the document to clear the document window (select **File**, **Close**).

Activity 2.2—View and Open a File; Edit a Memorandum

1. If necessary, launch the WordPerfect program.
2. View the files on your file disk and find the memorandum from Gene Hunter that was typed in Chapter 1, pages 29–30. Open the memorandum. (Select the **Open** button on the Power Bar; if necessary, click in the Drives box and click on the drive letter where your file disk is located; click on the first filename; select **View**; if necessary, select the next filename; select **OK** to open the file.)
3. Make the revisions shown.

Interoffice Correspondence

To: See Distribution Below — Date: (Use current date)

From: ~~Gene~~ G. Hunter and B. Wills — Subject: Reimbursement Rates

All offices have been provided with the new fuel reimbursement rates that should be placed into effect immediately. We are requesting that Each division office will photocopy a set of the rates and forward the rate sheets to all area representatives.

Also, the sales offices have been provided with the rates for all area offices under their authority. Please forward the ~~You will notice that an additional~~ ~~amount for the seasonal adjustment has been added to each rate.~~ rate sheets to your area operations manager.

If gasoline prices decline this fall, revised rates will be published to reflect any changes at that time.

xx (your initials)

Distribution:

S. Bentley
L. Jardine
W. Moyer Penny McManus Ed Salas

---

4. Proofread and correct any errors.
5. Use the *new* filename **2act2r** (Chapter 2, activity 2, revised) and save the revised file. (Select **File**, **Save As**; type the new filename; if necessary, click in the Drives box and click on the drive letter where the file disk is located; select **OK**.)
6. Print one copy (select the **Print** button on the Power Bar; choose **Print**).
7. Close the document to clear the document window (select **File**, **Close**).

Activity 2.3—Create and Edit a Memorandum

1. If necessary, launch the WordPerfect program.
2. Type the following memorandum. Use Memorandum—Style 1 (see Chapter 1, Figure 1.4).

Memorandum

To: See Distribution Below

From: D. P. Crenshaw

Date: (Use current date)

Subject: Employee Changes

Tim will end full-time employment with DPA at the end of the month. He will, however, continue working with us part-time.

Li Jean will be promoted to take over Tim's duties effective immediately.

On behalf of DPA, I want publicly to wish Tim the best of luck in his new life. By next month, we should all see one of his creations, HOW TO SURVIVE NETWORKS, in bookstores.

xx (your initials)

Distribution:

Bing Chiou
Isabel Fan
Mike Martinez
Darrell Russo

---

3. Save the file as **2act3** (Chapter 2, activity 3). (Select the **Save** button on the Power Bar; type the filename; if necessary, click in the Drives box and click on the drive letter where the file disk is located; select **OK**.)

4. Make the revisions shown.

Memorandum

To: See Distribution Below

From: Denise D. P. Crenshaw, Human Resources Director

Date: (Use current date)

Subject: Employee Changes

Tim will end full-time employment with DPA ~~at the end of the month~~. He will, however, continue working with us part-time.

Li Jean will be promoted to take over Tim's duties effective immediately. If you have training or graphic needs, please direct your request to Li Jean.

On behalf of DPA, I want publicly to wish Tim the best of luck in his new life. By next month, we should all see one of his creations, HOW TO SURVIVE NETWORKS, in bookstores .

¶ Tim's work at DPA contributed to our professional-looking courses and slides and to more knowledgeable coworkers on WordPerfect for Windows and PageMaker.

xx

Distribution:

Bing Chiou
Isabel Fan
Mike Martinez
Darrell Russo

---

5. Proofread and correct any errors.
6. Use the *new* filename **2act3r** (Chapter 2, activity 3, revised) and save the revised file. (Select **File**, **Save As**; type the new filename; if necessary, click in the Drives box and click on the drive letter where the file disk is located; select **OK**.)
7. Print one copy (select the **Print** button on the Power Bar, choose **Print**).
8. Close the document to clear the document window (select **File**, **Close**).

Challenge Your Skills

Skill 2.1—Create and Edit a Memorandum

1. If necessary, launch the WordPerfect program.
2. Use Memorandum—Style 1 (see Chapter 1, Figure 1.4) and the following information.
   a. Send the memorandum to All Jacobson Transport Drivers from T. D. Van Wetter. The subject of the memorandum is Vehicle Inspection.
   b. Use the current date; include your reference initials.

When delivering vehicles, it is important to inspect each vehicle thoroughly. The following are items to assist you with delivery inspections.

The floor mats will be coded. Codes are located in the trunk on a sticker, under the mat, or on the trunk lid. The codes begin with a "B." For example, B-36, B-37, etc.

Remember to submit the inspection checklists to your immediate supervisor. If you have any questions, please contact me by the end of next week at 555-6880.

---

3. Save the file; use the filename **2skill1** (Chapter 2, skill 1).
4. Use the following information to edit the memorandum:
   a. Change the T. in the From line to Theresa and add her title, Manager.
   b. Delete the last sentence in the second paragraph that begins "For example, . . ."
   c. Insert the following new paragraph between the last two paragraphs:
      The vans have fog lights. Check the fog light switch that is located on the left side of the dashboard.
   d. Change the phone number in the last paragraph to (408) 555-6999.
5. Proofread and correct any errors.
6. Use the *new* filename **2skill1r** (Chapter 2, skill 1, revised) and save the file.
7. Print one copy of the memo.

8. Close the document.

Skill 2.2—Create and Edit a Memorandum

1. If necessary, launch the WordPerfect program.
2. Use Memorandum—Style 2 (see Chapter 1, Figure 1.6) and the following information.
   a. Send the memorandum to Manuel Espinosa from J. C. Kornhaus. The subject of the memorandum is PLD Briefing.
   b. Use the current date; include your reference initials.

Thank you for your help in preparing the materials for the Jefferson County Board of Supervisors last week.

As a result of your work, our laboratory team was able to provide a well documented presentation that responded to our critics and answered the questions posed by the Supervisors. We hope to have results of the briefing before the next board meeting.

In the future, if I can be of any assistance to you, please contact me at (314) 555-6767.

---

3. Save the file; use the filename **2skill2** (Chapter 2, skill 2).
4. Use the following information to edit the memorandum:
   a. Change the subject of the memo to Preliminary Lab Data Briefing.
   b. In the first paragraph insert the words PLD Briefing before the word materials.
   c. Insert the following paragraph between the last two paragraphs:
      I deeply appreciate the extra effort you put forth to meet the many deadlines required in putting together this briefing package.
   d. Two returns after your reference initials, use the following format to indicate that a copy of the memo will be sent to another person.
      c: Jaimi Callegari, Lab Director
5. Proofread and correct any errors.
6. Use the *new* filename **2skill2r** (Chapter 2, skill 2, revised) and save the file.
7. Print one copy of the memo.
8. Close the document.

➾ Skill 2.3—Create and Edit a Memorandum; Language Arts

1. If necessary, launch the WordPerfect program.
2. Use Memorandum—Style 2 (Chapter 1, Figure 1.6) and the following information.

a. Send the memorandum to Local 70 Shop Stewards from Jane Avery. The subject of the memo is Contract Negotiations.

b. Use the current date; include your reference initials.

c. The memo is to be distributed to the following persons (alphabetize by last name): Tamis, D.; Kerdasha, P.; Metzger, A.; DuBoce, R.; Pham, N.; Giovanette, M.; and Taslim, E.

d. Correct three spelling words and two punctuation errors. Remember to check for the spelling words and grammar rules discussed in both Chapters 1 and 2.

Negotations on a new contract are set to begin next month. In order to avoid any pitfalls we need to have a well-prepared bargaining team. Last year's bargaining team did a comendable job and worked hard to negotiate a strong, well-written contract.

A new bargaining team will be selected by secret ballot at the membership meeting next week. A list of members who have been nomminated to serve on the bargaining team is available at the Union Hall.

Also a form requesting ideas on the contract issues to be negotiated can be picked up at the Union Hall. Some of the areas open for negotiation are: wages, eligibility for retirement benefits, medical benefits, conference reimbursements, and working conditions.

---

3. Save the file; use the filename **2skill3** (Chapter 2, skill 3).
4. Use the following information to edit the memorandum:
   a. Delete the second sentence of the first paragraph.
   b. Insert the following sentence at the end of the second paragraph:
      If desired, members can drop by and pick up the list before the meeting.
   c. Insert the following new paragraph after the last paragraph:
      Please remind union members at your location of the upcoming membership meeting. If a union member cannot be present, contact George Nazzaro for proxy forms. Let me know if I can be of further assistance.
5. Proofread and correct any errors.
6. Use the *new* filename **2skill3r** (Chapter 2, skill 3, revised) and save the file.
7. Print one copy and close the document.
8. If you have completed your work, exit WordPerfect (select **File**, **Exit**).

CHAPTER 3

Create Business Letters

Features Covered

- Use the automatic date feature
- Change justification
- Use bold, underline, and italic text attributes
- Change margins
- Change fonts
- Use Speller
- Use Page Zoom Full view

Objectives and Introduction

After successfully completing this chapter, you will be able to use the automatic date feature, change justification, use text attributes such as bold, italic, and underline, and change margins to create business letters. Convenient WordPerfect features such as fonts, Speller, and Page Zoom Full view are often used in preparing business letters.

Business Letters

A letter is formal written communication used to convey information from one business to another or from one individual to another. Business letters are one of the most important types of written communications.

Traditionally, letters have followed one of two styles: a modified block or block style. With the development of word processing machines and programs, the block style has become the most frequently used letter style. With the block style, all lines of the letter begin at the left margin (see Figure 3.1).

Another style of letter that is now being used is the AMS (Administrative Management Society) letter simplified style. The AMS simplified style omits the salutation and complimentary closing. A subject line and the typewritten signature are

FIGURE 3.1

Traditional style letter

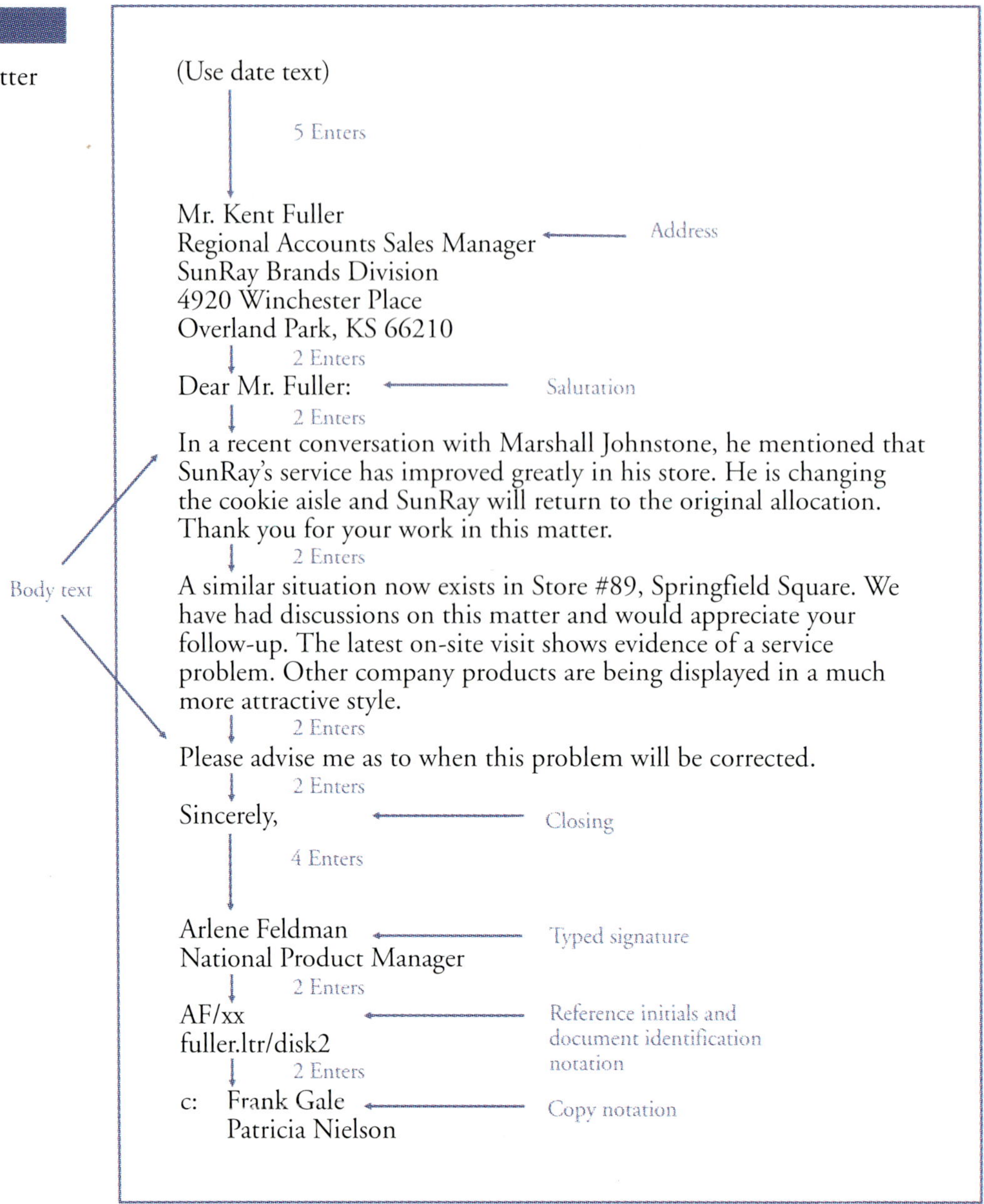
(Use date text)

5 Enters

Mr. Kent Fuller
Regional Accounts Sales Manager
SunRay Brands Division
4920 Winchester Place
Overland Park, KS 66210

2 Enters

Dear Mr. Fuller:

2 Enters

In a recent conversation with Marshall Johnstone, he mentioned that SunRay's service has improved greatly in his store. He is changing the cookie aisle and SunRay will return to the original allocation. Thank you for your work in this matter.

2 Enters

A similar situation now exists in Store #89, Springfield Square. We have had discussions on this matter and would appreciate your follow-up. The latest on-site visit shows evidence of a service problem. Other company products are being displayed in a much more attractive style.

2 Enters

Please advise me as to when this problem will be corrected.

2 Enters

Sincerely,

4 Enters

Arlene Feldman
National Product Manager

2 Enters

AF/xx
fuller.ltr/disk2

2 Enters

c: Frank Gale
Patricia Nielson

typed in uppercase letters. Like the traditional block style, all lines of the letter begin at the left margin (blocked). See Figure 3.2.

At the bottom of a letter the following information may be included:

- ☐ The author's initials in capital letters and the typist's initials in lowercase letters, e.g., AF/xx (the x's indicate where you type your initials).
- ☐ A document identification notation showing the filename and location of the document, e.g., fuller.ltr/disk2.
- ☐ If a photocopy of the letter is to be sent to another person(s), a copy notation is typed. Generally a photocopy is indicated by a lowercase "c" followed by a colon (c:). Press the **Tab** key once and type the name; press **Enter**.

  Note: *Always press the* ***Tab*** *key before each listed name; otherwise the names may not align when fonts are changed.*

FIGURE 3.2

AMS simplified style letter

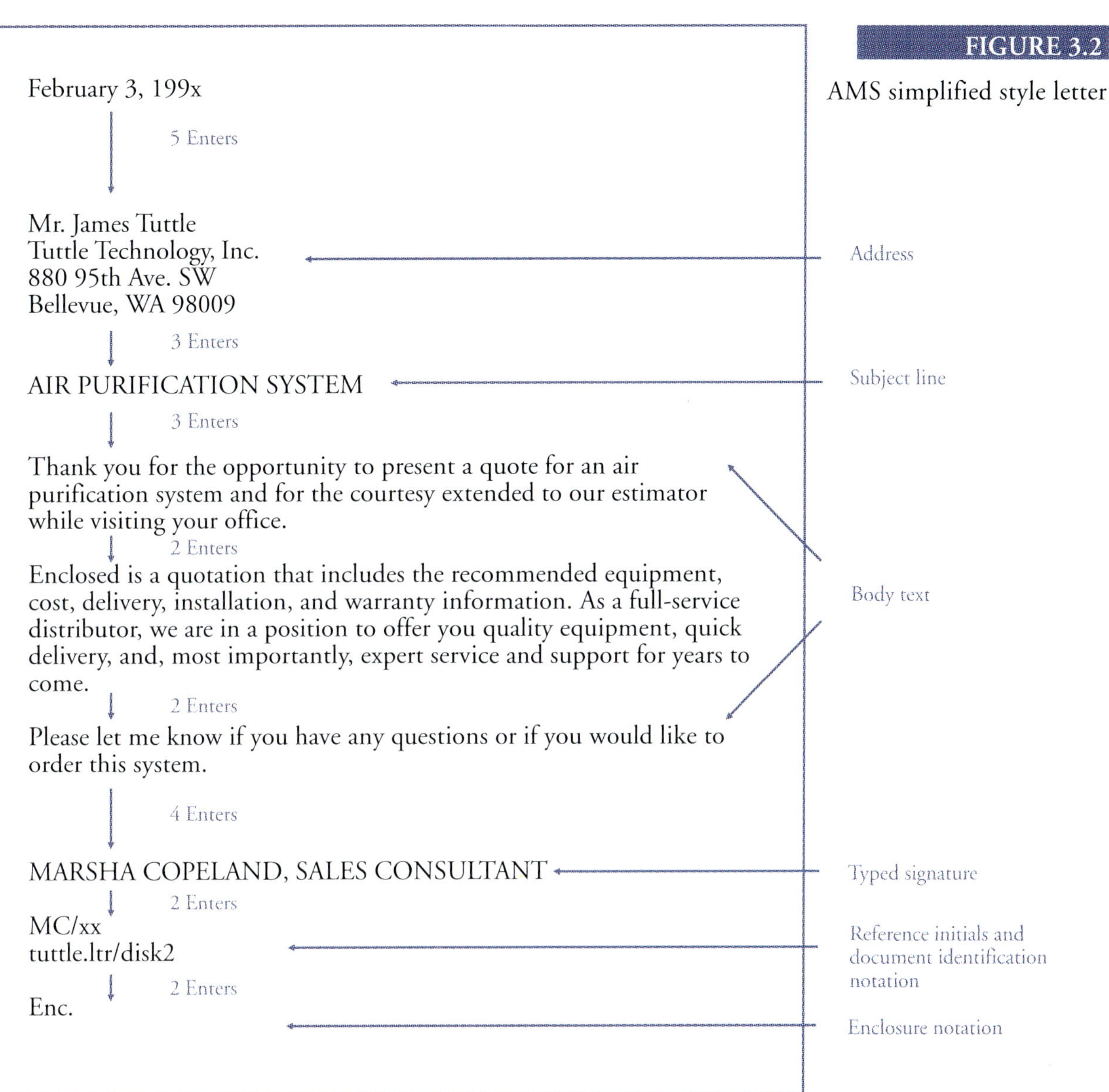
February 3, 199x

Mr. James Tuttle
Tuttle Technology, Inc.
880 95th Ave. SW
Bellevue, WA 98009

AIR PURIFICATION SYSTEM

Thank you for the opportunity to present a quote for an air purification system and for the courtesy extended to our estimator while visiting your office.

Enclosed is a quotation that includes the recommended equipment, cost, delivery, installation, and warranty information. As a full-service distributor, we are in a position to offer you quality equipment, quick delivery, and, most importantly, expert service and support for years to come.

Please let me know if you have any questions or if you would like to order this system.

MARSHA COPELAND, SALES CONSULTANT

MC/xx
tuttle.ltr/disk2

Enc.

- ☐ If the letter contains a statement that an item(s) is being enclosed, type an enclosure notation two **Enters** below the document identification notation or two **Enters** below a copy notation, e.g., type **Enc.**

After a business letter has been typed, formatted, reviewed, and proofread, a final copy is printed. A final letter is customarily printed on letterhead stationery. The letterhead information usually includes the company name, address, phone number, and fax number. Typically, the letterhead information is preprinted on company stationery. Today, however, many individuals who use word processing and desktop publishing programs create their own letterheads. In Chapter 13, a letterhead will be created. A letter printed on company letterhead in final form will look similar to Figure 3.3.

FIGURE 3.3

Traditional style letter printed on letterhead

SunRay Industries
580 Deharo Street, San Francisco, CA 94107
(415) 555-8303 FAX (415) 555-8318

April 2, 199x

Mr. Kent Fuller
Regional Accounts Sales Manager
SunRay Brands Division
4920 Winchester Place
Overland Park, KS 66210

Dear Mr. Fuller:

In a recent conversation with Marshall Johnstone, he mentioned that **SunRay's** service has improved greatly in his store. He is changing the cookie aisle and **SunRay** will return to the original allocation. ***Thank you for your work in this matter.***

A similar situation now exists in Store #89, Springfield Square. We have had discussions on this matter and would appreciate your follow-up. The latest on-site visit shows evidence of a service problem. Other company products are being displayed in a much more attractive style.

Please advise me as to when this problem will be corrected.

Sincerely,

Arlene Feldman
National Product Manager

AF/xx
fuller.ltr/disk2

c: Frank Gale
Patricia Nielson

Automatic Date Feature

WordPerfect provides two methods for automatically inserting the current date into a document: **Date Text** and **Date Code**. In order for the date to be inserted by WordPerfect, the current date must be stored in the computer's memory.

When **Insert, Date, Date Text** is selected, the current date is placed in the document by WordPerfect. If the document is opened on a different day, the date will not change unless edited manually. The current date can also be inserted into a document by selecting the **Date Text** button on the Button Bar.

When **Insert, Date, Date Code** is selected, a special code is inserted by WordPerfect. If the document is opened on a later date, the date is automatically changed to the current date.

Different formats for the current date can be inserted by selecting **Insert, Date, Date Format** and choosing a desired date format option in the Date Format dialog box. For example, the day can be printed followed by the month and year (2 May 1994).

Start-Up Instructions

- An empty document window should be displayed on the screen.

Use the Date Text Feature

1. Select the Date Text button on the Button Bar {Alt, i, d, t *or* Ctrl and d}.

   Note: *The current date is inserted at the location of the insertion point. If necessary, the date can be changed by the user.*

Finish-Up Instructions

- Type the traditional block style letter shown in Figure 3.1 on page 52 using the spacing shown. Use wordwrap to type the body text paragraphs of the letter.
- After typing the letter, use the filename **3drill1** and save the file (select the **Save** button on the Power Bar; type the filename; if necessary, click in the Drives box and click on the drive letter where the file disk is located; select **OK**).

Justification

The term *justification* in WordPerfect is used to describe the alignment of text in relation to the left and right margins. The five different types of justification are Left, Right, Center, Full, and All. (See Figure 3.4.) With Left justification, text is aligned at the left margin and is not aligned at the right margin (ragged right). Left justification is the default setting for WordPerfect 6.0. Right justification is the opposite of Left justification, i.e., text is aligned at the right margin and not at the left margin (ragged left). Center justification aligns text so that an equal amount of blank space displays left and right of the centered text. Full justification adjusts lines to begin and end exactly at the left and right margins. The All option is used to evenly space letters of a title or heading between the left and right margins.

When justification is changed, a code is inserted at the beginning of the paragraph where the insertion point is located. The selected justification remains in effect from that location forward in the document or until a different justification is chosen.

In addition to the Right justification type, WordPerfect provides a Flush Right alignment feature for aligning text at the right margin. The Flush Right alignment feature is used to right align a single line or a portion of a line. However, in WordPerfect, the Right justification type is used to right align multiple lines.

The Center alignment (see Chapter 1) and the Center justification are the two types of horizontal centering provided by WordPerfect. When the Center alignment command is used before text is typed, the line is centered and the insertion point returns to the left margin after the Enter key is pressed. The code displayed in Reveal

FIGURE 3.4

The five types of justification

This is an example of Left justification. The text is aligned at the left margin.	This is an example of Right justification. The text is aligned at the right margin.	This is an example of Center justification. An equal amount of blank space displays on the left and right of the centered text.
This is an example of Full justification. Text begins and ends exactly at the left and right margin, except for the last line of the paragraph.	The All justification option is used to evenly space letters between the left and right margins including short lines. This is used for titles and headings, e.g., W o r d P e r f e c t .	

Codes for Center alignment is *Hd Center on Marg.* However, if a group of lines is selected (and no codes or text follow) and the Center alignment command is used, the insertion point remains in the center of the document window.

When the Center justification command is used before text is typed, the line(s) is centered and after the Enter key is pressed the insertion point remains in the center of the document screen. However, if text is selected, only the blocked lines are centered. The expanded code *Just:Center* displays in Reveal Codes.

With Full justification, additional spaces are placed between words in order to align the text at both the left and right margins. The extra spaces between words may make the text difficult to read and may be visually unattractive. Therefore, Left justification is used for most business correspondence and Full justification may be used for documents such as books.

The All option places additional space between words and between letters in words and is useful when creating a heading for a newsletter (see Chapter 13). Also, the All justification option fully justifies the last line in a paragraph.

Start-Up Instructions

- The file named **3drill1.wpd** should be displayed in the document window.

Steps to Change Justification

1. The insertion point should be located where the justification is to be changed.

   For example, place the insertion point at the beginning of the document (**Ctrl** and **Home**).

2. Move the mouse pointer to the **Justification** button on the Power Bar. Press and hold the left mouse button {Alt, L, L, j}.

   Note: *A drop-down list of justification choices displays.*

3. Move the mouse pointer to highlight the desired justification type.

   For example, highlight **Full** {f}.

4. Release the mouse button.

Finish-Up Instructions

- Use the *new* filename **3drill1.ful** and save the file on your file disk (select **File**, **Save As**; type the filename; if necessary, click in the Drives box and click on the drive letter where the file disk is located; select **OK**).
- Print one copy (select the **Print** button on the Power Bar; choose **Print**).

Text Attributes

Emphasis can be added to text by using text attributes such as bold, underline, and italic. Text attributes can be set in the Font dialog box by selecting the desired attribute(s) in the Appearance box. In addition, text attributes can be set by using the **Bold**, **Underline**, and **Italic** options on the Power Bar. More than one text attribute can be applied to the same text characters, e.g., **bold and underline**.

The bold text attribute prints words darker on the page as compared to other printed words. Text to be printed in bold will be displayed darker than the other characters on the screen. When bold is selected, WordPerfect inserts a bold code on each side of the text. Display Reveal Codes to view the bold codes.

Words are underlined in printed text to show emphasis. Once the text to be underlined is selected and the underline feature is used, the text displays underlined in the document window. Traditionally, underlining was used in the place of italic because many typewriters were unable to create italic text. Since most printers now support italic, the trend is to replace underline with italic or bold to add emphasis.

The italic text attribute prints text somewhat slanted to the right. However, there are some dot matrix printers that do not print italicized text. Once the text to be italicized is selected and the italic attribute is applied, the text displays slightly slanted on the screen.

Start-Up Instructions

- The file named **3drill1.ful** should be displayed in the document window.

Steps to Bold Text

1. Select the text to be printed in bold (see Chapter 2, page 35 for information on selecting text).

   For example, select **SunRay's** in the first sentence of the letter.

2. Select the **Bold** button [B] on the Power Bar {Ctrl and b}.

Steps to Underline Text

1. Select the text to be underlined (see Chapter 2, page 35 for information on selecting text).

   For example, select **Store #89, Springfield Square** in the first sentence of the second paragraph.

2. Select the **Underline** button [U] on the Power Bar {Ctrl and u}.

Steps to Italicize Text

1. Select the text to be italicized (see Chapter 2, page 35) for information on selecting text).

   For example, select the final sentence of the first paragraph.

2. Select the **Italic** button on the Power Bar {Ctrl and i}.

Finish-Up Instructions

- Select the word SunRay in the second sentence of the first paragraph and bold the text.
- Select the final sentence in the first paragraph and bold the text. This sentence will be both bold and italic.
- Use the *new* filename **3drill1.txt** and save the file on your file disk (select **File, Save As**; type the new filename; if necessary, click in the Drives box and click on the drive letter where the file disk is located; select **OK**).

  Note: The following Steps to Remove Bold, Underline, or Italic Text Attributes are for your information.

Remove Bold, Underline, or Italic Text Attributes

1. Select the desired text.
2. Select the **Bold, Underline,** or **Italic** buttons on the Power Bar {Ctrl and b, Ctrl and u, *or* Ctrl and i}.

Change Margins

Generally, WordPerfect's default (preset) margins are used to print a final letter. If a letter is unusually short or long, however, it may be desirable to change the document's margins. Margins can be changed in the Margins dialog box or by using the Ruler Bar (see Chapter 7, page 158).

The top and bottom margins are preset to 1 inch. Using a standard size 8½ x 11-inch paper and a combined top and bottom margin of 2 inches, 9 inches remain for typed lines on a page. Depending on the information preprinted in a letterhead, the top margin can vary between 2 and 2½ inches. The bottom margin on an average length letter generally remains unchanged. The left and right document margins are preset for 1 inch. With these settings, 6.5 inches are available across the page.

When the margins are changed, codes display in the Reveal Codes window for each changed margin, for example, *Lft Mar, Rgt Mar, Top Mar.* When a margin code is highlighted in Reveal Codes, the code is expanded to show the margin measurement, e.g., *Lft Mar:1.5".*

Once the margins have been changed, the new margins remain effective from that location forward in the document or until different margins are selected. Therefore, if the margins are to be effective for the entire document, the insertion point should be located at the beginning of the document before the margins are changed.

The margins can be changed in the document at any time, i.e., before or after the document is typed. Changing the margins is best accomplished after the document is completed, because a decision can more easily be made as to whether margins should be changed depending on the length of the document. After typing a document, estimate the desired placement of the document. A letter should be printed on the page with the space around the edges of the letter evenly balanced.

The number of words in the letter body text and the depth of the letterhead are used to make decisions regarding margin changes. The following are some suggested margin settings for letters:

	Top Margin	**Left and Right Margins**
Short letter (under 100 words*)	2.5"	2.0"
Average letter (100–200 words)	2.0"	1.5"
Long letter (over 200 words)	1.75"	1.0"

*See Document Information in Chapter 9.

Before printing the final letter, preview the entire document on the screen by selecting the **Page Zoom Full** button on the Power Bar (see Page Zoom View later in this chapter).

Start-Up Instructions

- The file named **3drill1.txt** should be displayed in the document window, or type the letter shown in Figure 3.1.
- The insertion point must be located at the top of the document.

Steps to Change Margins

1. Place the insertion point at the location in the document where the margin change is to take effect.

   For example, locate the insertion point at the top of the document (**Ctrl** and **Home**).

2. Select **Layout, Margins** {Alt, L, m *or* Ctrl and F8}.

   Note: *The Margins dialog box displays.*

3. *To change the left margin,* move the mouse pointer to the box located beside the word **Left**; double-click to highlight the measurement and type the desired margin in inches {Alt and L, type desired margin, press Enter}.

   For example, type **1.5**. (Do not type the last period.)

   Note: *With the margin amount displayed in the measurement box highlighted, the new amount is typed, automatically replacing the existing figure(s). If the insertion point displays in the measurement amount box and the amount is not highlighted, the original amount must be deleted and the new amount typed. Typing the final zero and the quotation mark is not necessary.*

FIGURE 3.5

Margins dialog box

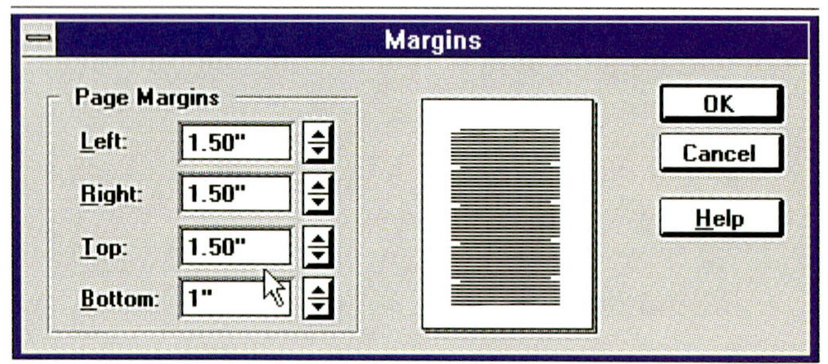

To change the right margin, move the mouse pointer to the box located beside the word **Right**, double-click to highlight the measurement, and type the desired margin in inches {Alt and r, type desired margin, press Enter}.

For example, type **1.5**. (Do not type the last period.)

To change the top margin, move the mouse pointer to the box located beside the word **Top**, double-click to highlight the measurement, and type the desired margin in inches {Alt and t, type desired margin, press Enter}. (See Figure 3.5.)

For example, type **1.5**. (Do not type the last period.)

To change the bottom margin, move the mouse pointer to the box located beside the word **Bottom**, double-click to highlight the measurement, and type the desired margin in inches {Alt and b, type desired margin, press Enter}.

For example, check that the default margin of 1" displays.

4. Select **OK** to accept the new margin settings {press Enter twice}.

Finish-Up Instructions

- Use the *new* filename **3drill1.mar** and save the file on your file disk (select **File**, **Save As**; type the filename; if necessary, click in the Drives box and click on the drive letter where the file disk is located; select **OK**).
- Print one copy (select the **Print** button on the Power Bar; choose **Print**).

Font Changes

By using a variety of typefaces (fonts) and sizes, the appearance of letters, reports, résumés, or other business documents can be enhanced. A typeface is a specific design of type (shape), such as Arial or Times New Roman. A font includes all the letters, numbers, symbols, and punctuation marks for a given typeface in one size and style. For example, Arial 14-point bold is one font and Times New Roman 10-point italic is another font.

Each printer has one or more built-in fonts. Many built-in fonts, such as Courier, are monospaced and fixed-pitch (i.e., each character is allocated the same amount of horizontal space).

WordPerfect provides additional fonts that can be used with any printer that can print graphics (if necessary, see your instructor). The fonts provided by WordPerfect, such as Arrus BT and Humanst521 Lt BT, are proportional and scalable (i.e., the horizontal space allocated for each character varies based on the width of the character and the characters can be printed in almost any size).

These scalable/proportional fonts are measured in points. There are approximately 72 points in an inch. A 24-point character is approximately one-quarter of an inch tall. A ruler at the back of this book shows the letter "E" in various point sizes and can be used to assist you in determining appropriate point sizes to use in different documents. Generally, a 10- to 12-point font is used for the text of business letters, memorandums, and reports.

Traditionally when using a typewriter with monospaced fonts, the Spacebar was pressed twice after a final punctuation mark. When using proportional spaced fonts, the Spacebar is pressed only once after a final punctuation mark, because a single space is sufficient to visually separate sentences.

Font characteristics such as font name, font size, and appearance (bold, underline, italics) can be changed by selecting the **Font** option on the Layout menu. In addition, the font can be changed by selecting the **Font Face** button on the Power Bar; the font size can be changed by selecting the **Font Size** button on the Power Bar; and the appearance of text can be changed by selecting the **Bold**, **Underline**, or **Italic** buttons on the Power Bar. When the **Font Face** button is selected, the last four fonts used are displayed at the top of the Font Face list.

The font change is effective from the location of the insertion point forward in the document or until another font is selected. However, if text is selected and the font is changed, the new font will be in effect for the selected text only. Font codes can be viewed in the Reveal Codes window.

Start-Up Instructions

- The file named **3drill1.mar** should be displayed in the document window.

Change Font Name, Size, and/or Appearance

Note: Changing fonts is most effectively accomplished using a mouse. Therefore, keystrokes have not been included with the following steps.

1. Place the insertion point at the location where the font change is to begin or select the text to be affected.

   For example, place the insertion point at the top of the document.

2. Move the mouse pointer to the **Font Face** button FFF on the Power Bar and click once.

   Note: A list of available fonts displays.

3. Move the mouse pointer to the desired font name and click once.

   For example, select **Arrus BT** or **make a decision of your own**.

   Note: The text has been changed to display the new font. Use Reveal Codes (Alt and F3) to view the font code.

To Change the Font Size and Appearance for Selected Text Only

4. Select the text for which the font is to be changed.

   For example, select the document notation (**fuller.ltr/disk2**).

5. Select **Layout, Font**.

   Note: The Font dialog box displays containing font names, font sizes, and text appearance.

6. Move the mouse pointer to the desired font size and click once.

   For example, select **10** in the Size box or **make a decision of your own**.

7. Move the mouse pointer to the desired text attribute in the Appearance box and click once.

   For example, select **Italic**.

   Note: *WordPerfect displays a sample of the chosen font name, size, and appearance in the Resulting Font box located below the font list. The displayed sample is only an approximate size and style.*

8. Select OK {press Enter}.

To Change Font Size Only

9. Move the insertion pointer to the location where the new font size is to take effect or select the text to be affected.

   For example, move the insertion point to the left of the **c** in the copy notation.

10. Move the mouse pointer to the **Font Size** button [‡A] on the Power Bar and click once.

11. Move the mouse pointer to the desired size and click once.

    For example, select **10**.

Finish-Up Instructions

- A final letter printed on letterhead is shown in Figure 3.3.
- Use the *new* filename **3drill1.fon** and save the file on your file disk (select **File, Save As**; type the new filename; if necessary, click in the Drives box and click on the drive where the file disk is located; select **OK**).
- Print one copy (select the **Print** button on the Power Bar; select **Print**).
- Close the document (select **File**, **Close**).

The Speller

The Speller is a WordPerfect feature that checks the spelling of each word and identifies duplicate words and irregular capitalization in a document. When a word is found that is not in one of WordPerfect's dictionaries, a list of words similar to the unrecognized word is displayed on the screen. If the correctly spelled word is displayed in the list of words, it can be selected. If the correctly spelled word is not displayed in the list, the word can be added to one of the WordPerfect dictionaries.

WordPerfect has two types of dictionaries: a main dictionary and supplemental dictionaries. The main dictionary is used to check the spelling of words for all documents. Supplemental dictionaries are created by individual users of WordPerfect and contain terms that an individual uses frequently. For example, a medical secretary might create a supplemental dictionary that contains medical terms. An unlimited number of supplemental dictionaries can be created.

If an entire document is to be checked for spelling accuracy, the insertion point can be located anywhere in the document. If only part of the document or a single word is to be checked, the desired portion of the document or the individual word is selected.

If the same word is typed twice, the Speller will identify the duplicated word. The duplicated word can be removed by selecting **Replace**. To leave both occurrences of the duplicated word, **Skip Once** is selected.

The Speller will also identify words that contain irregular capitalization, such as tHe or THe. When a word with irregular capitalization is identified, the Speller suggests that the word be changed to all uppercase letters, all lowercase letters, or initial capital, e.g., THE, the, or The.

Not all errors in a document are discovered by the spelling command. For example, words easily misspelled or mistyped, such as there/their, form/from, she/he, are not identified as incorrect words. Therefore, once the document is checked for spelling, it should also be carefully proofread for accurate meaning.

Start-Up Instructions

Note: The icon indicates that the data (text) is available on disk. The data disk is supplied to your instructor.

- Open the file named **3drill2.wpd** which is located on the data disk (select the **Open** button on the Power Bar; if necessary, click in the Drives box and click on the drive where the data disk is located; double-click on the filename).
- Use the following steps and spell-check the file named **3drill2.wpd**. After using the Speller, be sure to proofread the document.

Steps to Use the Speller

1. Select the Speller button on the Power Bar {Alt, t, s *or* Ctrl and F1}.

   Note: The Speller dialog box displays. The name of the document to be reviewed displays in the Title bar of the dialog box.

2. Select Start to begin the spell check {press Enter}.

   *Note: The first unrecognized word is highlighted in the document and displays to the right of the words "Not found" in the Speller dialog box (see Figure 3.6). WordPerfect displays the word that most closely matches the spelling of the unrecognized word in the **Replace With** box and the word is highlighted at the top of the list of suggested words.*

FIGURE 3.6

Speller dialog box

3. *To accept the highlighted word,* select Replace {Alt and r}. If desired, another word in the list of suggestions can be highlighted.

For example, select **Replace** to accept the suggested word "being."

If the correctly spelled word is shown in the list of suggestions, select the suggested word and select Replace {press the down arrow key to highlight the word, r}. The identified word is corrected on the screen and the spell check continues.

4. *To delete one occurrence of a duplicated word,* select Replace {Alt and r}.

For example, select **Replace** to delete one occurrence of the word "of."

To retain both occurrences of a duplicated word, select Skip Once {Alt and o}.

5. T*o correct irregular capitalization,* select the desired suggestion and choose Replace {Alt and r}.

For example, "and" should display in the Replace With box. Select **Replace.**

6. If the correct spelling of a word is not on the list, other options can be selected.

   a. Select Skip Once to skip the current instance of the word {Alt and o}.

      For example, select **Skip Once** to skip the reference initial "PJM" and continue with the spell check. Select **Skip Once** to skip the document name and file location.

   b. Select Skip Always to ignore the word throughout the remainder of the document {Alt and a}.

   c. Select Add to add the word to a WordPerfect supplemental dictionary {Alt and d}. The word will be added to the default supplemental dictionary. *To choose a different supplemental dictionary,* choose Add to and select the desired dictionary {Alt and t}.

   d. Click in the Replace With box and type the correct word in the document. Select Replace {Alt and w, type the correction, Enter}.

      Note: *To discontinue the Speller before completion, select* ***Close*** *{Alt and c}.*

7. When the entire document has been checked, the message "Spell-check completed. Close Speller?" displays. Select Yes {press Enter}.

Finish-Up Instructions

- Use the *new* filename **3drill2.spe** and save the file on your file disk (select **File, Save As**; type the new filename; if necessary, click in the Drives box and click on the drive where the file disk is located; select **OK**).
- Print one copy (select the **Print** button on the Power Bar; choose **Print**).

Page Zoom Full View

A full document page can be displayed by selecting the **Page Zoom Full** button on the Power Bar. Using Page Zoom Full view to display a document assists in making decisions concerning the alignment of text and the amount of blank space in the mar-

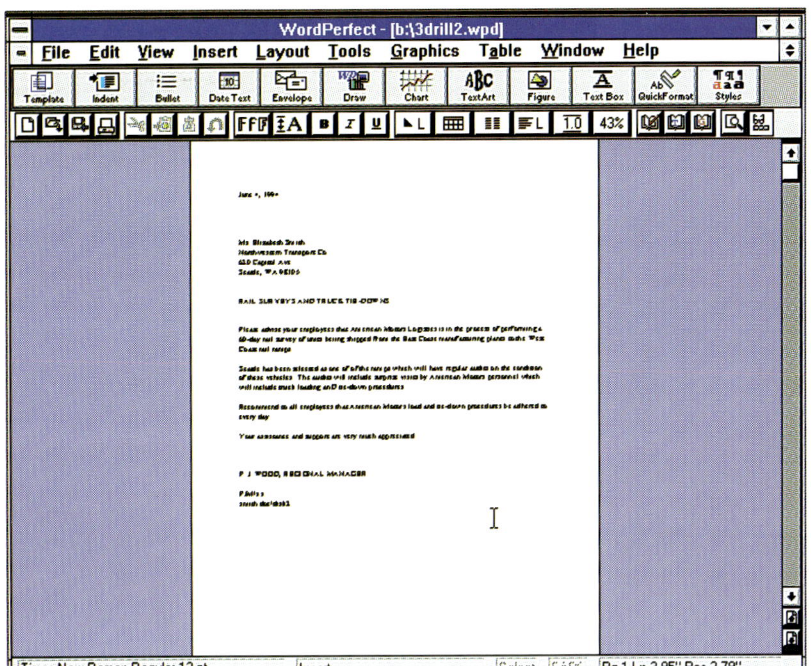

FIGURE 3.7

Page Zoom Full view

gins. When the Page Zoom Full button is selected a second time, the view returns to the original view size. Other zoom views can be selected by choosing the **Zoom** button on the Power Bar and choosing the desired view (see Steps to Use Zoom Feature, Chapter 14, page 337).

Start-Up Instructions

- A mouse must be used to complete the following steps.
- The file named **3drill2.spe** should be displayed in the document window.

Steps to Use Page Zoom Full View

1. Select the Page Zoom Full button on the Power Bar.

   Note: The entire document page displays on the screen. (see Figure 3.7).

2. To exit Page Zoom Full view, select the **Page Zoom Full** button again.

Start-Up Instructions

- Optional. Type the AMS simplified style letter shown in Figure 3.2. Use the Speller to review the document for spelling errors. After using the Speller, be sure to proofread the document. Use the filename **3drill3** and save the file.
- Print one copy (select the **Print** button on the Power Bar; choose **Print**).
- Close the document (select **File**, **Close**).

The Next Step

Chapter Review and Activities

Self-Check Quiz

T F 1. Once a font change is made for selected text, the changed font is effective from the location of the insertion point forward in the document or until another font is selected.

T F 2. When using the Speller, you can correct a word that is not found in any of the WordPerfect dictionaries.

T F 3. The document identification notation is typed above the reference initials.

T F 4. In the traditional letter style, the **Enter** key is pressed four times after typing the last paragraph.

5. The ______ button is selected to view an entire page in the document window.
   a. **Open**
   b. **Page Zoom Full**
   c. **Print**

6. WordPerfect's default margins are
   a. 1" top and bottom; 1.25" left and right.
   b. 1" left and right; 1.25" top and bottom.
   c. 1" left, right, top and bottom.

7. The current date can be placed in a document by selecting the ______
   a. **Date Text** button on the Power Bar.
   b. **Date Code** button on the Button Bar.
   c. **Date Text** button on the Button Bar.

8. List the top, left, and right margins that are suggested for an average letter (100–200 words).

9. List the five different types of justification.

10. Explain the difference between Right justification and the Flush Right alignment feature.

Enriching Language Arts Skills

Spelling/Vocabulary Words

telecommunications electronic transfer of information between two locations.

tailored made to fit a specific need.

existence having presence; being; having life.

description a verbal or written explanation.

Appositives

Appositives are words that immediately follow a noun and further identify the noun but usually are not necessary to the meaning of the sentence. Appositives are set off by commas.

Example:

Ester Tam, a copyeditor for eight years, will be our new senior editor.

Activities

Activity 3.1—Create a Traditional Style Letter; Use the Bold Text Attribute

1. Type the following letter using the traditional style letter (see Figure 3.1 on page 52).

(Use date text)

Hugh and Mary Ellis
752 Cherry Rd.
Newport News, VA 23602

Dear Mr. and Mrs. Ellis:

During the last six months, you have visited Horizon Estates on the Chesapeake Bay. You have experienced the panoramic views and the quiet country setting. And you have seen the large, family-oriented floor plans.

Now we have some exciting news! Horizon Estates is releasing seven new homes for sale. We invite you to revisit our sales office to choose from the home sites now available.

The moment you have been waiting for is NOW! It is time to own your own home at Horizon Estates.

Cordially,

Angela H. Santos
Sales Manager

AHS/xx
ellis.ltr/d1

---

2. Bold each occurrence of the words "Horizon Estates" (select the text; select the **Bold** button on the Power Bar).
3. Save the file on your file disk; use the filename **3act1** (Chapter 3, activity 1). (Select the **Save** button on the Power Bar; type the filename; if necessary, click in the Drives box and click on the drive letter where the file disk is located; select **OK**.)
4. Print one copy (select the **Print** button on the Power Bar; choose **Print**).
5. Close the document (select **File**, **Close**).

Activity 3.2—Create a Traditional Style Letter; Use Full Justification; Change Margins and Font

1. Type the following letter using the traditional style letter (see Figure 3.1 on page 52).

(Use date text)

Ms. Marcy Flores
Manager, Systems and Processing
Turtle Markets
850 W. Natanes Rd.
Phoenix, AZ 85017-4168

Dear Marcy:

Thank you for taking the time to speak with me yesterday. Please find enclosed a copy of our 8.1 Migration Seminar brochure.

As we discussed, Syncon Business Consulting will be holding Migration Seminars at the end of next month. I highly recommend that one of your team members plan to attend the Los Angeles seminar.

If SBC can be of any other service to Turtle Markets, please do not hesitate to give us a call.

Regards,

Louis Noble
Operations Manager

LN/xx
flores.ltr/d2

c: M. T. Silverman

Enc.

---

2. Change the left, right, and top margins to 1.5" (place the insertion point at the beginning of the document; select **Layout**, **Margins**; type the desired margins; select **OK**).
3. Change to **Full** justification (move the mouse pointer to the **Justification** button on the Power Bar; press and hold the mouse button; move the mouse pointer to **Full**; release the mouse button).
4. Change the font to **BernhardtMod BT** or make a choice of your own (with the insertion point located at the top of the document, select the **Font Face** button on the Power Bar; move the mouse pointer to **BernhardtMod BT**; click once).
5. Save the file on your file disk; use the filename **3act2** (Chapter 3, activity 2). (Select the **Save** button on the Power Bar; type the filename; if necessary, click in the Drives box and click on the drive letter where the file disk is located; select **OK.**)
6. Print one copy (select the **Print** button on the Power Bar; choose **Print**).
7. Close the document (select **File**, **Close**).

Activity 3.3—Create an AMS Simplified Style Letter; Use Bold and Italic; Change Margins and Font Size; Use Speller and Page Zoom Full View

1. Type the following letter using the AMS simplified style letter (see Figure 3.2 on page 53). Use the bold and italic text attributes as shown.

(Use date text)

Mr. Dennis Eaton
2295 Miranda Place
Alamo, CA 94507

SPRING MEMBERSHIP PROMOTION

As you are well aware, in the past year *Diablo Fitness Center* has made a great deal of progress in managing, rebuilding, and improving its facility and equipment.

With our spring membership promotion, you will receive **FREE** a beautiful, deluxe bathrobe and three months added to your present membership, compliments of *Diablo Fitness Center.* All you have to do is introduce two new members to the club during the next two months.

We are looking forward to your participation in this program!

MARIZE LOCKE, PRESIDENT

ML/xx
eaton.ltr/disk3

---

2. Change the left and right margins to 2" and the top margin to **1.75"** (place the insertion point at the beginning of the document; select **Layout**, **Margins**; type the desired margins; select **OK**).
3. Select the words "SPRING MEMBERSHIP PROMOTION" and change the font size to **14** point (select the **Font Size** button on the Power Bar; move the mouse pointer to **14;** click once).
4. Use the Speller to find and correct misspelled words. (Select the **Speller** button on the Power Bar; select **Start**. When the spell check is complete, select **Yes** to close the Speller.)
5. Use the Page Zoom Full view to display the entire document in the document window (select the **Page Zoom Full** button on the Power Bar; select the **Page Zoom Full** button again to return to normal view).
6. Save the file on your file disk; use the filename **3act3** (Chapter 3, activity 3). (Select the **Save** button on the Button Bar; type the filename; if necessary, click in the Drives box and click on the drive letter where the file disk is located; select **OK**.)
7. Print one copy (select the **Print** button on the Power Bar; choose **Print**).

8. Close the document (select **File**, **Close**).

Challenge Your Skills

Skill 3.1—Create and Edit a Traditional Style Letter

1. Use the traditional style letter and the following information.

   a. Use the current date.

   b. Send the letter to Mrs. Consuelo Sundheimer, 80 Patriot Place, Apt. #5, Downers Grove, IL 60515.

   c. Use Dear Mrs. Sundheimer for the salutation.

   d. Use an appropriate complimentary closing.

   e. The letter is from Debby Reiter, M.D.

   f. Include your reference initials and document identification notation.

   g. Make decisions regarding:

      Justification
      Margins
      Fonts
      Use of bold, italic, and underline text attributes

   h. The letter body text follows:

      At the end of the month, I will be leaving the Lincoln Medical Group in order to enter private practice in Des Plaines, Illinois.

      Our records indicate that you or a member of your family has been seen by me during the past year. Hopefully, you will not be inconvenienced by a change in physicians. I would like to assist you with the transition to a new health care provider.

      Your health is important to me, and Lincoln Medical is committed to assuring you continuity of care. My entire staff and I will be available to assist you with this transition. Please call if you have any questions or concerns.

2. Save the file on your file disk; use the filename **3skill1** and print one copy.

3. Use the following information to change the letter:

   a. Insert the following paragraph between the middle and last paragraphs:

      If you have specific concerns regarding a medical condition or are undergoing prenatal care, please give me a call directly at (708) 555-8900. Otherwise, you may call Celeste Renshaw or Bertha Lenhardt at (708) 555-6303 and they will be happy to help you select another physician.

4. Use the Speller to find and correct any misspelled words; also proofread carefully for accurate meaning.

5. Save the file on your file disk; use the filename **3skill1r** (Chapter 3, skill 1, revised).
6. Print one copy and close the document.

Skill 3.2—Create and Edit an AMS Simplified Style Letter

1. Use the AMS simplified style letter and the following information.
   a. Use the current date.
   b. Send the letter to Mrs. Sabrina Alvares, 77 Hazelwood Ln., Menomonee Falls, WI 53051.
   c. The subject of the letter is TAX PLANNING.
   d. The letter is from Tami Nguyen, C.P.A.
   e. Include your reference initials, document identification notation, and enclosure notation.
   f. Make decisions regarding:
      Justification
      Margins
      Fonts
      Use of bold, italic, and underline text attributes
   g. The letter body text follows:

      Enclosed is your new tax organizer. Although it may seem like you just finished last year's taxes, it is not too early to begin thinking about the preparation of this year's taxes.

      As for new law changes, the new 31 percent bracket kicks in, as well as the new "haircut" for itemized deductions. Remember that for federal tax purposes, capital gains are still taxed at 28 percent.

      As you thumb through your tax organizer, you will see that it contains the prior year's figures. Knowing your information from the prior year will help you to verify the accuracy and completeness of the current year information. Please include cost and purchase date of all assets sold.

      If you feel that your tax situation merits an appointment or that you need to discuss any matters with me, please call Bob to schedule an appointment.

2. Save the file on your file disk; use the filename **3skill2**.
3. Use the following information to change the letter:
   a. Insert the following paragraph above the last paragraph.

      Forward your estimated tax partnership papers to me as soon as possible. We do not need to delay the filing of your partnership taxes while you gather your individual information.

4. Use the Speller to find and correct any misspelled words; also proofread carefully for accurate meaning.

5. Save the file on your file disk; use the filename **3skill2r** (Chapter 3, skill 2, revised).
6. Print one copy and close the document.

Skill 3.3—Create and Edit a Traditional Style Letter; Language Arts

1. Use the traditional style letter and the following information.
   a. Use the current date.
   b. Send the letter to Mr. Clinton Nomura, Engineering Productivity Division, 18023 Shawsheen St., Andover, MA 01810-1086.
   c. The letter is from Josephine Reyes, Membership Chairperson.
   d. Include your reference initials, document identification, and enclosure notation.
   e. Make decisions regarding:

      Appropriate salutation
      Justification
      Margins
      Fonts
      Use of bold, italic, and underline text attributes

   f. Correct three spelling and two punctuation errors.
   g. The letter body text follows:

      The enclosed brochure is provided to inform you of the existence of a professional organization taylored to meet the specific needs of telecommuncation professionals.

      The NORAM Telecommunications Association is more than 15 years old and has more than 600 members. There are members from all 50 states and Canada.

      The membership brochure will provide you with a describtion of our programs and information on next month's conference. Our conference will be held in Chicago, Illinois. Hurry now to register and take advantage of the early registration reduced fee.

      If you have any questions feel free to contact me or my assistant Billie Detweiler, at (215) 555-8303. Thank you for taking time to consider becoming a member of the NORAM Telecommunications Association.

2. Use the Speller to find and correct any misspelled words; also proofread carefully for accurate meaning.
3. Save the file on your file disk; use the filename **3skill3**.
4. Print one copy.
5. If you have completed your work, exit WordPerfect (select **File**, **Exit**).

FIGURE 4.2

Find Text dialog box menu options

Type:	
Text	Tells WordPerfect to locate specific text.
Specific Code	Displays a list of codes, such as margins and justification, that WordPerfect can locate.
Match:	
Whole Word	Select the Whole Word option to locate the next occurrence of matching text that is a word by itself.
Case	Select the Case option to instruct WordPerfect to locate words that exactly match the case of the text typed in the Find box.
Font	Select the Font option to tell WordPerfect to locate text in a particular font name, size, and/or attribute.
Codes	Select Codes to display an extensive list of codes that can be located by WordPerfect.
Action:	
Select Match	Use Select Match to tell WordPerfect to highlight the specific text in the document window when a match is located.
Position Before	Select Position Before to place the insertion point to the left of the first character when a match is located.
Position After	Select Position After to place the insertion point to the right of the last character when a match is located.
Extend Selection	Use Extend Selection to select text from the location of the insertion point to the location of the next occurrence of the text to be found.
Options:	
Begin Find at Top of Document	Instructs WordPerfect to start the search beginning at the top of the document.
Wrap at Beg./End of Document	Instructs WordPerfect to begin the search at the location of the insertion point. When the end of the document is reached, the search continues at the beginning of the document and continues until the insertion point is reached.
Limit Find Within Selection	Instructs WordPerfect to limit the search to the selected text.
Include Headers, Footers, etc.	Instructs WordPerfect to search for specified text in headers, footers, footnotes, graphic boxes, etc.

3. Select each menu in the Find Text dialog box and check that the desired options are selected.

   For example, select **Type** and check that **Text** is selected (a checkmark displays beside a selected option) {Alt and t}. Select **Match** and check that **Whole Word** is selected {Alt and m}. Select **Action** and check that **Select Match** is selected {Alt and a}. Select **Options** and check that **Begin Find at Top of Document** is selected {Alt and o}.

4. Select **Find Next** {Alt and f}.

   Note: *The first occurrence of the specified text is highlighted in the document window.*

5. The text can be edited and the Find procedure continued.

a. Edit by deleting, inserting, or replacing.

For example, move the mouse pointer to the highlighted text in the document window and click once. Type **LaGrande Federal Savings** {Alt and c; Ctrl and Backspace; type the text and press the Spacebar once}.

b. To continue to search for the next occurrence of the same text, select **Find Next** in the Find Text dialog box {F2, Enter}.

For example, continue the Find process and change all occurrences of **LFS** to **LaGrande Federal Savings**.

Note: When the message "Not Found" displays, no additional occurrences of the specified text can be located.

6. Select **OK** {Enter}.
7. Select **Close** {Alt and c}.

Finish-Up Instructions

- When the entire text has been searched, use the *new* filename **4drill3.fin** and save the file on your file disk (select **File**, **Save As**; type the filename; if necessary, click in the Drives box and click on the drive letter where the file disk is located; select **OK**).
- Print one copy (select the **Print** button on the Power Bar; choose **Print**).
- Close the document (select **File**, **Close**).

Replace Text Automatically

Replacing text automatically is the process of locating and deleting specific text or codes and inserting new text or codes. The document is searched for a specific word/code or group of words/codes. Each occurrence of the specified text can be replaced automatically with new text. When the Replace command is accessed, the Find and Replace Text dialog box displays. Menu options in the Find and Replace Text dialog box are used to give WordPerfect more information on the text to be replaced. The Type, Match, and Options menus contain the same options that are available in the Find Text dialog box (see Figure 4.2 for information on these menu options). In addition, the Option menu contains an option that is not available in the Find Text dialog box, Limit Number of Changes. Two additional menus are available in the Find and Replace Text dialog box: Direction and Replace (see Figure 4.3 for an explanation of the Find and Replace menu options).

Start-Up Instructions

- Open the file named **4drill3.txt** located on the data disk (select the **Open** button on the Power Bar; if necessary, click in the Drives box and click on the drive letter where the data disk is located; double-click on the filename).

FIGURE 4.3

Find and Replace Text dialog box menu options. (See Figure 4.2 for Type, Match, and Options menu options.)

Options:	
Limit Number of Changes	Specify the number of times the designated text should be replaced. (See Figure 4.2 for explanation of other Option menu items.)
Replace:	*Note: This menu is available only when the insertion point is located in the Replace With box.*
Case	Select the Case option to instruct WordPerfect to replace text exactly as the text is shown in the Replace With box.
Font	Select the Font option to specify the font name, size, and/or attribute for the text shown in the Replace With box.
Codes	Select Codes to display an extensive list of codes that can be inserted in the Replace With box.
Direction:	
Forward	Instructs WordPerfect to find and replace the specified text from the insertion point to the end of the document.
Backward	Instructs WordPerfect to find and replace the specified text from the insertion point to the beginning of the document.

Replace Text Automatically

1. Select **Edit, Replace** {Alt, e, r *or* Ctrl and F2}.

   Note: The Find and Replace Text dialog box is displayed at the bottom of the screen. The insertion point is located in the Find box (see Figure 4.4).

2. In the Find box, type the text to be replaced.

   For example, type **LFS** in the Find box.

3. Select the **Type, Match, Direction,** and **Options** menu in the Find and Replace Text dialog box and check that desired options are selected.

   For example, select **Type** and check that **Text** is selected (a checkmark displays beside a selected option) {Alt and t}. Select **Match** and check that **Whole Word** is selected {Alt and m}. Select **Direction** and check that **Forward** is selected {Alt and d}. Select **Options** and check that **Begin Find at Top of Document** is selected {Alt and o}.

4. Click in the **Replace With** box {Tab}.

5. Type the new text in the Replace With box.

   For example, type **Landmark Financial Services**. (Do not type the period.)

FIGURE 4.4

Find and Replace Text dialog box

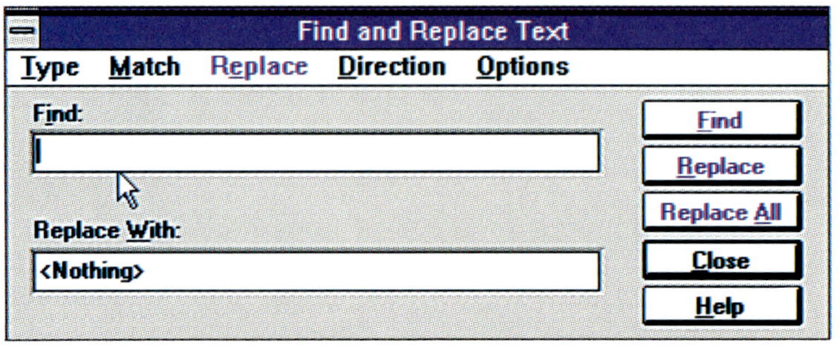

6. If desired, select the Replace menu and use the options to provide additional information about the replacement text.

   For example, change the font for the replacement text to bold by selecting **Replace, Font, Font Style, Bold, OK** {Alt and e, f; Alt and y; press the down arrow key to display Bold; Enter}.

7. Select Replace All {Alt and a}.

   Note: WordPerfect instantly changes the specified text.

8. When all occurrences of the specified text are replaced, text in the Find box of the Find and Replace dialog box is highlighted. Select **Close** {Alt and c}.

Finish-Up Instructions

- Use the *new* filename **4drill3.rep** and save the file on your file disk (select **File, Save As**; type the filename; if necessary, click in the Drives box and click on the drive letter where the file disk is located; select **OK**).
- Print one copy (select the **Print** button on the Power Bar; choose **Print**).
- Close the document (select **File, Close**).

Undo Replaced Text

Since WordPerfect replaces all occurrences of specified text rapidly, it may be necessary to undo the replaced text if word(s) are found that should not have been changed. To undo the replaced text, select **Edit**, **Undo** {Alt and e, u} before performing any other actions.

Create Text Using the Bullet, Indent, and Double Indent Features

Text can be indented to improve readability and enhance the document's appearance. If the Indent feature is used, all lines of a paragraph are indented from the left margin until the **Enter** key is pressed. The first time the **Indent** button is selected, the insertion point or text moves to the first preset tab and all text is indented at that position. If the **Indent** button is selected a second time the insertion point or text moves to the second preset tab which is used to indent the text.

Both sides of a paragraph or line can be indented using the Double Indent feature. Often a paragraph is double-indented in a letter to show emphasis (see Figure 4.6).

Numbers, letters, or bullets (special characters placed at the left of a paragraph) can be inserted to provide extra emphasis or to improve readability. The desired number, letter, or bullet style is chosen from a list of available styles displayed in the Bullets & Numbers dialog box. Various number styles are available such as 1., 2., 3., or I., II., III. Uppercase and lowercase letter styles are also available, i.e., A., B., C., or a., b., c. Some of the bullet styles available are small or large circles (• or ●), and a diamond (♦).

Numbers, letters, or bullets can be inserted as text is typed or after the text has been typed. If numbers, letters, or bullets are to be inserted as text is typed, the **New Bullet or Number on ENTER** option is selected in the Bullets & Numbers dialog box. If numbers, letters, or bullets are to be inserted after the text is typed, the text is selected before the **Bullet** button is selected.

Start-Up Instructions

- Open the file named **4drill4.obj** located on the data disk (select the **Open** button on the Power Bar; if necessary, click in the drives box and click on the drive letter where the data disk is located; double-click on the filename).

Steps to Create Paragraphs Using the Indent Feature

1. With the paragraph(s) to be indented displayed in the document window, place the insertion point to the left of the first character of the paragraph to be indented.

   For example, place the insertion point to the left of the **R** in the paragraph that begins Results-Oriented.

2. Select the Indent button on the Button Bar {Alt, L, a, i or F7}.

   Note: *All lines of the paragraph are indented.*

Finish-Up Instructions

- Repeat steps 1 and 2 and indent the last three paragraphs of the document.
- Use the new filename **4drill4.den** and save the file (select **File**, **Save As**; type the filename; if necessary, click in the Drives box and click on the drive letter where your file disk is located; select **OK**).
- Print one copy (select the **Print** button on the Power Bar; choose **Print**).
- Close the document (select **File**, **Close**).

Start-Up Instructions

- In a clear document window, type the salutation and the first paragraph of the letter shown in Figure 4.5. Press **Enter** twice after the first paragraph.

Steps to Create Paragraphs Using the Double Indent Feature

1. Select Layout, Paragraph, Double Indent to turn on the Double Indent feature {Alt, L, a, d *or* Ctrl and Shift and F7}.

2. Type the paragraph to be indented from both the left and right margins. Press **Enter** twice at the end of the paragraph.

   For example, type: **If you were to die as a result of an accident, the All-in-One Plan would cancel your mortgage debt and leave your family secure in a mortgage-free home.**

   Note: *When the* ***Enter*** *key is pressed, the insertion point returns to the left margin and the Double Indent feature is turned off.*

Dear Mortgage Customer:

Recently we wrote to you about a unique plan of insurance that would provide flexible protection for your family.

> If you were to die as a result of an accident, the All-in-One Plan would cancel your mortgage debt and leave your family secure in a mortgage-free home.

This insurance plan would also provide your family with an important financial cushion when they would need it most. After the plan pays off the mortgage balance, any remaining benefit goes to the beneficiary of your choice.

> You simply cannot be turned down, regardless of your health or occupation. No medical exam or answers to health questions are required.

Take action today. Send for your application form by filling out the enclosed, postage-paid card.

Sincerely,

Jean Silverburg
Vice President

JS/xx

FIGURE 4.5

Paragraphs indented using the Double Indent feature

Finish-Up Instructions

- Use the Steps to Create Paragraphs Using the Double Indent Feature and complete the document shown in Figure 4.5.
- Save the file on your file disk; use the filename **4drill5.all** (select the **Save** button; type the filename; if necessary, click in the Drives box and click on the drive letter where the file disk is located; select **OK**).
- Print one copy (select the **Print** button on the Power Bar, choose **Print**).
- Close the document (select **File**, **Close**).

Start-Up Instructions

- Open the file named **4drill6.txt** located on the data disk (select the **Open** button on the Power Bar; if necessary, click in the drives box and click on the drive letter where the data disk is located; double-click on the filename).

Steps to Create a Numbered or Bulleted List

1. Select all paragraphs to be numbered or bulleted.

   For example, select all paragraphs except for the title.

2. Select the **Bullet** button on the Button Bar (Alt, i, n}.

   Note: *The Bullets and Numbers dialog box displays (see Figure 4.6).*

FIGURE 4.6

Bullets & Numbers dialog box

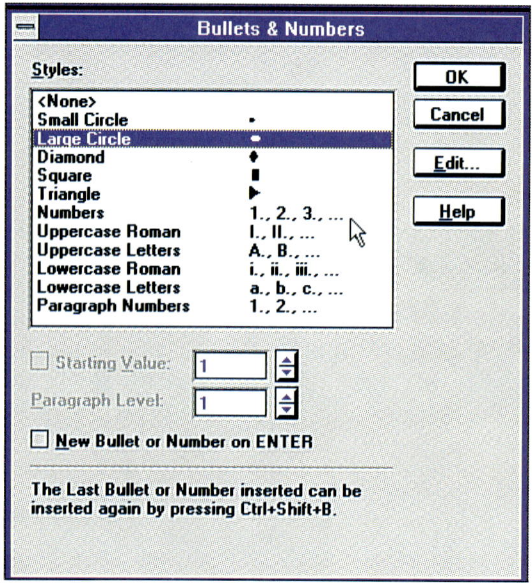

3. Select the desired number, letter or bullet style {press the up or down arrow key to highlight the desired style}.

   For example, select the **Numbers** style.

4. Select OK {Enter}.

   Note: Your document should look similar to Figure 4.7. If items in the numbered list are moved, the items are automatically renumbered.

Finish-Up Instructions

- Use the *new* filename **4drill6.num** (select **File**, **Save As**; type the filename; if necessary, click in the Drives box and click on the drive letter where the file disk is located; select **OK**).
- Print one copy (select the **Print** button on the Power Bar; choose **Print**).
- Change the numbered list to a bulleted list (select all numbered paragraphs; select the **Bullet** button; select the **Diamond** style; select **OK**).

FIGURE 4.7

Numbered paragraphs

Applicant Requirements--Air Conditioning Mechanic

1. Any combination equivalent to completion of high school and three years of increasingly responsible experience in the operation, repair, and maintenance of heating, ventilation, and cooling systems.

2. Hold a valid driver's license authorizing operation of motor vehicles.

3. Successful compliance with job-related medical standards as determined by a medical examination conducted by a company-approved physician.

4. Proof of U.S. citizenship or proof of legal authorization to work in the United States.

- Use the *new* filename **4drill6.dia** and save the file (select **File**, **Save As**; type the filename; if necessary, click in the Drives box and click on the drive letter where the file disk is located; select **OK**).
- Print one copy (select the **Print** button on the Power Bar; choose **Print**).
- Close the document (select **File**, **Close**).

Print Selected Text

Once a document has been typed, just a portion of the text can be printed if desired. The text to be printed is selected. The **Print** button is chosen. The selected text prints at the location on the page where the text would have printed had the entire document been printed. For example, if the selected text is located in the middle of the page, the text will print in the middle of the page.

Start-Up Instructions

- Open the file named **4drill6.num** located on your file disk (select the **Open** button on the Power Bar; if necessary, click in the Drives box and click on the drive letter where the file disk is located; double-click on the filename).

Print Selected Text

1. Select the text to be printed.

   For example, select the entire third paragraph.

2. Select the Print button on the Power Bar {Alt and f, p *or* F5}.

   Note: *When the Print dialog box displays, a black dot appears to the left of the Selected Text option in the Print Selection box.*

3. Select Print to print the selected text {Enter}.

Finish-Up Instructions

- Close the document (select **File**, **Close**).

The Next Step

Chapter Review and Activities

Self-Check Quiz

T F 1. The Find command is used to locate a word or group of words in a document.

T F 2. Moving text is the process of duplicating text.

T F 3. Before text can be copied or moved, the text is selected.

T F 4. To begin the Replace function, select **Edit**, **Replace**.

T F 5. A single paragraph cannot be selected and printed.

6. Bullet characters can be inserted to the left of selected paragraphs by choosing
   a. the **Bullet** button on the Button Bar.
   b. the **Bullet** button on the Power Bar.
   c. **Edit**, **Bullets and Numbering**.

7. When using the drag and drop method to move text,
   a. the text must be selected.
   b. a mouse must be used.
   c. keystrokes can be used.
   d. both a and b.

8. When the **Indent** button is selected
   a. the text is indented from both the left and right margins.
   b. a bullet character is inserted at the left of the selected paragraphs.
   c. all lines of a paragraph are indented from the left margin until the Enter key is pressed.

9. Which option in the Find and Replace Text dialog box should be selected in order to instruct WordPerfect to find only the whole word(s) typed in the Find box?

10. What is the difference between the Indent feature and the Double Indent feature?

Enriching Language Arts Skills

Spelling/Vocabulary Words

dues fees paid by members to an organization at regular intervals.
affiliation act of belonging or being connected to a specific group.
outweigh to be of more importance or value.
distinguished worthy of notice; excellent; outstanding.

Compound Adjectives and Coordinating Conjunctions

Hyphenate two words that precede and describe a noun and function as a single adjective.

Example:

The designer sent a well-defined sample of the proposed meeting area.

A comma is placed before a coordinating conjunction (e.g., *and, or, because*) that joins two independent clauses (i.e., clauses that are complete sentences). No comma is placed before a coordinating conjunction if *one* or both clauses are dependent.

Example:

We will respond promptly to the questionnaire, ***because*** *our company would like to maintain a good working relationship with our clients.* (Two independent clauses.)

We mailed 400 surveys yesterday ***and*** *expect to obtain a 3 percent response by the end of May.* (One independent and one dependent clause.)

Activities

Activity 4.1—Create a Numbered List and Move Text

1. Type the following paragraphs using the spacing shown.

Features of WordPerfect 6.0 for Windows

Button Bar and Power Bar--The Button Bar and Power Bar provide a quick and easy way to format, edit, save, and print documents. Commonly used features are represented by icons (pictures). When an icon is selected, the associated command is performed immediately.

Multiple documents--With WordPerfect 6.0, a user can have up to nine documents open at one time. Each document is placed in a separate window. Information can be copied or moved from one window to another as desired.

Bullets--The Bullet button can be selected to easily create bulleted lists.

Graphics--WordPerfect 6.0 for Windows provides more than 135 graphics images that can be placed in a document. Both text and graphics are displayed on the screen. With the use of the mouse, graphics can be positioned and sized interactively.

Drawing--The WP Draw button provides access to the drawing tools of the WordPerfect Presentations program. Illustrations can be created and existing images can be edited. The drawings can be incorporated into WordPerfect documents.

---

2. Number all paragraphs except the title (select all paragraphs to be numbered; select the **Bullet** button; select the **Number** style; select **OK**).
3. Save the file on your file disk; use the filename **4act1.wpw** (select the **Save** button; type the filename; if necessary, click in the Drives box and click on the drive letter where the file disk is located; select **OK**).
4. Print one copy (select the **Print** button on the Power Bar; choose **Print**).
5. Move the items as shown.

Features of WordPerfect 6.0 for Windows

1. Button Bar and Power Bar--The Button Bar and Power Bar provide a quick and easy way to format, edit, save, and print documents. Commonly used features are represented by icons (pictures). When an icon is selected, the associated command is performed immediately.

2. Multiple documents--With WordPerfect 6.0, a user can have up to nine documents open at one time. Each document is placed in a separate window. Information can be copied or moved from one window to another as desired.

3. Bullets--The Bullet button can be selected to easily create bulleted lists.

4. Graphics--WordPerfect 6.0 for Windows provides more than 135 graphics images that can be placed in a document. Both text and graphics are displayed on the screen. With the use of the mouse, graphics can be positioned and sized interactively.

5. Drawing--The WP Draw button provides access to the drawing tools of the WordPerfect Presentations program. Illustrations can be created and existing images can be edited. The drawings can be incorporated into WordPerfect documents.

---

6. Save the file on your file disk; use the filename **4act1.rev** (select **File**, **Save As**; type the filename; if necessary, click in the Drives box and click on the drive letter where the file disk is located; select **OK**).
7. Print one copy (select the **Print** button on the Power Bar; choose **Print**).
8. Close the document (select **File**, **Close**).

Activity 4.2—Create a Bulleted List and Replace Text Automatically

1. Use the traditional style and type the following letter.

(Use current date)

Mr. Austin Estes
55 Johnston Rd., #8
Albany, NY 12203

Dear Mr. Estes:

Enclosed is a copy of the GTA Constant Traveler newsletter highlighting our expanded world of service and membership benefits.

Our latest expansion opens new corners of the globe to you for mileage building and award opportunities. Wherever you fly on GTA, you will earn our minimum of 1,500 miles per flight segment. No airline offers more.

In addition to our expanded service, the newsletter highlights:

New fares for GTA business-class fliers.

Triple mileage for selected GTA intercontinental routes.

Special "GTA Partners Program" holiday promotion.

To increase your flexibility when traveling within North America, GTA has introduced upgrade awards for our business fliers. Also, members may continue to purchase a GTA First Class seat at reduced rates any time before departure through our paid upgrade program.

We at GTA thank you for flying with us and look forward to serving your air travel needs.

Sincerely,

Anna R. Ingram
Senior Vice President

ARI/xx
estes.ltr/disk4

Enc.

---

2. Select the three sentences that followed the third paragraph which begin "In addition to our expanded. . ." and create a bulleted list (select the **Bullet** button; select the **Small Circle** style; select **OK**).

3. Save the file on your file disk; use the filename **4act2.mae** (select the **Save** button; type the filename; if necessary, click in the Drives box and click on the drive letter where the file disk is located; select **OK**).
4. Print one copy (select the **Print** button on the Power Bar; choose **Print**).
5. Replace all occurrences of GTA with Global Trans Airline (select **Edit**, **Replace**; type **GTA** in the Find box; type **Global Trans Airline** in the Replace With box; select **Replace All**).
6. Save the file on your file disk; use the filename **4act2.rep** (select **File**, **Save As**; type the filename; if necessary, click in the Drives box and click on the drive letter where the file disk is located; select **OK**).
7. Print one copy (select the **Print** button on the Power Bar; choose **Print**).
8. Close the document (select **File**, **Close**).

Activity 4.3—Copy, Edit, and Print Selected Text

1. Open the file named **4drill6.num** or type the document shown on page 86 (Figure 4.7).
2. Change the numbered list to a bulleted list (select the numbered items, select the **Bullet** button on the Button Bar, move the mouse pointer to the **Diamond** bullet and click, select **OK**). Click once to deselect the list.
3. Add three **Enters** at the bottom of the document.
4. Select the entire document.
5. Copy the entire document by selecting **Edit**, **Copy**.
6. Move the insertion point to the blank line at the bottom of the document and select **Edit**, **Paste** to insert a copy of the document.
7. Make the changes shown to the pasted copy. (Do not change the line spacing.)

Applicant Requirements-~~Air Conditioning Mechanic~~ Maintenance Supervisor

1. Any combination equivalent to completion of high school and ~~three~~ five years of increasingly responsible experience in the operation of janitorial services, ~~repair, and maintenance of heating, ventilation, and cooling systems.~~ as well as supervising a staff of ten or more persons.
2. Hold a valid California state driver's license authorizing operation of motor vehicles.
3. Successful compliance with job-related medical standards as determined by a medical examination conducted by a company-approved physician.
4. Proof of U.S. citizenship or proof of legal authorization to work in the United States.

---

8. Save the file on your file disk; use the filename **4act3.app** (select **File**, **Save As**; type the filename; if necessary, click in the Drives box and click on the drive letter where the file disk is located; select **OK**).

9. Select the edited copy and print one copy of the selected text (select the **Print** button on the Power Bar; choose **Print**).

10. Close the document (select **File**, **Close**).

Activity 4.4—Create Paragraphs Using the Double Indent Feature

1. Use the traditional block style and type the following letter. Use the Double Indent feature to indent the second and third paragraphs from both the left and right margins (select **Layout, Paragraph, Double Indent**).

(Use current date)

Mr. Phil Emerson
P. O. Box 7526
London, KY 40741-9945

Dear Mr. Emerson:

We have great news for you! Your application for a ValueCard account has been preliminarily approved. However, before we can send you your new card, we need your assistance in verifying all income.

> Please send us a copy of your last two paycheck stubs issued within the last thirty (30) days. If you have listed other income, please provide verification.

> If we receive the requested information within thirty (30) days, we will be able to complete your evaluation.

We certainly hope to hear from you so that we can complete our approval process and you can begin to enjoy the many advantages that a ValueCard has to offer.

Sincerely,

Carol Shaw
Credit Card Director

CS/xx
emerson.ltr/d2

---

2. Save the file on your file disk; use the filename **4act4.pem** (select the **Save** button; type the filename; if necessary, click in the Drives box and click on the drive letter where the file disk is located; select **OK**).

3. Print one copy (select the **Print** button on the Power Bar; choose **Print**).
4. Close the document (select **File**, **Close**).

Challenge Your Skills

Skill 4.1—Create a Numbered List, Move, and Edit Text

1. Use the Memorandum—Style 1 and the following information:
   a. Send the memo to Sales Associates from Suzanne Boscacci, Division Manager.
   b. Use the current date; include your reference initials.
   c. The subject of the memo is Current Sales Promotion.
   d. Send copies to J. Matarazzo and G. Higgins.
   e. The unformatted memorandum body text follows:

      Enclosed are photographs to assist in building your current sales promotion displays.

      Please note the following:

      Wingits have been discontinued and Chocwiz quantities reduced in order to incorporate Ultimate Almonds and expand on the successful Cheesecake Minis. Chocwiz should be placed next to snack crackers for a common price point. Ultimate Almonds should be placed in the space previously occupied by Chocwiz.

      Order quantities will be communicated through the central ordering office and will be processed automatically. Sales associates will not key in any orders.

      Orders reflect only the quantities necessary to build displays. Make plans to order refill quantities when necessary.

      Stores will require extra service calls during this promotion. Let your stores know when you will be visiting their sites.

      Announcement to the stores of this promotion has already been distributed. Orders will now be processed electronically. The new electronic order processing will ensure accurate and timely delivery of products.

      Remember--proper point of sale, displays, and shelf!

2. Select and number the third, fourth, fifth, and sixth paragraphs.
3. Move items 3 and 4 above item number 2.
4. Delete the last paragraph and insert the following two paragraphs:

Advise stores now of their upcoming shipment and make plans to build displays. Stores resisting this promotion should be advised to call Leonard Koenig or Laura Gonzales (department buyers) at 555-3422.

LET'S SELL SOME PRODUCTS!

5. Save the file on your file disk; use the filename **4skill1.sas**.
6. Print one copy and close the document.

Skill 4.2—Copy and Edit Text

1. Create the following form using the format and spacing shown.

   Hint: *Press* ***Enter*** *twice after all lines of text, except press* ***Enter*** *three times after typing the store number and after typing the last line of the form. Use Flush Right justification to align items at the right margin.*

SALES INVENTORY SUMMARY

SALES ASSOCIATE: JACQUELINE VILLEGAS

STORE #: 286

Item Name	Amount Purchased
Cheesecake Minis	12 gross
Chocwiz	10 gross
Ultimate Almonds	20 gross

---

2. Copy the form below the original form. Change the data in the copied form as follows:

   Sales Associate: David Novak
   Store #: 235
   Cheesecake Minis: 10 gross
   Chocwiz: 5 gross
   Ultimate Almonds: 22 gross

3. Copy the original form again and place below the second form. Change the data in the copied form as follows:

   Sales Associate: Monie Lucero
   Store #: 182
   Cheesecake Minis: 15 gross
   Chocwiz: 8 gross
   Ultimate Almonds: 18 gross

4. Save the file on your file disk; use the filename **4skill2.sum.**
5. Print one copy and close the document.

➸ Skill 4.3—Replace Text Automatically; Language Arts

1. Use the Memorandum—Style 1 and the following information:

   a. Change both the left and right margins to **1.25"** and the top margin to **1.5"**.

   b. Send the memo to Consolidated Life Insurance Field Force from Juan Valdivia, Vice President.

   c. Use the current date; include your reference initials.

   d. The subject of the memo is IUA Membership.

   e. Correct three spelling and four punctuation errors.

To qualify for the National Quality, National Sales Achievement, Health Insurance, or the Million Dollar Roundtable Awards, your IUA membership dues must be current.

If you are a recent member of the Consolidated Life Insurance field force and were previously a member of IUA under another company's name, please write a letter to IUA National Headquarters and ask that your afilliation be changed to Consolidated Life Insurance.

Your IUA membership is important because of the awards or honors it can bring you personally. Additionally IUA has a long and distinguished history in representing professional agents in the Life, Health, and Financial Services industry. The benefits far outweight the membership dues. IUA provides information for agents to learn from each other and share sales ideas, and it serves as a platform for defending your interests in relation to state and federal legislation.

In order to help us fight legislative efforts to control the insurance industry we need your help by renewing or beginning your membership with IUA.

Consolidated Life Insurance takes great pride in the number of agents who are members of the IUA and the dissinguished service rendered by members of our field force. We here at Consolidated Life Insurance appreciate your services and applaud you for a well done job. If you are not a member of IUA please give this serious consideration.

---

2. Automatically replace all occurrences of IUA with Insurance Underwriters Association.
3. Automatically replace all occurrences of Consolidated Life Insurance with CLI.
4. Save the file on your file disk; use the filename **4skill3.iua**.
5. Print one copy.
6. If you have completed your work, exit WordPerfect (select **File**, **Exit**).

Part 1
Checking Your Step

Production Skill Builder Activities
Chapters 1-4

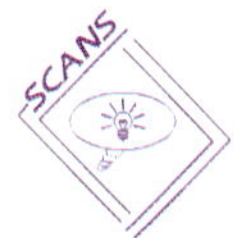

Production Activity 1.1—Create and Edit a Memorandum—Style 1

1. Use Memorandum—Style 1 and the following information to create a memorandum.

   a. Make decisions regarding:

      Margins
      Justification
      Memo date
      Use of Speller
      Reference initials

   b. Send the memorandum to All Administrative Support Staff from Chris Fosdahl.

   c. The subject of the memorandum is Alternative Work Schedules.

   d. Memorandum body text follows:

      For the past three years, we have been researching alternative work schedules such as flex time, shared time, and the four-day week. We appreciate your opinions and ideas concerning this matter.

      At its last meeting, the board of directors granted approval for a flex-time schedule in two departments and a shortened work week in a third department. Both of these plans will operate for a six-month trial period. Accounting, Marketing, and Quality Assurance are the three departments involved in this experiment. All other departments will remain on their normal schedules.

      At the end of the trial period, we will assess the results and determine whether we should stay with the old schedules or convert all departments to alternative work plans.

2. Save the file; use the filename **1pact1.aws**.

3. Revise the memorandum as shown:

For the past three years, we have been researching alternative work schedules such as flex time, shared time, and ~~the~~ [a] four-day week. ~~We appreciate~~ [Y]your opinions and ideas ~~concerning this matter~~ [have been very much appreciated].

At its last meeting, the board of directors granted approval for a flex-time schedule in ~~two~~ [three] departments and a shortened work week in a ~~third~~ [fourth] department. ~~Both~~ [All] of these plans will operate for a ~~six~~ [four]-month trial period. Accounting, Marketing, [Personnel,] and Quality Assurance are the ~~three~~ [four] departments involved in this experiment. All other departments will remain on their normal schedules.

[¶ Personnel in the affected departments should discuss their new work schedules with their respective managers. A survey will be sent out to all employees to obtain each individual's opinion concerning the new work schedules.]

At the end of the trial period, ~~we will assess~~ the results [will be assessed] and [a decision will be made to] determine whether we should stay with the old schedules or convert all departments to alternative work plans.

---

4. Use the *new* filename **1pact1.rev** and save the file.
5. Print one copy and close the document.

Production Activity 1.2—Create a Numbered List and Copy Text

1. Type the following information and use center and bold as shown.
2. Press **Enter** three times after the last item.
3. Center and bold as shown.

Golden Plan Realty Marketing Strategy

Enter the information about your home in the MLS computer.

Inform all GPR sales representatives about your home.

Develop a list of features and benefits of your home to be given to company sales agents and area brokers.

Develop a list of items to give your home more **curb appeal.**

Contact twenty homeowners in the surrounding area and ask if they know anyone who would like to purchase your home.

Hold **open houses** as needed.
Prepare and distribute **advertising** for your home.

---

4. Press the Enter key three times after the last paragraph.
5. Select all paragraphs except the title and create a numbered list using the Bullet button.
6. Select a font of your choice with a point size of 12 to 14 for the entire document.
7. Save the file; use the filename **1pact2.gpr**.
8. Print one copy.
9. Select and copy the entire document and place the copied text below the original copy.

   Note: Three Enters should follow the last item. Both the copy and the original will be on the same page. It may be necessary to center and bold the title of the copied list.
10. Save the file again using the same filename, **1pact2.gpr**.
11. Print one copy.
12. Close the document.

Production Activity 1.3—Create a Numbered List, Move, and Replace Text

1. Use Memorandum—Style 1 and the following information to create a memorandum.
   a. Make decisions regarding:
      Margins
      Justification
      Fonts
      Memo date
      Reference initials
      Indention
   b. Send the memorandum to Kirsten R. Muller, Regional Vice President.
   c. The memorandum is from P. W. Cooper, Sales Manager.
   d. The subject of the memorandum is Promotion of Jeanine Castello.
   e. Memorandum body text follows:

      As part of the Sales Compensation Program, the company will be setting up new job titles for all secretarial and clerical employees. The new job titles will be: Division Administrative Assistant, Division Secretary, and Sales Clerk.

nies. Therefore we are pleased to send you a copy of last year's annual report for Global Consolidated Life Insurance (GCL).

We have just experienced one of the most comendable years in the company's 93-year history. We had a record net income of $30 million on total revenues of almost $890 million. We actually held operating expenses below the previous year's level, and the company reached a new milestone last month--$5 billion in assets.

More than 95 percent of the company's assets are invested in bonds, short-term debt instruments, and first mortgage loans. At year end, not a single bond issue was in payment default, and not a single mortgage was in foreclosure.

When you need additional insurance or seek a high return on an individual anuity, we hope you will contact your GCL agent. Our company has been in existance for more than 90 years, and you can count on GCL being there when you need us.

2. Save the file; use the filename **1pact5.gcl**.
3. Use the following information to revise the letter.
   a. In the second paragraph change the word "company's" to GCL's and delete the word "the."
   b. Change the net income to $32.5 million and total revenues to $900 million.
   c. Delete the last sentence of the third paragraph and insert the following sentences:

      Based on the company's financial condition and operating performance, GCL continues to earn a superior rating. We have had a top rating recommendation since 1955.

   d. Insert the following paragraph above the third paragraph:

      Of course, the financial strength of the company really rests on the quality of our invested assets, and we believe that our invested assets are first-rate.

4. Use the *new* filename **1pact5.glo** and save the file again.
5. Print one copy and close the document.

Part 2
A Step Further

Work with Special Features

Chapters 5-8

- Create a table
- Join cells
- Change column widths
- Insert columns and rows
- Convert tabbed text to a table
- Set row height and fill (shade) cells
- Center a table horizontally and vertically
- Change the table borders and lines
- Set and customize the number type
- Align figures at the decimal point
- Move and delete a row or column
- Change table row margins
- Copy and delete a table
- Calculate column/row totals
- Copy a formula
- Omit table lines and borders
- Use single and double underlines
- Convert case
- Use a hard space
- Insert special characters
- Set tabs
- Change margins using the Ruler Bar
- Create newspaper style columns
- Place a border line between columns
- Change column definition
- Insert a column break
- Use hyphenation
- Create parallel columns
- Convert text in parallel columns to a table

CHAPTER 5

Create a Table

Features Covered

- Create a table
- Insert a row
- Join cells
- Change justification for multiple cells
- Insert a column
- Set row height
- Change column widths
- Set and customize the number type
- Align figures at the decimal point
- Center a table horizontally and vertically
- Convert tabbed text to a table
- Change table borders and lines
- Fill (shade) cells

Chapter Objectives and Introduction

After successfully completing this chapter, you will be able to create a table, increase and decrease column widths, insert columns and rows, join table cells, and align figures at the decimal point. In addition, you will be able to change row height, center a table horizontally and vertically, use the Tables Button Bar, and create a table using existing text. Traditionally, a table has been created by calculating the location of column tabs so that when the table is printed it will be centered horizontally on the page. Tables in this book will be created using the Table feature, which will determine the column widths automatically and display lines around each column and row.

The Table feature is used to organize information into columns and rows without using tab settings. A sample table containing information is shown in Figure 5.1. Table information can include either text or numbers or both.

FIGURE 5.1

Sample table

Software Requirements	
WordPerfect 6.0 for Windows	**Microsoft Word 6.0 for Windows**
386 or higher	286/386 or higher
6–8 Mb of RAM	4 Mb of RAM
Mouse or track ball device	Mouse or track ball device
28 Mb hard disk space	6–24 Mb hard disk space
Windows 3.1	Windows 3.1
DOS 3.1 or higher	DOS 3.1 or higher
VGA graphics adapter	Graphics adapter

Create a Table

A table can be easily created using the **Table Quick Create** button on the Power Bar. Also, text typed in columns can be converted to a table using the Convert Tabular Text feature. Once the number of table columns and rows are specified, lines for the columns and rows display in the document window. The table lines are set by default to print but can be omitted if desired (see Chapter 6, page 143).

The table lines form columns and rows. The columns are identified by letters A, B, C, etc., and the rows are numbered 1, 2, 3, etc. The intersection of each column and row is called a cell. Each cell is identified by an address. When the insertion point is located in the third column (column C) and row 2, the cell address is C2. The cell address displays in the bottom middle of the Status bar. When the mouse pointer is moved to a cell, the cell address also displays in the left side of the Title bar.

When the insertion point is located in a table cell, the Tables Button Bar displays (see Figure 5.4). If the insertion point is moved outside the table cells, the WordPerfect Button Bar automatically displays.

Text typed in each table cell wraps around in the cell. If the **Enter** key is pressed in a cell, the cell automatically increases in height. If text within a cell is to be indented, press the **Ctrl** and **Tab** keys to activate the tab or press the **F7** key.

The **Tab** key, **Shift** and **Tab** keys, or the arrow keys are used to move the insertion point from cell to cell. After text is typed in one cell, the **Tab** key or an arrow key is used to move the insertion point to the next cell. To return to the previous cell, press **Shift** and **Tab**.

Create a Table

1. Move the mouse pointer to the Table Quick Create button on the Power Bar. Press and hold the mouse button {Alt, a, c, *or* F12}.

   Note: A miniature grid displays at the location of the Table Quick Create button (see Figure 5.2).

2. Continue to press and hold the mouse button while dragging to highlight the desired number of columns and rows. Release the mouse button {type the number of columns, press Tab, type the number of rows, press Enter}.

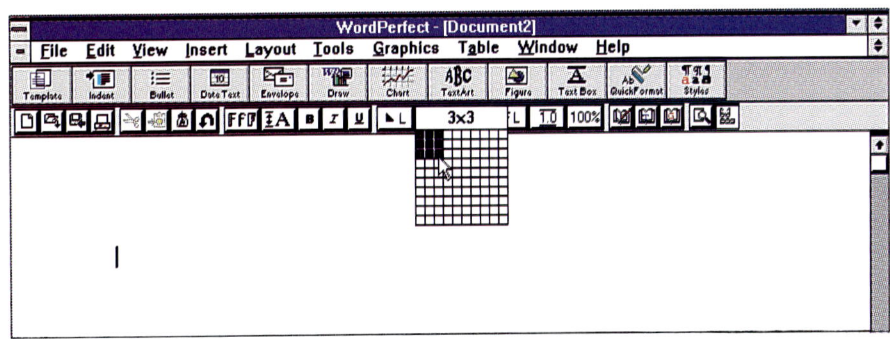

FIGURE 5.2

Miniature table grid

For example, drag to highlight a 3 x 3 table; release the mouse button.

Note: The empty columns and rows for the table and the Tables Button Bar display in the document window.

Finish-Up Instructions

- To type the unformatted information in each cell, press the **Tab** key or the arrow keys to move from cell to cell and row to row. Type the unformatted information shown in Figure 5.3.

  *Note: If the **Enter** key is mistakenly pressed while typing information into a table cell, press the **Backspace** key to delete the unwanted return. If the **Tab** key is pressed after the last cell entry, check that the insertion point is in a cell in the row to be deleted, then select the **Delete Tbl** button on the Tables Button Bar, check that "1" displays in the Rows option, and select **OK**.*
- Use the filename **5drill1.tbl** and save the file (select the **Save** button; type the filename; if necessary, click in the Drives box and click on the drive letter where the file disk is located; select **OK**).
- Optional. Print one unformatted copy.

Format and Modify a Table

Formatting a table is the process of completing such tasks as aligning figures at the decimal point, centering text in the cell, increasing or decreasing the column widths, and centering the table horizontally on the page. The primary goals of formatting a table are to present a pleasing appearance and to make reading easier. To produce a table that is formatted for an appealing appearance, *visually* adjust the width and height of cells and the alignment of text within the cells. (If desired, the ruler provided in the back of this book can be used to assist in estimating column width.)

The Tables Button Bar automatically displays when the insertion point is located in a table cell (see Figure 5.4). The Tables Button Bar contains many buttons that assist in the formatting and modification of tables.

Emma Croft	Western	155575.25
Tan Nguyen	Central	155295.95
Lloyd Guevara	Southern	155333.75

FIGURE 5.3

Unformatted table

FIGURE 5.4

Tables Button Bar

Modifying a table is the process of restructuring a table to include new columns or rows or to join cells. If the **Tbl Insert** button on the Tables Button Bar is selected, a new column or row can be inserted into an existing table before or after the cell that contains the insertion point.

Modifying a table can also include changing row height. Row height is the amount of space between the top and bottom cell lines. When row height is increased, the cell text will be placed at the top of the cell and the additional space will be added between the text and the bottom cell line. Two row height options are available: Auto and Fixed. Auto is the default row height setting.

With the Auto setting selected, WordPerfect will increase or decrease the row height to accommodate any amount and size of text typed in the cells. The height for the row will be adjusted to the maximum height needed for any cell in the row. When the Fixed setting is selected, an exact amount of space can be specified for each row. When text is added or deleted, the row height will not adjust automatically. If necessary, a new Fixed row height amount can be entered.

Two or more cells in a row can be joined in order to provide space for information that relates to more than one cell or column. Also, some or all of the cells in the column can be joined.

Table numbers can be formatted by selecting from a list of standard formats, such as Currency and Commas. When the Currency format is selected, WordPerfect automatically inserts a dollar sign in front of the table numbers and inserts commas to separate thousands within the table numbers ($12,652.00).

With the Commas format, the table numbers are formatted with commas to separate thousands (12,652.00). The default number of digits after the decimal for both the Currency format and Commas format is two. The number of digits after the decimal can be changed. For example, to eliminate the decimal point and zeros in the number 12,652.00, the number of digits after the decimal can be changed to zero.

WordPerfect provides QuickMenus for easy access to menu items related to a specific feature. The right mouse button is pressed to obtain a QuickMenu. For example, if several cells are selected and the right mouse button is pressed, the QuickMenu displays with various options such as Copy, Insert, Join Cells, etc.

Start-Up Instructions

- The file named **5drill1.tbl** should be displayed in the document window.

Insert a Table Row

1. Place the insertion point in the row that will be located before or after the inserted row.

   For example, place the insertion point in any cell in the first row.

2. Select the **Tbl Insert** on the Tables Button Bar {Alt, a, i}.

   Note: *The Insert Columns/Rows dialog box displays.*

3. Select the desired Insert option.

For example, check that the Rows option is selected and that the number displayed in the Rows box is highlighted. If necessary, select Rows {r}.

4. Type the number of rows to be inserted {type desired number of rows}.

   For example, type 2.

5. Select the desired Placement option.

   For example, check that **Before** is selected {press Tab *or* b}.

6. Select OK {press Enter}.

   Note: *Two new rows display at the top of the table.*

Finish-Up Instructions

- If necessary, press **Shift** and **Tab** to move the insertion point to the first cell in the table.
- Type the following text into the new cells as shown. (Remember: Press the **Tab** key to move from cell to cell and row to row.)

Semiannual Sales		
Names	Divisions	Sales

- Use the *new* filename **5drill1.ins** and save the file again (select **File**, **Save As**; if necessary, click in the Drives box and click on the drive letter where the file disk is located; type the new filename, select **OK**).

Start-Up Instructions

- The file named **5drill1.ins** should be displayed in the document window.

Steps to Join Table Cells

1. Select the cells to be joined by moving the mouse pointer to the left line of the first cell to be joined until the left selection arrow displays (see Figure 5.5). Double-click to highlight the desired row of cells {place the insertion point in the first and/or left cell to be selected; press and hold the Shift key and tap F8 and then tap the End key; continue to hold the Shift key and press the right or down arrow key to extend the highlighting}.

   For example, select the cells in row one.

2. Select Table, Join {Alt, a, j}.

Left selection arrow

Semiannual Sales		
Names	Divisions	Sales
Emma Croft	Western	155575.25
Tan Nguyen	Central	155295.95
Lloyd Guevara	Southern	155333.75

FIGURE 5.5

Table with left selection arrow

3. Select Cell {c}.

Note: All cells in row 1 are now one cell. Continue with the following Steps to Change Justification in Multiple Cells.

Shortcut

1. With the cells to be joined selected, click the *right* mouse button to display the QuickMenu.
2. Select Join Cells.

Start-Up Instructions

- The table named **5drill1.ins** should be displayed in the document window.

Change Justification for Multiple Cells

1. Select the cells where justification is to be changed by moving the mouse pointer to the left line of the top left cell to be selected until the left selection arrow displays. Press and hold the left mouse button while dragging to highlight the desired cells and rows {see Step 1 in the Steps to Join Table Cells on page 109}.

   For example, select all cells in rows 1 and 2.

2. Move the mouse pointer to the Justification button. Press and hold the mouse button while dragging the mouse pointer to the desired justification. Release the mouse button {Alt, a, o *or* Ctrl and F12; e, j, press the down arrow key until Center displays, press Enter}.

   For example, select Center.

Finish-Up Instructions

- If necessary, click once to deselect the table cells.
- Use the *new* filename **5drill1.jus** and save the file again (select **File**, **Save As**; if necessary, click in the Drives box and click on the drive letter where the file disk is located; type the new filename, select **OK**).

Start-Up Instructions

- The file named **5drill1.jus** should be displayed in the document window.

Insert a Table Column

1. Place the insertion point in the column that will be located before or after the inserted column.

   For example, place the insertion point in any cell in column C.

   Note: Check that the cell address in the middle of the Status bar displays with a "C" followed by a number, e.g., TABLE A Cell C3).

2. Select the Tbl Insert button on the Tables Button Bar {Alt, a, i}.

   Note: The Insert Columns/Rows dialog box displays

3. Select Columns {c}.

Note: The number in the Columns box is highlighted.

4. Type the number of columns to be inserted.

   For example, check that "1" is displayed. If necessary, type "1."

5. Select the desired Placement option {press Tab}.

   For example, check that the **Before** option is chosen. (If necessary, select **Before**.)

6. Select OK {press Enter once}.

Finish-Up Instructions

- Type the following information into the new column cells.

Office
Los Angeles
Kansas City
Atlanta

Note: The original Center justification is in effect in the cell containing the column heading, while the remaining column cells are left aligned.

- Save the file again using the same filename **5drill1.jus** (select the **Save** button).

Start-Up Instructions

- The file named **5drill1.jus** should be displayed in the document window.

Steps to Change Table Row Height

1. Select and highlight the rows where the row height is to be changed. (If necessary, see Step 1 of the Steps to Join Table Cells on page 109.)

   For example, select the first two table rows.

2. Select the Format Tbl button on the Tables Button Bar {Alt, a, o *or* Ctrl and F12}.

   Note: The Format dialog box displays.

3. Select the desired Format option.

   For example, check that **Row** is selected. (If necessary, select **Row** {o}.)

4. Select the Row Height Fixed option {x}.

   Note: The figures in the Fixed box are highlighted.

5. Type the desired row height.

   For example, type .4. (Do not type the final period.)

6. Select OK {press Enter once}.

   Note: Rows 1 and 2 are increased in height.

Change Table Borders and Lines and Fill (Shade) Cells

The lines and borders that display around the table cells can be changed by choosing a border, line, or fill style. The default line style for all the table lines (left, right, top, bottom, inside, and outside) is "Single." The preset border line style is "No Border." There are various types of line and border styles, such as dashed, dotted, thick, thin-thick, etc. (see Figure 5.8). The line styles can be designated to print around all table cells or only specific cells, and table border can be designated to print around an entire table. Lines can also be omitted (see Chapter 6).

The fill style is a pattern (or gradient) that includes foreground and background colors (see Figure 5.8). The foreground or background colors are shaded percentages of a color. For example, the 10% Shaded Fill appears light gray. A sample of the selected fill displays in a sample box in the Table Line/Fill dialog box. If a color monitor is being used, various colors or shades can be chosen and displayed on the screen.

If the table lines are changed to "None," the table structure can still be shown in the document by selecting the **TblGrid** button on the Tables Button Bar or by choosing **View**, **Table Gridlines**. The table gridlines visually replace the border, line, and fill styles and display as small dots around all table cells. The table gridlines do not print.

Start-Up Instructions

❖ Open the file named **5drill3.wpd** located on the data disk (select the **Open** button; if necessary, click in the Drives box and click on the drive letter where the file disk is located; double-click on the filename).

Change the Table Border

Note: When changing the table border, the insertion point can be located in any table cell.

1. Select the TblLineFill button on the Tables Button Bar {Alt, a, L *or* Shift F12}.

   Note: The Table Lines/Fill dialog box displays showing the options for changing a cell border line or fill style.

2. Select the desired option.

   For example, select **Table** {a}.

   *Note: When **Table** is selected, different options display in the Table Lines/Fill dialog box.*

3. Click on the NO BORDER button in the Border Lines box {Alt and b, Spacebar}.

   Note: A palette of border styles displays (see Figure 5.8).

4. Move the mouse pointer to the desired border style and click once {press the arrow keys until the desired border style is selected; Enter}.

   For example, move the mouse pointer to the double border (first border in the third row) and click once.

5. Select OK {press Enter}.

   Note: The table displays with double borders on the top, bottom, left, and right sides.

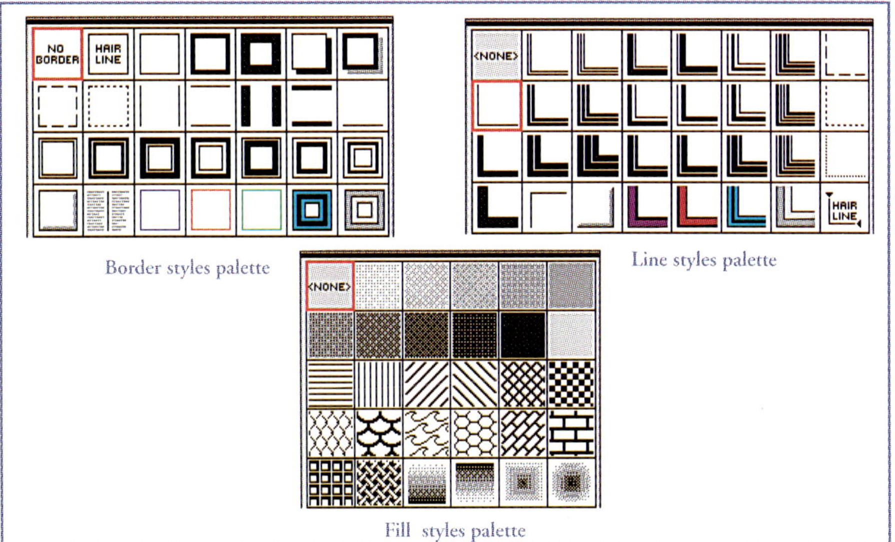

FIGURE 5.8

Line, Border, and Fill styles palettes

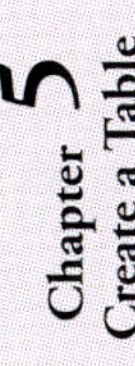

Steps to Change Table Lines

1. Select the cell(s) where the line(s) is to be changed. (If necessary, see Step 1 of the Steps to Join Table Cells on page 109 for selecting cells.)

   For example, select all cells in row 2 where the column headings are located.

2. Select the TblLineFill button on the Tables Button Bar {Alt, a, L *or* Shift and F12}.

   Note: The current Cell or Selection option is chosen.

3. Click once on the desired Line Styles option button.

   For example, click on the **Bottom** button {Alt and b, Spacebar}.

   Note: A palette of line styles displays (see Figure 5.8).

4. Move the mouse pointer to the desired line style and click once {press the arrow keys until the desired line style is selected; Enter}.

   For example, move the mouse pointer to the double line option (first row, to the right of "None") and click once.

5. Select OK {press Enter}.

   Note: The bottom line of row 2 displays with a double line.

Steps to Fill (Shade) Table Cells

1. Select the cells to be shaded. (If necessary see Step 1 in the Steps to Join Table Cells on page 109.)

   For example, select all cells with money amounts.

2. Select the TblLineFill button on the Tables Button Bar {Alt, a, L *or* Shift and F12}.

3. Click on the NONE button in the Fill Options box {Alt and f, Spacebar}.

   Note: A palette of fill options displays (see Figure 5.8).

4. Move the mouse pointer to the desired fill option and click once {press the arrow keys until the desired option is selected; Enter}.

   For example, move the mouse pointer to the lightest shaded sample, 10% fill (first row, to the right of <NONE>) and click once.

   Note: A 10% fill displays in the Fill style box.

5. Select OK {Enter}.

   Note: Click once to deselect the cells and display the 10% fill.

Finish-Up Instructions

- Select the title and column headings in rows 1 and 2 and change the font to Swiss721 BlkEx BT, 14-point.
- Use the *new* filename **5drill3.fil** and save the file (select **File**, **Save As**; type the filename; if necessary, click in the Drives box and click on the drive letter where the file disk is located; select **OK**).

Center a Table or Text Vertically

Table rows or lines of text can be centered vertically on a page between the top and bottom margins. On an 8½ by 11-inch sheet of paper, approximately 66 lines (6 lines per inch) or approximately 33 table rows (3 lines per inch) can be printed. Text that occupies fewer than 54 lines (66 – 12 = 2" top/bottom margins) and tables that occupy fewer than 27 rows will usually display more attractively on a page if the lines/rows are centered between the top and bottom margins. The tables typed in this book will be fewer than 20 rows; therefore, vertical centering will be useful.

Start-Up Instructions

- The file named **5drill3.fil** should be displayed in the document window.

Center a Table or Text Vertically

1. With the insertion point located in any table cell, select Layout, Page, Center {Alt and L, p, c}.
2. Select the Current Page {p}.
3. Select OK {Enter}.

   *Note: Select the **Page Zoom Full** button to view the table centered vertically on the page. Select the **Page Zoom Full** button again to return to the normal view. Select **View, Draft** to display the table at the top of the document window.*

Finish-Up Instructions

- Save the file again using the same filename **5drill3.fil** (select the **Save** button).
- Print one copy (select the **Print** button; choose **Print**).
- Close the document (select **File**, **Close**).

The Next Step

Chapter Review and Activities

Self-Check Quiz

T F 1. A table can be created using the **Tables Quick Create** button on the Power Bar.

T F 2. The intersection of each column and row is called a cell.

T F 3. The **Enter** key is pressed in a cell in order to insert a new table row.

T F 4. Formatting a table can include increasing or decreasing the table column widths.

T F 5. Text that is separated by tabs and hard returns can be converted to a table.

6. When the **Decimal** justification option is selected, figures are aligned
   a. at the left digit.
   b. at the right digit.
   c. at the decimal point.
   d. either b or c.

7. To use the **Tab** key to indent text in a cell, press
   a. Tab.
   b. Shift and Tab.
   c. Ctrl and Tab.
   d. none of the above.

8. A table or text can be centered vertically on a page by selecting **Layout**, **Page**, **Center**, and choosing
   a. **Current Page**.
   b. **Current and Subsequent Pages**.
   c. **Center Page(s)**.

9. State the primary purpose for formatting a table.

10. Give one reason for joining table cells.

Enriching Language Arts Skills

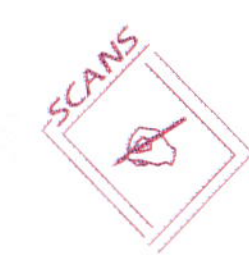

Spelling/Vocabulary Words

initiative readiness to begin action.
strategic pertaining to the importance of accomplishing a plan.
alliances a joining together to meet a common goal.

Dollar Amounts Formats

Use a comma to separate the number digits into groups of thousands. No space is placed between a number and the dollar sign. If even numbers are used in the body of a document or if a column of numbers has even dollar amounts, the zeros are omitted. Even dollar amounts can either be right justified or decimal justified in a column in order to align the numbers on the right.

Example:

```
$28,655,342
      1,389
     10,843
```

Activities

Activity 5.1—Create and Format a Table and Change Table Number Type

1. Create a table with 3 columns and 4 rows (select the **Table Quick Create** button on the Power Bar, press and hold the mouse button and drag to highlight a 3 x 4 table, release the mouse button).
2. Type the unformatted text as shown.

Federated Growth Trust	Yearly increase	1453.55
Colonial Growth Shares	Bi-annual increase	675.67
Fidelity Set Energy	Quarterly increase	420.25
Global Income Trust	Yearly increase	1600.75

3. Use the filename **5act1.tbl** and save the file.
4. Use the following instructions to format the table:
   a. Change the justification for the text in column B to **Right**. (Select all cells in column B. Select the **Justification** button and choose **Right**. Click once to deselect the cells.)
   b. Change the justification for the figures in column C to **Decimal**. (Select all cells in column C. Select the **Justification** button and choose **Decimal**. Click once to deselect the cells.)
   c. Change the number type for cell C1 to **Currency**. (Select cell C1, choose the **Tbl # Type** button, and select **Currency**, **OK**.)
   d. Change the number type for cells **C2** through **C4** to **Commas**. (Select cells **C2** through **C4**, choose the **Tbl # Type** button, and select **Commas**, **OK**.)
   e. Visually estimate and decrease columns B and C to approximately 2 inches wide each. (Place the mouse pointer on the column line between columns B and C until the double-headed arrow displays. Press

and hold the mouse button while dragging the line to the left. Release the mouse button. Repeat for the column line at the right of the table.)

f. Position the table centered horizontally on the page (select **Format Tbl**, **Table**, **Table Position**, **Center**, **OK**).

*Note: Your table should look **similar** to the following:*

Federated Growth Trust	Yearly increase	$1,453.55
Colonial Growth Shares	Bi-annual increase	675.67
Fidelity Set Energy	Quarterly increase	420.25
Global Income Trust	Yearly increase	1,600.75

5. Use the same filename, **5act1.tbl**, and save the file again (select the **Save** button).
6. If desired, select the **Page Zoom Full** button to view the table horizontally centered. Select the **Page Zoom Full** button again to return to the normal view.
7. Print one copy (select the **Print** button; choose **Print**).
8. Close the document (select **File**, **Close**).

Activity 5.2—Create and Format a Table, Insert Rows, Join Cells, Change Table Number Type, and Change Row Height

1. Create a table with 2 columns and 5 rows (select the **Table Quick Create** button on the Power Bar, press and hold the mouse button while dragging to highlight a 2 x 5 table, release the mouse button).
2. Type the unformatted text as shown.

Alaska	402500
Iowa	2993000
New York	18499500
Oklahoma	3188000
Texas	14555000

3. Change the number type for column B to Commas and set the digits after the decimal to zero. (Select cells **B1** through **B5**. Choose the **Tbl # Type** button and select **Commas**, select **Custom**, click twice on the down triangle beside the Digits after Decimal box to display zero (0), and select **OK** twice.)
4. Change the justification of column B to Decimal. (With column B selected, move the mouse pointer to the **Justification** button, press and hold the mouse button while dragging to select **Decimal**. Release the mouse button.)
5. Click to deselect the formatted figures.

6. Insert three rows (place the insertion point in either cell in row 1, select the **Tbl Insert** button, click on **Rows**, type **3**, select **OK**).
7. Join the row 1 cells (select the cells in row 1; select **Tables**, **Join**, **Cell**).
8. Join the second row cells.
9. Center all cells in rows 1, 2, and 3. (Select all cells in rows 1, 2, and 3. Move the mouse pointer to the **Justification** button, press and hold the mouse button while dragging to select **Center**. Release the mouse button. Click once to deselect the cells.)
10. Change the row height for the first two rows to **.5**. (Select the first two rows, select the **Format Tbl** button, select **Row Height**, select **Fixed**; type **.5**; **OK**. Click once to deselect the cells.)
11. In row 1, type the title **State Populations** in the top row. Notice that the text is centered.
12. In row 2, type the subtitle **(Approximately)**.
13. Type the column headings **State** and **Population** in the third row cells.
14. Visually estimate and decrease the width of columns A and B to approximately 2". (Place the mouse pointer on the column line between columns B and C until the double-headed arrow displays. Press and hold the mouse button while dragging the line to the left. Release the mouse button. Repeat for the column line at the right of the table.).

    Note: *Your table should look similar to the following table:*

State Populations	
(Approximately)	
State	Population
Alaska	402,500
Iowa	2,993,000
New York	18,499,500
Oklahoma	3,188,000
Texas	14,555,000

15. Center the table horizontally on the page (select the **Format Tbl** button; select **Table**, **Table Position**, **Center**, **OK**).
16. Use the filename **5act2.spa** and save the file (select the **Save** button; type the filename; if necessary, click in the Drives box and click on the drive letter where the file disk is located; select **OK**).
17. Print one copy (select the **Print** button; choose **Print**).
18. Close the document (select **File**, **Close**).

Activity 5.3—Create and Format a Table, Insert a Column, Shade Cells, and Change Table Number Type

1. Create a table with 2 columns and 5 rows (select the **Tables Quick Create** button on the Power Bar, press and hold the mouse button while dragging to highlight a 2 x 5 table, release the mouse button).

2. Type the unformatted text as shown.

Mortgage Affordability	
Annual Income	Mortgage Amount
25000	55000
45000	115000
65000	166000

3. Use the following information to format the table shown:

   a. Select and join the cells in row 1 (select **Table, Join, Cell**).

   b. Select and center the title and column heading cells in rows 1 and 2. (With rows 1 and 2 selected, move the mouse pointer to the **Justification** button, press and hold the mouse button while dragging to select **Center**. Release the mouse button.)

   c. With all cells in rows 1 and 2 selected, shade the cells. (Select the **TblLineFill** button, click on the **None** button in the Fill Options box, click on the lightest fill style, **OK**.)

   d. Select all cells that contain dollar amounts and set the number type to **Commas** and the digits after the decimal to zero. (Select the **Tbl # Type** button, select **Commas**; select **Custom**, click twice on the down triangle twice beside the Digits after Decimal box to display zero (0), select **OK** twice.)

   e. With the cells containing amounts highlighted, select the **Justification** button and choose **Decimal**. Click once to deselect the cells.

   f. Insert one new table column between columns A and B (place the insertion point in column B, select the **Tbl Insert** button, select **Columns, OK**).

   g. Type the following information into the new column cells:

Home Price
68,500
136,700
205,200

   h. Visually estimate and adjust each table column width to approximately 2". (Move the mouse pointer to the desired column line until the double-headed arrow displays, press and hold the mouse button and drag the mouse left to decrease the column width.)

i. Change the number type for all cells in row 3 to Currency and change the digits after the decimal to zero. (Select the cells in row 3, select the **Tbl#Type** button, choose **Currency**; select **Custom**, click twice on the down triangle beside the Digits after Decimal box to display zero (0), and select **OK** twice).

j. Center the table horizontally (select the **Tbl Fmt** button on the Tables Button Bar, choose **Center** in the Table Position box, **OK**).

Note: Your table should look similar to the following:

Mortgage Affordability		
Annual Income	Home Price	Mortgage
$25,000	$68,500	$55,000
45,000	136,700	115,000
65,000	205,200	166,000

4. Use the filename **5act3.mag** and save the file (select the **Save** button; type the filename; if necessary, click in the Drives box and click on the drive letter where the file disk is located; select **OK**).
5. Print one copy (select the **Print** button; choose **Print**).
6. Close the document (select **File**, **Close**).

Activity 5.4—Create and Format a Table, Change Table Lines

1. Create a table with 4 columns and 6 rows (select the **Table Quick Create** button Power Bar, press and hold the mouse button while dragging to highlight a 4 x 6 table, release the mouse button).
2. Type the unformatted text as shown.

Daily Summary of Sales Calls			
July 21	General	Agency	Total
Calls offered	5393	971	6364
Calls lost	121	10	131
Inquiries	1877	896	2773
Bookings	650	251	901

3. Use the following information to format the table:

a. Select and join the cells in row 1 (select **Table, Join**, **Cell**).

b. Center the title in row 1. (Move the mouse pointer to the **Justification** button, press and hold the mouse button while dragging to select **Center**. Release the mouse button.)

c. Select cells B2 through D6 and use **Right** justification. (Move the mouse pointer to the **Justification** button, press and hold the mouse button while dragging to select **Right**. Release the mouse button.)

d. Visually estimate and decrease the column width of columns B, C, and D to approximately 1.25". (Move the pointer to the desired column line until the double-headed arrow displays, press and hold the mouse button and drag the mouse left to decrease the column width.)

e. Select all table cells and set the row height to .5". (Select the **Format Tbl** button, select **Row**, select **Row Height**, select **Fixed**; type .5, select **OK**. Click to deselect the cells.)

f. Center the table horizontally (select the **Format Tbl** button, select **Table**, choose **Center** in the Table Position box, select **OK**).

g. Select all cells in row 2 and choose double lines for the top and bottom. (Select the **TblLineFill** button, click on the line style button beside the word **Top**, click on the double-line style; click on the line style button beside the word **Bottom**, click on the double-line sample; select **OK**.)

h. Center the table vertically (select **Layout**, **Page**, **Center**, **Current Page**, **OK**).

*Note: If desired, select the **Page Zoom Full** button on the Power Bar to view the centered table. Select the **Page Zoom Full** button again to return to normal view. Your table should look similar to the following:*

Daily Summary of Sales Calls			
July 21	General	Agency	Total
Calls offered	5,393	971	6,364
Calls lost	121	10	131
Inquiries	1,877	896	2,773
Bookings	650	251	901

4. Use the filename **5act4.dss** and save the file (select **Save** button; type the filename; if necessary, click in the Drives box and click on the drive letter where the file disk is located; select **OK**).

5. Print one copy (select the **Print** button; choose **Print**).

6. Close the document (select **File**, **Close**).

Challenge Your Skills

Skill 5.1—Create and Format a Table, Insert a Column, Change Row Height, and Shade Cells

1. Create a table with 3 columns and 12 rows.
2. Type the unformatted text as shown.

Parts List		
Item	Description	Part No.
A	Left upright	3307-6
B	Right upright	3308-4
C	Top shelf	3310-5
D	Rail	3311-7
E	Bottom shelf	3314-2
F	Adjustable shelf	4400-1
G	Kick panel	4415-8
H	Back panel	4418-2
I	Screw	4420-2
J	Dowel	4422-6

3. Use the following information to format the table:
   a. Join the cells in row 1.
   b. Select and center the title and column heading cells in rows 1 and 2.
   c. Use **Center** justification in all cells of column A except the title and column heading. Use **Right** justification in all the cells of column C except the column heading.
   d. Insert a column between columns B and C.
   e. Set **Center** justification for all cells of the new column C, including the column heading.
   f. Use a light fill (shading) for rows 1 and 2.
   g. Set the row height for rows 1 and 2 to .4".
   h. Type the text as shown into the new column.

Quantity
1
1
1
3

1
2
1
1
8
12

i. Change the font for the entire table to **Arrus BT, 14-point.**

j. Adjust the widths of the columns so that the table information is appealing and easy to read.

k. Center the table horizontally and vertically.

4. Use the filename **5skill1.pal** and save the file.
5. Print one copy.
6. Close the document.

Skill 5.2—Create and Format a Table and Insert Rows and a Column

1. Create a table with 2 columns and 8 rows and type the unformatted text as shown.

Cost/Expense Items	Amount Budgeted
Salaries, programmers	96000
Salaries, system designers	106000
Salaries, computer operators	120000
Salary, manager	68000
Computer supplies	35000
Miscellaneous expenses	5500
Insurance	12500

2. Use the following information to format the table:

a. Insert a row at the top of the table. Join the cells in row 1. Set the row height for row 1 to .5".

b. Type the title **R & A Consulting Services** and use **Center** justification.

c. Select cells B2 through B9 and set **Decimal** justification (including the column heading cell).

d. Insert a new row above "Miscellaneous expenses."

e. Type the following information into the new row:
Depreciation, furniture; 6,500

f. Insert a column between columns A and B.

g. Type the following information into the new column cells:
   Actual Amount Spent; 95060.25; 85081.16; 129882.43; 73247.20; 43463.50; 6500.00; 6700.00; 13240.00

3. Make decisions regarding number type format and the digits after the decimal for the cells containing figures.
4. Make decisions regarding border, line, and fill styles for cells, font changes, table lines, and column widths so that the table information appears pleasing and easy to read.
5. Use the filename **5skill2.rac** and save the file.
6. Print one copy.
7. Close the document.

Skill 5.3—Create and Format a Memorandum with a Table; Language Arts

1. Use Memorandum—Style 1 and the following information:
   a. The memo should be sent to Abby Foods Group from Helen Millard.
   b. The subject of the memo is New Vice President.
   c. Use the current date; include your reference initials.
   d. Correct three spelling errors, one punctuation error, and one dollar amount format error.
   e. After creating the table, format cells as desired (e.g., increase or decrease column widths, change the justification of column headings, choose fill style for desired cells, change table lines, and set the number type, digits after decimal, and justification for dollar amounts.
   f. The memorandum body text follows:

Douglas Bartlett has been appointed to the position of Vice President, Business Development and National Accounts--Grocery, Sales & Integrated Logistics Division.

The role of Business Development continues to grow in importance as the cornerstone of Sales & Integrated Logistics' intiative to pursue strategic customer aliances. In this new position Douglas will be responsible for developing and directing startegic programs and partnership alliances with national and regional account grocery customers. He will report to Gayleen Kirkland, Senior Vice President, Sales & Integrated Logistics Division, Abby Foods Group.

Reporting to Douglas are:

Name	Accounts	Account Value
Santiago Cruz	Business Development & National Accounts	390000
Veronica Johnson	Business Development & Eastern Region	135000
Richard Epstein	Business Development & Midwestern Region	96000
Connie Jimenez	Business Development & Southern Region	78000.00

Douglas assumes his new responsibilities from the position of Regional Vice President, Broker Sales, Central Region. His office is located at 2022 Oakton Street, Des Plaines, IL 60018, and the telephone number is (708) 555-9009.

---

2. Use the filename **5skill3.nat** and save the file.
3. Print one copy.
4. Close the document.
5. If you have completed your work, exit WordPerfect.

CHAPTER 6

Edit a Table

Features Covered

- Move a row and column
- Delete a row and column
- Change table row margins
- Copy a table
- Delete a table
- Calculate column and row totals
- Copy a formula
- Omit table lines and borders
- Print double underlines

Chapter Objectives and Introduction

After successfully completing this chapter, you will be able to move and delete a table row and column, change table row margins, and copy and delete a table. You will also be able to calculate a column or row total, set the number type and digits after the decimal, omit table lines and borders, and use double underlines. Once a table has been typed and printed, the table information can be edited. Changes can include moving or deleting columns and rows, changing row margins, and omitting table lines. A formula can be used to total a column or row, and can be copied to other cells. An entire table can also be copied or deleted.

Move a Table Column or Row

A table column or row can be moved to another column or row location within a table. When a column or row is moved, the column or row is deleted from the original location and relocated. When a column or row is copied, the column or row displays in the original location *and* the new location.

Delete a Table Column or Row

When editing a table, a column or row can be deleted. A column or row is deleted by first placing the insertion point in the column or row to be deleted and then choosing the **Delete Tbl** button on the Tables Button Bar and selecting **Rows** or **Columns**. A row or column can also be deleted by selecting the row or column and choosing the **Cut** button on the Power Bar.

If a column or row is deleted by mistake, **Edit**, **Undo** can be selected (or select the **Undo** button on the Power Bar) to retrieve and display the deleted column or row. However, **Edit**, **Undo** must be selected before another action is performed.

Start-Up Instructions

- The file named **6drill2.row** should be displayed in the document window.

Steps to Delete a Table Column

1. Place the insertion point in any cell in the column to be deleted.

   For example, place the insertion point in any cell in column B. (Check the Status bar to confirm the cell address.)

2. Select the Delete Tbl button on the Tables Button Bar {Alt, a, d}.

   Note: The Delete dialog box displays.

3. Select the desired delete option.

   For example, select **Columns** {c}.

   Note: The number "1" displays.

4. Select OK to delete one column {press Enter}.

   Note: If a table column is deleted by mistake, select the ***Undo*** *button to retrieve the deleted column.*

Finish-Up Instructions

- Use the *new* filename **6drill2.del** and save the file on the file disk (select **File**, **Save As**; type the filename; if necessary, click in the Drives box and click on the drive letter where your file disk is located; select **OK**).
- Print one copy (select the **Print** button; choose **Print**).

Start-Up Instructions

- The file named **6drill2.del** should be displayed in the document window.

Delete a Table Row

1. Place the insertion point in any cell in the row to be deleted.

   For example, place the insertion point in any cell in row 3.

2. Select the Delete Tbl button on the Tables Button Bar {Alt, a, d}.

3. Select the desired delete option.

   For example, check that Rows is selected and that the number "1" displays.

4. Select OK {Enter}.

   Note: If a table row is deleted by mistake, select the ***Undo*** *button to retrieve the deleted row.*

Finish-Up Instructions

- Use the *new* filename **6drill2.dtr** and save the file on the file disk (select **File, Save As**; type the filename; if necessary, click in the Drives box and click on the drive letter where your file disk is located; select **OK**).
- Print one copy (select the **Print** button; choose **Print**).

Change Table Row Margins

Another WordPerfect editing feature is the capability to change any or all table row margins. The row margins are the spaces that are placed between the cell text and the top, bottom, left, and right table cell lines. For example, the space placed between the top table line and the cell text is the top row margin. The cell margins are measured in fractions of inches. An example of a top row margin is .1 inches.

Row margins are changed by using the Table Format dialog box. Before setting row margins, select the cell(s) where margins are to be changed. The **Row** option is chosen to display the Row Margin options. The desired row margins can be typed or the up and down triangles can be selected to increase or decrease the amount displayed in the Top/Bottom option boxes.

Start-Up Instructions

- The file named **6drill2.dtr** should be displayed in the document window.

Change Table Row Margins

1. Select the row(s) where the row margin is to be changed.

   For example, select all table cells by moving the mouse pointer to the top or left side of any cell until the top or left selection arrow displays and triple-click {place the insertion point in the first table cell, press and hold the Shift key, then press the down arrow key until all rows are highlighted}.

2. Select the Format Tbl button on the Tables Button Bar {Alt, a, o *or* Ctrl and F12}.

3. Select Row {o}.

   Note: The Format dialog box changes to display only the row format options.

4. Double-click in the desired Row Margins box.

   For example, double-click in the **Top** option box {p}.

5. Type the desired margin for the table row(s).

    For example, type .2. (Do not type the final period.)

6. Double-click in the desired Row Margins box.

    For example, double-click in the **Bottom** option box {press Tab}.

7. Type the desired margin for the table row(s).

    For example, type .2. (Do not type the final period.)

    *Note: Check that the **Auto** option is selected in the Row Height box.*

8. Select OK {press Enter}.

    Note: The top and bottom cell margins in all cells are changed. If desired, click once to deselect the table cells.

Finish-Up Instructions

- Use the *new* filename **6drill2.mar** and save the file on the file disk (select **File**, **Save As**; type the filename; if necessary, click in the Drives box and click on the drive letter where your file disk is located; select **OK**).
- Print one copy (select the **Print** button; choose **Print**).
- Continue with the following Steps to Copy a Table or close the document.

Copy a Table

An entire table can be copied to another window or to another location within the current document window. A table is often copied for the purpose of making changes to the copied table without changing the original table, for the purpose of saving paper by placing two items on a page, or for the purpose of using the table information in another letter, memorandum, or report.

Start-Up Instructions

- The file named **6drill2.mar** should be displayed in the document window.

Steps to Copy a Table

1. Select the entire table by moving the mouse pointer to the top or left of any cell to obtain the up or left selection arrow and triple-click {place the insertion point in the first cell of the table, press and hold the Shift key while tapping the down arrow key}.

2. Select the Copy button on the Power Bar {Alt, e, c *or* Ctrl and x}.

    Note: The Table Cut/Copy dialog box displays.

3. Select Column or Row {c or r}.

4. Select OK {Enter}.

    Note: A copy of the table is placed in the Clipboard.

5. Locate the insertion point at the desired position.

For example, move the mouse pointer below the table and click once {press the down arrow key repeatedly}. Press the **Enter** key once to place a hard return after the table.

6. Select the **Paste** button on the Power Bar {Alt, e, p *or* Ctrl and v}.

   Note: *A copy of the table is inserted at the location of the insertion point.*

Finish-Up Instructions

- Use the *new* filename **6drill3.cop** and save the file on the file disk (select **File, Save As**; type the filename; if necessary, click in the Drives box and click on the drive letter where your file disk is located; select **OK**).
- Optional. Print one copy (select the **Print** button; choose **Print**).
- Continue with the Steps to Delete a Table or close the document.

Delete a Table

A table can be deleted by selecting the entire table. If a table is deleted by mistake, select the **Undo** button on the Power Bar to retrieve and display the table on the screen again. The **Undo** button must be selected before any other operation is performed.

Start-Up Instructions

- The file named **6drill3.cop** should be displayed in the document window.

Delete a Table

1. Select the table to be deleted.

   For example, select the first table by moving the mouse pointer to the top or left of any cell in the table until the up or left selection arrow displays and triple-click {place the insertion point in the first cell of the table, press and hold the Shift key while tapping the down arrow key}.

2. Select the **Delete Tbl** button on the Table Button Bar {Alt, a, d}.

   Note: *The Delete Table dialog box displays with the Entire Table option selected.*

3. Select **OK** {Enter}.

Finish-Up Instructions

- Close the document and do not save the file.

Calculate a Column or Row Total

Table cells containing numbers (values) can be calculated by using formulas to add, subtract, multiply, or divide. A value number is a number used to obtain a mathematical result. A text number is a number that will not be used to compute a result. Examples of text numbers are a social security number or a year (e.g., 1995).

Columns and rows are totaled by using a table formula. Table formulas are easily created in the Edit Formula box located in the Table Formula Feature Bar. The Tables Formula Feature Bar is displayed by selecting the **TblFormBar** on the Tables Button Bar. The insertion point is first placed in the cell that will contain the column or row sum and then is placed in the Edit Formula box. The formula is typed or selected from the list of table functions. The table cells to be summed are typed or selected using the mouse. An example of a formula to add a column is *SUM(B3:B7).*

A shortcut for summing a column is to locate the insertion point in the desired cell, then click in the Edit Formula box and select the **Sum** button. The Sum button shortcut method can also be used to total a single row; however, the row must be the first row containing numbers in the table.

With the Tables Button Bar displayed, a formula is deleted from a cell by placing the insertion point in the cell and selecting **Delete Tbl** and choosing **Cell Contents.** Also, a formula can be deleted by selecting the cell and choosing **Edit, Cut** or by selecting the **Cut** button on the Power Bar.

If numbers (values) are changed in the table cells, the cells that contain formula results will need to be recalculated. One method to recalculate is to select the **Calculate** button on the Tables Formula Feature Bar. When the **Calculate** button is selected on the Tables Formula Feature Bar, all formulas in every table in the document are recalculated.

A second method to recalculate is to select the **Calculate** button on the Tables Button Bar. When the **Calculate** button on the Tables Button Bar is chosen, the Calculate dialog box displays. The **Calc Table** button is selected to recalculate the formula(s) in the current table or the **Calc Document** button is selected to recalculate the formulas in every table in the document.

Also in the Calculate dialog box, the **Calculate Table** and **Calculate Document** options can be used to turn on the automatic recalculate feature. If the **Calculate Table** option is selected, the formula(s) in the current table are automatically recalculated. If the **Calculate Document** option is selected, formulas in every table in the document are automatically recalculated. The automatic recalculation takes place after a number is changed and the insertion point is moved to another cell.

Start-Up Instructions

- Open the file named **6drill4.exp** located on the data disk.

Steps to Use a Formula to Calculate the Sum of a Column

1. Select the TblFormBar button on the Tables Button Bar {Alt, a, r}.

   Note: *The Table Formula Feature Bar displays below the Power Bar (see Figure 6.3).*

2. Place the insertion point in the cell where the calculated sum will be placed.

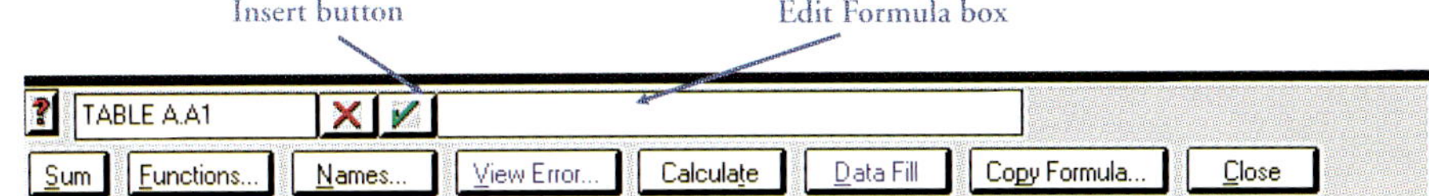

FIGURE 6.3

Table Formula Feature Bar

Chapter 6
Edit a Table

For example, place the insertion point in cell B8. (Check the Status bar to confirm the cell address.)

3. Move the mouse pointer to the Edit Formula box in the Table Formula Feature Bar and click once {Alt and Shift and e}.

   Note: *The insertion point displays in the Edit Formula box. The message "Formula Edit mode is on" displays in the right side of the Table Formula Feature Bar.*

4. Select the **Functions** button located in the Table Formula Feature Bar {Alt and Shift and f}.

   Note: *The Table Functions dialog box displays.*

5. Click on the scroll box in the Function box to scroll down until the desired function displays. Move the mouse pointer to the desired function and double-click {type the letters of the desired function until the function name is highlighted}.

   For example, scroll down the list of functions until SUM(List) displays. Move the mouse pointer to **SUM(List)** and double-click {type sum, press Enter}.

   Note: *The SUM(List) function displays in the Edit Formula box with the word List highlighted.*

6. Select the cells to be calculated {type the cell addresses to be calculated separated by a colon or period.

   For example, select cells B3 through B7 {type B3:B7}.

   Note: *When the mouse is used to select the cells, the cell addresses B3:B7 display in the Edit Formula box and the cells are highlighted in the table.*

7. Select the **Insert** button (✓) located to the left of the Edit Formula box to insert the formula and results in the current cell (where the insertion point is located) {press Enter}.

   Note: *The Column sum displays in cell B8. The formula for cell B8 displays in the Status bar at the bottom middle of the document window, e.g., TABLE A Cell B8 = SUM(B3:B7). TABLE A indicates that this is the first table in a document.*

Shortcut

1. With the Table Formula Feature Bar displayed, place the insertion point in the cell where the calculated sum will be placed.
2. Click once in the Edit Formula box to locate and display the insertion point.
3. Click on the **SUM** button on the Table Formula Feature Bar.

Finish-Up Instructions

- Place the insertion point in cell C8 and use the shortcut to total the values in column C.

FIGURE 6.4

Edited table

Division Expenses		
Expense Category	Eastern Division	Western Division
Indirect labor	$34,500	$38,600
Materials	14,800	15,200
Supplies	15,800	16,200
Utilities	17,400	18,200
Insurance	12,500	13,700
TOTALS	$95,000	$101,900

- Use the filename **6drill4.cal** and save the file on the file disk (select **File**, **Save As**; type the filename; if necessary, click in the Drives box and click on the drive letter where your file disk is located; select **OK**).

Start-Up Instructions

- The file named **6drill4.cal** should be displayed in the document window.
- The Table Formula Feature Bar should be displayed (if necessary, select the **TblFormBar** button on the Tables Button Bar).
- Edit the table as shown in Figure 6.4.

Edit Table Figures and Recalculate

1. After the table figures have been changed, place the insertion point in any table cell.

   Note: To change any number, select the original number, then type the revised number.

2. Select the Calculate button on the Table Formula Feature Bar to automatically recalculate the table column totals {Alt, e, a}.

   Note: If the ***Calculate*** *button is selected on the Tables Button Bar, the Calculate dialog box displays. Select the* ***Calc Table*** *button to automatically update the column totals.*

3. If desired, select Close on the Table Formula Feature Bar.

Finish-Up Instructions

- Use the *new* filename **6drill5.rev** and save the file on the file disk (select **File**, **Save As**; type the filename; if necessary, click in the Drives box and click on the drive letter where your file disk is located; select **OK**).
- Print one copy (select the **Print** button; choose **Print**).

Start-Up Instructions

- The file named **6drill5.rev** should be displayed in the document window.
- Insert one table column after column C (place the insertion point in any cell in column C, select the **Tbl Insert** button, select **Columns**, select **After, OK**).
- Select and join the cells in row 1 (select **Table**, **Join**, **Cell**).

- Type the column heading **Total Expenses** in cell D2. Visually estimate and decrease the column widths so they appear approximately the same width. The first row total will be calculated in the following Steps to Total a Row.

Steps to Total a Row

1. Place the insertion point in the cell where the row total is to be inserted.

   For example, place the insertion point in cell D3.

2. If necessary, select the **TblFormBar** button on the Tables Button Bar {Alt, a, r}.

   Note: *The Table Formula Feature Bar displays below the Power Bar.*

3. Move the mouse pointer to the Edit Formula box in the Table Formula Feature Bar and click once {Alt and Shift and e}.

   Note: *The insertion point displays in the Edit Formula box.*

4. Select the **Functions** button located in the Table Formula Feature Bar {Alt and Shift and f}.

5. Click on the scroll box in the Function box to scroll down until the desired function displays. Move the mouse pointer to the desired function and double-click {type the letters of the desired function until the function name is highlighted}.

   For example, scroll down the list of functions until SUM(List) displays. Move the mouse pointer to **SUM(List)** and double-click {type sum, press Enter}.

6. Select the cells to be calculated {type the cell addresses to be calculated separated by a colon or period}.

   For example, select cells B3 through C3.

   Note: *When the mouse is used to select cells, the cell addresses B3:C3 display in the Edit Formula box and the cells are highlighted in the table.*

7. Select the Insert button (✓) located to the left of the Edit Formula box to insert the formula and results in the current cell {press Enter}.

   Note: *The row sum displays in cell D3. The formula for cell D3 displays in the Status bar, e.g., TABLE A Cell D3 = Sum (B3:C3). TABLE A indicates that this is the first table in a document.*

8. Select **Close** on the Table Formula Feature Bar {Alt and Shift and c}.

Finish-Up Instructions

- Use the *new* filename **6drill6.tro** and save the file on the file disk (select **File**, **Save As**; type the filename; if necessary, click in the Drives box and click on the drive letter where your file disk is located; select **OK**).
- Continue with the Steps to Copy a Formula.

Copy a Formula

After a formula is placed in a table cell, the formula can be copied to one or more cells. A formula can be copied to a single cell, down a column, or right across a row. A formula is copied to multiple cells by indicating direction (down or right) and the desired number of cells in which the formula should appear. For example, to copy a formula to five rows, the **Down** option is selected and the number 5 is placed in the Down option box.

After the formula is copied, the results are displayed immediately in the cell(s) where the formula was copied. When a formula is copied, the row and column cell addresses in the formula are automatically changed to reflect the cell addresses where the formula was copied.

Start-Up Instructions

- The file named **6drill6.tro** should be displayed in the document window.
- The Table Formula Feature Bar should be displayed. (If necessary, select the **TblFormBar** button on the Tables Button Bar.)

Copy a Formula

1. Place the insertion point in the cell that contains the formula to be copied.

   For example, place the insertion point in cell D3.

2. Select the Copy Formula button on the Table Formula Feature Bar {Alt and Shift and m}.

   Note: The Copy Formula dialog box displays. The Source box and the To Cell box both display the cell address, i.e., D3.

3. Select the Destination option.

   For example, select **Down** {Alt and d}.

   Note: The number "1" is highlighted in the Down box.

4. Select the up triangle to display the number of cells in which to copy the formula {type the desired number}.

   For example, click on the up triangle repeatedly until the number 5 displays.

   Note: The number in the Down option box will not accept a figure greater than the number of empty cells below the cell to be copied.

5. Select OK {press Enter}.

   Note: WordPerfect immediately copies the formula into each cell in column D and displays the total results for each row.

6. Select the Close button on the Table Formula Feature Bar {Alt and Shift and c}.

Finish-Up Instructions

- If necessary, visually estimate and change the column widths to appear approximately the same width.

- Use the *new* filename **6drill6.for** and save the file again (select **File**, **Save As**; type the filename; if necessary, click in the Drives box and click on the drive letter where your file disk is located, select **OK**).
- Print one copy (select the **Print** button; choose **Print**).

Omit Table Lines

The single lines that display around each cell are defaulted (preset) to print. The table lines and/or border can be omitted from table rows and cells. After the table lines or border are omitted, the table's row and column structure remains in effect.

Start-Up Instructions

- The file named **6drill6.for** should be displayed in the document window.

Steps to Omit All Table Lines

1. Place the insertion point in any table cell.
2. Select the TblLineFill button on the Tables Button Bar {Alt, a, L *or* Shift and F12}.

   Note: The Table Lines/Fill dialog box displays.
3. Select the Table option {a}.

   Note: The Table Lines/Fill options display.
4. Select the button to the right of the Line Style option {Alt and L, Spacebar}.

   Note: A palette of available line styles displays.
5. Click on <NONE> {press the arrow keys until NONE is selected; Enter}.
6. Select OK {press Enter}.

   Note: The table lines no longer display in the document window; however, the table's column and row structure remain in effect.

Finish-Up Instructions

- Select the row that contains the column headings; choose the **Underline** button on the Power Bar.
- Use the *new* filename **6drill6.omt** and save the file on the file disk (select **File**, **Save As**; type the filename; if necessary, click in the Drives box and click on the drive letter where your file disk is located; select **OK**).
- Optional. Print one copy (select the **Print** button; choose **Print**).

Print Double Underlines Below the Total Amount

Double underlines are placed under a column total amount in order to emphasize the total. Generally, if double underlines are used, table lines are not printed. When a column is totaled, a single underline is used to separate the last column amount from the total amount.

The single underline traditionally has been formatted to extend the width of the total amount. Therefore, one or more spaces were placed to the left of the last column number in order to extend the underline. Because WordPerfect's number type format feature does not allow a space(s) to be used to extend the underline, the additional space(s) will not be effective unless the General number format is used.

Traditionally, the dollar sign ($) in the first figure and the last figure of a column have been formatted to align. Since there is often an additional digit(s) in the total amount, an extra space(s) would be placed between the dollar sign and the first digit in the first column entry. However, WordPerfect's Table Number type feature does not allow a space to be placed between a dollar sign and an amount when the Currency format is selected.

Once the column total has been calculated, the amount is selected and the **Double Underline** attribute is selected in the Cell Format dialog box. An example of text with double underlines displays at the bottom of the Format dialog box.

Start-Up Instructions

- The file named **6drill6.omt** should be displayed in the document window.
- Select cells B7 to D7 in the row above the row containing the total amounts. Select the **Underline** button on the Power Bar.

Print Double Underlines

1. Select the cells that contain the total amounts.

   For example, select cells **B8, C8,** and **D8.**

2. Select the **Format Tbl** button on the Tables Button Bar {Alt, a, o *or* Ctrl and F12}.
3. Select the desired option.

   For example, check that **Cell** is selected. If necessary, select **Cell** {e}.

4. Select the **Double Underline** option in the Appearance box {d}.

   Note: *An X displays beside the Double Underline option. Also, a sample of text with double underlines displays at the bottom of the Format dialog box.*

5. Select **OK** {Enter}.

Finish-Up Instructions

- If necessary, click once to deselect the selected row.
- Use the *new* filename **6drill6.und** and save the file on the file disk (select **File, Save As**; type the filename; if necessary, click in the Drives box and click on the drive letter where your file disk is located; select **OK**).

- Print one copy (select the **Print** button; choose **Print**).
- Close the document (select **File**, **Close**).

The Next Step

Chapter Review and Activities

Self-Check Quiz

T F 1. A table row or column can be moved.

T F 2. Before deleting a table column, place the insertion point in any cell in the column to be deleted.

T F 3. An entire table can be copied to another document window or another location in the current document window.

T F 4. If table cell values or formulas are changed, the column or row totals can be recalculated and updated by selecting the **Calculate** button on the Table Formula Feature Bar.

5. A row or column can be deleted by choosing the ______ button on the Tables Button Bar and selecting **Rows** or **Columns**, **OK**.
   a. **Format Tbl**
   b. **TblCellForm**
   c. **Delete Tbl**
   d. **Tbl # Type**

6. A moved column is deleted from the original location and _______ a new location.
   a. duplicated in
   b. relocated to
   c. copied to
   d. reproduced in

7. When using the Table Formula Feature Bar, the _____ button is used to create a formula to total cells.
   a. **Sum**
   b. **Function**
   c. **Calculate**
   d. Either a or b.

8. The _______ table lines are defaulted to print.
   a. Single
   b. Double
   c. Thick/Thin 1
   d. None of these.

9. Write down the formula for adding three cells in row 4. The cells are located in columns C, D, and E.

10. Describe a table row margin.

7. Print one copy and close the document.

Activity 6.2—Move Columns, Change Row Margins, Copy a Table and Delete a Table

1. Create a table with 4 columns and 8 rows.
2. Type the following unformatted information into the table cells as shown. (Remember: Text will automatically wrap around in cells.)

Norton Products			
Annual Conference Costs			
Item	1992	1993	1994
Conference facilities	3600	4000	5000
Demonstration materials	2500	3400	4000
Accommodations	35500	36800	37600
Meals	25000	26000	26700
Travel	31900	32300	35400

3. Use the following instructions to format the table:
   a. Move column D (i.e., 1994 information) between columns A and B (move the mouse pointer to the top of any cell in column D to obtain the top selection arrow, double-click, select the **Cut** button, select **Column**, **OK**; place the insertion point in any cell in column B, select the **Paste** button).
   b. Move the now column D (1993 information) between columns B and C (see step 3a, if necessary).
   c. Select and join the cells in row 1.
   d. Select and join the cells in row 2.
   e. Select rows 1 and 2 and center the title and subtitle.
   f. Increase the width of column A so the words display on one line.
   g. Select the entire table and change the top and bottom row margins to .15 (move the mouse pointer to the top or left of any cell until the up or left selection arrow displays, triple-click; select the **Format Tbl** button, select **Row**, double-click in the **Top** Row Margins option box, type **.15**, double-click in the **Bottom** Row Margins option box, type **.15**, select **OK**).
   h. Select cells **B3** through **D8** and set **Decimal** justification (move the mouse pointer to the **Justification** button, press and hold the mouse button while dragging to select **Decimal**, release the mouse button).
   i. Select cells **B4** through **D4** and set the number type to **Currency** and the digits after the decimal to zero (select the **Tbl # Type** button, se-

lect **Currency**, select **Custom**, click twice on the down triangle beside the Digits after Decimal box, select **OK** twice).

j. Select cells **B5** through **D8** and set the number type to **Commas** and the digits after the decimal to zero (select the **Tbl # Type** button, select **Commas**, select **Custom**, click twice on the down triangle beside the Digits after Decimal box, select **OK** twice).

Note: Your table should look similar to the following table:

Norton Products			
Annual Conference Costs			
Item	1994	1993	1992
Conference facilities	$5,000	$4,000	$3,600
Demonstration materials	4,000	3,400	2,500
Accommodations	37,600	36,800	35,500
Meals	26,700	26,000	25,000
Travel	35,400	32,300	31,900

4. Copy the table.

   a. Select the entire table by moving the mouse pointer to the top or left of any cell in the table until the up or left selection arrow displays and triple-click.

   b. Select the **Copy** button.

   c. Move the mouse pointer below the table and click once; press the **Enter** key twice.

   d. Select the **Paste** button.

   ***Note:** To view both tables on the screen, select the **Page Zoom Full** button. Select the **Page Zoom Full** button again to return to the normal view.*

5. Save the file on the file disk; use the filename **6act2.nor**.

6. Print one copy.

7. Delete the first table.

   a. Repeat step 4a and select the entire table.

   b. Select the **Delete Tbl** button; select **OK**.

   ***Note:** Select the **Page Zoom Full** button to view the single remaining table. Select the **Page Zoom Full** button again to return to the normal view.*

8. Optional. Print the single table.

9. Close the document (do not save the modified file).

Activity 6.3—Copy a Formula, Delete a Row and Column and Omit Table Lines

1. Open the file named **6act3.mac** located on the data disk.
2. Calculate the sum of column B (select the **TblFormBar** button, place the insertion point in cell B10, click in the Edit Formula box, select **Sum**).
3. Copy the formula in cell B10 to C10 and D10 (place the insertion point in cell B10, select the **Copy Formula** button, select **Right**, type **2**, **OK**). Select the **Close** button on the Table Formula Feature Bar.
4. Select cells **B10** through **D10** and set the number type to **Currency** and set the digits after the decimal to zero (select the **Tbl # Type** button, select **Currency**, select **Custom**, click twice on the down triangle beside the Digits after Decimal box, select **OK** twice).

   Note: *Your table should look similar to the following table:*

MAINTENANCE COSTS			
Ardenwood Condominiums			
Job	April	May	June
Landscaping	$1,500	$1,500	$1,500
Pool cleaning	300	450	700
Roof repairs	8,670	4,200	3,700
Light fixtures	50	50	50
Deck repairs	5,000	4,600	4,950
Tennis courts	175	225	380
TOTALS	$15,695	$11,025	$11,280

5. Use the new filename **6act3.ard** and save the file on the file disk.
6. Print one copy.
7. Edit the table as follows:
   a. Delete row 8 (i.e., Deck repairs). (Place the insertion point in any cell in row 8, select the **Delete Tbl** button, check that **Rows** is selected, **OK**).

      Note: *The total amounts are automatically recalculated.*
   b. Delete column D (place the insertion point in any cell in column D, select the **Delete Tbl** button, select **Columns**, **OK**).
   c. Select the entire table and omit table lines (select the **TblLineFill** button, select **Table**, select the **Line Style** button, select **None**, **OK**).
   d. Select row 3 and underline the column headings (select the **Underline** button on the Power Bar).

e. Select and underline the figures in cells B8 and C8 (select the **Underline** button on the Power Bar).

f. Select and double underline the total amounts in cells B9 and C9 (select the **Format Tbl** button, select **Double Underline**, **OK**).

g. Center the table horizontally on the page (select the **Format Tbl** button, select **Table**, **Table Position**, **Center**, **OK**).

8. Use the *new* filename **6act3.con** and save the file on the file disk.

9. Print one copy and close the document.

Challenge Your Skills

Skill 6.1—Create a Table and a Formula

1. Create a two-column table using the following information:

   a. The title of the table is TOTAL PRINTER STAND COST.

   b. The price of the Premium Printer Stand is $99.99.

   c. Shipping and Handling will be $5.50.

   d. The charge for Express Delivery is $15.00.

   e. Calculate the total amount due.

2. Make decisions regarding:

   Justification for table columns
   Row margins
   Column widths
   Placement of the table on the page (vertically and horizontally)
   Table lines and border
   Shading cells
   Single and double underlines

3. Use the filename **6skill1.tot** and save the file.

4. Print one copy and close the document.

Skill 6.2—Calculate Column Totals; Language Arts Skills

1. Use the traditional style letter and the following information:

   a. The letter should be addressed to Mr. N. G. Specht, Branch Manager, Tucker-Haynes Corporation, 206 Midvale Blvd., Madison, WI 53705.

   b. The letter is from Loreen K. Faulkner, District Manager.

   c. Make decisions regarding:

      Margins
      Justification
      Date
      Salutation

Closing
Justification for table columns
Number type and digits after the decimal
Formulas
Table lines and border
Shading cells
Reference initials
Document identification

d. Correct three spelling, two punctuation, and one dollar amount format errors.

e. Letter body text follows:

Changes in our corporate travel reimbursement rates are necessary because of increased capital expenditures. The current travel rates remain in effect until the first of next month.

The following table shows the current and new rates.

Per Diem Amounts		
Item	Current Rate	New Rate
Lodging	95.00	105.00
Breakfast	9.00	6.00
Lunch	10.50	8.75
Dinner	28.00	23.00
Car rental	36.00	28.00
Total Per Deim		

As you will note while the amount allowed for lodging has been increased by $ 10, the amount allowed for meals and car rental has decreased. Please let me know by the first of the month if you feel that these changes will adverseily affect your personnel.

Please remind all employees that receipts for every item must be submitted before a reinbursement check can be written. As of the first of the month, no out-of-pocket expenses will be reimbursed unless preapproved by a branch manager.

If you have any questions regarding these rate changes please call me.

2. Use the filename **6skill2.per** and save the file.
3. Print one copy.
4. If you have completed your work in WordPerfect, exit the program.

CHAPTER

Create a Résumé

Features Covered

- Insert special characters
- Convert case
- Use a hard space
- Change margins using the Ruler Bar
- Set tabs

Chapter Objectives and Introduction

After successfully completing this chapter, you will be able to insert special WordPerfect characters, change the case for characters to all lowercase, all uppercase, or initial capitals, use a hard space to keep words on the same line, change left and right margins using the Ruler Bar, and set tabs in order to format an attractive, easy-to-read résumé.

A résumé is a document that summarizes a person's education, work experience, and work skills. A résumé is submitted to a prospective employer when applying for a job. Because a résumé serves as a person's introduction to a prospective employer, it is important that the résumé be attractive and easy to read. A résumé may be formatted using the Tab and Indent features, or the Table feature may be used to arrange information in parallel columns.

Tab settings can be changed so that paragraphs can be indented in an attractive manner. Emphasis can be added to text by using text attributes such as bold, underline, and italics. Special characters, such as the accent marks in résumé, can be inserted into a document. In addition, special emphasis can be given by placing symbols in front of desired paragraphs. (See Figure 7.1.)

Special Characters

Special text characters, such as the é's in résumé, and symbols, such as ❖ and ✰, can be inserted into a document by accessing WordPerfect's character sets. The Word-

Tables feature can be used to type and format each column of information (see Chapter 5 for information on converting existing tabbed text into a table).

After tabs are changed, the new tab settings can be viewed by turning on Reveal Codes. If necessary, all tab set codes can be deleted to return to the default tab settings.

Start-Up Instructions

- The file named **7drill1.mar** should be displayed in the document window.
- The Ruler Bar should be displayed on the screen.

Set Tabs Using the Ruler Bar

Note: A mouse must be used to set tabs using the Ruler Bar.

1. Place the insertion point at the location where the tabs are to be set, or select the text for which tabs are to be set.

   For example, select the three bulleted items.

2. To clear all existing tabs, move the mouse pointer to a tab marker on the Ruler Bar, click the *right* mouse button once and select Clear All Tabs.

3. Check the letter that displays in the Tab Set button on the Power Bar. (If necessary, select a different tab type by pressing and holding the mouse button and dragging to select the desired tab type; release the mouse button.)

   For example, check that **L** displays in the Tab Set button.

4. Move the mouse pointer to the bottom of the Ruler Bar at the desired tab location and click once.

   For example, move the mouse pointer to **1.75"** on the Ruler Bar and click.

Note: A left tab marker displays on the Ruler Bar.

Insert a New Tab with Dot Leaders

5. Move the mouse pointer to the Tab Set button on the Power Bar. Press and hold the mouse button and drag to select the desired dot leader type.

   For example, select the **...Right** tab type.

Note: The Dot Right tab type displays in the Tab Set button on the Power Bar.

6. Move the mouse pointer to the bottom of the Ruler Bar at the desired tab location and click once.

   For example, move the mouse pointer to 7" and click.

Note: A right tab marker with dot leader characters displays on the Ruler Bar. Continue with the following Finish-Up Instructions to complete the typed information.

Finish-Up Instructions

- Place the insertion point to the right of the last character in the word *Writer.* Press the **Tab** key once.

❖ Technical Writer . . . . June 199x
❖ Copyeditor . . . . May 1993
❖ Assistant Copyeditor . . . . November 1990

FIGURE 7.5

Document with dot leader characters

Note: Dot characters display from the end of the word ***Writer*** *to the right margin, and the insertion point is located at the right margin.*

- Type **June 199x**.
- Move the insertion point to the right of the last character in the next line, *Copyeditor*. Press the **Tab** key and type **May 1993**.
- Move the insertion point to the right of the last character in the final line, *Assistant Copyeditor*. Press the **Tab** key and type **November 1990**.
- The last several lines of your document should look similar to Figure 7.5.
- Use the *new* filename 7**drill1.tab** and save the file on your file disk.
- Close the document. If necessary, remove the Ruler Bar from the screen (select **View**, **Ruler Bar**).

Chapter 7
Create a Résumé

Start-Up Instructions

- Open the file named 7**drill2.wpd** located on the data disk.

Steps to Set Tabs Using the Tab Set Dialog Box

1. Place the insertion point where tabs are to be set, or select the text for which tabs are to be set.

   For example, place the insertion point in the blank line after the title.

2. Select **Layout, Line, Tab Set** {Alt, L, L, t}.

   Note: The Tab Set dialog box displays (see Figure 7.6).

3. Select the **Clear All** button to delete all the preset tabs {Alt and a}.
4. To set a tab, move the mouse pointer to the Position box and double-click. Type the desired tab location {Alt and p, type the desired tab location}.

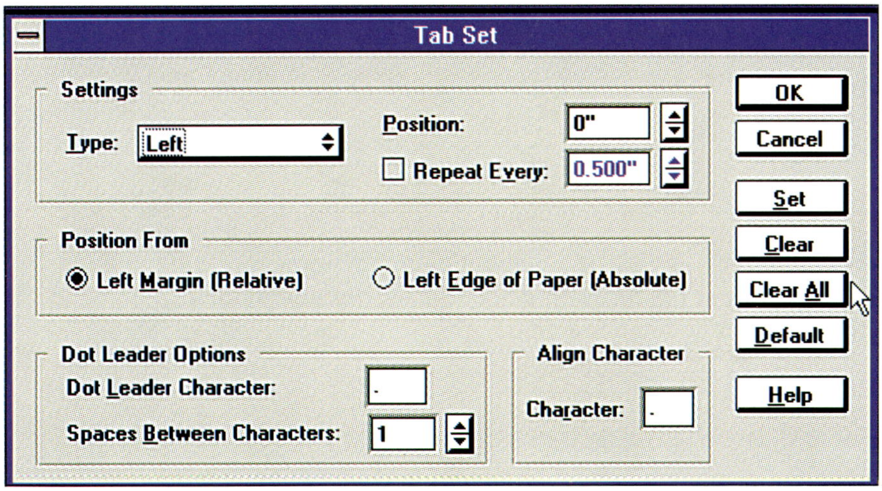

FIGURE 7.6

Tab Set dialog box

For example, type **.25**. (Do not type the final period.)

Note: Check that Left displays in the Type box.

5. Select **Set** {Alt and s}.
6. Repeat step 4 and type the desired tab location {Alt and p, type the desired tab location}.

   For example, type **2.5**. (Do not type the final period.)
7. To select a different tab type, move the mouse pointer to the Type box, press and hold the mouse button, and drag to select the desired type; release the mouse button {Alt and t, press the up or down arrow keys until the desired tab type displays}.

   For example, select the **Center** tab type.
8. Select **Set** {Alt and s}.
9. Repeat step 4 and type the desired tab location {Alt and p, type the desired tab location}.

   For example, type **4.5**. (Do not type the final period.)
10. Repeat step 7 to select the desired tab type.

    For example, select the **Right** tab type.
11. Select **Set** {Alt and s}.
12. Repeat step 4 and type the desired tab location {Alt and p, type desired tab location}.

    For example, type **5.5**. (Do not type the final period.)
13. Repeat step 7 to select the desired tab type.

    For example, select the **Decimal** tab type.
14. Select **Set** {Alt and s}.
15. Select **OK** to exit the Tab Set dialog box {Enter}.

    Note: The columns are aligned at each tab.

Finish-Up Instructions

- Use the *new* filename **7drill2.set** and save the file.
- Print one copy
- Close the document.

Steps to Create Evenly Spaced Tabs

Note: The following Steps to Create Evenly Spaced Tabs and the Steps to Delete Tab Set Code are for your information.

1. Place the insertion point at the location where the evenly spaced tabs are to be in effect.
2. Select **Layout, Line, Tab Set** {Alt, L, L, t}.
3. Select **Clear All** to delete all existing tabs {Alt and a}.

4. Select the Repeat Every option {Alt and v}.
5. Double-click in the Repeat Every box and type the spacing desired between tabs {press Tab and type the desired spacing}.
6. Select OK {press Enter}.

Delete Tab Set Code

1. Turn on Reveal Codes (**Alt** and **F3**).
2. Place the red or shaded block to the left of the tab set code *(Tab Set)*.
3. Press Delete.

Chapter 7 Create a Résumé

Create a Résumé

- ❖ Use the following information to create the résumé shown in Figure 7.1 on page 154.
- ❖ Change the font to **Arrus BT, 12-point**, or **make a font choice of your own**. Use bold, italic, and underline text attributes as shown.
- ❖ Use the Ruler Bar and change the left margin to 1.25" and the right margin to 7.25".
- ❖ Use the Ruler Bar and set a left tab at 1.5" and a right tab with dot leaders at 7.25".
- ❖ Use special text and bullet characters as shown. The *é* is found in the Multinational character set and the (❖) is found in the Iconic Symbols character set.
- ❖ Remember to use the **Indent** button to indent paragraphs.
- ❖ Save the file on your file disk; use the filename **7drill3.swa**.
- ❖ Print one copy.
- ❖ Close the document.

Create a Résumé Using the Table Feature

A résumé can also be created using the Table feature to format the information in two columns. Sideheads, such as EMPLOYMENT EXPERIENCE, EDUCATIONAL BACKGROUND, HONORS, and REFERENCES, can be typed in the first column and related information can be placed in the second column. The widths of the table columns can be adjusted to accommodate headings and text. Some of the advantages of using a table to format a résumé are ease of setup and formatting, ease of reading, and visual attractiveness.

Create a Résumé Using the Table Feature

- ❖ Use the following information to create the résumé shown in Figure 7.7.

- Change the font to **Arrus BT, 10-point**, or **make a font choice of your own**. Use bold and italic text attributes as shown.
- Type and center the heading information.
- Create a table with two columns and seven rows. Decrease the width of column 1 and increase the width of column 2. Omit all table lines. (If necessary, see Chapters 5 and 6 for information on changing the width of table columns and omitting table lines.)
- Save the file on your file disk; use the filename **7drill4.wen**.
- Print one copy and close the document.

FIGURE 7.7

Résumé created using the Table feature

RÉSUMÉ
MAXINE WENRICH
45 BLACKSTONE DRIVE
AVENEL, NJ 07001
(201) 555-4828

EMPLOYMENT EXPERIENCE	*Berkhard Newsletter*, Hillside, New Jersey. Full-time editor/reporter. Responsible for reporting and editing several industry newsletters. March 1991 to present.
	The Trentonian, Trenton, New Jersey. Part-time reporter. Responsibilities included covering municipal meetings and developing feature articles. November 1988 to March 1991.
EDUCATIONAL BACKGROUND	Camden Community College, Cherry Hill, New Jersey. A.A. Communications; specialized in journalism. Computer courses studied: Microsoft Word for Windows, WordPerfect, PageMaker, and Paradox.
	High School Diploma, Camden High School, Cherry Hill, New Jersey.
HONORS	Dean's Scholar, 1988. Member Beta Gamma, Honorary Scholastic Society.
REFERENCES	Available upon request.

The Next Step

Chapter Review and Activities

Self-Check Quiz

T F 1. Tabs are set by default every inch.

T F 2. The eight tab types are left, center, decimal, right, dot left, dot center, dot right, and dot decimal.

T F 3. A hard space between words instructs WordPerfect to always print both words on the same line.

T F 4. When a relative tab is set, the tab location changes when the right margin is changed.

T F 5. The WordPerfect Characters dialog box is accessed by selecting **Font**, **Character**.

6. WordPerfect can convert the case of letters to
   a. all uppercase.
   b. all lowercase.
   c. initial capitals.
   d. any of the above.

7. The Ruler Bar can be used to
   a. set left and right margins.
   b. set top and bottom margins.
   c. set tabs.
   d. both a and c.

8. List two advantages of using a table when creating a résumé.

9. In which WP character set are the following symbols found?

   é ❖ ➟ ✐ ©

10. What is the difference between a relative and an absolute tab?

Enriching Language Arts Skills

Spelling/Vocabulary Words

implement to carry out; to set in motion.

RÉSUMÉ
W. KEVIN KINCAID
172 VINE STREET, APT. 12
ATLANTA, GA 30314

Education	Georgia State, Atlanta, Georgia *B.S. Business Administration*, Minor in Psychology Studied microcomputer applications: Lotus, dBase IV, WordPerfect, and Ventura. Also studied BASIC, PASCAL, and C programming languages. 5/93
Experience	Goldman Research, Hapeville, Georgia (part-time) Responsible for interviewing prospective panel members for the firm. Handled public relations as a host and supervised numerous focus groups. 9/92-4/93
	GTE Service Corporation, Macon, Georgia Worked with a small group of individuals on a project to develop a computer-based *Vertical Services* costing model used to develop costs of a new company telephone service. Summer 1992
	Southern National Bank, Atlanta, Georgia (part-time) Worked in the *Customer Service Department.* Answered phones, distributed mail, and researched microfiche documents to verify answers to customer questions. 10/89-5/92
Activities	Member of Voyagers Club, Newton Math Society, and Tau Sigma Kappa (Computer Honor Society).
References	Available upon request.

2. Use the filename **7act2.kin** and save the file.
3. Use the following information and edit the résumé.
   a. Change the sideheadings to all uppercase letters.
   b. Insert and center the phone number (404) 555-2438 beneath the city, state, and zip code.
   c. Delete the words "Available upon request" that follow the References sideheading.
   d. Insert the following two references:

Cynthia Bates, Office Supervisor
Goldman Research
390 Walker St.
Hapeville, GA 30354
(404) 555-8901

Rubin Cortez, Bank Manager
Southern National Bank
2012 Spring NW
Atlanta, GA 30318
(404) 555-2200

4. Use the filename **7act2.rev** and save the file.
5. Print one copy and close the document.

Activity 7.3—Create Your Own Résumé

1. Create your own résumé using Figure 7.1 or Figure 7.7 as a guide.
2. If necessary, use margin changes to increase or decrease the amount of text that will fit on a page. For example, if your résumé is short, it may be desirable to increase the left, right, and top margins. If your résumé is long, decrease the top, bottom, left, and right margins.
3. Remember to insert special characters for the word *résumé*.
4. Use one or two fonts to enhance the appearance of your résumé.
5. Use the Speller and proofread carefully.
6. Use the filename **7act3.res** and save the file.
7. Print one copy and close the document.

Challenge Your Skills

Skill 7.1—Create a Résumé, Set Tabs, and Insert Special Characters

1. Use the following information to type the résumé shown.
   a. Change the top margin to .75" and the bottom margin to .5"; reduce the left and right margins by .25" each.
   b. Clear all tabs. Use the Ruler Bar to set a left tab at 1" and set a dot right tab at the right margin.
   c. Use the bold and italic text attributes as shown.
   d. Select a symbol from the Iconic Symbols character set. Insert the chosen symbol in front of each job title.

Résumé
Randall McChesney
3845 West 23rd Place
Chicago, IL 60623
(312) 555-3841

EDUCATIONAL BACKGROUND

Northwestern University, Evanston, Illinois 6/93
Candidate for *Masters of Management degree.* Concentration in marketing and finance. Member of the Finance Club and Black Management Association.

B.A. Economics, Spelman College, Atlanta, Georgia 5/91
Sun Oil Scholar, Avon Scholar, and recipient of four-year Honors Program Scholarship. President of Economics Club.

EMPLOYMENT EXPERIENCE

Wyle Services, Inc., Chicago, Illinois
Corporate Planning Assistant 8/93-Present
Review and analyze the strategic plans, prepare presentations for senior management, and evaluate Wyle's presence in Japan with respect to imports, exports, and net income.

Stein, Roe & Farnham Mutual Funds, Inc., Chicago, Illinois
Summer Intern 1991
Prepared new account reports and analyzed the flow of dollars into the funds. Utilized Microsoft Excel and MacDraw microcomputer programs for the Macintosh computer.

Prudential Insurance Co., Chicago, Illinois
Claims Representative 6/88-8/90
Initiated correspondence between the company and municipalities, made arrangements for outside adjusters to inspect cars and homes, and settled claims over the telephone.

REFERENCES

Mrs. Roberta Anzac, Manager
Prudential Insurance Co.
1290 Michigan Ave.
Chicago, IL 60600
(312) 555-5000 ext. 3423

Mr. Benjamin Harpreet
Wyle Services, Inc.
121 Adams West
Chicago, IL 60604
(312) 555-6200

2. Use the filename **7skill1.rmc** and save the file.
3. Print one copy.
4. Close the document.

Skill 7.2—Create a Résumé with Special Characters; Language Arts Skills

1. Create a résumé for Carlene Quevedo using the following information.
   a. Make decisions regarding:
      Résumé format
      Margins
      Tab settings and indentions
      Fonts
      Hard spaces
      Uppercase and lowercase headings
      Bold and italic text attributes
      Special characters
      References
   b. Correct four spelling and two punctuation errors
   c. Carlene lives at 570 Betner Dr., Mansfield, OH 44907 (419) 555-8387.
   d. Carlene graduated in 1988 with a B.A. in Political Science from Ohio State University, Columbus, OH. She is currently a master's degree candidate in Business Administration at Ohio State University, Columbus, OH.
   e. Carlene's work experience is as follows:

   Hayden Services, Network Services Department, Mansfield, OH
   Product Developer
   7/90-Present

   Job responsibilities include: develop and impliment the insentive program for the Smart Ring product line. Specifically, develop the tracking systems and implementation booklet for the program.

   J.M. Smucker Company, Orrville, OH
   District Sales Manager
   9/88-6/90

   Job responsibilities included managing food brokers over a five-state region, including training for office and sales staff. Assisted in sales presentations and customer relations. Responsible for personal selling to large restaurants, hotels and food service chains.

   Also at J.M. Smucker Company, Carlene worked as a part-time sales representative in the Columbus district from 6/86-9/88. Her responsibilities were: direct contact with grocery retailers and wholesalors; introduction of new products, presentation of promottional deals, and maintenance of customer relations.

f. Carlene's references are:

Marly Lawson, Hayden Services, 30 Park Ave. West, Mansfield, OH 44902 (419) 555-4550

Norman P. Costello, Jr., J.M. Smucker Company, 689 Main St., Orrville, OH 44667 (216) 555-8799

2. Use the filename **7skill2.cq** and save the file.
3. Print one copy.
4. If you have completed your work, exit WordPerfect.

CHAPTER

Create Newspaper and Parallel Text Columns

Features Covered

- Newspaper-style columns
- The Columns Define button
- Change column definitions
- Balanced newspaper columns
- Column breaks
- Hyphenation
- Parallel columns
- Convert text in parallel columns to a table

Objectives and Introduction

After successfully completing this chapter, you will be able to use the **Columns Define** button to format text in newspaper-style columns and to use the Columns feature or the Table feature to create parallel columns. In addition, you will also learn how to control the flow of text in newspaper columns using the balanced newspaper column feature and column breaks, and how to use the hyphenation feature to improve the look and readability of columnar text.

Columns of text can be arranged in newspaper style or parallel style. Text in newspaper columns wraps around from line to line, column to column, and page to page. Paragraphs of related text can be arranged in parallel columns so that information can be read from left to right. The Hyphenation feature can be used to improve the readability of columnar text by reducing the amount of space at the end of lines.

Newspaper Columns

Newspaper columns are created by placing a column definition code at the beginning of the text that will be arranged in columns either before or after the text is typed. The simplest method for creating columns is to place the code in the document *after* the text is typed. When the column code is inserted, the column arrangement displays instantly on the screen.

A quick way to create columns using WordPerfect's default column settings (equal width newspaper column with .5 inch space between columns) is to select the **Columns Define** button on the Power Bar and choose the desired number of columns. WordPerfect automatically calculates even column widths based on the page margins, inserts a .5-inch gutter (blank space between columns), and displays the text in columns in the document window.

If column settings different from the default are desired, select **Layout**, **Columns**, **Define** or select the **Columns Define** button on the Power Bar and choose the **Define** option. The Columns dialog box displays and the column type, number of columns, space between columns and column widths can be specified (see Figure 8.3).

The *Type* section is used to specify newspaper, balanced newspaper, or parallel columns (the default is newspaper). The *Number of Columns* box is used to specify the number of desired columns (the default is 2). Parallel columns are discussed later in this chapter.

The *Spacing Between Columns* box in the Columns dialog box is used to specify the amount of space (in inches) to be placed between the columns. The default setting is .5 inches and can be changed. (The distance between columns is often referred to as the gutter space.)

Once the number of columns is specified, WordPerfect automatically calculates equal widths for each column and determines the left and right margins for each column. The width of each column and the distance between each column displays in the *Custom Widths* box. If the number of columns or distance between columns is changed, the column margins are automatically recalculated when **OK** is selected.

A border line can be placed between columns or borders can be placed around text by selecting **Layout**, **Columns**, **Border/Fill** and choosing the desired border style. WordPerfect provides many styles of borders including a single line between columns, hairline, double, dashed, and extra thick. In this chapter, we will work with the single line between columns style. Borders are also discussed in chapters 5 and 13.

Once all the column settings are set, **OK** is chosen and the text displays in columns on the screen. Turn on Reveal Codes to view the column definition code *Col Def.* When the red or shaded block is located to the left of the column definition code, the code expands to show the column type and number of columns, e.g., *Col Def: Newspaper, Total: 2, Col[Adj], Gut [0.5"], Col[Adj].*

When newspaper columns have been defined, the text flow can be controlled by inserting a column break to force text to the next column or page. A column break is inserted by pressing **Ctrl** and **Enter**. Once newspaper columns are turned on, pressing **Ctrl** and **Enter** moves the insertion point and any text that follows the insertion point to the top of the next column. If the insertion point is located in the final column of the page when **Ctrl** and **Enter** are pressed, the text is forced to the top left column of the next page.

Text in newspaper and balanced newspaper columns automatically flows from the bottom of one column to the top of the next column and flows from the bottom of one page to the top left column of the next page (see Figure 8.2). The term *snaking* is often used to describe columnar text that wraps from column to column and page to page.

When the **Balanced Newspaper** type is selected, the flow of text is adjusted so that each column is approximately the same length. This method provides a more balanced appearance on the page and is often used when text does not completely fill the last column on a page.

After newspaper columns are typed, extra space may display at the end of lines, making the columnar information difficult to read. Hyphenation can be used to align words more evenly at the margin and to improve the appearance and readability of the columnar text.

A column off code can be placed at the end of the columnar text in order to change the number of columns, e.g., to return to a single-column layout. To end a multicolumn layout, insert a column off code by selecting the **Columns Define** button on the Power Bar and choosing the **Columns Off** option.

Start-Up Instructions

- Open the file named **8drill1.wpd** located on the data disk.

Steps to Create Newspaper Columns

1. Place the insertion point to the left of the first character in the text to be placed in columns.

   For example, place the insertion point to the left of T in the word "The" (first word of the first paragraph).

2. Move the mouse pointer to the **Columns Define** button on the Power Bar. Press and hold the mouse button {Alt, L, c, d}.

3. Move the mouse pointer to the desired number of columns and release the mouse button {type desired number of columns, Enter}.

   For example, select **2 Columns.**

   Note: The text is displayed in columns on the screen.

Finish-Up Instructions

- Turn on Reveal Codes (select **View**, **Reveal Codes**). Move the red or shaded block in the Reveal Codes window to the left of the column definition code, *Col Def,* to display the expanded code. Turn off Reveal Codes (select **View**, **Reveal Codes**).
- Use the *new* filename **8drill1.new** and save the file on your file disk.

Start-Up Instructions

- The file named **8drill1.new** should be displayed in the document window.

Steps to Place a Border Line Between Newspaper Columns

1. With the insertion point located anywhere in the newspaper columns, select **Layout, Columns, Border/Fill** {Alt, L, c, b}.

   Note: The Column Border dialog box displays.

2. Select the **Border Style** button {Alt and b, Spacebar}.

FIGURE 8.1

Column Border dialog box

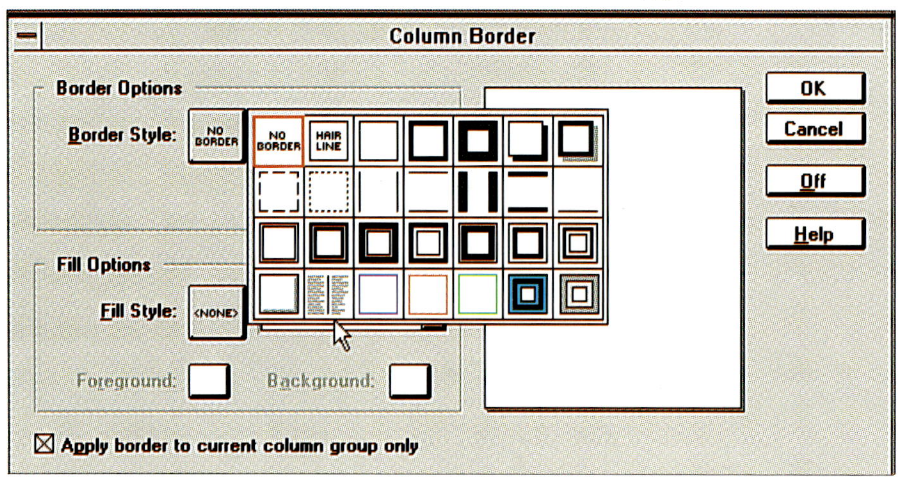

Note: A palette of available border styles displays (see Figure 8.1).

3. Move the mouse pointer to the desired border style and click the mouse button once {press the arrow keys until the desired border style is selected; Enter}.

   For example, click on the **Column Between** (the second button in the bottom row) border style.

   Note: A sample of the border style displays on the Border Style button and on the right side of the Column Border dialog box. Also, the words "Column Between" displays in the box to the right of the Border Style button.

4. Select OK to exit the Column Border dialog box {Enter}.

   *Note: Your document should look similar to Figure 8.2. Select the **Page Zoom Full** button on the Power Bar to view the entire page; select the **Page Zoom Full** button again to return to the normal view.*

Finish-Up Instructions

- Save the file again using the same filename, **8drill1.new**.
- Print one copy.

Start-Up Instructions

- The file named **8drill1.new** should be displayed in the document window.

Steps to Change the Column Definition

1. Place the insertion point at any location in the newspaper columns.

   Note: The insertion point must be located to the right of the Col Border and Col Def codes. If necessary, turn on Reveal Codes and position the insertion point after the column codes.

2. Move the mouse pointer to the Columns Define button in the Power Bar. Press and hold the mouse button {Alt, L, c}.

3. Move the mouse pointer to Define and release the mouse button {d}.

FIGURE 8.2

Text arranged in multiple columns

SAVING AND INVESTING TRENDS

The pattern for saving and investing money during the next ten years will be drastically different than in the years past. Several distinct areas are the driving forces of the changes predicted for the next decade.

Healthy Savings Attitudes

Americans' attitudes towards saving and investment are improving. During the past few years, the average savings rate for Americans was 5% of after-tax income--far less than the previous decade. However, last year Americans had a healthy increase in savings to 6.5%

Demographics

The baby boom generation is fast approaching middle age. They are planning for their children's education, their own retirement, and their own leisure activities. In addition, Americans have increased their wealth dramatically and are recognizing the need to save and invest wisely.

Products

During the past decade, Americans began to achieve their savings goals by investing in nontraditional products. For example, mutual funds, money market funds, and annuities have been selected for investments because they provide an opportunity for higher returns with limited risks. In the next decade, demand for unconventional investments will be even more noticeable.

Demand for Change

The American people are telling the financial institutions that they want more products, more security, and honest advisors. Such requests are driving financial institutions to look inward and re-evaluate their philosophies in order to make primary changes in the way they conduct business.

Financial Institutions

Traditionally, individuals have used Savings and Loan associations for many of their savings needs and turned to brokerage firms for investments. Since the Savings and Loan industry has experienced great difficulties, many people have lost confidence and seek a more secure place for their savings.

Note: The Columns dialog box displays (see Figure 8.3).

4. Make the desired changes to the type of columns, number of columns, distance between columns, etc.

For example, place the insertion point at the beginning of the third paragraph to the left of the **B** in the word *Before.*

2. Press **Ctrl** and **Enter**.

   Note: *The text following the insertion point is immediately moved to the second column.*

Finish-Up Instructions

- Center the text vertically on the page (select **Layout**, **Page**, **Center, Current Page**, **OK**).
- Use the *new* filename **8drill2.brk** and save the file on your file disk.
- Print one copy.
- Close the document.

Hyphenation

Hyphenation is the process of dividing a word at the right margin so that the first part of the word prints at the end of the line and the remainder of the word prints at the beginning of the next line. Hyphenating words is used to make line endings at the right margin look more even (less ragged) or to avoid large gaps between words in a line with full justification. Hyphenation can be controlled by using the Prompt for Hyphenation *When Required* or Prompt for Hyphenation *Always* options.

When text is typed, regular, soft, and hard hyphens and hyphenation soft returns can be inserted. Regular hyphens break compound words at the right margin when necessary. For example, the hyphenated word *well-qualified* will split after the hyphen if the hyphen is at the right margin.

A hard hyphen, such as the hyphen in the compound name *Jones-Meyer,* is inserted between words that should always appear on the same line of text. A hard hyphen is inserted by pressing the **Ctrl** and hyphen (-) keys (**Ctrl** and -). The hard hyphen is also referred to as a required hyphen.

A soft hyphen can be inserted by placing the insertion point to the left of the character that will follow the hyphen, pressing and holding the **Ctrl** and **Shift** keys while tapping the hyphen key once. When a word that contains a soft hyphen does not break at the end of line, the hyphen is hidden. In other words, a soft hyphen will display in the document window only if the hyphenated word needs to break at the end of the line. However, the soft hyphen code always displays in the Reveal Codes window.

A hyphenation soft return is used for words that are separated by slashes, e.g., administrator/director. If the words separated by a slash reach the right margin, WordPerfect separates the words after the slash only if a hyphenation soft return has been inserted after the slash. The hyphenation soft return is actually a code, *Hyph Srt,* and, similar to a soft hyphen, affects the document only when words separated by slashes need to be broken at the right margin.

WordPerfect uses a hyphenation zone to determine which words need to be hyphenated. The hyphenation zone includes an area to the left of the right margin and also an area to the right of the right margin. If a word begins before the left area and extends beyond the right area, hyphenation of the word is desirable. The default hyphenation zone is 10 percent left and 4 percent right. This means that WordPerfect

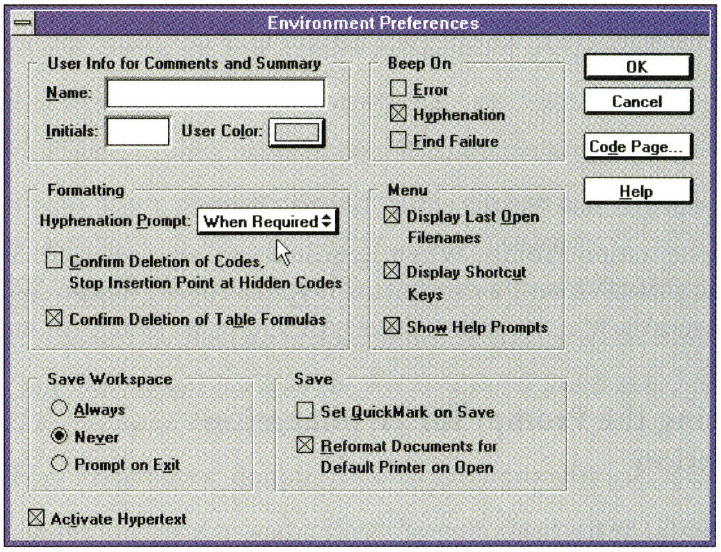

FIGURE 8.4

Environment Preferences dialog box

will determine an area that is 10 percent of the line length as the left area and 4 percent of the line length as the right area. A small hyphenation zone will produce more hyphenated words; a larger hyphenation zone will reduce the number of hyphenated words. Generally, the default hyphenation zone will produce a visually acceptable hyphenation area.

There are three options for controlling the hyphenation process. The hyphenation options are found in the Hyphenation Prompt section of the Environment Preferences dialog box (see Figure 8.4). The Environment Preferences dialog box is displayed by selecting **File**, **Preferences**, and double-clicking on **Environment**.

The three hyphenation options, *Never*, *When Required*, and *Always*, are used to control how and when WordPerfect will hyphenate words. The default setting is Hyphenation Prompt When Required. With *When Required* in effect, words found in the WordPerfect main dictionary are automatically hyphenated. However, if a word is not found in the dictionary, the program will pause and ask the user to select the appropriate hyphenation point.

When Hyphenation Prompt *Never* is selected, WordPerfect hyphenates words found in the main dictionary without pausing. However, if a word is not found in the dictionary, WordPerfect determines a hyphenation point and does not pause to allow the user to make a hyphenation decision. The Hyphenation Prompt *Never* and *When Required* settings are not recommended, because the main dictionary words may not include all the words that need to be hyphenated and the hyphenation decisions made by WordPerfect may not follow basic word division guidelines (see page 182).

If the Hyphenation Prompt *Always* is selected, WordPerfect will pause at each word to be hyphenated and allow you to confirm the displayed hyphenation suggestion. The hyphenation point can be changed if desired by pressing the left or right arrow keys.

Turn on hyphenation only after a document has been proofread, edited, and is being prepared for final form. Use one of the hyphenation procedures only if there are gaps between words or large spaces at the right margins. If the gaps or spaces are small, hyphenation may be unnecessary.

Once hyphenation has been turned on, WordPerfect begins looking for words that can be hyphenated. Typically, WordPerfect decides where to divide a word, then

Part 2
Checking Your Step

Production Skill Builder Activities
Chapters 5-8

Production Activity 2.1—Create and Copy Table Formulas, Insert a Row, and Recalculate

1. Create the table shown. Type the following unformatted information into the table cells.

   Note: *The text may wrap around in the cells differently than shown because of the fonts and point sizes selected on your computer.*

PROPERTY SALES			
1st Quarter			
Location	Original Purchase Price	Appraised Value	Price Realized
30661 W. Elliot Ave.	145000	185000	182950
895 Garden Rd.	108000	191000	193450
309 Talco Ave.	220000	259000	256500
73 Walnut St.	179000	299000	293750
Totals			

2. Block and join the cells in row 1. Also join the cells in row 2.
3. Make decisions regarding:

   Justification for title, subtitle, and column heading cells
   Justification for columns containing dollar amounts
   Table lines
   Shading cells
   Column widths

4. Insert a formula into cell B8 to calculate the column total.

5. Copy the formula in cell B8 to cells C8 and D8.
6. Set the number type format for cells B4 through D4 to **Currency**. Set the number of digits after the decimal to zero.
7. Set the number type format for cells B5 through D7 to **Commas**. Set the number of digits after the decimal to zero.
8. Set the number type format for cells B8 through D8 to **Currency**. Set the number of digits after the decimal to zero.
9. Insert a row between row 6 and 7. Type the following information into the new row table cells: 652 Parkland; 89000; 169000; 168200. Recalculate the table column totals.
10. Save the file; use the filename **2pact1.tbl**.
11. Print one copy.
12. Close the document.

Production Activity 2.2—Create a Résumé, Set Tabs, and Insert Special Characters

1. Use the following information to type the résumé shown.
   a. Change the top margin to .75" and the bottom margin to .5".
   b. Use the Tab Set dialog box and clear all tabs; set left tabs at **.5** and **.75** and set a right tab with dot leaders at **6**.
   c. Make decisions on the use of bold, underline, and italic text attributes.
   d. Select a font of your own choice in a point size of 12.
   e. Use special characters to create the é's in Résumé.
   f. Choose an appropriate bullet character to replace the asterisks shown.

Résumé
Robert N. Ortiz
341 Maple Ave.
Paterson, NJ 07509
(201) 555-4582

EMPLOYMENT EXPERIENCE

Crowe Communications, Inc., Wyckoff, New Jersey
*	Technical Writer 10/91-Present
	Write and edit technical journals and procedure manuals for computer systems and applications on a contract basis.

Newpark Software, Boston, Massachusetts
*	Copyeditor 5/87-10/91
	Copyedited documentation for software applications.

* Assistant Copyeditor 8/86-5/87
  Assisted with the copyediting of company newsletters, internal procedure manuals, and some advertising information. Was promoted to Copyeditor on May 1, 1987.

Law Offices of Adam T. Cusick, Takoma Park, Maryland
* Clerical Assistant (part-time) 1/85-5/86
  Duties included typing, photocopying, faxing, and mail distribution.

EDUCATIONAL BACKGROUND

Rutgers University, Newark, New Jersey (part-time) 2/91-Present
A.A. English, Montgomery Jr. College, Takoma Park, Maryland 9/84-5/86
High School Diploma, Denbigh High School, Denbigh, Virginia 6/84

REFERENCES

Jason Heller, Supervisor
Newpark Software
230 Franklin St., Suite 25
Boston, MA 02110
(617) 555-6721

Tom Yim, Paralegal
Law Offices of Adam T. Cusick
7629 Carroll Ave.
Takoma Park, MD 20912
(301) 555-3990

---

2. Use the filename **2pact2.res** and save the file.
3. Print one copy and close the document.

Production Activity 2.3—Create Parallel Columns

1. Create the following document using parallel columns. Make decisions regarding:

   Margins
   Justification
   Fonts
   Method to use to create the parallel columns (i.e., Columns feature or Table feature)
   Width of columns
   Bold/underline/capitalization of title, subtitle, and sideheads
   Hyphenation

Engineer's property inspection report
306 West 98th St.
July 18, 199x

general	The property is known as 306 West 98th Street and is located on the north side of West 98th Street.
construction	The building was built in 1920 under the new building application NB-584. It is constructed of wood floors and roof beams of masonry bearing and is classified as Class 3, non-fireproof construction, under the Indianapolis City Administrative Building Code.
occupancy	The building is classified as a Class A multiple dwelling. The occupancy, room, and apartment counts have not changed since the building was constructed.
street	The front building abuts West 98th Street, which is a publicly owned and maintained street with a single sidewalk on the north side of the street. The street is paved with asphalt and is in good condition.
utilities	Water is supplied to the building from an Indianapolis City water main in the bed of 98th Street from a curb box at the edge of the sidewalk at the south property line. Gas for domestic cooking ranges is supplied from a main in the bed of 98th Street maintained by the Consolidated Gas Co. The gas is metered and billed to each occupant separately. Electricity is supplied and individually metered and billed to each apartment occupant from a main line in the bed of 98th Street maintained by Consolidated Gas Co.

2. Save the file; use the filename **2pact3.pir**.
3. Print one copy.
4. Close the document.

Production Activity 2.4—Create Newspaper Columns; Language Arts Skills

1. Open the document with the filename **2pact4.txt** located on the data disk.
2. Use newspaper columns and the following information to complete the document.

a. Make decisions regarding:

   Margins and font size to fit document on one page
   Number of columns
   Type of columns
   Space between columns
   Border line between columns
   Justification
   Fonts
   Spacing before and after sideheadings
   Bold/underline/capitalization of title, subtitle, and sideheads

b. Correct two spelling errors and four punctuation errors.

3. Use the filename **2pact4.fin** and save the file.
4. Close the document.

Part 3
A Step Up

Create Reports and Special Documents

Chapters 9-12

- Document information
- Change vertical line spacing
- Thesaurus
- Grammatik
- Standard paragraphs
- Copy text between windows
- Print page numbers
- Create headers and footers
- Keep text together (widow/orphan)
- Create footnotes and endnotes
- Search for codes
- Print specific pages
- Create form files and data files
- Determine field names
- Merge files
- Edit data files and form files
- Mark a record(s)
- Create an envelope address
- Create an envelope definition
- Create mailing labels
- Sort table data file records

CHAPTER

Create a One-Page Document

Features Covered

- Document information
- Thesaurus
- Grammatik
- Standard paragraphs
- Copy text between windows
- Change vertical line spacing

Objectives and Introduction

After successfully completing this chapter, you will be able to create a one-page document with vertical line spacing of one and left justification and use Document Information to determine the word count. You will also be able to create a one-page document with vertical line spacing of two and full justification and use the Thesaurus to find alternative words (synonyms). In addition, you will learn to assemble personalized documents using standard paragraphs, to copy text between document windows, and to use the Grammatik program to check a document for correct grammar.

A one-page document can be an article, essay, minutes, agenda, report, or any type of document that describes an event or provides information. Investment, insurance, sales, real estate, and medical documents are examples of one-page business documents.

Create a One-Page Document

A document can be created with vertical line spacing of one (single spacing) or vertical line spacing of two (double spacing). If a document is typed with vertical line spacing of one, the paragraphs begin at the left margin with one blank line space between paragraphs (see Figure 9.1). If a document is typed with vertical line spacing

Document Information

2041	Character Count
326	Word Count
42	Line Count
23	Sentence Count
11	Paragraph Count
1	Page Count
6	Average Word Length
14	Average Words Per Sentence
35	Maximum Words Per Sentence

OK

FIGURE 9.2

Document Information dialog box

clude total the number of characters, words, lines, sentences, paragraphs, and pages contained in a document or selected text. The average word length, average words per sentence, and maximum words per sentence also display in the Document Information dialog box.

When a portion of a document is selected and the statistics are listed, the statistics displayed in the dialog box relate only to the selected text. A total word, character, or line count is useful when preparing a document that must meet specific guidelines, for example, a school research paper or an article submitted for publication.

Start-Up Instructions

- The file named **9drill1.tsm** should be displayed in the document window.

Use Document Information

1. Select File, Document Info {Alt, f, i}.

   Note: A Document Information dialog box similar to Figure 9.2 displays.

2. Select OK to return to the document window {Enter}.

Finish-Up Instructions

- Optional. At the top of the printed document, handwrite the total number of words.
- Optional. If any changes are made to the document, save the file again using the same filename, **9drill1.tsm**.
- Close the document.

Change Vertical Line Spacing

Additional space can be created between lines of text by changing the vertical line spacing. The added space can be used, for example, to accommodate handwritten changes to draft letters or reports. Also, a report set for line spacing of two may be easier to read.

The **Line Spacing** button on the Power Bar can be used to change the line spacing to 1 (single), 1.5, or 2 (double). The **Other** option in the **Line Spacing** button drop-down list is selected to display the Line Spacing dialog box. In the Line Spacing dialog box, a specific line spacing amount can be typed or selected by clicking on the up or down triangles to display the desired line spacing amount.

When the line spacing is changed, a line spacing code is inserted in the document. In Reveal Codes, the line spacing code is shown as *Ln Spacing*. When the insertion point is located to the left of the line spacing code, the expanded code displays with the amount of line spacing selected (e.g., *Ln Spacing: 2.0*).

Start-Up Instructions

- Open the file named **9drill2.ann** located on the data disk.

Change the Vertical Line Spacing

1. Place the insertion point at the beginning of the text where the vertical line spacing is to be changed.

   For example, place the insertion point at the beginning of the document.

2. Move the mouse pointer to the **Line Spacing** button 1.0 on the Power Bar. Press and hold the mouse button and drag to select the desired line spacing option. Release the mouse button {Alt, L, L, s; delete the existing line spacing amount, type the desired line spacing amount, Enter}.

   For example, move the mouse pointer to the **Line Spacing** button, press and hold the mouse button and drag to select **2**. Release the mouse button.

Finish-Up Instructions

- Move the mouse pointer to the left of the first character in the first paragraph and select **Full** justification (move the mouse pointer to the **Justification** button on the Power Bar, press and hold the mouse button and drag to select **Full**, release the mouse button).

  Note: *Your document should look similar to Figure 9.3.*

- Use the filename **9drill2.v2** and save the file.
- Print one copy.

Use the Thesaurus

A list of words that have the same or similar meaning (synonyms) are stored in the WordPerfect Thesaurus. An author writing a letter or other information attempts to use words that will effectively communicate ideas. A thesaurus assists a writer by providing synonyms that may more clearly convey his/her message. The WordPerfect Thesaurus can be used during the writing process or after a document is written.

When the Thesaurus command is selected, a dialog box displays containing a list of synonyms with subgroups of nouns, verbs, and/or adjectives. Words marked with a bullet character are called "headwords." By double-clicking on a headword, additional synonyms can be displayed. A list of *antonyms* (words with opposite meanings) may display at the bottom of the synonyms list.

FIGURE 9.3

One-page document with vertical line spacing of two and full justification

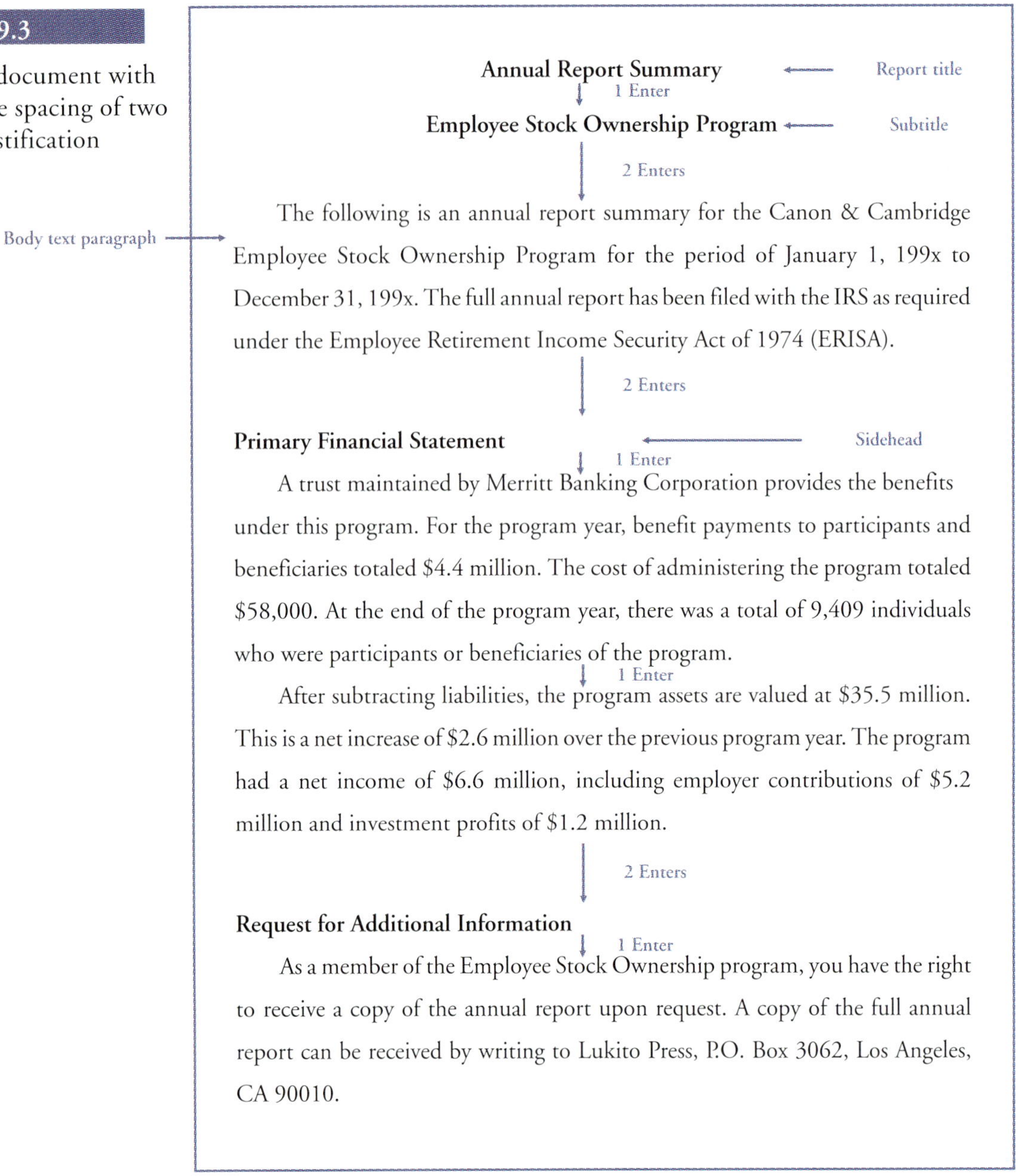

Annual Report Summary

Employee Stock Ownership Program

The following is an annual report summary for the Canon & Cambridge Employee Stock Ownership Program for the period of January 1, 199x to December 31, 199x. The full annual report has been filed with the IRS as required under the Employee Retirement Income Security Act of 1974 (ERISA).

Primary Financial Statement

A trust maintained by Merritt Banking Corporation provides the benefits under this program. For the program year, benefit payments to participants and beneficiaries totaled \$4.4 million. The cost of administering the program totaled \$58,000. At the end of the program year, there was a total of 9,409 individuals who were participants or beneficiaries of the program.

After subtracting liabilities, the program assets are valued at \$35.5 million. This is a net increase of \$2.6 million over the previous program year. The program had a net income of \$6.6 million, including employer contributions of \$5.2 million and investment profits of \$1.2 million.

Request for Additional Information

As a member of the Employee Stock Ownership program, you have the right to receive a copy of the annual report upon request. A copy of the full annual report can be received by writing to Lukito Press, P.O. Box 3062, Los Angeles, CA 90010.

In the Thesaurus, the author can replace the word, look up a listed word, view the text in the document window, or close. (If the selected word cannot be found, the message "Word not found..." displays at the bottom left of the Thesaurus dialog box.) The author can choose a word from the displayed list, type a different word to be looked up, or double-click on a listed word that is marked with a bullet.

After double-clicking on a marked word, a list of related synonyms and antonyms displays in the next column in the Thesaurus dialog box. Words that are not marked with a bullet are not included in the WordPerfect Thesaurus or are not included in the form requested (e.g., the word *seasonal* that displays for the requested adjective *season* is not marked because the requested word is for an adjective, not a noun). However, if you double-click on an unmarked word, another form of the word may display (e.g., *face* displays after double-clicking on the unmarked word *facing*).

Start-Up Instructions

- The filename **9drill2.v2** should be displayed in the document window.

Steps to Select Synonyms From the Thesaurus

1. Place the insertion point between any characters in the word to be looked up in the Thesaurus.

   For example, place the insertion point between any character in the word *full* in the second sentence of the first paragraph.

2. Select the **Thesaurus** button on the Power Bar {Alt, t, t *or* Alt and F1}.

   ***Note:** The Thesaurus dialog box displays (see Figure 9.4).*

3. Place the mouse pointer on the down arrow in the scroll bar to the right of the listed words. Press the left mouse button repeatedly to scan through the listed words until the desired word displays {press the Tab key four times, then press the down arrow keys repeatedly until the desired word displays}.

   For example, press the left mouse button repeatedly until the word *complete* displays.

4. Move the mouse pointer to the desired replacement word and click once {press the up or down arrow key to highlight the desired word}.

5. Select **Replace** {Alt and r}.

6. Place the insertion point between any character in the next word to be looked up.

   For example, place the insertion point between any characters in the word *benefit* in the second sentence of the second paragraph.

7. Select the **Thesaurus** button on the Power Bar {Alt, t, t *or* Alt and F1}.

8. Scan through the words listed on the screen and determine if there is a suitable replacement. If no suitable replacement word displays, select **Close** {Alt and c}.

   For example, because there is no suitable replacement for the word *benefit*, select **Close**.

9. Place the insertion point in the next word to be looked up.

Chapter 9 Create a One-Page Document

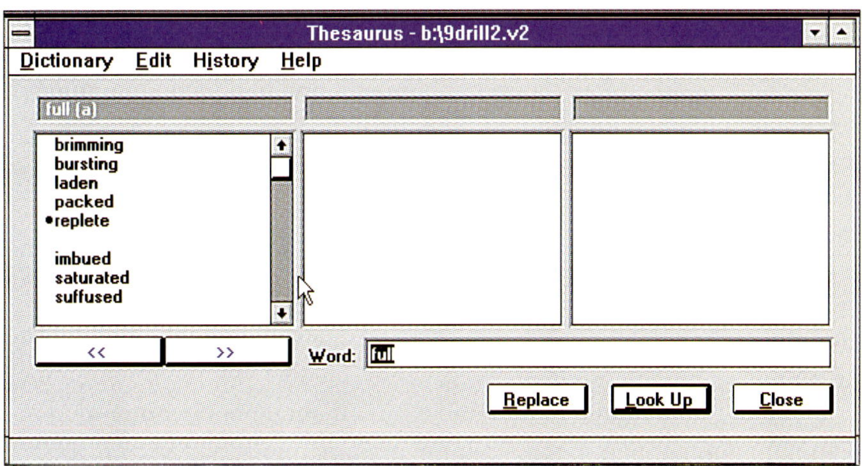

FIGURE 9.4

Thesaurus dialog box

For example, place the insertion point between any character in the word *administering* in the third sentence of the second paragraph.

10. Select **the Thesaurus** button and scan the listed words. If a suitable replacement word exists, select the word and choose **Replace** {Alt and r}.

    For example, choose the word **manage**. Select **Replace.**

    Note: *The Thesaurus does not include the "ing" suffix when the word administering is replaced. Continue with the Finish-Up Instructions.*

Finish-Up Instructions

- Delete the **e** in *manage* and type **ing**.
- Place the insertion point in the word *assets* in the first sentence of the third paragraph; select the **Thesaurus** button and scroll down the list of words until the word *holdings* displays; select **holdings**; select **Replace**.
- Place the insertion point in the word *receive* in the first sentence of the fourth paragraph; select the **Thesaurus** button and scan the list of words. Select **obtain**; choose **Replace**.

  Note: *Normally, the file with the new synonyms is saved and, if desired, renamed.*
- Use the *new* filename **9drill2.the** and save the file.
- Print one copy.
- Continue to the Steps to Use the Grammatik program or close the document.

Use the Grammatik Program

Grammatik (rhymes with *dramatic*) is a grammar-checking program that checks a document for grammatical, spelling, and writing-style errors. When the **Grammatik** button is selected, the text is checked against a list of grammar rules such as passive voice, subject-verb agreement, double negatives, repetitive expressions, and capitalization.

The grammar rules used to check text can be viewed or changed by selecting **Options, Writing Style** in the Grammatik dialog box. Select a writing style option such as Business Letter, Memo, or Report. The formality level (*i.e.,* Standard, Formal or Informal) can be selected also. The default settings for the General writing style and Standard Formality are used in this book.

When Grammatik checks a document, suggested changes are displayed. The suggested grammar change can be accepted, ignored, or rewritten. The grammar suggestions provided should be used only as a guide, because the grammar information may or may not be correct according to other grammatical sources.

The Options menu in the Grammatik dialog box provides choices for changing various grammar-checking defaults. For example, a proofreading mode for Grammar, Mechanics, Style, and Statistics as well as writing style and formality level can be selected in the Options menu. If desired, a custom writing style can be created by selecting the Edit button in the Writing Style dialog box (see Figure 9.5).

If Statistics is selected in the list of Options, the word, syllable, paragraph, and sentence (long and short) count display along with the average number of sentences

Rule Classes		Styles	
Grammar	Uses rules relating to the correct use of parts of speech, e.g., subject and verb agreement, possessive forms, homonyms, etc.	Business Letter	For writing that requires a formal tone and precise use of grammar and style rules.
Mechanical	Uses rules relating to errors in spelling, capitalization, transposed letters, punctuation, etc.	Memo	Appropriate for informal, interoffice correspondence.
Style	Uses rules relating to style and word choice, such as passive voice, jargon, wordiness, etc.	Report	Appropriate for formal business reports and college papers

FIGURE 9.5

Custom writing style options

in a paragraph, words per sentence, and syllables per word. Also listed in the statistics is the Flesch Reading Ease readability number. The number displayed by the Flesch Reading Ease option indicates a grade level in school, for example, a number under 30 is considered college level while a number over 90 is considered fourth grade level. Any readability number between 50 and 80 is considered an effective reading level for most individuals.

Start-Up Instructions

- The file named **9drill2.the** should be displayed in the document window.

Use the Grammatik Program

Note: Using the mouse is the most effective way to perform the Steps to Use the Grammatik Program. A mouse must be available to perform the following steps.

1. The document to be grammar checked must be saved and displayed on the screen.
2. Select the **Grammatik** button on the Power Bar.

   Note: The Grammatik dialog box displays.
3. Select **Start**.

   *Note: The first occurrence of a word, phrase, or sentence to be checked is displayed. The item to be checked is highlighted in the document window. For example, **for the period of** and the advice, "Simplify," displays in the Rule Class box (see Figure 9.6).*
4. View the suggested words listed in the bottom left of the dialog box. Double-click on the desired replacement option.

   For example, double-click on **from**.

   Note: The next item to be checked (ERISA) is highlighted.
5. Select the **Ignore Word** button because the acronym (ERISA) is spelled correctly.

   *Note: The next item to be checked is highlighted, e.g., **has been filed**.*

FIGURE 9.7

Standard paragraphs document (9drill3.stn)

Standard Seminar Information

Seminar Locations and Dates

March 5-6, 199x--Park Plaza, Boston, Massachusetts
March 14-15, 199x--Four Ambassadors, Miami, Florida
March 19-20, 199x--Hyatt Regency, Phoenix, Arizona
March 21-22, 199x--Seattle Hilton, Seattle, Washington

Session Descriptions

New Technologies--This session provides a preview of new technologies, including wireless communications and interactive television. Hand-held pen devices and voice user interfaces will be demonstrated.

Electronic Distribution--This session discusses the best way to distribute sophisticated print documents in electronic form that can be viewed on a screen and printed out when needed.

The Future of Electronic Delivery--This session includes the impact of developments that are predicted to take place over the next decade: online delivery using telephone, cable, and satellite services.

Telecommunications for Print Production--This session begins with a summary of the status of high-speed digital communications around the world. Specific user examples illustrating methods in which print publishers are using the technology will be discussed.

Advertising in a Digital World--This session will be a panel discussion on the impact of online interactive services and the effect the digital world will have on advertising.

For example, type the current date, inside address, salutation, and first two paragraphs of the letter shown in Figure 9.8. Press **Enter** twice after the second paragraph.

3. Save the personalized document.

   For example, save the file on your file disk; use the filename **9nunes.ltr.**

Steps to Copy Text Between Windows

1. Select Window {Alt, w}.
2. Select the name of the document that contains the standard paragraphs {press the down arrow key as many times as needed to highlight the desired filename, press Enter}.

   For example, click once on the file named **9drill3.stn.**

   Note: *The file containing the standard paragraphs displays on the screen. The file containing the new document is still open in memory but is currently hidden.*
3. Select the desired text to be copied to the personalized document.

(Use current date)

Mr. Theodore Nunes
4808 Cameron Creek, Apt. 8
Fort Worth, TX 76132

Dear Mr. Nunes:

Your registration has been received to attend the upcoming Communications Conference.

The conference date, location, and description of your selected session(s) is as follows:

Copy the following paragraphs from the list of Standard Seminar Information (**9drill3.stn**).

March 19-20 conference date and location information

New Technologies

Telecommunications for Print Production

If you need additional information about the seminar or hotel accommodations, please call 1-800-555-1800.

Sincerely,

Howard Walsh
Seminar Coordinator

HW/xx
nunes.ltr/disk1

FIGURE 9.8

Personalized document assembled using standard paragraphs (9nunes.ltr)

For example, select **March 19-20, 199x--Hyatt Regency, Phoenix, Arizona.**

4. Select the **Copy** button on the Power Bar {Alt, e, c *or* Ctrl and c}.

   Note: *A copy of the selected text has been placed in the clipboard.*

5. Select **Window** {Alt, w}.

6. Choose the filename of the personalized document.

   For example, click once on the file named **9nunes.ltr.**

   Note: *In the personalized letter, the insertion point should be located at the left margin one blank line space below the second paragraph.*

7. Select the **Paste** button on the Power Bar {Alt, e, p *or* Ctrl and v}.

   Note: *The copied text is retrieved from the clipboard and displays on the screen.*

8. If necessary, press the **End** key to locate the insertion point at the end of the line, and press **Enter** one or two times in order to locate the insertion point one blank line space below the copied text.

9. Select **Window** {Alt, w}; choose the filename of the document that contains the standard paragraphs.

For example, choose **9drill3.stn.**

10. Select the text to be copied to the personalized document.

For example, select the paragraph that begins **New Technologies--.**

11. Select the **Copy** button on the Power Bar {Alt, e, c *or* Ctrl and c}.

12. Select **Window** {Alt, w}. Choose the filename of the personalized document.

For example, choose **9nunes.ltr.**

Note: *The insertion point should be located at the left margin one blank line below the conference date information.*

13. Select the **Paste** button on the Power Bar {Alt, e, p *or* Ctrl and v}.

14. If necessary, place the insertion point at the end of the paragraph. Press **Enter** one or two times to locate the insertion point one blank line space below the copied paragraph.

Finish-Up Instructions

- Repeat steps 9–14 and copy the paragraph that begins **Telecommunications for Print Production--.**
- Type the final paragraph, complimentary closing, typed signature, title, reference initials, and document identification as shown in Figure 9.8.
- Save the personalized document file using the same filename, **9nunes.ltr.**
- Print one copy.
- Close the document

The Next Step

Chapter Review and Activities

Self-Check Quiz

T F 1. A Tab is used to indent the first line of a paragraph for a document with vertical line spacing of one.

T F 2. A thesaurus contains synonyms that assist a writer in communicating clearly.

T F 3. A document typed with vertical line spacing of two is always printed with full justification.

T F 4. The advice presented by the Grammatik program should always be used to correct the grammar in a document.

5. The standard paragraphs file must be ____ before copying text that will be pasted in an individualized document.
   a. open in a document window
   b. displayed in the Viewer window
   c. closed
   d. either a or b

6. If a document is typed with vertical line spacing of two, one or _____ blank lines precede the first paragraph.
   a. three
   b. two
   c. one
   d. none of these

7. A document title is often centered and printed in ____.
   a. italic
   b. a different font
   c. uppercase letters
   d. both a and c

8. The text copied from an open document or from the Viewer window is placed in the _____.
   a. clipboard
   b. Viewer window
   c. document window
   d. Page Zoom window

9. List the names of the menu and submenu selected in order to display the Document Information dialog box.

10. State one purpose for using standard paragraphs to assemble individualized documents.

Enriching Language Arts Skills

Spelling/Vocabulary Words

partnership a legal association of individuals joined together, often for business purposes.

accrual method an accounting technique that reports income when earned. In contrast, the cash accounting method records income when payment is received.

maturity the date when a financial exchange is due, e.g., the day a promissory note or bond is to be paid.

depreciation reduction in the value of an asset; decrease in price.

liability a debt owed; a disadvantage.

amortized the method of distributing the cost of an asset over the life of the debt.

Speller Hint

The Speller approves words that are correctly spelled; however, a correctly spelled word can be incorrectly used in a sentence. After using the Speller, proofread the document for words used incorrectly.

Examples:

of, off	you, your, you're	is, it, in, if	to, too, two	its, it's
no, not	for, from, form	a, as, an	there, their	used, sued

Activities

Activity 9.1—Create a One-Page Document and Use Document Information

1. Type the following document with vertical line spacing of one and left justification.
2. Use the default left, right, top, and bottom margins.

Telephone System

Enhanced Phone System

Flextex Health Care has improved its telephone system. The phone changes enhance previous improvements made to the system and, as a result, have increased ease of use for our customers' convenience.

The new system features direct dial access to the Client Services Department for all client inquiries. Client representatives are available to provide information and assistance Monday through Friday from 9:00 a.m. to 4:00 p.m. and on Saturday from 9:00 a.m. to 3:00 p.m.

Who to Call

All questions should be directed to the Client Services Department. If the staff is unable to answer your particular question at the time of your call, they will research the answer and call you with a response.

Where to Call

Next week you will be provided with a list of numbers to call for specific inquiries. One set of numbers is for claims and referral information; the other is for benefits information. It is important that you use the new department extension numbers because the new phone system replaces all previous telephone extension numbers. All calls to Client Services will be answered in the order that the calls are received.

Clients calling Flextex's main phone number, (505) 555-2310, will reach the automated phone system with a current list of options. Callers can access the list by using a touch-tone telephone. Clients with rotary telephones can remain on the line for an operator's assistance.

Current Telephone Numbers

Please use the following information about the current telephone numbers.

Call 1 + (800) 555-4554 or (505) 555-7878 for information concerning bills, medical referrals, reimbursements, and third-party liability.

Call 1 + (800) 555-8322 or (505) 555-4849 for information concerning copayments, benefits, changing a primary care physician, replacing identification cards, enrollment eligibility information, group coverage, and notification of address or telephone changes.

---

3. Use the filename **9act1.tel** and save the file.
4. Print one copy.
5. Select **File, Document Info** to determine the total number of words in the document. Handwrite the number of words at the top of your printed copy. Select **OK**.
6. Close the document.

Activity 9.2—Create Personalized Letters Using Standard Paragraphs

1. Open the file named **9drill3.stn** that was created previously in this chapter, or create the standard paragraphs document shown in Figure 9.7.
2. Create a new file and type the following personalized letter. Copy the standard paragraphs from the file named **9drill3.stn** as indicated.

(Use current date)

Ms. Mary Sinclair
951 David Ross Road
W. Lafayette, IN 47906

Dear Ms. Sinclair:

Thank you for your interest in attending our Communications Conferences. Below is a listing of the upcoming conference dates and a description of the two seminars in which you have expressed an interest.

> Copy the following standard paragraphs from the list of seminar information in the file named **9drill3.stn.**
>
> Copy all four seminar locations and dates.
>
> Copy the paragraph that begins "Advertising in a Digital World."
>
> Copy the paragraph that begins "The Future of Electronic Delivery."

7. Save the personalized document as **9skill3.yum**.
8. Print one copy.
9. If you have completed your work, exit WordPerfect.

CHAPTER 10

Create a Multiple-Page Document

Features Covered

- Print page numbers
- Create headers and footers
- Keep text together (widow/orphan)
- Create footnotes and endnotes
- Search for codes
- Print specific pages

Objectives and Introduction

After successfully completing this chapter, you will be able to create a multiple-page document, print page numbers on each page, and use the widow/orphan feature. Also, you will be able to create and edit headers, footers, footnotes, and endnotes as well as print a specific page(s) and search for codes.

A multiple-page document is comparable to a one-page report and can be an article, essay, minutes, agenda, or any type of document that describes an event or provides information. A multiple-page document consists of two or more pages. Examples of multiple-page business documents are investment, insurance, legal, medical, and sales documents.

Create a Multiple-Page Document

Like a one-page document, a multiple-page document can be created with vertical line spacing of one (single spacing) or two (double spacing). Pages of a multiple-page document are formatted the same as a one-page document with 1-inch top, bottom, left, and right default margins. (See Chapter 9, Figures 9.1 and 9.3.)

Each page of a multiple-page document is separated by a soft page break. When the number of available vertical lines on the page are filled, the text automatically

FIGURE 10.1

Hard page break in Page view mode

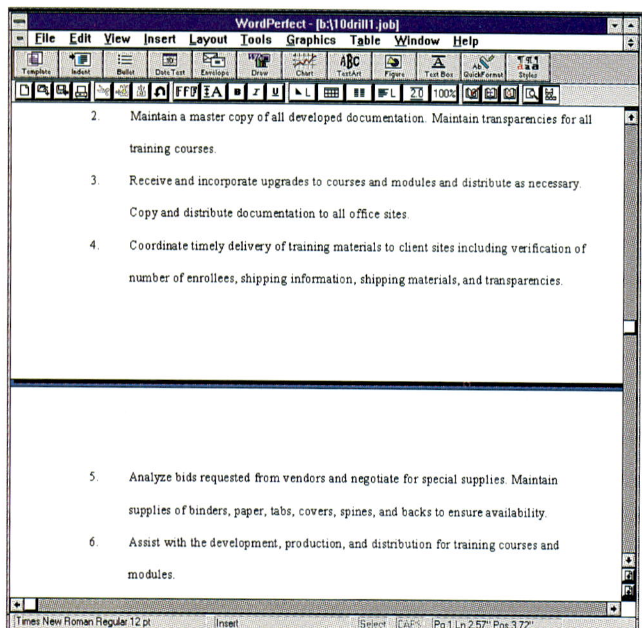

wraps to the next page. The soft page break is also referred to as an automatic page break. In Reveal Codes, a soft page break is identified with an *SPg* code.

If a new page is desired before the available lines on the page are filled, a hard page break is used to create the new page. A hard page break is placed in a document by pressing the **Ctrl** and **Enter** keys. The hard page break is also known as a required page break. In Reveal Codes, a hard page break is identified with an *HPg* code.

WordPerfect provides several modes to view text in the document window, namely, Page, Two Page, and Draft views. The Page view mode is referred to as a WYSIWYG (what you see is what you get) display because the page elements such as margins, fonts, text attributes, headers/footers, and footnotes display in the document window as they will print. A graphical representations of the top and bottom of each page and space that indicates margins display in the document window (see Figure 10.1).

The Two Page view mode, similar to the Page view mode, displays two consecutive pages side by side in the same document window. The Two Page view mode is useful for evaluating the page layout and the text is usually too small to read.

The Draft view mode is also similar to the Page view mode; however, headers/footers, footnotes, and top and bottom margins do not display in the document window. A soft page break displays as a single horizontal line placed across the width of the document window. A hard page break may display as two single horizontal lines or as a thick single line.

The pages of a multiple-page document can be viewed on the screen to see the placement of the lines and page numbers. The current page is viewed by using either the Page View or the Page Zoom Full feature. In Page View, additional pages can be viewed by pressing the **Page Up** and **Page Down** keys. Also, in Page Zoom Full, additional pages can be viewed by selecting the **Previous Page** and **Next Page** buttons, which are located at the bottom of the vertical scroll bar (see Figure 1.7 in Chapter 1). If desired, two pages can be displayed on the screen at one time by selecting **View, Two Page.**

Print Page Numbers

Each page of a multiple-page document should be numbered. If the pages are numbered at the bottom, number 1 is printed at the bottom of the first page. If pages are numbered at the top, the first page may or may not be numbered. WordPerfect's default is to print with no page numbers.

Page numbers can be instructed to print at the top or bottom of the page and at the left margin, centered, or at the right margin as well as alternating on the top or bottom of pages. The default position for page numbers is 1 inch from the top of the page or 1 inch from the bottom of the page. The **Position** option in the Page Numbering dialog box is used to indicate the placement of page numbers. The **Options** button in the Page Numbering dialog box can be selected to format the page numbers and to specify text that will be included with the page number. For example, the page numbering format could be changed to uppercase Roman numerals or the word *Page* can be printed along with the page number (e.g., Page 1).

Page numbers can be set to print as lowercase letters (a, b, c, etc.) or uppercase letters (A, B, C, etc.), lowercase Roman numerals (i, ii, iii, etc.), uppercase Roman numerals (I, II, III, etc.), or numbers (1, 2, 3, etc.). If text will accompany the page number, type the desired text in the Format and Accompanying Text box before or after the page number code (*[Pg#]*).

A different beginning page number can be set by selecting the **Value** button in the Page Numbering dialog box. For example, to begin numbering pages with page 4, type 4 in the New Page Number box in the Page Settings category.

A header or footer can also be used to print page numbers. (See Headers and Footers later in this chapter.)

Start-Up Instructions

- Open the file named **10drill1.job** located on the data disk.

Steps to Number Pages

1. With the insertion point located at any position on page one, select Layout, Page, Numbering {Alt, L, p, n}.

   Note: The Page Numbering dialog box displays.

2. Move the mouse pointer to the Position box, press and hold the mouse button and drag to select the desired page number position option {Alt and p, press the up or down arrow keys until the desired position option is highlighted}.

   For example, move the mouse pointer to the Position box, press and hold the mouse button and drag to select **Bottom Center**; release the mouse button.

   Note: A sample of the page number location displays below the Position box (see Figure 10.2).

3. Select OK {press Enter}.

   *Note: Select **View, Two Page** to display both pages on the screen. Select **View, Page** to return to the normal view.*

FIGURE 10.2

Page Numbering dialog box

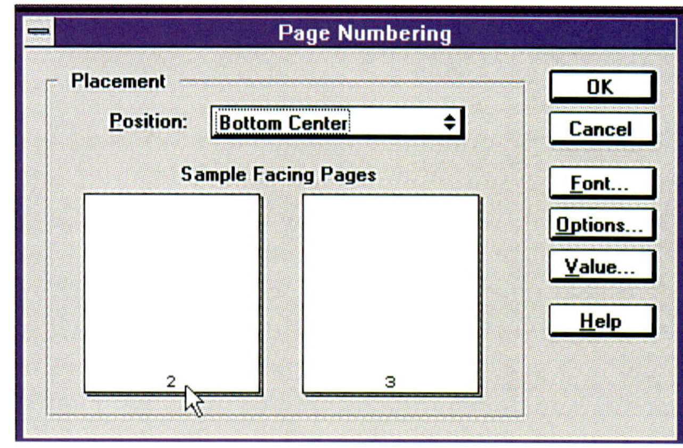

Finish-Up Instructions

- Turn on Reveal Codes (select **View, Reveal Codes**). With the insertion point located at the beginning of the document, place the red or shaded block to the left of the *Pg Num Pos* code and view the expanded page numbering code, e.g., *Pg Num Pos: Bottom Center.* Turn off Reveal Codes (select **View, Reveal Codes**).
- Use the *new* filename **10drill1.num** and save the file.
- Print one copy.

Start-Up Instructions

- The file named **10drill1.num** should be displayed in the document window.

Steps to Change the Page Numbering Method

1. With the insertion point located at any position on page one, select **Layout, Page, Numbering** {Alt, L, p, n}.
2. Select **Options** {o}.
3. Move the mouse pointer to the Page box; press and hold the mouse button and drag to select the desired number type. Release the mouse button {Alt and p, press the up or down arrow until the desired option displays}.

   For example, select **Uppercase Roman.**
4. Select **OK** to return to the Page Numbering dialog box {Enter}.
5. Select **OK** {press Enter}.

Finish-Up Instructions

- Turn on Reveal Codes (select **View, Reveal Codes**). With the insertion point at the beginning of the document, place the red or shaded block to the left of the *Pg Num Meth* code and view the expanded page numbering method code, e.g., *Pg Num Meth: Lev 1;4.* Turn off Reveal Codes (select **View, Reveal Codes**).
- Use the filename **10drill1.rom** and save the file.
- Print one copy.

Start-Up Instructions

- The file named **10drill1.rom** should be displayed in the document window.

Delete Page Numbers by Deleting the Page Numbering Position Code

1. If necessary, turn on Reveal Codes (select **View, Reveal Codes**).
2. Place the red or shaded block to the left of the page number code.

   For example, place the red or shaded block to the left of the code *Pg Num Pos: Bottom Center.*
3. Press the Delete key.
4. Turn off Reveal Codes (select **View**, **Reveal Codes**).

Finish-Up Instructions

- In Page View, scroll to the bottom of each page. Notice that the page numbers no longer display at the bottom of the document pages.
- Close the document. Do not save the file.

Headers and Footers

Generally, a multiple-page document includes headers or footers. A header is a title or information that prints in the top margin of the second and following pages (see Figures 10.3 and 10.5). A footer is a title or information that prints in the bottom margin of each page (see Figure 10.5). Headers and footers can consist of more than one line of text. Once created, headers and footers can be edited, suppressed for a single page, discontinued, or deleted.

When a header is used, the header information is normally not printed on the first page of a document but prints at the top of the second and following pages. When a footer is used, the title information along with the page number (optional) prints at the bottom of every page. The default position for headers is 1" from the top of the page, and the default position for footers is 1" from the bottom of the page. A header or footer can be viewed by selecting **View**, **Page** or by choosing the **View**, **Two Page** option.

Two different headers or footers can be created. Header A & B and Footer A & B are options available in the Headers/Footers dialog box. Usually, only Header A or Footer A is used. However, if a document is set up to display different headers/footers on left and right pages, Header/Footer A would be used to create a left-page header or footer and Header/Footer B would be used to create a right-page header or footer. The footers in this textbook are examples of different left- and right-page footers.

If the format of a document is changed, the format of the header or footer must also be altered to match the changed document format. For example, if the margins or fonts are changed for the entire document, the margins or fonts for the header and/or footer must also be changed.

For example, type **J. Russell Mason, The President's Report to the Board of Directors, Spring 1990, p. 2.**

4. Select **Close** on the Footnote/Endnote Feature Bar {Alt and Shift and c}.

   Note: *The footnote number displays at the location of the insertion point. To display the footnote, select **View, Two Page** and/or scroll to the bottom of the page.*

Finish-Up Instructions

- Place the insertion point after the last period in the third paragraph that ends with the word *methods.*
- Use steps 2-4 to create the following footnote:

  Ibid., p. 3.
- Place the insertion point after the last period in the final paragraph that ends with the word *centers.*
- Use steps 2-4 to create the following footnote:

  Lois Hodges, "Contribution to Community Education," *The Times Crier*, 3 May 1991, p. 10.
- Use the *new* filename **10drill2.fnt** and save the file.
- Print one copy.

Start-Up Instructions

- The file named **10drill2.fnt** should be displayed in the document window.

Edit a Footnote or Endnote

Note: *The same method is used to edit footnotes and endnotes. For information on creating endnotes, see page 241.*

1. Select **Insert, Footnote** or **Endnote, Edit** {Alt, i, f or e, e}.

   For example, select **Insert, Footnote, Edit** {Alt, i, f, e}.

   Note: *The Edit Footnote dialog box displays.*

2. Type the number of the footnote/endnote to be edited.

   For example, check that the number **3** displays. If necessary, type **3**.

3. Select **OK** to locate the insertion point at the beginning of the footnote/endnote {Enter}.

4. Make corrections using the customary edit methods.

   For example, change p. 10 to **p. 24**.

5. Select **Close** on the Footnote/Endnote Feature Bar {Alt and Shift and c}.

Finish-Up Instructions

- Save the file again using the same filename, **10drill2.fnt**.

Start-Up Instructions

- The file named **10drill2.fnt** should be displayed in the document window.

Delete a Footnote or Endnote

Note: The same method is used to delete footnotes and endnotes. For information on creating endnotes, see the following Steps to Create Endnotes.

1. Select the footnote or endnote reference number in the document.

    For example, select the footnote reference number **2** that displays after the third paragraph.

2. Press the **Delete** key once. The footnote/endnote number and the footnote/endnote information are both deleted.

    Note: If other footnotes/endnotes follow the deleted footnote or endnote, the remaining footnotes/endnotes are automatically renumbered.

Finish-Up Instructions

- Use the *new* filename **10drill2.fin** and save the file.
- Print one copy.
- Close the document.

Start-Up Instructions

- Open the file named **10drill2.foo** located on the data disk.

Steps to Create Endnotes

1. Place the insertion point to the right of the text to be referenced.

    For example, place the insertion point to the right of the period after the last sentence in the first paragraph that ends with the word *annually*.

2. Select **Insert, Endnote, Create** {Alt, i, e, c}.

    Note: The Endnote Feature Bar displays below the Power Bar, and the endnote number is shown at the bottom of the screen after the last paragraph in the document.

3. Press the **Tab** key once; type the endnote information.

    For example, type **J. Russell Mason, The President's Report to the Board of Directors, Spring 1990, p. 2.**

4. Select the **Close** button on the Endnote Feature Bar {Alt and Shift and c}.

    Note: The insertion point returns to the referenced text, and the number 1 displays at the end of the paragraph. In Page view mode, scroll down to display the last page of the document and view the endnote.

Finish-Up Instructions

- Place the insertion point after the last period in the third paragraph that ends with the word *methods.*
- Use steps 2-4 to create the second endnote:

  Ibid., p. 3.
- Place the insertion point after the last period in the final paragraph that ends with the word *centers.*
- Use steps 2-4 to create the third endnote:

  Lois Hodges, "Contribution to Community Education," ***The Times Crier,*** **3 May 1991, p. 24.**

  Note: If necessary, select ***Close*** *on the Endnote Feature Bar.*
- With the insertion point to the right of the footnote number located after the last paragraph that ends with the word *centers,* press **Ctrl** and **Enter** to create a hard page break.
- Type the title **Notes**; press **Enter** once.
- Select and center the title.
- Use the *new* filename **10drill2.end** and save the file.
- In order to view all endnotes in Page view mode, it may be necessary to scroll down the page.
- Print one copy.

Search for Codes

To quickly locate a specific place in a document, the user can search for text or codes. Searching for codes is quite similar to searching for specific text (see Chapter 4). Locating a code is useful for deleting or moving a code or for finding a specific area of the document.

A code can be located by matching a code listed in the Codes dialog box. A code can also be found by designating a specific value or a specific code such as *Font, Just* or *Bot Mar.*

To find a code that has been assigned a specific value (e.g., a font size code), choose **Type** in the Find Text dialog box, select **Specific Codes,** double-click on **Font Size**, select the up or down triangles to increase or decrease the number until the desired size displays and select **Find Next**; select **Close** (or move the Find Font Size box to the top of the document window—see Chapter 16). Turn on Reveal Codes to display the found code. The red or shaded block is located to the right of the found code.

Start-Up Instructions

- The file named **10drill2.end** should be displayed in the document window.

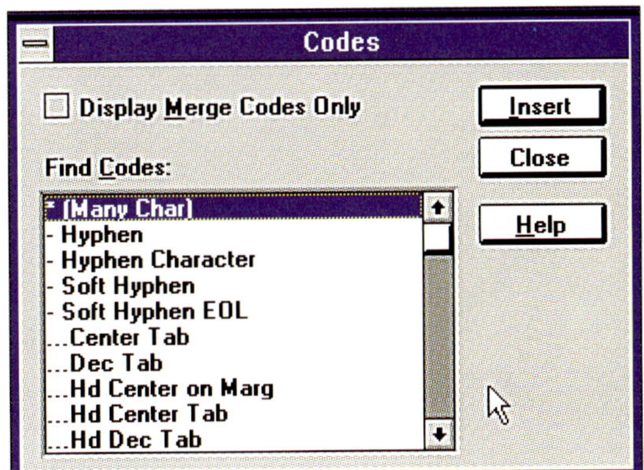

FIGURE 10.7

Codes dialog box

Steps to Search for a Code

Note: The insertion point should be located at the top of the document to be searched.

1. Select Edit, Find {F2}.
2. Select Match, Codes {Alt and m, o}.

   Note: The Codes dialog box displays (see Figure 10.7).
3. Begin typing the desired code or use the scroll bars to display the desired code.

   For example, type **Endn.**

   *Note: The code Endnote is highlighted after typing **endn**.*
4. Double-click on the desired code {press Enter}.

   For example, double-click on the **Endnote** code.

   Note: The code Endnote is placed in the Find box in the Find Text dialog box.
5. Select Find Next in the Find Text dialog box {Alt and f}.

   Note: The endnote number is highlighted in the text.
6. Select Close {Alt and c}.

Finish-Up Instructions

- Press the **Backspace** key to delete the endnote code in the document.

  Note: The endnotes are automatically renumbered in the document but are not renumbered on the last page of the document.
- Select **Insert**, **Endnote**, **Edit**, select **OK** or type **1**, press the **Delete** key, type **1**, select **Close**.

  Note: If desired, scroll to the end of the document to view the renumbered endnote(s).
- Save the file again using the same filename, **10drill2.end**.

Chapter 10
Create a Multiple-Page Document

Print Specific Pages

After printing a multiple-page document, one or more of the pages may need to be edited and only those pages will need to be reprinted. To specify the exact pages to print, the Multiple Pages option is selected in the Print dialog box, and the desired pages are entered as follows:

- Place a comma or space between nonconsecutive pages, e.g., 1,3 or 2 4 6.
- Place a dash between the beginning and ending page numbers to print a consecutive range of pages, e.g., 5-9.
- Place a dash after the beginning page number to print from a specific page to the end of the document, e.g. 5-.
- Place a dash before the page number to print from the beginning of a document up to a specific page, e.g., -6.

A combination of these methods can be used, e.g., 4,5, 8-11 *or* 2-4 6. Page numbers must be typed in numerical order. If, for example, the specified pages are 8, 2-5, only page 8 will print.

Also, a single page can be printed by typing the page number in the Page(s) box or by placing the insertion point anywhere on the page, selecting the **Print** button on the Power Bar, choosing the **Current Page** option, and selecting **Print**. When the **Current Page** option is selected, only the page where the insertion point is located will print.

Start-Up Instructions

- The document containing the pages to print should be displayed in the document window. For example, the file named **10drill2.end** should be displayed in the document window.

Print Specific Pages

1. Select the **Print** button on the Power Bar {Alt, f, p *or* F5}.
2. Select the **Multiple Pages** option in the Print dialog box {Alt and m}.
3. Select **Print** {Alt and p}.

   *Note: The Multiple Pages dialog box displays with the word **all** highlighted in the Page(s) box (see Figure 10.8).*

4. In the Page(s) box, type the page numbers to be printed.

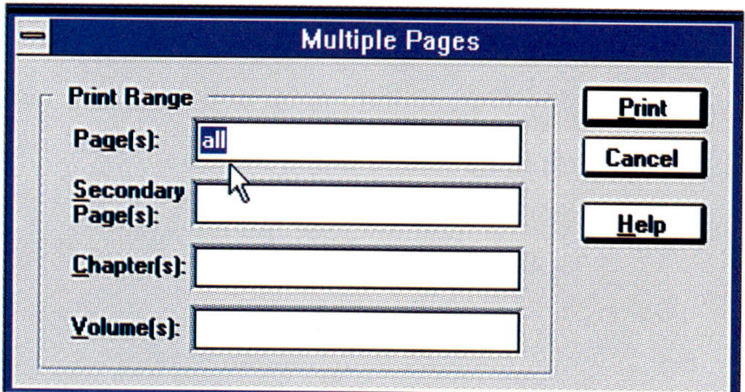

FIGURE 10.8

Multiple Pages dialog box

For example, type **1,3** to print pages 1 and 3 only.

5. Select **Print** {Alt and p}.

   Note: *A message, "Preparing document for printing," displays briefly.*

Finish-Up Instructions

- Close and do not save the document.

The Next Step

Chapter Review and Activities

Self-Check Quiz

T F 1. A multiple-page report is printed with vertical line spacing of one or two.

T F 2. A footer is typed once but prints on all pages of a multiple-page document.

T F 3. A header is normally printed on all pages of a document.

T F 4. Footnotes are consecutively numbered and printed on the page where the information is referenced.

5. Press _____ and **Enter** to place a hard page break in a document.
   a. **Ctrl**
   b. **Alt**
   c. **Shift**
   d. **Home**

6. Using the Page Numbering options, numbers can be set to print as ______
   a. lowercase or uppercase letters.
   b. lowercase or uppercase Roman numerals.
   c. numbers (1, 2, 3, etc.).
   d. any of these.

7. The _____ feature of the keep text together function can be used to prevent a table or chart from being printed on two pages.
   a. widow/orphan
   b. block protect
   c. conditional end of page
   d. none of the above

8. A code in a document can be found by ________________
   a. matching a code listed in the Codes dialog box.
   b. designating a specific value.
   c. indicating a specific code such as *Bot Mar.*
   d. any of these.

9. State the difference between a footnote and a footer.

Exploration and Human Evolution," *Spacefaring Gazette*, August 1988, p. 9.

5. Number the document pages at the top right corner.
6. Use the *new* filename **10skill3.fin** and save the file.
7. Print one copy.
8. If you have completed your work, exit WordPerfect.

CHAPTER

Create a Form Letter and Mailing List

Features Covered

- Create a form (primary) file
- Create a data (secondary) file
- Merge files
- Determine field names
- Edit data files and form files
- Mark a record(s)

Objectives and Introduction

After successfully completing this chapter, you will be able to create and merge a data file with a form file. You will also understand fields and records and learn how to remove the blank line that results from an empty field. In addition, you will be able to edit data and form files, mark records, and sort by fields.

A form letter is a standard letter that is sent to many individuals or companies. The same letter can be typed once, merged with a list of names and addresses, and printed. A form letter can be used for collecting overdue accounts, requesting donations, presenting product information, etc. The form letter is referred to as the form file. The list of names and addresses is referred to as the data file.

Create a Data File

The *data file* is a group of variables and field names. A variable is the information that changes in each form letter and can include names, addresses, dollar amounts, dates, special comments, etc. The variable information is referred to as data. The data file can be either a text or a table file. If a text data file is used, each variable displays on a separate line followed by a code. If a table data file is used, the variable information displays in table cells (see Figure 11.1). A table data file is recommended,

FIGURE 11.1

A data file with field names and data

title	first	last	co	address	city	state	zip	acct#
Ms.	Roxanne E.	Peterson		P.O. Box 96	Cathlamet	WA	98516	4182
Mr.	Mark	Koch, Jr.	Abby, Inc.	25 Jones Lane	Mt. Juliet	TN	37122	3198
Ms.	Esther	Emerson		40 E. 56th St., #5	New York	NY	10022	2186

because it is easier to create, proofread, and edit. (In earlier versions of WordPerfect the data file was called the secondary file.)

A *field* is the name given to a variable; for example, a dollar amount field can be named "dollar." A field name should be determined for each unit of information before beginning the process to create a data file. The field names in the data file must correlate exactly with the field names in the form file. A collection of all desired units (fields) is a record. In other words, a record is a single "set" of information that pertains to one entity, for example, one individual's first name, last name, company, address, city, state, and zip code.

When the table data file and records are created and displayed on the screen, the Merge Feature Bar automatically shows below the Power Bar. The Merge Feature Bar is used to insert fields, the Date code, and merge codes, and to display the Merge dialog box. If the data file is displayed, the **Go to Form** button shows on the Merge Feature bar. This button provides a quick way to create or open a form letter.

Create a Table Data File

1. Select Tools, Merge {Alt, t, e *or* Shift and F9}.

   Note: The Merge dialog box displays (see Figure 11.2).

2. In the Data File area, select Place Records in a Table option {p}.

   Note: An X displays in the box beside the Place Records in a Table option.

FIGURE 11.2

Merge dialog box

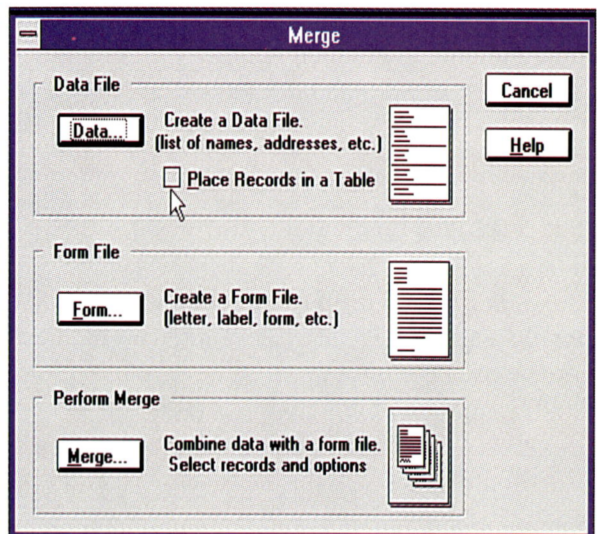

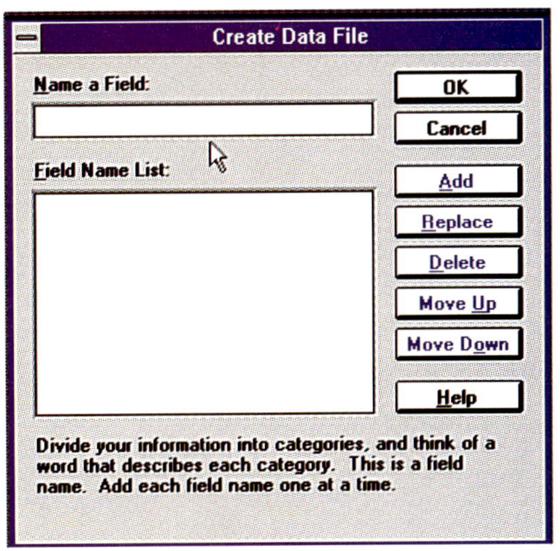

FIGURE 11.3

Create Data File dialog box

3. Select the **Data** button {d}. The Create Data File dialog box displays (see Figure 11.3).

   Note: If the Create Merge File dialog box displays, select the ***New Document Window*** *option.)*

4. Decide on a name for each data file field.

   For example, **title**, **first**, **last**, **co**, **address**, **city**, **state**, **zip**, and **acct#**.

5. Create each field name as follows:

   a. Type the name of the first field in the Name a Field box.

      For example, type **title**. (Do not type the final period.)

   b. Select **Add** or press **Enter** to display the field name in the Field Name List box.

   c. Type the next field name in the Name a Field box.

      For example, type **first**. (Do not type the final period.)

   d. Select **Add** or press **Enter** to display the field name in the Field Name List box.

6. Repeat steps 5a-b to add the remaining field names.

   For example, type the field names **last**, **co**, **address**, **city**, **state**, **zip**, and **acct#**. (Do not type the final period.)

   Note: If changes are desired, move the mouse pointer to the field name to be changed in the Field Name List box and click once. Use the Add, Replace, Delete, Move up, or Move down button options.

7. Select **OK** {Enter once}.

   Note: The Quick Data Entry dialog box with a list of the first eight field names displays for one record (see Figure 11.4). Also, a table with the field names displays in the document window.

8. With the insertion point in the first field name box, type the variable information.

   For example, type the recipient's title: **Ms.** (Type the final period.)

9. Press the **Tab** key to move the insertion point to the next field name box.

FIGURE 11.4

Quick Data Entry dialog box

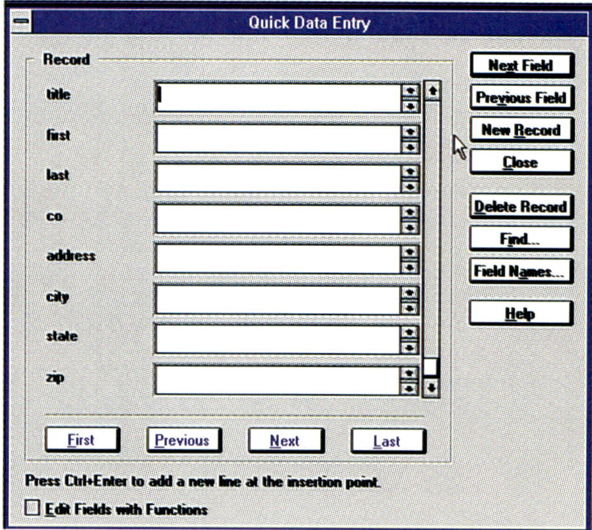

Note: If desired, point to the desired field name box and click once.

10. Type the the second field name data.

    For example, type the recipient's first name and, if available, middle initial: **Roxanne E.** (Type the final period.)

11. Press the Tab key to move the insertion point to the next field name box.

12. Type the third field name data.

    For example, type the recipient's last name: **Peterson**. (Do not type the final period.)

13. Press the Tab key to move the insertion point to the next field name box.

14. Type the the next field name data.

    For example, type the company name. No company name is available; therefore, press the **Tab** key.

    *Note: When information for a field is not available, press the **Tab** key to skip to the next field name box.*

15. Type the next field name data and press the Tab key.

    For example, type **P.O. Box 96** and press the **Tab** key.

16. Repeat step 17 and type the remaining data for the record.

    For example, type the following data:

Cathlamet	Tab
WA	Tab
98612-0096	Tab
4182	Do not press Tab.

17. Select the New Record button {Alt and r}.

    *Note: When the **New Record** button is selected, the data for the record just completed displays in the table in the document window.*

18. Repeat steps 8-17 and enter the field data for the following two records.

Mr.	Tab
Mark	Tab
Koch, Jr.	Tab
Abby, Inc.	Tab
25 Jones Lane	Tab
Mt. Juliet	Tab
TN	Tab
37122	Tab
3198	Select New Record.

Ms.	Tab
Esther	Tab
Emerson	Tab
	Tab
40 E. 56th St., #5	Tab
New York	Tab
NY	Tab
10022	Tab
2186	Do not press Tab.

19. When all the records have been completed, select Close {Alt and c}.
20. A message displays, "Save the changes to disk?" Select Yes {Enter}. Type the drive letter where the disk is located followed by the filename.

    For example, type **a:11drill1.dat**; select **OK**.

    Note: *The data displays in a table; the first row contains the field names. The Merge Feature bar displays below the Power Bar (see Figure 11.5).*

Finish-Up Instructions

- Continue with the Steps to Create a Form File.

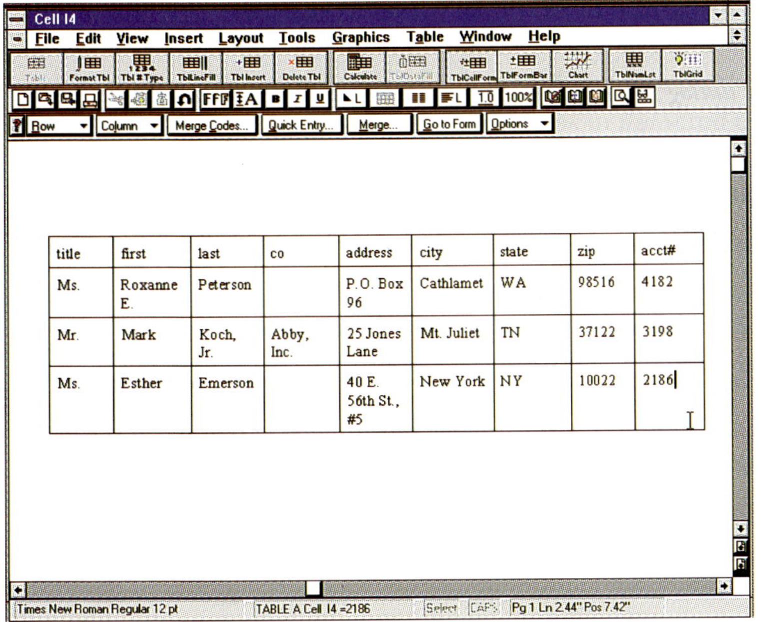

title	first	last	co	address	city	state	zip	acct#
Ms.	Roxanne E.	Peterson		P.O. Box 96	Cathlamet	WA	98516	4182
Mr.	Mark	Koch, Jr.	Abby, Inc.	25 Jones Lane	Mt. Juliet	TN	37122	3198
Ms.	Esther	Emerson		40 E. 56th St., #5	New York	NY	10022	2186

FIGURE 11.5

Table Data File with Merge Feature Bar displayed

(DATE)

FIELD(first) **FIELD**(last)
FIELD(company)
FIELD(address)
FIELD(city), **FIELD**(state) **FIELD**(zip)

Dear **FIELD**(title) **FIELD**(last):

It is a pleasure to answer your recent letter requesting current information about **FIELD**(vendor). Credit was extended to **FIELD**(vendor) on **FIELD**(date),with a limit of $**FIELD**(amount).

Their invoices have always been paid promptly, many times taking advantage of the cash discount.

This information is to be held in strict confidence. We are glad to be of service to you. If you have any further questions, please do not hesitate to contact us.

Sincerely,

T. W. Loyden
Credit Division Manager

TWL/xx

---

6. Save the form file; use the filename **11act3.frm**.
7. Select the **Close** button in the Insert Field Name or Number dialog box.
8. Select the **Merge** button on the Merge Feature bar, select **Merge**.
9. If necessary, type or select the Form File or Data File names(s) needed in the Perform Merge Dialog box.
10. Select **Options**, check that Remove Blank Line displays. If necessary, press and hold the mouse button and drag to highlight **Remove Blank Line**. Release the mouse button. Select **OK**.
11. Select **OK** to Perform Merge.
12. Print one copy of each merged letter.
13. Optional. Save the file of merged letters; use the filename **11act3.mer**.
14. Close the file containing the merged letters.
15. To edit the data file, use the following information:
    a. To display the data file named **11act3.dat**, select the **Go to Data** button on the Merge Feature Bar.

b. Change D. L. Ibbaro's initials to **Daniel Louis.**

c. Add the company name **Foodland, Inc.** to Roy E. Dunhill's record.

d. Delete the column that contains dollar amounts (place the insertion point in the desired column, select **Table, Delete,** select **Columns, OK**).

e. Save the edited data file using the same filename, **11act3.dat.**

16. To edit the form file, use the following information:

a. To display the form file named**11act3.frm**, select the **Go to Form** button on the Merge Feature Bar.

b. Delete **FIELD(amount)** and replace with **14,000.**

c. Save the file using the same filename, **11act3.frm.**

17. Merge **11act3.frm** with **11act3.dat.** (If necessary, see steps 8, 9, and 11 for specific instructions.)

18. Print one copy of each merged letter.

19. Optional. Save the file of merged letters; use the filename **11act3.me2.** Close all documents.

Challenge Your Skills

Skill 11.1—Create, Merge, and Edit a Form File and Data File; Mark Specific Data Records to Print

1. Use the following information to create a table data file.

a. The field names for the table data file are: first, last, address, city, state, zip, title, date, and amounts

b. The information for each record follows:

Lowell S.	Sharlene	Rudolph P.
Grizoffi	Kelterman	Lehman
72 Cobbs Creek Circle	572 Tiyunga Blvd.	1370 North Avenue
New Gloucester	North Hollywood	Miami
ME	CA	FL
04260	91600	33139
Mr.	Ms.	Mr.
October 24, 199x	November 5, 199x	September 12, 199x
$15,000, $40,000, or $65,000	$25,000, $60,000, or $100,000	$10,000, $25,000, or $50,000

2. Save the tabe data file; use the filename **11skill1.dat.**

3. Create the following form file. Make decisions regarding:

Margins
Justification
Fonts
Tab settings for indention of enumerated items

(DATE)

FIELD(first) **FIELD**(last)
FIELD(address)
FIELD(city), **FIELD**(state) **FIELD**(zip)

Dear **FIELD**(title) **FIELD**(last):

Thank you for your request for information on our special group term life plans. A brochure describing the special group life plans and an application for coverage are enclosed. In order for you to be eligible for the special group life rates, the enclosed application must be received by **FIELD**(date). After that date, this special group plan will no longer be available.

Based on your age, there are three amounts of group term life insurance that you can apply for--**FIELD**(amounts). With the special group plan, you are guaranteed:

1. **No medical exam.** A medical exam is not automatically required--your insurability can usually be determined based on the information in your application.

2. **Personal rate protection.** Once your application has been accepted, the only time your rates will change is when you move into a different age group.

3. **Credit card convenience.** Your monthly premiums can be conveniently billed to your UniCard account. You will never have to worry about paying the premium on time.

Please fill out, sign, and return the enclosed application in the postage-paid envelope. Remember, the signed application must be received in our office by **FIELD**(date).

Sincerely,

Marshall K. Piazzola
Executive Vice President

MKP/xx

Enc.

---

4. Save the form file; use the filename **11skill1.frm**.
5. Merge **11skill1.frm** with **11skill1.dat**.
6. Print one copy of each merged letter.
7. Optional. Save the file of merged letters; use the filename **11skill1.mer**.
8. Edit the table data file using the following information:
   a. Delete the **amounts** field column.

b. Use the following information to add two new records to the table data file named **11skill1.dat**:

Peter N.	Art
Hurtado	Mansano
1469 Wilshire Blvd.	887 Hardow Drive
Los Angeles	Las Vegas
CA	NV
90023	89106
Mr.	Mr.
November 2, 199x	October 1, 199x

c. Save the changed table data file.

9. Edit the form file using the following information:

a. Delete the first sentence of the second paragraph that begins "Based on . . ."

b. Delete the last sentence in the last paragraph that begins "Remember . . ."

c. Save the changed form file.

10. Mark and merge the two new records.

11. Print a copy of the two new merged letters and close all documents.

Skill 11.2—Create and Merge a Form File and Data File with Blank Fields; Language Arts

1. Use the following information to create a table data file.

a. The field names for the data file are: title, first, lastname, address1, address2, city, state, zip, name, and amount

b. The information for each record follows:

Mr.	Ms.	Mr.	Mrs.
Yohannes	Paige	Joseph R.	June A.
Wohlenberg	Ybarra	Nevitt	Penning
Gardenwood Terrace			Shore Apartments
36 Hill Rd., #16	2606 Auburn Way	313 36th St.	28 Addison Way, #6
York	Weatherford	Arlington	Springfield
PA	TX	VA	NJ
17403	76087	22203	07081
Yohannes	Paige	Joseph	June
5,000	7,000	6,000	5,000

2. Save the table data file; use the filename **11skill2.dat**.

3. Create the following form file. Make decisions regarding:

Margins
Justification
Fonts
Reference initials, document identification, and enclosure notation

4. Correct three spelling errors, two misused words, and two punctuation errors.

(DATE)

FIELD(title) **FIELD**(first) **FIELD**(lastname)
FIELD(address1)
FIELD(address2)
FIELD(city), **FIELD**(state) **FIELD**(zip)

Dear **FIELD**(title) **FIELD**(lastname):

First things first, **FIELD**(name). You can receive a credit card that is free forever.

You have been pre-approved to receive a Continental Omni card with a credit line of $**FIELD**(amount). All you need to do is use the card at least once a year and its yours--free from annual fees for life. Simply apply by the expiration date on the enclosed confirmation card.

That's not the only savings you will receive. You can save on interest, to. Ninety million people are currently paying 16% or more in credit card interest. The Continental Omni card offers a variable Annual Percentage Rate that is only 15.4% (prime rate plus 9.4%). And if the prim rate drops, your interest rate drops, too.

Your Continental Omni card which includes your picture, is accepted worldwide. So you can shop, dine, travel and make calls--with one card. You will also have the only Omni card that comes with the TWT Customer Service network. You can reach us anytime--24 hours a day, 365 days a year--from virtualy anywhere. And you will receive the responsive, personal service you would expect from TWT.

The fastest way to receive your card is to call 1-800-555-8222 or complete and return the enclosed confirnation card in the postage-paid envelope provided.

Sincerely,

Rachael G. Hunsberger
President

5. Save the form file; use the filename **11skill2.frm**.
6. Merge **11skill2.frm** with **11skill2.dat**.

   Hint: Remember to use the ***Remove Blank Line*** *option.*
7. Print one copy of each merged letter.
8. Optional. Save the file of merged letters; use the filename **11skill2.mer**.
9. If you have completed your work, exit WordPerfect.

CHAPTER 12

Create and Print Mailing Labels

Features Covered

- Create an envelope address
- Create an envelope definition
- Create mailing labels
- Sort records in a table data file

Objectives and Introduction

After successfully completing this chapter, you will be able to create envelope addresses, an envelope definition, and mailing labels using predefined labels. In addition, you will be able to sort records in a table data file.

Once a form file is merged with a data file, envelope addresses or mailing labels can be created for each document. Using existing data file addresses or letter addresses to create envelope addresses or mailing labels can assist in expediting the process of setting up and printing addresses on envelopes or labels.

Create Envelope Addresses

Envelope addresses are easily created by selecting the **Envelope** button on the WordPerfect Button Bar or by using the **Layout**, **Envelope** command. WordPerfect reviews the file in the current document screen and automatically identifies the address information.

Once WordPerfect has identified the address information, the Envelope dialog box displays (see Figure 12.1). The address information displays in the Mailing Addresses box. If WordPerfect has incorrectly identified the address information, the correct address can be typed. If no address information is found in the current file, the Mailing Addresses box of the Envelope dialog box will be empty.

A previously typed return address may display in the Return Addresses box. Return or mailing addresses can be typed and added to a list of addresses. The list of re-

FIGURE 13.3

Sample letterhead with graphic line

Precision Information Systems

30 East Seventh Street
St. Paul, Minnesota 55101

Voice: (612) 555-1622
Fax: (612) 555-3879

5. Move the mouse pointer to the button to the right of the words "Line Style" and click once to display the Line Style palette {Alt and L, Spacebar}.
6. Move the mouse pointer to the desired line style and click once {press the arrow keys until the desired line style is selected; Enter}.

   For example, move the mouse pointer to the **Thick/Thin 2** line style (fourth line style on the second row) and click once.

   Note: *A sample of the Thick/Thin 2 line displays beside the Line Style box.*
7. Select **OK** {Enter}.

   Note: *Your letterhead should look similar to Figure 13.3.*

Finish-Up Instructions

- Use *new* the filename **13drill1.lth** and save the file.
- Print one copy and close the document.

Create a Flier with a Graphic Image

Creating a flier in WordPerfect is similar to creating a flier on a typewriter. The flier, however, can include graphic lines, graphic images, and text printed in different font styles and point sizes (see Figure 13.4 on page 306).

Once the flier text is typed, the text is formatted with the desired fonts, point sizes, justification, and appearance. When a graphic image is retrieved, the image is placed in a graphic Figure box. Graphics can be sized or repositioned on the page, the border lines around the graphic Figure box can be removed or changed, and a border can be placed around the entire page.

Start-Up Instructions

- Open the file named **13drill2.wpd** located on the data disk.

Steps to Retrieve a Graphic Image

1. With the insertion point located at the beginning of the document, select the **Figure** button on the Button Bar {Alt, g, f}.

   Note: *The Insert Image dialog box displays. A list of graphic files with the filename extension .wpg displays. The graphic files are stored in the default WordPerfect graphics directory (e.g., c:\wpwin60\graphics).*

2. Scroll through the list of files and click on the desired filename {Alt and n, Tab, press the down arrow key to highlight the desired filename}.

   For example, click once on **hotair.wpg**.

3. To view the graphic image before retrieving the image into the document, select the View button {Alt and w}.

   Note: The hot air balloon graphic image displays in the Viewer window.

4. Select OK to retrieve the selected graphic image {Enter}.

   Note: The hot air balloon graphic image is placed in a graphic Figure box and displays in the right corner of the document window. A border displays around the graphic Figure box that contains the graphic image. Small black handles (boxes) at the edges and corners of the graphic Figure box indicate that the graphic Figure box is selected. Also, the Graphics Box Feature Bar displays below the Power Bar. If the mouse pointer is located within the graphic box, it displays as a four-headed arrow.

5. Move the mouse pointer away from the graphic box and click once to deselect the box.

Finish-Up Instructions

- Use the *new* filename **13drill2.fli** and save the file.

Start-Up Instructions

- The file named **13drill2.fli** should be displayed on the screen.
- The Graphics Box Feature Bar should be displayed. If necessary, select **Graphics**, **Edit Box** to display the Graphics Box Feature Bar.

Steps to Position a Graphic Box

1. Move the mouse pointer anywhere in the graphic box and click once to select the box {Alt, g, e}.

   For example, move the mouse pointer anywhere in the graphic Figure box containing the **hotair.wpg** graphic image and click once.

   Note: Small black handles display at the edges and corners of the box indicating that the graphic box is selected.

2. Select the **Position** button the Graphics Box Feature Bar {Alt and Shift and p}.

   Note: The Box Position dialog box displays.

3. In the Vertical area of the Position Box dialog box, move the mouse pointer to the box beside the word "Place" and double-click {Alt and a}.

4. Type the desired vertical position for the graphic box.

   For example, type **2.5** to place the graphic figure box 2.5" below the first line of text in the flier.

   Note: The graphic figure box moves down the page 2.5 inches below the first line of text.

5. Select OK {Enter}.

FIGURE 13.4

Flier with a graphic image

FIRST ANNUAL
HOT AIR BALLOON RACE
AND COMPETITION

WHERE: Camelback Inn

WHEN: Saturday and Sunday
April 13 and 14

WHAT: Action in the Air

COST: $100 Entry Fee

PRIZES: $1,000 First Place
$500 Second Place
$250 Third Place

ACTIVITIES

20K Air Race

Balloon Design Contest

Balloon Rides

Ballooning Lessons

PROCEEDS WILL BENEFIT THE SCOTTSDALE YOUTH PROGRAM

Remove the Border from a Graphic Box

6. With the graphic box selected, choose the **Border/Fill** button on the Graphics Box Feature Bar {Alt and Shift and b}.

   Note: *The Box Border/Fill Styles dialog box displays.*

7. Move the mouse pointer to the button to the right of the words "Border Style" and click once to display the Border Style palette {Alt and b, Spacebar}.

8. Click once on the **<NO BORDER>** border style to remove the graphic box border {press the arrow keys until <NO BORDER> is selected; Enter}.

   Note: *The words "Spacing Only" display in the box to the right of the Border Style button.*

9. Select **OK** {Enter}.

   Note: *If desired, scroll down to view the graphic image. The graphic image displays at the new position, and the graphic Figure box border has been removed. If the mouse has not been clicked in the document screen, the small black handles (boxes) remain around the graphic Figure box. Your document should look similar to Figure 13.4.*

Finish-Up Instructions

- Move the mouse pointer away from the graphic Figure box and click once to deselect the graphic Figure box.
- Use the same filename, **13drill2.fli**, and save the file.

Start-Up Instructions

- The file named **13drill2.fli** should be displayed in the document window.

Create a Page Border

1. With the insertion point located at any position on the page, select **Layout, Page, Border/Fill** {Alt, L, p, b}.
2. Move the mouse pointer to the button to the right of the words "Border Style" and click once to display the Border Style palette {Alt and b, Spacebar}.
3. Move the mouse pointer to the desired border style and click {press the arrow keys until the desired border style is selected; Enter}.

   For example, click once on the second double-line border style on the third row (i.e., Thick Double).

4. Select **OK** {Enter}.

   *Note: To view the page border, select the **Page Zoom Full** button. Select the **Page Zoom Full** button again to return to the normal view.*

Finish-Up Instructions

- Use the *new* filename **13drill2.fin** and save the file.
- Print one copy and close the document.

Text with Graphic Overlay

A graphic image can be placed over text to create a graphic overlay. WordPerfect provides several graphic images suitable for creating documents with graphic overlays. (See Figure 13.7 and Appendix C.) By default, when a graphic box containing a graphic image is placed in a document, text is moved to make room for the graphic box. However, WordPerfect can be instructed to place the graphic box over the text.

Start-Up Instructions

- Open the file named **13drill3.txt** located on the data disk.

Steps to

Create Text with a Graphic Overlay

1. Place the insertion point at the location where the graphic image should be inserted.

   For example, the insertion point should be located at the beginning of the document.

2. Select the **Figure** button on the Button Bar {Alt, g, f}.

3. Scroll through the list of graphic files and double-click on the desired graphic filename {press the Tab key once, press the down arrow key to highlight the desired filename, press Enter}.

   For example, double-click on the file named **bord11L.wpg**.

   Note: The graphic image displays in the document window. A border displays around the graphic box that contains the graphic image. Small black handles (boxes) at the edges and corners of the graphic box indicate that the graphic box is selected. Also, the Graphics Box Feature Bar displays below the Power Bar.

Change the Size of the Graphic Box

4. Select the **Size** button on the Graphics Box Feature Bar {Alt and Shift and s}.

   Note: The Box Size dialog box displays.

5. In the Width box, select the desired option.

   For example, select **Full** {f}.

6. In the Height box, select the desired option.

   For example, select the **Set** option and type **4** in the Set option box {e, type 4}.

7. Select **OK** {Enter}.

   Note: The graphic box displays the full width of the document window and the text moves to the bottom of the document window.

Flow the Text Through the Graphic Box

8. Select the **Wrap** button on the Graphics Box Feature Bar {Alt and Shift and w}.

   Note: The Wrap Text dialog box displays.

9. Select the **No Wrap (through)** option {o}.

10. Select **OK** {Enter}.

    *Note: The text displays within the graphic box, because the wrapping type option of flow text **through** was chosen.*

Remove the Border Around the Graphic Box

11. Select the **Border/Fill** button on the Graphics Box Feature Bar to display the Box Border Fill Styles dialog box {Alt and Shift and b}.

12. Move the mouse pointer to the button to the right of the words "Border Style" and click once to display the Border Style palette {Alt and b, Spacebar}.

13. Select the **NO BORDER** border style to remove the graphic box border {press the arrow keys until NO BORDER is selected; Enter}.

    Note: The words "Spacing Only" display in the box to the right of the Border Style button.

14. Select **OK** {Enter}.

    Note: The border line is removed. The small black handles continue to display at the edges and corners of the graphic box to indicate that the graphic box is selected.

Finish-Up Instructions

- Move the mouse pointer away from the graphic box and text and click once to deselect the box.
- Use the *new* filename **13drill3.ovr** and save the file.
- Print one copy. Keep the **13drill3.ovr** file in the document window to use with the following Steps to Edit a Graphic Image Using the WP Draw Program.

Use WP Draw

Graphic images can be created and/or edited using the drawing tools available in the WP Draw program that is provided with WordPerfect 6.0 for Windows. The color, size, location, and rotation of an existing graphic image can be changed, and new graphic images can be drawn or created by combining existing graphic images. Text can be typed and formatted in the WP Draw program and placed into a document as a graphic image.

When a graphic image is placed into a document, a link is established between the graphic image and the WP Draw program. This link is established through the Windows Object Linking and Embedding (OLE) feature. The OLE feature permits the changes made to the graphic image in the WP Draw program to be reflected in the graphic image located in the WordPerfect document. The WP Draw program can be accessed by double-clicking on a graphic image in a document, by selecting the **WP Draw** button on the Button Bar, or by choosing **Graphics**, **Draw**. When the WP Draw program is loaded, the graphic image displays in the WP Draw window.

A graphic image may contain many separate pieces. Each piece of a graphic image is referred to as a graphic item. It is often a good idea to group all the graphic items that make up a single graphic image so that the items can all be edited at one time (e.g., moved, sized, copied, or rotated).

Start-Up Instructions

- The file named **13drill3.ovr** should be displayed in the document window.
- The Graphic Box Feature Bar should be displayed. If necessary, select **Graphics**, **Edit Box** to display the Graphics Box Feature Bar.

Steps to Edit a Graphic Image Using the WP Draw Program

Note: A mouse is required to complete the following steps.

1. Select the graphic box containing the graphic image to be edited.

   For example, if necessary, select the **Prev** button on the Graphics Box Feature Bar to select the graphic box containing the **bord11L.wpg** graphic image.

2. Move the mouse pointer anywhere in the desired graphic image and double-click.

   Note: After a few moments, the WP Draw program window displays with only the graphic image contained in the selected graphic box (see Figure 13.5).

FIGURE 13.5

WP Draw window

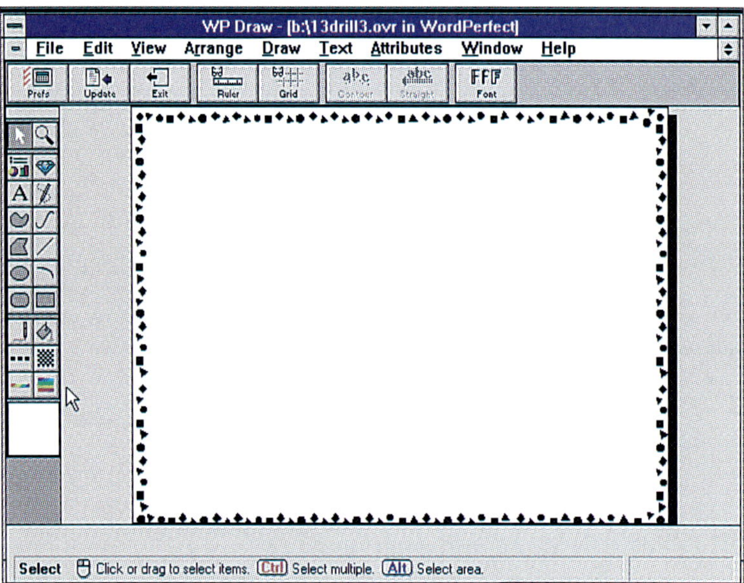

Group Graphic Items

3. Select the graphic items to be affected.

   For example, select **Edit, Select, All** to select all the graphic items that make up the border graphic image.

   Note: A small black handle displays at the left center edge of the graphic image. You will need to look carefully to see the small black handle because the handle is small and looks very similar to the border items. All the graphic items that make up the border graphic image are now considered one item.

4. Select **Arrange, Group**.

Change the Color of the Graphic Image

5. Select the **Set Fill Color** button located at the left of the WP Draw window. ("Set Fill Color" displays in the Title bar when the mouse pointer is located on the Set Fill Color button.)

   Note: A palette of colors displays.

6. Move the mouse pointer to the desired color and click once.

   For example, move the mouse pointer the to royal blue color square in the center of the first color palette line (row) or make a choice of your own. Click to select the color.

   Note: The fill color for the selected graphic items changes to the selected color.

Insert a Second Graphic Image into an Existing Graphic Image

7. Select **File, Insert File**.

   Note: The Insert File dialog box displays containing a list of available WordPerfect graphic files (.wpg).

8. Scroll through the list of filenames and double-click on the desired filename.

   For example, double-click on the file named **trumpt.wpg**.

   Note: The trumpet graphic image displays within the existing graphic image.

9. Select the desired graphic items.

For example, to select all the graphic items that make up the trumpet graphic image, move the mouse pointer approximately 1" above the left edge of the trumpet mouthpiece. Press and hold the mouse button and drag down and to the right to encompass the entire trumpet. Release the mouse button.

Note: Black handles display around the trumpet graphic image. Also, small handles display on each graphic item making up the trumpet graphic image.

10. Select **Arrange, Group**.

Note: All the graphic items that make up the trumpet graphic image are now considered a single item.

Size a Graphic Item

11. Move the mouse pointer to the black handle at a corner of the graphic image until a double-headed arrow displays.

For example, move the mouse pointer to the black handle at the lower left corner of the trumpet graphic image until the double-headed arrow displays.

12. Press and hold the mouse button and drag to size the graphic item.

For example, drag up and to the right to reduce the size of the graphic image to approximately 1.5" x .5".

13. Release the mouse button.

Move a Graphic Item

14. Move the mouse pointer anywhere inside the selected graphic item, press and hold the mouse button, and drag the item to the desired location.

For example, move the mouse pointer inside the trumpet graphic, press and hold the mouse button, and drag the trumpet down to approximately ½" from the bottom right corner of the border graphic image (see Figure 13.6).

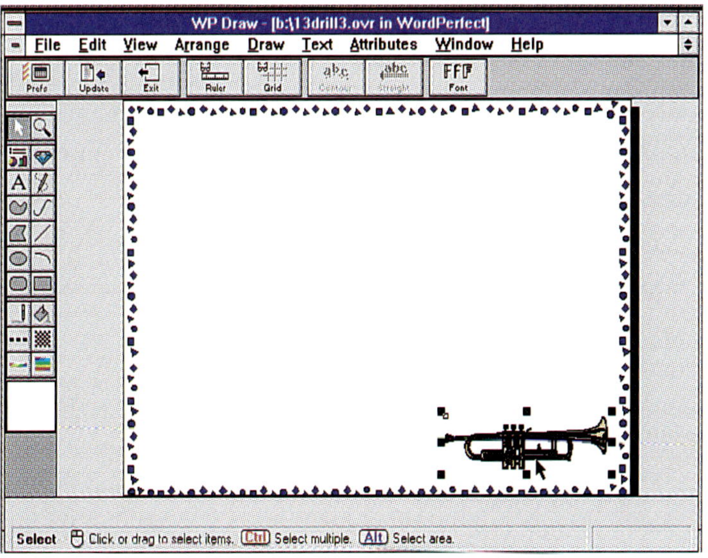

FIGURE 13.6

Move a graphic item in the WP Draw program

FIGURE 13.7

Text with graphic overlay

Rotate a Graphic Item

15. Select Edit, Rotate.

Note: Small rotation handles are added to the black handles at the edges and corners of the selected graphic item.

16. Move the mouse pointer to a rotation handle until a double-headed arrow displays.

For example, move the mouse pointer to the rotation handle at the bottom left corner of the trumpet graphic.

17. Press and hold the mouse button while dragging to rotate the graphic item. Release the mouse button.

For example, drag down approximately 1/4" to rotate the trumpet graphic approximately 30 degrees.

Exit WP Draw and Place the Modified Graphic into the Document Window

18. Select File, Exit and Return to . . .

19. Select Yes to the message "Save changes to. . ."

Finish-Up Instructions

- Move the mouse pointer away from the graphic box and text and click once to deselect the graphic box. Your document should look similar to Figure 13.7.
- Use the *new* filename **13drill3.inv** and save the file.

Copy a Graphic Image

A graphic image can be selected and copied into the same document or, if desired, into a different document. If all the text and graphic images in a document are to be copied, the **Edit, Select, Page** command can be used to ensure that everything in the document (e.g., text, margins codes, or graphic box codes) is selected. Once selected, the text and graphic images can be copied by using either of the methods of copying text discussed in Chapter 4, pages 77-79.

Start-Up Instructions

- The file named **13drill3.inv** should be displayed in the document window.

Copy a Graphic Image and Text

1. Select the graphic image and/or text to be copied.

   For example, select **Edit, Select, Page** to select all text and the graphic image.

   Note: *The entire text and graphic image are highlighted.*

2. Select the Copy button {Alt, e, c *or* Ctrl and c}.
3. Move the mouse pointer below the selected graphic image and/or text and click once to deselect.
4. Move the insertion point to the desired location.

   For example, move the insertion point to the bottom of the document and press the **Enter** key six times.

5. Select the Paste {Alt, e, p *or* Ctrl and v}.

   Note: *A copy of the graphic image and text is inserted into the document.*

Finish-Up Instructions

- Select the **Page Zoom Full** button to view both copies of the text and graphic image. Select the **Page Zoom Full** button again to return to the normal view.
- Use the *new* filename **13drill3.cop** and save the file.
- Print one copy and close the document.

Create a Newsletter

A typical newsletter includes text columns, graphics, and borders. Different fonts and point sizes can be used for the newsletter text (see Figure 13.9). A graphic Text box can be used to create the heading portion (nameplate) of the newsletter. The default settings for a graphic Text box include horizontal graphic lines at the top and bottom of the box. If desired, the graphic lines can be changed and a fill (shading) can be created for the Text box.

The **Columns Define** button on the Power Bar can be used to specify the desired number of columns for the newsletter body text. (See Chapter 8, Steps to Create Newspaper Columns on page 175.) Graphic images can be placed in the document to add visual appeal.

Graphic boxes (e.g., Figure boxes, Text boxes, and User boxes) can be *attached* to a paragraph, a page, a fixed position on a page, or a character. A graphic box that is attached to a paragraph remains with the paragraph if the paragraph is relocated. A graphic box that is attached to a page remains at a fixed position on the page relative

2. Select the company name and change the font to **EngraversGothic BT, 14-point**. Select the address, city, state, zip, voice, and fax numbers and change the font to **EngraversGothic BT, 10-point**.
3. Place a single horizontal graphic line above the company name (move the insertion point to the blank line above the company name, select **Graphics, Horizontal Line**).
4. Place a Thick/Thin 2 horizontal graphic line below the company name (move the insertion point to the blank line below the company name, select **Graphics**, **Custom Line**, select the **Line Style** button, click on the desired line style, select **OK**).
5. Use the filename **13act2.lth** and save the file.
6. Print one copy and close the document.

Activity 13.3—Create a Flier with Text and a Graphic Overlay

1. Change the left, right, top, and bottom margins to .25".
2. Type and format the text as shown in the flier shown below.

3. Place the insertion point at the top of the document.

4. Retrieve the graphic image file named **bord17.wpg** (select the **Figure** button on the Button Bar, double-click on **bord17.wpg**).

5. With the graphic box containing the border graphic image selected, make the following changes:

   a. Select the **Size** button on the Graphics Box Feature Bar. In the Width box, select the **Full** option and choose **OK**.

   b. Select the **Wrap** button on the Graphics Box Feature Bar and choose the **No Wrap (through)** option. Select **OK**.

   c. Select the **Border/Fill** button on the Graphics Box Feature Bar. Click on the Border Style button and select **No Border**. Choose **OK**.

   d. Move the mouse pointer away from the graphic box and click once to deselect the box.

   e. Select the **Close** button on the Graphics Box Feature Bar to remove the feature bar.

6. If desired, select the **Page Zoom Full** button to view the entire flier. Select the **Page Zoom Full** button again to return to the normal view.

7. Use the filename **13act3.des** and save the file.

8. Print one copy and close the document.

Activity 13.4—Create a Newsletter with a Graphic Image

1. Open the file named **13act4.txt** located on the data disk. Use the following information and the newsletter style shown in Figure 13.9 to create an employee newsletter for Campanella Systems.

   a. Place the insertion point at the top of the document and create the nameplate using a Text box. (If necessary, see pages 314-315.)

   b. Place the insertion point to the left of the E in "Eastern" and create two newspaper style columns.

   c. Place a column border between the two columns (select **Layout, Columns, Border/Fill,** select the **Border Style** button, select the **Columns Between** border style, **OK**).

   d. Place the insertion point to the left of the first character in the first paragraph.

   e. Retrieve the graphic file named **group.wpg** (select the **Figure** button on the Button Bar, double-click on **group.wpg**).

   f. With the graphic box containing the *group.wpg* graphic image selected, click on the **Position** button on the Graphics Box Feature Bar. Move the mouse pointer to the From box in the Horizontal area, press and hold the mouse button, and drag to select **Left Margin**. Release the mouse button. Double-click in the Place box below the word "Vertical" and type .75. Select **OK**.

For example, select **COMPUTER TERMINOLOGY** and the following two blank lines.

2. Select the **Copy** button {Alt, e, c *or* Ctrl and c}.
3. Select the next text to be accumulated in the Clipboard.

   For example, select **Access** and the following blank line.

4. Select **Edit, Append** {Alt, e, d}.
5. Repeat steps 3 and 4 and accumulate any other desired text in the Clipboard.

   For example, append the terms **Access Time**, **Back-up Drive**, **Back-up File**, **Buffer**, **Command**, **Execute**, **Kilobyte**, and **Megabyte** to the Clipboard.

6. When all desired text has been selected and appended to the Clipboard, open an existing file or select the **New Document** button to create a new file.

   For example, select the **New Document** button.

7. Select the **Paste** button to insert the text appended to the Clipboard {Alt, e, p *or* Ctrl and v}.

Finish-Up Instructions

- If necessary, center the title **COMPUTER TERMINOLOGY.**
- Change the font for all the text to **Swiss721 BlkEx BT, 24-point.**
- Use the filename **14drill3.app** and save the document.
- Print one copy.
- Close both documents (**14drill3.app** and **14drill3.ter**).

Create Superscripts and Subscripts

Superscripts are characters that are printed a fraction above the text line, and subscripts are characters that are printed a fraction below the text line (see Figure 14.3). Superscripts and subscripts are used, for example, when printing chemical formulas, algebraic equations, or degrees of temperature.

When working with superscripts and subscripts, it is sometimes desirable to enlarge the display of the text on the screen in order to see better the superscripted or subscripted text. With the Zoom feature, text and graphics can be displayed as large as 400% or as small as 25%. WordPerfect also provides Margin Width, Page Width, and Full Page zoom options. The Margin Width option displays a complete line of text in the document window regardless of the font size selected. The Page Width option displays the page including the margins within the document window. The Full Page option displays the entire page. The Zoom feature can be accessed by selecting the **Zoom** button on the Power Bar or by selecting **View, Zoom.**

Start-Up Instructions

- An empty document window should be displayed. (If necessary, select the **New Document** button.)

$(x + 4)^2$	NH_4
$(c - d)^2$	Na_2PO_4

FIGURE 14.3

Superscripts and subscripts

Steps to Create a Superscript

1. Type the desired text.

   For example, type **(x + 4)2**. (Do not type the period.)

2. Select the character to be a superscript.

   For example, highlight the **2**.

3. Select **Layout**, **Font** {Alt, L, f *or* press F9}.
4. Move the mouse pointer to the **Position** box, press and hold the mouse button, and drag to highlight **Superscript**. Release the mouse button {Alt and p, press the up arrow key to display Superscript}.
5. Select **OK** {Enter}.

   Note: The highlighted character displays as a superscript on the screen.

6. Before continuing to type, press the right arrow key once.

   For example, press the right arrow key once and then press the **Tab** key twice.

Steps to Create a Subscript

1. Type the desired text.

   For example, type **NH4**.

2. Select the character to be a subscript.

   For example, highlight the **4**.

3. Select **Layout**, **Font** {Alt, L, f, *or* press F9}.
4. Move the mouse pointer to the **Position** box, press and hold the mouse button, and drag to highlight **Subscript**. Release the mouse button {Alt and p, press the down arrow key to display Subscript}.
5. Select **OK** {Enter}.

   Note: The highlighted character displays as a subscript on the screen.

6. Before continuing to type, press the right arrow key once.

   For example, press the right arrow key once and then press the **Enter** key twice.

Steps to Use the Zoom Feature

1. Move the mouse pointer to the **Zoom** button 100% on the Power Bar. Press and hold the mouse button and drag to highlight the desired Zoom option. Release

the mouse button {Alt, v, z; press the up or down arrow keys to select the desired Zoom option, Enter}.

For example, select **200%**.

Note: *The Zoom button displays 200%, and the text in the document window is enlarged to 200%.*

2. If desired, return to the normal Zoom view by moving the mouse pointer to the **Zoom** button, pressing and holding the mouse button and dragging to highlight **100%**; release the mouse button {Alt, v, z; press the up arrow key to select 100%, Enter}.

Finish-Up Instructions

- Using the Steps to Create a Superscript and Steps to Create a Subscript, type the equation and formula in the second line of Figure 14.3. If desired, select **200% Zoom** view.
- Use the filename **14drill4.sup** and save the file.
- Print one copy and close the document.

Use the Equation Editor

WordPerfect provides an Equation Editor window that can be used to create (but not solve) scientific and mathematical equations/formulas. When an equation/formula is created, the equation/formula is placed in either an Equation or Inline Equation graphic box. Both Equation and Inline Equation graphic boxes are defaulted to display and print without borders or shading. An equation box can be moved, sized, or shaded in the same way as discussed using a Figure box or Text box in Chapter 13 and it can be attached to a paragraph, page, or character. An Inline Equation box is inserted within a line of text and moves with that line of text when a document is edited.

When the Equation Editor is accessed, a separate window displays, which is divided into three main sections: the editing window, the palette, and the display window (see Figure 14.4). The *editing window* is the area in which an equation/formula is displayed as it is being created or edited. Text and/or numbers are typed in the editing window, and commands, functions, or symbols are either selected from the palette or are typed in order to build an equation/formula. The tilde (~) is used to insert space between characters instead of the Spacebar.

The *palette* contains commands, functions, or symbols that are used to create a formula. For example, the SQRT command is selected to insert a square root ($\sqrt{\ }$) symbol. The left and right braces ({ }) are used to create a group that will act as a single unit. For example, to create $(\frac{2y}{4x})^2$, the commands and text { ({2y} OVER {4x}) } SUP 2 would be placed in the editing window. Also, commands, functions, and symbols can be typed directly into the editing window. For example, to superscript text in the Equation Editor window, select the **SUP or** ^ command or type **SUP** in the editing window.

The *display window* is the area in which WordPerfect shows the equation/formula as it will appear when printed. The **Redisplay** button is selected to view the format-

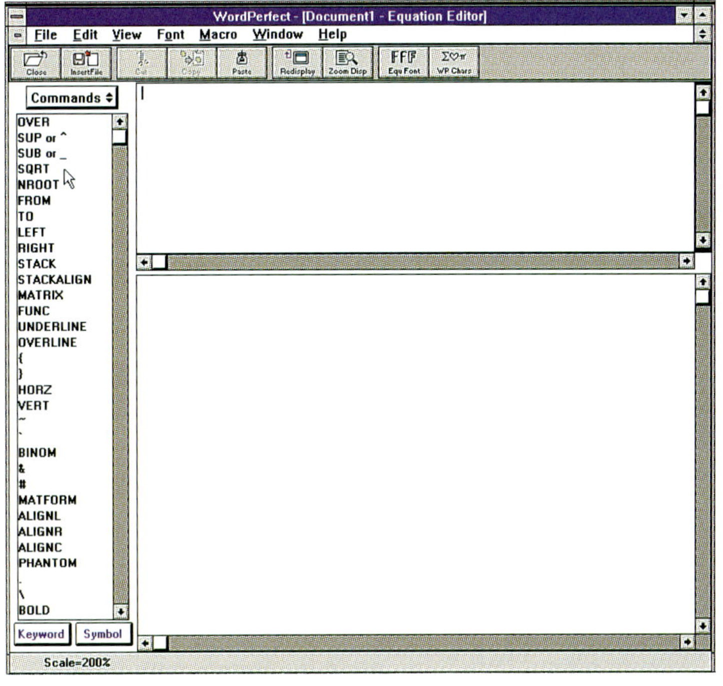

FIGURE 14.4

Equation Editor window

ted equation/formula. An error message, *Incorrect syntax*, displays if an error is made when creating an equation/formula.

After the equation/formula is created, the **Close** button is selected in the Equation Editor window. WordPerfect places the equation/formula in an Equation box or Inline Equation box in the regular document window at the location of the insertion point. (*Note:* A graphic box is inserted even if the editing window is empty when the **Close** button is selected.) To exit the Equation Editor window without inserting the equation and equation graphic box into the document screen, select **File**, **Cancel.** To edit the equation or formula, double-click on the equation/formula and make the desired changes in the Equation Editor window.

Chapter 14 Create Document with Special Features

Start-Up Instructions

- An empty document window should be displayed. If necessary, select the **New Document** button.
- The following Steps to Create an Equation/Formula will be used to create the formula shown in Figure 14.5.

Steps to Create an Equation/Formula Using the Equation Editor

Note: The insertion point should be located in the document at the place where the equation/formula will be inserted.

1. Select Graphics, Equation {Alt, g, q}.

   Note: The Equation Editor window displays (see Figure 14.4).

2. Select or type the desired command.

   For example, double-click on **SQRT** (square root) {type **SQRT** and press the **Spacebar** once}.

   Note: The command SQRT displays in the editing window.

3. Select or type the next command or text.

   For example, double-click on the left brace ({) {type a left brace ({) and press the Spacebar once}. Repeat to place a second left brace in the editing window.

4. Select or type the next command or text.

   For example, type an **x**. Type a left parenthesis [(] followed by another **x**.

5. Select or type the next command or text.

   For example, double-click on the **SUP or ^** command {press the Spacebar, type SUP, and press the Spacebar again}.

6. Select or type the next command or text.

   For example:

   a. Type a **2**. (Do not type the period.)
   b. Select the ~ (Tilde) command or type a tilde (~) to insert a space.
   c. Type a hyphen (-) to represent a minus symbol.
   d. Select the ~ (Tilde) command or type a tilde (~) to insert a space.
   e. Type a **y**.

7. Select or type the next command or text.

   For example, double-click on the **SUP or ^** command {press the Spacebar once, type SUP, and press the Spacebar again}.

   Type a **2** followed by a right parenthesis [)].

8. Select or type the next command or text.

   For example, double-click on the right brace (}) {type a right brace (})}.

9. Select or type the next command or text.

   For example, double-click on the **OVER** command {press the Spacebar once, type OVER, and press the Spacebar again}.

10. Select or type the next command or text.

    For example, double-click on the left brace ({) {type a left brace ({) and press the Spacebar once}.

    Type **4x**.

11. Select or type the next command or text.

    For example, scroll down the list of commands and double-click on the right brace (}) {press the Spacebar once and type a right brace (})}. Repeat to insert a second right brace.

    Note: *The equation displays on one line and should look similar to the equation shown in the editing window in Figure 14.5.*

12. Select the **Redisplay** button {Alt, v, r *or* Ctrl and F3}.

    Note: *The formatted equation displays in the display window. However, if the equation command or text was entered incorrectly, an equation error message displays in the*

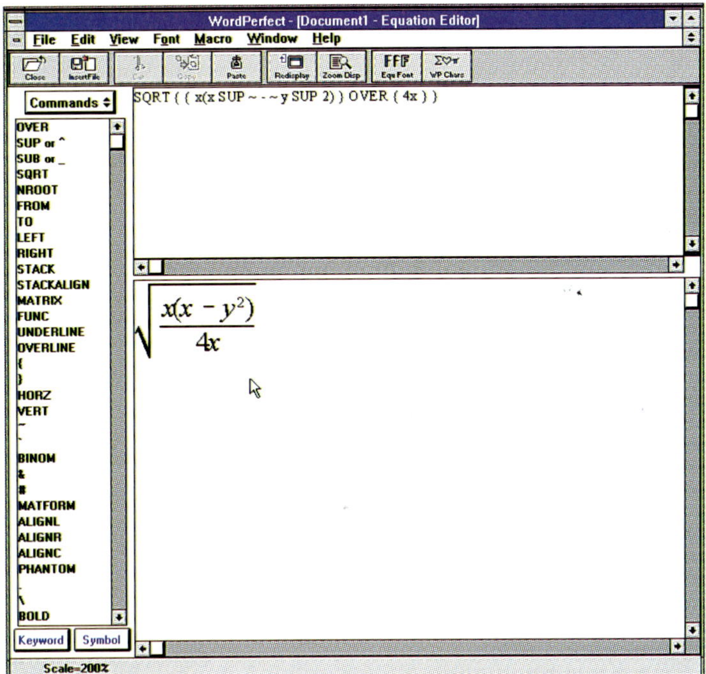

FIGURE 14.5

Equation Editor with completed equation

Status bar. If the commands were typed (and not selected from the palette), a blank space should both precede and follow the commands.

13. Select the Close button to exit the Equation Editor window and place the equation in the regular document window {Alt, f, c *or* Ctrl and F4}.

    Note: The equation displays in the middle of the document window.

Finish-Up Instructions

- Use the filename **14drill5.equ** and save the file.
- Print one copy and close the document.

  Note: The following Steps to Edit an Equation/Formula are for your information.

Steps to Edit an Equation/Formula

1. Move the mouse pointer to the equation in the document window and double-click {Alt, g, e; Alt and Shift and o, e}.

   Note: The Equation Editor window and equation/formula display.

2. Make the desired changes.
3. Select the Redisplay button {Alt, v, r *or* Ctrl and F3}.
4. Select the Close button to exit the Equation Editor window {Alt, f, c *or* Ctrl and F4}.

   Note: The corrected equation/formula displays in the document window.

Start-Up Instructions

- On a clear screen, type the following text that will precede the Inline Equation box:

The formula for finding the area of a triangle when the lengths of the three sides are known is

- Press the **Spacebar** once after the last character.

Steps to Create an Inline Equation Graphic Box

1. Select Graphics, Custom Box {Alt, g, c}.

   Note: The Custom Box dialog box displays.

2. In the Style Name box, double-click on Inline Equation {press the down arrow key to highlight Inline Equation Box, press Enter}.

   Note: An empty Inline Equation graphic box is inserted in the document window and the Graphics Box Feature Bar displays below the Power Bar. Small black handles display indicating that the Inline Equation box is selected; no borders display around the Inline Equation box.

3. Select the Content button on the Graphics Box Feature Bar {Alt and Shift and o}.

   Note: The Box Content dialog box displays.

4. Select the Edit button {e}.

5. Select or type the desired commands and text needed to create the equation.

   For example, create the equation $A=\sqrt{s(s-a)(s-b)(s-c)}$ by typing and selecting the following text and commands: **A= SQRT** {**s(s-a)(s-b)(s-c)**}. (A space should follow the SQRT command and the right brace.)

6. Select Redisplay {Alt, v, r *or* Ctrl and F3}.

7. Select Close to display the equation in the document window {Alt, f, c *or* Ctrl and F4}.

8. Continue typing any text that follows the Inline Equation box.

   For example, type a period (.) to complete the sentence.

Finish-Up Instructions

- Use the filename **14drill6.inl** and save the file.
- Print one copy and close the document.

The Next Step

Chapter Review and Activities

Self-Check Quiz

T F 1. To set the line height, select **Layout**, **Line**, **Height**, choose **Fixed,** and, if desired, change the line height and select **OK**.

T F 2. Information placed in the Clipboard can be viewed and/or deleted in the Clipboard Viewer window.

T F 3. Once an equation has been created in the Equation Editor window, select the **Close** button to place the formula/equation in the regular document window.

T F 4. Letterspacing is used to increase or decrease the amount of space between letters in selected text.

T F 5. The **Zoom** button can be used to enlarge the display of text up to 1000%.

6. Letterspacing is also referred to as __________.
   a. tracking
   b. kerning
   c. word spacing
   d. none of these

7. A superscript is a character that prints a fraction ____ the text line.
   a. above
   b. below
   c. on
   d. both b and c

8. List two advantages for changing the initial font in a document.

9. Explain the difference between word spacing and letterspacing.

10. Write an example in which you personally might use the Append feature.

Enriching Language Arts Skills

Spelling/Vocabulary Words

derogatory tending to belittle; negative.

inclusion the act of containing, encompassing, consisting of.

propaganda information spread to help or harm a group, institution, or nation.

rendered to have performed, to have done, supplied.

surreptitious obtained or performed in a secretive or devious manner.

Independent Adjectives

Two adjectives that modify the same noun are separated by a comma.

Example:

The small, blue chair will be used for guests when they visit the president.

Activities

Activity 14.1—Set Initial Font and Use Leading Adjustment

1. Set the initial font for the current document to **Arrus BT, 12-point**, or choose a font of your own (select **Layout**, **Document**, **Initial Font**, choose desired font, **OK**).
2. Use the following information and type the document shown.
   a. Press the **F7** key three times after typing the lead words **Medical Care**, **Rehabilitation**, and **Disability Income**.
   b. Bold and center the title and bold the lead words.
   c. Press **Enter** twice after the title and after each paragraph as shown.

NOTICE TO EMPLOYEES

If a work injury occurs, you are automatically entitled to workers' compensation. Texas law provides certain benefits to employees who are injured or become ill because of a job-related activity.

Medical Care All medical treatment required to cure the injury or illness will be performed without cost to the employee. The employee chooses the physician and facility. The facility must be located within a reasonable geographical area. The employee should never see a bill because all costs are paid directly by the employer or its agents.

Rehabilitation If the injury or illness prevents return to the employee's usual job, the employee may receive vocational rehabilitation. All costs are paid by the employer.

Disability Income Employees disabled by job injury or job illness receive disability income while unable to work. The payments are two-thirds of the employee's average weekly pay, up to a maximum set by state law.

---

3. Use the filename **14act1.emp** and save the file.
4. Change the font size to **24-point** for the title.
5. Change the word spacing for the title to 200% and letterspacing for the title to 150% of optimal (block the title, select **Layout**, **Typesetting**,

Word/ Letterspacing, choose **Percent of Optimal** in the Word Spacing box, double-click in the Percent of Optimal box and type **200**, choose **Percent of Optimal** in the Letterspacing box, double-click in the Percent of Optimal box and type **150**, **OK**).

6. Select each lead word and change the font size to **18-point**.
7. Check the alignment of paragraphs and make adjustments as needed.

   Hint: *Delete or insert indent code(s) between the lead words and indented paragraphs, as needed.*
8. Locate the insertion point at the beginning of the first paragraph and set the line height to **Fixed** (select **Layout**, **Line**, **Height**, **Fixed**, select **OK**).
9. Select **Layout**, **Typesetting**, **Word/Letterspacing**, **Adjust Leading**, double-click in the Between Lines box and type **.15**, select **OK**.
10. Use the filename **14act1.fin** and save the file.
11. Print one copy and close the document.

Activity 14.2—Use Append to Create an Overhead Transparency

1. Open the file named **14act2.pd** located on the data disk.
2. Select the title **PAID LEAVES** and the following two blank lines.
3. Select the **Copy** button.
4. Select the first heading **VACATION** and the following blank line.
5. Select **Edit**, **Append**.
6. Select the next heading and the following blank line.
7. Select **Edit**, **Append**.
8. Repeat steps 6 and 7 to append the remaining headings to the Clipboard.
9. When all of the remaining headings have been appended to the Clipboard, select the **New Document** button.
10. Select the **Paste** button to insert the appended text into the new document.
11. Center the title and format the text for use as an overhead transparency (use a large font size).
12. Use the filename **14act2.ovr** and save the file.
13. Print one copy and close both documents.

Activity 14.3—Use the Equation Editor

1. Use the Equation Editor (select **Graphics**, **Equation**) to create the following equations. Select the **Redisplay** button to view the typed equation. Make any corrections necessary. Select the **Close** button after completing each equation/formula to transfer the equation/formula to the document window. (Each equation will display on a separate line.)

b. Move the mouse pointer to the button under the words **Sort Order**, press and hold the mouse button and drag to select **Ascending**, release the mouse button {Tab to select the Sort Order button, press a}.

c. Double-click in the **Cell** box and type **1** (to sort by the first column) {Tab to select the Cell box contents, type 1}.

d. Check that 1 displays in the Line and Word boxes.

Create a Second Key Definition

5. Select the **Add Key** button {Alt and a}.

   Note: Key 2 displays below Key 1.

6. Select the desired sort criteria for the new key.

   For example, check that the following sort criteria display for Key 2:

Type:	Alpha
Sort Order:	Ascending
Cell:	1
Line:	1

   Double-click in the Word box and type 2 to sort by the second word in cell 1 (i.e., the first name).

7. Select **OK** {Enter}.

   Note: The salespeople's names are listed alphabetically. Notice that the first names were used to sort the people with the same last name.

Finish-Up Instructions

- Use the *new* filename **15drill1.alp** and save the file.
- Print one copy and close the document.

Start-Up Instructions

- Open the file named **15drill2.txt** located on the data disk.

Steps to Sort Paragraphs

1. Select all the paragraphs to be sorted.

   For example, select all paragraphs in the document.

2. Select **Tools, Sort** {Alt, t, r *or* Alt and F9}.

3. Check that **Paragraph** displays in the Sort By box.

4. In the Key Definitions area, select the desired sort criteria for Key 1.

   For example, to sort by last names, edit the Key 1 definition as follows:

   a. Check that **Alpha** displays in the Type button. If necessary, move the mouse pointer to the **Type** button, press and hold the mouse button and drag to select **Alpha**, release the mouse button {Tab to select the Type button, press a}.

b. Check that **Ascending** displays in the Sort Order button. If necessary, move the mouse pointer to the **Sort Order** button, press and hold the mouse button and drag to select **Ascending**, release the mouse button {Tab to select the Sort Order button, press a}.

c. Check that 1 displays in the Line, Field, and Word boxes.

Note: *If a second key is displayed, move the mouse pointer to the second key definition and click once on any item in the definition, Then select the **Delete Key** button {Alt and 2, Alt and d}.*

5. Select **OK** {Enter}.

Note: *The text is sorted by only the first line of each paragraph (section). For the purpose of sorting, a paragraph is defined as any text followed by two hard returns (two Enters).*

Finish-Up Instructions

- Check the spacing between each section. A single blank line should display between each section. If necessary, delete extra blank lines.
- Use the *new* filename **15drill2.par** and save the file.

Start-Up Instructions

- The file named **15drill2.par** should be displayed in the document window.

Steps to Sort Lines

1. Select the lines of text to be sorted.

   For example, select the four lines under the first line "Delete."

2. Select **Tools, Sort** {Alt, t, r *or* Alt and F9}.
3. Check that **Line** displays in the Sort By box.
4. In the Key Definitions area, select the desired sort criteria.

   For example, check that the following are selected for Key 1:

Type:	Alpha
Sort Order:	Ascending
Field:	1
Line:	1
Word:	1

5. To create additional keys, select the **Add Key** button and select the desired sort criteria for each key.

   For example, create two more keys and check or select the following sort criteria:

   Key 2

Type:	Alpha
Sort Order:	Ascending
Field:	1

	Line:	1
	Word:	2
Key 3		
	Type:	Alpha
	Sort Order:	Ascending
	Field:	1
	Line:	1
	Word:	3

6. Select OK {Enter}.

Finish-Up Instructions

- Repeat steps 1–6 to sort the lines under each section in the document.
- Use the *new* filename **15drill2.sor** and save the file.
- Print one copy and close the document.

Use Macros

Macros are shortcuts that eliminate repetitious action. Macros are especially useful when your actions involve selecting several menus and submenus or making changes in dialog boxes. For example, to create a horizontal graphic line with the Thick/Thin 2 line style and .1" of space above and below the line, the following steps must be performed: select **Graphics**, **Custom Lines**, click on the **Line Style** button, select the **Thick/Thin 2** line style, double-click in the **Above** box, type **.1**, double-click in the **Below** box, type **.1**, and choose **OK**. Using a macro, the instructions to create the horizontal graphic line could be reduced to only six steps or less. Also, macros can be used to eliminate repetitious typing. For example, creating a standard closing paragraph with a typed signature line, reference initials, and enclosure notation can be reduced to six mouse clicks.

WordPerfect supplies a number of macros, which are stored in the macros subdirectory and are identified by the filename extension *.wcm.* A supplied macro is played (activated) by selecting the desired macro and responding to prompts displayed on the screen. These supplied macros can be used to view the contents of the Clipboard; print a list of available fonts, convert footnotes to endnotes, and many other tasks.

In addition to the macros supplied by WordPerfect, new macros can be created. First, the macro is given a name. Every keystroke and mouse selection is then recorded and finally the recording is stopped and automatically saved.

Because WordPerfect remembers each keystroke and mouse selection made while Record is turned on, plan the macro before selecting **Tools**, **Macro**, **Record.** Write down each step needed to create the macro. Once Record is turned on, Macro Record displays in the Status bar. When all the desired keystrokes and mouse selections have been completed, stop the recording of the macro by selecting **Tools**, **Macro**, **Record** for a second time. The macro is automatically saved.

Once a macro is recorded, the macro can be played as often as needed by selecting **Tools**, **Macro**, **Play**, typing or selecting the desired macro filename, and selecting **OK**. The macro performs each recorded step. When all the recorded steps have been completed, you can edit, save, print, or close the file using normal procedures.

Changes to a document created by a macro do not alter the macro. The macro can be used again and again.

WordPerfect remembers the last macro played and the macro name is displayed on the Macro menu when **Tools**, **Macro** is selected. Macros can be added to the Macro menu by selecting **Tools**, **Macro**, **Menu**, **Insert**, typing or selecting the macro name and choosing **Select**, **OK**. A macro listed on the Macro menu can be played instantly by clicking on the listed macro name.

Start-Up Instructions

- A new document window should be displayed. (If necessary, select the **New Document** button.)

Steps to Use a Supplied Macro

1. Select Tools, Macro, Play {Alt, t, m, p *or* Alt and F10}.

   Note: *The Play Macro dialog box displays. The insertion point is located in the Name box.*

2. Click on the List Files button (the small button with a picture of a file folder) to display a list of macros {F4}.

   Note: *The Select File dialog box displays. The macros stored in the default macro directory (e.g., c:\wpwin60\macros) are shown.*

3. Double-click on the desired macro {Tab, press the down arrow key to highlight desired macro name, Enter}.

   For example, double-click on **allfonts.wcm**.

   Note: *The selected filename and the full path displays in the Name box of the Play Macro dialog box.*

4. Select Play {Enter}. Wait a few moments. If necessary, respond to any prompts that display on the screen.

   Note: *In a few moments, the macro creates a document containing a list of available fonts with samples of each font. The macro is now finished.*

Finish-Up Instructions

- Use the filename **15drill3.fon** and save the list of available fonts.
- Print one copy and close the document.

Start-Up Instructions

- A new document window should be displayed. (If necessary, select the **New Document** button.)

Steps to Record a Macro

1. In a clear document window, select Tools, Macro, Record {Alt, t, m, r *or* Ctrl and F10}.

   Note: *The Record Macro dialog box displays.*

FIGURE 15.3

Template Information dialog box

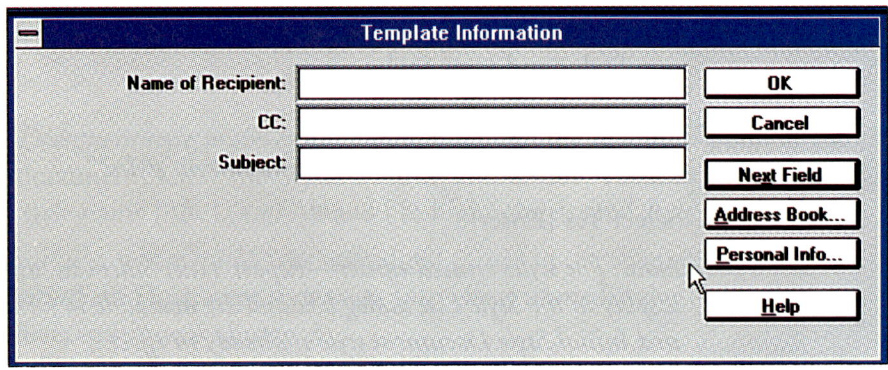

clude a recipient's name, address, phone number, fax number, subject, or copy notation.

Use an ExpressDoc Template

1. Select the **Template** button on the Button Bar {Alt, f, t *or* Ctrl and t}.

   Note: The Templates dialog box displays containing a list of available templates.

2. Double-click on the desired template name {press the up or down arrow key to highlight the desired template name, press Enter}.

   For example, scroll up the list of templates and double-click on **memo5**.

   Note: After a few moments, the Template Information dialog box displays (see Figure 15.3). In the document window, a portion of the template with formatted text and codes is visible.

   *Note: If personal information has not been entered for your WordPerfect program, a message displays requesting information. Select **OK**, then skip to step 4 and fill in the personal information as shown. Return to step 3 and continue with the steps.*

3. Type the requested information into the appropriate boxes.

   For example, type the following information into the boxes:

Name of Recipient:	**Alice Boyd** (press **Tab**)
CC:	**Vivian Raley** (press **Tab**)
Subject:	**Software Updates**

4. To change the personal information that was created the first time the Template feature was used, select the **Personal Info** button and make the appropriate changes {Alt and p}.

   For example:

   a. In the Name box, type your name and press **Tab**.

   b. In the Title box, type **Software Coordinator** and press **Tab**.

   c. In the Company box, type **Holt & Associates** and press **Tab**.

   d. In the Address box, type **1274 Pennsylvania Ave.** and press **Tab**.

   e. In the City, State Zip box, type **York, PA 17404** and press **Tab**.

   f. In the Telephone box, type **717-555-4800** and press **Tab**.

FIGURE 15.4

Memorandum created using the *memo5* ExpressDoc template

INTEROFFICE MEMORANDUM

To: Alice Boyd

CC: Vivian Raley

From: Your Name

Date: June 26, 1994

Subject: Software Updates

Yesterday, Sara Martin requested that we research the possibility of updating our database and spreadsheet programs. Several people in her department have noted that the current database and spreadsheet programs are lacking some much-needed features.

I would like to meet with you on Tuesday to discuss changing to the latest versions of Paradox and Quattro Pro. Let's meet for lunch at the Blue and Red Diner on Birch Avenue at 11:45 a.m. Please let me know by Monday if you are available to meet at that time.

FROM THE DESK OF...

YOUR NAME
SOFTWARE COORDINATOR
HOLT AND ASSOCIATES
1274 PENNSYLVANIA AVE.
YORK, PA 17404

717-555-4800
Fax: 717-555-4823

g. In the Fax box, type 717-555-4823.

5. Select OK to return to the Template Information dialog box {Tab, Enter}.
6. Select OK {Tab, Enter}.

   Note: *In a few moments, the top portion of a memorandum displays in the document window including the information typed in the Template Information and Personal Information dialog boxes. Notice that the buttons on the Button Bar have changed. The insertion point is located two blank lines below the Subject line. If desired, select the* ***Page Zoom Full*** *button to view the entire memorandum. Select the* ***Page Zoom Full*** *button again to return to the normal view.*

Finish-Up Instructions

- Type the body text of the memorandum as shown in Figure 15.4.
- Use the filename **15drill7.tem** and save the document.
- Print one copy and close the document.

9. Use the filename **15skill1.alp** and save the sorted file.
10. Print one copy and close the document.

Skill 15.2—Create and Apply Styles

1. Type the following unformatted presentation text.

WORDPERFECT 6.0 FOR WINDOWS
Features Presentation

1. MENU BAR
a. File
b. Edit
c. View
d. Layout
e. Tools
f. Graphics
g. Table
h. Window
i. Help

2. BUTTON BAR
a. Template
b. Indent
c. Bullet
d. Date Text
e. Envelope
f. Draw
g. Chart
h. TextArt
i. Figure
j. Text Box
k. QuickFormat
l. Styles

---

2. Use the filename **15skill2.txt** and save the unformatted file.
3. Edit the *InitialStyle* as follows:

Margins:	**Left and Right—1.75"; Top—1.25"**
Font:	**Arrus BT, 16-point**

4. Create the following styles.

Name:	**P-Title**
Description:	**Title for presentations**
Type	**Paragraph (paired)**
Justification:	**Center**
Font:	**Humanst521 Cn BT, Bold, 24-point**
Spacing Between Paragraphs:	**2**

Name:	**P-Subtitle**
Description:	**Subtitle for presentations**
Type:	**Paragraph (paired)**
Justification:	**Center**
Font:	**Humanst521 Cn BT, Bold, 20-point**
Spacing Between Paragraphs:	**2**

Name:	**P-Level 1**
Description:	**Topic level 1--presentations**
Type:	**Paragraph (paired)**
Spacing Between Paragraphs:	**1.5**

Name:	**P-Level 2**
Description:	**Topic level 2--presentations**
Type:	**Paragraph (paired)**
Special:	Press **F7** once to indent paragraphs

5. Apply the new styles to the document paragraphs.

   Hint: *A style can be applied to multiple paragraphs by selecting the desired paragraphs before choosing the* ***Styles*** *button.*

6. Use the filename **15skill2.for** and save the formatted presentation.

7. Print one copy and close the document.

Skill 15.3—Create a Macro; Use an ExpressDoc Template

1. Create a macro that when played produces the following distribution list. Name the macro **dist_lst** . ***Hint:*** *Type the drive letter where your disk is located followed by the macro name to save the macro to your file disk.*

   Distribution:

   S. F. Acevedo
   V. A. Butler
   J. P. Delaney
   M. T. Epranian
   E. D. Rindfleish
   R. P. Schueler
   C. T. Zornosa

   Hints: *Plan the macro by creating the document before selecting* ***Tools, Macro, Record****. Write down the steps needed to create the macro.*

2. When the macro is complete, close the document.

3. Use the following information to create a memorandum using an ExpressDoc template.

   a. The *memo1* ExpressDoc template should be used.

   b. The following information should be inserted into the box in the Template Information dialog box.

Recipient:	**See Distribution List**
CC:	**P. S. Perkins**
Subject:	**Company-Funded Retirement Gifts and Luncheons**

c. Change the Personal Information as follows:

Name:	**Pattie Zuecher**
Title:	**Manager, Human Resources**
Organization:	**Digital MicroComputer Products**
Address:	**242 Congress Ave.**
City, State, Zip:	**Austin, TX 78701**
Telephone:	**512-555-6030**
Fax:	**512-555-2846**

d. The following is the text of the memorandum.

This memo is in response to inquiries regarding the Company's policy concerning luncheons and/or gifts to employees who are retiring. Please use the following guidelines to ensure consistent, equitable, and uniform application for such expenditures.

- The equivalent of all luncheon costs for up to 12 individuals may be charged to the Company.
- A reasonable gift may be purchased for the individual. Funds contributed by fellow employees usually cover such expenses; however, a Company contribution towards the cost of a reasonable gift, not to exceed $100, may be charged to the Company.
- All such expenditures are to be charged to individual department accounts.

Please contact me if further clarification is needed.

e. Place the insertion point two lines below the final paragraph and play the **dist_lst** macro to insert the distribution list.

4. Use the filename **15skill3.mem** and save the file.
5. Print one copy and close the document.

Skill 15.4—Sort Table Columns; Language Arts

1. Open the file named **15skill4.mem** located on the data disk.
2. Make decisions regarding:

   Margins
   Justification
   Fonts (the final letter should fit on one page)
   Date of letter
   Table format (including cell widths, alignment of text, table borders)
   Reference initials, document identification, and enclosure notation
3. Correct four spelling errors and two punctuation errors
4. Sort the table cells alphabetically by the Item column.
5. Use the filename **15skill4.fin** and save the file.
6. Print one copy.
7. If you have completed your work, exit WordPerfect.

CHAPTER 16

Managing Document Windows and Files

Features Covered

- Cascade, tile, maximize, minimize, move, restore, and resize document windows
- Create, revise, and print a document summary
- Use File Options to copy, move, rename, and delete files and to create directories
- Use QuickList
- Convert files to and from other word processing formats
- Assign a password
- Use DOS without exiting WordPerfect
- Insert (retrieve) an existing file into a document on the screen
- Use Print Manager to cancel the printing of a document

Objectives and Introduction

After successfully completing this chapter, you will be able to cascade, tile, maximize, minimize, move, restore, and resize document windows as well as create, revise, and print document summary information. You will also learn to use WordPerfect's File Options to open, delete, rename, move, and locate files and to create and delete directories and subdirectories. In addition, you will learn to use WordPerfect's QuickList, QuickMenu, file conversion, and password features. You will learn to access DOS without exiting WordPerfect in order to perform tasks such as checking your hard disk or formatting a new disk. Finally, you will learn to use the Print Manager and to insert an existing file into a document on the screen.

WordPerfect provides tools to manage, organize, access, and secure files. Files can be accessed or managed by using the Windows, Document Summary, and QuickList features. Passwords can be created and used to secure files. Also, files from other word processing programs can be converted to or from the WordPerfect format. If desired, WordPerfect can be temporarily exited in order to accomplish tasks at the DOS prompt or to cancel the printing of a document.

The Windows in WordPerfect

The WordPerfect document window displays after the WordPerfect program is launched. When a new file is created or an existing file is opened, a new window displays. Nine document windows can be open at one time. As each new file is opened, WordPerfect sequentially numbers the document windows, for example, Document1, Document2, etc. The document number displays in the Title bar. If the document has been saved, the filename displays in the Title bar. Any document window can be cascaded, tiled, maximized, minimized, copied/moved, restored, resized, or closed. Manipulating the windows in WordPerfect is called *windowing*.

Start-Up Instructions

- Create five files as follows:
  a. In a new file, type **This is file 1.**; press **Enter** twice.
  b. Use the filename **16file.1** and save the file on your disk.
     Note: Do not close the file.
  c. Select the **New Document** button; type **This is file 2.**; press **Enter** twice.
  d. Use the filename **16file.2** and save the file on your disk.
  e. Select the **New Document** button; type **This is file 3.**; press **Enter** twice.
  f. Use the filename **16file.3** and save the file on your disk.
  g. Select the **New Document** button; type **This is file 4.**; press **Enter** twice.
  h. Use the filename **16file.4** and save the file on your disk.
  i. Select the **New Document** button; type **This is file 5.**; press **Enter** twice.
  j. Use the filename **16file.5** and save the file on your disk.

Cascade Document Windows

1. Select Window, Cascade {Alt, w, c}.

   *Note: When **Cascade** is selected, all open document windows overlap each other so that only the Title bar of each inactive window displays. The active window displays in front of the cascaded windows. In an active window, the Title bar displays in color or is highlighted.*

Tile Document Windows

1. Select Window, Tile {Alt, w, t}.

   *Note: When **Tile** is selected, all opened document windows are visible. The active window displays at the top or top left of the screen with the Title bar highlighted (see Figure 16.1).*

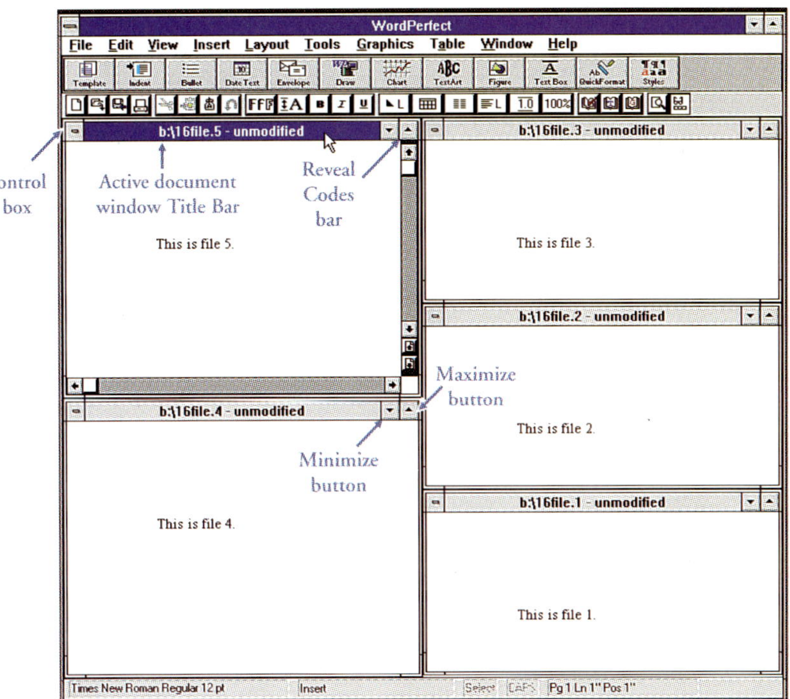

FIGURE 16.1

Tiled document windows with maximize and minimize buttons, control box, and Reveal Codes bar

Steps to Activate/Change the Active Window

1. Place the mouse pointer in the desired window and click once to activate the window {Alt, w, type the number of the desired window *or* Ctrl and F6 until the desired window is activated}.

   For example, move the mouse pointer to the various open windows and click.

Note: Remember, a window is active when the Title bar is highlighted or displayed in a color.

Steps to Maximize a Window

1. If more than one window is displayed on the screen, activate the desired window and select the **Maximize** button (up triangle) to view the window in full size {activate the desired window; Alt and hyphen, x}.

   For example, maximize the window containing the file named **16file.4**.

*Note: The document window containing the file named **16file.4** displays in full size in the document window.*

Steps to Restore a Window

Note: Restoring a document window is the process of returning the document window to its previously determined size.

1. With the document window maximized on the screen, select the **Restore** button located at the right end of the Menu bar of the desired window to return the window to its previous size {Alt and hyphen, r}.

Chapter 16 Managing Document Windows and Files

FIGURE 16.2

Minimized document window

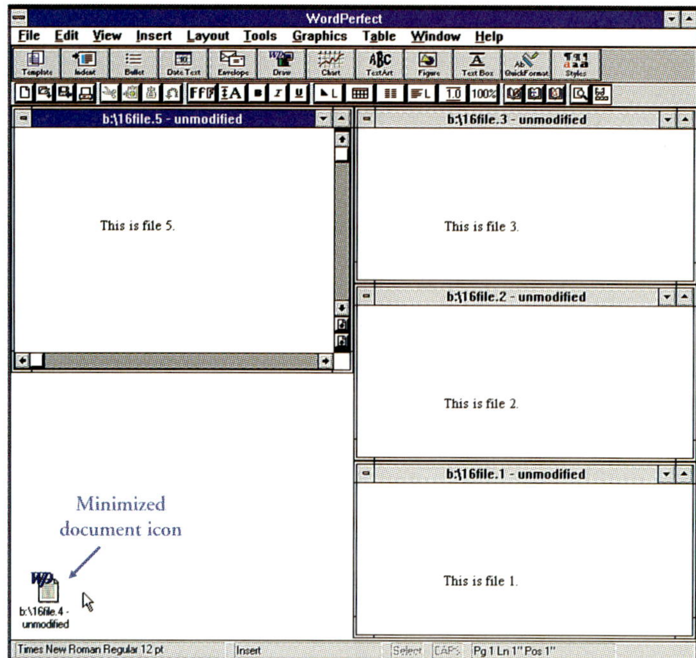

For example, select the **Restore** button in the window containing the file named **16file.4**.

Note: The file is returned to its previous size (before it was maximized).

Steps to Minimize a Window

Note: Minimizing a document window reduces the document window to a small icon (see Figure 16.2).

1. Activate the desired window, select the **Minimize** button located in the Title bar of the document window {Alt and hyphen, n}.

   For example, minimize the window containing the file named **16file.4**.

   Note: The document window is changed to a small icon and displays in the bottom left corner of the screen. The document name displays below the icon.

Steps to Restore a Minimized Window

1. Double-click on the icon that contains the desired window {Alt, w, type the number of the windows to be restored}.

   For example, double-click on the icon containing the file named **16file.4**.

Move a Window

Note: The window to be moved must be smaller than the full, maximized size.

1. Locate the mouse pointer in the desired document window Title bar; press and hold the left mouse button {Alt and hyphen, m}.

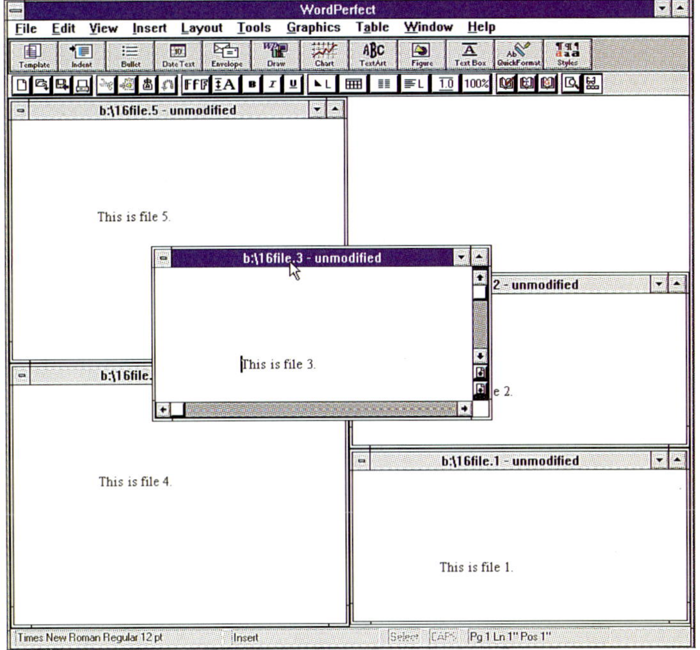

FIGURE 16.3

Moving a document window

For example, move the mouse pointer to the Title bar of the document window containing the file named **16file.3**; press and hold the mouse button.

Note: *A dashed outline appears around the document window.*

2. Drag the dashed window outline to the desired position and release the mouse button {press the up, down, left, or right arrow keys to move the window to the desired location, press Enter}.

   For example, drag the dashed outline for the document window containing the file named **16file.3** to approximately the center of the screen and release the mouse button (see Figure 16.3).

Resize a Window

Note: *The window must be smaller than the full, maximized size.*

1. Locate the mouse pointer on the document window's left, right, or bottom edge until a double-headed arrow displays. Press and hold the left mouse button and drag the dashed outline to the desired size, release the mouse button {Alt and hyphen, s, press the left, right, up, or down arrow keys to obtain the double-headed arrow at the desired document window's edge; press the chosen arrow key again repeatedly until the desired size displays, press Enter. Repeat to change the window size at any edge}.

   For example, move the mouse pointer to the bottom edge of the document window containing the file named **16file.2** and enlarge and reduce the window height.

Close All Windows

1. Select **File, Close** {Alt, f, c}.

   For example, close the windows that contain **16file.1**, **16file.2**, **16file.3**, and **16file.4**. (Do not close the file named **16file.5**.)

   Note: *When a document window is closed, the next opened window is displayed with the Title bar highlighted. However, if there is no other open window, an empty screen displays with the words "Document1- unmodified" in the Title bar. Each open window must be closed separately one at a time.*

Start-Up Instructions

- Maximize the file named **16file.5**.
- Reveal Codes should not be displaying in the document window. If necessary, turn off Reveal Codes (select **View, Reveal Codes**).

Use the Mouse to Display the Reveal Codes Window

1. Point to the small, dark rectangular bar at the top or bottom of the vertical scroll bar until a double-headed arrow displays (see Figure 16.1).

   For example, point on the small, dark bar at the top of the vertical scroll bar until the double-headed arrow displays.

2. Press and hold the mouse button while dragging the mouse downward; release the mouse when the dividing bar is positioned at the desired location in the document window.

   For example, press and hold the mouse button while dragging the dividing bar below the sentence "This is file 5."

   Note: *When the Reveal Codes window displays, the window size can be changed by pointing to the dividing bar (anywhere along the top edge of the Reveal Codes window) until the double-headed arrow displays and dragging up or down to obtain the desired size.*

Finish-Up Instructions

- Remove the Reveal Codes window from the document window by pointing to the dividing bar until the double-headed arrow displays. Press and hold the mouse button and drag down until the dividing bar touches the vertical scroll bar. Release the mouse button.

Document Summary Information

A document summary can be created to provide specific information about a file, such as a descriptive name, document type, and the name of the document author and typist (see Figure 16.4). The document summary is created by selecting **File,**

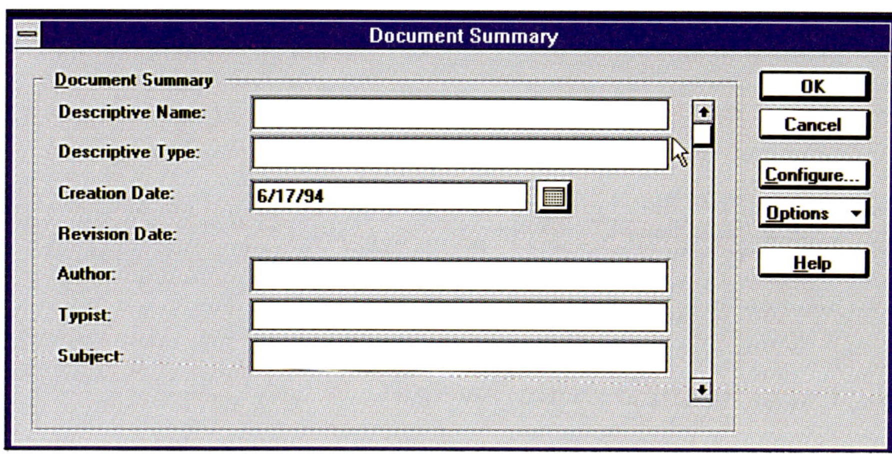

FIGURE 16.4

Document Summary dialog box

Document Summary and typing the desired information into the option boxes in the Document Summary dialog box. If desired, WordPerfect can be instructed to automatically display the Document Summary dialog box the first time a document is saved.

Once the document summary information is typed, the information can be changed and the updated information saved. If desired, the document summary can be printed. The document does not print when the document summary is printed.

Start-Up Instructions

❖ The file named **16file.5** should be displayed in the document window.

Create a Document Summary After a Document Is Saved

1. Select File, Document Summary {Alt, f, y}.

   Note: The Document Summary dialog box displays. The current date displays in the Creation Date box to indicate the date the Document Summary was/is created. If desired, the Creation Date can be changed to another date. The Revision Date is the date the document was last revised. See Figure 16.4. This date is saved and updated automatically by WordPerfect and cannot be changed by the user.

2. Check that the insertion point is located in the Descriptive Name box and type words that identify the file {press Tab to locate the insertion point in the desired box, type the information}.

   For example, type **This is a sample file.**

3. Click in the Descriptive Type box and type words that identify the document category {see step 2}.

   For example, type **Sample.**

4. Click in the Typist box and type the name of the typist {see step 2}.

   For example, type your name.

5. If desired, type any additional information desired into the option boxes.

6. Select OK {press Enter}.

Steps to Revise a Document Summary

1. Select **File, Document Summary** {Alt, f, y}.
2. Select the option(s) to be changed and type the updated information.

   For example, in the Author box, type the name of a friend.

3. Select **OK** to save the updated document summary {Enter}.

Steps to Print the Document Summary Information

1. Select the **Print** button, select **Document Summary** {Alt, f, p, a *or* F5, a}.
2. Select **Print** {p}.

   Note: The document summary prints; the document does not print.

Steps to Create a Document Summary When a New Document Is Saved

Note: The following steps are for your information only. If these steps are followed, the Document Summary dialog box will display ***every*** *time a new document is saved or exited.*

1. Select **File, Preferences** {Alt, f, e}.
2. Double-click on the **Summary** icon {Alt and s}.
3. Select the **Create Summary on Save/Exit** option {Alt and c}.
4. Select **OK** {Enter}.
5. Select **Close** to return to the document window {Alt and c}.

   Note: If the Create Summary on Save/Exit option is selected, the Document Summary dialog box displays when a new document is saved or exited.

Insert (Retrieve) an Existing File Into a Document on the Screen

Note: The file named ***16file.5*** *should be displayed in the document window.*

1. Place the insertion point in the document window at the desired location.

   For example, place the insertion point on the second blank line below the sentence "This is file 5."

2. Select **Insert, File** {Alt, i, i}.

   Note: The Insert File dialog box displays.

3. Double-click on the desired file.

   For example, double-click on the file named **16file.1**.

   Note: The message "Insert file into current document?" displays.

4. Select **Yes** {Enter}.

   Note: The information from the selected file displays on the screen.

Finish-Up Instructions

- Close the document window. (It is not necessary to save the file.)

Use File Options

The File Options in the Open and Save As dialog boxes are used to perform the usual disk maintenance tasks of copying, moving, renaming, and deleting files. Additional options include changing file attributes, printing files, printing a file list, creating directories/subdirectories, and removing directories.

Changing file attributes are functions that traditionally have been accomplished by using DOS (the disk operating system). In WordPerfect for Windows, the attributes can be changed by selecting **File Options** in the Open or Save As dialog box. One attribute that can be assigned to a file is Read-Only. This attribute allows a file to be read (opened), but the file cannot be overwritten (saved with the same name). When a Read-Only file displays on the screen, the Title bar shows the filename followed by the words "(Read-Only)."

Start-Up Instructions

- The files named **16file.1**, **16file.2**, **16file.3**, **16file.4**, and **16file.5** must be available on your disk.
- A mouse is the most efficient method for performing actions when using File Options. A mouse must be used to perform the File Options functions that follow.

Print a List of Files

Note: The drive containing the list of files to be printed should be highlighted in the Directories box. If necessary, select the drive in the file box where your file disk is located.

1. Use the desired Open or Save As dialog box.

   For example, select the **Open** button.

2. Select **File Options**.
3. Select **Print File List**.

   Note: The Print File List dialog box displays.

4. Select **Print Entire List**.

   For example, check that the Print Entire List is selected.

5. Select **Print**.
6. Select **Cancel** to exit the Open dialog box.

Steps to

Create a Directory

1. Use the Open or Save As dialog box.

   For example, select **File, Save As**.

2. If necessary, double-click on the desired drive letter in the Drives box.

   For example, check that the drive where your file disk is located displays in the Drives box.

3. If necessary, in the Directories box highlight the drive letter where the new directory is to be located.

   For example, check that the drive letter where your file disk is located (a: or b:) is highlighted in the Directories box. If necessary, click once on the drive letter in the Directories box.

4. Select **File Options**.

5. Select **Create Directory**.

   Note: *The Create Directory dialog box displays.*

6. Type the new directory name in the New Directory box.

   For example, type your last name (up to eight characters).

7. Select **Create**.

   Note: *The directory name displays beneath the disk drive letter shown in the Directories box. Notice the file folder icon displaying next to the directory name.*

Create a Subdirectory

8. Repeat steps 4 and 5 under Create a Directory.

9. Type the drive letter followed by a colon, directory name, backslash, and the desired subdirectory name.

   For example, type a: followed by your last name, a backslash, and your first name (a:smith\laura).

10. Select **Create**.

Finish-Up Instructions

- Double-click on your last name directory to display the new first name subdirectory.

Start-Up Instructions

- Double-click on the drive letter in the Directories box to display the list of files on your file disk.

Copy/Move a File(s)

1. In the Open or Save As dialog box, highlight the name of the file(s) to be copied.

   For example, in the Save As dialog box, select the first file to be copied, i.e., **16file.1**. To select multiple files, point to the last file to be copied, i.e., **16file.5**, press and hold the Shift key while clicking the mouse button once.

   Note: *All files between **16file.1** and **16file.5** are selected.*

2. Select **File Options**.

3. Select **Copy** or **Move**.

For example, select **Copy**.

Note: The Copy/Move Files dialog box displays.

4. In the Copy/Move Selected Files To box, type the drive location where the files are to be copied or moved and, if necessary, type the directory name.

   For example, type a:your lastname (a:smith).

5. Select **Copy** or **Move**.

   Note: The files are copied or moved and the dialog box displays. If files are copied, the filenames remain highlighted. If the files are moved to a different drive location, the filenames no longer display in the current list of filenames.

Finish-Up Instructions

- When the copy process is completed, double-click on your last name directory to display a list of the copied files. If the message "Open marked files?" displays, select **No** {Enter}.
- Select **16file.2**. To select a nonconsecutive file, point to the file name e.g., **16file.4**, press the **Ctrl** key while clicking the left mouse button once.
- Use the steps 2-4 of the Steps to Copy/Move a File(s) and move the files named **16file.2** and **16file.4** to your first name subdirectory. In the Move Selected Files To box, type your subdirectory name, select **Move**.

  Note: The two moved files no longer display in your last name directory. Double-click on your first name. The two copied files display in the Filename list.

Start-Up Instructions

- The files in your first name subdirectory should be displayed in the Save As dialog box.

Steps to Delete a File(s)

1. In the Open or Save As dialog box, highlight the name of the file(s) to be deleted.

   For example, highlight the files named **16file.2** and **16file.4** located in your first name directory.

2. Select **File Options**.
3. Select **Delete**.

   Note: The Delete File(s) dialog box displays with the message "Do you want to delete selected files?" If only one filename is selected, the Delete File dialog box displays with the name of the file to be deleted highlighted.

4. Select **Delete**.

   Note: The deleted files no longer display in the Filename list.

Steps to Remove a Directory (or Subdirectory)

1. In the Open or Save As dialog box and in the Directories box, highlight the name of the directory or subdirectory to be removed.

For example, highlight your first name subdirectory.

2. Select **File Options**.
3. Select **Remove Directory.**

   Note: The Remove Directory dialog box displays and the directory name to be removed is highlighted.

4. Select **Remove.**

   *Note: The directory/subdirectory is removed from the file list. If the directory/subdirectory is not empty (files and/or subdirectories are listed under the directory/subdirectory name) when Delete is selected, a message displays, "WARNING! Directory ... contains files. Remove directory anyway?". Select **Yes**.*

Steps to Rename a File

1. In the Open or Save As dialog box, highlight the name of the file to be renamed.

   For example, highlight the file named **16file.3** in your last name directory.

2. Select **File Options**.
3. Select **Rename**.

   Note: The Rename File dialog box displays with the file location and filename displayed in the From box.

4. In the To: box, type the drive location and new filename or edit the name displayed.

   For example, change the filename to **16file3.ren**. (Do not type the final period.)

5. Select **Rename**.

   *Note: The new filename, **16file3.ren**, displays in your last name directory list and the filename **16file.3** no longer displays.*

Start-Up Instructions

- Double-click on the drive letter in the Directories box to display the list of files on your file disk.

Steps to Print a File from the Open or Save As Dialog Box

1. In either the Open or Save As dialog box, highlight the name of the file to be printed.

   For example, highlight a file of your choice.

2. Select **File Options**.
3. Select **Print**.

   Note: The Print File dialog box displays with the name of the file to be printed highlighted.

4. Select **Print**.

Note: A message "Preparing Document for Printing" displays briefly. The document prints.

Finish-up Instructions

- Select **Cancel** to close the Open or Save As dialog box.
- Close all open documents.

Steps to Copy Text from the Viewer to the Clipboard

1. Use the Open or Save As dialog box.

   For example, select the **Open** button.

2. Highlight the desired filename.

   For example, highlight the file named **16file.3**.

3. Select the **View** button.

   Note: The document displays in the Viewer.

4. Select the desired text.

   For example, select the sentence "This is file 3." Point the mouse pointer at the top of the T and drag to the right and/or downward to highlight.

5. Press the *right* mouse button to display the QuickMenu; select **Copy to Clipboard**.

   Note: The text remains highlighted.

6. Select **Cancel** in the Open or Save As dialog box to return the insertion point to the document window.
7. Select the **Paste** button.

   Note: The text copied from the Viewer displays on the screen.

Finish-Up Instructions

- Close the document (do not save).

Steps to Open Multiple Files

1. Select the **Open** button and choose the first file to be opened.

   For example, highlight the file named **16file.1**.

2. Press and hold the **Ctrl** key while selecting the next file to be opened.

   For example, select the file named **16file.2**.

3. Repeat step 2 and highlight any additional file(s) to be opened.

   For example, highlight the file named **16file.4**.

   Note: A maximum of nine files can be opened at one time.

4. Select **OK**.

Note: WordPerfect opens each file into a separate document window. The last file opened displays on the screen.

Finish-Up Instructions

- Select **Window**, **Tile** to display all open document windows.
- Close all document windows.

The QuickList

The QuickList feature provides a fast and easy method to access frequently used directories and subdirectories. Directories and subdirectories can be assigned descriptive names by using the QuickList feature. Instead of typing the full path name for the desired directory/subdirectory when opening or saving files, the descriptive name can be selected from the QuickList box. The QuickList feature can be accessed from either the Open or Save As dialog boxes.

For example, letters authored by B. Smith of the Personnel Department might be saved in the subdirectory c:\persnl\letters\smith. A QuickList entry could be created that identified the subdirectory as B. Smith Letters. To open a file saved in the subdirectory c:\persnl\letters\smith, you would select B. Smith Letters in the QuickList box in the Open File dialog box. A list of all files in the subdirectory would display immediately.

Start-Up Instructions

- The file disk with your last name directory must be available.

Create a QuickList Directory Entry

Note: The Steps to Create a QuickList Directory Entry can also be accomplished from the Save As dialog box.

1. Select the **Open** button {Alt, f, o *or* Ctrl and o}.
2. Select **QuickList** {Alt and L, Alt and Shift and down arrow}.
3. Select **Add Item** {a}.

   Note: The Add QuickList Item dialog box displays.
4. If necessary, type the name and location of the directory to be added to the QuickList.

   For example, type **a:** or **b:** and your last name directory.
5. To locate the insertion point in the Description box, press the **Tab** key once or click in the Description box.

   Note: When the insertion point is placed in the Description box, the information in the Directories/Filename box is automatically inserted in the Description box.
6. Delete any information in the Description box and type a descriptive name of the directory (or subdirectory).

For example, type **Sample Files.** (Do not type the period.)

7. Select **OK** {Enter}.

   Note: The Sample Files entry is added to the QuickList box and is highlighted.

8. Select **Cancel** to return to the document window {Esc}.

Steps to Access a Directory Using the QuickList

Note: The Steps to Access a Directory Using the QuickList can also be accomplished from the Save As dialog box.

1. Select the **Open** button {Alt, f, o *or* Ctrl and o}.
2. Double-click on the desired name in the QuickList box {Alt and q, use the up or down arrow key to highlight the desired item, Enter}.

   For example, double-click on **Sample Files.**

   Note: The list of files displays in the Filename list. Your last name directory is highlighted in the Directories box. If desired, open a file.

Finish-Up Instructions

- Select **Cancel** to exit the Open dialog box to return to the document window {press Esc}.

Steps to Delete a QuickList Entry

Note: The Steps to Delete a QuickList Entry can also be accomplished from the Save As dialog box.

1. Select the **Open** button {Alt, f, o *or* Ctrl and o}.
2. In the QuickList box, highlight the name to be deleted {Alt and q, press the up or down arrow key to highlight the desired item name}.

   For example, highlight **Sample Files** in the QuickList box.

3. Select **QuickList** {Alt and L, Alt and Shift and down arrow}.
4. Select **Delete Item** {L}.

   Note: The message displays "Delete item... from the QuickList?".

5. Select **Yes** {Enter}.

   Note: The Sample Files item no longer displays in the QuickList box.

6. Select **Cancel** to return to the document window {press Esc}.

Chapter 16 Managing Document Windows and Files

Converting Files

WordPerfect for Windows provides a method to change the file format of a document. A document can be saved to another file format or converted from a different file format. For example, a document originally saved in Microsoft Word for Windows can be converted to a WordPerfect file format. Also, a WordPerfect document can be saved in another format, such as WordStar.

Start-Up Instructions

- Open the file named **16file.1**.

Save a File in a Different File Format

1. Select **File, Save As** {Alt, f, a *or* F3}.
2. Type the desired filename in the Filename box.

   For example, type **16conver.fil**. (Do not type the final period.)
3. Select the down arrow button in the Format box {Alt and t; Alt and Shift and down arrow key}.
4. Scroll through the list of file formats and double-click on the desired format {press the up or down arrow keys until the desired file format is highlighted}.

   For example, scroll up the list of file formats and click once on **MS Word for Windows 2.0c.{*.doc}**.
5. Select **OK** {press Enter twice}.

   Note: *The message "Conversion in Progress" displays briefly. The file named* ***16conver.fil*** *is now saved in the MS Word for Windows format. The file named* ***16file.1*** *is still available on your file disk and is saved in the WordPerfect 6.0 for Windows file format.*

Finish-Up Instructions

- Close the document.

Open a File Created in a Different Program

1. Select the **Open** button and double-click on the desired file.

   For example, double-click on the file named **16conver.fil**.

   Note: *The Convert File Format dialog box displays. MS Word for Windows 2.0c displays in the Convert File Format From box because WordPerfect has attempted to determine the format of the file.*
2. If necessary, select a different file format by selecting the down arrow and clicking on the desired file format.
3. Select **OK** {Enter}.

   Note: *A "Conversion in Progress" message displays. After a few moments, the converted file displays. The displayed file has been converted to the WordPerfect 6.0 for Windows format. The file must be saved to retain the WordPerfect for Windows format and to record it on the disk.*

Finish-Up Instructions

- Use the *new* filename **16conv.wp** and save the file.
- Close the document.

File Security

Once a file is created, the file can be saved and given a password. Each time the saved file is opened, the password is requested. The password must be remembered by the user because there is no method available for finding a forgotten password. A password can be removed or changed at any time (but only if you remember the current password).

WordPerfect provides two protection options. One option, called Enhanced Password Protection, uses case-sensitive protection but is not compatible with earlier versions of WordPerfect. The second option, called Original Password Protection, is not case-sensitive but is compatible with earlier versions of WordPerfect.

Start-Up Instructions

- Select the **New Document** button.
- Type the following sentence:

  This is a very secret file that no one but me should ever see.

Steps to Create or Change a Password

1. Select **File, Save As** {Alt, f, a *or* F3}.
2. Type the desired filename.

   For example, type **16secret.fil**. (Do not type the final period.)
3. Select **Password Protect** located at the bottom right corner of the dialog box {Alt and p}.

   Note: *An X displays in the Password Protect box.*
4. Select **OK** {Enter}.

   Note: *The Password Protection dialog box displays.*
5. Type the desired password in the Type Password for Document box.

   For example, type **007**. (Do not type the period.)

   Note: *To ensure privacy, the typed characters are displayed as X's on the screen. A password can be 1 to 23 characters and can contain spaces, uppercase and lowercase letters, or any characters found on the keyboard.*
6. Select **OK** {Enter}.
7. Retype the password to confirm.
8. Select **OK** to confirm the password and save the file {Enter}.

Finish-Up Instructions

- Close the document.

Steps to Open a File That Has Been Protected with a Password

1. Select the **Open** button {Alt, f, o *or* Ctrl and o}.

2. Select the desired filename.

   For example, double-click on **16secret.fil.**

   Note: *The Password dialog box displays.*

3. Type the password exactly as typed when the password was created.

   For example, type **007**. (Do not type the period.)

   Note: *As the password is typed, X's display on the screen.*

4. Select OK {Enter}.

Steps to Remove a Password

1. With the password-required document open, select **File, Save As** {Alt, f, a *or* F3}.
2. Select **Password Protect** {Alt and p}.

   Note: *An X no longer displays beside the Password Protect option.*

3. Select OK {Enter}.

   Note: *If the file is not saved after the Password is removed, the password will still be needed to open the file.*

4. A message displays "File . . . already exists. Do you want to replace it?"; select Yes {y}.

Finish-Up Instructions

- Close the document window.

Using DOS Without Exiting WordPerfect

DOS commands such as format, chkdsk (check disk), dir (directory), date, erase, and diskcopy can be accessed without exiting the WordPerfect program. Windows allows multiple programs to run at the same time. The names of the programs that are currently running can be viewed by pressing and holding the **Alt** key while tapping the **Tab** key repeatedly to display the program names. When the desired program name displays, release the **Alt** key to switch to the program.

Use DOS Without Exiting WordPerfect

1. Press and hold the Alt key while tapping the Tab key until the Program Manager option displays. Release the Alt key.
2. Double-click on the MS-DOS prompt icon located in the Main group.

   Note: *After a few moments, the DOS prompt displays.*

3. Type and execute the desired DOS command.

   For example, type **ver** and press **Enter.**

   Note: *After typing **ver**, the number of the DOS version in use displays.*

4. If desired, type another DOS command or type **exit** to return to the Program Manager and close the DOS window.

   For example, type **exit** and press **Enter.**

5. Press and hold the **Alt** key while tapping the **Tab** key until the WordPerfect option displays. Release the **Alt** key.

   Note: *The WordPerfect document window displays.*

Cancel the Printing of a Document

Once a document has been sent to print, the printing may be stopped or canceled. After **Print** is selected in the Print dialog box, the "Preparing Document for Printing" message displays briefly on the screen. As long as the Preparing Document For Printing message displays on the screen, the print job can be canceled if the **Esc** key is pressed immediately. However, once the "Preparing Document for Printing" message disappears from the screen, the print job must be canceled by using the WordPerfect Print Job dialog box or the Windows Print Manager.

The WordPerfect Print Job dialog box monitors the progress of a print job. While a document is being printed, the number of the page that is currently printing, the name of the printer, and the number of the copy (copy one, two, three, etc.) being printed display in the WordPerfect Print Job dialog box. If the job being printed contains multiple pages and/or multiple copies, the printing can be canceled by selecting the **Cancel Print Job** option. However, once the print job has been processed by WordPerfect, the WordPerfect Print Job dialog box immediately leaves the screen and the document prints. Access the WordPerfect Print Job dialog box by selecting the **Print** button and choosing the **Control** button. To cancel the printing of a document, select the **Cancel Print Job** option (in the WordPerfect Print Job dialog box).

To use the Windows Print Manager to cancel the printing of a document, press and hold the **Alt** key while tapping the **Tab** key until the Print Manager box displays; release the **Alt** key. If a document is to be canceled from the print queue (list of filenames), highlight the name of the print job to be canceled, select **Delete,** and select **OK** to the message "Do you want to quit printing the document . . . ?".

If a document does not print, check that the printer is turned on and the printer cables are securely connected. Also, if a printer is shared, check the switch box or Local Area Network (LAN) connection (see your instructor). Before resending a print job, check the Windows Print Manager for any filenames of documents waiting to print. If necessary, delete these filenames.

Access Print Manager

Note: *The following steps are for your information only.*

1. After a document has been sent to print, press and hold the **Alt** key while tapping the **Tab** key repeatedly until Print Manager displays.

   Note: *The Print Manager dialog box displays.*

2. *To delete a file from the print queue,* highlight the name of the desired document, select the **Delete** button.

Note: If the document is in the process of printing, a message displays "Do you want to quit printing the document. . .?". Select ***OK.***

3. *To resume the printing of a document,* select the printer name and select **Resume.**
4. *To exit Print Manager,* select **View, Exit.**
5. *To return to WordPerfect without exiting the Print Manager,* press and hold the **Alt** key while tapping the **Tab** key until WordPerfect displays. Release the **Alt** key.

The Next Step

Chapter Review and Activities

Self-Check Quiz

T F 1. When multiple document windows are open, select **Window, Tile** to display all the documents on the screen.

T F 2. The **Maximize** button can be selected to reduce the size of a document window.

T F 3. A tiled document window can be moved but not resized.

T F 4. When the document summary is printed, the document does not print.

5. ____ is the maximum number of document windows that can be open at one time.
   a. Nine
   b. Ten
   c. Eleven
   d. Twelve

6. The maximum number of characters that can be used in a password is ___.
   a. 20
   b. 21
   c. 22
   d. 23

7. Text can be ____ from the Viewer and placed in the clipboard.
   a. deleted
   b. copied
   c. moved
   d. none of these

8. The QuickList provides easy access to _________.
   a. directories
   b. subdirectories
   c. a document window
   d. both a and b

9. List five tasks that can be accomplished by using the File Options available in the Open and Save As dialog boxes.

10. List the five steps to access and use DOS without exiting WordPerfect.

Enriching Language Arts Skills

Proofreading Hints

When proofreading a document, read the document twice: once for content and meaning and once to check grammar, spelling, and punctuation. When proofing your own work, place the original document/draft beside the screen and read across comparing line by line. Read aloud with a second person to compare the printed copy with the original document/draft.

Examples of types of errors to look for when proofreading:

Repeated words	The wedding reception will be held on Sunday *at the at the* Jamestown Country Club.
Misused or missing words	The transaction is *not* legal. The transaction is *now* legal.
Missing punctuation	The cost was *$2516.* (should be *$25.16*)
Misspelled names	Kathryn or Catherine
Transposed letters/ numbers	The *item* is 10:00 a.m. (*time*) The report is due October *21.* (should be October *12*)

Activities

Activity 16.1—Cascade, Tile, and Maximize Document Windows

1. Open four files of your choice from your file disk.
2. Cascade the document windows.
3. Tile the document windows to observe all open windows.
4. Maximize one of the document windows.
5. Close all document windows.

Activity 16.2—Print a List of Files

1. Using File Options, print a list of the files on your file disk (select the **Open** button, select **File Options**, **Print File List**, select **Print Entire List**, **Print**. Choose **Cancel** to exit the menu).

Activity 16.3—Create and Print a Document Summary

1. Open one of the files from your file disk and review the document to determine the document's subject.

2. Create a document summary for your chosen file. Fill in the Descriptive Name, Descriptive Type, and Typist boxes with the appropriate information.
3. Print the document summary.
4. Save and close the document.

Challenge Your Skills

Skill 16.1—Create and Delete Directories, Copy, Move, and Delete Files; Create a QuickList Entry

1. Create two directories on your file disk using the directory names **dir1** and **dir2**.
2. Select and copy four **.wpg** files (WordPerfect graphics files) from the *c:\wpwin60\graphics* subdirectory to **dir1**. (If necessary, check with your instructor or instructional assistant for the drive and/or directory where the WordPerfect graphics files are located.)
3. Move two of the graphics files from dir1 to dir2.
4. Optional. Print the list of files in the dir1 and dir2 directories.
5. Delete the files in the dir2 directory.
6. Delete the dir2 directory.
7. In the dir1 directory, rename one of the graphics files using the filename **graphics2.wpg**.
8. Optional. Print the list of files in the dir1 directory.
9. Create a QuickList entry for the dir1 directory (make a choice of your own for the QuickList entry name).
10. If you have completed your work, exit WordPerfect.

Part 4
Checking Your Step

Production Skill Builder Activities
Chapters 13-16

Production Activity 4.1—Newsletter with Table and Graphics; Sorting

1. Use the following information to create the two-page newsletter shown on pages 398 and 399.
   a. Change the top and bottom margins to .75"; change the left and right margins to .5".
   b. Create a footer that includes the newsletter name, issue date, and page number.

      Hint: *When creating the footer, change the left and right margins to .5".*
   c. Use letterspacing and word spacing to adjust the spacing in the title.
   d. Use the ☞ and ➢ characters that are located in the Iconic Symbols character set.
   e. When creating the table, set the table position to Right to place the table in the right column.
   f. The graphics files are named **sun_dsg.wpg** and **medical1.wpg** and are located in the *wpwin60/graphics* directory.
   g. If space is available, create TextArt to call attention to a specific topic in the newsletter. Review the document to determine a topic that should be given more emphasis.
2. Optional. After completing the newsletter, sort the table of upcoming classes by class name or by date.
3. Optional. After completing the newsletter, use paragraph sorting to sort the locations of Bright Medical Center by name.
4. Use the filename **4pact1.new** and save the file.
5. Print one copy and close the document.

COMMUNITY HEALTH BULLETIN

Spring, 199x **Bright Medical Center**

Sunning Health Tips

Summer is almost here and it's time to start thinking about protecting your skin from burns and ultraviolet rays. Take a moment to review the following tips:

- ☞ Avoid being outside during midday hours (10 a.m. to 2 p.m.) on sunny days.
- ☞ Wear sunscreen for all outdoor activities year round. Apply sunscreen at least one hour before going out into the sun and again after swimming or perspiring heavily.
- ☞ If you are taking medication, check with your doctor before going out into the sun. Antihistamines, antibiotics, estrogens, tranquilizers, or birth control pills may cause a photosensitive skin reaction.
- ☞ Avoid using indoor sunlamps, tanning booths, sun reflectors, tan accelerators, or tanning pills.

Upcoming Health Education Classes

Bright Medical Center offers many health education classes. These classes are held at the Community Center. The fee to attend each class is $15. This fee covers handouts, a community health T-shirt, and refreshments. Your ideas for additional classes are welcome and can be sent to Dr. Deanna Berninger at Rose Valley Hospital. The following table is a listing of upcoming classes.

Cooking for a Healthy Heart	6/19	1:00 p.m.
Anxiety & Phobias	5/15	7:00 p.m.
CPR	4/14	7:30 p.m.
Senior Care Issues	4/20	3:00 p.m.
Food, Fitness & Fun	5/20	9:00 a.m. & 5:30 p.m.
Nutrition	6/11	6:00 p.m.
Stop Smoking	6/10	6:30 p.m.
Sports Injury	4/30	7:30 p.m.

Walking--The Right Exercise

Walking is becoming the exercise of choice for many people, mainly because it's so easy to do. Find a pair of comfortable shoes, a friend, and a park or walking trail and this exercise will lead to a healthier life.

What are the benefits of walking?

- ➢ Improved cardiovascular fitness
- ➢ Toned muscles
- ➢ Reduced stress and tension
- ➢ Reduced cholesterol
- ➢ Increased metabolic rate, helping you to keep weight off

Community Health Bulletin **Spring, 199x** **Page 1**

Carpal Tunnel Syndrome

Individuals who keyboard for long periods of time are at risk of developing the painful hand disorder known as "Carpal Tunnel Syndrome." Repetitive motions of the hand such as excessive wrist movement or holding the wrists in a stationary position for long periods of time can irritate nerves, tendons and arteries in the narrow area of the wrist known as the "carpal tunnel." Carpal tunnel syndrome has been very prevalent in careers such as secretarial, word processing, data entry, and cashiering.

Although the actual injury occurs in the wrist area, the pain from the injury is usually felt in the hand. Carpal tunnel syndrome may also cause numbness in the fingers.

Below are a few suggestions for avoiding carpal tunnel syndrome:

- ☞ Maintain good posture--straight back, shoulders relaxed, elbows alongside the body, wrists straight, and arms parallel to the floor.
- ☞ Adjust the angle of the keyboard for comfort.
- ☞ Use a wrist rest to provide support for the wrists and to assist in maintaining the straight wrist position.
- ☞ Before beginning a job that requires repetitive wrist action, practice a few wrist stretching and strengthening exercises.
- ☞ Avoid over-reaching with fingers.
- ☞ Take frequent short breaks, perform other types of activities, or practice wrist stretching exercises.
- ☞ Avoid pounding on the keys.
- ☞ Take advantage of computer program features that are designed to reduce repetitive keystrokes. Usually these features allow you to record a set of keystrokes then play them back using only one or two keystrokes. Look for features with such names as "Recorder," "Macro," or "Playback."

Bright Medical Center Locations

For your convenience, Bright Medical Centers are located throughout the city. Please check for the location nearest you.

East Valley Center **555-7800**
9900 Jefferson Avenue

Clearlake Center **555-4200**
1435 Clearlake Plaza, Suite 1000

Paradise Center **555-5800**
4500 Paradise Road, Suite 255

Lakeport Center **555-4425**
#525 Lakeport Mall

Production Activity 4.2—Superscripts, Subscripts, and Equations

1. Create the following document using superscripts, subscripts, and equations.

SUPERSCRIPTS, SUBSCRIPTS, AND EQUATIONS

COMPLEMENTARY ANGLES

40° 50°   27° 63°
35° 55°   10° 80°

CHEMICAL FORMULAS

Sodium Hydrosulfite = $Na_2S_2O_4$ Sodium Sulfite = Na_2SO_3

Sodium Phosphate = NaH_2PO_4 Sodium Ethylate = C_2H_5ONa

ALGEBRAIC EQUATIONS

$\frac{1}{y}+\frac{1}{2}=\frac{1}{y-2}$ $\frac{(2a^2c)^2}{5m}$ $\sqrt{\frac{1}{20}}$ $\sqrt{\frac{49a^2}{64b^2}}$

---

2. Use the filename **4pact2.sse** and save the file.
3. Print one copy and close the document.

Production Activity 4.3—Text with Graphic Overlay and Line Sorting; Word Spacing and Letterspacing

1. Use the following information and create a flier similar to the one shown on page 401.
   a. The graphics file is named **marsh.wpg** and is stored in the *wpwin60\graphics* directory.
   b. Use word spacing and letterspacing to adjust the spacing between the words and letters if needed.
   c. Optional. Use line sort to sort the *General Information* items alphabetically.
   Hint: *Perform line sort before formatting (bolding, indenting, etc.) the text.*
2. Use the filename **4pact3.fli** and save the file.
3. Print one copy and close the document.

Where you can enjoy shopping,
tennis, bicycling, biking, or
just relaxing on the beach.

General Information

Full, hearty breakfast included
Afternoon tea and refreshments
Free use of bicycles
Smoking permitted on verandas only
Check-in between 2:00 p.m. and 10:00 p.m.
Check-out time at 12:00 noon
Off-season and mid-week specials
Cocktails available after 5:00 p.m.

Production Activity 4.4—Use Append to Create an Overhead Transparency

1. Open the file named **4pact4.pos** located on the data disk.
2. Use the Append feature and create an overhead transparency consisting of the document title and sideheads contained in the file named **4pact4.pos**.
3. When the title and sideheads have been appended to the Clipboard, create a new document and paste the appended text into the new document.
4. Format the new document as an overhead transparency. Make decisions regarding:

Fonts and point sizes
Justification
Spacing between paragraphs

5. Use the *new* filename **4pact4.ovr** and save the overhead transparency file.
6. Print one copy and close the documents.

Production Activity 4.5—Create and Modify Styles

1. Open the file named **4pact5.doc** located on the data disk.
2. Edit the *InitialStyle* style as follows:

Font:	Arrus BT, 11-point or make a choice of your own
Margins:	Left and Right—1.25"
Page:	Center Current Page

3. Create the following styles:

Style name:	Doc. title
Description:	Style for job description title
Style type:	Paragraph (paired)
Font:	Humanst521 Cn BT, Bold, 14-point or make a choice of your own
Spacing Between Paragraphs:	2
Justification:	Centered
Style name:	Sidehead
Description:	Style for sideheads
Style type:	Paragraph (paired)
Font:	Humanst521 Cn BT, Bold, 13-point or make a choice of your own
Spacing Between Paragraphs:	1.5
Style name:	TV Prog Name
Description:	Changes TV program name font
Style type:	Character
Font:	Use Arrus BT, Bold, Italic, 11-point or make a choice of your own

4. Apply the styles to the document title, sideheads, and TV program name.
5. Correct two spelling errors, two punctuation errors, and one repeated word error.
6. Use the *new* filename **4pact5.for** and save the formatted document.
7. If you have completed your work, exit WordPerfect.

Part 5
A Giant Step

Use Desktop Publishing

Chapters 17–19

- Landscape layout
- Shadow boxes
- Insert previous created text into a document or graphic box
- Insert a Lotus PIC file into a graphic box
- Scale a graphic image within a graphic box
- Use Advance to position text
- Rotated text and reversed taxt
- Shadow text attribute
- Create unequal width columns
- Create headers/footers for odd and even pages
- Edit border line style settings
- Create a drop cap
- Automatically indent the first line of all paragraphs
- Create a graphic box that extends across multiple columns
- SmartQuotes
- Subdivide pages
- Use WP Draw to create and eidt graphic images
- Create a watermark
- Print a booklet

Use Special Desktop Publishing Features

Features Covered

- Landscape orientation
- Create shadow boxes and customize border color
- Insert previously created text into a document or graphic box
- Insert a Lotus PIC file into a graphic box
- Scale a graphic image within a graphic box
- Add captions to graphic boxes
- Use Advance to position text
- Rotate text
- Reverse text

Objectives and Introduction

After successfully completing this chapter, you will be able to use landscape orientation, multiple columns, and graphic boxes to create a two-sided, tri-fold mailer brochure. You will also learn how to create special effects using shadow boxes, rotated text, and reversed text.

Brochures come in all shapes and sizes. One of the most common brochures is the tri-fold mailer. Information is printed on both sides of the page. Generally, a three-column format is used and the pages are printed in landscape orientation (i.e., 11 inches by 8.5 inches) as shown in Figures 17.1 and 17.2. Often a tri-fold mailer will include graphic images, graphic lines and borders, and special effects such as shadow boxes, rotated text, and reversed text. The features presented in this chapter will be used to develop the tri-fold mailer brochure shown on page 421.

FIGURE 17.1

Mock-up of a tri-fold mailer brochure

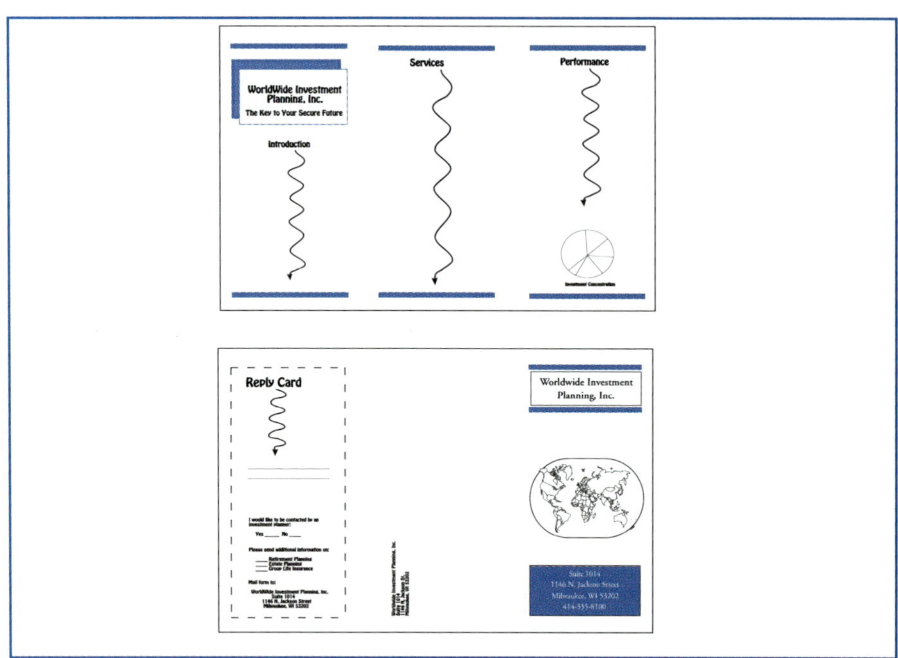

Format a Brochure

Before beginning to create a brochure in WordPerfect, it is a good idea to create a mock-up—a hand-drawn representation of how the final brochure will look. From the mock-up you can decide on the paper orientation (landscape or portrait), number of columns, margins, types of borders to be used, where graphic images will be placed, and what special effects will be used. The mock-up can also show where text will be placed in each column (see Figure 17.1).

One of the first decisions that must be made is what paper orientation will be used—portrait or landscape. Until now, all of the documents that have been created in this book have used portrait orientation (e.g., 8.5 inches by 11 inches). WordPerfect can also be used to create documents using landscape orientation (11 inches by 8.5 inches) See Figure 17.2. When landscape orientation is selected, WordPerfect automatically rotates text when the document is printed so that text prints horizontally in relation to the long (11-inch) side of the page.

Once a decision has been made on the paper orientation, the number of columns is set. For example, if a tri-fold mailer is to be created, three columns are set. Margins can also be set. Small margins generally are used so that as much information as possible can be placed on the page. If a laser printer will be used to print the brochure, margins greater than .25 inches are used because the printer cannot place text closer than about ¼ of an inch from the edges of the page. (Note: The area that cannot be printed varies from printer to printer but generally a .25-inch margin can be used.)

To enhance the appearance of a brochure, the color of graphic lines and borders, page borders, and text can be changed. If a color printer is available, WordPerfect can print text, graphic images, and graphic lines and borders in the specified color. Any Windows-supported color printer can be used (e.g., HP Deskjet 500C Series, IBM Color Printer, and HP Paintjet XL).

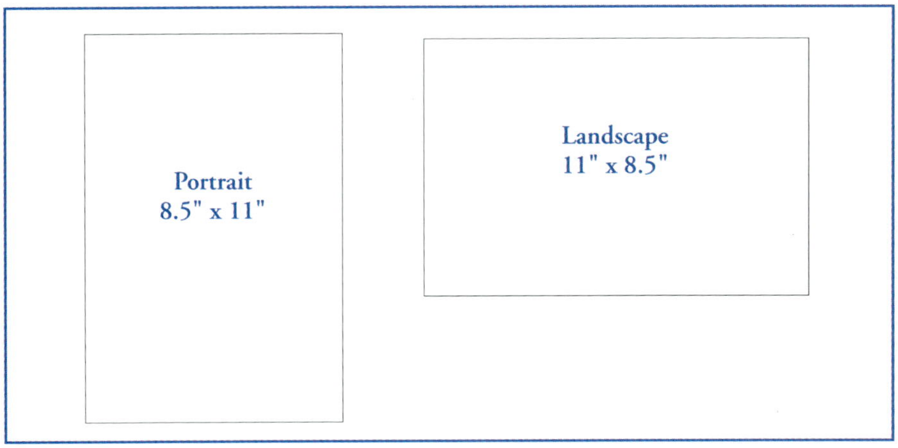

Portrait
8.5" x 11"

Landscape
11" x 8.5"

FIGURE 17.2

Portrait and landscape orientation

Start-Up Instructions

- An empty document window should be displayed. If necessary, select the **New Document** button to obtain an empty document window.
- Set the left and right margins to .35"; set the top and bottom margins to .75".

Create Landscape Layout

1. Select Layout, Page {Alt, L, p}.
2. Select Paper Size {s}.

   Note: The Paper Size dialog box displays.
3. Scroll down the list of paper definitions to display Letter Landscape. Double-click on Letter Landscape {press the down arrow key to highlight Letter Landscape, Enter}.

   *Note: No change displays on the screen. However, if Reveal Codes is turned on, a Paper Sz/Typ code displays. If the red or shaded block is moved to the left of the Paper Sz/Typ code, the expanded code **Paper Sz/Typ: 11" by 8.5": Letter Landscape** displays.*

Finish-Up Instructions

- Use the Columns Define button, select **Define** and set the number of columns to **3** and the spacing between columns to .7".
- Use the filename **17drill1.lan** and save the file.

Chapter 17 Use Special Desktop Publishing Features

Create a Shadow Box

The shadow box special effect is created by choosing the **Customize Style** option in the Box Border/Fill Styles dialog box and selecting the desired drop shadow type. The color and width of the shadow can be changed if desired. Another special effect changes the corners of a graphic box from square to rounded. When rounded corners are used, the radius of the curve can be set; the corners become more circular as the radius increases.

Start-Up Instructions

- The file named **17drill1.lan** should be displayed in the document window.

Steps to Create a Shadow Box

1. Select the **Text Box** button on the Button Bar {Alt, g, t}.
2. Select the **Size** button on the Graphics Box Feature Bar {Alt and Shift and s}.
3. In the Width area, double-click in the **Set** box and type the desired width for the graphic box {Alt and s, type desired width}.

   For example, type **3**.
4. In the Height area, select the **Set** option and type the desired height of the graphic box {Alt and e, type desired height}.

   For example, type **1.5**.
5. Select **OK** {Enter}.
6. Select the **Border/Fill** button on the Graphics Box Feature Bar {Alt and Shift and b}.
7. Select the **Border Style** button and choose the desired border style {Alt and b, Spacebar, press the arrow keys to select desired border style, Enter}.

   For example, select the **Thick** single border style (the fourth button in the first row).
8. Select **Customize Style** {c}.

   Note: The Customize Border dialog box displays.
9. In the Drop Shadow area, select the **Type** button {y, Spacebar}.

   Note: A palette of drop shadow types displays.
10. Select the desired drop shadow type {press the up or down arrow key to select the desired drop shadow type, Enter}.

    For example, select the ■ drop shadow type.

Change Color of the Drop Shadow Box

11. In the Drop Shadow area, select the **Color** button {c, Spacebar}.
12. Click on the desired color {press the arrow keys to select the desired color, Enter}.

    For example, select the **royal blue** color in the first row.

Change Color of Graphic Box Border

13. In the Change Color area, select the **Border Color** box {b, Spacebar}.
14. Click on the desired color {press the arrow keys to select the desired color, Enter}.

    For example, select the **royal blue** color in the first row.
15. Select **OK** twice {Enter, Tab, Enter}.

Place Text in the Shadow Box

16. With the insertion point displayed in the shadow box, type and format the desired text.

For example,

a. Change the font to **Arrus BT** and **Bold**.

b. Type and center the following:
WorldWide Investment Planning, Inc. (Press **Enter** twice.)
The Key to Your Secure Future

c. Select the words **WorldWide Investment Planning, Inc.** and change the point size to **14 point**.

Note: If the insertion point is not displayed in the shadow box, move the mouse pointer inside the shadow box and click once to select the box. Click the ***right*** *mouse button and choose* ***Edit Text*** *from the QuickMenu.*

Finish-Up Instructions

- Move the mouse pointer away from the shadow box and click once to deselect the box.
- Use the same filename, **17drill1.lan**, and save the file.

Insert Previously Created Text into a Document or Graphic Box

Text that has been previously created and saved can be inserted into a document or graphic box. When a previously saved file is inserted into a document or graphic box, the original text file remains untouched and a copy of the text is placed into the document or graphic box. The copy of the text can be formatted and changed as desired. Formatting or editing the text that has been inserted into a document or graphic box does not affect the original text file.

Text is inserted into a document by using the **Insert File** command and choosing the desired file. The **Insert File** command is very useful if several people are creating text files that will be combined to create a final document. For example, each person might create a different portion of a brochure. When all the sections are complete, the **Insert File** command can be used to place each text file into the brochure document.

Another method to insert previously created text into a graphic box is to select the **Content** button on the Graphics Box Feature Bar, type or select the desired filename, and choose **OK**.

Start-Up Instructions

- The file named **17drill1.lan** should be displayed in the document window.
- The insertion point should be located below the shadow box in the first column.

Insert Previously Created Text into a Document or Graphic Box

1. Select **Insert, File** {Alt, i, i}.
2. Type or select the location and name of the desired file.

   For example, select the file named **17drill1.co1** located on the data disk.
3. Select **Insert** {Enter}.
4. Select **Yes** to the message "Insert file into current document?" {y}.

   *Note: The text contained in the file named **17drill1.co1** displays in the first column of the document.*

Finish-Up Instructions

- Move the insertion point below the last line of text in the first column.
- Press **Ctrl** and **Enter** to insert a hard column break and move the insertion point to the top of the second column.
- Repeat steps 1–4 of the Steps to Insert Previously Created Text into a Document or Graphic Box and insert the file named **17drill1.co2** located on the data disk.
- Move the insertion point below the last line of text in the second column.
- Press **Ctrl** and **Enter** to insert a hard column break and move the insertion point to the top of the third column.
- Repeat steps 1–4 of the Steps to Insert Previously Created Text into a Document or Graphic Box and insert the file named **17drill1.co3** located on the data disk.
- Use the *new* filename **17drill1.pg1** and save the file.

Insert a Lotus PIC File into a Graphic Box

Graphic images created in many different programs can be retrieved into graphic boxes. For example, a graph created in Lotus 1-2-3 (filename extension *.pic*) or a drawing created in PC Paintbrush (filename extension *.pcx*) can be retrieved into a graphic box and placed in a WordPerfect document.

When a graphic image saved in a format other than WordPerfect's graphic format (filename extension *.wpg*) is retrieved, WordPerfect converts the image to the *.wpg* format so that the graphic image can be placed in a WordPerfect document. Although WordPerfect can convert graphic images created in many different graphic programs, some of the original colors, shading, fonts, or other attributes may not be converted precisely as they appear in the original image.

Captions can be added to graphic boxes. WordPerfect automatically inserts a figure or box number when a caption is created. The figure or box number can be deleted, if desired, by pressing the **Backspace** key once. The default position for the caption is at the bottom and outside the border of the graphic box. However, if desired, the position of the caption can be changed by selecting the **Caption** button on the Graphics Box Feature Bar and choosing a different caption position.

Start-Up Instructions

- The file named **17drill1.pg1** should be displayed in the document window.
- The insertion point should be located in the blank line below the last line of text in the third column.

Insert a Figure Box Containing a Lotus PIC File

1. Select the **Figure** button on the Button Bar {Alt, g, f}.
2. Click on the down arrow located to the right of the List Files of Type box {Alt and t, press the down arrow key to display the list of file types}.
3. Scroll up or down the list of file types until the desired file type displays. Click on the desired file type {press the up or down arrow key to highlight the desired file type, Enter}.

   For example, scroll up the list of file types until Lotus PIC (*.pic) displays. Click on the **Lotus PIC (*.pic)** file type.
4. If necessary, click in the Drives box and click on the drive letter where the desired file is located {Alt and v, press the arrow keys to highlight drive letter, Enter}.

   For example, if necessary, click in the Drives box and click on the drive letter where the data disk is located.
5. Double-click on the desired filename {Alt and n, Tab, press the arrow keys to highlight the desired filename, Enter}.

   For example, double-click on the file named **17pie.pic**.

Remove the Figure Box Border

6. If necessary, move the mouse pointer inside the graphic box and click once to select the graphic box {Alt, g, e, Enter}.

   For example, if necessary, move the mouse pointer inside the graphic box containing the *17pie.pic* graphic image and click once.
7. Select the **Border/Fill** button on the Graphics Box Feature Bar {Alt and Shift and b}.
8. Select the **Border Style** button and click on NO BORDER {Alt and b, Spacebar, press the arrow keys to select the NO BORDER style, Enter}.
9. Select **OK** {Enter}.

Create a Caption for a Graphic Box

10. Select the **Caption** button on the Graphics Box Feature Bar {Alt and Shift and a}.

    Note: The Box Caption dialog box displays.
11. Select the **Edit** button {Alt and e}.

    Note: The words "Figure 1" display below the graphic box containing the Lotus PIC file. The insertion point is located at the right of the number 1.

12. Type and format the caption information.

For example:

a. Press the **Backspace** key once to remove the word and number "Figure 1."

b. Change the font to **Arrus BT, 10 point**.

c. Type and center **Investment Concentration**.

Finish-Up Instructions

- Move the mouse pointer away from the graphic box containing the pie chart and click once to deselect the box.
- Save the file again using the same filename, **17drill1.pg1**.

Scale a Graphic Image Within a Graphic Box

The size of a graphic image within a graphic box can be scaled (enlarged or reduced) by using the scaling tools available on the Image Tools palette. When the Scale button is selected, the scaling tools display. The first scaling tool is used to enlarge a selected portion of the graphic image to fill the graphic box. The second scaling tool is used to enlarge or reduce the entire graphic image. The third scaling tool is used to return or reset the graphic image to its original size within the graphic box.

Start-Up Instructions

- The file named **17drill1.pgl** should be displayed in the document window.
- The Graphics Box Feature Bar should be displayed. If necessary, move the mouse pointer inside any graphic box and click once. Click the *right* mouse button once and choose the **Feature Bar** option on the Graphics QuickMenu.

Scale a Graphic Image Within a Graphic Box

Note: *The following steps require a mouse.*

1. Move the mouse pointer inside the graphic box containing the graphic image to be scaled (enlarged or reduced) and click once to select the graphic box.

   For example, move the mouse pointer inside the graphic box containing the *17pie.pic* graphic image and click once.

2. Select the Tools button on the Graphics Box Feature Bar.

   Note: *The Image Tools palette displays beside the selected graphic box.*

3. Select the Scale button on the Image Tools palette.

   Note: *Three scaling tools display beside the Scale button.*

4. Select the desired scaling tool.

   For example, select the scaling tool.

Note: A scroll bar displays to the right of the selected graphic box. Scroll up to reduce the graphic image and scroll down to enlarge the graphic image.

5. Scroll up or down the scaling scroll bar to enlarge or reduce the graphic image.

   For example, scroll down the scaling scroll bar to enlarge the graphic image so that the image fills the graphic box.

   Note: If the image becomes too large, scroll up the scaling scroll bar to reduce the size of the image.

6. When the graphic image is the desired size, move the mouse pointer away from the graphic box and click once to deselect the box.

   Note: The Image Tools palette and scaling scroll bar are removed from the screen.

Finish-Up Instructions

- Save the file again using the same filename, **17drill1.pg1**.
- If desired, print one copy.

Use Advance to Position Text

The Advance feature is used to position text at a specific location on the page or within a graphic box. The position of the text can be measured vertically and/or horizontally either from the location of the insertion point or from the top and/or left edge of the page. The Advance feature is used instead of pressing the Enter, Spacebar, or Tab keys to change the location of the text.

Start-Up Instructions

- The file named **17drill1.pg1** should be displayed in the document window.

Use Advance to Vertically Position Text

1. Place the insertion point to the left of the first character in the text to be positioned.

   For example, press **Ctrl** and **Home** to place the insertion point at the beginning of the document.

2. Select **Layout, Typesetting** {Alt, L, t}.

3. Select **Advance** {a}.

   Note: The Advance dialog box displays.

4. In the Vertical Position box, select the **Up from Insertion Point, Down from Insertion Point,** or **From Top of Page** option.

   For example, select **From Top of Page** {t}.

5. Double-click in the Vertical Distance box and type the number of inches or fraction of inches that the text should be moved from the insertion point or top of the page {v, type the amount the text should be moved}.

   For example, type **1.25**. (Do not type the final period.)

Chapter 17 Use Special Desktop Publishing Features

6. Select **OK** {Enter}.

Finish-Up Instructions

- Place the insertion point to the left of the S in the word "Services" at the top of the second column.
- Repeat steps 2–6 to advance the text from the top of the page 1.25".
- Place the insertion point to the left of the P in the word "Performance" at the top of the third column.
- Repeat steps 2–6 to advance the text from the top of the page 1.25".
- Use the same filename, **17drill1.pg1**, and save the file again.

Start-Up Instructions

- The file named **17drill1.pg1** should be displayed in the document window.
- Place the insertion point below the graphic box containing the pie chart in the third column.

Create Page Two of the Brochure

1. If desired, select the **Page Zoom Full** button so that the entire page can be viewed {Alt, v, z, f, Enter}.
2. Press **Ctrl** and **Enter** to move the insertion point to the top of the first column on page two.

   Note: Col 1 and Pg 2 display in the Status bar.

Finish-Up Instructions

- Use the *new* filename **17drill1.pg2** and save the file.

Create a Dashed Box for a Tear Sheet

1. Select the **Text Box** button on the Button Bar {Alt, g, t}.
2. Select the **Border/Fill** button on the Graphics Box Feature Bar {Alt and Shift and b}.
3. Select the **Border Style** button and click on **Dashed Border** style (first button in the second row) {Alt and b, Spacebar, press the arrow keys to highlight the desired border style, Enter}.
4. Select **OK** {Enter}.
5. Select the **Size** button on the Graphics Box Feature Bar {Alt and Shift and s}.
6. In the Width area, double-click in the Set box and type the desired box width {Alt and s, type desired width}.

   For example, type **3**.
7. In the Height area, select **Full** {Alt and u}.
8. Select **OK** {Enter}.

9. Select **OK** in response to the message *If you change the box size to "Full." the box placement will change to "Page."* {Enter}.

   Note: *The dashed box is moved to the right column. That's OK. The next steps will select the correct position for the graphic box.*

10. Select the **Position** button on the Graphics Box Feature Bar {Alt and Shift and p}.
11. In the Horizontal area, move the mouse pointer to the box located to the right of the word "from." Press and hold the mouse button and drag to highlight **Left Margin**. Release the mouse button {Alt and L, Tab twice, press the Spacebar, press the up arrow key to highlight Left Margin, Enter}.
12. Select **OK** {Enter}.

Finish-Up Instructions

- Insert the text file named **17drill1.co4** located on the data disk into the dashed graphic box (with the insertion point located in the dashed graphic box, select **Insert**, **File**, type the name and location of the file, select **Insert**, **Yes**).

  Note: *If necessary, see the Steps to Insert Previously Created Text into a Document or Graphic Box on page 410.*

- Move the mouse pointer away from the graphic box and click once to deselect the graphic box.
- Use the same filename, **17drill1.pg2**, and save the file.

Rotate Text and Reverse Text

Two special effects that can be created using WordPerfect are rotated text and reversed text. WordPerfect can rotate text in 90 degree increments (e.g., 90, 180, or 270 degrees). In order to rotate text, the text must be placed in a graphic box.

Reversed text (white text on a dark background) is accomplished by choosing a black or dark, solid fill for a graphic box, changing the color of the text to white, and typing the desired text. Reversed text is also referred to as "reversed type" or "reverses."

If Windows System Colors are used to display text and other items on the screen, the white text will continue to display as black in the document window. However, when the document is printed, the text will be white. To determine whether Windows System Colors are being used to display text and other items, select **File**, **Preferences**, double-click on **Display**. In the Show area, check to see if Windows System Colors is selected (an X displays beside a selected option). If desired, click on the Windows System Colors options to deselect. Select **OK**, **Close** to return to the document window.

Start-Up Instructions

- The file named **17drill1.pg2** should be displayed in the document window.
- The insertion point should be located at the top of the second column on page 2.

Steps to Create Rotated Text

1. Select **Graphics, Custom Box, User, OK** {Alt, g, c, press the up or down arrow key to highlight User, Enter}.
2. Select the **Position** button on the Graphics Box Feature Bar {Alt and Shift and p}.
3. In the Box Placement area, select **Put Box on Current Page (Page Anchor)** {p}.
4. In the Horizontal area, select **Across Columns** {r}.
5. Double-click in the **Across Columns** box and type the number of the column in which the graphic box should be placed {Tab, type column number}.

   For example, type **2** and check that 2 displays in the "through" box.
6. Move the mouse pointer to the box located below the Across Columns option and to the right of the word "from." Press and hold the mouse button and drag to highlight **Left Edge of Column**. Release the mouse button {Alt and a, Tab, Spacebar, press the up arrow key to highlight Left Edge of Column, Enter}.
7. In the Vertical area, move the mouse pointer to the box located to the right of the word "from." Press and hold the mouse button and drag to highlight the desired vertical position for the graphic box {Alt and c, Tab, Spacebar, press the up or down arrow key to highlight desired position, Enter}.

   For example, select **Bottom Margin**.
8. Select **OK** {Enter}.
9. Select the **Size** button on the Graphics Box Feature Bar {Alt and Shift and s}.
10. In the Width area, double-click in the **Set** box and type the desired width of the graphic box {Alt and s, type desired width}.

    For example, type **1.5**.
11. Select **OK** {Enter}.
12. Select the **Content** button on the Graphics Box Feature Bar {Alt and Shift and o}.

    Note: *The Box Contents dialog box displays.*
13. Move the mouse pointer to the **Content** box, press and hold the mouse button, and drag to highlight **Text**. Release the mouse button {c, Spacebar, press the down arrow key to highlight Text, Enter}.
14. In the Rotate Contents Counterclockwise area, select the desired rotation.

    For example, select **90 Degrees** {Alt and 9}.
15. Select **Edit** {e}.

    Note: *The Text Box Editor window displays. If necessary, select the* ***Zoom*** *button on the Power Bar and choose* ***100%****.*
16. Type and format the desired text.

    For example:

    a. Change the font to **Arrus BT, 10 point**.

    b. Type the following:

WorldWide Investment Planning, Inc.
Suite 1014
1146 N. Jackson St.
Milwaukee, WI 53202

17. Select the **Close** button {Alt and Shift and c}.

Note: The text is rotated in the document window.

Finish-Up Instructions

- Use the *new* filename **17drill1.rot** and save the file.

Start-Up Instructions

- The file named **17drill1.rot** should be displayed in the document window.
- Press **Ctrl** and **Enter** to move the insertion point to the top of the third column on page two.

Steps to Create the Front Panel of the Brochure

1. Select the **Text Box** button on the Button Bar {Alt, g, t}.
2. Type and format the desired text.

   For example:

   a. Change the font to **Arrus BT, Bold, 14 point.**

   b. Type and center the following:
   WorldWide Investment Planning, Inc.
3. Select the **Size** button on the Graphics Box Feature Bar {Alt and Shift and s}.
4. In the Width area, double-click in the **Set** box and type the desired width for the graphic box {Alt and s, type desired width}.

   For example, type **3.**
5. Select **OK** {Enter}.
6. Select the **Border/Fill** button on the Graphics Box Feature Bar {Alt and Shift and b}.
7. Select **Customize Style** {c}.
8. In the Change Color area, select the **Border Color** button {b, Spacebar}.
9. Select the desired color {press the arrow keys to select the desired color, Enter}.

   For example, select the **royal blue** color in the first row.
10. Select **OK** twice {Enter, Enter}.
11. Move the mouse pointer below the graphic box and click once to deselect the box {Alt and Shift and c}.

Import a Graphic Image

12. Select the **Figure** button on the Button Bar {Alt, g, f}.

13. If necessary, click in the Drives box and click on the drive letter where the *wpwin60* directory is located. Also, if necessary, select the *graphics* subdirectory in the Directories box.

14. Double-click on the desired graphic filename.

    For example, double-click on **world.wpg**.

Create Rounded Corners for a Graphic Box Border

15. Select the **Border/Fill** button on the Graphics Box Feature Bar {Alt and Shift and b}.

16. Select **Customize Style** {c}.

17. In the Corners area, click on the **Square Corners** option to deselect the option {q}.

    Note: An X no longer displays in the Square Corners option box.

18. Click on the up triangle to the right of the Radius box to increase the amount the corners are rounded {d, press the up arrow key to increase the amount the corners are rounded}.

    For example, click on the up triangle until **.500** displays.

    Note: The sample border in the Customize border dialog box changes to an oval shape as the up triangle is selected.

19. Select **OK** twice {Enter, Enter}.

20. Select the **Position** button on the Graphics Box Feature Bar {Alt and Shift and p}.

21. In the Box Placement area, select **Put Box on Current Page (Page Anchor)** {p}.

22. In the Vertical area, double-click in the **Place** box and type **0** (zero) {Alt and c, type 0}.

23. In the Vertical area, move the mouse pointer to the box located to the right of the word "from." Press and hold the mouse button and drag to highlight the desired vertical position. Release the mouse button {Tab, Spacebar, press the arrow keys to highlight the desired vertical position, Enter}.

    For example, select **Center of Margins**.

24. Select OK {Enter}.

25. Select the Size button on the Graphics Box Feature Bar {Alt and Shift and s}.

26. In the Width area, double-click in the Set box and type the desired box width {Alt and s, type desired width}.

    For example, type **3**.

27. Select **OK** {Enter}.

28. Move the mouse pointer away from the graphic box and click once to deselect the box {Alt and Shift and c}.

Finish-Up Instructions

- Save the file again using the same filename, **17drill1.rot**.

Start-Up Instructions

- The file named **17drill1.rot** should be displayed in the document window.
- Locate the insertion point below the graphic box containing the *world.wpg* graphic image. (If necessary, press the **Enter** key several times to locate the insertion point below the graphic box.)

Steps to Create Reversed Text

1. Select the **Text Box** button on the Button Bar {Alt, g, t}.
2. Select the **Border/Fill** button on the Graphics Box Feature Bar {Alt and Shift and b}.
3. Select the **Border Style** button and click on the desired border style {Alt and b, Spacebar, press the arrow keys to select the desired border style, Enter}.

   For example, select NO BORDER.
4. Select the **Fill Style** button and click on the desired fill style {Alt and f, Spacebar, press the arrow keys to select the desired fill style, Enter}.

   For example, click on the **solid fill** style (100% Fill) in the second row.
5. Select the **Foreground** button and choose the desired foreground color {r, Spacebar, press the arrow keys to select the desired color, Enter}.

   For example, select the **royal blue** color in the first row.
6. Select **OK** {Enter}.
7. Type and format the desired text.

   For example:

   a. Select **Layout, Font.** In the Color Options area, select the **Color** button and click on the white square at the end of the first row {Alt, L, f, Alt and L, Spacebar, press the arrow keys to select the desired color, Enter}. Change the font to **Arrus BT, Bold, 12 point.** Select **OK.**

   Note: If the message box displays regarding the text color change, select OK. *The text will display as black type, but will print white.*

   b. Type and center the following:

   Suite 1014
   1146 N. Jackson Street
   Milwaukee, WI 53202
   414-555-8100
8. Select the **Position** button on the Graphics Box Feature Bar {Alt and Shift and p}.
9. In the Box Placement area, select **Put Box on Current Page (Page Anchor)** {p}.
10. In the the Vertical area, double-click in the **Place** box and type **0** (zero) {Alt and c, type 0}.
11. In the Vertical area, move the mouse pointer to the box located to the right of the word "from." Press and hold the mouse button and drag to highlight the desired position. Release the mouse button {Tab, Spacebar, press the arrow keys to highlight the desired position, Enter}.

For example, select **Bottom Margin.**

12. Select **OK** {Enter}.
13. Select the **Size** button on the Graphics Box Feature Bar {Alt and Shift and s}.
14. In the Width area, double-click in the **Set** box and type the desired box width {Alt and s, type desired width}.

    For example, type **3.**

15. Select **OK** {Enter}.

Finish-Up Instructions

- Move the mouse pointer away from the graphic box and click once to deselect the box.
- Use the *new* filename **17drill1.fin** and save the document.

Start-Up Instructions

- The file named **17drill1.fin** should be displayed in the document window.
- The insertion point should be located at the top of the document. If necessary, press **Ctrl** and **Home** to move the insertion point to the top of the document.

Create a Page Border and Change the Border Color

1. Select **Layout, Page, Border/Fill** {Alt, L, p, b}.
2. Select the **Border Style** button {Alt and b, Spacebar}.
3. Select the desired border style {press the arrow keys to select the desired border style, Enter}.

    For example, select the **Thick Top/Bottom** border style (the sixth button in the second row).

4. To place the page border on the current (first) page only, check that an X displays beside the **Apply border to current page only** option. If necessary, select the **Apply border to current page only** option {Alt and p}.

Change the Border Color

5. Select **Customize Style** {c}.
6. In the Change Color area, select the **Border Color** button {b, Spacebar}.
7. Select the desired color {press the arrow keys to select the desired color, Enter}.

    For example, select the **royal blue** color in the first row.

8. Select **OK** twice {Enter, Enter}.

Finish-Up Instructions

- Use the same filename **17drill1.fin** and save the document.
- Print one copy of the tri-fold mailer brochure. Your final brochure should look similar to the tri-fold mailer shown on page 421.

WorldWide Investment Planning, Inc.

The Key to Your Secure Future

For over 25 years, WorldWide Investment Planning, Inc., has assisted individuals in developing a secure and prosperous financial future through sound investments.

WorldWide Investment Planning, Inc., strives to uphold a long tradition of superior quality investment opportunities for our clients. Our investments are high quality, widely diversified, and have good call protection—all key factors in sound risk management.

WorldWide Investment Planning, Inc., has over $3.5 billion in assets. The pre-tax return on assets for the last three years has averaged 8.95 percent.

Services

WorldWide Investment Planning, Inc., provides services to meet the needs of each individual.

- ✓ Retirement Planning
  - ✓ Tax-deferred annuities and pension plans
  - ✓ Pension administration for small businesses and individuals
- ✓ Estate Planning
  - ✓ Living trusts
  - ✓ Trust funds
  - ✓ Transfer of family business assets
- ✓ Group Life Insurance

WorldWide Investment Planning, Inc., also provides a quarterly newsletter, *The Investment Report*, to keep our clients informed about investment opportunities and economic conditions that may affect their investments.

Performance

The management of WorldWide Investment Planning, Inc., constantly monitors the economic conditions around the world to ensure the best protection for our clients' investments. Currently, approximately 30 percent of our investments are in North America, 22 percent in Europe, 34 percent in the Pacific Rim, and 11 percent in Central and South America.

Our firm invests in a wide variety of products, industries, and services including banking, capital equipment, real estate, and investment-quality bonds.

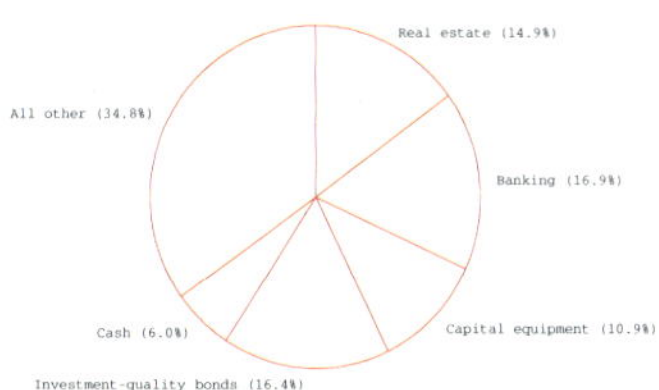

Investment Concentration

To receive additional information about WorldWide Investment Planning, Inc., or to be contacted by an investment planner, please complete and return this form.

Name ______________________

Address ______________________

City __________ State ____ Zip ____

Phone ______________________

I would like to be contacted by an investment planner:

Yes ______ No ______

Please send additional information on:

____ Retirement Planning

____ Estate Planning

____ Group Life Insurance

Mail form to:

WorldWide Investment Planning, Inc.
Suite 1014
1146 N. Jackson Street
Milwaukee, WI 53202

WorldWide Investment Planning, Inc.
Suite 1014
1146 N. Jackson St.
Milwaukee, WI 53202

WorldWide Investment Planning, Inc.

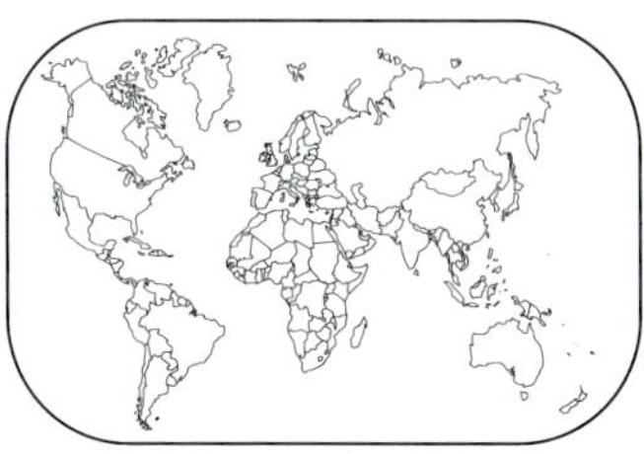

Suite 1014
1146 N. Jackson Street
Milwaukee, WI 53202
414-555-8100

Chapter 17
Use Special Desktop Publishing Features

The Next Step

Chapter Review and Activities

Self-Check Quiz

T F 1. Information is printed on both sides of a tri-fold mailer brochure.

T F 2. When text is printed in landscape layout, the top of the page is the 11-inch side.

T F 3. Previously created text can be inserted into a document, but cannot be inserted into a graphic box.

T F 4. The horizontal position of a graphic box can be specified; however, the vertical position cannot be changed.

T F 5. The corners of a graphic box can be changed from square to rounded.

6. WordPerfect can rotate text in ________.
   a. 10-degree increments
   b. 45-degree increments
   c. 90-degree increments
   d. 30-degree increments

7. To insert existing text into a document, select ______, **File**, type or select the name and location of the desired file, and choose **Insert**.
   a. **Insert**
   b. **Open**
   c. **File**
   d. **Window**

8. Instead of pressing the Enter, Spacebar, or Tab keys, the _____________ feature can be used to position text.

9. Create the shadow box effect by selecting **Customize Style** in the Box Border and Fill Styles dialog box, selecting the _____ option, and choosing the desired shadow type.

10. List the steps to create a caption for a graphic box.

Enriching Language Arts Skills

Spelling/Vocabulary Words

brochure a small pamphlet, leaflet.

paramedic person with medical training who responds to medical emergencies or assists physicians.

typography a description of the features of a place or region; the art of graphically representing the physical features of a place or region.

Parentheses

Parentheses can be used to set off nonessential expressions that might otherwise confuse the reader. The information within the parentheses provides supplemental information that has no direct bearing on the main idea of the sentence or paragraph. Words, phrases, or clauses can be enclosed within parentheses. Unless a comma, colon, or semicolon is necessary to the text within the parentheses, place the punctuation outside the closing parenthesis. If the text within the parentheses is a complete sentence, the final period is placed within the parentheses.

Examples:

The actual gross sales for the quarter were $1,050,000 (compared with projected sales of $795,000).

If you are planning to attend the next sales conference (March 5), please contact the travel department immediately.

Several staff members will attend the sales conference next month. (The conference will be held in Hawaii.)

Activities

Activity 17.1—Create a Tri-Fold Mailer Brochure

1. Use the skills learned in this chapter and the following information to create the tri-fold mailer brochure shown on page 424.

   a. Change the paper orientation to **Letter Landscape** (select **Layout**, **Page**, **Paper Size**, double-click on **Letter Landscape**).

   b. Set the left and right margins to **.3"**. Set the top and bottom margins to **.75"**. Set the number of columns to three and the spacing between columns to **.6"**.

   c. Set the width of graphic boxes to **3"** and make decisions on colors for graphic lines, borders, and shadow boxes.

   d. The text for each column has been created and saved on the data disk. Insert the following text files into the appropriate columns or graphic boxes:

Column 1	**17act1.co1**
Column 2	**17act1.co2**
Column 3	**17act1.co3**
Column 1, page 2	**17act1.co4**

   e. In the second column on the second page, set the graphic box to a width of **1.5"**. Rotate the text 90 degrees.

   f. The graphic file in the third column of the second page is named **skipper.wpg** and is usually located in the *wp60win\graphics* directory.

Small Business Owners Forum

Fall Series

Nine years ago, the Small Business Owners Forum was developed to provide an information resource for local small businesses. The forum provides a setting in which valuable business relationships can be developed and information on common problems can be shared.

This fall's Forum series, entitled ***Personal Development: Focus and Flexibility—Keys to Success***, will address many of the most challenging issues faced by small business owners including:

- Defining and focusing on objectives
- Meeting ever-changing economic and business challenges
- Turning failures into successes
- Finding the tools and resources needed to succeed

IF AT FIRST. . .

Learning to create new successes from past mistakes

October 8, 199x
Woodridge Clubhouse
3300 Woodridge Road
7:00 - 9:00 p.m.

Find reserves of energy, courage, and brilliance you never knew you possessed. Sharpen your focus and jump-start your motivation. Develop the skills to maintain your enthusiasm and motivation through the difficult times.

A panel of several local small business people will share their actual "near death" business experiences and recoveries. They will explain how it is that our attitude is often our biggest enemy or largest asset.

The panel moderator will be Deirdre Sacks, Vencon Technologies. Ms. Sacks will share management tips on how to turn around an ailing business and implement strategies for greater success.

AM I THERE YET?

Learn how to stay focused when all else is chaos

November 12, 199x
Woodridge Clubhouse
3300 Woodridge Road
7:00 - 9:00 p.m.

Phone calls, customer demands, employee problems—how do you cope? To find out, we have assembled a panel of local business people who know firsthand how to prioritize, organize, delegate, and SUCCEED.

Sheila Craighead, president of First Progressive Bank and chairperson of the Belle Mead Chamber of Commerce, will share with us how she keeps everything going.

Alfredo Belli, a customer relations consultant and owner of Belli Consultants, will share with us the common "success" traits.

Lucille Nugent, managing partner of Nugent, Dunkle, and Ponte, CPAs, works daily with owners of medium and small businesses. Nugent built her own successful business after overcoming several potentially lethal business circumstances.

Small Business Owners Forum
Registration

I plan to attend the following session(s):

____ October 8, 199x

____ November 12, 199x

Cost: $15.00 per session

Name: ____________________

Company: ____________________

Address: ____________________

City/State/Zip: ____________________

Phone: ____________________

Make check payable to:

Belle Mead Chamber of Commerce

and mail to:

1428 Township Line Road
Belle Mead, NJ 08502

Belle Mead Chamber of Commerce
1428 Township Line Road
Belle Mead, NJ 08502

Small Business Owners Forum

Fall Series

1428 Township Line Road
Belle Mead, NJ 08502
201-555-3400

2. Use the filename **17act1.fin** and save the final brochure.
3. Print one copy.
4. Close the document.

Challenge Your Skills

Skill 17.1—Create a Tri-Fold Mailer Brochure

1. Use the following information to create the tri-fold mailer brochure shown on page 426.
   a. Make decisions regarding:
      Margins
      Number of columns
      Color and shading for borders/lines and shadow
      Corners for shadow box and other graphic boxes
      Font sizes for text
   b. The graphic image is named **buck.wpg** and is usually located in the *wp60win\graphics* directory.
   c. The text for columns 1, 2, 3, and 4 are saved on the data disk under the filenames **17skill1.co1**, **17skill1.co2**, **17skill1.co3**, and **17skill1.co4**.

   Hint: *Retrieve, size, and position the* ***buck.wpg*** *graphic image in the third column of page one before inserting the text file. The height of the graphic box containing the* ***buck.wpg*** *graphic image should be approximately 1.5".*
2. Correct three spelling and one parentheses error.
3. Use the filename **17skill1.fin** and save the file.
4. Print one copy.
5. If you have completed your work in WordPerfect, exit the program.

Deer Haven—Douglas County Fire Protection District

Board of Directors

Robert Bradley, Chairperson
Vivian Baker
Terry Eliasen
Elena Morgan
Danny Griffin

Fire Chief

Arthur Bischoff

The District

The district serves all of Douglas County, an area of nearly 100 square miles. The population is approximately 20,000.

The district operates four fire stations, two of which are staffed by career personnel. Station 24 in Minden is staffed by a Captain and an Engineer assigned to Engine 24. Station 23 in Gardnerville is staffed by two Firefighters/ Paramedics assigned to Medic 23. Stations 25 and 26 in Genoa and Zephyr Cove, respectively, are staffed by volunteer personnel.

The district owns and operates four fire engines, one truck, one squad, one water tender, and one medic unit.

Insurance Service Office Rates the District

The district has received a new rating from the Insurance Service Office, which rates fire departments for insurance companies. We were previously rated as a 5 (on a scale of 1 to 10, 1 being the best for structures within 1,000 feet of a hydrant and 8 for structures farther than 1,000 feet from a hydrant. The new rating is 3 for structures within 1,000 feet of a hydrant and 5 for structures farther than 1,000 feet from a hydrant. This could mean a reduced insurance premium if your insurance company uses the ISO rating schedule.

Questions? Comments?

The Deer Haven Fire Protection District Board of Directors meets at 7:00 p.m. on the second Wednesday of each month at Station 24 in Minden. The public is encouraged to attend.

We welcome any comments/suggestions you may have. We can be contacted at the address and phone number listed on the front of this broshure.

New Engine in Service in Minden

Last year we purchased a new fire engine to be assigned at Minden Station 24.

The engine was placed in service at the end of the 1993 fire season. It was built by Hi Tech Fire Apparatus in Oakdale. The new machine features a 1,500 gallon per minute pump and all the tools necessary to combat structural and wildland fires. We feel it is an excellent addition to our organization.

The engine is different from what you might see on a city street. As you are well aware, the layout and topografy of the Deer Haven Fire Protection District offer many challenges to large trucks such as fire engines. The new engine is considerably shorter than most structural fire engines and features higher angles of approach and departure to accommodate our rough and narrow roads.

The new engine with its tools and equipment represents a $250,000 investment. We saved for a long time and paid for it in cash.

A Message from Medic 23

Two of the four firefighters on duty each day are Firefighters/Parimedics assigned to Medic 23 at Station 23.

Medic 23 is part of the Douglas County Emergency Medical System funded by County Service Area 16. Currently, there are six primary response medic units in service. All are operated by fire districts, and each district hires paramedics off a common hiring list.

Firefighters/Paramedics in the Service Area 16 system all have at least one year of paramedic experience prior to coming to Douglas County. Almost all come from areas that have very high call volumes.

Our system allows our medics to serve a dual role as firefighters. With the ability to use paramedics in any situation to which we respond, the public gets the most for its tax dollar.

Most of us came here to be part of the Douglas County community. We have chosen to live here for many of the same reasons that you have. We participate in community events, send our children to school here, and serve our communities as volunteer firefighters when not on duty.

We are proud to be part of your community and appreciate more than you know the support you give us.

Deer Haven—Douglas County
Fire Protection District
P.O. Box 684
Minden, NV 89423

DEER HAVEN—DOUGLAS COUNTY

Fire Protection District
Serving you 24 hours a day
P.O. Box 684
Minden, NV 89423
702-555-1000

CHAPTER 18

Create a Magazine Article

Features Covered

- Use the shadow text attribute
- Create unequal column widths
- Edit border line style settings
- Create drop caps
- Indent the first line of all paragraphs automatically
- Create a graphic box that spans multiple columns
- Place (nest) a graphic box within a graphic box
- Enable SmartQuotes and insert em dashes
- Create headers/footers for odd and even pages

Objectives and Introduction

After successfully completing this chapter, you will be able to use the shadow text attribute, create columns of unequal widths, edit border line styles, and create drop caps. In addition, you will learn to automatically indent each paragraph of a document, create a graphic box that spans multiple columns, "nest" a graphic box within a graphic box, and use typographical symbols for quotation marks and em dashes. Also, creating different footers for odd and even pages will be covered.

WordPerfect 6.0 for Windows has continued to incorporate and enhance many of the functions that have traditionally been accomplished only through the use of typesetting or desktop publishing programs. In this chapter, you will perform many desktop publishing functions that are used to enhance publications such as a magazine article.

Create a Magazine Article

Before beginning to create a magazine article, decisions need to be made regarding the graphic images to be included, the number of columns, and the widths of columns.

Decisions will also need to be made about the use of special text attributes and other effects.

Many articles also include pull quotes and sidebars. A pull quote is a small portion of the article text that is excerpted from the article and placed in a separate box. The purpose of a pull quote is to attract attention to the article. Therefore, the font of the pull quote text is often changed and/or enlarged. Also, borders are usually placed above, below, or around the text to set the quote off from the article text.

A sidebar is a box or area that contains information related to the article text. The purpose of a sidebar is to further explain a subject covered in the article or to provide additional statistics or information that may interest the reader.

One of the main purposes of a magazine article's format is to entice people to read the article. Therefore, special text effects and attributes such as shadow text, rotated text, drop caps, and leading adjustments are used to add visual interest. Graphic images or pictures are often included in a magazine article to enhance page appearance or to illustrate the article's key points.

Start-Up Instructions

- Open the file named **18drill1.txt** located on the data disk.
- Turn on widow/orphan control (select **Layout**, **Page**, **Keep Text Together**, **Prevent the first and last lines of paragraphs from being separated across pages**, **OK**).
- Change the initial font to **BernhardMod BT** (select **Layout**, **Document**, **Initial Font**; in the Font Face box, highlight **BernhardMod BT**, **OK**).

Use Shadow Text Attribute

1. Select the desired text.

   For example, select the words **Don't Knot Up.**
2. Select **Layout, Font** {Alt, L, f *or* Alt and F9}.
3. In the Appearance box, select **Shadow** {Alt and w}.
4. Select **OK** {Enter}.

   Note: A gray shadow is placed around the letters in the selected text.

Increase Leading for Title and Subtitle Lines

5. Select the desired text.

   For example, select both the title and subtitle lines.
6. Select **Layout, Typesetting, Word/Letterspacing** {Alt, L, t, w}.
7. Select **Adjust Leading** {L}.
8. Double-click in the **Between Lines** box and type the desired amount of additional space to be placed between the lines of the selected text {t, type amount}.

   For example, type **.10**. (Do not type the final period.)
9. Select **OK** {Enter}.
10. Click once to deselect the text.

Finish-Up Instructions

- ❖ Place the insertion point at the beginning of the document (**Ctrl** and **Home**).
- ❖ Insert a graphic image as follows:
  - a. Select the **Figure** button on the Button Bar.
  - b. If necessary, select the drive and directory where the WordPerfect graphic files are located, e.g., *c:\wpwin60\graphics*. Double-click on **humbird.wpg**.
  - c. Select the **Position** button on the Graphics Box Feature Bar. Select **Put Box on Current Page (Page Anchor)**.
  - d. In the Horizontal area, move the mouse pointer to the box located to the right of the word "from," press and hold the mouse button, and drag to highlight **Left Margin**. Release the mouse button. Select **OK**.
  - e. *To turn the graphic image around to face the opposite direction*, select the **Tools** button on the Graphics Box Feature Bar and select the **Mirror Vertical** button located on the Image Tools palette.
  - f. Select the **Border/Fill** button on the Graphics Box Feature Bar, select the **Border Style** button, click on NO BORDER, select **OK**.
  - g. Move the mouse pointer away from the graphic image and click once to deselect the graphic box and to remove the Image Tools palette from the screen.
- ❖ Select **Close** on the Graphics Box Feature Bar.
- ❖ Use the *new* filename **18drill1.new** and save the file

Create Unequal Column Widths

Until now, only equal width newspaper columns have been created. However, it is also possible to create columns of different widths. When creating columns of different widths, it is important to remember that the total of the widths of all columns and the space between columns should equal the width of the page minus the margins. For example, if default 1" margins are used, the total of all columns plus the space between columns should equal 6.5 inches.

Column widths can be specified in the Columns dialog box. In the Columns dialog box, the width of each column and the space between columns display in the Column Widths area. Different columns widths can be entered, and the space between columns can be changed. When columns widths or space between columns are changed, WordPerfect recalculates the width(s) of the other column(s). If the width of a column should not be changed when other column widths or the space between columns are altered, selected the Fixed option located to the right of the column width box.

The width of each column can be changed using the Ruler Bar after the number of columns has been selected. To adjust the width of a column using the Ruler Bar, move the mouse pointer to the area between the column width markers, press and hold the mouse button, drag to the desired width, and release the mouse button. To change the space between two columns, place the mouse pointer on the left or right

FIGURE 18.1

Text Columns dialog box

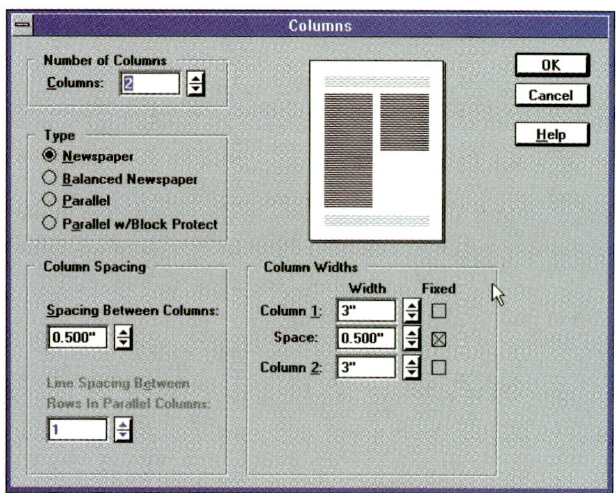

column width marker, press and hold the mouse button, and drag left or right to increase or decrease the space between the two columns.

Start-Up Instructions

- The file named **18drill1.new** should be displayed in the document window.

Steps to Create Unequal Column Widths

1. Place the insertion point at the location where the columns are to begin.

   For example, place the insertion point to the left of the first character in the body text (the C in Constant).

2. Move the mouse pointer to the **Columns Define** button, press and hold the mouse button, and drag to select the **Define** option. Release the mouse button {Alt and L, c, d}.

   Note: The current widths of each column and the space between each column display in the Column Widths area (see Figure 18.1). Currently, column 1 and column 2 are each 3 inches wide with a space of .5 inches between columns. If desired, the number of columns and type of columns can be changed.

3. To change the width of a column, double-click in the desired column width box and type the desired width.

   For example, double-click in the **Column 1** width box and type **2** {Alt and 1}.

   *Note: WordPerfect will automatically recalculate the width for column 2 when the insertion point is moved out of the Column 1 width box or **OK** is selected.*

4. Move the mouse pointer to the **Fixed** box located to the right of the Column 1 width box and click once {no keystrokes}.

   Note: An X displays in the Fixed box. When Fixed is selected, WordPerfect will not change the width of the column when other column widths or the spacing between columns is changed.

5. To change the amount of space between columns, double-click in the **Space** box and type the desired spacing between columns {Tab, type desired amount of space}.

For example, double-click in the **Space** box and type **.25**. (Do not type the final period.)

Note: To see the new column width for Column 2, click once in the Column 2 width box. Notice that WordPerfect has recalculated the width of Column 2, and 4.25" now displays in the Column 2 width box. A visual representation of the column widths appears above the Column Widths area.

6. When all column widths have been set, select **OK** {Enter}.

   Note: Scroll down to observe the text displayed in two columns. The first column is 2" wide and the second column is 4.25" wide.

Finish-Up Instructions

- Use the same filename, **18drill1.new**, and save the file again.
- Continue with the Steps to Create Headers/Footers for Odd and Even Pages.

Create Headers/Footers for Odd and Even Pages

Multiple headers and footers can be placed in a WordPerfect document. Each page of a document can contain a maximum of two headers and two footers (e.g., Header A, Header B, Footer A, and Footer B). If desired, different headers and/or footers can be created for each page of a document. Also different headers and/or footers can be created for odd and even pages. For example, Footer A could be used to create a footer that will appear on odd-numbered pages (1, 3, 5, etc.) and Footer B could be used to create a footer that will appear on even-numbered pages (2, 4, 6, etc.).

Start-Up Instructions

- The file named **18drill1.new** should be displayed in the document window.

Create Headers/Footers for Odd and Even Pages

1. Move the insertion point to the page on which the footer is to begin.

   For example, move the insertion point to the top of the document (**Ctrl** and **Home**).

2. To create a header/footer for odd pages, select **Layout, Header/Footer** {Alt, L, h}.
3. Select the desired header or footer option.

   For example, select **Footer A** {f}.

4. Select **Create** {c *or* press Enter}.
5. Select the **Placement** button on the Header/Footer Feature Bar. Choose the desired placement option {Alt and Shift and e, choose the desired placement option, Enter}.

   For example, select **Odd Pages** to create a footer for odd-numbered pages {Alt and Shift and e, o, Enter}.

Chapter **18**
Create a Magazine Article

6. Select OK {Enter}.
7. Type and format the header/footer text.

   For example:

   a. Change the font size to **10 point**.
   b. Type **Health Magazine Weekly**. (Do not type the period.)
   c. Press **Alt** and **F7** to move the insertion point to the right margin.
   d. Insert the page numbering code by selecting the **Number** button on the Header/Footer Feature Bar and choose **Page Number** {Alt and Shift and m, p}.
8. Select **Close** on the Header/Footer Feature Bar {Alt and Shift and c}.
9. To create a header/footer for even pages, select **Layout, Header/Footer** {Alt, L, h}.
10. Select the desired header or footer option.

    For example, select **Footer B** {o}.
11. Select **Create** {c *or* press Enter}.

    Note: *Although Footer B has been selected, the Footer A text displays. That's OK.*
12. Select the **Placement** button on the Header/Footer Feature Bar. Choose the desired placement option {Alt and Shift and e, choose the desired placement option, Enter}.

    For example, select **Even Pages** to create a footer for even-numbered pages {Alt and Shift and e, e, Enter}.
13. Select **OK** {Enter}.

    Note: *The Footer A text continues to display until you begin to type the text for Footer B. That's OK. If desired, turn on Reveal Codes to see the Footer B code.*
14. Type and format the desired header/footer text.

    For example:

    a. Change the font size to **10 point**.
    b. Insert the page numbering code by selecting the **Number** button on the Header/Footer Feature Bar and choosing **Page Number** {Alt and Shift and m, p}.

       Note: *The number 1 displays. That's OK.*
    c. Press **Alt** and **F7** to move the insertion point to the right margin.
    d. Type the article name, **Don't Knot Up**. (Do not type the period.)
15. Select **Close** on the Header/Footer Feature Bar {Alt and Shift and c}.

Finish-Up Instructions

- Use the same filename, **18drill1.new**, and save the file again.
- Continue with the Steps to Create a Graphic Box for Pull Quote Text.

Edit Border Line Style Settings

Each graphic box type (Figure, Table, Text, etc.) contains settings for border lines (see Figure 13.1, page 302). For example, by default a Table box has a thick border line at the top and bottom of the box. If desired, the style of the border line(s) can be changed and/or the thickness of the border line(s) can be edited. For example, the top border line of a Table box can be changed to the thin-thick line style and the bottom border line can be changed to a thick-thin line style. Also, the thickness of each border line can be set and, if the border line style contains more than one line, the space between the lines can be changed.

Start-Up Instructions

- The file named **18drill1.new** should be displayed in the document window.
- The insertion point should be located to the left of the first character in the body text (e.g., the C in Constant).
- Select the **Page Zoom Full** button to display all of page 1 in the document window.

Steps to Create a Graphic Box for Pull Quote Text

1. Select the **Text Box** button on the Button Bar {Alt, g, t}.
2. Use the sizing handles (black boxes at corners and edges of the graphic box) and size the graphic box.

   For example, move the mouse pointer to the sizing handle that is located at the bottom center of the Text box until the double-headed arrow displays. Press and hold the mouse button and drag down until the bottom of the text box is just below the last line of text in the first column. (Do not include the footer.) Release the mouse button {Alt and Shift and s, e, type 4.7, press Enter}.

   Note: The text is moved to the second column.
3. With the insertion point located in the Text box, type or insert the desired text.

   For example, select **Insert, File,** and double-click on the file named **18drill1.pul** that is located on the data disk. Select **Yes.**

Finish-Up Instructions

- Continue with the Steps to Change the Border Line Style Settings.

Change Border Line Style Settings

1. With the graphic box selected, click on the **Border/Fill** button on the Graphics Box Feature Bar {Alt and Shift and b}.
2. Select **Customize Style** {c}.

   Note: The Customize Border dialog box displays (see Figure 18.2). In the ***Select sides to modify*** *area, the Top and Bottom options are selected. Current, any changes made to*

FIGURE 18.2

Customize Border dialog box

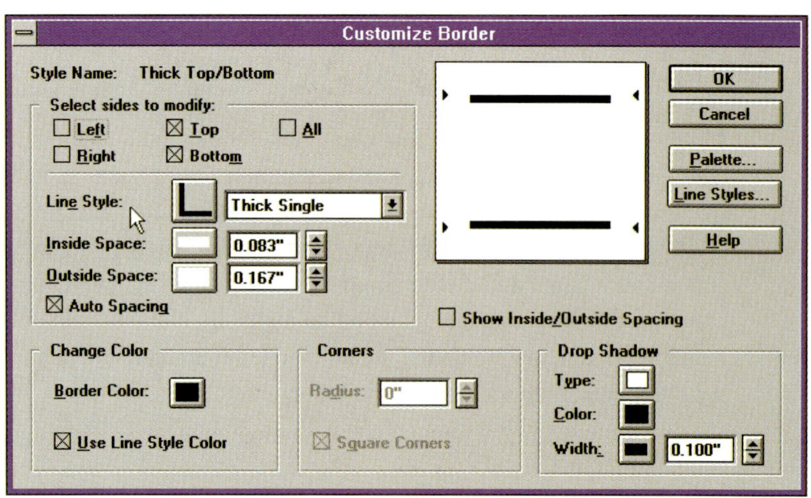

the line style will affect both the top and bottom lines. If you want to change only one border, deselect the box(es) that is not to be changed.

3. Modify the border lines as desired.

   For example, modify the Top and Bottom border lines as follows:

   a. Select the **Line Style** button located at the left of the Customize Border dialog box and click on the **Thick/Thin 1** line style (fourth button in the first row) {e, Tab, press the down arrow key repeatedly until Thick/Thin 1 displays}.

   b. To change the amount of space between the border lines and/or the thickness of the border lines, select the **Lines Styles** button located on the right side of the Customize Border dialog box {Alt and L}.

   c. Select **Edit** {Alt and e}.

      Note: *The Edit Line Style dialog box containing a sample of the selected line style displays (see Figure 18.3). If the line style consists of more than one line, an arrow points to the line that will be edited.*

   d. Change the thickness of the thinner line by double-clicking in the Width box and typing **.03** or by clicking on the up triangle located to the right of the Width box until **0.030"** displays {w, Tab, press the up arrow key to display 0.030"}.

   e. Change the spacing between the lines by double-clicking in the **Spacing Below Line** box and typing **.03** or by clicking on the up triangle

FIGURE 18.3

Edit Line Style dialog box

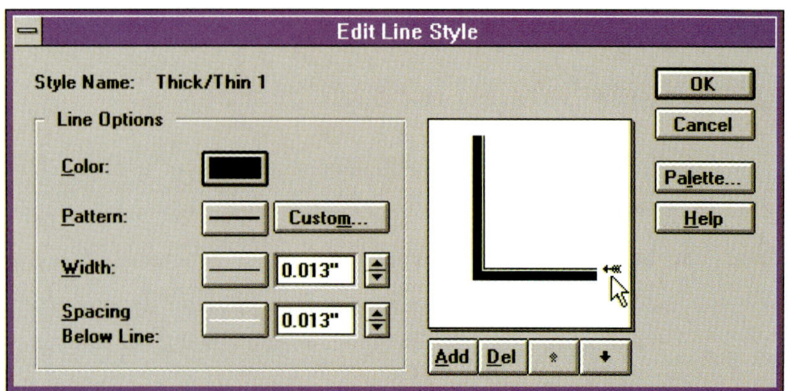

located to the right of the Spacing Below Line box until **0.030"** displays {Alt and s, Tab, press the up arrow key to display 0.030}.

f. To change the thickness of the next line, move the mouse pointer to the thick line and click once to move the arrow {press the Tab key repeatedly until a dotted outline displays around the down arrow button below the sample lines, press the Spacebar once}.

g. Change the thickness of the thick line to **0.083"** (see step 3d).

h. Select **OK** {Enter}.

i. Choose **Select** {Alt and s}.

4. When all changes have been made to the line style, select **OK** twice {Enter twice}.

Finish-Up Instructions

- Move the mouse pointer away from the graphic box and click once to deselect the box. If necessary, select the **Close** button on the Graphics Box Feature Bar.
- Select the **Page Zoom Full** button to return to the normal view. Scroll down to observe the graphic box border lines.
- Use the *new* filename **18drill1.lin** and save the file.

Create a Drop Cap

A drop cap is a special effect that is often used in the first paragraph of an article. The first character of the first word in the paragraph is enlarged. WordPerfect provides a macro, *dropcap.wcm*, that automates the process of creating drop caps. When the dropcap macro is used, the drop cap letter is placed in a User box. If desired, a border or fill can be added to the User box.

Start-Up Instructions

- The file named **18drill1.lin** should be displayed in the document window.

Create a Drop Cap

1. Place the insertion point to the left of the character that will become a drop cap.

For example, place the insertion point to the left of the first character in the body text (the C in Constant).

2. Select **Tools, Macro, Play** {Alt, t, m, p}.

3. Select the **List** button located at the right of the Name box {F4 *or* Alt and the down arrow key}.

Note: The Select File dialog box containing a list of macro (.wcm) files displays.

4. Double-click on **dropcap.wcm** {Tab, press the down arrow key to the highlight desired macro name, Enter}.

5. Select **Play** {Alt and p}.

Chapter 18
Create a Magazine Article

Note: In a few moments, the Drop Cap Options box displays showing the current font and size for the drop cap and asking if you want to change these options.

6. Select **No** to accept the current options or select **Yes** to change the drop cap font or size.

   For example, select **Yes** {Enter} and change the font to **Brush738 BT, 52 point**. Select **OK** {Enter}.

   Note: The drop cap letter displays in the document window. (The drop cap letter is automatically placed in a User box.)

Finish-Up Instructions

- To increase the space between the drop cap letter and the paragraph text, select the User box containing the drop cap letter by moving the mouse pointer to the letter and clicking once. Move the mouse pointer to the sizing handle at the right center of the User box until a double-headed arrow displays. Press and hold the mouse button and drag to the right approximately 1/8".
- Move the mouse pointer away from the User box containing the drop cap letter and click once to deselect.
- Use the same filename, **18drill1.lin**, and save the file again.

Automatically Indent the First Line of All Paragraphs

To save space, the first line of each paragraph is indented so that an extra blank line is not needed between paragraphs. The first line of each paragraph can be indented manually by moving the insertion point to the beginning of each paragraph and pressing the Tab key. However, WordPerfect can be instructed to automatically indent the first line of each paragraph. If the Tab key is pressed to indent the first line of a paragraph, the line is indented to the first tab stop. If the first line of a paragraph is automatically indented, an indention amount can be specified, e.g., .25".

Start-Up Instructions

- The file named **18drill1.lin** should be displayed in the document window.

Automatically Indent the First Line of All Paragraphs

1. Place the insertion point to the left of the first character in the first paragraph to be indented.

   For example, place the insertion point to the left of the quotation mark (") that precedes the word **The** in the second paragraph of the document.

2. Select **Layout, Paragraph, Format** {Alt, L, a, f}.

   Note: The number 0" displays in the First Line Indent box and is highlighted.

3. Type the desired indent amount.

For example, type .25. (Do not type the final period.)

4. Select **OK** {Enter}.

Note: Scroll through the document and notice that the first line of each paragraph is indented.

Finish-Up Instructions

- Use the same filename, **18drill1.lin**, and save the file.

Create a Graphic Box That Extends Across Multiple Columns

Until now, a graphic box in a multicolumn document has been placed within a single column. A graphic box can also be set to extend across (cover) more than one column. For example, if a two-column format is used, a graphic box can be set to extend across both columns.

A graphic box that extends across more than one column in a magazine article can be used to hold a graphic image, sidebar information, or both. If desired, multiple columns can be created within a graphic box. To place a graphic image in a graphic box that contains text, a second graphic box is created within the first graphic box. This is sometimes referred to as *nesting* a graphic box.

Start-Up Instructions

- The file named **18drill1.lin** should be displayed in the document window.

Steps to Create a Graphic Box That Extends Across Multiple Columns

1. Move the insertion point to the page on which the graphic box will be located.

   For example, place the insertion point to the left of the first character of the second paragraph on page 2 (column 1).

2. Select the **Text Box** button on the Button Bar {Alt, g, t}.
3. Select the **Position** button on the Graphics Box Feature Bar {Alt and Shift and p}.
4. Select **Put Box on Current Page (Page Anchor)** {p}.
5. In the Horizontal area, select **Across Columns** {r}.

   Note: When the Across Columns option is selected, the number 1 displays in the box to the right of the words "Across Columns" and the number 2 displays in the box to the right of the word "through" (see Figure 18.4). These boxes are used to specify the number of the columns over which the graphic box will be located. Because this graphic box will be placed over both columns, no change is necessary.

6. In the Vertical area, move the mouse pointer to the box to the right of the word "from," press and hold the mouse button, and drag to highlight the desired vertical position.

   For example, highlight **Bottom Margin** {c, Tab, down arrow key}.

7. Select **OK** {Enter}.

FIGURE 18.4

Box Position dialog box

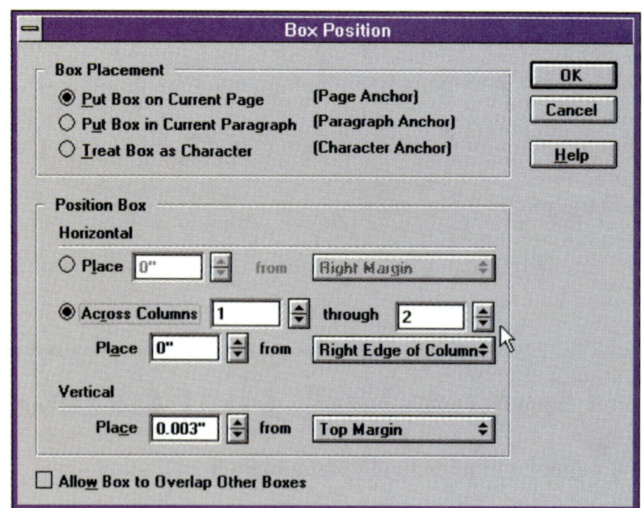

8. Select the **Size** button on the Graphics Box Feature Bar {Alt and Shift and s}.
9. In the Width area, select **Full** {f}.
10. In the Height area, select **Set** and type the desired box height {Alt and e, type desired height}.

    For example, select **Set** and type **5**.
11. Select **OK** {Enter}.
12. With the insertion point in the Text box, type or insert the desired text.

    For example, select **Insert, File** and double-click on the file named **18sbar.txt** located on the data disk. Select **Yes.**

    *Note: If desired, move the mouse pointer away from the Text box and click to deselect the box. Select **Page Zoom Full**. Select **Page Zoom Full** again to return to the normal view.*

Create Multiple Columns Within a Graphic Box

13. Move the insertion point to the location where the multiple column layout should begin.

    For example, place the insertion point to the left of the T in the word **These** (the first word of the first paragraph in the graphic box).

    Note: *If necessary, to obtain the insertion point, click in the graphic box, press the* right *mouse button and select* Edit Text. *Then place the insertion point at the desired location in the text.*
14. Move the mouse pointer to the **Columns Define** button, press and hold the mouse button, and drag to highlight **Define**. Release the mouse button {Alt L, c, d}.
15. Select the desired type of columns and type the number of columns in the Number of Columns box.

    For example, check that Newspaper columns is selected and type **3** in the Number of Columns box {3}.

16. To change the amount of space between columns, double-click in the **Spacing Between Columns** box and type the desired amount of space between columns {Alt and s, type desired amount, Enter}.

    For example, double-click in the **Spacing Between Columns** and type **.25**. (Do not type the final period.)

17. Select **OK** {Enter}.

Finish-Up Instructions

- Continue with the Steps to Place (Nest) a Second Graphic Box Containing a Graphic Image Within a Graphic Box.

Place (Nest) a Second Graphic Box Containing a Graphic Image Within a Graphic Box

1. Place the insertion point at the location where the second graphic box will be inserted.

    For example, press **Ctrl** and **End** to locate the insertion point on the blank line below the last paragraph in the graphic box.

2. Select the **Figure** button on the Button Bar {Alt, g, f}.

3. If necessary, select the drive and directory where the graphic image is located. Double-click on the filename of the desired graphic image {Tab, press the down arrow key to highlight desired filename, Enter}.

    For example, double-click on **humbird.wpg**.

    Note: It may be necessary to scroll up to view the graphic box containing the **humbird.wpg** *graphic image.*

4. Select the **Border/Fill** button on the Graphics Box Feature Bar {Alt and Shift and b}.

5. Select the **Border Style** button and click on the desired border style {Alt and b, Spacebar, press the arrow keys to highlight desired border style, Enter}.

    For example, select the **NO BORDER** style.

6. Select **OK** {Enter}.

Finish-Up Instructions

- To deselect the graphic boxes, scroll up the document and click outside the graphic boxes.
- If necessary, select **Close** on the Graphics Box Feature Bar.
- Use the *new* filename **18drill1.sid** and save the file.

Use Typographically Correct Symbols for Quote Marks and Em Dashes

In the past when using a typewriter, the quotation mark (") has been used in place of the correct opening (“) and closing (”) quotation marks. Also, two hyphens (--) have been used to indicate a dash in place of the correct em dash (—). Because the “, ” , and — characters are not available on keyboards, often " and -- are still used when creating text on the computer.

The SmartQuotes feature can be used to convert straight single or double quotation marks (' or ") to paired single or double quotation marks (‘ ’ and “ ”). If the SmartQuotes feature is enabled before typing the text, the quotation marks are automatically converted as text is typed. If the SmartQuotes feature is enabled after text has been typed, the Find feature can be used to search for straight quotation marks (either ' or "). When a straight quotation mark is located in the document, delete the quotation mark. Then type the ' or " character and WordPerfect will replace the straight quotation mark with an opening or closing quotation mark.

The Replace feature can be used to search for double hyphens (--) and to replace them with the em dash (—) character.

Start-Up Instructions

❖ The file named **18drill1.sid** should be displayed in the document window.

Enable SmartQuotes and to Use Find to Insert Correct Typographic Symbols

1. Select **Tools, QuickCorrect** {Alt, t, q}.
2. Select **Enable SmartQuotes** {Alt and e}.
3. Select **Close** {c}.
4. Place the insertion point at the beginning of the text to be searched.

   For example, press **Ctrl** and **Home** to place the insertion point at the beginning of the document.
5. Select **Edit, Find** {Alt, e, f *or* F2}.
6. In the Find What box, type a quotation mark (").
7. Select **Find Next** {Alt and f}.

   Note: *The first occurrence of a “ is highlighted in the document.*
8. Move the mouse pointer to the right of the highlighted quotation mark (") and click once. Press the **Backspace** key to delete the quotation mark (") {Alt and c, Backspace}.
9. Type a quotation mark (").

   Note: *WordPerfect inserts an opening (“) quotation mark in the document. To view the quotation mark, move the mouse pointer to the **Zoom** button, press and hold the mouse button, and drag to highlight **200%**. Release the mouse button.*

10. Select **Find Next** in the Find Text dialog box {F2, Alt and f}.

11. Repeat steps 8-10 until all straight quotation marks (") have been changed to the correct opening (“) and closing (”) quotation marks.

    Note: When the Find box displays with the message "Not Found," select ***OK****. Select* ***Close*** *to exit the Find Text dialog box. If desired, change the Zoom view to* **100%**.

Disable SmartQuotes

12. Select **Tools, QuickCorrect** {Alt, t, q}.

13. Select **Enable SmartQuotes** to deselect the option {Alt and e}.

14. Select **Close** {c}.

Finish-Up Instructions

- Use the same filename, **18drill1.sid**, and save the file again.

Steps to Convert Typed Characters to Correct Typographic Symbols

1. Place the insertion point at the beginning of the text to be searched.

    For example, press **Ctrl** and **Home** to place the insertion point at the beginning of the document.

2. Select **Edit, Replace** {Alt, e, r *or* Ctrl and F2}.

3. Type the character(s) to be replaced.

    For example, type -- (two hyphens).

    Note: When the two hyphens are typed, the codes [-Hyphen][-Hyphen] display in the Find box.

4. Click once in the **Replace With** box {Tab}.

5. To replace text with a character from a WordPerfect Character set, press **Ctrl** and **w** to display the WordPerfect Characters dialog box.

6. Move the mouse pointer to the **Character Set** box, press and hold the mouse button and drag to highlight the set that contains the desired character; release the mouse button {Alt and s, Spacebar, press the down arrow key to highlight the desired set, press Enter}.

    For example, select **Typographic Symbols**.

7. Click on the desired character and then select **Insert and Close** {Alt and r, press the arrow keys to move the dotted outline to the desired character, Alt and a}.

    For example, scroll down and click on the — character (4,34 displays in the Number box) and select **Insert and Close**.

8. Select **Replace All** {Alt and a}.

9. Select **Close** {Alt and c}.

    Note: The insertion point is located beside the last occurrence of the em dash in the document window.

Don't Knot Up

Remember to Stop and Smell the Flowers

Each person has unique stress triggers:

- memories
- relationships
- boredom
- physical threats from the environment

Constant stress is bad for you. It is so bad that some health experts call it the deadliest environmental toxin of this age. Whatever else you may be doing—or not doing—for your health, consider what you must do about stress.

"The mind talks to the body and the body talks back and sometimes it is a fatal conversation." That's a Russian proverb quoted by Robert Eliot, MD, a cardiologist who studies stress. He teaches people how to stop "the self-destructive chatter" of stress in *Is It Worth Dying For?* (Bantam, 1984) and *From Stress to Strength—How to Lighten Your Load and Save Your Life* (coming from Bantam in October).

Stress comes from inside as the mind/body prepares to fight with or flee away from something that is taken as a threat. Each person has unique stress triggers: memories, relationships, boredom, and physical threats from the environment.

Even though stress feels only like an emotion, its life-long effects are destructive—heart disease, stroke, substance abuse, injury, and depression. Stress makes the immune system less effective as well, and many experts suspect it makes cancer and infectious diseases more likely to take hold. You have to stop this from happening to you.

Just as stressors are different from person to person, there is no one way for everyone to cope. Yet medical science has noted that people with certain habits cope with stress better. Research

has tried to measure the effects of two approaches in particular: exercise and relaxation (or meditation theory).

The Russian proverb predates what physiologists now understand. Nature designed the mind and body as one unit: "there is no separation," Dr. Eliot says. Constant stress changes every cell's function as neuropeptide hormones from the brain fire off to and are received by receptors in every organ. Even the immune system is wired to the emotions. The system simply wasn't meant to take constant strain.

A low level of exercise interrupts the harmful effects of stress. The easy explanation is that muscle action "burns up" the hormones that keyed you up. In other words, when the system has prepared for a fight, exercise gives it what it needs. Exercising also reverses fight or flight effects. Dr. Eliot points out, for instance, that stress hormones make blood vessels squeeze tighter to prevent bleeding if you get hurt in a fight. Smaller blood vessels raise blood pressure, but exercise forces them open and reduces the pressure.

People who are somewhat fit receive a bonus, in addition to having healthier reactions to everyday stress, according to Mark Sothman, PhD. When they meet a new challenge "or any novel threatening task, they have an enhanced response," Dr. Sothman says. Research he has led at the University of Wisconsin suggests that if you're fit, you have greater stamina and response at times of peak stress.

Calm—You Know it Won't Be Easy

These measures are not simple. That's why so few people can chill out at will. But make the effort. Exercise and/or relaxation will change the way you handle stress.

Exercise to save your life. Keep trying—walking, running, swimming, bicycling, dancing—until you find things you can fit into your schedule and which you can face daily. The biggest health gains occur when you go from being a couch potato to moving around for a steady 20 minutes a day, even at a low rate. Exercise will not relieve stress, however, if you turn exercising into another form of stress.

Learn to clear your mind through your lungs. Relaxation training is best taught by an experienced instructor. It requires persistence to clear your mind of distractions and release muscle tension. It also requires 20 minutes a day.

Whatever makes you anxious, tense or stressed, your experience is like everyone else's in one way: Stress means you fell out of control. "Whatever technique you use, if you get a sense of control, you'll do better with the stress," says Paul Rosch, MD, Director of the American Institute of Stress in Westchester, Connecticut.

You don't have to be super-fit to experience this advantage, but it's important not to ignore fitness for too long. "You also need to exercise regularly for something more than six months; it should be ongoing," Dr. Sothman says.

Meditation, the seeming opposite of exercise, overcomes stress by cutting "the self-destructive chatter" between thought patterns and cellular reaction. Meditation affects a system that works without your conscious control—the autonomic nervous system (ANS). One function of the ANS revs you up for a fight. But relaxation turns on the opposite function, the one that keeps you on an even keel when there is no threat.

Relaxing meditation is deceptively simple: Inhale and exhale slowly as you repeat a word, sound, or phrase of a prayer. Gently draw your thoughts back if they stray from thinking about anything other than your word and, perhaps, your breathing. According to Herbert Benson, MD, at The Mind/Body Medical School at Deaconess Hospital, when meditation "breaks the chain of everyday thinking, it simply turns off the fight or flight response." In his pioneering 1975 book, *The Relaxation Response* (in paperback from Avon), Dr. Benson summarizes how meditation lowers your pulse, blood pressure, breathing rate, and metabolism.

Although survival depends on your nervous system's being fired up when times are wild, health comes from calmly flowing along the rest of the time. Meditation opens that flow. It's just the relief a tense mind/body requires to live a healthy life.

Reprinted by permission from Health Signs, a quarterly publication by Washington Township Hospital District, Fremont, California.

Finish-Up Instructions

- Select the **Page Zoom Full** button if desired. Scroll upward to display each page of the document.
- Use the *new* filename **18drill1.fin** and save the file.

  Note: Your final document should look similar to the magazine article shown on page 442.
- Print one copy and close the document.

The Next Step

Chapter Review and Activities

Self-Check Quiz

T F 1. By default, a Table box has a thick border line at the top and thick thin border lines at the bottom of the box.

T F 2. The Spacing Below Line option in the Edit Line Style dialog box is used to change the spacing between two lines.

T F 3. The first line of paragraphs can be automatically indented by selecting **Layout**, **Paragraph**, **Format**, typing the desired indent amount in the First Line Indent box, and selecting **OK**.

T F 4. Multiple columns cannot be created within a graphic box.

T F 5. The SmartQuotes feature can be used to change the quotation mark (") to typographically correct opening (“) and closing (”) quotation marks.

6. The __________ macro is used to automate the process of creating drop cap letters.
   a. *dropcap.wpg*
   b. *dropcap.wcm*
   c. *allfonts.wcm*

7. Columns of unequal widths can be created by ______________.
   a. specifying the widths of columns in the Columns dialog box
   b. using the Ruler Bar to adjust the column widths
   c. selecting **Layout**, **Margins**, and typing the margins for each column
   d. either a or b

8. List the four steps to use the shadow text attribute.

Chapter **18**
Create a Magazine Article

9. Placing a second graphic box within another graphic box is often referred to as ________ a graphic box.

10. Write a brief explanation of why two different footers might be used in a document.

Enriching Language Arts Skills

Spelling/Vocabulary Words

compatibility able to exist together in harmony; consistent; suitable.
promulgated to have made known publicly; to have published; announced.
standards habits or customs established by an authority; example; paradigms.

Em and En Dashes

The em dash (—), a typographic symbol about the width of the character m, is often used in place of a comma. Press the hyphen key twice (--) to create a dash on a typewriter or computer keyboard. Many software programs provide a method to create typographically correct em dashes (see page 440). The en dash (–), a typographic symbol about the width of the character n, is used as a hyphen or as a substitute for the word to, e.g., July–September. The correct typographic symbols for em and en dashes have traditionally been used for books, newspapers, and advertisements and are recommended for use when creating a professional-looking document.

Example:

em dash *Our notebook sales have increased 20 percent since last year—from $10,000 to $12,000.*

en dash *The annual report for the first year 1994–95 will be available at the end of March.*

Activities

Activity 18.1—Create a Magazine Article

1. Open the file named **18act1.txt** located on the data disk.
2. Select the title and choose the **Shadow** text attribute (select **Layout, Font, Shadow**).
3. With the insertion point located at the top of the document, create a graphic box and retrieve the graphic image named **trumpt.wpg.** (Select the **Figure** button, double-click on **trumpt.wpg.**)
4. Change the horizontal position of the graphic box to **Left** (select the **Position** button, select **Put Box on Current Page**; in the Horizontal area, select the "from" box and choose **Left Margin**; select **OK**).
5. Remove the graphic box border (select the **Border/Fill** button, select the **Border Style** button, click on NO BORDER, select **OK**).

6. Place the insertion point at the beginning of the first paragraph in the body text and create two columns. Set the width of column 1 to **2.25"**. Set the space between columns to **.25"**. Set the width of column 2 to **4"**.

   Note: *For assistance, see Steps to Create Unequal Column Widths on page 430.*

7. With the insertion point located at the top of the document, create footers for the odd and even pages of the article using the following information:

   Note: *For assistance, see Steps to Create Headers/Footers for Odd and Even Pages on page 431.*

   a. Use Footer A to create the footer for the odd-numbered pages. Change the font to **Arrus BT, 10 point**. The text for the footer follows:

      Today's PC Magazine **Page (insert page number code)**

   b. Use Footer B to create the footer for the even-numbered pages. Change the font to **Arrus BT, 10 point**. The text for the footer follows:

      Page (insert page number code) **Sound Boards**

8. Create a graphic box for the pull quote text.

   Note: *For assistance, see Steps to Create a Graphic Box for Pull Quote Text on page 433.*

   a. Place the insertion point to the left of the E in Early.

   b. Select the **Text Box** button.

   c. Move the mouse pointer to the sizing handle at the bottom center of the Text box until a double-headed arrow displays. Press and hold the mouse button and drag down until the bottom of the Text box is just below the last line of text in the first column. (Do not include the footer.)

   d. Insert the file named **18act1.pul** located on the data disk into the Text box (select **Insert**, **File**, double-click on the file named **18act1.pul**, select **Yes**).

   e. Change the line style for the border lines to **Thick/Thin 1** (select the **Border/Fill** button, select **Customize Style**, select the **Line Style** button located on the left side of the dialog box, click on the **Thick/Thin 1** line style [fourth button in the first row]).

   f. Change the thickness of the thin line to **.02"** and the Spacing Below Line to **.03"** (select the **Line Styles** button located on the right side of the dialog box, select **Edit**, double-click in the **Width** box and type **.02**, double-click in the **Spacing Below Line** box and type **.03**).

   g. Change the thickness of the thick line to **.04"** (click on the thick line, double-click in the **Width** box and type **.04**, select **OK**, choose **Select**, select **OK** twice).

9. Use the dropcap macro to create a drop cap for the first character of the first paragraph. Change the font for the drop cap to **Brush738 BT, 52 point** (place the insertion point to the left of the **E** in **Early**, select **Tools**, **Macro**, **Play**, select the **List** button, double-click on **dropcap.wcm**, select **Play**, select **Yes**, select the desired font and size, select **OK**).

Note: For assistance, see Steps to Create a Drop Cap on page 435.

10. Automatically indent the first line of all the remaining paragraphs **.35"** (place the insertion point to the left of the **O** in **One**, select **Layout**, **Paragraph**, **Format**, type **.35**, select **OK**).

    Note: For assistance, see Steps to Automatically Indent the First Line of All Paragraphs on page 436.

11. Place the insertion point to the left of the first character of the first paragraph on the second page (first column)and use the following information to create a graphic Text box that spans both columns.

    a. Select the **Text Box** button.

    b. Select the **Position** button. Choose the **Put Box on Current Page (Page Anchor)** option.

    c. In the Horizontal area, select **Across Columns**.

    d. In the Vertical area, select the "from" box and choose **Bottom Margin**. Select **OK**.

    e. Select the **Size** button. In the Width area, select **Full**. In the Height area, select **Set** and type 5.5. Select **OK**.

    f. Insert the file named **18act1.bar** located on the data disk.

    g. Define a three-column format for the sidebar text (place the insertion point to the left of the **I** in **In**, select the **Columns Define** button, and choose **3 Columns**.

    h. Deselect the Text box (move the mouse pointer away from the Text box and click once).

    i. Select the **Close** button on the Graphic Box Feature Bar.

12. Enable SmartQuotes and use Find to convert the quotation marks (") contained in the document to typography quotation marks (" and "). (Place the insertion point at the beginning of the document. Select **Tools**, **Quick Correct**, **Enable SmartQuotes**, **Close**. Select **Edit**, **Find**, type a ". Select **Find Next**. Move the mouse pointer to the right of the highlighted " mark and click once. Press the **Backspace** key and type a " mark. Select **Find Next**. Repeat until all occurrences of the " mark have been converted. Select **Tools**, **Quick Correct**, **Enable SmartQuotes**, **Close**.)

13. Use the filename **18act1.fin** and save the file.

    Note: *Your final document should look similar to the magazine article shown on page 447.*

14. Print one copy and close the document.

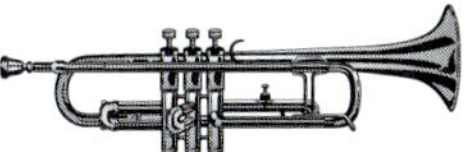

Sound Boards

By Darrel Dorsett

A sound board converts digital data sent to the board into sound. . .

The quality of the sound depends on the digital input, the design of the board, and the audio amplifiers. Better sound usually means more bytes of digital data and more expensive cards and amplifiers.

Early computer builders were anxious to give their creations a voice. Many of us have heard the sound of an early Bell Labs computer singing "Daisy" from "A Bicycle Built for Two." Many attempts were made to give the computer voice. Early attempts only produced the sounds that are associated with science fiction computers. When the personal computers were marketed, sound was still in the minds of the designers and users. The ill-fated Texas Instrument TI-99A and the Commodore 64 even had limited sound capabilities built in. It would be natural to expect the later IBM PCs to have an ability to produce sounds. Early sound programs were written to use the internal speaker. It did not take long for the early PC users to appreciate the inadequacy of a PC speaker as a sound device. The I/O ports were also used to send analog sound signals to external audio amplifiers. This only showed the inability of the basic computer to generate the complex waveforms that constitute any sounds other than pure tones.

One early sound board was the IBM Music Feature board. This board had an eight-voice FM stereo synthesizer. By using four of the music feature boards, 32 voices could be generated. This was an expensive way to add sound to games. The card's MIDI (Musical Instrument Digital Interface) capabilities were limited. The Roland board was also available, but was, and still is, primarily a professional MIDI sound board.

Creative Labs built a board called the Game Blaster. The Game Blaster was a sound board to add vitality to games. The board had 12 voices that played through an AM synthesizer. Later the Sound Blaster was produced which used the same Yamaha FM synthesizer as the competitive AdLib board. Mediavision is another builder of similar sound boards.

A sound board converts digital data sent to the board into sound which is analog in nature. This uses circuitry called a Digital Analog Converter (DAC). The quality of the sound depends on the digital input, the design of the board and the audio amplifiers. Better sound usually means more bytes (megabytes) of digital data (larger files) and more expensive cards and amplifiers.

Sound is converted into digital form through software using circuitry called an Analog Digital Converter (ADC). Not all sound boards can perform this function, but most boards today do so. Only casual game players would look for a board without this function. The choice of which board to buy will depend on your current and future use of the board as well as how much money you want to invest in a sound board.

Sound boards may interface with a (MIDI). This is a standard interface initially created by Kawai, Korg, Roland, Sequential Circuits and Yamaha. The MIDI interface allows the computer to generate music in a manner similar to earlier analog synthesizers, but much less expensively.

Sound boards usually have a joystick port because it was the support of sound in games that provided the market that brought about the proliferation of less expensive, more capable sound boards.

Many sound boards also provide support for CD-ROMs. This allows music and other sound sources to be integrated into programs and attached to data files in the computer. CDs with a library of sounds and sound effects are available.

The first step to installing a sound board is to follow the instructions from the maker of the board. If the board has two sets of connector fingers along its bottom, it should go into a motherboard slot with two openings (16-bit slot.) Generally, use the default values the manufacturer set up. The IRQ (interrupt request) value is often 5 or 7. The base I/O address is often 220H or 240H. The DMA (direct memory access) is usually 1. These are not the only choices and you may have to change these settings. Usually the sound board has accompanying diagnostic software to aid you in setting the correct values if you experience conflicts. You should try using several of the board's capabilities with its own software before trying to access the board through WordPerfect. Always write down the various settings of the sound board.

Once the sound board is installed, you will have the capability of inserting sound files in your WordPerfect documents (see the sidebar entitled Driving Your Sound Board).

Driving Your Sound Board

In order for a sound board to function with a software program such as WordPerfect 6.0 for Windows, a driver (a file that contains software instructions for using a sound board) must be installed to run under Windows.

Depending on the sound board installed in your computer, two types of sound files, MIDI and WAV, can be used with WordPerfect 6.0 for Windows. In order to create your own sound files, you need a microphone or other input device connected to your computer.

A sound file can be stored in a document or a link can be established to a sound file on disk. If a sound file is stored in the document, the document size is greatly increased. However, the document containing the sound file can be transported and played on any computer that contains a compatible sound board. If a link is established to a sound file on the computer's hard disk, the sound file is not stored as part of the document. The document size is not increase. However, if the document file is transferred to a different computer, the sound file is not transferred and will not be available.

To place a sound file into a WordPerfect 6.0 for Windows document, select Insert, Sound, type or select the name of the sound file. Choose the Link to File on Disk or Store in Document option. Select OK. An icon displays in the left margin of your document to mark the location of the sound clip. To play a sound clip, double-click on the sound clip icon in the document.

Challenge Your Skills

Skill 18.1—Create a Magazine Article

1. Open the file named **18skill1.txt** located on the data disk. Review the text and determine appropriate pull quote text.
2. The graphic file named **fax.eps** is provided on the data disk for use in the article.
3. Make decisions regarding:

   Initial font for the document
   Font for article title, subtitle, and sideheads
   Leading adjustment for title
   Number and widths of columns as well as space between columns
   Placement and text for pull quotes
   Use of a drop cap
   Indention for paragraphs
   Hint: *If the first line of each paragraph will be automatically indented, remove the indention from sidehead paragraphs by blocking each paragraph and selecting* ***Layout, Paragraph, Format, 0*** *(zero),* ***OK****.*
   Placement and format of sidebar information
   Footers for odd and even pages of the article
4. The sidebar text is contained in a file named **18skill1.bar**.
5. Correct three spelling and four punctuation errors.
6. Use the filename **18skill1.fin** and save the file.
7. Print one copy.
8. If you have completed your work in WordPerfect, exit the program.

CHAPTER

Create a Booklet

Features Covered

- Create subdivided pages
- Use WP Draw to create and edit graphic images
- Create a watermark
- Page number subdivided pages
- Print a booklet

Objectives and Introduction

After successfully completing this chapter, you will be able to subdivide a physical page into two or more logical pages, create a watermark that appears on all pages of a document, insert page numbers for subdivided pages, and print the subdivided pages in booklet form.

WordPerfect's Subdivide Page feature is used to divide a physical page into two or more logical pages. Each logical page can contain text, graphics, a header and/or footer, a page number, etc. Subdividing pages is useful for creating booklets, tickets, or other documents that do not require a full page. WordPerfect also provides the capability to print subdivided pages in booklet form. WordPerfect's Watermark feature is used to print text or a graphic image in the background of pages in a document.

Subdivide Pages

WordPerfect's Subdivide Page feature can be used to create documents such as booklets and programs. With the Subdivide Page feature, a single sheet of paper can be divided into multiple pages. The piece of paper is referred to as a *physical page.* The subdivided pages are referred to as *logical pages.* See Figure 19.1.

When subdivided pages are created, the physical page can be divided vertically (by columns) and/or horizontally (by rows). For example, when creating a booklet, the physical page is divided into two columns and one row. If tickets are being created,

FIGURE 19.1

Physical page vs. logical pages

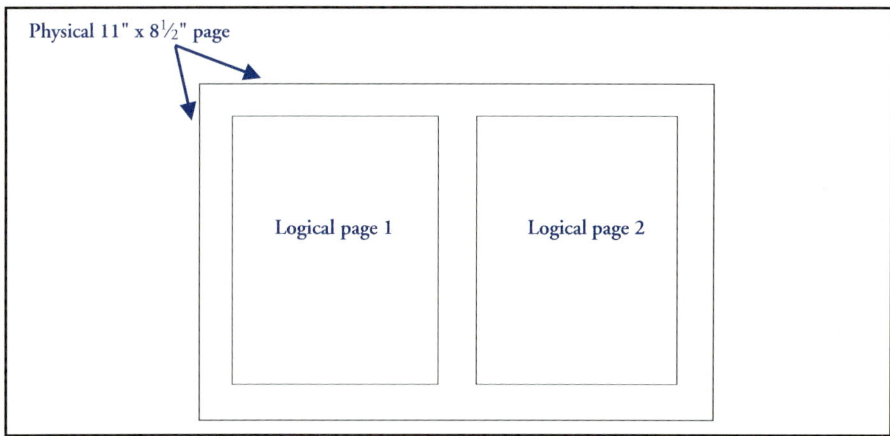

the physical page could be divided into two columns and five rows (ten logical pages) to create ten tickets per physical page.

When pages are subdivided, each logical page is treated by WordPerfect as a separate page of the document and can contain headers and/or footers, page numbers, and other page items. Text can be centered vertically and horizontally relative to the margins of the logical page. To view the logical pages on the screen side by side, the **Page Zoom Full** button is selected or the **Zoom** button is selected and a 50% or 75% view is chosen.

Start-Up Instructions

- Open the file named **19drill1.txt** located on the data disk.
- Change the initial font for the document to **Arrus BT, 11 point** (select **Layout, Document, Initial Font**, select desired font and size, select **OK**).

Steps to Create Subdivided Pages

1. Select **Layout, Page** {Alt, L, p}.
2. Select **Subdivide Page** {v}.

   Note: The Subdivide Page dialog box displays (see Figure 19.2).
3. Type the number of columns and/or rows that will be on one physical page of paper.

   For example, type **2** in the Number of Columns box.
4. Select **OK** {Enter}.

Change to Landscape Paper Type

5. Select **Layout, Page, Paper Size** {Alt, L, p, s}.

FIGURE 19.2

Subdivide Page dialog box

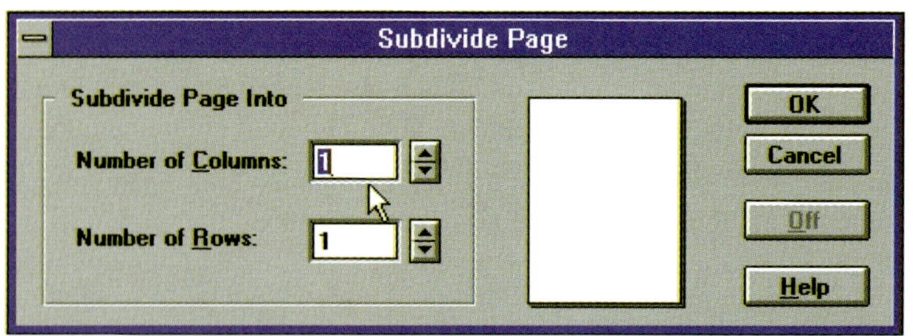

6. Click on the desired paper size/type.

   For example, scroll down and click on **Letter Landscape** {press the down arrow key to highlight Letter Landscape}.

7. Choose **Select** {Enter}.

Center Text Vertically on All Pages

8. Select **Layout, Page, Center** {Alt, L, p, c}.

   Note: *The Center Page(s) dialog box displays.*

9. Select **Current and Subsequent Pages** {s}.

10. Select **OK** {Enter}.

Finish-Up Instructions

- To view both logical pages with vertically centered text, select the **Page Zoom Full** button. Select the **Page Zoom Full** button again to return to the normal view.
- Use the following information and place the graphic image named **ender01.wpg** on the first page of the document.
  a. The insertion point should be located to the left of the first character on page 1 (the **C** in **Customer**).
  b. Select the **Figure** button on the Button Bar. Double-click on **ender01.wpg.**

     Note: *Some of the text is moved over to page 2. That's OK.*
  c. Select the **Position** button on the Graphics Box Feature Bar.
  d. Select **Put Box on Current Page (Page Anchor)**.
  e. In the Horizontal area, move the mouse pointer to the box located to the right of the word "from," press and hold the mouse button, and drag to highlight **Center of Paragraph**. Release the mouse button.
  f. In the Vertical area, double-click in the box located to the right of the word "Place." Type **1.5**.
  g. In the Vertical area, move the mouse pointer to the box located to the right of the word "from," press and hold the mouse button, and drag to highlight **Top of Page**. Release the mouse button.
  h. Select **OK**.
  i. Select the **Size** button. In the Height area, select **Set** and type **3**. Select **OK**.
  j. Select the **Border/Fill** button on the Graphics Box Feature Bar, select the **Border Style** button and click on NO BORDER. Select **OK**.
- Move the mouse pointer away from the graphic box and click once to deselect the box.
- Select the **Close** button on the Graphics Box Feature Bar.
- Use the *new* filename **19drill1.sub** and save the file on your file disk.

Use WP Draw to Create and Edit Graphic Images

The WP Draw program can be used to create and edit graphic images. The drawing tools, such as the **Line**, **Ellipse**, and **Freehand** tools, can be used to create graphic items. The **Set Line Color**, **Set Fill Color**, and **Set Line Style** tools are used to specify the appearance of the graphic item(s).

The **Text** tool can be used to insert text into a graphic image. Also,the text can be contoured to the shape of a graphic item. For example, text can be contoured to flow around the shape of an ellipse.

The **Select item(s)** tool is used to select graphic items or text in the WP Draw window. Multiple items can be selected using the **Select item(s)** tool by holding down the **Shift** key while clicking on each item to be selected.

An existing graphic image can be imported into the WP Draw program, and the WP Draw tools can be used to edit the graphic image.

Once a graphic image has been created or edited, the graphic image can be saved. The saved graphic image can also be retrieved into other documents.

Start-Up Instructions

- The file named **19drill1.sub** should be displayed in the document window.

Edit a Graphic Image Using the WP Draw Program

Note: A mouse is required to complete the following steps.

1. Double-click on the graphic image to be edited.

   For example, double-click on the **ender01.wpg** graphic image.

   Note: In a few minutes, the graphic image displays in the WP Draw program window.

2. Select Edit, Select, All.
3. Select Arrange, Group.
4. Select View, Ruler to display a horizontal ruler across the top of the drawing window and a vertical ruler along the left side of the drawing window.

   Note: When the mouse pointer is moved within the drawing window, light gray lines move in the rulers to indicate the location of the mouse pointer.

Move an image in the drawing window

5. Move the mouse pointer to any part of the graphic image, press and hold the mouse button, and drag to move the graphic image.

   For example, move the mouse pointer to the center of the graphic image, press and hold the mouse button, and drag down and to the right approximately $\frac{1}{8}$". Release the mouse button.

   Note: Small, black sizing handles display at the top and left side of the drawing window.

Size the graphic image

6. Move the mouse pointer to a black sizing handle, press and hold the mouse button, and drag to size the image.

   For example, move the mouse pointer to the sizing handle at the upper left corner until a double-headed arrow displays. Press and hold the mouse button and drag down and to the right until the red or light gray line reaches approximately 2.5" on the vertical ruler (ruler along the left side of the drawing window) and the red or light gray line reaches approximately 2" on the horizontal ruler (ruler across the top of the drawing window). Release the mouse button.

7. Move the mouse pointer within the graphic image, press and hold the mouse button, and drag to center the image in the drawing window.

Add Text

8. Select the **Text** tool [A] from the Tools palette.

9. Move the mouse pointer to the drawing window and click once to obtain an insertion point.

   For example, move the mouse pointer to the empty area at the top of the drawing area and click once.

   Note: *The insertion point is placed on the left side of the Text Editor box (see Figure 19.3).*

10. Type and format the desired text.

    For example:

    a. Change the font to EngraversGothic BT, 45 point by selecting **Text, Font**, choosing **EngraversGothic BT** in the Font Face box, selecting 45 in the Font Size box, and selecting **OK**.

    b. Type **Crown Plastics, Inc.**

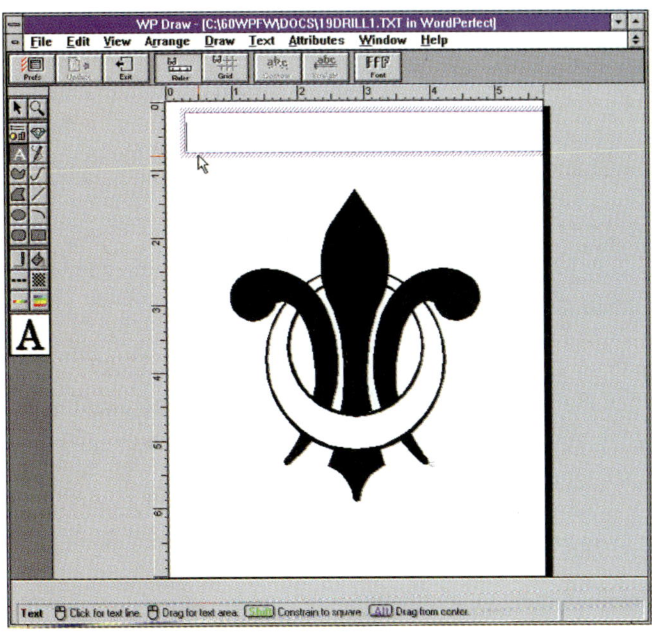

FIGURE 19.3

Insertion point in a Text Editor box (WP Draw)

Chapter 19
Create a Booklet

Note: Because the EngraversGothic BT font was selected, the text will display as CROWN PLASTICS, INC.

Contour Text to the shape of a drawing object

11. Draw the object to which the text should contour.

For example:

a. Select the **Ellipse** tool from the Tools palette.

b. Move the mouse pointer to the drawing window at approximately .75" on the vertical ruler and .25" on the horizontal ruler.

c. Press and hold the mouse button and drag down and to the right until the ellipse covers the graphic image and the graphic image is centered within the ellipse. Release the mouse button.

***Note:** The Ellipse is filled with black or a color and covers the graphic image. That's OK. The next steps will change the fill.*

d. Select the **Select item(s)** tool from the Tools palette and click on the Ellipse that was just drawn.

e. Select the **Set Fill Color** tool on the Tools palette and choose **White** (top right corner of the color palette).

***Note:** The graphic image is still hidden behind the Ellipse. That's OK.*

f. Select **Arrange, Back** to send the Ellipse behind the graphic image.

12. Click on the text to be contoured.

For example, click on the words **CROWN PLASTICS, INC.**

13. Press and hold the **Ctrl** key, move the mouse pointer to the graphic item that will be used to contour the text, and click once.

For example, press and hold the **Ctrl** key, move the mouse pointer to the edge of the Ellipse and click once.

14. Select **Arrange, Effects, Contour Text.**

***Note:** The Contour Text dialog box displays.*

15. Move the mouse pointer to the **Position** box, press and hold the mouse button, and drag to highlight the desired position for the contoured text. Release the mouse button.

For example, select **Top Center.**

16. Check that the **Display Text Only** option is selected.

***Note:** When the Display Text Only option is selected, the drawing object used to contour the text will not display when the OK button is selected.*

17. Select OK.

***Note:** The text is contoured to the shape of the ellipse at the top of the graphic image. The ellipse no longer displays because the Display Text Only option was selected in the Contour Text dialog box.*

Save the Edited Graphic Image

18. Select File, Save Copy As.

19. Type the desired filename in the Filename box.

For example, type **crown.wpg**.

20. Select the drive and/or directory where the graphic image should be saved.

For example, click in the Drives box and click on the drive letter where your file disk is located.

21. Select **Save**.

Finish-Up Instructions

- Select the **Ellipse** tool from the Tools palette.
- Move the mouse pointer to approximately 1" on the vertical ruler and .5" on the horizontal ruler. Press and hold the mouse button and drag down and to the right until the ellipse covers the graphic image and the graphic image is centered in the ellipse.
- Select the **Select item(s)** tool from the Tools palette. Move the mouse pointer to the ellipse and click once to select the ellipse.
- Select the **Set Fill Color** tool on the Tools palette and click on white.
- Select **Arrange, Back**.
- Select the **Set Line Style** tool on the Tools palette and choose the third line width button in the far left column.
- Save the graphic image using the same filename, **crown.wpg** (select **File, Save Copy As**, double-click on **crown.wpg**, select **Yes**).
- Select **File, Exit and Return to . . . .**
- Select **Yes** to the message "Save changes to . . . "
- Move the mouse pointer away from the graphic box and click once to deselect the graphic box.
- Use the same filename, **19drill1.sub**, and save the file again.

Create a Watermark

A watermark is a type of graphic box that is repeated on each page of a document. Text and/or a graphic image can be placed in a watermark box. The watermark text or graphic image is displayed and prints in a light gray or light color and other text and/or images can be placed on top of the watermark image. If a graphic image is used as a watermark, it may be necessary to lighten the image even more, so that overlying text can be easily read. The darkness of a graphic image can be changed by adjusting the contrast between the dark and light areas of the image. The contrast is changed by selecting the **Contrast** button on the Image Tools palette, and selecting a contrast option.

Start-Up Instructions

- The file named **19drill1.sub** should be displayed in the document window.

Steps to Create a Watermark

1. Place the insertion point on the first page where the watermark is to be located.

   For example, place the insertion point to the left of the first word (First) in paragraph one on the second logical page.

2. Select **Layout, Watermark** {Alt, L, w}.

   Note: *The Watermark dialog box displays. The WaterMark A option is selected.*

3. Select **Create** {c}.

   Note: *An empty document window displays. The words "Watermark A" display in the Title bar and the Watermark Feature Bar displays below the Power Bar.*

Place a graphic image in the Watermark window

4. Select the **Figure** button on the Watermark Feature Bar {Alt and Shift and f}.

5. If necessary, select the drive and/or directory where the desired graphic image is stored.

   For example, if necessary, click in the Drives box and click on the drive letter where your file disk is located.

6. Double-click on the desired filename.

   For example, double-click on **crown.wpg.**

   Note: *Because the graphic image is in a Watermark graphic box, the image is light. Also, notice that the Watermark Feature Bar has been replaced by the Graphics Box Feature Bar.*

7. To select the Watermark graphic box, press the right arrow key once and then select the **Prev** button on the Graphics Box Feature Bar.

   Note: *The right arrow key is pressed so that the insertion point is located to the right of the graphic box code.*

Change the contrast between the light and dark areas of the graphic image

8. Select the **Tools** button on the Graphics Box Feature Bar {Alt and Shift and L}.

   Note: *The Image Tools palette displays.*

9. Select the **Contrast** tool from the Image Tools palette.

   Note: *A contrast palette displays.*

10. Select the desired contrast option.

    For example, select the third option in the fourth row.

    Note: *The graphic image is much lighter.*

11. Select **Close** on the Graphics Box Feature Bar {Alt and Shift and c}.

12. Select **Close** on the Watermark Feature Bar {Alt and Shift and c}.

    Note: *The watermark displays in the document window. The watermark image is a light gray and the text is placed on top of the graphic image. The watermark displays on each page from this page forward in the document.*

Finish-Up Instructions

- Use the *new* filename **19drill1.wat** and save the file on your file disk.

Page Number the Subdivided Pages

Page numbers can be added to subdivided pages using the normal procedure to insert page numbers. In the case of a booklet, however, the cover page is generally not included in the page numbering. Therefore, the page numbering code is placed at the top of the second logical page and the page number reset to page 1. For page numbering purposes, page 2 is now page 1.

Start-Up Instructions

- The file named **19drill1.wat** should be displayed in the document window.

Number Subdivided Pages

1. Place the insertion point on the page on which the first page number should be located.

   For example, place the insertion point to the left of the first word (First) in paragraph one on the second logical page.

2. Select **Layout, Page, Numbering** {Alt, L, p, n}.
3. To set a new starting page number, select the **Value** button, type the beginning page number in the New Page Number box, and select **OK** {Alt and v, type beginning page number, press Enter}.

   For example, type **1** in the New Page Number box and select **OK**.

4. Move the mouse pointer to the **Position** box, press and hold the mouse button, and drag to highlight the desired position. Release the mouse button {Alt and p, Spacebar}.

   For example, select **Bottom Center** {o}.

5. Select **Close** {Alt and c].

Finish-Up Instructions

- If desired, scroll down to view the page numbers.
- Use the same filename **19drill1.wat** and save the file again.

Chapter **19** Create a Booklet

Print the Booklet

When a document has been created using the Subdivide Page feature, WordPerfect can print the document in a booklet format. When the **Booklet Printing** option is selected, WordPerfect automatically arranges the pages in the correct order. For example, the first and last page of the booklet are printed on one piece of paper. Also when Booklet Printing is selected, only half of the pages are printed. These pages are then reinserted into the printer and the other half of the pages are printed on the back. When the second half of the pages have been printed, the pages can be folded in the middle to form a booklet.

Start-Up Instructions

- The file named **19drill1.wat** should be displayed in the document window.

Print the Booklet

1. Select the **Print** button {Alt, f, p *or* F5}.
2. Select the **Options** button {o}.

   Note: *The Print Output Options dialog box displays.*
3. Select **Booklet Printing** {b}.
4. Select **OK** {Enter}.
5. Select **Print** {Enter}.
6. When the first page(s) has been printed, place the printed page back into the paper tray and resume printing.

   Note: *Check with your instructor or instructional assistant for information on reloading the printed pages into your printer. Your completed booklet should look similar to the booklet below.*

FIGURE 19.4

Completed booklet with watermark

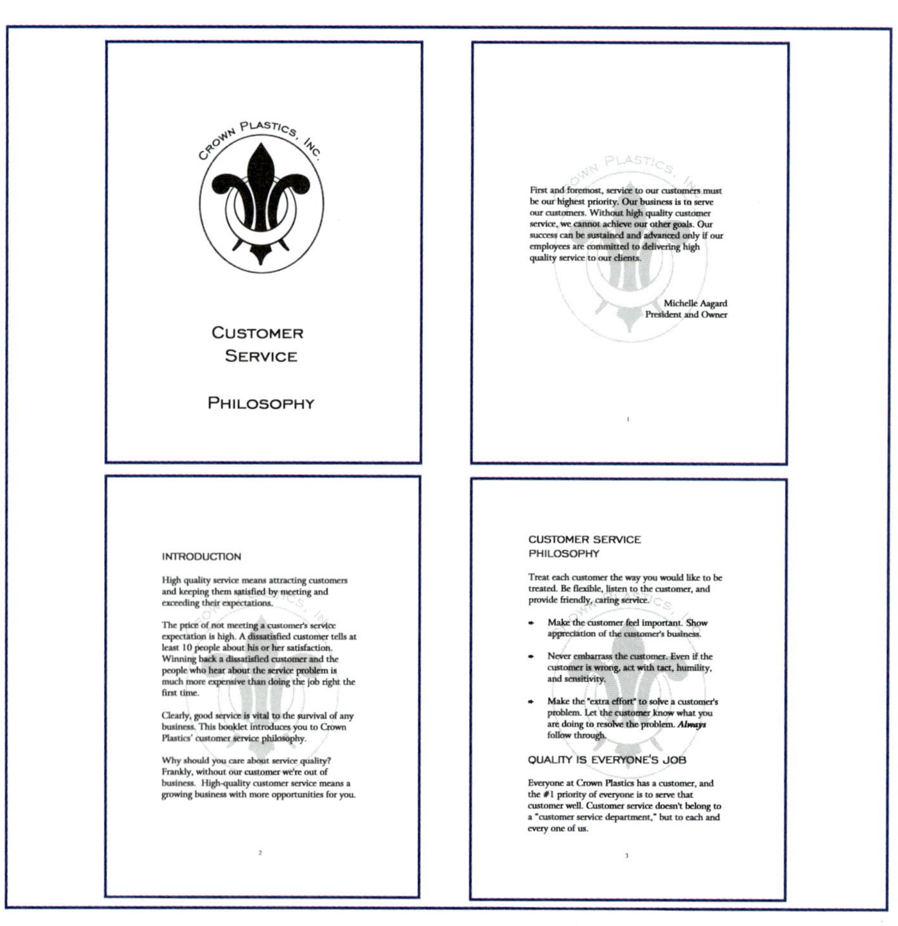

First and foremost, service to our customers must be our highest priority. Our business is to serve our customers. Without high quality customer service, we cannot achieve our other goals. Our success can be sustained and advanced only if our employees are committed to delivering high quality service to our clients.

Michelle Aagard
President and Owner

1

INTRODUCTION

High quality service means attracting customers and keeping them satisfied by meeting and exceeding their expectations.

The price of not meeting a customer's service expectation is high. A dissatisfied customer tells at least 10 people about his or her satisfaction. Winning back a dissatisfied customer and the people who hear about the service problem is much more expensive than doing the job right the first time.

Clearly, good service is vital to the survival of any business. This booklet introduces you to Crown Plastics' customer service philosophy.

Why should you care about service quality? Frankly, without our customer we're out of business. High-quality customer service means a growing business with more opportunities for you.

2

CUSTOMER SERVICE PHILOSOPHY

Treat each customer the way you would like to be treated. Be flexible, listen to the customer, and provide friendly, caring service.

- Make the customer feel important. Show appreciation of the customer's business.
- Never embarrass the customer. Even if the customer is wrong, act with tact, humility, and sensitivity.
- Make the "extra effort" to solve a customer's problem. Let the customer know what you are doing to resolve the problem. ***Always*** follow through.

QUALITY IS EVERYONE'S JOB

Everyone at Crown Plastics has a customer, and the #1 priority of everyone is to serve that customer well. Customer service doesn't belong to a "customer service department," but to each and every one of us.

3

The Next Step

Chapter Review and Activities

Self-Check Quiz

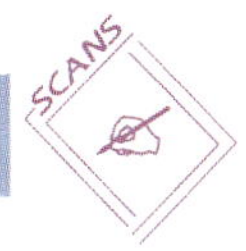

T F 1. A physical page can only be subdivided into two logical pages.

T F 2. A watermark is light gray when printed.

T F 3. Only a graphic image can be used as a watermark.

T F 4. In a document with subdivided pages, each logical page is treated as a separate page of the document.

T F 5. Page numbers cannot be printed on subdivided pages.

T F 6. The WP Draw program can be used to create and edit graphic images.

7. To contour text to the shape of a graphic item, select the text to be contoured, press and hold the _____ key and click on the graphic item to be used to contour the text.
   a. **Shift**
   b. **Enter**
   c. **Ctrl**
   d. **Alt**

8. A document can be printed as a booklet by selecting the _______ option in the Print Output Options dialog box.
   a. **Print in Reverse Order**
   b. **Print Multiple Pages**
   c. **Print Odd/Even Pages**
   d. **Booklet Printing**

9. In two sentences, state the difference between the physical page and logical page(s).

10. In a document with subdivided pages, the piece of paper is referred to as the _________ page.

Enriching Language Arts Skills

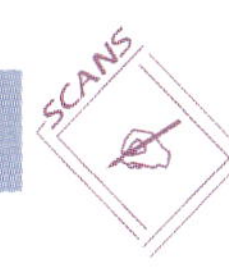

Spelling/Vocabulary Words

coaching providing instruction and direction.

evaluation the appraisal of a person or thing; formal review of a person's job performance.

feedback response to a question or request for information or input; e.g., information on the progress of meeting company goals.

Colons, Capitalization, and Punctuation for Bulleted and Enumerated Lists

Place a colon after an independent clause that introduces a bulleted or enumerated (numbered) list. An introductory clause frequently includes words such as "the following" and "as follows." When creating a bulleted or enumerated list, capitalize the first word and insert a final punctuation mark (period, question mark, or exclamation point) after each item that is a complete sentence or phrase. Do not capitalize the first word or insert final punctuation when bulleted or enumerated lists are not complete thoughts.

Example:

The following qualifications are suggested for an air conditioning mechanic applicant:

1. *high school or equivalent, plus three years' experience*
2. *hold a valid driver's license*
3. *successful compliance with job-related medical standards*
4. *proof of U.S. citizenship*

Activities

Activity 19.1—Create a Booklet, Use WP Draw to Edit a Graphic Image, and Create a Watermark

1. Open the file named **19act1.txt** located on the data disk.
2. With the insertion point at the top of the document, subdivide the physical page into two logical pages (select **Layout**, **Page Subdivide Page**, type **2**, select **OK**).
3. Change the paper size to Letter Landscape (select **Layout**, **Page**, **Paper Size**, click on **Letter Landscape**, choose **Select**).
4. Vertically center the contents of all pages (select **Layout**, **Page**, **Center**, **Current and Subsequent Pages**, **OK**).
5. Change the initial font to **BernhardMod BT** (select **Layout**, **Document**, **Initial Font**, select **BernhardMod BT**, **12 point**, select **OK**).
6. Use the following information to create a graphic box on the first page of the booklet containing the graphic image named **horse_j.wpg**.
   a. Select the **Figure** button and double-click on **horse_j.wpg**.
   b. Select the **Border/Fill** button. Select the **Border Style** button, click on NO BORDER, and select **OK**.
   c. Select the **Position** button. Select **Put Box on Current Page (Page Anchor)**. In the Horizontal area, select **Center of Paragraph** in the "from" box. In the Vertical area, double-click in the **Place** box and type **0**. Select **OK**.
   d. Deselect the graphic box.

7. Use the following information to edit the **horse_j.wpg** graphic image to create a logo for the Royal Equestrian Center.

   a. Double-click on the **horse_j.wpg** graphic image to access the WP Draw program.

   b. Select and group all the graphic items that are elements of the **horse_j.wpg** graphic image (select **Edit**, **Select**, **All**; select **Arrange**, **Group**).

   c. Flip the **horse_j.wpg** graphic image (select **Arrange**, **Flip Left/Right**).

   d. Turn on the horizontal and vertical rulers (select **View**, **Ruler**).

   e. Reduce the graphic image by 1" horizontally and vertically. (Move the mouse pointer to the sizing handle at the upper left corner of the drawing window until a double-headed arrow displays, press and hold the mouse button, and drag down and to the right until the red or light gray lines are at approximately 1" on both the horizontal and vertical rulers. Release the mouse button.)

   f. Center the graphic image in the drawing window (move the mouse pointer into the graphic image, press and hold the mouse button, and drag to center the graphic image in the drawing window).

   g. Select the **Elliptical Arc** tool. Move the mouse pointer into the drawing window so that the red or light gray line is at 4.5" on the vertical ruler and ¼" on the horizontal ruler. Press and hold the **Alt** key and the mouse button while dragging up and to the right until the red or light gray line is at ½" on the vertical ruler and 8" on the horizontal ruler. Release the **Alt** key and the mouse button.

   h. Add the text **Royal Equestrian Center** to the graphic image. Use the **ShelleyVolante BT** font in **52 point**, **Bold** or make a choice of your own (select the **Text** tool, click in an empty area of the drawing window, select **Text**, **Font**, choose the desired font, size, and appearance, select **OK**, type the desired text).

   i. Contour the text to the elliptical arc. (Select the **Select item(s)** tool, click on the text, press and hold the **Ctrl** key and click on the arc, select **Arrange**, **Effects**, **Contour Text**. Check that the **Display Text Only** option is selected. In the Position box, select **Top Center**, **OK**.)

   j. Use the filename **royal.wpg** and save the edited graphic file to your file disk (select **File**, **Save Copy As**, type the filename; if necessary, click in the Drives box and click on the drive letter where your file disk is located, select **Save**).

   k. Return to the document window (select **File**, **Exit and Return . . .**, **Yes**).

   l. Deselect the graphic box.

8. Create a watermark for the second and following pages using the **royal.wpg** graphic image created in step 7.

   a. Move the insertion point to the left of the first word (The) in paragraph 1 on the second page of the booklet.

   b. Select **Layout**, **Watermark**, **Create**.

c. Select the **Figure** button on the Watermark Feature Bar. Click in the Drives box and click on the drive letter where your file disk is located. Double-click on **royal.wpg.**

d. Select the **Close** button on the Graphics Box Feature Bar.

e. Select **Close** on the Watermark Feature Bar.

9. Use the following information and place page numbers on the booklet pages.

a. With the insertion point located on page 2 of the booklet, select **Layout, Page, Numbering.**

b. Select the **Value** button, type **1** in the New Page Number box. Select **OK.**

c. Select the **Position** box and choose **Bottom Center.**

d. Select **Close.**

10. Use the *new* filename **19royal.bkl** and save the file on your file disk.

11. Print the document as a booklet (select the **Print** button, choose **Options, Booklet Printing, OK, Print**).

Remember: *After the first physical page of the booklet prints, reinsert the paper into the printer and resume printing. Your completed booklet should look similar to the booklet below.*

SAFETY GUIDELINES

INTRODUCTION

The Royal Equestrian Center is committed to the safety of our employees. Each year many employees are injured while on the job. Most of these on-the-job injuries can be prevented or minimized by observing the safety practices outlined in this booklet. Two of the most common safety hazards are trips, falls, and slips and back injuries.

If you find a safety hazard, inform your supervisor immediately. A safe work area benefits everyone.

Review these safety guidelines and apply them to your everyday activities, both on and off the job.

1

TRIPS, FALLS, AND SLIPS

Trips, falls, and slips are the most common types of accidents. Always be aware of your surroundings and remember the following:

✓ Always wipe up spills immediately.

✓ Pick up debris around your work area.

✓ Keep boxes, low-level carts, etc., out of doorways and away from traffic areas.

✓ Make sure that telephone and electrical cords are under desks or along walls.

✓ Watch for objects in your path.

✓ Open doors slowly. Watch for oncoming traffic.

✓ Report torn carpets, cracked tiles, etc.

2

BACK INJURIES

Back sprains usually result from improper lifting, bending, standing, or sitting. Your back is a complex mechanism that needs respectful handling.

PROTECT YOUR BACK

✓ Practice good posture.

✓ Don't turn, twist, or bend to pick up objects even if they are light.

✓ Avoid slouching or slumping. Sit firmly against the back of chairs.

✓ Lift with your legs, not your back.

✓ Don't carry anything heavier than you can manage with ease.

3

Activity 19.2—Create a Booklet and Create a Watermark

1. Open the file named **19act2.txt** located on the data disk.
2. With the insertion point located at the top of the document, subdivide the physical page into two logical pages (select **Layout, Page Subdivide Page** and type 2, **OK**).
3. Change the paper size/type to Letter Landscape (select **Layout, Page, Paper Size**, click on **Letter Landscape**, choose **Select**).
4. Vertically center the contents of all pages (select **Layout, Page, Center, Current and Subsequent Pages, OK**).
5. Change the initial font to **Arrus BT, 12 point** (select **Layout, Document, Initial Font**, select **Arrus BT, 12 point**, select **OK**).
6. Use the following information to create a graphic box on the first page of the booklet containing the graphic image named **hotrod.wpg**.
   a. Select the **Figure** button. Double-click on **hotrod.wpg**.
   b. Select the **Border/Fill** button. Select the **Border Style** button, click on NO BORDER, select **OK**.
   c. Select the **Tools** button. Select the **Mirror Vertical** button on the Image Tools palette.
   d. Deselect the graphic box.
7. Create a watermark for the second and following pages using the **hotrod.wpg** graphic image.
   a. Place the insertion point to the left of the first word (Today's) on the second logical page of the booklet.
   b. Select **Layout, Watermark, Create**.
   c. Select the **Figure** button on the Watermark Feature Bar. Double-click on **hotrod.wpg**.
   d. To select the Watermark graphic box, press the right arrow key once, then select the **Prev** button.
   e. Select the **Tools** button. Choose the **Contrast** button on the Image Tools palette. Click on the fourth contrast option on the fourth row.
   f. Select the **Mirror Vertical** button on the Image Tools palette.
   g. Select the **Close** button on the Graphics Box Feature Bar.
   h. Select the **Close** button on the Watermark Feature Bar.
8. Use the following information to place page numbers on the booklet pages.
   a. With the insertion point located on page 2 of the booklet, select **Layout, Page, Numbering**.
   b. Select the **Value** button and type **1** in the New Page Number box. Select **OK**.
   c. Select the **Position** box and choose **Bottom Center**.

   d. Select **Close**.

9. Use the *new* filename **19hotrod.bkl** and save the file on your file disk.

10. Print the document as a booklet (select the **Print** button, select **Options**, **Booklet Printing**, **OK**, **Print**).

    Remember: *After the first physical page of the booklet prints, reinsert the paper into the printer and resume printing. Your completed booklet should look similar to the booklet below.*

HOT CARS!!!

HOT MUSIC!!!

CAR SHOW
and
SADIE HAWKINS DANCE

June 21, 199x
Culter Park

Today's events are sponsored by the Holbrook Cruisers, the Marshall Chamber of Commerce, and the Marshall First Street Program. Events will include a Car Show and Awards, booths, food, entertainment, and a Sadie Hawkins dance. All proceeds will benefit all three organizations and youth programs in Marshall and the surrounding area.

An event such as this is aimed at bringing visitors to historic downtown Marshall. The event is being held in the downtown area to give downtown business exposure to the many visitors who will attend the Car Show and the dance that follows in the park.

Our wish this evening is for your enjoyment--the sheer pleasure of recapturing feelings of days gone by.

Thank you for sharing this evening with us.

Tonight's performance includes the following:

1

The Cruis'n Coasters

The Cruis'n Coasters is a popular "Oldies" dance party band based in the Bay Area. The group features three outstanding vocalist/instrumentalists with a song list focusing on favorite tunes from the late 50s through the 60s and into the 70s. Three-part harmony arrangements, coupled with hi-tech equipment and the immense popularity of the oldies, have contributed to the group's 10-year success story.

Members of The Cruis'n Coasters have appeared in concert with such artists as The Legendary Rockin' Rockets and Flash Cadillac.

2

Richie Cymbol

Growing up in New Orleans, Richie was exposed to a variety of music which included a strong dose of classic blues. He formed his own band which, in addition to playing blues venues, played many clubs around town using different repertoires that included Rock & Roll, Soul, Pop, and Country Music. After settling in the Bay Area, Richie began freelancing in nightclubs from Los Angeles to Portland satisfying what has become an enormous appetite for different music styles. Richie has established his reputation by playing with a variety of notable artists in concert, nightclub, television, and radio appearances.

3

Challenge Your Skills

Skill 19.1—Create a Booklet

1. Create a booklet using the following information:

   a. The booklet text is contained in a file named **19skill1.txt** located on the data disk.

   b. Make decisions regarding:

Initial font for the booklet
Font, size, text attributes and alignment for the booklet title and sideheads
Use and placement of appropriate graphic image(s)
Use of WP Draw to edit/create graphic image(s)
Use of watermark
Page numbers for the booklet
Conversion of dashes (--) to the typographically correct em dash (—)

2. Correct three spelling errors, one misused word, and three punctuation errors.
3. Use the *new* filename **19ski.bkl** and save the file on your file disk.
4. Print one copy of the document as a booklet.
5. If you have completed your work, exit WordPerfect.

Part 5
Checking Your Step

Production Skill Builder Activities
Chapters 17-19

Production Activity 5.1—Create a Tri-Fold Brochure

1. Create a tri-fold brochure using the following information:
   a. The brochure describes the features of the Umpqua Lighthouse and Conference Center. Decide on a color for the border lines and shadow.
   b. The column text is contained in the following files which are located on the data disk:

Column 1	5pact1.co1
Column 2	5pact1.co2
Column 3	5pact1.co3
Column 1, page 2	5pact1.co4

   c. Make decisions regarding:
      Margins
      Font and point size for text
      Use of shadow boxes
      Use of rounded or square corners for shadow boxes
      Appropriate graphic image(s)
      (Suggested graphic images: **marsh.wpg**, **humbird.wpg**, **sun_dsg.wpg**, or **skipper.wpg**)
      Graphic box for first column on second page
      Rotated text for second column of page 2 (return address)
      Use of graphic image(s), reverse text, and borders for the third column of page 2 (the cover of the brochure)
2. Use the filename **5pact1.bro** and save the file.
3. Print one copy.
4. Close the document

Production Activity 5.2—Magazine Article (Group Project)

1. In groups of 3–5 people, write a magazine article that contains pull quote(s), sidebar information, different left and right page footers, columns with different widths, and graphic images.
2. Suggested article topics:

   Favorite features in WordPerfect 6.0 for Windows
   WordPerfect 6.0 for Windows vs. Word 6.0 for Windows
   Incorporating sound and/or animation in documents
   Desktop publishing features in WordPerfect 6.0 for Windows
3. Make decisions regarding:

   Margins
   Initial font for document
   Font and point size for article title
   Use of shadow text attribute
   Column widths
   Pull quote information, format, and placement
   Appropriate graphic image(s)
   Sidebar information, format, and placement
   Indentation for first line of paragraphs
   Footer text
4. Save the final magazine article using the filename **5pact2.fin**.
5. Print one copy and close the document.

Production Activity 5.3—Create a Booklet; Language Arts

1. Open the file named **5pact3.txt** located on the data disk.
2. Make decisions regarding:

   Subdividing pages to create a booklet
   Paper size and type
   Page numbering
   Initial font for the document
   Font and point size for booklet title
   Graphic image for cover of booklet and watermark
   Use of correct typographical symbols for quotation marks and em dashes
   Text to appear on each page
3. Correct four spelling errors, one misused word, three punctuation errors, and one missing parenthesis
4. Use the *new* filename **5pact3.fin** and save the file.
5. Print one copy as a booklet and close the document.

Part 6
Step Right Up

Create Special Documents

Chapters 20-22

- Line Numbering
- Redline and strikeout
- Compare documents
- Comments
- Hidden text
- Bookmarks
- Hypertext links
- Outlines
- Table of contents
- Index
- Table of Authorities
- Create paragraph styles containing borders and graphic images
- Create a style based on an existing style
- Link styles
- Cross-references
- Create, expand, condense, and save master documents

CHAPTER

Advanced Editing Techniques and Hypertext

Features Covered

- Turn on line numbering
- Use strikeout and redline text attributes
- Use the Compare Documents feature
- Insert a comment into a document
- Mark hidden text
- Create a bookmark
- Create hypertext links

Objectives and Introduction

After successfully completing this chapter, you will be able to turn on line numbering, use redline and strikeout text attributes to mark inserted or replaced and deleted text, and use the Compare Documents feature to mark the differences between two documents. You will also be able to use the Comments and Hidden Text features to insert notes into a document. Once you have learned to electronically mark a specific portion of text by using the Bookmark feature, you will then be able to link text by creating hypertext links.

WordPerfect's line numbering feature can be turned on to print a line number beside each line of text in a document. This feature is often used when creating legal documents. The redline and strikeout text attributes can be used to mark inserted or replaced and deleted text as a document is edited. The Compare Documents feature is used to mark the differences between two documents. The Redline, Strikeout, and Compare Documents features are used to help track the changes made to a document. The Comments and Hidden Text features are used to insert notes into a document. These features are often used when a document is reviewed by more than one person. Each person reviewing the document inserts hidden text or comments that suggest changes, ask additional questions, or add remarks on the document's contents. The author of the document can then review the comments or hidden text and determine the changes that need to be made to the document. Bookmarks are used to mark text, and hypertext links allow you to jump to and from the marked text.

Line Numbering

A number can be placed beside each line of text in a document. Line numbering is often used for legal documents and other documents in which text needs to be referenced by line number.

The Line Numbering dialog box is used to turn on line numbering and to control how line numbers are printed (see Figure 20.1). A preview of the numbering format displays in the sample numbering box. If changes are made to the **Numbering Method, Starting Line Number, First Printing Line Number**, or **Numbering Interval** options, the sample box will reflect the changes.

The default Numbering Method is Number (i.e., 1, 2, 3). However, the **Numbering Method** can be changed to lowercase letters (a, b, c), uppercase letters (A, B, C), lowercase roman numerals (i, ii, iii), or uppercase roman numerals (I, II, III). The **Starting Line Number** option is used to change the number of the first line. For example, instead of beginning the line numbers at number 1, line numbers can be set to begin at number 100. Generally, WordPerfect begins printing line numbers at the first line of the paragraph that contains the insertion point when line numbering is turned on. However, the **First Printing Line Number** option can be used to instruct WordPerfect to begin printing the line numbers on a line other than line 1. For example, if a document contains two blank lines at the top of the document, WordPerfect can be instructed to begin printing line numbers on line 3. A number can be placed either beside each line of a document or at intervals. The **Numbering Interval** option is used to specify the interval at which numbers will be printed. For example, WordPerfect can be instructed to print line numbers at every fifth line.

The position of the line numbers can also be changed. By default, line numbers are printed .6 inches from the left edge of the page. If margins are changed, it may be desirable to change the position of the line numbers. The position of the line numbers can be measured either from the left edge of the page or from the left margin.

When the **Restart Numbering on Each Page** option is selected in the Line Numbering dialog box, the line numbers begin counting again on each page from the number designated in the Starting Line Number box. If Restart Numbering on Each Page is not selected, the lines on all pages will be numbered continuously.

Blank lines can be counted or ignored by selecting or deselecting the **Count Blank Lines** option. If desired, the lines of each newspaper column can be counted by choosing the **Number all Newspaper Columns** option. Also, the font, color, or text attributes (bold, italic, etc.) for the line numbers can be changed by selecting the **Font** button in the Line Numbering dialog box.

After line numbering has been turned on, the numbers can be viewed in the document window. However, it may be necessary to use the horizontal scroll bar to view the left margin of the page. Also, the **Page Zoom Full** button can be selected to view the placement of the line numbers on the page.

Start-Up Instructions

❖ Open the file named **20drill1.txt** located on the data disk.

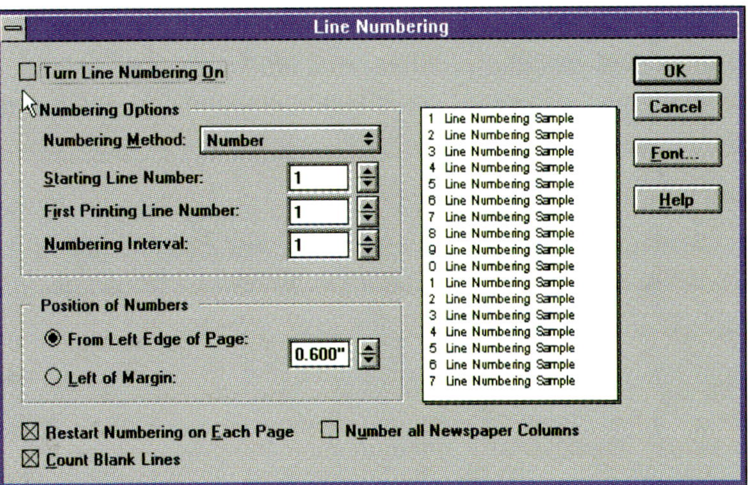

FIGURE 20.1
Line Numbering dialog box

Steps to Turn On Line Numbering

1. Place the insertion point at the location at which the line numbering should begin.

   For example, place the insertion point at the beginning of the document.

2. Select **Layout, Line, Line Numbering** {Alt, L, L, n}.

   Note: The Line Numbering dialog box displays (see Figure 20.1).

3. Select **Turn Line Numbering On** {o}.

4. Select any options desired.

   For example, select the **Font** button {f} and change the font to **Arial**. Select **OK** {Enter}.

5. Select **OK** {Enter}.

   *Note: If necessary, use the horizontal scroll bar to scroll to the left to view the line numbers. Line numbers can also be viewed by selecting the **Page Zoom Full** button. To return to the normal view, select the **Page Zoom Full** button again.*

Finish-Up Instructions

- Use the *new* filename **20drill1.num** and save the file on your file disk.
- Print one copy and close the document.

Redline and Strikeout

The redline and strikeout text attributes can be used to mark revisions in a document. The redline text attribute is used to mark inserted or replaced text. The strikeout text attribute is used to mark text to be deleted. When text is formatted with the strikeout attribute, a line is placed through the text (i.e., ~~strikeout~~).

Depending on the monitor used, text marked with the redline attribute will display in red or gray on the screen. When redlined text is printed, the text will print with a shaded gray background or, if a color printer is available, the text will print in red.

The method of marking and printing redlined text can be changed. For example, a vertical bar (|) placed in the left margin is often used to identify redlined text. A redlined character in the margin draws the reader's attention to the lines that contain inserted/replaced text.

After an edited document has been reviewed, the redline and/or strikeout marks can be removed. When redline marks are removed, the text changes to normal text (e.g., not red or gray). When strikeout marks are removed, the strikeout text is deleted from the document. At times, redline marks are not removed from a document so that inserted or replaced text is clearly identified.

Start-Up Instructions

- Open the file named **20drill1.txt** located on the data disk.

Use Strikeout

1. Select the desired text.

   For example, in the second sentence of paragraph two, select the text from the first comma to the second comma (include both commas in the selected text).

2. Select **Layout, Font** {Alt, L, f *or* F9}.
3. In the Appearance box, select **Strikeout** {Alt and k}.
4. Select **OK** {Enter}.
5. Click once to deselect the text {press the up or down arrow key}.

   Note: A line is placed through the text.

Use Redline

1. Place the insertion point at the location at which text will be inserted.

   For example, place the insertion point to the right of the "e" in the word "state" (near the end of the first sentence in paragraph three).

2. Select **Layout, Font** {Alt, L, f *or* F9}.
3. In the Appearance box, select **Redline** {Alt and r}.
4. Select **OK** {Enter}.
5. Type the text to be inserted.

   For example, press the **Spacebar** once and then type **composed of unrelated persons who live together for reasons of economy and safety**. (Do not type the period.)

   Note: The inserted text displays in red on color monitors and in gray on monochrome monitors.

Finish-Up Instructions

- In the last paragraph, change *one million* to *eight hundred thousand*.

a. Select *one million* and select **Layout**, **Font**, **Strikeout**. Select **OK**.

b. Click to the left of the comma following the words "one million." Turn on Reveal Codes and check that the insertion point is located to the right of the Strikeout code.

c. Select **Layout**, **Font**, **Redline**, **OK** and type **eight hundred thousand**. (Do not type the period.)

- Use the *new* filename **20drill1.red** and save the file on your file disk.

Start-Up Instructions

- The file named **20drill1.red** should be displayed in the document window.

Steps to Change the Method of Marking Redline Text

1. With the insertion point located anywhere in the document, select **Layout, Document, Redline Method** {Alt, L, d, r}.
2. Select the desired option.

   For example, select **Mark Left Margin** to place a redline character in the left margin beside each line that contains inserted/revised text {L}.
3. Select **OK** {Enter}.

   Note: The redline character (|) has been placed in the left margin beside each line that contains redline text. If necessary, scroll to the left side of the document to view the redline character (|). The redlined text will continue to display in red in the document window.

Remove Strikeout Text

1. Select **File, Compare Documents** {Alt, f, r}.
2. Select **Remove Markings** {r}.
3. Select **Remove Strikeout Text Only** {s}.
4. Select **OK** {Enter}.

   Note: The strikeout text has been deleted. However, redline characters still display to indicate where text has been inserted or replaced.

Finish-Up Instructions

- Use the *new* filename **20drill1.fin** and save the file on your file disk.
- Print one copy.
- Select **Layout**, **Document**, **Redline Method**, **Printer Dependent**, and **OK** to return to the default redline setting {Alt, L, d, r, p, Enter}.
- Save the file again using the same filename, **20drill1.fin**.
- Close the document.

Compare Documents

The Compare Documents feature is used to identify the differences between the text in two files. When documents are compared, WordPerfect marks inserted or replaced text with the redline text attribute and deleted text with the strikeout text attribute. If text has been moved, the words "THE FOLLOWING TEXT WAS MOVED" displays before the moved text and the words "THE PRECEDING TEXT WAS MOVED" displays after the moved text. (These phrases are formatted as strikeout text.)

WordPerfect can compare documents by **Word**, **Phrase**, **Sentence**, or **Paragraph**. Word, Phrase, Sentence, and Paragraph are defined as follows:

Word	Text that ends with a space, any punctuation mark, hard return, hard page break, or end of document.
Phrase	Text that ends with any punctuation mark, hard return, hard page break, or end of document.
Sentence	Text that ends with any final punctuation mark, a hard return, a hard page break, or end of document.
Paragraph	Text that ends with a hard return, hard page break, or end of document.

Using the **Word** option provides the most precise results because only the inserted, replaced, deleted, and moved text is marked. When the **Phrase**, **Sentence**, or **Paragraph** options are selected, whole segments of text may be marked making it unclear as to the specific word(s) that have been changed.

After the documents have been compared, the redlined and/or strikeout text can be accepted by removing markings. When markings are removed, redlined text is changed to normal text and strikeout text is deleted.

Start-Up Instructions

❖ Open the file named **20drill2.txt** located on the data disk.

Use Compare Documents

1. Make desired revisions.

   For example, make the revisions shown in Figure 20.2.

2. Select **File, Compare Documents, Add Markings** {Alt, f, r, a}.

   *Note: The Add Markings dialog box displays. The name of the saved file displays in the **Compare Current Document to** box. To compare the current document to a different saved file, type the desired filename (including the drive letter and directory) in the **Compare Current Document to** box or select the **List** button and double-click on the desired filename.*

3. Select the desired Compare by option.

   For example, check that **Word** is selected. (If necessary, select **Word** {Alt and w}.)

4. Select **OK** {Enter}.

SMALL CLAIM FILING INSTRUCTIONS

The small claim filing fee form is used to tell the Court how many small claims filings you have had in the past 12 months. This information is used to determine your filing fee. If you have had less than 12 filings in the past 12 months, the charge is $6.00 8; if 12 or more the charge is $12. 15

This filing fee and a reasonable cost for serving the defendant are reimbursable to you if your case is rewarded with a judgment against the defendant. Reasonable cost of personal service is usually considered to be $14 20 per individual served. Amounts in excess of ~~this amount~~ $20 may be denied at the discretion of the judge hearing the case.

FIGURE 20.2

Revised text

Note: In a moment, the document displays with redline and strikeout marks showing the inserted and deleted text.

Finish-Up Instructions

- Use the *new* filename **20drill2.com** and save the file.
- Print one copy.

Start-Up Instructions

- The file named **20drill2.com** should be displayed in the document window.

Steps to Remove Strikeout Text and Redline Markings

1. Select **File, Compare Documents** {Alt, f, r}.
2. Select **Remove Markings** {r}.
3. Check that **Remove Redline Markings and Strikeout Text** is selected.
4. Select **OK** to remove redline markings and strikeout text {Enter}.

   Note: The text that was marked with the strikeout attribute has been deleted and the text that was marked with the redline attribute has been changed to normal text.

Finish-Up Instructions

- Use the *new* filename **20drill2.fin** and save the file on your file disk.
- Print one copy.
- Close the document.

Insert Comments

Nonprinting notes (comments) can be placed within a document using the Comments feature. Comments can remind you of special formatting or printing requirements or other tasks that need to be accomplished. For example, a comment might remind you to load letterhead paper into the printer before printing the document or to call to verify the title of the addressee before sending a letter. The Comments feature can also be used to collect the responses of people who review a document. For example, a proposal can be sent via e-mail (electronic mail) to several people asking for their input. The reviewers can insert their comments into the document and return the document to the originator of the document.

These comments can be edited and, if desired, converted to text and inserted into the document. To delete a comment, turn on Reveal Codes, place the insertion point to the left of the *Comment* code and press the **Delete** key.

Start-Up Instructions

❖ Open the file named **20drill3.txt** located on the data disk.

Note: A comment icon displays in the left margin.

Steps to

View a Comment

1. Move the mouse pointer to the **Comment icon** in the left margin and click once.

   Note: The Comment caption box displays containing the comment text. The comment text can be edited by double-clicking on the Comment icon. After editing the comment, select **Close** *to return to the document.*

2. To remove both the Comment caption box and text from view, click once.

Insert a Comment

1. Place the insertion point at the location at which the comment should be inserted into the document.

   For example, place the insertion point after the final period in the item number 1 paragraph.

2. Select **Insert, Comment** {Alt, i, m}.
3. Select **Create** {c}.

   Note: The Comments Feature Bar displays below the Power Bar.

4. Type the comment text.

   For example, type the following:

   I think this should be changed to three consecutive periods and 95% of sales objective.

   Also, should a copy of the meeting report be forwarded to the

Personnel department to be placed in the sales representative's personnel record?

(insert your name)

5. If desired, select the **Date** {Alt and Shift and d} and/or **Time** {Alt and Shift and t} button to insert the current date and/or time into the comment text.

   For example, press the **Enter** key once and select the **Date** button. Press **Enter** again and select the **Time** button.

6. Select the **Close** button on the Comments Feature Bar.

   Note: Scroll to view the Comment icon located in the left margin beside the last line of the item number 1 paragraph.

Finish-Up Instructions

- If desired, turn on Reveal Codes to view the *Comment* code.
- Place the insertion point after the final period in the item number 2 paragraph.
- Repeat steps 2–6 and create the following comment:

  Will a copy of the meeting report and written plan be forwarded to the Personnel department?

  (insert your name)

  Select the **Date** button.
- Use the *new* filename **20drill3.cmt** and save the file.
- Close the document.

Mark Hidden Text

The Hidden Text feature is useful for creating notes, questions, messages, or confidential information that can display (be visible on the screen and print) or be hidden (not display on the screen and not print). By using hidden text, a single document can be used for more than one purpose. For example, a list of employee names, departments, business phone numbers, home phone numbers, and home addresses can be created. The home phone numbers and home addresses can be marked as hidden text. The complete document, including the hidden text, can be printed for managers; a second document containing only the employee names, departments, and business phone numbers can be printed for everyone else.

Start-Up Instructions

- Open the file named **20drill4.txt** located on the data disk.

Use the Hidden Text Attribute

1. Select the text to be hidden.

Chapter 20 Advanced Editing Techniques and Hypertext

For example, move the mouse pointer to the column heading Minimum Price until the up arrow displays and double-click.

2. Select **Layout, Font** {Alt, L, f}.
3. Select **Hidden** in the Appearance area {Alt and e}.
4. Select **OK** {Enter}.

   Note: *The hidden text no longer displays in the document window. However, if Reveal Codes is turned on, the* ***Hidden*** *code and some of the text can be viewed.*

Finish-Up Instructions

- Use the *new* filename **20drill4.hid** and save the file.

Start-Up Instructions

- The file named **20drill4.hid** should be displayed in the document window.

View Hidden Text

1. Once text has been marked as hidden, select **View, Hidden Text** {Alt, v, x}.

   Note: *The text marked as hidden displays in the document window and will print. If hidden text is displayed, selecting* **View, Hidden Text** *will remove the hidden text from the document window.*

Finish-Up Instructions

- Print one copy.
- Close the document.

Create Bookmarks

The Bookmark feature enables you to electronically mark a specific portion of text in a document in a manner similar to placing a paper bookmark within a book to mark a reference or page. Several bookmarks can be placed in a document. Each bookmark is given a unique name. When a bookmark is created, WordPerfect automatically suggests using the characters following the insertion point as the bookmark name. The suggested name, however, can be changed by deleting the original characters and typing a new name. Once a bookmark is created, the insertion point can be moved quickly (jumped) from any location in the document to the bookmark location.

A special bookmark called a QuickMark can also be set. Only one QuickMark can be set in a document. The location of the QuickMark is set by selecting **Insert, Bookmark, Set QuickMark.** Once the QuickMark has been set, the insertion point can be moved quickly to the QuickMark by selecting **Insert, Bookmark, Find QuickMark.**

Start-Up Instructions

- Open the file named **20drill5.txt** located on the data disk.

Steps to Create a Bookmark

1. Place the insertion point at the location where the bookmark will be inserted.

   For example, place the insertion point at the beginning of the heading **Apartment Complexes** on page 2 of the document.

2. Select **Insert, Bookmark** {Alt, i, b}.
3. Select the **Create** button {Alt and e}.

   Note: The Create Bookmark dialog box displays. The text "Apartment Complexes" displays in the Bookmark Name box. The bookmark name can be accepted or a different name can be typed.

4. Select **OK** to accept the bookmark name displayed.

   Note: If desired, use Reveal Codes to display the ***Bookmark*** *code. Turn off Reveal Codes.*

Finish-Up Instructions

- Place the insertion point at the beginning of the heading **Shopping Malls** on page 3 of the document.
- Repeat steps 2–4 to create a bookmark named **Shopping Malls.**
- Place the insertion point at the beginning of the heading **Light Industrial and Warehouse/Distribution Properties** on page 4.
- Repeat steps 2–4 and change the bookmark name to **Light Industrial** (in the Bookmark Name box, press the **Delete** key and type **Light Industrial**).
- Use the *new* filename **20drill5.bkm** and save the file on your file disk.

Start-Up Instructions

- The file named **20drill5.bkm** should be displayed in the document window.

Steps to Jump to a Bookmark

1. Select **Insert, Bookmark** {Alt, i, b}.
2. Double-click on the desired bookmark name {use the arrow keys to highlight the desired bookmark name, press Enter}.

   For example, double-click on **Apartment Complexes.**

   Note: The insertion point moves to the heading Apartment Complexes on the second page of the document.

Finish-Up Instructions

- Repeat steps 1–2 and jump to the **Light Industrial** bookmark.

Create Hypertext Links

The Hypertext feature is used to link a part of a document to another part of the same document (via a bookmark), to another document, or to a macro. In order to use hypertext to link sections of a document, bookmarks must be created. The Hypertext feature uses the bookmark names to establish the connection or link between sections in a document.

When creating a link, a portion of text is selected to function as *hypertext*. Text marked as hypertext displays bold and is underlined on the screen, or it can be placed in a shaded rectangular box resembling a button.

After all hypertext links have been established, the Hypertext feature must be activated in order to jump from the marked hypertext to the linked bookmark. After a hypertext jump has been made, the insertion point can be returned to the original position in the document by selecting the **Back** button on the Hypertext Feature Bar. If the marked hypertext is to be edited, the Hypertext feature must be deactivated.

Start-Up Instructions

- The file named **20drill5.bkm** should be displayed in the document window.

Create Hypertext Links

1. Select the text to be used as a hypertext link.

   For example, in the first sentence of the document, select the text **apartment complexes** in the first paragraph of the document.

2. Select **Tools, Hypertext** {Alt, t, h}.

   Note: *The Hypertext Feature Bar displays below the Power Bar.*

3. Select the **Create** button on the Hypertext Feature Bar {Alt and Shift and t}.

   Note: *The Create Hypertext Link dialog box displays. The bookmark name "Apartment Complexes" displays in the Go to Bookmark box.*

4. To display a list of bookmarks in the document and select a bookmark name, select the down arrow located to the right of the **Go to Bookmark** box, move the mouse pointer to the bookmark name, and click once {press the down arrow key to highlight the bookmark name.

   For example, because the bookmark name Apartment Complexes displays in the Go to Bookmark box, skip to step 5.

5. Select the desired appearance for the hypertext link text.

   For example, select **Button** in the Appearance area.

6. Select **OK** {Enter}.

   Note: *The hypertext link displays in a shaded rectangular box in the document window.*

Finish-Up Instructions

- Select the text **shopping malls** in the first sentence of the document. Repeat Steps 3–6 and select the **Shopping Malls** bookmark.

- Select the text **light industrial** in the first sentence of the document. Repeat steps 3–6 and select the **Light Industrial** bookmark.
- Use the *new* filename **20drill5.hyp** and save the file on your file disk.

Start-Up Instructions

- The file named **20drill5.hyp** should be displayed in the document window.
- The Hypertext Feature Bar should be displayed in the document window. If necessary, select **Tools**, **Hypertext** to display the Hypertext Feature Bar.

Use Hypertext

1. Check that the **Deactivate** button displays in the Hypertext Feature Bar. If the **Deactivate** button is not displayed, select the **Activate** button. The button name changes to **Deactivate**.
2. Move the mouse pointer to the desired hypertext and click once {move the insertion point to the hypertext and press Enter}.

   For example, move the mouse pointer to the hypertext **apartment complexes** and click.

   Note: *The insertion point moves to the location of the Apartment Complexes bookmark.*

To Return the Insertion Point to the Original Position in the Text

3. Select the **Back** button on the Hypertext Feature Bar {Alt and Shift and b}.

Finish-Up Instructions

- Move the mouse pointer to the hypertext link **shopping malls** and click.
- Return the insertion point to the original position in the text.
- Move the mouse pointer to the hypertext link **light industrial** and click.
- Return the insertion point to the original position in the text.
- Select the **Close** button on the Hypertext Feature Bar.
- Close the document.

Turn Off Hypertext

Note: *The following step is for your information only.*

1. Select the **Deactivate** button on the Hypertext Feature Bar {Alt and Shift and a}.

   Note: *The button name changes to* **Activate***. To edit the text, double-click on the text and make the desired changes using normal editing procedures.*

The Next Step

Chapter Review and Activities

Self-Check Quiz

T F 1. The position of line numbers cannot be changed.

T F 2. The redline text attribute can be used to mark inserted or replaced text.

T F 3. To remove strikeout text only, select **File, Compare Documents, Remove Markings, Remove Strikeout Text Only, OK**.

T F 4. WordPerfect can compare documents by word, phrase, or paragraph, but not by sentence.

T F 5. Comments created using WordPerfect's Comments feature can be printed.

6. In order to use hypertext to link sections of a document, ________ must be created.
   a. bookmarks
   b. comments
   c. hidden text
   d. buttons

7. Once a _________ is created, the insertion point can be jumped from any location in the document to the marked location.
   a. bookmark
   b. line number
   c. comment
   d. strikeout

8. The Hypertext feature can be used to link a part of a document to _____________.
   a. another part of the same document
   b. another document
   c. a macro
   d. all of the above

9. Write a brief description of how you might use the Hidden Text or Comments feature.

10. Which Compare by option is used to obtain the most precise results when using the Compare Documents feature?

Enriching Language Arts Skills

Spelling/Vocabulary Words

demonstrate to prove; to display or operate.

mentor a teacher or guide.

realistic practical, obtainable.

Contractions

An apostrophe is used to indicate where a letter(s) has been omitted when two words are combined to form a verb contraction. Generally, contractions are not used in formal business writing. Contractions can be used in personal letters or informal business documents.

Examples:

it's (it is)	*you're (you are)*
I've (I have)	*don't (do not)*
we'll (we will)	*they're (they are)*

Activities

Activity 20.1—Use Line Numbering

1. Open the file named **20act1.txt** located on the data disk.
2. Turn on line numbering at the beginning of the document. Change the font for line numbers to **Arial, 10 point** (select **Layout**, **Line**, **Numbering**, **Turn Line Numbering On**, **Font**, **Arial**, **10**, **OK** twice).
3. Use the *new* filename **20act1.num** and save the file.
4. Print one copy.
5. Close the document.

Activity 20.2—Use Redline and Strikeout

1. Open the file named **20act2.txt** located on the data disk.
2. Make the changes shown. Use the redline attribute to mark inserted or replaced text. Use the strikeout attribute to mark text to be deleted.

A current challenge in offices today is the need to provide individuals with a sense of accomplishment and a feeling of control over how their job is performed.

One solution is to ensure that the system increases the user's capability by delivering professional results and functions needed for the job. For example, voice has been overlooked in many systems; telephone integration and voice mail are being added to office systems.

A second solution is to give the user more control over the system resources by providing personal tools. Personal computers are turning out to be a powerful motivator for office personnel. A laptop computer especially provides flexibility for travel and home use as well as connecting easily to the company's local area network.

Individual satisfaction and motivation are the critical components of working life quality and productivity improvement. Computers and software applications that are designed to provide ~~Design that addresses the user's personal concerns by providing~~ intuitive and efficient interfaces, needed functions, and resource control can improve job satisfaction and motivation.

---

3. Use the *new* filename **20act2.red** and save the file on your file disk.
4. Print one copy.
5. Remove the strikeout text (select **File**, **Compare Documents**, **Remove Markings**, **Remove Strikeout Text Only**, **OK**).
6. Change the redline method to **Mark Left Margin** (select **Layout**, **Document**, **Redline Method**, **Mark Left Margin**, **OK**).
7. Save the document again.
8. Print one copy.
9. Close the document.

Activity 20.3—Create Bookmarks and Hypertext Links

1. Open the file named **19act1.txt** located on the data disk.
2. Create the following bookmarks:
   a. Place the insertion point at the beginning of the heading **TRIPS, FALLS, AND SLIPS** on page 3 of the document.
   b. Select **Insert**, **Bookmark**, **Create**. Select **OK** to accept the suggested bookmark name of Trips, Falls, and Slips.
   c. Place the insertion point at the beginning of the heading **BACK INJURIES** on page 4 of the document.
   d. Select **Insert**, **Bookmark**, **Create**. Select **OK** to accept the suggested bookmark name.
3. Create the following hypertext links:
   a. Highlight the text **trips, falls, and slips** in the first paragraph under the heading Introduction on page 2 of the document.
   b. Select **Tools**, **Hypertext**. Select the **Create** button on the Hypertext Feature Bar.
   c. Click on the down arrow beside the **Go to Bookmark** box.

d. Click on the **Trips, Falls, and Slips** bookmark name.

e. In the Appearance area, select **Button**.

f. Select **OK**.

g. Highlight the text **back injuries** in the first paragraph under the heading Introduction on page 2 of the document.

h. Select **Tools**, **Hypertext**. Select the **Create** button on the Hypertext Feature Bar.

i. If necessary, click on the down arrow beside the **Go to Bookmark** box and click on the the **Back Injuries** bookmark name.

j. In the Appearance area, select **Button**.

k. Select **OK**.

4. Check that the **Deactivate** button displays in the Hypertext Feature Bar.
5. Move the mouse pointer to the hypertext link **back injuries** and click to jump to the **Back Injuries** bookmark. Return from the jump (select the **Back** button).
6. Use the *new* filename **20act3.hyp** and save the file on your file disk.
7. Optional. Print one copy.
8. Close the document.

Challenge Your Skills

Skill 20.1—Use Compare Documents; Language Arts

1. Type the following document.
2. Make decisions regarding:

    Margins
    Fonts
    Indentation for enumerated items

3. Correct three spelling errors, three contractions, and two punctuation errors.

STEPS TO ATTRACT A MENTOR

Attracting the support and encouragement of older professionals in your career field is the basis of mentoring. A good menter offers excellent insights and introductions to people higher up. It is a great way to learn about a companys unspoken rules. You'll need to develop several skills in order to attract a mentor.

1. Learn how to listen. Never interrupt others before they have completed their comments. Look for opportunities to deminstrate that you're listening carefully.

2. Develop a presentation that demonstrates your personal pride. Walk straight, keep your head up, shake hands firmly and establish eye contact whenever you're in a conversation.

3. Be persistent. People who persist develop excellence in their fields faster than those who settle for second best.

4. Be willing to accept failure as easily as you accept success. Learn from your mistakes.

5. Set realitic career goals. Without a career map, it's easy to drift aimlessly from one job to another.

---

4. Use the filename **20skill1.txt** and save the file to your file disk.
5. Print one copy.
6. Make the following changes. (**Do not save the changes at this time.**)

STEPS TO ATTRACT A MENTOR

a more experienced professional

Attracting the support and encouragement of ~~older professionals~~ in your career field is the basis of mentoring. A good menter offers excellent insights and introductions to

professional individuals

~~people higher up~~. It is a great way to learn about a companys unspoken rules. You'll need to develop several skills in order to attract a mentor.

1. Learn how to listen. Never interrupt others before they have completed their

Learn listening skills by observing other good listeners.

comments. ~~Look for opportunities to deminstrate that you're listening carefully.~~

body language that demonstrates self-confidence.

2. Develop ~~a presentation that demonstrates your personal pride~~. Walk straight, keep

when conversing with others.

your head up, shake hands firmly and establish eye contact ~~whenever you're in a conversation.~~

3. Be persistent. People who persist develop excellence in their fields faster than those who settle for second best.

4. Be willing to accept failure as easily as you accept success. Learn from your mistakes.

Setting specific career objectives will enable

5. Set realitic career goals. ~~Without a career map, it's easy to drift aimlessly from one~~

you to make decisions that lead to your desired goal.

~~job to another.~~

---

7. Use the Compare Documents feature to show inserted or replaced and deleted text.
8. Print one copy.
9. Remove all redline and strikeout markings to accept the changes to the document.
10. Use the *new* filename **20skill1.fin** and save the edited document on your file disk.
11. Print one copy.
12. If you have completed your work, exit WordPerfect.

CHAPTER 21

Outlines, Table of Contents, Indexes, & Table of Authorities

Features Covered

- Create an outline
- Change outline definitions
- Hide/show an outline family
- Show/hide outline levels
- Move an outline family
- Mark, define, and generate a table of contents, index, and table of authorities

Objectives and Introduction

After successfully completing this chapter, you will be able to display the Outline Feature Bar and create, number, and edit an outline. In addition, you will learn to mark, define, and generate a table of contents, an index, and a table of authorities.

Creating an outline is often very useful when writing reports, manuscripts, or other multiple-page documents. An outline assists a writer in organizing thoughts and grouping related information. Once a document is written, WordPerfect provides tools to assist the writer in creating a table of contents and/or an index. A table of authorities is used to list the citations (sources) of statements made in a legal document.

Create an Outline

An outline is a list of ideas expressed in phrases or sentences. The outline can provide a brief summary for writing a document such as a report. The ideas in an outline are enumerated in levels. WordPerfect's outline numbering feature can automatically number eight outline levels. In addition, body text (text that is not numbered) can be included in an outline style. An example of a WordPerfect enumerated outline style with body text and eight levels is shown in Figure 21.1.

FIGURE 21.1

Sample outline with body text and eight levels

Sample Outline Levels

↓ 3 Enters

I. Level one—first major idea
  A. Level two
  B. Second idea at level two
    1. Level three
      a. Level four
      This is an example of body text in an outline. The body text is not numbered.
        (1) Level five
          (a) Level six
          (b) Second idea at level six
            i) Level seven
              a) Level eight
              b) Second idea at level eight
II. Level one—second major idea

When the **Outline** command is selected, the Outline Feature Bar displays below the Power Bar. The Outline Feature Bar contains buttons that can be used to quickly format and edit the outline displayed.

The WordPerfect outline definitions provide various format styles for numbering outlines, paragraphs, legal documents, and documents with headings. These style formats can be chosen after selecting the **Outline Definitions** button on the Outline Feature Bar. The Outline definition style is illustrated in Figure 21.1. Once an outline is created, a different definition can be selected and immediately applied to the outline displayed in the document window. For example, an outline defined as legal can be converted to an outline defined as bullets.

An idea and indented related ideas and body text below the idea are a *family.* A family can consist of one or more ideas (levels). Outline families can be hidden so that only the first item in a family is visible. Hiding the related ideas helps a writer organize main ideas. If a main idea is moved, the hidden family is also moved. Families can be hidden on an individual level or by level for the entire outline. For example, to hide all families below level three, select the **Show 3** button on the Outline Feature Bar. Families are hidden on an individual level by choosing the **Hide Family** button on the Outline Feature Bar. The capability to hide and show outline families is often referred to as *collapsible* outlining.

Start-Up Instructions

- Type the outline title **Sample Outline Levels.** Press **Enter** three times. Select and center the title. Press **Ctrl** and **End** to place the insertion point in the third blank line below the title.

Steps to Display the Outline Feature Bar and Create an Outline

1. Select **Tools, Outline** {Alt and t, o}.

   Note: *The Outline Feature Bar, the level indicator icon, and the outline item number display in the document window (see Figure 21.2). The insertion point is located at the first default tab. Also, Level 1 displays in the Status Bar. Turn on Reveal Codes (Alt and F3) to view the outline code,* **Para Style: Level 1 Style.**

FIGURE 21.2

Outline Feature Bar, level indicator icons and outline item number

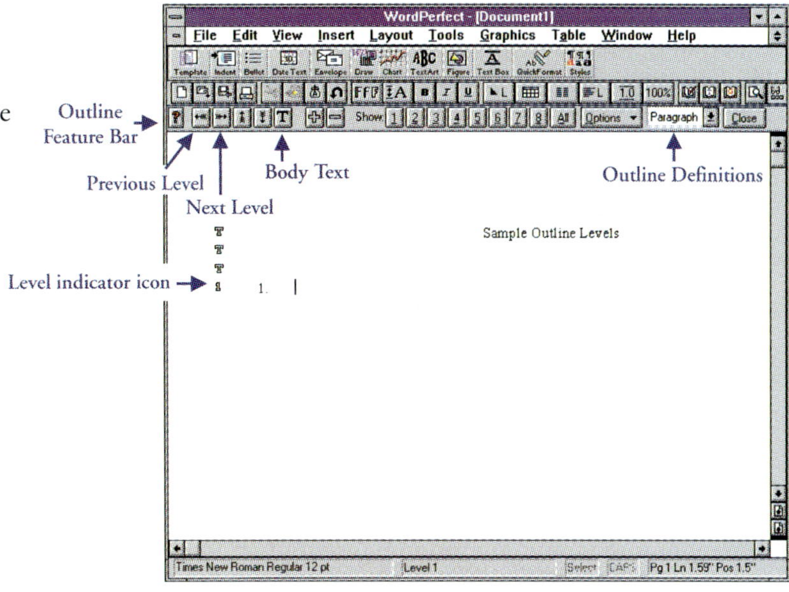

2. Click in the **Outline Definitions** box [Paragraph] on the Outline Feature Bar {Alt and Shift and d}.
3. Select the desired outline definition {press the up or down arrow key to highlight the desired style, Enter}.

   For example, choose **Outline**.

   Note: *The outline item number 1 is now displayed as Roman numeral I.*
4. Type the desired information.

   For example, type **Level one—first major idea**. (Do not type the period.) Press **Enter** once.

   Note: *The level 1 indicator icon and the Roman numeral II display.*
5. Press the **Tab** key once or select the **Next Level** button on the Outline Feature Bar.

   Note: *An A is displayed, replacing the Roman numeral II, the level 2 indicator icon displays in the left margin, and Level 2 displays in the Status bar. A plus (+) displays beside the level 1 icon to indicate that one or more levels follow.*
6. Type the desired information.

   For example, type **Level two**. (Do not type the period.) Press **Enter** once.

   Note: *The letter B displays.*
7. Type the desired information.

   For example, type **Second idea at level two** and press **Enter** once.

   Note: *The letter C displays.*
8. Press the **Tab** key once or select the **Next Level** button on the Outline Feature Bar.

   Note: *The number 1 displays, replacing the letter C.*
9. Type the desired information.

For example, type **Level three** and press the **Enter** key once.

10. Press the **Tab** key once or select the **Next Level** button on the Outline Feature Bar.

    Note: The lowercase a displays.

11. Type the desired information.

    For example, type **Level four** and press **Enter** once.

To Create Outline Body Text

12. Select the **Body Text** button on the Outline Feature Bar {Alt and Shift and t}.

    Note: The insertion point moves to the left and the body text icon "T" displays in the left margin.

13. Type the body text.

    For example, type **This is an example of body text in an outline. The body text is not numbered**. Press the **Enter** key once.

To Change the Outline Level

14. Select the **Options** button on the Outline Feature Bar {Alt and Shift and o}.

15. Select the desired option.

    For example, select **Change Level** {c}.

    Note: The Change Outline Level dialog box displays.

16. Click repeatedly on the up triangle until the desired level number displays or type the desired level number.

    For example, type **5**.

17. Select **OK** {Enter}.

18. Type the desired information.

    For example, type **Level five** and press the **Enter** key once.

19. Press the **Tab** key once or select the **Next Level** button on the Outline Feature Bar.

    Note: An (a) displays.

20. Type the desired information.

    For example, type **Level six** and press the **Enter** key once.

    Note: A (b) displays.

21. Type the desired information.

    For example, type **Second idea at level six** and press the **Enter** key once.

22. Press the **Tab** key once or select the **Next Level** button on the Outline Feature Bar.

    Note: An i) displays.

23. Type the desired information.

    For example, type **Level seven** and press the **Enter** key once.

24. Press the **Tab** key once or select the **Next Level** button on the Outline Feature Bar.

Note: An a) displays.

25. Type the desired information.

For example, type **Level eight** and press the **Enter** key once.

26. Type the desired information.

For example, type **Second idea at level eight** and press the **Enter** key once.

27. *To return the insertion point to the left margin*, select the **Options** button in the Outline Feature Bar, select **Change Level**, type **1**, and select **OK** {Alt and Shift and o, c, 1, Enter}.

Note: The Roman numeral II displays.

28. Type the desired information.

For example, type **Level one—second major idea.** (Do not type the period.)

29. To end the automatic outline numbering, select the **Options** button on the Outline Feature Bar and choose **End Outline** {Alt and Shift and o, e}.

Note: *The insertion point moves down and to the left and the body text icon "T" displays in the left margin to indicate that the outline numbering is no longer active. Notice that no new Roman numeral displays.*

Finish-Up Instructions

- Optional. Place the insertion point in front of the first word in the body text (i.e., This). Press **F7** three times to indent the body text under Level four.
- Use the filename **21drill1.out** and save the file.
- Optional. Print one copy.

Start-Up Instructions

- The file named **21drill1.out** should be displayed in the document window.

Steps to Change the Outline Definition

1. With the insertion point located in any line of the outline, click in the **Outline Definitions** box Paragraph on the Outline Feature Bar {Alt and Shift and d}.
2. Click on the desired style {press the up or down arrow key to highlight desired style, Enter}.

For example, scroll up and click on **Legal**. Select the **Outline Definitions** button again and scroll up and click on **Bullets**.

Note: Your outline with the Bullets definition should look similar to Figure 21.3.

Steps to Turn Off/On Level Icons

1. Select the **Options** button on the Outline Feature Bar {Alt and Shift and o}.

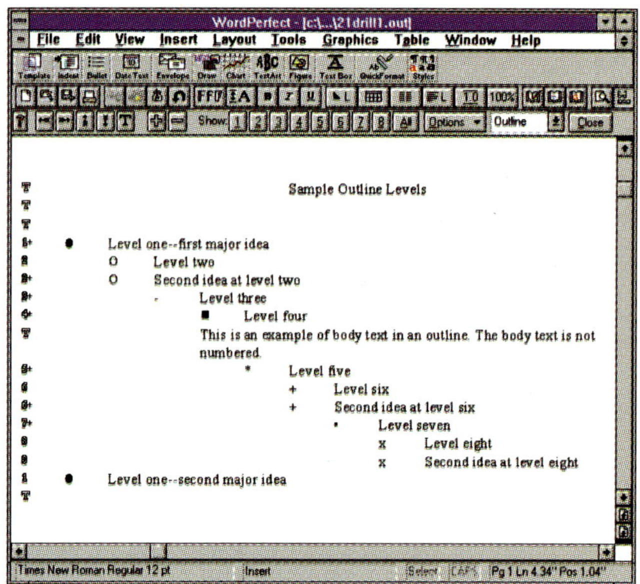

FIGURE 21.3

Outline using Bullets definition

2. Select the desired option.

   For example, select **Show Level Icons** {i}.

   *Note: If a checkmark displays beside Show Level Icons, selecting **Show Level Icons** will remove the level icons from the document window.*

Finish-Up Instructions

- With the insertion point located in any line of the outline, change the Outline Definition to **Outline** (click in the **Outline Definitions** box, choose **Outline**).
- Continue with the Steps to Insert a New Item(s) in an Outline.

Start-Up Instructions

- The level icons should be displayed. If necessary, select the **Options** button and click on **Show Level Icons.**

Insert a New Item(s) in an Outline

1. Place the insertion point to the right of the final character in the item that will precede the new item.

   For example, place the insertion point to the right of the "r" in four (Level four).

2. Press **Enter** once to obtain the next outline number.

   Note: The level 4 icon and the level letter b display.

3. Type the desired outline item.

   For example, type **Second idea at level four.** (Do not type the period.)

Finish-Up Instructions

- Use the same filename, **21drill1.out** and save the file.
- Continue with the Steps to Hide or Show an Outline Family.

Steps to Hide or Show an Outline Family

1. Place the insertion point in the first item of the family to be hidden.

   For example, place the insertion point anywhere in Level five.

2. Select the **Hide Family** button on the Outline Feature Bar {Alt and Shift and i}.

   *Note: All **indented** items below Level five no longer display in the document window. A minus sign displays at the right of the level 5 icon to indicate that the family below level five is hidden.*

3. To show a hidden family, place the insertion point in the desired family item and select the **Show Family** button on the Outline Feature Bar {Alt and Shift and s}.

   For example, place the insertion point in Level five; select the **Show Family** button.

Steps to Show or Hide Outline Levels

1. Place the insertion point in any line of the outline.

2. Select the desired Show number button on the Outline Feature Bar.

   For example, select the **Show 2** button {Alt and Shift and 2}.

   Note: Only levels one and two display. Levels three through eight are removed temporarily from the document window. Notice the level icons are only 1's and 2's. A minus sign displays at the right of the level 2 icon to indicate that the family below level two is hidden. To show all hidden levels, select the **Show All** *button on the Outline Feature Bar {Alt and Shift and a}.*

Finish-Up Instructions

- Select the **Show All** button to display all outline levels.

Steps to Move an Outline Family

1. Place the insertion point in the first item of the family to be moved and select the **Hide Family** button {Alt and Shift and i}.

   For example, place the insertion point in Level seven and select the **Hide Family** button.

2. Move the mouse pointer to the minus sign located at the right of the level indicator until a double-headed arrow displays; press and hold the mouse button and drag the thin horizontal line to the desired location.

   For example, move the mouse pointer to the minus sign beside the level indicator 7 until a double-headed arrow displays; press and hold the mouse button and drag the thin horizontal line up until it displays between Second idea at level two and Level three. Release the mouse button.

   Note: Level seven now displays between Level two and Level three. The family is still hidden and the level icon is 7. That's OK.

3. To renumber the moved family, locate the insertion point in the desired line, select the **Previous Level** button or **Next Level** button until the desired level displays.

For example, press the up arrow key once to locate the insertion point in the moved Level seven line, and then click on the **Previous Level** button four times until the level indicator 3 displays {press Alt and Shift and p until the desired level displays}.

4. Show the moved family by selecting the **Show All** button {Alt and Shift and a}.

Note: The family of Level seven displays and is renumbered.

Finish-Up Instructions

- Use the *new* filename **21drill1.rev** and save the file on your file disk.
- Optional. Print one copy.
- Close the document.

Change an Outline Level

Note: The following steps are for your information only.

1. *To change an outline item to the previous level,* select the **Previous Level** button on the Outline Feature Bar or press the **Shift** and **Tab** keys.
2. *To change an outline item to the next level,* select the **Next Level** button on the Outline Feature Bar or press the **Tab** key.

Create a Table of Contents

A table of contents lists the main topics in a report, newspaper, book, etc. The topic is usually followed by *leader characters* (periods) and the page number where the topic is located (see Figure 21.4). Buttons on the Table of Contents Feature Bar provide easy access to many of the table of contents commands.

Creating a table of contents is a four-part process:

1. The document is typed.
2. The table of contents entries are marked.
3. The table of contents is defined.
4. The table of contents is generated.

The table of contents entries are identified (marked) in a document that has been previously typed. The main topics in a document are usually typed centered or at the left margin and are referred to as major headings. Under each major heading, there can be one or more subheadings.

Table of contents entries are marked by selecting the appropriate Table of Contents level **Mark** button on the Table of Contents Feature Bar. When all the table of contents entries have been marked, the table of contents is defined. Usually, a table of contents is placed on a separate page at the beginning of the document. The insertion point is moved to the beginning of the document and a new page is created by

CONTENTS

FIGURE 21.4

Sample table of contents

pressing **Ctrl** and **Enter**. After **Ctrl** and **Enter** are pressed, the page number on page 2 must be reset to 1. The first page of text must be renumbered to 1 so that the table of contents will show the correct page numbers. The insertion point is then moved to the new first page and the table of contents title is typed.

Once the title for the table of contents is typed, the table of contents is defined by indicating the number of levels for the table of contents in the Define Table of Contents dialog box. If desired, the numbering format for each level of the table of contents can be selected by clicking on the Position box and choosing the desired format. WordPerfect places the message <<Table of Contents will generate here>> in the document at the location of the insertion point. In Reveal Codes, the generate message displays between two *Gen Txt* codes.

Once the table of contents is generated by selecting the **Generate** button on the Table of Contents Feature Bar, the table of contents text is placed at the location of the message <<Table of Contents will generate here>>. When the default table of contents numbering format is used, the table of contents text displays with dot leader characters and the page number aligned at the right margin. Second-level entries are indented .5 inches from the left margin (see Figure 21.4).

If a document is modified after the table of contents has been generated, the table of contents can be updated to show new page numbers. Also, new table of contents entries can be marked or existing entries can be deleted. When all changes to the document and entries have been completed, the document is saved and the **Generate** button is selected again. The original table of contents is replaced by the updated table of contents.

Start-Up Instructions

- Open the file named **21drill2.txt** located on the data disk.
- Turn on Reveal Codes.

Mark Table of Contents Entries

1. Select **Tools, Table of Contents** {Alt, t, c}.

   Note: *The Table of Contents Feature Bar displays below the Power Bar (see Figure 21.5).*

2. Select a level 1 table of contents entry (major heading).

   For example, select the heading **PRESIDENT'S ANNOUNCEMENT**.

FIGURE 21.5

Table of Contents Feature Bar

3. Select the **Mark 1** button on the Table of Contents Feature Bar {Alt and Shift and 1}.

   Note: The table of contents codes, ***Mrk Txt ToC****, display before and after the selected text.*

4. Select a level 2 table of contents entry (subheading).

   For example, select **Operation Changes.**

   Note: In the Reveal Codes window, check that the underline codes are not included in the selected text.

5. Select the **Mark 2** button on the Table of Contents Feature Bar {Alt and Shift and 2}.

Finish-Up Instructions

- Repeat steps 2–3 to mark the remaining level 1 table of contents entries—**A JOINT VENTURE** and **RAW LAND.**
- Repeat Steps 4–5 to mark the remaining level 2 table of contents entries—**Market Conditions** and **Raw Land/Joint Ventures.**
- Use the *new* filename **21drill2.mrk** and save the file on your file disk.

Start-Up Instructions

- The file named **21drill2.mrk** should be displayed in the document window.
- The Table of Contents Feature Bar should be displayed. (If necessary, select **Tools, Table of Contents.**)

Steps to Define a Table of Contents

1. Move the insertion point to the top of the document (press **Ctrl** and **Home** twice).

2. Press **Ctrl** and **Enter** to insert a hard page break at the top of the document to create a new page for the table of contents.

   Note: Page 1 of the original document is now page 2 and must be renumbered to become page 1 again.

3. Select **Layout, Page, Numbering** {Alt, L, p, n}.

4. If necessary, select the desired position for the page numbers.

   For example, move the mouse pointer to the Position box, press and hold the mouse button and drag to highlight Bottom Center. Release the mouse button.

5. Select **Value**. In the **New Page Number** box, type **1** {Alt and v, 1}.

6. Select **OK**. Select **Close** {Enter, Alt and c}.

Note: Pg 1 displays in the Status bar.

7. Press the up arrow key to move the insertion point to the new empty page.

8. Type and format a title for the table of contents page.

   For example, type **CONTENTS**. Press **Enter** three times. Select the word **CONTENTS** and choose **Center** justification.

9. Place the insertion point at the location at which the table of contents will be inserted.

   For example, place the insertion point on the third blank line below the word CONTENTS.

10. Select the **Define** button on the Table of Contents Feature Bar {Alt and Shift and d}.

    Note: The Define Table of Contents dialog box displays.

11. Check that the number in the **Number of Levels (1-5)** box is highlighted. [If necessary, double-click in the Number of Levels (1-5) box {Alt and n}.]

12. Type the number of table of contents levels used when marking the document.

    For example, type **2**.

    Note: Level 1 and Level 2 are now active and display in the Level, Style, and Position area. A sample of the table of contents displays below the Styles and Page Numbering boxes (see Figure 21.6).

13. Select **OK** {Enter}.

    *Note: A message displays "<<Table of Contents will generate here>>." Use Reveal Codes to view the **Gen Txt** codes that display before and after the generate message. When the table of contents is generated, the table of contents will be placed between the **Gen Txt** codes.*

Finish-Up Instructions

- Use the same filename, **21drill2.mrk**, and save the file again.

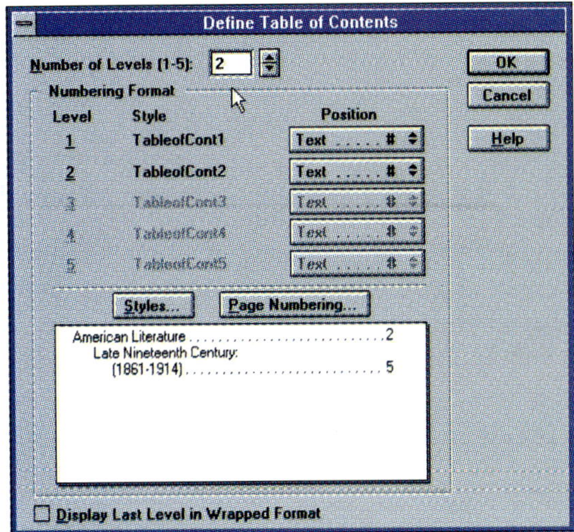

FIGURE 21.6

Define Table of Contents dialog box

Chapter 21 Outlines, Table of Contents, Indexes & Table of Authorities

Start-Up Instructions

- The file named **21drill2.mrk** should be displayed in the document window.
- The table of contents entries must be marked and the location, page number format, and number of levels must be defined before the table of contents can be generated.
- The Table of Contents Feature Bar should be displayed. If necessary, select **Tools, Table of Contents.**

Generate a Table of Contents

1. Select the **Generate** button on the Table of Contents Feature Bar {Alt and Shift and g}.

   Note: The Generate dialog box displays.

2. Select **OK** {Enter}.

   Note: The Please Wait message box displays briefly. Then the table of contents displays in the document window.

Finish-Up Instructions

- Use the *new* filename **21drill2.toc** and save the file on your file disk.
- Print one copy and close the document.

Create an Index

An index is an alphabetical listing of topics contained in a document. Entries in the index usually include a page number to indicate the location of the topic. Once a document is typed, the main index heading and subheading entries can be marked, the index numbering format can be defined, and the index can be generated. The Index Feature Bar is used to access quickly the index commands (see Figure 21.7).

Once the index heading and subheading entries have been marked, the index format is defined. An index is usually placed on a separate page at the end of the document. A hard page break is inserted at the end of the document and an index page title is typed. When the numbering format of the index is defined, the message <<Index will generate here>> displays. In Reveal Codes, the generate message displays between two *Gen Txt* codes.

After the index heading and subheading entries have been marked and the index numbering format has been defined, the index is generated. The generated index organizes all topics alphabetically and inserts the page number(s) on which the topic is located in the document. The generated index displays at the location of the <<Index will generate here>> message.

If a document is modified after the index has been generated, the index can be updated to show new page numbers. New heading and subheading entries can also be marked. When all changes to the document and entries have been complete and the document is saved, the **Generate** button is selected, replacing the original index with the updated index.

FIGURE 21.7

Index Feature Bar

Start-Up Instructions

- Open the file named **21drill2.txt** located on the data disk.

Mark Index Entries

1. Select **Tools, Index** {Alt, t, x}.

   Note: The Index Feature Bar displays below the Power Bar (see Figure 21.7).

Mark Heading Index Entries

2. Select the text to be a heading index entry.

   For example, select **limited partnership** in the first sentence of the first paragraph.

3. Click in the **Heading** box on the Index Feature Bar {Alt and Shift and e}.

   Note: The selected text displays in the Heading box.

4. Edit the heading entry text as needed.

   For example, press the **Home** key and capitalize the "l" in the word "limited."

5. Select the **Mark** button on the Index Feature Bar {Alt and Shift and m}.

   Note: If desired, use Reveal Codes to view the Index code.

6. Select the text to be a heading index entry.

   For example, select **joint venture** in the first sentence of the third paragraph.

7. Click in the **Heading** box on the Index Feature Bar {Alt and Shift and e}.
8. Edit the heading entry text as needed.

   For example, press the **Home** key and capitalize the "j" in the word "joint."

9. Select the **Mark** button on the Index Feature Bar {Alt and Shift and m}.

Mark Subheading Index Entries

10. To select the heading index entry that the subheading index entry will be under, move the mouse pointer to the down arrow located to the right of the Heading box, click once to display a list of headings, click on the desired heading {Alt and Shift and e, press the up or down arrow key to display the desired heading}.

    For example, check that **Joint venture** displays in the Heading box. (If necessary, click on the down arrow to the right of the Heading box and click on **Joint venture**.)

11. Select the text to be a subheading index entry.

    For example, select the words **form of partnership** located in the first sentence of the third paragraph.

12. Click in the **Subheading** box on the Index Feature Bar {Alt and Shift and s}.

    Note: The selected text "form of partnership" displays in the subheading box and will be a subheading index entry under the main heading, Joint venture.

13. Edit the subheading text as needed.

    For example, the subheading words already begin with lowercase letters. Therefore, no editing is needed.

14. Select the **Mark** button on the Index Feature Bar {Alt and Shift and m}.

Finish-Up Instructions

- Select the words **Market Conditions**. Repeat steps 3–5 to mark the selected text as a heading index entry. The "C" in *Conditions* should be changed to lowercase.
- Select the words **raw land** in the first sentence of the last paragraph. Repeat steps 10–14 to mark the selected text as a subheading index entry under the main heading, *Joint venture.*
- Use the *new* filename **21drill3.ind** and save the file on your file disk.

Start-Up Instructions

- The filename **21drill3.ind** should be displayed in the document window.
- The Index Feature Bar should be displayed. (If necessary, select **Tools, Index.**)

Steps to Define an Index

1. Move the insertion point to the bottom of the document (**Ctrl** and **End**).
2. Press **Ctrl** and **Enter** to insert a hard page break.
3. Type and format a title for the index page.

    For example, type INDEX. Press **Enter** three times. Select the word **INDEX** and select **Center** justification.

4. Place the insertion point at the location where the index will be inserted.

    For example, place the insertion point on the third blank line below the title INDEX.

5. Select the **Define** button on the Index Feature Bar {Alt and Shift and d}.

    Note: The Define Index dialog box displays (see Figure 21.8).

6. Select the desired Numbering Format Position.

    For example, move the mouse pointer to the **Position** button, press and hold the mouse button and drag down to highlight the **Text, #** option. Release the mouse button {Spacebar, x}.

    Note: A sample of the index displays.

7. Select **OK** {press Enter}.

    *Note: A message displays "<<Index will generate here>>." Use Reveal Codes to view the **Gen Txt** codes that display before and after the generate message. When the index is generated, the index will be placed between the **Gen Txt** codes.*

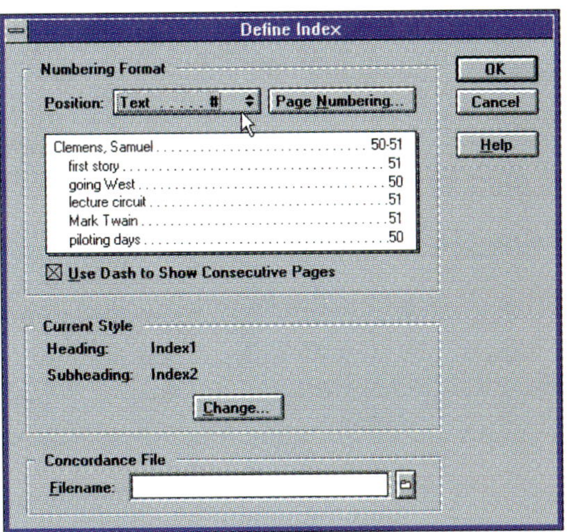

FIGURE 21.8

Define Index dialog box

Finish-Up Instructions

- Use the same filename, **21drill3.ind**, and save the file again.

Start-Up Instructions

- The file named **21drill3.ind** should be displayed in the document window.
- The index entries must be marked and the index numbering format and location defined before the index can be generated.
- The Index Feature Bar should be displayed. (If necessary, select **Tools**, **Index**.)

Steps to Generate an Index

1. Select the **Generate** button on the Index Feature Bar {Alt and Shift and g}.

   Note: The Generate dialog box displays.

2. Select **OK** {Enter}.

   Note: The Please Wait message box displays briefly, then the index displays in the document window.

Finish-Up Instructions

- Place the insertion point at the top of the index page and change the line spacing to one.
- Use the *new* filename **21index.lan** and save the file on your file disk.
- Print one copy of the index page only. Close the document.

Create a Table of Authorities

A table of authorities is a list of the specific sources used to substantiate a statement(s) in a legal document. A source can include information such as a case name, volume, reporter, page, court and jurisdiction, and date. The source information is referred to as a citation. The most common sources cited are statutes and cases. Headings, such as Cases, Other Sources and Statutes, are used to group the listed sources

FIGURE 21.9

Sample Table of Authorities

Table of Authorities

Cases	**Page**
FDIC v. Air Florida System, Inc. 822 F 2d 833, 843	2
Jannis v. Ellis (1957) 308 P 2d 750, 149 CA 2d 751 CCP 1287	2, 3
Sandler v. Casale (1981) 125 CA 3d 707,178 CR 265	2
Other Sources	
CP 86 (a) (10)	3

(see Figure 21.9). A table of authorities is used predominately for cases being heard at an upper level court.

Creating a table of authorities is similar to creating a table of contents, i.e., the document is typed, the entries are created (marked), the table of authorities is defined and then generated. The Table of Authorities Feature Bar is used to create a table of authorities (select **Tools**, **Table of Authorities**).

When a table of authorities entry is first marked, the Create Full Form dialog box is used. In the Create Full Form dialog box, the Section Name and a Short Form name are typed or selected. The section name is used to indicate the section in the table of authorities where the source information (citation) will be placed. For example, Sandler v. Casale . . . is a case source and is listed under the heading "Cases" (see Figure 21.9)

The Short Form name is created and used only if the same source is used at another location(s) in the document. When a source is used again, the insertion point is placed in or beside the source information in the document, the Short Form name is selected in the Short Form box, and the **Mark** button is selected. Using the Short Form name and the **Mark** button is a quick method to mark the second and following references to the same source.

Once the table of authorities entries are created, the entries can be edited by selecting the **Edit Full Form** button on the Table of Authorities Feature Bar. The Short Form and Section Name for each entry is listed in the Edit Full Form dialog box. Double-click on the desired entry to obtain the Table of Authorities Full Form Feature Bar and editing window. Make any needed changes to the section, short form or source information. Select **Close** to return the insertion point to the document.

After the table of authorities entries are created, the table of authorities page is created. The table of authorities page includes the title, **Table of Authorities**, section head(s) (Cases, etc.), and the heading, Page (see Figure 21.9). After the title and headings are typed, the insertion point is placed where the citations are to be listed. For example, the insertion point is placed one blank space after the heading **Cases**. The table of authorities is then defined to setup the numbering format for each section and location of the list of citations. Various numbering formats are available. For example, the numbering format can include the text, dot leaders, and the page number, or the format can include only the text and page number. The default numbering format is text with dot leaders and a page number as seen in Figure 21.9. After the numbering format is defined and the **Insert** button is selected, the message <<Table of Authorities will generate here>> displays in the document window.

Once the table of authorities entries are created and the format numbering defined, the table of authorities is generated. Use the **Generate** button on the Table of Authorities Feature Bar to generate the citations with page numbers.

Start-Up Instructions

- Open the file named **21drill4.lgl** located on the data disk.
- Turn on Reveal Codes.

Steps to Create Full and Short Form Table of Authorities Entries

1. Select **Tools, Table of Authorities** {Alt, t, a}.

   Note: *The Table of Authorities Feature Bar displays below the Power Bar.*

2. Select the desired citation, including any necessary codes.

   For example, select the complete citation that begins **Sandler v. Casale . . .** on page two, in the first paragraph under Part III, Law and Argument and include the italic code. (Do not select the comma at the end of the citation.)

3. Select the **Create Full Form** button on the Table of Authorities Feature Bar {Alt and Shift and r}.

   Note: *The Create Full Form dialog box displays.*

4. Type the desired section name in the Section Name box.

   For example, type **Cases.**

5. Press the **Tab** key to enter the Short Form box.
6. Type the desired short form name.

   For example, type **Sandler.**

   Note: *The Create Full Form dialog box will look similar to Figure 21.10.*

7. Select **OK.**

   Note: *The full citation displays below the Table of Authorities Full Form Feature Bar.*

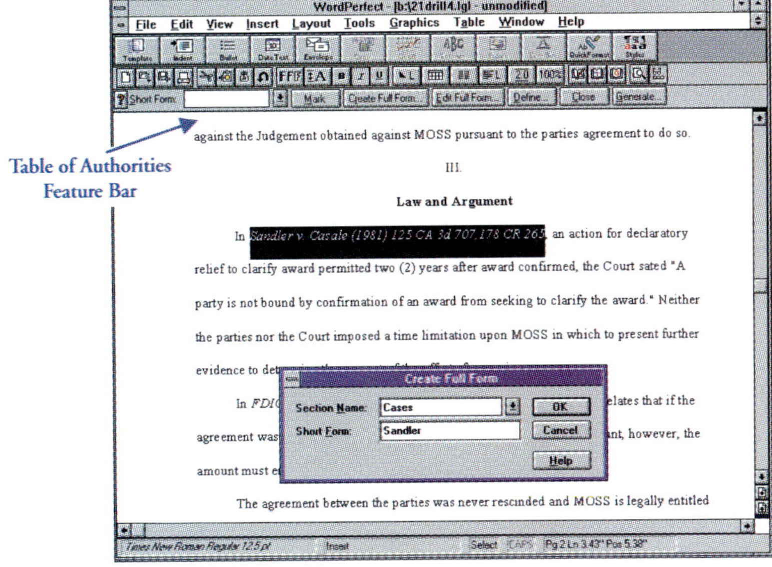

FIGURE 21.10

Table of Authorities Feature Bar and Create Full Form dialog box

Chapter 21 Outlines, Table of Contents, Indexes & Table of Authorities

8. Edit the citation if needed.

   For example, check that the citation is italicized. (If necessary, select the text and choose the **Italic** button.)

9. Select **Close** {Alt and Shift and c}.

   Note: In Reveal Codes, the expanded code ToA code shows the Section Name—Cases—the Short Form—Sandler—and the words Full Form.

Finish-Up Instructions

- Repeat steps 2–9 and use the following information to create the Table of Authorities full and short form entries.
- Select the citation that begins **FDIC v. Air Florida**, including the italics code, in the second paragraph under Part III, Law and Argument. The Section Name is **Cases**. The Short Form name is **FDIC**.
- Select the citation that begins **Jannis v. Ellis** in the fourth paragraph under Part III. The Section Name is **Cases**. The Short Form name is **Jannis**.
- Select the citation that begins **CP 86** at the end of the one-line paragraph that starts with the words "Jurisdiction remains." The Section Name is **Other Sources**. The Short Form name is **CP 86**.
- Use the *new* filename **21drill4.toa** and save the file on your file disk.
- Continue with the Steps to Use a Short Form to Create a Table of Authorities Entry.

Start-Up Instructions

- The file named **21drill4.toa** should be displayed in the document window.

Use a Short Form to Create a Table of Authorities Entry

1. Place the insertion point in the desired citation information.

   For example, place the insertion point to the left of the first character in the word "Jannis" on the line above the quoted paragraph that begins "The so-called . . .".

2. Click on the down arrow to the right of the **Short Form** button and select the desired Short Form name {Alt and Shift and s, press the up or down arrow key to display the desired short form name}.

   For example, select **Jannis** in the Short Form box.

3. Select the **Mark** button on the Table of Authorities Feature Bar {Alt and Shift and m}.

   Note: No change displays in the document window. Use Reveal Codes to view the Table of Authorities code, e.g., ToA: , Jannis.

Finish-Up Instructions

- Use the same filename **21drill4.toa** and save the file.

Start-Up Instructions

- ❖ The file named **21drill4.toa** should be displayed in the document window.
- ❖ The Table of Authorities Feature Bar should be displayed. (If necessary, select **Tools, Table of Authorities.**)

Define a Table of Authorities

1. Follow steps 1-7 in the Steps to Define a Table of Contents beginning on page 500.
2. Type and format the title for the Table of Authorities.

    For example, type the title **Table of Authorities**. Press **Enter** three times. Select the title. Select **Bold** and choose **Center** justification.

3. Locate the insertion point two blank lines below the title, type and format the column headings for the Table of Authorities.

    For example, press the down arrow key three times; type **Cases**; press **Alt** and **F7**. Type **Page**; press **Enter** twice. Bold the headings **Cases** and **Page**. Move the insertion point to the second blank line below the headings Cases and Pages.

4. Select the **Define** button on the Table of Authorities Feature Bar {Alt and Shift and d}.
5. Highlight the desired Section Name.

    For example, check that **Cases . . .** is highlighted.

6. Select the **Insert** button {Alt and i}.

    Note: The message <<Table of Authorities will generate here>> displays in the document window.

7. Press **Enter** once and type the next Table of Authorities heading. Press **Enter** twice.

    For example, type and bold the words **Other Sources**. Press **Enter** twice.

8. With the insertion point one blank line below the second Table of Authorities heading, select the **Define** button on the Table of Authorities Feature Bar {Alt and Shift and d}.

    For example, press the down arrow key twice and select the **Define** button.

9. Highlight the desired Section Name {press the up or down arrow key}.

    For example, click on **Other Sources**.

10. Select the **Insert** button {Alt and i}.

    Note: The message <<Table of Authorities will generate here>> displays in the document window. If desired, use Reveal Codes to view the **Gen Txt** *codes.*

Finish-Up Instructions

- ❖ Use the same filename, **21drill4.toa**, and save the file again.

Start-Up Instructions

- The file named **21drill4.toa** should be displayed in the document window.
- The table of authorities entries must be marked and the table of authorities defined.
- The Table of Authorities Feature Bar should be displayed. (If necessary, select **Tools**, **Table of Authorities**.)

Steps to Generate a Table of Authorities

1. Select the **Generate** button on the Table of Authorities Feature Bar {Alt and Shift and g}.

   Note: *The Generate dialog box displays.*

2. Select **OK** {Enter}.

   Note: *The Please Wait message box displays briefly. Then the table of authorities with the list of citations and the headings Cases, Other Sources, and Pages displays in the document window.*

Finish-Up Instructions

- With the insertion point in the Table of Authorities page, set the page numbering format to lowercase Roman numerals. (Select **Layout**, **Page**, **Numbering**, **Position**, **Bottom Center**, **Options**, **Page**, **Lowercase Roman**, **OK** twice.)
- Place the insertion point on the first page of text and set the page numbering format to Numbers. (Select **Layout**, **Page**, **Numbering**, **Options**, **Page**, **Numbers**, **OK** twice.)
- Use the *new* filename **21drill4.aut** and save the file.
- Print one copy and close the document.

The Next Step

Chapter Review and Activities

Self-Check Quiz

T F 1. WordPerfect can number nine outline levels automatically.

T F 2. Legal is one of WordPerfect's Outline definitions.

T F 3. To obtain the next outline level, press the **Tab** key.

T F 4. After the text is marked and the table of contents is defined, the generated table of contents will be placed at the location of the message "<<Table of Contents will generate here>>."

T F 5. All items in a numbered outline, including body text, are numbered.

6. An outline family can include ______________.
   a. an idea
   b. indented related ideas
   c. body text
   d. all of the above

7. The table of authorities is ________ to setup the numbering format and location for the table of authorities entries.
   a. defined
   b. generated
   c. marked
   d. none of the above

8. Creating a table of contents is a four-part process. List the four parts.

9. A generated index is usually placed on a separate page at the _____ of a document.

10. List the five steps to mark an index subheading.

Enriching Language Arts Skills

Spelling/Vocabulary Words

appreciation the increase in the value of property or goods.
dissolution the act of breaking apart or terminating.
irrevocable not to be canceled or reversed.
valid sound, authentic, just.

Percentage Amounts

Use figures for numbers that are followed by the word *percent*. Spell out the word *percent* unless the percentage amount is used in a headline/title or in a table that contains statistical information.

Examples:

Salaries are 30 percent of the total budget. (Percent is spelled out.)

Percentage of Males and Females		
Age Group	Male	Female
20-29	68.0%	65.0%
30-39	18.5%	19.5%
40-49	13.5%	15.5%

(Statistical information in a table)

PRICES ARE SLASHED 40% STOREWIDE!!! (Headline information)

Activities

Activity 21.1—Create an Outline

1. Type the following outline title followed by three Enters:

   Estate and Financial Management Planning
2. Select and center the title.
3. Display the Outline Feature Bar (select **Tools**, **Outline**).
4. Use the Outline definition (select the **Outline Definitions** button, choose **Outline**).
5. Define and create the following outline. (If necessary, see the Steps to Display the Outline Feature Bar and Create an Outline on pages 492-495).

I. Tools of estate planning
   A. Financial
   B. Legal

II. Estate planning is money
   A. Creation/investment
   B. Reinvestment
   C. Distribution

III. Why financial planning?
   A. Financial security
      1. Obstacles
      2. Concerns
   B. Financial life improvement
      1. Lower income taxes
      2. Investments
      3. Retirement income
         a. Early retirement
         b. Retirement at age 65

IV. Financial security
   A. Financial check-up
   B. Professional consultation

---

6. Use the filename **21act1.out** and save the file on your file disk.
7. Print one copy.
8. Close the document.

Activity 21.2—Create a Table of Contents and Index

1. Open the file named **21act2.txt** located on the data disk.

2. Display the Table of Contents Feature Bar (select **Tools**, **Table of Contents**).
3. Mark all sideheads as a level 1 table of contents entry (select the sidehead, choose the **Mark 1** button).
4. Move the insertion point to the beginning of the document and create a new page for the table of contents (press **Ctrl** and **Home** twice; press **Ctrl** and **Enter**).
5. With the insertion point on page 2, insert page numbers and reset the page number to 1 (select **Layout**, **Page**, **Numbering**; select **Value**; in the New Page number box, type **1**, select **OK**; select **Position**, **Bottom Center**, **Close**).
6. Press the up arrow key once to move the insertion point to the new page. Type the title **CONTENTS**; press **Enter** three times. Select and center the title.
7. With the insertion point on the third line below the title, define the table of contents (select **Define**, check that the **Number of Levels(1-5)** is **1**, select **OK**).
8. Display the Index Feature Bar (select **Tools**, **Index**).
9. Mark the first occurrence of the following index entries. If necessary, see Steps to Mark Index Entries beginning on page 503.

   Member meetings
      annual meetings
      special meetings
   Executive Committee
   Proxies
   Quorum
10. Move the insertion point to the end of the document (press **Ctrl** and **End**). Insert a hard page break to create a new page for the index (**Ctrl** and **Enter**).
11. Change the line spacing to one for the index page.
12. Type the title **Index** and press **Enter** three times. Select and center the title.
13. With the insertion point on the third line below the title, define the index (select **Define**, choose **Position**, **Text**, **#**, select **OK**).
14. Use the filename **21act2.fin** and save the file.
15. Generate the table of contents and index (select the **Generate** button, **OK**).

    Note: *The table of contents and index will generate at the same time.*
16. Save the file again using the same filename, **21act2.fin**.
17. Print one copy.
18. Close the document.

Activity 21.3—Create a Table of Authorities

1. Open the file named **21act3.txt** located on the data disk.
2. Display the Table of Authorities Feature Bar (select **Tools**, **Table of Authorities**).
3. Create the Full and Short Form Table of Authorities entries using the following information. (Select the desired citation and necessary codes, choose the **Create Full Form** button, type the desired section name in the Section Name box, press **Tab**, type the Short Form name, select **OK**. Check citation information and choose **Close**.)
   a. Select the citation **Civil Code section 1354** located on page 1 in the first sentence of the second paragraph. The Section Name is **Statutes**. The Short Form name is **CC 1354**.
   b. Select the citation **Civil Code section 1355** located on page 2 in the paragraph that begins "Under former . . ." The Section Name is **Statutes**. The Short Form name is **CC 1355**.
   c. Select the citation **Civil Code section 1351, et seq** located on page 2 after the second sentence in the paragraph that begins "Under former . . . ". The Section Name is **Statutes**. The Short Form name is **CC 1351**.
   d. Select the citation that begins **W. Hyatt, Condominium and Homeowner . . .** at the top of page 3. The Section Name is **Statutes**. The Short Form name is **W. Hyatt**.
   e. Select the citation that begins **Laguna Royale Owners . . .** located on page 3 in the paragraph that begins "The presumption of reasonableness . . .". The Section Name is **Cases**. The Short Form name is **Laguna Royale**.
   f. Select the citation that begins **Hidden Harbor Estates . . .** located on page 3 at the end of the paragraph that begins "The presumption of reasonableness . . . ". The Section Name is **Cases**. The Short Form name is **Hidden Harbor**.
   g. Select the citation that begins **Oceanside v McKenna** located on page 4. The Section Name is **Cases**. The Short Form name is **Oceanside**.
4. Use a short form to create table of authorities entries using the following information. (Place the insertion point in the citation to be marked, select the down arrow to the right of the **Short Form** button, click on the desired Short Form name, select **Mark**.)
   a. Place the insertion point in the citation **Civil Code section 1354** located on page 1 in the paragraph that begins "The questions of whether . . . ". The Short Form is **CC 1354**.
   b. Place the insertion point in the citation **Civil Code section 1354** located on page 2 in the paragraph numbered 1 below the Argument heading. The Short Form is **CC 1354**.

c. Place the insertion point in the citation that begins **Laguna Royale** located on page 4 at the end of the paragraph that begins "Oceanside v McKenna . . . ". The Short Form name is **Laguna Royale.**

5. Use the *new* filename **21act3.toa** and save the file on your file disk.
6. Define the Table of Authorities as follows:

   a. Press **Ctrl** and **Home** twice, press **Ctrl** and **Enter**, select **Layout**, **Page**, **Numbering**, **Value**, **1**, **OK**, **Close**.

   b. Press the up arrow key once. Type, center, and bold the title **Table of Authorities.** Press **Enter** three times after the title and select **Left** justification.

   c. Type **Statutes**. Press **Alt** and **F7**. Type **Page**. Press **Enter** twice. Bold the headings **Statutes** and **Page**.

   d. Place the insertion point on the second blank line below the headings. Select the **Define** button. Click on **Statutes**. Select **Insert**. Press **Enter** once.

   e. Type and bold the heading **Cases**. Press **Enter** twice.

   f. Select the **Define** button. Click on **Cases**. Select **Insert**.

7. Generate the Table of Authorities (select the **Generate** button, **OK**).
8. With the insertion point in the Table of Authorities page, change the page numbering format to lowercase roman numerals (select **Layout**, **Page**, **Numbering**, **Position**, **Bottom Center**, **Options**, **Page**, **Lowercase Roman**, **OK**, **Close**).
9. With the insertion point in the first page of text, set the page numbering format to Numbers (select **Layout**, **Page**, **Numbering**, **Options**, **Page**, **Numbers**, **OK**, **Close**).
10. Use the same filename, **21act3.toa**, and save the file.
11. Print one copy and close the document.

Challenge Your Skills

Skill 21.1—Create and Edit an Outline

1. Use the Outline feature and create the following outline. The paragraphs have been indented to show levels for outline numbering. Make decisions regarding:

   Margins
   Justification
   Fonts *(**Hint:** Use Arrus BT, 11 point or a similar font.)*
   Outline numbering and spacing

Bancroft Owners' Conditions and Restrictions

- Definitions
  - Association
  - Owner
- Property rights
  - Owner's easements of enjoyment
  - Parking rights
  - Easements
    - For private sidewalk, yard, and patio use
    - For encroachments of overhanging eaves and decks
- Annual and special assessments
  - Liens and personal obligations of assessments
  - Maximum annual assessments
    - No more than 15 percent increase without a vote
    - Increased assessments with a written consent of 60 percent of members
  - Due dates for assessments
    - Approved operating budget 60 days before beginning of year
      - Estimate revenue and expenses on accrual basis
      - Identify total cash reserves
    - Financial statements prepared with accepted accounting principles
- Exterior maintenance
  - Common area maintenance
  - Exterior maintenance on lots

2. Use the filename **21skill1.ban** and save the file on your file disk.
3. Edit the outline as follows:
   a. Insert the following items:

      Under item I:

      C. Properties
      D. Common areas

   b. Insert the following first-level and second-level items above Roman numeral III (i.e., Annual and special assessments):

      Membership and voting rights
          Every lot owner is an Association member
          All owners are entitled to one vote

   c. Hide the outline family now numbered IV. B.

   d. Select the **Bullets** outline definition.
4. Once changes are made, use the *new* filename **21skill1.rev** and save the file again.
5. Print one copy.

6. Close the document.

Skill 21.2—Create and Edit a Table of Contents and an Index; Language Arts

1. Open the file named **21skill2.txt** located on the data disk and make decisions regarding:

   Margins
   Justification
   Fonts
   Widow/Orphan control
   Page numbering format and placement
   Spacing before and after headings and subheadings
   Bold, underline, and capitalization of title, headings, and subheads
   Format of table of contents
   Format of index

2. Correct two spelling errors, one misused word, one percent error, and two punctuation errors.
3. The title of the document is Pocatello College Agreement.
4. Use the Table of Contents Feature Bar and mark the first- and second-level table of contents entries.
5. Define the table of contents.

   Hint: *Remember to reset the page number for the first page of the document (after the table of contents page) to page 1.*

6. Use the Index Feature Bar and mark all occurrences of the following main heading and subheading entries.

   Hint: *Use the Find command to locate index entry text. If the index entry text appears in a paragraph more than once, only mark the first occurrence of the text.*

   Preamble
   Recognition
   Leaves
      Sick leave
      Industrial accident or illness leave
      Jury duty
   Transfers and Reassignments
   Professional Education Program
      Multicultural program
      Learning styles program
   Layoffs
   Performance Evaluation Procedures
      Contract employees
      Regular employees

7. Define the index.
8. Use the *new* filename **21skill2.fin** and save the file on your file disk.
9. Generate the table of contents and index.

10. Print one copy.

11. Revise the document as follows:

    a. Insert the following paragraph after the first paragraph under the **LEAVES** heading:

        Immediate Family Illness Leave

        An employee may be granted three (3) days of paid leave per year in the event of the serious illness of a member of his or her immediate family.

    b. Insert the following paragraph after the first paragraph under the **RECOGNITION** heading.

        ORGANIZATIONAL RIGHTS

        The Union shall have the right to use institutional bulletin boards and mail services, subject to reasonable regulations, and the right to use institutional facilities for the purpose of conducting Union business.

    c. Determine the appropriate table of contents and index entries for the inserted text and mark those entries.

12. Use the new filename **21skill2.rev** and save the file on your file disk.

13. Generate the table of contents and index.

14. Use page numbering to insert a lowercase roman numeral for the table of contents page. (The page numbering format for all other pages should be Numbers.)

15. Use the same filename, **21skill2.rev**, and save the file again.

16. Print one copy and close the document.

CHAPTER

Advanced Features and Master Documents

Features Covered

- Create a paragraph style containing a paragraph border and graphic image
- Create a style based on an existing style
- Link styles
- Create cross-references
- Create a master document
- Expand and condense a master document
- Use cross-references in a master document
- Save a master document and subdocuments

Objectives and Introduction

After completing this chapter, you will be able to create a paragraph style containing a paragraph border and a graphic image. You will also be able to create a style based on an existing style as well as be able to link styles. You will learn to create cross references and master documents. In addition, you will expand, condense, and use cross references in a master document as well as save the master document and subdocuments.

In addition to format codes (see Chapter 15), text and graphic elements can be included in styles. Also, WordPerfect's Cross-Reference and Master Document features promote easy use when creating multiple-page documents.

Advanced Styles

In Chapter 15, basic styles that contain formatting such as margins, font changes, and justification were created. In addition, many other formatting elements, such as graphic lines, borders, and graphic images, can also be incorporated into a style. If desired, text that is used often can be inserted into a style. For example, a letterhead style can be created that contains text, font changes, graphic lines, and/or a graphic image. The letterhead style can be saved in a style file and used each time a letter is being created.

Styles that contain graphic elements, such as graphic lines, page/paragraph borders, and graphic boxes, can be created. Graphic elements are inserted into a style in a manner similar to inserting a graphic element in a regular document window.

In addition to creating styles by placing codes in the Contents box of the Styles Editor dialog box, styles can be created based on an existing style. Using an existing style to create a new style can greatly expedite the process of create styles. When a new style is based on another style, the name of the existing style displays in the Contents box. Additional formatting options are selected to modify the new style. For example, the font or justification of the new style may be changed.

A style can be linked to another style. When styles are linked, the first style is in effect until the **Enter** key is pressed. When the **Enter** key is pressed, the first style is turned off and the next (linked) style is turned on.

Once created, the styles are saved in a style file so that they are available when formatting other documents (see Chapter 15).

Start-Up Instructions

❖ Open the file named **22drill1.txt** located on the data disk.

Create a Paragraph Style Containing a Paragraph Border

1. Place the insertion point in the paragraph where the new style will be applied.

   For example, place the insertion point in the first sidehead, **Always Ask Questions.**

2. Select the **Styles** button on the Button Bar {Alt, L, s *or* Alt and F8}.

3. Select **Create** {Alt and r}.

4. In the Style Name box, type a name for the new style.

   For example, type **sidehead.** (Do not type the period.)

5. Click in the Description box and type a description of the style {Alt and d}.

   For example, type **style for sideheads.** (Do not type the period.)

6. Choose the desired style type {Alt and y, Spacebar, press the up or down arrow key to highlight the desired style, Enter}.

   For example, check that **Paragraph (paired)** displays in the Type box.

7. Click in the Contents box {Alt and c}.

8. To change the font, appearance, or size, select **Layout, Font** in the Styles Editor dialog box, then make the desired changes, and select **OK.**

   For example, select **Layout, Font,** change the font to **Engravers-Gothic BT, 14 point, Bold** and select **OK.**

   Note: *A Font, Font Size, and Bold code display in the Contents box.*

To Place a Paragraph Border Below the Paragraph

9. Select **Layout, Paragraph, Border/Fill** {Alt, L, a, b}.
10. Select the **Border Style** button and click on the desired border style {Alt and b, Spacebar, use the arrow keys to highlight the desired border style, Enter}.

    For example, select the **Thin Bottom** border style (second row, last button).
11. Select the **Customize Style** button and make desired changes {c}.

    For example:

    a. Select the **Line Style** button (located on the left side of the dialog box) {e}.

    b. Select the **Thick Double** border style (second button in the second row) {Spacebar, use the arrow key to highlight the Thick Double border style, Enter}.

    c. Select **OK** twice {Enter twice}.

    Note: The ***Para Border*** *code displays in the Contents box.*
12. When all the style formats have been specified, select **OK** {Tab, Enter}.

    Note: The new style named "sidehead" displays in the Style List dialog box.
13. With the desired style name highlighted, choose **Apply** to apply the new style to the paragraph containing the insertion point {Alt and a}.

    For example, with the **sidehead** style name highlighted, choose **Apply**.

Finish-Up Instructions

- Place the insertion point in the sidehead *Listen to Advice But Make Your Own Decision.*
- Select the **Styles** button.
- Double-click on the style named **sidehead** to apply the style to the sidehead paragraph.
- Place the insertion point in the sidehead *There Are No Shortcuts to Success.*
- Select the **Styles** button.
- Double-click on the style named **sidehead** to apply the style to the sidehead paragraph.
- Use the *new* filename **22drill1.for** and save the file.

Start-Up Instructions

- The file named **22drill1.for** should be displayed in the document window.

Steps to Create a Paragraph Style Containing a Graphic Image

1. Place the insertion point in the paragraph to be formatted with the new style.

For example, place the insertion point in the paragraph that begins "To succeed as an entrepreneur . . ."

2. Select the **Styles** button on the Button Bar {Alt, L, s *or* Alt and F8}.
3. Select **Create** {Alt and r}.
4. In the Style Name box, type a name for the new style.

   For example, type **graphic par.** (Do not type the period.)
5. Click in the Description box and type a description of the style {Alt and d}.

   For example, type **style containing a graphic image.**
6. Choose the desired style type {Alt and y, Spacebar, press the up or down arrow key to highlight the desired type, Enter}.

   For example, check that **Paragraph (paired)** displays in the Type box.
7. Click in the Contents box {Alt and c}.
8. Select the **Graphics** menu in the Styles Editor dialog box {Alt and g}.
9. Select **Figure** {f}.
10. Double-click on the desired filename {Tab, press the down arrow key to highlight filename, press Enter}.

    For example, double-click on **drtbord.wpg.**

    Note: *The Graphics Box Feature Bar displays at the bottom of the document window and the* ***Box*** *code displays in the Contents box.*
11. Edit the graphic box as needed.

    For example:

    a. Select the **Position** button. In the Horizontal area, move the mouse pointer to the "from" box, press and hold the mouse button, and drag to select **Left Margin**. Release the mouse button. Select **OK** {Alt and Shift and p, L, Tab, Spacebar, use arrow keys to highlight Left Margin, Enter twice}.

    b. Select the **Size** button. In the Width area, double-click in the **Set** box and type **.5**. Select **OK** {Alt and Shift and s, s, type .5, Enter}.

    c. Select the **Border/Fill** button. Click on the **Border Style** button and click on the NO BORDER. Select **Customize Style**, double-click in the **Outside Spacing** box and type **.04**. Select **OK** twice. {Alt and Shift and b, Spacebar, use the arrow keys to highlight NO BORDER, Enter; c, o, Tab, type .04, Enter twice}.
12. Select **OK** {Tab, Enter}.
13. With the desired style name highlighted, choose **Apply** to apply the new style to the paragraph containing the insertion point {Alt and a}.

    For example, with the graphic par style name highlighted, choose **Apply**.

Finish-Up Instructions

- Move the insertion point to the paragraph that begins "The successful entrepreneur has a . . ."
- Select the **Styles** button. Double-click on the style named **graphic par**.
- Move the insertion point to the paragraph that begins "A successful entrepreneur gives a . . ."
- Select the **Styles** button. Double-click on the style named **graphic par**.
- Use the same filename, **22drill1.for**, and save the file.

Start-Up Instructions

- The file named **22drill1.for** should be displayed in the document window.
- Create a title style using the following information.
    a. Move the insertion point to the top of the document.
    b. Select the **Styles** button and choose **Create**.
    c. In the Style Name box, type **title**.
    d. In the Description box, type **style for title**. Check that **Paragraph (paired)** displays in the Type box.
    e. Click in the Contents box.
    f. Change the font to **EngraversGothic BT**, **18 point**, **Bold** (select **Layout**, **Font**, select the desired font, size, and appearance, select **OK**).
    g. Change the justification to **Center** (select **Layout**, **Justification**, **Center**).
    h. Add two lines of space between paragraphs (select **Layout**, **Paragraph**, **Format**, click on the up triangle beside the **Spacing Between Paragraphs** box until 2 displays, select **OK**).
    i. Choose **OK**.
- Continue with the Steps to Create a Style Based on an Existing Style.

Steps to Create a Style Based on an Existing Style

1. In the Style List dialog box, select **Create** and type the name for the new style {r}.

   For example, type **subtitle**.

2. In the Description box, type a description of the style {Alt and d}.

   For example, type **style for subtitle paragraphs**.

3. Choose the desired style type {Alt and y, Spacebar, press the up or down arrow key to highlight the desired type, Enter}.

   For example, check that **Paragraph (paired)** displays in the Type box.

4. Click in the Contents dialog box {Alt and c}.
5. Select **Layout, Styles** {Alt, L, s}.

Note: The Style List dialog box displays.

6. Double-click on the style to be used as the basis for the new style.

   For example, double-click on the style name **title.**

   *Note: The code **Para Style: title Style** displays in the Contents box.*

7. Make additional selections to modify the new style.

   For example, change the font size to 16 point by selecting **Lay-out, Font, 16, OK.**

8. When all modifications are complete, select **OK.**

Finish-Up Instructions

- Continue with the following Steps to Link Styles.

Link Styles

1. In the Style List dialog box, highlight the name of the style that will be linked to another style.

   For example, click once on the style name **title.** ·

2. Select **Edit** {Alt and e}.

3. Click on the down arrow below the **Enter Key will Chain to** option {press the Tab key until the box below the "Enter Key will Chain to" option is highlighted}.

   Note: A list of style names displays.

4. Scroll through the list of style names and click on the style to be linked {press the down arrow key to display the desired style name}.

   For example, click on **subtitle.**

5. Select **OK** {Enter}.

Finish-Up Instructions

- Using the following information, save the new styles using the filename **22drill1.sty**.
  a. In the Style List dialog box, select **Options**, **Save As**.
  b. Type the name of the new style file including the drive letter and/or directory name. For example, type **a:22drill1.sty**.
  c. Check that the **Both** option in the Style Types section is selected.
  d. Select **OK**.
  e. Select **Close** to exit the Style List dialog box.
- With the insertion point at the top of the document, type the following text:

  Becoming a Successful Entrepreneur (do not press Enter).
- Select the **Styles** button. Double-click on the style named **title.**
- Press **Enter** to activate the linked style.
- Type the following text.

Key Points to Remember

- Use the *new* filename **22drill1.fin** and save the file on your file disk.
- Print one copy and close the document.

Create Cross-References

The Cross-Reference feature is used to *direct* readers from one area of a document to another area of the document. For example, in this textbook cross-references are often used to direct readers from the text to a related figure. Cross-references can connect pages, figures, notes, captions, etc.

Creating a cross-reference requires two parts: a reference and a target. The *reference* is the location in the document where the cross-reference information is inserted. The *target* is the location in the document where the reader is directed. For example, in the cross-reference information "See Table 3 on page 596," the reference is the location where the page number is inserted and the target is the table that appears on page 596.

A target is identified by a target name. A single target name can be used for cross-referencing multiple references. For example, a target name given to a figure can be used to reference the figure one or more times.

A reference can be linked to multiple targets, e.g., see pages 22, 30, and 46. When the cross-reference is created for multiple targets, each target is marked separately using the same target name.

Once a reference(s) and target(s) are marked, the Generate feature is used to insert the cross-reference number. If a target is moved or deleted, the Generate feature must be used to update the cross-references.

Start-Up Instructions

- To complete the drills, activities, and skills in this chapter, copy the following files located on the data disk to your file disk. For information on copying files, see Chapter 16, page 384.

22chap1.sub	22sub1.skl
22chap2.sub	22sub2.act
22chap3.sub	22sub2.skl
22chap4.sub	22sub3.act
22chap5.sub	22sub3.skl
22skill1.txt	22sub4.act
22sub1.act	22sub4.skl

- Open the file named **22chap1.sub** located on your file disk.

Create a Cross-Reference

1. Place the insertion point where the reference is to be located in the document.

For example, place the insertion point directly to the left of the period in the last sentence, which begins "See Figure 1.1 . . . "

2. Select **Tools, Cross-Reference** {Alt, t, f}.

   Note: The Cross-Reference Feature Bar displays.

3. Select the desired reference type.

   For example, check that **Page** displays to the right of the Reference button.

4. Click in the **Target** box in the Cross-Reference Feature Bar and type the desired target name {Alt and Shift and t, type target name}.

   For example, click in the **Target** box and type **first figure**.

5. Select the **Mark Reference** button on the Cross-Reference Feature Bar {Alt and Shift and e}.

   Note: A question mark displays at the location of the insertion point in the document. That's OK. The question mark will be replaced by a page number after a target is marked and the **Generate** *button is selected.*

6. Move the insertion point to the desired target location.

   For example, press the down arrow key approximately three times to locate the insertion point below the captioned box.

7. Select the **Mark Target** button on the Cross-Reference Feature Bar {Alt and Shift and a}.

   Note: No change displays in the document window. However, in Reveal Codes, a ***Target*** *code displays at the location of the insertion point.*

8. Select the **Generate** button on the Cross-Reference Feature Bar {Alt and Shift and g}.

   Note: The Generate dialog box displays.

9. Select **OK** {Enter}.

   Note: Scroll up the document to view the cross-reference page number that has been inserted on page 1.

10. Select the **Close** button on the Cross-Reference Feature Bar {Alt and Shift and c}.

Finish-Up Instructions

- Save the file using the same filename **22chap1.sub**.
- Print one copy and close the document.
- Open the file named **22chap2.sub** located on your file disk.
- Create a cross-reference using the following information:
  - a. Place the insertion point to the left of the period in the sentence that begins "See Figure 2.1 . . . ".
  - b. Repeat steps 2–10. Use the target name **second figure**.
- Save the file using the same filename, **22chap2.sub**.
- Print one copy and close the document.

Create a Master Document

The Master Document feature in WordPerfect is useful for managing large documents such as a book with chapters. The master document is a file containing codes that link other files (called subdocuments) to the master document file. The master document file also includes any formatting codes that will apply to the entire document such as page numbering and initial font. The subdocuments are the files that will be placed together with other files to become one (master) document. The subdocuments are saved as separate files and when desired are assembled together into one (master) file.

After the subdocument files are created and saved, the master document file is created. First, the formatting that applies to the entire document such as page numbering, margins, font type, and size are placed in the new document. If a title page is desired, the title information is typed. Usually a hard page break is placed after the title. Second, the subdocument links are inserted. When a subdocument link is inserted, a subdocument icon displays in the master document. (If the draft view is selected, the subdocument information displays with a gray background.) The name and location of the subdocument can be displayed by clicking once on the subdocument icon. In the Reveal Codes window, a *Subdoc* code is inserted. A subdocument link can be deleted by deleting the *Subdoc* code in the Reveal Codes window.

To display or print the subdocument text, the master document must be *expanded*. When the master document is expanded, the text of each subdocument displays between the subdocument icons.

After displaying or printing the expanded master document, the document can be *condensed* to remove the subdocument text from the document window. When a master document is condensed, only a subdocument icon displays for each subdocument. The advantage of a condensed document is the saving of space on a disk, because the text of the subdocuments is not saved with the master document.

Formatting and editing changes can be made to a subdocument or a master document. A format code remains in effect until WordPerfect encounters a new code either in the master document or in a subdocument. Changes made to the text in the master document and subdocuments can be saved. A master document, however, must be condensed before saving.

Start-Up Instructions

- Open a new document window.
- Type and center the title **WordPerfect 6.0 Made Easy**. Press **Enter** once.
- Select the title and change the font to **CaslonOpnface BT, 24 point**. Click once to deselect the text.
- Center the current page vertically (top to bottom). (Select **Layout**, **Page**, **Center, Current Page**, **OK**.)
- Insert page numbers at the bottom center; suppress the page number on page one (select **Layout**, **Page**, **Numbering**, **Position**, **Bottom Center**, **OK**, **Layout**, **Page**, **Suppress**, **Page Numbering**, **OK**).
- Press **Ctrl** and **Enter** to create a hard page break. (If necessary, change the justification to **Left**.)

Steps to Create a Master Document

1. Display the Generate Button Bar by moving the mouse pointer into the Button Bar, then clicking the *right* mouse button, and clicking on **Generate.**
2. Select the **Subdoc** button on the Generate Button Bar {Alt, f, d, s}.
3. Type or select the location at which the subdocuments are located.

   For example, if necessary, click in the Drives box and click on the drive letter where your file disk is located (a: or b:).
4. Double-click on the desired filename {Tab, press the down arrow key to highlight the desired filename, Alt and i}.

   For example, select **22chap1.sub**.

   Note: A subdocument icon is placed in the left margin at the top of page 2. To display the name and location of the subdocument, move the mouse pointer to the subdocument icon and click once. The name and location of the subdocument display in a comment box. To remove the comment box from the document window, click on the subdocument icon again.
5. To place the next subdocument (chapter) of the master document on a separate page, press **Ctrl** and **Enter**.

   *Note: Because **Ctrl** and **Enter** will create a new page, a new sheet of paper will feed through the printer when printed. Do not press **Ctrl** and **Enter** after the last subdocument code.*

Finish-Up Instructions

- Repeat steps 2–5 and select the following subdocuments located on your file disk:

  22chap2.sub
  22chap3.sub
  22chap4.sub
  22chap5.sub
- Use the filename **22master.doc** and save the master document on your file disk.

Start-Up Instructions

- The file named **22master.doc** should be displayed in the document window.
- The Generate Button Bar should be displayed.

Expand a Master Document

1. With the master document in the document window, select the **ExpandMst** button on the Generate Button Bar {Alt, f, d, e}.

   Note: The Expand Master Document dialog box displays with a list of the subdocuments marked, showing the file location of each subdocument.
2. Select **OK** {Enter}.

Note: A Please Wait message box displays briefly. In a moment, the contents of each subdocument display in the document window; press ***Ctrl*** *and* ***Home****, then scroll down through the document. Notice that a subdocument icon displays at the beginning and end of each subdocument.*

Finish-Up Instructions

- Select the **Page Zoom Full** button to view each page of the document.

  Note: The cross-references in Chapters 1 and 2 will display incorrect page references at this time. This problem will be corrected in a later step.
- Select the **Page Zoom Full** button again to return to the normal view.
- Continue with the Steps to Condense a Master Document

Start-Up Instructions

- The expanded master document named **22master.doc** should be displayed in the document window.
- The Generate Button Bar should be displayed.

Steps to Condense a Master Document

1. Select the **Condense** button {Alt, f, d, c}.

   Note: The Condense/Save Subdocuments dialog box displays. Each subdocument is listed twice: once for condensing and once for saving. An X displays beside each listed file indicating that all files are to condensed and saved. If desired, files can be deselected for condensing and/or saving.
2. Select **OK** to condense and save all marked files {Enter}.

   Note: In a moment, only the subdocument icons and the title page remain in the document window.

Finish-Up Instructions

- Continue with the Steps to Create a Cross-Reference in a Master Document.

Create Cross-References in a Master Document

To use the Cross-Reference feature to reference items in different documents, the files that will contain references and targets must be subdocuments in a master document. The Generate feature is used to update the cross-references to reflect the correct page numbers in the master document.

Start-Up Instructions

- The master document named **22master.doc** should be displayed in the document window.

Chapter 22 Advanced Features and Master Documents

- The Generate Button Bar should be displayed.
- Expand the master document named **22master.doc** (select the **ExpandMst** button, **OK**).

Steps to Create a Cross-Reference in a Master Document

1. With the expanded master document on the screen, place the insertion point at the location at which the cross-reference is to be inserted.

   For example, in the Chapter 3 subdocument, place the insertion point to the left of the period in the final paragraph.

2. Create a cross-reference:

   a. Select **Tools, Cross-Reference** or select the **Cross-Ref** button on the Generate Button Bar {Alt, t, f}.

   b. Check that **Page** displays to the right of the Reference button in the Cross-Reference Feature Bar.

   c. Click in the Target box and type the desired target name {Alt and Shift and t, type target name}.

      For example, click in the Target box and type **business letters**.

   d. Select the **Mark Reference** button {Alt and Shift and e}.

   e. Move the insertion point to the desired target location.

      For example, in the Chapter 4 subdocument, place the insertion point to the right of the final period in the last paragraph.

   f. Select the **Mark Target** button {Alt and Shift and a}.

   g. Select the **Generate** button on either the Cross-Reference Feature Bar or the Generate Button Bar {Alt and Shift and g}.

   h. Select **OK** {Enter}.

Finish-Up Instructions

- Scroll up the document to view the cross-reference in the Chapter 3 subdocument. Also, scroll up to see that the cross-references in the Chapter 1 and Chapter 2 subdocuments have been updated.
- Select the **Close** button on the Cross-Reference Feature Bar.
- Optional. Print the master document.

Save an Edited Master Document and Subdocuments

1. Select the **Save** button {Alt, f, s}.

   Note: *The message "Document is expanded. Condense?" displays.*

2. Select **Yes** {y}.

Note: The Condense/Save Subdocuments dialog box with the marked subdocuments displays. All subdocuments are marked for both condensing and saving.

3. Select **OK** {Enter}.

Finish-Up Instructions

- Display the WordPerfect Button Bar (move the mouse pointer into the Generate Button Bar, click the *right* mouse button, click on **WordPerfect**).
- Close the document.

The Next Step

Chapter Review and Activities

Self-Check Quiz

T F 1. A style can be created based on an existing style.

T F 2. The target is the location in a document at which the cross-reference information displays.

T F 3. A reference cannot be linked to multiple targets.

T F 4. A master document must be expanded before the document is printed.

T F 5. When a master document is condensed, the subdocument text displays in the document window.

6. The ________ feature is used to insert or update cross-references.
   a. Mark Reference.
   b. Mark Target.
   c. Expand Master document.
   d. Generate.

7. A style can contain ______________.
   a. graphic lines.
   b. page or paragraph borders
   c. graphic boxes
   d. all of the above

8. Creating a cross-reference requires two parts: a ________ and a _________.

9. Define a subdocument.

10. What is the purpose of a cross-reference?

Enriching Language Arts Skills

Spelling/Vocabulary Words

cuisine a style of cooking or preparing food.

duty-free free from a government tax that is usually applied to imports.

traditional of or pertaining to the statements, beliefs, customs, etc., that are handed down through oral communication from one generation to another.

Basic Rules for Numbers

Generally, in written text numbers one through ten are spelled out as are numbers used in approximation, at the beginning of a sentence, or that are rounded. Related numbers in the same document should be expressed in the same form, i.e., numbers one through ten are written as figures when used with related numbers above ten.

Examples:

We will pick up eight additional passengers at the next bus stop. (Numbers one through ten are spelled out.)

Thirty-one people are enrolled in the television course for Real Estate Appraisals. (Spell out a number at the beginning of a sentence.)

Samuel reported that around sixty people attended the luncheon. (Spell out a number used in approximation.)

Out of the 23 questionnaires returned, 7 indicated that new stereo systems would be purchased this year. (Related number is written as a figure when used with a number above ten.)

Activities

Activity 22.1–Create a Master Document and Cross-References

1. Open a new document window.
2. Type and center the title **Tips for Saving the Environment**; use **Arrus BT, 18 point, Bold**. Press **Enter** once after the title. Select **Left** justification.
3. Center the current page vertically (select **Layout**, **Page**, **Center, Current Page**, **OK**).
4. Insert page numbers at the bottom center; suppress the page number on page 1.
5. If necessary, press **Ctrl** and **End** to move the insertion point to the bottom of the document. Press **Ctrl** and **Enter** to create a hard page break.
6. Display the Generate Button Bar (move the mouse pointer into the Button Bar, click the *right* mouse button, click on **Generate**).
7. Create a master document containing the following subdocuments that are located on your file disk. Remember to place a hard page break be-

tween each subdocument (do not press Ctrl and Enter after the last subdocument). If necessary, see the Steps to Create a Master Document on page 528.

22sub1.act
22sub2.act
22sub3.act
22sub4.act

8. Use the filename **22act1.mtr** and save the master document.

9. With **22act1.mtr** in the document window, expand the master document. If necessary, see Steps to Expand a Master Document on page 528.

10. Select the **Cross-Ref** button on the Generate Button Bar. Create the following cross-references:

    a. Place the insertion point in the space between the words "page" and "and" in the last paragraph of Chapter 1.

    b. Check that **Page** displays to the right of the Reference button.

    c. Click in the **Target** box and type **energy**.

    d. Select the **Mark Reference** button.

    e. Scroll down to Chapter 3 and place the insertion point after the period in the last paragraph.

    f. Select the **Mark Target** button.

    g. To mark the next cross-reference, place the insertion point to the left of the period in the last paragraph of Chapter 1.

    h. Check that the **Page** displays to the right of the Reference button.

    i. Double-click in the **Target** box and type **saving.**

    j. Select the **Mark Reference** button.

    k. Scroll down to Chapter 4 and place the insertion point to the left of the first character in the first paragraph.

    l. Select the **Mark Target** button.

    m. To mark the last cross-reference, place the insertion point to the left of the period in the last sentence of the first paragraph in Chapter 4.

    n. Check that **Page** displays to the right of the Reference button.

    o. Double-click in the **Target** box and type **table.**

    p. Select the **Mark Reference** button.

    q. Move the insertion point between the table and the text "Table 4.1" on the following page.

    r. Select the **Mark Target** button.

    s. Select the **Generate** button, **OK.**

11. Print one copy.

12. Condense the master document (select the **Condense** button, **OK**).

13. Use the same filename, **22act1.mtr**, and save the file on your file disk.
14. Display the WordPerfect Button Bar (move the mouse pointer into the Generate Button Bar, click the *right* mouse button, click on **WordPerfect**).
15. Close the document.

Activity 22.2–Create Advanced Styles in a Master Document

1. Open the master document named **22act1.mtr** that was created in Activity 22.1.
2. Expand the master document (select **File**, **Master Document**, **Expand Master**, **OK** or select the **ExpandMst** button on the Generate Button Bar).
3. Create a chapter heading style using the following information:
   a. Place the insertion point at any position in the title, Chapter 1—Save Energy.
   b. Select the **Styles** button. Choose **Create**.
   c. In the Style Name box, type **chapter head**.
   d. In the Description box, type **style for chapter opening**. Check that **Paragraph (paired)** displays in the Type box.
   e. Click in the **Contents** box and change the font to **Arrus BT**, **13 point**, **Bold** (select **Layout**, **Font**, select the desired font, size, and appearance, select **OK**).
   f. Change the justification to Center (select **Layout**, **Justification**, **Center**).
   g. Create a paragraph border (select **Layout**, **Paragraph**, **Border/Fill**, click on the **Border Style** button, click on the **Thin Bottom** border style [last button on the second row], select **OK**).
   h. Select **OK**. With the *chapter head* style highlighted, choose **Apply**.
4. Create a paragraph style containing a graphic image.
   a. Place the insertion point at any location in the first paragraph of Chapter 1.
   b. Select the **Styles** button. Choose **Create**.
   c. In the Style Name box, type **graphic par**.
   d. In the Description box, type **style for paragraph containing a graphic image**. Check that **Paragraph (paired)** displays in the Type box.
   e. Click in the **Contents** box.
   f. Select **Graphics**, **Figure**.
   g. Double-click on the filename **sun_dsg.wpg**.
   h. Select the **Position** button. In the Horizontal area, move the mouse pointer to the "from" box, press and hold the mouse button, and select **Left Margin**. Release the mouse button. Select **OK**.

i. Select the **Size** button. In the Width area, double-click in the **Set** box and type **.5**. Select **OK**.

j. Select the **Border/Fill** button. Click on the **Border Style** button and click on NO BORDER. Select **Customize Style**. Double-click in the **Outside Spacing** box and type **.03**. Select **OK**.

k. Select **OK** twice.

5. Save the style file on your file disk. (In the Style List dialog box, select **Options**, **Save As**. Type the name of the style file including the drive letter and/or directory name. Use the filename **22act2.sty**. Check that the **Both** option is selected. Select **OK**).
6. Select **Apply**.
7. Apply the **graphic par** and **chapter head** styles to Chapters 2, 3, and 4.
8. Print one copy of the master document.
9. Save and condense the master document using the *new* filename **22act2.mtr**.
10. Close the document.

Challenge Your Skills

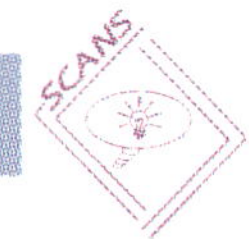

Skill 22.1—Create a Master Document, Cross-References, and Advanced Styles; Language Arts

1. Open the file named **22skill1.txt** located on your file disk.
2. Insert page numbers at the bottom center of each page; suppress the page number on page 1.
3. With the insertion point on page 2, create a master document containing the following subdocuments located on your file disk:

   22sub1.skl
   22sub2.skl
   22sub3.skl
   22sub4.skl

4. Use the filename **22skill1.mtr** and save the file.
5. Expand the master document.
6. Correct two spelling, two punctuation, and two number rule errors.
7. Create and generate cross-references for the four sentences on the title page and for the cross-reference in section 3.
8. Print one copy.
9. Create a section title style. Make decisions for the style name, description, font type, size, alignment, and paragraph borders. Apply the title style to each of the four section titles.

10. Create a style that contains a graphic image of your choice. Make decisions for the style name, graphic position and size, and the graphic box border and outside spacing. Apply the graphic style to each of the four sections.
11. Save the style file on your file disk. Use the filename **22skill1.sty**.
12. Print one copy.
13. Save and condense the master document. Use the same filename, **22skill1.mtr.**
14. If you have completed your work, exit WordPerfect.

Checking Your Step
Part 6

Production Skill Builder Activities
Chapters 20-22

Production Activity 6.1—Create a Multiple-Page Outline

1. Create the following outline. The paragraphs have been indented to show levels for outline numbering. Make decisions regarding:

    Margins
    Fonts
    Header/footer text and placement
    Outline definition
    Spacing above and below outline levels
    Proper capitalization of outline levels

COMPUTER SYSTEMS
Hardware Components and Maintenance

Analysis of system features and memory architecture
- Types of systems
- The system memory map
    - DOS program memory
    - Video memory adapter ROM and RAM
    - Motherboard ROM memory
    - Industry-adopted memory definitions
        - Conventional memory
        - Extended memory
        - Expanded memory
- Documentation
    - Types of documentation
        - *Guide to Operations and Quick Reference*
        - *Technical Reference Manuals*
        - *Hardware Maintenance Manuals*
    - Obtaining the documentation

- System teardown and preventive maintenance
    - Using the proper tools
        - Hand tools
        - Test equipment
    - Developing a preventive maintenance program
    - Reformatting hard disks
    - Operating environment
        - Heating and cooling
        - Static electricity
        - Power line noises
        - Dust and pollutants
    - Using power protection systems
        - Surge protectors and line conditioners
        - Backup power
            - Standby power supplies (SPS)
            - Uninterruptible power supplies (UPS)
    - Warranty and service contracts
- System diagnostics
    - Diagnostic software
        - Power-on self test (POST)
        - System diagnostics disk
- Detailed example of primary system components
    - Motherboards
        - Types of motherboards
        - Microprocessors
            - Data bus and address bus
            - Speed ratings of microprocessors
        - Math coprocessor upgrades
        - Memory
            - Upgrading the ROM BIOS
            - Motherboard memory
                - Memory banks
                - Memory chips
                - SIMMS
            - Speed ratings
    - The power supply
        - Power supply ratings
        - Power supply voltage and output testing
- Hard disk drives
    - Theory and operation
        - Drive components
            - Head actuator
            - Spindle ground strap
            - Cables and connectors
    - Types of hard disks
        - Interfaces
        - Head actuator mechanisms
    - Hard disk controllers
        - Standard controllers
        - After-market controllers

Hard disk upgrades
Repairing hard disk drives

---

2. Use the filename **6pact1.out** and save the outline.
3. Print one copy.
4. Close the document.

Production Activity 6.2—Create a Master Document with a Cross-Reference, Advanced Styles, Table of Contents, and Index

Note: If desired, this activity can be assigned as an individual project or as a group project with one group completing Part 1, the master document and cross-reference, a second group completing Part 2, creating and applying styles to the master document, and a third group completing Part 3, creating a table of contents and index.

Part 1—Create a Master Document and a Cross-Reference

1. Create a master document using the following information:
   a. Open a new document.
   b. Type and center the master document title, **Today's Health**. Make decisions regarding a font and a point size, justification, and centering the title vertically on the page.
   c. Insert page numbers. Make decisions on suppressing the page number on page one and on the location of the page numbers for the second and following pages.
   d. Place the following subdocuments into the master document. Each subdocument should be placed on a separate page. The following files are on the data disk.

      6psub1.txt
      6psub2.txt
      6psub3.txt
      6psub4.txt

   e. Use the filename **6pact2.mtr** and save the master document.
2. Expand the master document.
3. Create and generate a cross-reference for the table referenced on the first page of the Part 3 subdocument.
4. If desired, print one copy.
5. Save and condense the master document using the same filename, **6pact2.mtr**.

Part 2—Create and Apply Styles to the Master Document

1. Expand the master document named **6pact2.mtr** and create appropriate styles for the part headings and text. Make decisions on the following:

Use and placement of a graphic image in a style
Use of graphic lines or paragraph borders in a style
Style names and descriptions
Fonts
Justification

2. Save the styles using the filename **6pact2.sty**.
3. Apply the styles to each of the four subdocuments in the master document.
4. If desired, print one copy.
5. Save and condense the master document using the same filename, **6pact2.mtr**.

Part 3—Create a Table of Contents and Index for the Master Document

1. With the master document named **6pact2.mtr** displayed and expanded in the document window, mark appropriate table of contents entries and define the table of contents location and levels. (If necessary, see Chapter 21 for instructions on marking and defining a table of contents.)
2. Mark the following index entries. Also, define the location and format for the index.

   Health Insurance Plan of Missouri
   Immunization
   Osteoporosis
   Calcium
   Exercising

3. Generate the table of contents and index.
4. Print one copy.
5. Save and condense the master document using the same filename, **6pact2.mtr**.
6. If you have completed your work, exit WordPerfect.

Part 7
A Final Step

Advanced Techniques

Chapters 23-25

- Split cells
- Create formulas using spreadsheet-like functions
- Ignore cells when calculating
- Lock cells
- Use data fill
- Name a cell
- Create a floating cell
- Create a chart using WordPerfect Draw
- Import a spreadsheet
- Header rows
- Use IFBLANK...ELSE...ENDIF merge commands
- Merge a range of records
- Merge records based on conditions
- Form files with graphic images
- Output merged letters to a file or printer
- Import data
- User input in a merged letter
- Edit and correct (debug) macros
- Request user input in a macro
- Use variables
- Create IF-ELSE statements in macros
- Use glossary abbreviations

CHAPTER 23

Advanced Tables

Features Covered

- Split cells
- Create a formula
- Display negative numbers
- Set alignment position from right of cell
- Set vertical alignment in a table cell
- Ignore cells when calculating
- Lock cells
- Place a graphic image in a table
- Use data fill
- Name a cell
- Create a floating cell
- Create a chart using WP Draw
- Import a spreadsheet
- Create a header row
- Create a spreadsheet link

Objectives and Introduction

After successfully completing this chapter, you will be able to create a form using the Table feature. While creating the table form, you will learn to split cells, create a formula, display negative numbers between parentheses, and set the decimal alignment position from the right of the cell. You will learn to ignore cells when calculating, lock cells, and place a graphic image in a table using a graphic box. You will also learn to use data fill, name a cell, create a floating cell, import or link a spreadsheet, and create a header row for a multiple-page table. Finally, you will use the WP Draw program to create a chart based on a WordPerfect table.

In addition to the basic table features that are discussed in Chapters 6 and 7, other functions are available to format and display table numbers in cells. Also, a table can be enhanced by using any of the available WordPerfect graphics.

Create a Form Using the Table Feature

Many business forms, such as expense reports and invoices, can be created easily using the Table feature. Table cells can be split horizontally and vertically, numbers in cells can be positioned and displayed in many different ways, and formulas can be used for calculating.

A single table cell can be split into columns or rows. Usually, a cell is split into 2 columns or rows but can be split in up to 60 columns/rows if space is available.

Formulas are created in a cell in which the result of a calculation is desired. The formulas created in WordPerfect include symbols that indicate various math functions known as arithmetic operators. The arithmetic operator symbols used in formulas are as follows:

+ addition	- subtraction or negative number
* multiplication	/ division

When a column of numbers is added, a formula is used to avoid typing the cell address of each cell to be added. For example, if cells B1 through B8 are to be added, the formula Sum(B1:B8) can be used. The cells shown in between the parentheses will be added and the result placed in the cell where the formula is located. The colon is used to indicate a block of cells, the word "Sum" is used to signify addition, and the parentheses are used to set apart the cell addresses from the word "Sum."

When a formula is used, all numbers in the cells referenced in the formula are included in the calculation. Sometimes numbers represent information that should not be included in a column/row calculation. For example, if the date 5/26/95 was placed in a cell of a column to be calculated, the date should not be included in the total amount. By using the **Ignore Cell When Calculating** option in the Cell Format dialog box, cell information can be disregarded when calculated.

A minus sign (hyphen) is typed to indicate a negative number. The **Custom** option in the Number Type dialog box can be selected to obtain the Negative Numbers Formats. Select the **Parentheses** or the **CR/DR Symbol** (credit or debit) option to indicate a negative number. If the digits after the decimal option is set for two or more, decimal justification is chosen, and the parenthesis is used to display a negative number, the right parenthesis will wrap around to the next line. With **Column** selected in the Format dialog box, the **Position from Right** option is chosen to set the amount of space (distance) between the decimal and the right side of the column cells. To allow ample space for two decimal places and the right parenthesis, set the **Position from Right** to 0.35 inches.

If the row height is increased, the cell text or numbers can be defaulted to display at the top of the cell. Using the **Cell, Vertical Alignment** option in the Format dialog box, the text and/or numbers can be changed to display at the bottom or center of the cell.

Because a form will be used repeatedly, the information that remains constant in a table cell should be protected so that the cell contents will not accidentally be altered. Cells can be locked by selecting the **Cell, Lock** option in the Format dialog box. The insertion point cannot be placed in a locked cell. Locked cell(s) can be selected and formatted, however. For example, with the locked cell(s) selected, decimal justification can be chosen.

A table form can be enhanced by placing a graphic image in a table cell. After placing a graphic image in a table, the borders are usually removed.

Start-Up Instructions

- Open the file named **23expens.uf1** located on the data disk.
- If necessary, display the Tables Button Bar (move the mouse pointer into the Button Bar, click the *right* mouse button, click on **Tables**).

Split a Cell

Note: A mouse must be used for the following instructions to split a cell.

1. Place the insertion point in the cell to be split.

   For example, place the insertion point in cell A9.

   Note: Check the Status bar to see that A9 displays.

2. With the mouse pointer in any table cell, press the *right* mouse button once.

   Note: The Table QuickMenu displays.

3. Select the **Split Cell** option.

   Note: The Split Cell dialog box displays (see Figure 23.1).

4. Select the **Columns** or **Rows** option.

   For example, check that **Columns** is selected.

5. Point to the up or down triangle beside the Columns box to increase or decrease the number displayed.

   For example, check that **2** displays beside the Columns box.

6. Select **OK**.

   Note: The cell is divided into two columns, A9 and B9. The original column B (Week Ending) is now column C.

Finish-Up Instructions

- Repeat steps 1–6 and split cell A9 into 2 rows.
- Type **.29** (the payment rate for mileage) in cell B9.
- Use the *new* filename **23expens.fm1** and save the file on your file disk.

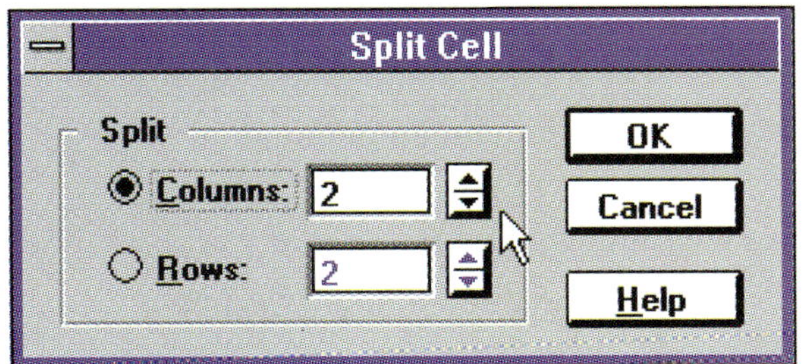

FIGURE 23.1

Split Cell dialog box

Start-Up Instructions

❖ The file named **23expens.ufl** and the Tables Button Bar should be displayed in the document window.

Create a Formula

1. Select the **TblFormBar** button on the Tables Button Bar.

Note: The Table Formula Feature Bar displays below the Power Bar (see Figure 6.3 on page 139).

2. Locate the insertion point in the cell in which the results of the formula are to be placed.

For example, locate the insertion point in cell **C9**.

3. Point to the **Edit Formula** box in the Table Formula Feature Bar and click once to relocate the insertion point.

*Note: The message, "Formula Edit Mode is On," displays to the right of the Edit Formula box. When the Formula Edit Mode is on, the WordPerfect menus and Button Bar can not be utilized. If a cell or range of cells is selected, the cell address(es) is inserted into the Edit Formula box. The Formula Edit Mode is turned off by selecting the **Insert** button on the Table Formula Feature Bar or by pressing the **Esc** key.*

4. Type the desired formula in the Edit Formula box.

For example, to multiply the number of miles by the mileage rate (.29), type **A10*B9**. (Do not type the period.)

5. Select the **Insert** button (✓) on the Table Formula Feature Bar or press **Enter**.

*Note: The result of the multiplication formula, zero (0), displays in cell C9 and the formula =A10*B9 displays in the Status bar. The result is zero because no data (values) have been typed into cell A10.*

Finish-Up Instructions

❖ Repeat steps 2–5 and type the formulas into the designated cells as follows:

cell D11	sum(C5:C10)
cell D16	sum(C12:C15)
cell D17	sum(D3:D16)
cell D19	D17+D18

Note: The amount in cell D18 will be subtracted from the amount in cell D17 because the amount in D18 will be entered as a negative (minus) number.

❖ Use the same filename, **23expens.fm1**, and save the file.

Note: Your form should look similar to the form in Figure 23.2.

❖ Continue with the Steps to Display Negative Number(s) Between Parentheses.

Start-Up Instructions

❖ The file named **23expens.fm1** and the Tables Button Bar should be displayed in the document window.

Windmill Foods, Inc. Weekly Expense Report			
Item		Week Ending:	1/x/9x
Lodging			
Meals			
Ground Transportation			
Car Rental			
Airfare			
Parking			
Mileage	.29	0	
Total Transportation			0
Miscellaneous			
Shipping/Postage			
Telephone			
Copying/Faxing			
Total Miscellaneous			0
Grand Total			0
Advance Received			
Total Payment/Reimbursement			0
Printed Name:		Signature:	Date:
*Original receipts required for all expenses.			

FIGURE 23.2

Table with split cells and formulas

Steps to Display Negative Number(s) Between Parentheses

1. Place the insertion point in the cell or select the cells in which a negative number(s) is to display between parentheses.

   For example, place the insertion point in cell **D18**.

2. Select the **Tbl#Type** button on the Tables Button Bar.
3. Choose the desired Select Type For option.

   For example, check that Cell is selected {c}.

4. Select the **Custom** button {u}.
5. In the Negative Numbers box, select **Parentheses** {p}.
6. Select **OK** twice {press Enter twice}.

   Note: No change displays in the document window at this time. The parentheses display only when a negative number is typed in the cell.

Finish-Up Instructions

- ❖ Continue with the Steps to Set Alignment Position From Right.

Start-Up Instructions

- ❖ The file named **23expens.fm1** and the Tables Button Bar should be displayed in the document window.

Steps to Set Alignment Position From Right

1. Place the insertion point in any cell in the column in which the alignment position will be set.

   For example, place the insertion point in any cell in column D.
2. Select the **Format Tbl** button on the Tables Button Bar {Alt and a, o *or* Ctrl and F12}.
3. Select **Column** {L}.
4. Select the **Position from Right** option in the Alignment area and type the desired amount of space {g}.

   For example, type **.35**. (Do not type the final period.)
5. Select **OK** {Enter}.

   Note: *No change displays in the document window. The distance between the decimal and the right of the cell can only be verified when a number is typed in a column cell.*

Finish-Up Instructions

- ❖ Continue with the Steps to Set the Vertical Alignment in a Table Cell.

Start-Up Instructions

- ❖ The file named **23expens.fm1** and the Tables Button Bar should be displayed in the document window.

Set the Vertical Alignment in a Table Cell

1. Locate the insertion point in the desired cell(s).

   For example, select all cells in row 2.
2. Select the **Format Tbl** button on the Tables Button Bar {Alt and a, o *or* Ctrl and F12}.
3. Select the desired Format option.

   For example, select **Cell** {e}.
4. Point to the option box located beside Vertical Alignment, press and hold the mouse button, and select the desired option {v, select desired option}.

   For example, select **Bottom** vertical alignment {b}.
5. Select **OK** {Enter}.

Note: If the cell height has not been increased, the cell contents may not display with the changed vertical alignment.

Finish-Up Instructions

- Repeat steps 1–5 in Steps to Set the Vertical Alignment in a Table Cell and set the vertical alignment to **Bottom** for cells B9 and C9.
- Use the same filename, **23expens.fm1**, and save the file.
- Continue with the Steps to Ignore Cells When Calculating.

Start-Up Instructions

- The file named **23expens.fm1** and the Tables Button Bar should be displayed in the document window.

Ignore Cells When Calculating

1. Place the insertion point in the cell or select the cells to be ignored when calculating.

   For example, place the insertion point in cell D2.

2. Select the **Format Tbl** button on the Tables Button Bar {Alt and a, o *or* Ctrl and F12}.
3. Select the desired Format option.

   For example, check that **Cell** is selected {e}.

4. Select the **Ignore Cell When Calculating** option in the Cell Attributes area {g}.
5. Select **OK** {Enter}.

   Note: A quotation mark is placed in front of the cell address in the Status bar, e.g., "Cell D2.

Finish-Up Instructions

- Use the same filename, **23expens.fm1**, and save the file.
- Continue with the Steps to Lock Cells.

Start-Up Instructions

- The file named **23expens.fm1** and the Tables Button Bar should be displayed in the document window.

Lock Cells

1. Place the insertion point in the cell or select the cells to be locked.

   For example, select cells A2 through C2, i.e., the first and second column headings.

2. Select the **Format Tbl** button on the Tables Button Bar {Alt and a, o *or* Ctrl and F12}.
3. Select the desired Format option.

   For example, check that **Cell** is selected {e}.

4. Select the **Lock** option in the Cell Attributes area {c}.
5. Select **OK** {Enter}.

   Note: *Brackets are placed around the cell address in the Status bar, e.g., [C2]. The insertion point cannot be placed in locked cells.*

Finish-Up Instructions

- Repeat steps 1–5 and lock the following cells:
  A3–A8, A9, B9, A11–A21, and C20–D20
- Use the *new* filename **23expens.fm2** and save the file.
- If necessary, select **Close** to remove the Table Formula Feature Bar from the document window.

Start-Up Instructions

- The file named **23expens.fm2** and the Tables Button Bar should be displayed in the document window.

Place a Graphic Image in a Table

1. In the document window, place the insertion point at the location where the graphic image is to be placed.

   For example, place the insertion point to the left of the "W" in the word Windmill in cell A1.
2. Select **Graphics, Figure** {Alt and g, f}.
3. Double-click on the desired filename {press Tab, use the up or down arrow key to highlight filename, press Enter}.

   For example, double-click on **windmill.wpg**.

   Note: *The graphic displays to the right of the table title and subtitle.*
4. Select the **Size** button on the Graphics Box Feature Bar {Alt and Shift and s}.
5. In the Width area, double-click in the **Set** box and type the desired amount {s, type desired amount}.

   For example, type **1.5**. (Do not type the final period.)
6. Check that the **Size to Content** option in the Height area is selected. If necessary, select the **Size to Content** option {z}.
7. Select **OK** {Enter}.
8. Select the **Wrap** button on the Graphics Box Feature Bar {Alt and Shift and w}
9. Select the **No Wrap (through)** option {o}.
10. Select **OK** {Enter}.

Finish-Up Instructions

- Use the *new* filename **23expens.for** and save the file.

- Select the windmill.wpg graphic image by choosing **Graphics**, **Edit Box**. Remove the borders (select the **Border/Fill** button on the Graphics Box Feature Bar, select the **Border Style** button, select **No Border**, **OK**).
- Select cells C3–D19 and set the cells for the Commas number type with 2 digits after the decimal (select **Tbl#Type**, **Commas**, **OK**). Use the Justification button and select **Decimal**.

  Note: *Zeros (0.00) display in the cells where formulas are located.*
- Place the insertion point in cell A20 and change the row height to **Fixed**, **.6** inches (select **Format Tbl**, **Row**, **Fixed**, type **.6**, **OK**).
- Select and join cells A11–C11.
- Select and join cells A16–C16.
- Select and join cells A17–C17.
- Select and join cells A19–C19.
- Select and join all the cells in row 21.
- Format cell D19 for currency number type.

  Note: *A dollar sign displays to the left of the zeros (e.g., $0.00).*
- Select all cells in row 2 and change the fill to Button Fill Style and the bottom line style to Double (select **TblLineFill** button, select the **Fill Style** button, select **Button Fill** in the second row—the last style button, select **Bottom** Line Styles button, select the **Double Lines** button to the right of the <None> button, select **OK**).
- Select cells D3–D19 and use 10% Shaded Fill (select **TblLineFill** button, select the **Fill Style** button, select the **10% Fill** button to the right of the <None> button, select **OK**).
- Type the following figures into the table cells:

cell D2 (Week Ending:)	9/24/9x
cell D3 (Lodging)	536.82
cell D4 (Meals)	138.93
cell C5 (Ground Transportation)	39
cell C6 (Car Rental)	157
cell C7 (Airfare)	795.32
cell C8 (Parking)	39.87
cell A10 (Mileage)	565
cell C12 (Miscellaneous)	15.60
cell C13 (Shipping/Postage)	22
cell C14 (Telephone)	14.68
cell C15 (Copying/Faxing)	28.99
cell D18 (Advance Received)	-1800

- Select the **Calculate** button on the Tables Button Bar; select **Calc Table**.
- Use the *new* filename **23expens.924** and save the file.

  Note: *Your form should look similar to the form in Figure 23.3.*
- Print one copy and close the document.

FIGURE 23.3

Final expense report form

Windmill Foods, Inc. Weekly Expense Report			
Item		Week Ending:	9/24/9x
Lodging			536.82
Meals			138.93
Ground Transportation		39.00	
Car Rental		157.00	
Airfare		795.32	
Parking		39.87	
Mileage	.29	163.85	
565			
Total Transportation			1,195.04
Miscellaneous		15.60	
Shipping/Postage		22.00	
Telephone		14.68	
Copying/Faxing		28.99	
Total Miscellaneous			81.27
Grand Total			1,952.06
Advance Received			(1,800.00)
Total Payment/Reimbursement			152.06
Printed Name:		Signature:	Date:
*Original receipts required for all expenses.			

Use the Data Fill, Name Cell, and Floating Cell Features

WordPerfect provides many features that assist in expediting the creation of tables and formulas. Data fill, cell naming, and floating cells are three features that can simplify your work with tables.

When the data fill feature is used, the information in the first few cells in a column or row are observed and the pattern of the values or words contained in the cells is determined. For example, if the first several table cells containing Sunday, Monday, and Tuesday are highlighted along with the four following cells and the **TblDataFill** button is chosen, WordPerfect automatically fills the following cells with Wednesday, Thursday, Friday, and Saturday. Also, if the first several cells contain values in increments of 5 (i.e., 5, 10, and 15), WordPerfect fills the following cells with 20, 25, 30, etc.

A name can be given to a cell and/or range of cells. The cell name can contain letters, numbers, underscores, spaces, WordPerfect characters, and any of the symbols #, $, ? or @. Also, a name can be given to a cell and used in a formula rather than using the cell address. If cell D8 (named Pay Rate) contains an hourly pay rate and cell D9 (named Amount of Hours) contains an hourly amount, a formula could be created to multiply the two cells by typing Pay Rate*Amount of Hours instead of D8*D9.

Also, a name can be given to a table. When a table is created, WordPerfect automatically assigns the name "Table A." The name can be changed by selecting the **Names** button on the Table Formula Feature Bar, highlighting the table name, and selecting **Edit**. Type the new name and select **OK**. The new table name displays in the Table/Floating Cell list in the Table Names in Current Document dialog box. When the insertion point is located in a table cell, the name of the table displays in the middle of the Status bar at the bottom of the document window and in the Address box if the Table Formula Feature Bar is displayed.

A floating cell is a one-cell table. A floating cell often references a table or another cell from which its value is obtained. Using a floating cell is a quick method for inserting calculated values into a document. For example, a letter containing a table may state that there has been an increase in sales and a cell in the letter table contains a formula that calculates the increase/decrease in sales. The figure displayed in the amount of increase/decrease is inserted in the floating cell located in the letter. The major advantage of using a floating cell is that if any values change in the table and the **Calculate Document** option is selected in the Calculate dialog box, the table values and the floating cell value in the letter are updated automatically.

Start-Up Instructions

- Open the file named **23saleun.flo** located on the data disk.
- The Tables Button Bar should be displayed in the document window.

Steps to Use Data Fill

1. Select the cells that contain the pattern of increasing numbers and the blank cells to be filled with the numbering pattern.

   For example, select cells A3 through A14.

2. Select the **TblDataFill** button on the Tables Button Bar.

   Note: *The numbers 4 through 12 display in the previously blank cells in column A.*

Finish-Up Instructions

- Select cells D3–D14 and repeat the Steps to Use Data Fill.
- Select the **Calculate** button and select **Calc Table** to update the total amount in cell D15.
- Copy the formula in cell E5 to E6 through E15 (select the **TblFormBar** button, select **Copy Formula**, type **E6**, select **Down**, **10** times, **OK**).
- Use the *new* filename **23sales.fl1** and save the file to your file disk.

Start-Up Instructions

- The file named **23sales.fl1**, the Tables Button Bar, and the Table Formula Feature Bar should be displayed in the document window.

FIGURE 23.4

Table Names in Current Document dialog box

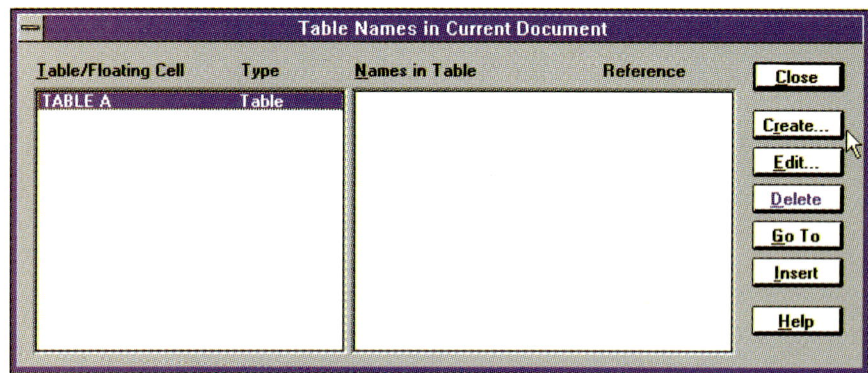

Steps to

Name a Cell

1. Place the insertion point in the cell to be named.

   For example, place the insertion point in Cell E15.

2. Select the **Names** button on the Table Formula Feature Bar {Alt and Shift and n}.

   Note: The Table Names in Current Document dialog box displays with TABLE A highlighted (see Figure 23.4).

3. Select the **Create** button {Alt and r}.

4. With the insertion point located in the **Enter Name Manually** box, type the desired cell name.

   For example, type **percent**.

5. Select **OK** {Enter}.

   Note: The cell name Percent displays below Names in Table and E15 displays below Reference.

6. Select **Close** {Enter}.

Finish-Up Instructions

- Continue with the Steps to Create a Floating Cell.

Create a Floating Cell

Note: The Tables Button Bar should be displayed.

1. Locate the insertion point in the text where the floating cell is to be inserted.

   For example, locate the insertion point between the words "are" and "over" in the first paragraph.

2. Select the **Table** button on the Tables Button Bar {Alt and a, c}.

   Note: The Create Table dialog box displays.

3. Select the **Floating Cell** option in the Create area {Alt and f}.

4. Select **OK** {Enter}.

   *Note: The words "Floating Cell A" display in the Address box in the Table Formula Feature Bar and in the Status bar. If desired, use Reveal Codes to see the **Flt Cell** codes.*

Finish-Up Instructions

- Use the same filename, **23sales.fl1**, and save the file.
- Continue with the Steps to Insert a Named Cell into a Floating Cell.

Start-Up Instructions

- The file named **23sales.fl1 and** the Tables Button Bar should be displayed in the document window.
- If necessary, turn on Reveal Codes. The red or shaded block should be located between the two Flt Cell (floating cell) codes. (If necessary, move the insertion point in the document window to relocate the red or shaded block in the Reveal Codes window.)
- Set zero decimals in the floating cell (select the **Tbl#Type** button, select **Percent**, select **Custom**, change **Digits after Decimal** to zero, select **OK** twice).

Steps to Insert a Named Cell into a Floating Cell

Note: The Table Formula Feature Bar and Reveal Codes should be displayed in the document window.

1. With the insertion point located between the two Flt Cell codes, point and click in the **Edit Formula** box to relocate the insertion point.
2. Select **Names** on the Table Formula Feature Bar.
3. Select the desired table.

   For example, select **Table A.**
4. Select the desired name in the Names in Table list.

   For example, select **PERCENT.**
5. Select the **Insert** button.

   Note: The Table A.Percent formula displays in the Edit Formula box.
6. Select the **Insert** button (✓) on the Tables Formula Feature Bar.

   Note: The total increase for the quarter, 13%, displays in the paragraph.

Finish-Up Instructions

- Use the same filename, **23sales.fl3**, and save the file.
- Print one copy and close the document.

Use WP Draw to Create a Chart

Data from a table can be visually displayed in a chart by using the WP Draw feature. Data from an existing WordPerfect table can be used to create a chart or new data can be typed in the worksheet area of the Chart Editor. If data in a WordPerfect table will be used to create a chart, the insertion point must be located in a table cell before the **Chart** button is selected. When the **Chart** button is selected, the table data is placed in the worksheet area of the Chart Editor and a bar chart graphically illustrating the table data displays (see Figure 23.5).

If the insertion point is not in a table cell when the **Chart** button is selected, sample data and a sample chart display. The sample data can be cleared by selecting **File**, **Clear**. Typing new data in the worksheet cells is similar to entering data in a WordPerfect table. The data can be formatted but cannot be calculated. In other words, column widths and number types can be changed, but a formula cannot be entered to add a column.

Once data is displayed in the worksheet area of the Chart Editor, the chart titles, legend, and labels can be entered and/or formatted. The data for a chart legend are obtained from the first column of the worksheet. The data for the chart labels are obtained from the top row of the worksheet. The titles, i.e., title, subtitle, Y1, Y2, and X Axis are typed in the titles dialog box. (The Y1 Axis refers to the left side of the chart, the Y2 Axis refers to the right side of the chart, and the X Axis refers to the bottom side of the chart.)

In addition to the bar chart, different types of charts are available such as line, pie, Hi-Lo, etc. Also, other chart examples are available for each chart type in the Chart Gallery (see Figure 23.6). For example, a bar chart can be stacked, cluster, or overlap.

The data in the Chart Editor worksheet can be changed. However, if the Chart Editor worksheet data are modified, the data is not modified in the original table located in the document window. When changes are made to the data in the Chart Editor worksheet data, the **Redraw** button is chosen to redisplay the chart with the revised information.

After a chart is setup, select the **Return** button to insert the chart into the WordPerfect document. The chart displays in a graphic box. The position, size, and border or fill style for the graphic box containing the chart can be edited using the options on the Graphic Box Feature Bar.

To edit a chart, double-click on the chart in the document window. The Chart Editor displays. Make desired changes. Select the **Update** button to incorporate the changes in the chart located in the document window without exiting the WP Draw program.

Start-Up Instructions

- Open the file named **23divisn.d3** located on the data disk.

Steps to

Create a Chart

1. With the insertion point located in any table cell, select the **Chart** button from the WordPerfect or Tables Button Bar {Alt and g, r}.

   Note: The Chart Editor displays with a bar chart that visually illustrates the table information (see Figure 23.5).

2. Select the **Titles** button {Alt and o, t}.

   Note: The Titles dialog box displays.

3. Type the desired chart title, then press the **Tab** key once.

   For example, type **Division Expense Report** and press **Tab**.

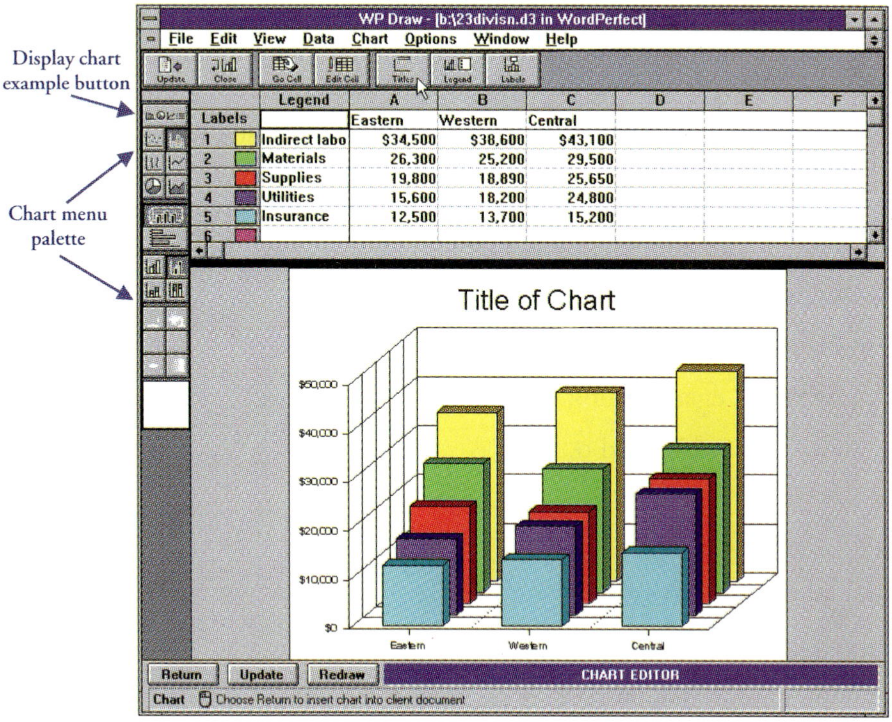

Display chart example button

Chart menu palette

FIGURE 23.5

Chart Editor

4. Type the desired chart subtitle, then press the **Tab** key once.

For example, type **Third Quarter** and press **Tab**.

5. Type the desired Y1 Axis information, then press the **Tab** key once.

For example, type the current year and press **Tab**.

6. Type the desired X Axis information.

For example, type **Divisions**.

*Note: If desired, select the **Preview** button to view the titles {Alt and v}.*

7. Select **OK** to exit the Titles dialog box {Enter}.

8. Select the **Legend** button {Alt and o, e}.

Note: The Legend dialog box displays.

9. Select the **Display Legend** option {y}.

Note: An X should display in the Display Legend box.

10. In the Placement area, select the desired option.

For example, select **Outside Chart** {o}.

11. Select the desired Placement Position {p, Spacebar, press the up or down arrow to highlight the desired option, Enter}.

For example, move the mouse pointer to the Position box, press and hold the mouse button and drag to highlight **Middle Right**. Release the mouse button.

12. In the Title area, double-click in the **Name** box and type the desired name {Alt and n}.

For example, type **Expense Categories**.

13. In the Box option area, select the desired option {Alt and a}.

For example, select **Attributes.**

Note: The Box Attributes dialog box displays.

14. Select the desired Box Style {b, Spacebar, press the up or down arrow key to highlight the desired option, Enter}.

For example, move the mouse pointer to the Box Style box, press and hold the mouse button and drag to highlight **Rounded Rectangle.** Release the mouse button.

15. Select **OK** to exit the Box Attributes dialog box {Enter}.

16. Select **OK** to exit the Legend dialog box {Enter}.

17. Select the **Labels** button {Alt and o, b}.

Note: The Labels dialog box displays.

18. Select the desired Label option.

For example, select **X Axis** {x}.

19. In the Options area, select the desired option.

For example, select **Stagger** {s}.

Note: An X displays beside the Stagger and Display options.

20. Select **OK** {Enter}.

21. Select the **Return** button on the bottom left side of the Chart Editor bar {Alt and f, x}.

Note: The WP Draw message box displays with the message, "Save changes...in WordPerfect?".

22. Select **Yes** {Enter}.

Note: In a few moments, the bar chart displays under the table in the document window.

Finish-Up Instructions

- Use the mouse to select and move the chart to the middle of the document window. Increase the size of the graphic box in order to read the label and legend information easily. (If necessary, see Chapter 13 for Steps to Change the Size and Position of a Graphic Box Using the Mouse, p. 320.)
- To deselect the chart, click outside the chart.
- Use the *new* filename **23divisn.cht** and save the file.
- Print one copy.

Start-Up Instructions

- The file named **23divisn.cht** should be displayed in the document window.

Use the Chart Gallery

1. Double-click on the chart graphic {Alt, g, e, Alt and Shift and o, e}.

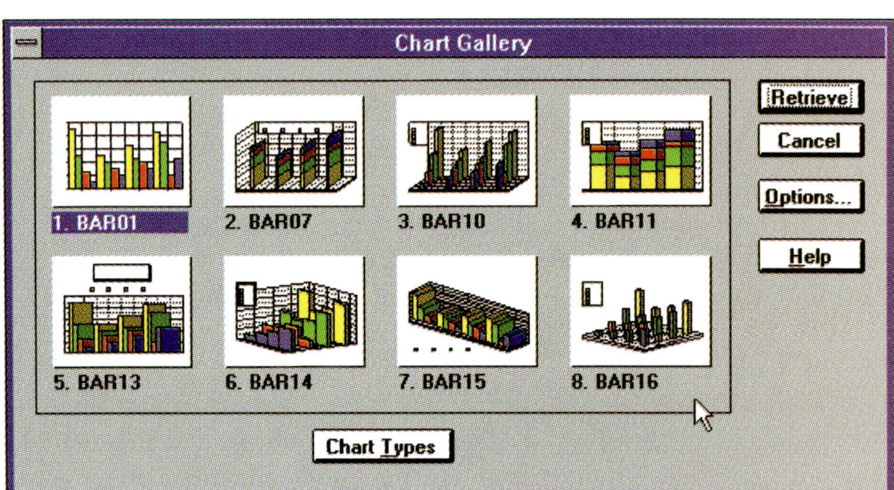

FIGURE 23.6

Chart Gallery

2. Select **Chart, Gallery** or select the **Display chart examples** button at the top of the Chart menu palette {Alt and c, g}.

   Note: The Chart Gallery displays containing several different bar chart styles (see Figure 23.6).

3. Select the desired bar chart.

   For example, select **Bar07** {press Tab five times, press the right arrow key once}.

4. Select **Retrieve** {Tab, Enter}.

   Note: The selected bar chart displays in the Chart Editor window.

Finish-Up Instructions

- Select **Return** and save the changes in WordPerfect.
- To deselect the chart, move the mouse pointer away from the chart and click once.
- Use the *new* filename **23divisn.c2** and save the file.
- Print one copy and close the document.

Import a Spreadsheet

A spreadsheet file can be imported easily into a WordPerfect document window. WordPerfect can open or import spreadsheet files from programs such as Excel, Lotus 1-2-3, and Quattro Pro.

When a spreadsheet file is imported, *all* or *part* of the file information is *copied and inserted* into a new or existing file. If a portion of a spreadsheet file is imported, a range (block of cells) can be typed to indicate the exact rows and columns to be copied. An imported file exists as a separate copy (file) from the original spreadsheet file.

A spreadsheet file can be imported by selecting the **Open** button on the Power Bar or selecting **Insert**, **Spreadsheet/Database**, **Import**. If the **Open** button is selected to import a spreadsheet file, the data is converted to a WordPerfect table and placed in a new document window. If the **Insert**, **Spreadsheet/Database**, **Import** option is used, the data is converted to a WordPerfect table and placed in the current document window at the location of the insertion point.

When the spreadsheet file is opened or inserted, the Import Data dialog box displays. The name and location of the file to be imported is selected or typed. When the **OK** button is chosen, the spreadsheet range indicating the top left and the bottom right table cell addresses displays in the Named Ranges and the Range boxes. The cell addresses can be changed if desired. The entire spreadsheet file can be inserted into an existing document by placing the insertion point at the desired location and then using the desired Open or Insert import procedure.

The spreadsheet file can be imported as a table, text, or a merge data file. If the spreadsheet is imported as a table, WordPerfect copies the spreadsheet information (up to 64 columns) into a WordPerfect table. The formulas and spreadsheet format are converted to WordPerfect math functions and format; however, checking for accuracy is always recommended. If the spreadsheet is imported as text, WordPerfect copies the information into columns separated by tabs. No formulas are imported when the text option is selected. When a spreadsheet file is imported as a merge data file, the file can be merged with a form file. (See form and data files in Chapters 11 and 12.)

Once a file is imported, additional formatting may be desired. For example, the column widths may need to be increased or decreased and cells may need to be joined. Also, the number type can be changed to display a dollar sign, commas, etc., in the cell amounts.

Start-Up Instructions

- Open the file named **23ltr.car** located on the data disk.

Steps to Import a Spreadsheet

1. The insertion point should be placed at the location where the spreadsheet file is to be inserted.

   For example, place the insertion point in the blank space between the two paragraphs.

2. Select **Insert, Spreadsheet/Database** {Alt and i, r}.
3. Select **Import** {i}.

   Note: If the filename **23dril2f.xls** *and location display correctly in the filename box, skip to step 8.*

4. Select the **List** button located beside the Filename box.
5. In the Drives box, select the location where your spreadsheet file is located.

   For example, select the drive letter where your data disk is located (a: or b:).

6. Double-click on the desired filename {Alt and n, use the arrow keys to highlight the filename and press Enter}.

   For example, double-click on the file named **23dril2f.xls**.

   Note: *The Import Data dialog box displays with the Data Type as a Spreadsheet and the Import As option as a Table.*

7. Select **OK**.

   Note: In the Named Ranges box, A1:E44 displays.

8. Select **OK**.

   Note: The "Conversion in progress" message displays and in a few moments the imported spreadsheet displays in a WordPerfect Table format.

Finish-Up Instructions

- If desired, view both pages of the document in the document window (place the insertion point in page 1 and select **View**, **Two Page**. Select **View**, **Page** to return to the normal view).
- Select the entire table (move the mouse pointer to the left edge of any cell until the left selection arrow displays, triple-click). Change the font to **Times New Roman**. Select the **TblLineFill** button (or choose **Table**, **Lines/Fill**), select the **Left**, **Right**, **Top**, and **Bottom** Line Style buttons, and choose the **Single** line style. Select **OK**.
- Select and join cells A1 through E4. Choose **Center** justification.
- Use the *new* filename **23drill3.ss** and save the file.
- Print one copy.
- Continue with the Steps to Create a Header Row(s).

Create a Header Row(s) for a Multiple-Page Table

The second and following pages of a multiple-page table should contain header information that identifies the table and/or column titles. A row or consecutive rows from the first page of a multiple-page table can be designated as a header row(s). A header row(s) prints as the top row(s) of the second and following pages of a multiple-page table.

The **Header Row** option is selected from the Format Table dialog box. An asterisk is displayed to the right of the cell address in the Status bar to indicate that the cell is part of a row that will print as a header row.

Any row or consecutive rows can be selected as a header row(s). If more than one row is selected, however, the multiple rows must be consecutive.

Start-Up Instructions

- The file named **23drill3.ss** and the Tables Button Bar should be displayed in the document window.

Create a Header Row(s)

1. Select the row(s) to be used as a header row(s).

   For example, select rows 2 and 3.

2. Select the Format Tbl button on the Tables Button Bar {Alt a, o}.

3. Choose the desired option.

   For example, check that Row is selected.

4. Select Header Row {d}.

   Note: An X is placed beside the Header Row option.

5. Select OK {Enter}.

   Note: In the Status bar an asterisk displays to the right of the cell address, i.e., ...A2.*

Finish-Up Instructions

- Use the *new* filename **23ltr.ss** and save the file.
- Print one copy and close the document.

Create a Spreadsheet Link

A spreadsheet file can be imported and linked simultaneously. When a spreadsheet is linked, the copied spreadsheet information in the WordPerfect document is updated to reflect any changes made to the original spreadsheet file. The link provides a connection between the WordPerfect document and the original spreadsheet file.

A link is created by selecting the **Spreadsheet/Database** option from the **Insert** menu and choosing **Create Link**. The filename of the spreadsheet to be imported and linked can be selected after choosing the File List button or by typing the filename in the Filename option box. When typing the filename, include the location of the file and the filename extension. For example, if the spreadsheet file is located on the disk in drive B, type *b:\budget.xls*. If only a portion of the spreadsheet is to be linked and imported, type the range of cells in the **Range** option box. The **OK** button is selected to create a link and import the spreadsheet. The "Conversion in progress" message displays and in a few moments the spreadsheet displays.

Link icons and codes display at the beginning and end of the imported/linked spreadsheet. The beginning link icon displays as two documents with a small arrow pointing downward. The ending link icon also displays as two documents but with the small arrow pointing upward. Click on the beginning link code to display the location, filename, and cell range of the imported/linked spreadsheet. For example, the code *Link b:\budget.xls, Spread:A1:D30* displays. Click on the ending link code to display the location and filename of the linked file. Link icons do not print and can be hidden on the screen. To hide the link icons, select **Spreadsheet/Database** from the **Insert** menu, choose **Options**, and deselect **Show Link Icons**.

A linked spreadsheet can be updated automatically upon document retrieval or can be updated manually. To automatically update a linked spreadsheet, select **Insert, Spreadsheet/Database, Options**. When the Link Options dialog box displays, select **Update on Retrieve** and choose **OK**. To manually update a linked spreadsheet file, select **Insert, Spreadsheet/Database, Update**. In the Update dialog box, select **Yes** to **Update All Data Links**.

The Next Step

Chapter Review and Activities

Self-Check Quiz

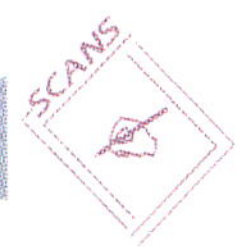

T F 1. If a cell is split into two columns, a formula cannot be used in either cell.

T F 2. The asterisk in the cell formula D8*E8 indicates multiplication.

T F 3. Using the WP Draw feature, a chart can be created to illustrate data from a WordPerfect table.

T F 4. When the row height is increased, text or numbers can be positioned at the top, center, or bottom of the cell.

T F 5. The insertion point cannot be placed in a locked cell, but a locked cell can be selected and formatted.

6. A floating cell is a ______-cell table.
   a. one
   b. two
   c. three
   d. None of these

7. In the Customize Number Type dialog box, negative numbers can be displayed with ________________.
   a. a minus sign
   b. a parentheses
   c. a CR/DR symbol
   d. all of these

8. A cell name can contain __________.
   a. numbers
   b. spaces
   c. WordPerfect characters
   d. all of these

9. Give two reasons for using the **Ignore Cell When Calculating** option.

10. In three sentences or less, state the differences between importing a spreadsheet file and linking a spreadsheet file.

Enriching Language Arts

Spelling/Vocabulary Words

quarter one of four parts into which something is divided; one-quarter of a year is three months, or $^1/_4$ of 12 months.

UPC Universal Product Code; a series of black lines of different widths used on packages to mark prices for electronic checkout.

versus as compared to; against. Common abbreviations are *v.* and *vs.*

Abbreviations in Table Column Headings

When creating tables and forms, abbreviations are often used in subtitles and/or column headings because of limited space. However, abbreviations should be used sparingly. If you are unsure of how to abbreviate a word, consult a dictionary.

Common abbreviations:

account	*acct.*	*department*	*dept.*
amount	*amt.*	*incorporated*	*inc.*
attention	*attn.*	*ounce*	*oz.*
dozen	*dz. or doz.*	*received*	*recd.*

Activities

Activity 23.1—Create and Format a Form Using the Table Feature; Create Formulas

1. Create a table with five columns and ten rows.
2. Use the following information to format the table similar to the table shown on page 565.
   a. Join cells A1–C1 and A2–C2.
   b. Split cells D1–E1 into two rows.
   c. Join cells D2–E2.
   d. Join cells D3–E3.
   e. Split cell D3 into two rows.
   f. Type the information shown in the table cells on page 565. Do not type the zeros in the Total Price column.
   g. Format the text in the table cells. Use your choice of fonts and font sizes.
   h. Select cells **A5–E12**. Set the row height to **.42** inches. Change the vertical alignment for the selected cells to **Bottom**.
   i. Select and right justify the cells in the columns below the Quantity and Stock No. column headings.

j. Set the number type to commas and two digits after decimal and use decimal justification for the cells in the columns below the Unit Price and Total Price column headings.

k. In the bottom row right cell (E12), set the number type for currency and two digits after the decimal.

3. Use the following information to format and place formulas in the form:

   a. Create a formula in the first cell of the Total Price column (E6) to multiply the Quantity times the Unit Price, e.g., **A6*D6**. Copy the formula to the next two rows.

   b. In the cell at the intersection of the Subtotal row and the Total Price column (E10), create a formula to add the top three cells of the Total Price column, e.g., **sum(E6:E8)**.

   c. In the cell at the intersection of the Sales Tax row and the Total Price column (E11), create a formula to multiply the subtotal times the sales tax. e.g., **E10*.0825**. (Do not type the final period.)

   d. In the cell at the intersection of the Total row and the Total Price column (E12), type a formula to add the subtotal and sales tax, e.g., **E10+E11**.

4. Use the filename **23act1.frm** and save the file.

5. Optional. Print one copy of the form.

Purchase Order **ABC Discount Supply** **2018 Winter St.** **Binghamton, NY 13909**			P.O. No.:	Date:
			Deliver To:	
To:			Delivery Date:	
			Ship By:	
Quantity	Stock No.	Description	Unit Price	Total Price
				0.00
				0.00
				0.00
		Subtotal		0.00
		Sales Tax (8.25%)		0.00
		Total		$0.00

Activity 23.2—Type Data into a Form and Use Calculate

1. Open the file named **23act1.frm** created in Activity 23.1.
2. Type the following information into the appropriate cells.

   Hint: *To indent information in a table cell, press the F7 key.*

   To: Longman Construction Co.
   9822 Keystone Blvd.
   Pittsburgh, PA 15227
   P.O. No.: 14022
   Date: Use current date (mm/dd/yy).
   Deliver To: Shane
   Delivery Date: Use a date one week from the current date.
   Ship By: UPS

Quantity	Stock No.	Description	Unit Price	Total Price
15	3455	Porcelain switches	1.50	
10	4822	Switch boxes	1.20	
50	4801	Switch plates	1.15	

3. Select the **Calculate** button on the Tables Button Bar and select **Calc Table** to compute and display the results of the formulas.
4. Use the *new* filename **23act2.po** and save the file.
5. Print one copy and close the document.

Activity 23.3—Use Data Fill and Create a Chart

1. Open the file named **23act3.sal** located on the data disk.
2. If necessary, display the Tables Button Bar.
3. Select cells **A2–A7**; select the **TblDataFill** button on the Tables Button Bar. Move the mouse pointer to any cell outside the selected cells and click once to deselect the cells.
4. With the insertion point in any table cell, select the **Chart** button on the Tables Button Bar.
5. Select **Chart**, **Gallery** and double-click on **Bar11**.
6. Select the **Titles** button and type the following information:

   Title: Andrea's Styling Salon
   Subtitle: Daily Receipts
   Y1 Axis: (use the current year)
   X Axis: December

7. Select **Options** and set the Y1 Axis position to **Vertical**; select the **X Axis** and set the position to **Horizontal**. Select **OK** twice.

8. Select the **Legend** button and type **Days of Week** in the Title Name box. Select **Display Legend**, **Outside Chart** with the position at the **Bottom Left**. Select **OK**.
9. Select the **Return** button and choose **Yes** to save changes.
10. Select the graphic box containing the chart and move the chart to the middle of the document window. Increase the size of the graphic box containing the chart so that the legend and labels can be read easily.
11. Click outside the graphic box containing the chart to deselect the box.
12. Use the *new* filename **23act3.cht** and save the file.
13. Print one copy and close the document.

Challenge Your Skills

Skill 23.1—Name Cells and Create a Floating Cell

1. Open the file named **23skill1.rap** located on the data disk.
2. Name the cells in the totals row as follows:

B7	Gross Salary
C7	Tax
D7	SSI
E7	Insurance
F7	Total net pay

3. In cell F7, create a formula (using the named cells) to add the deductions and subtract the total deductions from the Gross Salary.

   Hint: *Use a formula similar to the formula located in cell F6. Remember to use the cell names.*
4. Place the insertion point between the words "of" and "are" in the first memorandum paragraph and create a floating cell.
5. With the insertion point between the *Flt Cell* codes, insert the cell named "TOTAL NET PAY" into the floating cell.

   Hint: *Remember to click on the* ***Insert*** *button on the Table Formula Feature Bar.*
6. Format the floating cell to **Currency** number type.
7. Use the *new* filename **23skill1.flo** and save the file.
8. Print one copy and close the document.

Skill 23.2—Import a Spreadsheet File and Edit the Spreadsheet; Language Arts

1. Open the file named **23skill2.mem** located on the data disk.

2. Locate the insertion point on the second blank line below the first paragraph.
3. Insert and import the Excel spreadsheet file named **23bando.xls** located on the data disk.
4. In the memo and spreadsheet, correct two spelling errors and one punctuation error.
5. Make the following changes to the table:
   a. Change the font for the entire table to **Times New Roman**.
   b. Change the line style for all lines to **Single**.
   c. Join all cells in rows 1, 2, and 3; center the text in row 1.
   d. In rows 1 and 4, use **10% Fill**.
   e. Set row 4 for a header row.
   f. Use right justification for the cells containing amounts in columns A and E. Use decimal alignment for the cells containing amounts in columns D and H.
   g. Change the right column margin for the cells containing amounts in columns A and E to **.1**.
6. Insert page numbers at the bottom center.
7. Use the *new* filename **23skill2.imp** and save the file.
8. Print one copy.
9. If you have completed your work in WordPerfect, exit the program.

CHAPTER

Advanced Merging

Features Covered

- Use IFBLANK, ELSE, and ENDIF merge commands
- Merge a range of records
- Merge records based on conditions
- Create form files with graphic images
- Output merged letters to a file or printer
- Import data
- Request user input in a merged letter

Objectives and Introduction

After successfully completing this chapter, you will be able to use IFBLANK, ELSE, and ENDIF merge commands when merging a form and data file and print specific records by using a range of records or by setting merge conditions. Also, you will learn to designate the file location of graphic images, to output merged letters to a file or printer, and to import data into a data text file. In addition, you will learn to place a Keyboard command (a special command) in a form letter to allow user input as letters are merged.

The basic structure of WordPerfect's merge program, which combines form files and data files to produce individualized letters and mailing labels, was introduced in Chapters 11 and 12. In addition to the basics, the merge program has options and commands that can make merged documents look more professional, make the merge operation more flexible and efficient, and allow WordPerfect to use data from mainframe or database programs.

Improve the Appearance of Merged Documents

Many times data files will contain fields that are empty in some records. For example, Alan's Ads is a company that sends advertising for various clients to an interna-

FIGURE 24.1

Form file without IF statements

FIELD(title) FIELD(firstname) FIELD(lastname)
FIELD(company)
FIELD(address)
FIELD(city), FIELD(state/province) FIELD(zipcode)
FIELD(country)

Dear FIELD(title) FIELD(lastname):

George Santana

2544 Morris Road
London,
England

Dear Santana:

Merged letter address and salutation with extra space and a blank line that resulted from empty fields.

tional market. Their prospects' database contains the following fields: title, firstname, lastname, company, street address, city, state/province, country, zipcode, requestdate.

However, Alan soon finds out that some people do not check the title box on their information form, some companies fill out the form without including a person's name, and some foreign countries do not use the state/province field. If the inside address in the form letter uses all fields, some letters will print with blank spaces as shown in Figure 24.1.

One way of eliminating a blank line was discussed in Chapter 11, page 262. If the potentially blank field is on a line by itself, selecting the option **Remove Blank Line** during the merge operation will eliminate the blank line when the field is empty. Similarly, a question mark after the field name, i.e., FIELD(company?) will eliminate a blank line. However, these techniques are not applicable to the title field, because the title field leaves a blank horizontal space, not a blank line, if the title field is empty. Instead, WordPerfect uses the merge commands, IFBLANK...ELSE...ENDIF, to eliminate the blank horizontal space when a field is empty.

The IFBLANK command tells the Merge feature that: "If the field is empty (blank), print everything between here and the ELSE command that follows." An ELSE command is included to tell the Merge feature what to do if the field is not empty. The ENDIF command tells the Merge feature that this ends the IF statement. For an example of the IFBLANK, ELSE, and ENDIF merge commands, see Figure 24.3 on page 573. When an IFBLANK command is used, the ELSE and ENDIF commands must also be used to complete the command statement.

Start-Up Instructions

- Open the file named **24form1.frm** located on the data disk.
- Change to Draft view (select **View, Draft**).
- Locate the insertion point on the fourth blank line after the date.

Insert IFBLANK...ELSE...ENDIF Merge Commands

Note: If the Merge Feature Bar displays below the Power Bar, skip to step 5.

1. Select **Tools, Merge**.

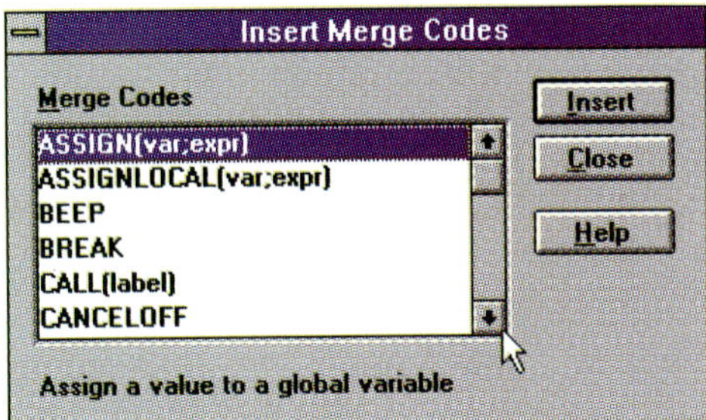

FIGURE 24.2

Insert Merge Codes dialog box

2. Select the desired Merge option.

    For example, select the **Form** option.

3. In the Create Merge File dialog box, select the **Use File in Active Window** option.

4. Select **OK**.

    Note: The Merge Feature Bar displays below the Power Bar.

5. To link a data file to the form file or to verify the name and location of the data file associated with the form file, select the **Go to Data** button on the Merge Feature Bar. If the message "Cannot open/retrieve. . ." displays, select **OK**. In the Associate dialog box, choose **Select**, select the desired drive and/or directory and double-click on the desired filename. Select the **Go to Form** button to return to the form file.

    For example, in the Associate dialog box, select the drive letter where the data disk is located, double-click on **24drill1.df**, and select the **Go to Form** button.

6. Select the **Merge Codes** button on the Merge Feature Bar.

    Note: The Insert Merge Codes dialog box displays (see Figure 24.2). The list of merge codes is alphabetized.

7. Use the scroll bar to display the desired merge code (command); then double-click on the merge code.

    For example, double-click on the **IFBLANK(field)** merge command.

    Note: The Insert Merge Code dialog box displays requesting the name of the field that may be empty.

8. Type the desired field name.

    For example, type **title**. (Do not type the period.)

9. Select **OK**.

    Note: The IFBLANK merge command followed by the field name (title) displays in the document window. The Insert Merge Codes dialog box remains on the screen. That's OK. The dialog box will be used again in a few steps.

10. Select the **Insert Field** button on the Merge Feature Bar .

    Note: The Insert Field Name or Number dialog box with the data filename and field names displays. The Insert Field Name or Number dialog box may be placed on top of the Insert Merge Codes dialog box.

11. To move the Insert Field Name or Number dialog box, point to the dialog box Title Bar, then press and hold the mouse button while dragging the dialog box to the bottom left of the document window.

12. To move the Insert Merge Codes dialog box, point to the dialog box Title Bar, press and hold the mouse button while dragging the dialog box to the bottom right of the document window.

    Note: The Insert Merge Codes dialog box may overlap the Insert Field Name or Number dialog box. That's OK.

13. In the Insert Field Name or Number dialog box, double-click on the desired field name.

    For example, double-click on **firstname.**

    Note: FIELD(firstname) has now been added to the document and is the first field that will be printed when the title field is blank.

14. Key any punctuation or spacing needed between fields *after* the field has been entered.

    For example, press **Spacebar** once.

    Note: A space will be placed between the first name and the last name when the files are merged.

15. In the Insert Field Name or Number dialog box, double-click on the next field to be inserted.

    For example, double-click on **lastname.**

16. In the Insert Merge Codes dialog box, double-click on the desired merge command.

    For example, double-click on **ELSE.**

    Note: The ELSE command will appear in the document window immediately followed by a nonprinting space. The ELSE command tells the Merge feature what to do if the field is not empty. To express what the IFBLANK...ELSE merge commands are accomplishing, one could say, "If the title field is blank, insert the firstname and lastname here, ELSE (otherwise) insert the title, firstname, and lastname here."

17. In the Insert Field Name or Number dialog box, double-click on the fields needed to complete the ELSE statement.

    For example, double-click on the **title**, **firstname**, and **lastname** fields. Press the **Spacebar** once between the title and firstname fields and between the firstname and lastname fields.

    Note: The merge codes may wrap around to the next line. That's OK.

18. In the Insert Merge Codes dialog box, double-click on the **ENDIF** merge command. Press **Enter** once to begin the second line of the address.

    Note: All IF statements **must** *have an ENDIF merge command.*

19. Complete the form file inserting merge commands and fields as needed.

    For example, use any of the steps 1–18 as needed and the following guidelines to complete the inside address and salutation codes, spacing, and punctuation as shown in Figure 24.3:

    a. The merge commands IFBLANK, ELSE, and ENDIF cannot be typed and must be selected from the Insert Merge Codes box.

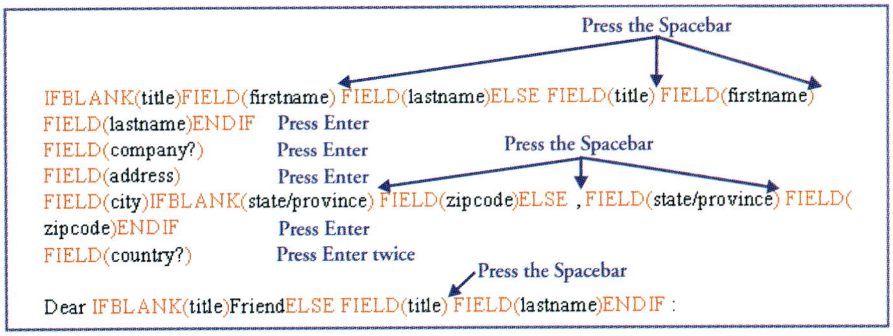

Press the Spacebar

IFBLANK(title)FIELD(firstname) FIELD(lastname)ELSE FIELD(title) FIELD(firstname)
FIELD(lastname)ENDIF Press Enter
FIELD(company?) Press Enter
FIELD(address) Press Enter
FIELD(city)IFBLANK(state/province) FIELD(zipcode)ELSE , FIELD(state/province) FIELD(
zipcode)ENDIF Press Enter
FIELD(country?) Press Enter twice

Dear IFBLANK(title)FriendELSE FIELD(title) FIELD(lastname)ENDIF :

FIGURE 24.3

Form file address and salutation with IFBLANK...ELSE...ENDIF commands

b. Press **Enter** only when a hard return is needed to make the next character start on a new line. WordPerfect will automatically wrap long statements such as the IFBLANK...ELSE...ENDIF statements.

c. Press the **Spacebar** only when a space is needed between two field names. WordPerfect will automatically place a nonprinting space between any two commands, such as between the ELSE and FIELD commands.

d. After FIELD(company) displays in the document window, move the insertion point to the right of the *y* in *company* and type a question mark.

e. Note that the comma and space that normally follow the CITY field are used as part of the next command. In this way, the comma and space print only if there is a state.

Finish-Up Instructions

- Type the salutation with the merge codes and fields as shown in Figure 24.3.
- Close the Insert Merge Codes and Insert Field Name or Number dialog boxes.
- Replace the x in the year in the first paragraph with the current year.
- Use the *new* filename **24drill1.frm** and save the form file on your file disk.
- Close the document.
- Test the form file by merging it with the data file **24drill1.df**. (If necessary, see Chapter 11, page 262 for Steps to Merge a Form File and Data File.)
- Check each letter to make sure that the information merged correctly and print one copy of each merged letter.
- If desired, use the filename **24drill1.mr** and save the merged letters on your file disk.
- Close all documents.

Improve Efficiency and Increase Flexibility with Merges

When a small data file is used, it is possible to send a mailing to everyone on the list, even though the mailing is applicable to only a few or to only those in a certain region.

As the data file grows, however, it rapidly becomes too wasteful and time-consuming to send a letter to all persons in the data file.

WordPerfect offers several ways to merge only specific records in the data file with the form letter. In Chapter 11, specific records were marked to be merged. WordPerfect also has two other methods: (1) selecting a range of records and (2) setting merge conditions.

Another problem that occurs with large data files is that the computer may not have enough memory to store all the merged letters at one time. This can cause the merge process to stop before it has merged all the letters. Using the range of records method to limit the merge to specific records may be helpful, or it may be more efficient to use the **Output File** option and output the information to the printer or a file to avoid an out-of-memory error.

Select a Range of Records

Specifying a range of records is useful in a situation in which new records are added at the beginning or end of the data file. Selecting records that are grouped in a certain order can also be useful, e.g., all records grouped by a specific zip code.

To merge all records after specific records have been selected, it may be necessary to deselect the record number Range option. Choose the **Reset All Records** button in the Perform Merge dialog box to deselect the Record Number Range option.

Start-Up Instructions

- Begin the merge operation by selecting **Tools**, **Merge**, **Merge**.
- Select the List box located to the right of the Form File box, click on **Select File**, select the drive letter where the data disk is located, and double-click on the filename **24drill2.frm**.
- Select the List box located to the right of the Data File box, click on **Select File**, select the drive letter where the data disk is located, and double-click on the filename **24drill2.df**.
- Select the **Options** button and check that **Remove Blank Line** displays in the If Empty Field in Data File box. Select **OK**.

Select Range of Records When Merging

1. Choose the **Select Records** button {Alt and s}.

   Note: The Select Records dialog box displays (see Figure 24.4).

2. Select the **Record Number Range** option {r}.

   Note: An X should display in the Record Number Range box.

3. In the From box, click repeatedly on the up or down arrow until the number of the first data record to be merged displays, or double-click in the From box and type the desired number {o, type the desired number}.

   For example, click repeatedly on the up or down arrow until **7** displays.

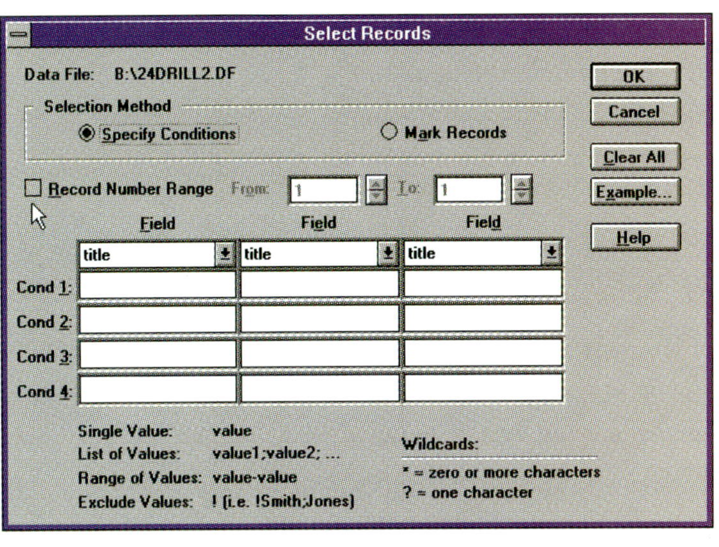

FIGURE 24.4

Select Records dialog box

4. In the To box, click repeatedly on the up or down arrow until the number of the last data record to be merged displays, or double-click in the To box and type the desired number {press Tab once, type the desired number}.

   For example, click repeatedly on the up arrow until 9 displays.

   Note: Only records 7, 8, and 9 will merge with the form letter.

5. Select **OK** {press Enter}.

6. Select **OK** {Tab repeatedly until an outline displays around the word OK, press Enter}.

   Note: A message, "Merging Record . . .", displays and the number of each selected record displays briefly one at a time. The merged letters display in the document window.

Finish-Up Instructions

- If desired, open and view or print the data file named **24drill2.df** so you can check that only records 7, 8, and 9 were merged with the form file.
- Optional. Print one copy of each merged letter.
- Close all documents. (Do not save the merged letters.)

Select Records Based on Conditions

Another way to select records is to base the selection on a condition that occurs in the data file. For example, you might need to send a letter to everyone who lives in a certain geographical area, e.g., California. If the data file has been set up with the state as a separate field, it is easy to select only those records in which the state is CA.

Start-Up Instructions

- To begin the merge operation, select **Tools**, **Merge**, **Merge**.
- Select the List button located to the right of the Form File box, click on **Select File**, select the drive letter where the data disk is located, and double-click on the filename **24drill3.frm**.

- Select the List button located to the right of the Data File box, click on **Select File**, select the drive letter where the data disk is located, and double-click on the filename **24drill3.df**.
- Select the **Options** button and check that **Remove Blank Line** displays in the If Empty Field in Data File box. Select **OK**.

Steps to Select Records Based on Conditions When Merging

1. Choose the **Select Records** button {Alt and s}.

   Note: The Select Records dialog box displays. Check that the ***Specify Conditions*** *option is selected in the Selection Method area. If necessary, select the* ***Specify Conditions*** *option.*

2. Click on the down arrow in the first Field box {Alt and f}.

   For example, click on the down arrow beside the name "title" displayed in the first Field column to show the field name list.

3. Click on the field name on which the condition will be based {press the up or down arrow key to display the field name}.

   For example, click on **state/province.**

   Note: The field state/province displays. (Some of the options for entering conditions are shown at the bottom of the dialog box.)

4. Click in the **Cond 1** box and type the condition(s) to be met {Alt and 1, type the desired condition}.

   For example, type **CA;NV** in the first box of the Cond 1 row.

   Note: Any record with CA or NV in the state/province field will be merged.

5. Click on the down arrow beside the middle Field box {Alt and e}.

   For example, click the down arrow beside the name "title" displayed in the middle Field column.

6. Click on the field name on which the next condition will be based {press the up or down arrow key to highlight the field name}.

   For example, click on **Workshop**.

7. Click in the **Cond 1** box below the field name. Type the conditions to be met {Alt and 1, Tab, type the desired condition}.

   For example, type **N** in the Cond 1 box below the field name Workshop.

   Note: Your screen should look similar to Figure 24.5. Conditions placed in the same row are AND conditions. That means the record must meet all of the conditions (the state/province must be CA or NV ***and*** *there must be an N (representing No) in the Workshop field). When conditions are placed in separate rows, an OR condition is created. For example, if the Workshop field is shown in the second row, any record with CA or NV in the state/province field* ***or*** *any record with the letter N in the Workshop field (regardless of the state) would be included in the merge.*

8. Select **OK** {Enter}.
9. Select **OK** {Tab repeatedly until an outline displays around the word OK, Enter}.

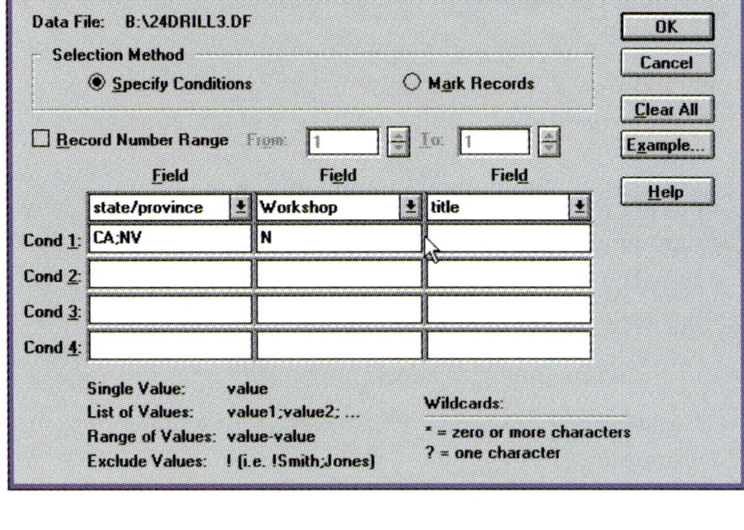

FIGURE 24.5

Defined conditions in the Select Record dialog box

Note: A message "Merging Record . . .", displays and the number of each selected record displays briefly one at a time. The merged letters display in the document window.

Finish-Up Instructions

- If desired, open and view or print the data file named **24drill3.df** so you can check that only records with CA and NV in the state/province field **and** the letter N in the Workshop field were merged with the form letters.

  Hint: Only two records will meet both conditions.

- Optional. Print one copy of each merged letter.
- Close all documents.

Form Files with Graphic Images

The merge operation will need less memory and less storage space if the option to use an **Image on Disk** has been selected as the Content option in the Box Content dialog box. When the **Image on Disk** option is chosen, each merged letter references the graphic file on the disk instead of saving a copy of the graphic within each letter.

Start-Up Instructions

- Open the form file named **24drill3.frm** located on the data disk.

Designate the File Location of a Graphic Image

1. To select the graphic image and display the Graphics Box Feature Bar, move the mouse pointer into the graphic image, click the left mouse button once, click the *right* mouse button once and select **Feature Bar** {Alt, g, e, *or* Shift and F11}.

   Note: The Graphics Box Feature Bar displays and the graphic is selected.

2. Select the **Content** button on the Graphics Box Feature Bar {Alt and Shift and o}.

   Note: The Box Content dialog box displays.

3. Select the desired Content option.

   For example, check that **Image on Disk** displays in the Content box. (If necessary, move the mouse pointer to the Content box, press and hold the mouse button while dragging to highlight **Image on Disk**. Release the mouse button {Alt and c, Spacebar, press the arrow keys to highlight desired option, Enter}.)

4. Check that the filename and location of the file display in the Filename box. If necessary, select or type the location and name of the graphic.

   For example, check that **b:\ender03.wpg** displays.

5. Select **OK** to return to the document window.

   Note: Each merged letter is directed to the graphic file on the disk rather than saving a copy of the graphic within each letter.

Finish-Up Instructions

- If necessary, deselect the graphic box.
- Save the file using the same filename, **24drill3.frm**.
- Close the file.

Use Output Options

The output options can be used to reduce the memory needed during the merge operation. Normally, the output is set to "Current or New Document," causing WordPerfect to place the merged letters either in the window currently displayed on the screen or in a new document window.

Start-Up Instructions

- Select **Tools**, **Merge**, **Merge**.
- Select the List box located to the right of the Form File box, click on **Select File**, select the drive letter where the data disk is located, and double-click on the filename **24drill3.frm**.
- Select the List box located to the right of the Data File box, click on **Select File**, select the drive letter where the data disk is located, and double-click on the filename **24drill4.df**.
- Select the **Options** button and check that **Remove Blank Line** displays in the If Empty Field in Data File box. Select **OK**.
- Select the **Reset** button to ensure that all previously defined merge conditions are cleared.

Output Merged Letters to a File

1. In the Perform Merge dialog box, select the arrow button beside the **Output File** box {Alt and u, Alt and the up or down arrow key}.

2. Choose the desired Output File option {press the up or down arrow key to highlight the desired option, Enter}.

   For example, choose **Select File.**

   Note: The Select Output File dialog box displays.

3. In the Filename box, type the desired drive location followed by a colon and the filename for the merged letters.

   For example, type the drive letter where your file disk is located followed by a colon and the filename **24drill3.mr** (**a:24drill3.mr**).

4. Select **OK** {press Enter}.

   Note: The Perform Merge dialog box displays with the desired Output File drive location and filename.

5. Select **OK** {press Enter}.

   *Note: The message "Merging Record . . ." displays in the document window. The merging message disappears when the merge is complete but the merged documents do not display in the document window. The merged letters are located on your file disk in the file named **24drill3.mr**.*

Finish-Up Instructions

- Open the file named **24drill3.mr** located on your file disk to display the merged letters.
- It is not necessary to print the letters.
- Close the document.

Start-Up Instructions

- Check that the printer is on and connected to the computer.
- Select **Tools, Merge, Merge.**
- Select the List button located to the right of the Form File box, click on **Select File**, select the drive letter where the data disk is located, and double-click on the filename **24drill3.frm**.
- Select the List button located to the right of the Data File box, click on **Select File**, select the drive letter where the data disk is located, and double-click on the filename **24drill1.df**.
- Select the **Options** button and check that **Remove Blank Line** displays in the If Empty Field in Data File box. Select **OK**.

Steps to Output Merged Letters to a Printer

1. Select the arrow button beside the **Output File box** {Alt and u, Alt and the up or down arrow key}.
2. Select **<Printer>** {press the down arrow key until <Printer> is highlighted, Enter}.
3. Select **OK** {press Enter}.

Note: The message "Merging Record . . ." displays in the document window. The merging message disappears when the merge is complete and the letters are sent to the printer.

Finish-Up Instructions

- Check the letters as they print to make sure the letters are correct. Sending the merged letters directly to the printer can avoid some memory problems but should be used only with data files and form files that have been merged and checked previously. Otherwise, a lot of paper can be wasted!

Text Data Files

In addition to placing data records in a table file format, data files can be created in a text data file format. One advantage of using the text data file format is to avoid difficult-to-read table columns when each record has many fields or characters in each field. Also, if the data file has numerous records and additional records are added periodically, the text data file format may be faster to work with than a large table. The text data file format was the only format available until WordPerfect 6.0, therefore, data files created with earlier versions of WordPerfect are in the text data file format. When data files are created, the default is to create a text data file format. Also, WordPerfect automatically places data file information imported from other programs into the text data file format.

In a text data file, the field names are placed at the beginning of the document. The records are then typed with each field in the same order as shown at the beginning of the document. Each field in a record must end with an ENDFIELD code. Each record must end with an ENDRECORD code. If a field does not have any data, for instance, if there is no company name, the ENDFIELD code is placed on the line by itself (see Figure 24.6). As the insertion point scrolls through a text data file, the Status bar at the bottom of the screen will show the field name. Check the Status bar frequently when typing data in a text data file to make sure that the information is being entered in the correct field.

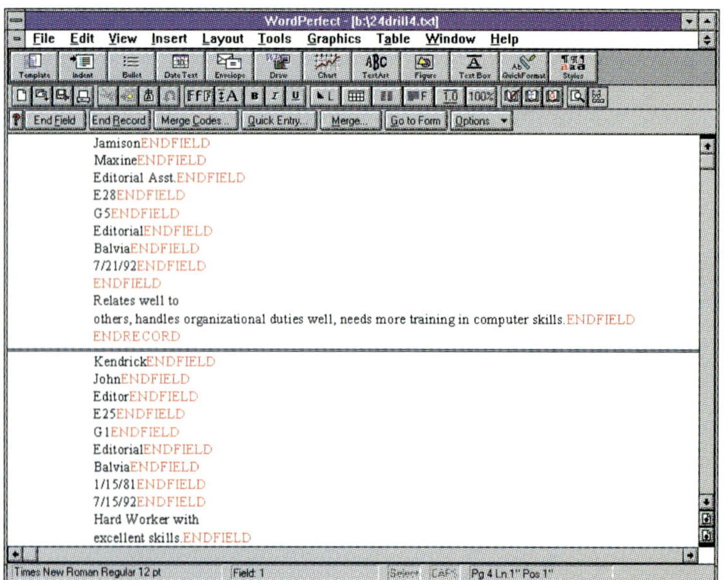

FIGURE 24.6

Text data file

"Jamison","Maxine","Editorial Asst.","E28","G5","Editorial","Balvia",7/21/92,
"Kendrick","John","Editor","E25","G1","Editorial","Balvia",1/15/81,7/15/92,
"Leong","Wendell","Oper. Mgr.","E32","G1","Admin.","Peterson",3/25/77,9/15/91,

FIGURE 24.7

Sample ASCII delimited file

Import Data

The data to be imported from the mainframe or database program must be in an ASCII (DOS) delimited file. Typically, each field in a delimited file is separated by a comma, each record ends with a CR/LF (carriage return/line feed), and character strings (text) are enclosed in quotation marks. Figure 24.7 shows a sample delimited file. When WordPerfect imports the delimited file, ENDFIELD and ENDRECORD codes will be inserted automatically. Before the data file can be merged with a form letter, however, field names must be added to the beginning of the file.

Start-Up Instructions

- The file named **24drill4.txt** located on the data disk will be used while performing the following Steps to Import Data into a Merge Data File.

Import Data into a Merge Data File

1. Select the **Open** button {Ctrl and o}.
2. Select or type the location, and type or highlight the name of the desired file, then select **OK** {press Enter}.

   For example, type the drive letter where the data disk is located followed by a colon and the filename **24drill4.txt** (**b:24drill4.txt**).

   Note: The Convert File Format dialog box displays with the ASCII (DOS) Text file format highlighted.
3. Click on the down arrow beside the Convert File Format From box to display the list of file formats; scroll up or down to display the desired option; click on the desired option file format {press the up or down arrow key until the desired format displays}.

   For example, scroll up and click on **ASCII DOS Delimited Text.**
4. Select **OK** {Enter}.

   Note: The Import Data dialog box displays.
5. In the Import As box, press and hold the mouse button while dragging to highlight the desired option; release the mouse button {Alt and i, press the up or down arrow key to display the desired option}.

   For example, choose **Merge Data File.**
6. Also, in the Import Data dialog box, check that the appropriate characters are entered for the Field and Record Delimiter, and the Encapsulated Characters options.

   For example, the WordPerfect defaults shown in Figure 24.8 should be displayed.

FIGURE 24.8

Import Data dialog box

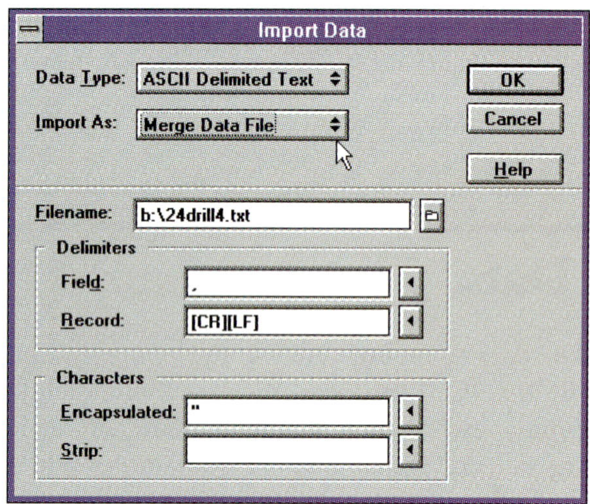

7. Select **OK** {press Enter}.

   Note: Depending on the size of the data file, WordPerfect may take a few moments to format the imported data into a merge data file. The text will display in the document window in a form similar to that in Figure 24.6. No field names will display at the top of the document. The Merge Feature Bar displays below the Power Bar.

8. Select **File, Save As** {Alt, f, a *or* F3}.

9. Type the new filename. If necessary, click in the Drives box and click on the drive letter where the file should be saved.

   For example, type the filename **24drill4.df**. (If necessary, click in the Drives box and click on the drive letter where your file disk is located.)

10. Select the desired Format option.

    For example, in the Save Data File As dialog box, check that the **WordPerfect 6.0...** format option is displayed in the Format box at the bottom of the dialog box.

11. Select **OK** {Enter}.

12. To add the field names to the data file, determine the field names and write down the exact order of the fields in a record.

    For example, the field names and order are: **lastname, firstname, position, mailstop, grade, department, supervisor, startdate, last-promo,** and **evaluation**.

13. Place the insertion point at the beginning of the document (**Ctrl** and **Home**).

14. Select the **Merge Codes** button on the Merge Feature Bar {Alt and Shift and c}.

    Note: The Insert Merge Codes dialog box displays.

15. Double-click on the desired Merge Codes option {press the down arrow key repeatedly or type the first few letters of the desired code until the code is highlighted, press Enter}.

    For example, double-click on **FIELDNAMES(name1;...;nameN)**.

    Note: The Create Data File dialog box displays.

16. Type the field names in the order in which they appear in the data file, pressing **Enter** (or selecting **Add**) after each field name.

For example, type the following:

lastname
firstname
position
mailstop
grade
department
supervisor
startdate
lastpromo
evaluation

Note: *If a mistake is made while typing the field names, click on the incorrect name in the Field Name List box and select* ***Delete****.*

17. When all the field names have been added and are in the correct order, select **OK** to display the field names in the document window {press Tab until an outline displays around the OK button, press Enter}.

18. Select **Close** to remove the Insert Merge Codes dialog box from the screen {Alt and Shift and c, Alt and c}.

Note: *The field names display in the document window at the top of the merge data file.*

Finish-Up Instructions

- Use the same filename, **24drill4.df**, and save the merge data file.
- Close the file.

  Note: *The imported data can now be used with form files containing the same field names.*

- Continue with the Steps to Request User Input in a Merged Letter on page 584.

Request User Input in a Merged Letter

Confidential data that may be used only once in a document is often not saved in a data file. A special command, **Keyboard**, can be inserted in the form file to instruct the program to pause and request the user to type the needed information. The Keyboard command is placed in the form file at the position in which the specific information will be located.

When the form file containing the Keyboard command is merged with a data file, the program will pause during the merging of each letter to allow the user to type the specific information. Once the information is typed, select **Continue** to resume the merge operation.

Start-Up Instructions

- Alan, of Alan's Ads, is giving a special bonus to various employees because of the work accomplished on the PCCA International campaign. Because the bonus is a one-time occurrence, it is not included in a data file.
- The data file created in the Steps to Import Data into a Merge Data File on page 581 should be available (**24drill4.df**).
- Open the file named **24drill4.frm** located on the data disk.

Steps to Request User Input in a Merged Letter

1. Place the insertion point at the location at which the user will enter information.

   For example, scroll down the page until the two-row table displays. Place the insertion point in the first cell of row 2 in the table (cell A2).

2. Select the **Keyboard** button on the Merge Feature Bar {Alt and Shift and k}.

   Note: The Insert Merge Codes dialog box displays. A Keyboard command is always followed by a prompt requesting information from the user.

3. Type the desired prompt message.

   For example, type **Enter vacation dates:**. (Do not type the period.)

4. Select **OK** {Enter}.

   Note: *The prompt message displays immediately in the table cell.*

Finish-Up Instructions

- Repeat steps 1–4 to place a Keyboard code in the second cell of row 2 (cell B2). Type the prompt message, **Enter vacation resort:**. (Do not type the period.)
- The x's below the last paragraph should be replaced with your initials.
- Use the *new* filename **24dril4k.frm** and save the form file on your file disk.

Start-Up Instructions

- Begin the merge process for the form file **24dril4k.frm** and the data file **24drill4.df** located on your file disk. (If necessary, see the Steps to Merge a Form File and Data File in Chapter 11 on page 262.)

Merge a Form File with User Input

Note: During the merging of the form file and the data file, a Merge Message prompt will appear in the document window when user input is needed in the merged letter.

1. When the Merge Message box displays, type the requested information.

   For example, when "Enter vacation dates:" displays in the Merge Message box, type **August 1-7**.

2. To continue the merge operation, select the **Continue** button on the Merge Feature Bar {Alt and Shift and c}.

Maxine Jamison	August 1-7	Sunnyside Resort
John Kendrick	December 5-12	Lake Tahoe Bed & Breakfast
Wendell Leong	July 15-22	Cape Cod Anglers Inn

FIGURE 24.9

Data for user input

Note: *The next prompt displays in the Merge Message box.*

Finish-Up Instructions

- Use the data in Figure 24.9 and continue to type the requested information at each prompt. To determine which letter is currently being merged, check the page number (1, 2, etc.) displayed in the Status bar.
- When all letters have been merged, the insertion point displays at the bottom of the final letter.
- Print one copy of each letter.
- Optional. Use the filename **24drill4.mr** and save the merged letter file.
- Close all documents.

The Next Step

Chapter Review and Activities

Self-Check Quiz

T F 1. The IFBLANK...ELSE...ENDIF merge commands are used in the form file to control extra horizontal spacing when fields are empty.

T F 2. When inserting merge commands, IFBLANK or ELSE, in a form file, the commands can be typed or selected from the Insert Merge Codes dialog box.

T F 3. Data imported from a database or a mainframe program must be in an ASCII (DOS) delimited file.

T F 4. A Keyboard command is used to request user input during the merge operation.

T F 5. To eliminate the blank line that will result from an empty field, a question mark can be inserted at the end of the field name, e.g., FIELD(company?).

6. Imported data can be placed in a _____ file.
   a. table
   b. graphic
   c. merge data file
   d. all of these

7. The output file for merged letters can be _____.
   a. the current document
   b. a new document
   c. the printer
   d. any of the above

8. In the Select Records dialog box, conditions placed in the same row are _____ conditions.
   a. AND
   b. OR
   c. either a or b
   d. none of these

9. Give one example of why you would use the KEYBOARD command in a form file.

10. List two options that could be used if the merge operation stopped because there was not enough memory to hold all the merged letters.

Enriching Language Arts Skills

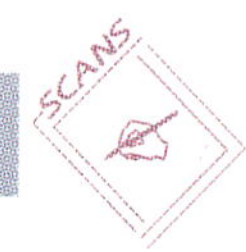

Spelling/Vocabulary Words

bonus money or other compensation given to an employee in addition to regular pay.

suitable acceptable, appropriate.

Abbreviations for Time

Type a.m. and p.m. with lowercase letters and no spaces. Only one period is used if the abbreviation is the last element in a sentence.

Example: The planning meeting will begin at 9:00 a.m. and adjourn at 3:00 p.m.

Activity

Activity 24.1—Create a Form Letter with IFBLANK...ELSE...ENDIF Merge Commands

1. Open the file named **24act1.lh** located on the data disk.
2. Using the following guidelines, create the letter address and salutation:
   a. Select the **Image on Disk** option in the Box Content dialog box (select the graphic image, click the *right* mouse button and select **Feature Bar**, select the **Content** button, select **Image on Disk** in the Content box, select **OK**).

b. Deselect the graphic box; press **Ctrl** and **End** to move the insertion point four lines below the date.

c. To display the Merge Feature Bar and create a link to a data file, select **Tools**, **Merge**, **Form**, select **Use File in Active Window**, **OK**. In the Associate a Data File box, type the drive letter where the data disk is located followed by a colon and the filename **24drill3.df**. Select **OK**.

d. Select the **Merge Codes** button, double-click on **IFBLANK(field)**, type **title**, **OK**.

e. Select the **Insert Field** button, double-click on **firstname**; continue to insert the merge codes and fields as shown. Include spaces and punctuation as needed.

IFBLANK(title)**FIELD**(firstname) **FIELD**(lastname)**ELSE FIELD**(title)
FIELD(firstname) **FIELD**(lastname)**ENDIF**
FIELD(company?)
FIELD(address)
FIELD(city)**IFBLANK**(state/province) **FIELD**(zipcode)**ELSE** , **FIELD**(state/province)
FIELD(zipcode) **ENDIF**
FIELD(country?)

Dear **IFBLANK**(title)Friend**ELSE FIELD**(title) **FIELD**(lastname)**ENDIF** :

---

3. Press **Enter** once after the salutation line.
4. Close the Insert Field Name or Number dialog box and the Insert Merge Codes dialog box.
5. To complete the letter, insert the text from the file named **24act1.txt** located on the data disk (select **Insert**, **File**, double-click on the **24act1.txt**, **Yes**).
6. Edit the letter as follows:

   a. Replace the x in the year in the second paragraph with the current year.

   b. Replace the x's after the author's initials with your initials.
7. Use the new filename **24act1.frm** and save the form letter to your file disk.
8. Merge the form letter **24act1.frm** with the data file **24drill3.df** using the following information:

   a. Select the **Merge** button. Choose **Merge**.

   b. Use the **Select Records** option to set the first condition to the letter **Y** in the Workshop field (choose the **Select Records** button, select the down arrow beside the word "title" in the first Field column, select **Workshop**, click in the **Cond 1** box below the word "Workshop," type a **Y**, select **OK**).

c. Select the **Options** button and check that **Remove Blank Lines** displays in the If Empty Field in Data File box. Select **OK.**

d. Set the Output File option for **Select File.** Use the filename **24act1.mr.** (Select the arrow button beside the **Output File** box, choose **Select File,** type or select the location and name of file, select **OK** twice.)

9. Open the file named **24act1.mr** and check the merged letters. Make sure only those records with a Y in the Workshop field were merged and that all address and salutation information was merged correctly. If necessary, print a copy of the file named **24drill3.df.**

10. Print one copy of the merged letters.

11. Close all documents.

Challenge Your Skills

Skill 24.1—Create a Form File That Contains a Keyboard Merge Command; Language Arts

1. Open the file named **24drilk4.frm located** on your file disk. Insert the following paragraph containing a Keyboard command after the table showing the vacation information. Correct two spelling and two punctuation errors.

   If you would rather have a cash bonus, your bonous would be **KEYBOARD(Enter cash bonus amount:).** Please let me know by 5:00 PM on Friday whether you want the vacation or cash bonus and confirm that the vacation dates shown will be suitible.

2. Use the *new* filename **24skill1.frm** and save the form file.

3. Merge the form file **24skill1.frm** with the data file **24drill4.df** located on your file disk. Use the information below to respond to the prompts:

Maxine Jamison	August 1-7	Sunnyside Resort	$2,000
John Kendrick	December 5-12	Lake Tahoe Bed & Breakfast	$3,000
Wendell Leong	July 15-22	Cape Code Anglers Inn	$2,500

   Hint: *Select the **Reset** button in the Perform Merge dialog box to ensure that any previous merge conditions are cleared.*

4. Optional. Use the filename **24skill1.mer** and save the merged documents.

5. Print the merged documents.

6. Close all documents.

7. If you have completed your work, exit WordPerfect.

CHAPTER 25

Advanced Macros

Features Covered

- Edit macros
- Correct (debug) macros
- Find a macro command's purpose, syntax, and parameters
- Record mouse actions and keystrokes while editing a macro
- Request user input in a macro
- Use variables in a macro
- Use a conditional statement in a macro
- Test a macro
- Use the abbreviation macro

Objectives and Introduction

After successfully completing this chapter, you will be able to better understand macro terminology, edit a macro using Edit Macro, and record keystrokes or additional mouse actions while editing a macro. You will also learn how to find the correct syntax and parameters for macro commands and how to use GETSTRING, variables, and a conditional statement while editing a macro. In addition, you will learn to debug (correct) macro errors and "test" a macro. Also, you will learn to set up and use the abbreviation macro.

Macros can be a useful tool to avoid repetitious keystrokes, to ensure that work is accurate, and to set up tasks to be accomplished automatically. In addition to using the macros supplied by WordPerfect and recording simple keystroke macros, macros can be created starting with the first command or by using a combination of *direct* editing and recording.

Useful Terminology

WordPerfect uses a macro language that is based on commands.Two types of commands are used—product comands and programming commands. Product commands are commands that produce a result and are used to record your actions in a macro. For example, to position the insertion point up one row in a table, the product command PosCellUp is used.

The programming commands are commands that direct and control the running of a macro in WordPerfect and other applications. For example, when a macro is being played, the PAUSE command will stop a macro temporarily and allow the user to take control of the computer.

A brief explanation of key macro terms is given in Figures 25.1 and 25.4. Also, if the WP Online Macros Manual is available on your computer, select **Help**, **Macros**, and **Macro Command Index** to display a list of all macro commands.

Suggestions for Writing and Editing Macros

Use spaces, tabs, indents, and hard returns to make the macro easier to read. "White space" is ignored by the macro, which sees spacing commands only when they are in character strings enclosed in quotation marks. DO NOT put spacing codes or characters in the middle of command names, parameter names, or parameter values. If you need to put a space in a long command so that WordPerfect can wrap the line, place it after a semicolon.

Many times macros printed in magazines or books will have numbered lines. These numbers are for reference only and are not to be typed in the macro. If desired, line numbering can be turned on by selecting Layout, Line, Numbering and choosing the Turn Line Numbering On option.

Comments are explanations about the macro and should be used liberally when creating or editing a macro. Inserting comments will make it much easier to change or update the macro and are very helpful if someone else must figure out how the macro works. To place a comment in the macro, start the line with two slashes (//). A hard return (Enter) will end the comment.

Edit a Macro

Many times macros must be changed after they have been created. For instance, you might have a macro that prints your name and return address to create personal stationery. When you move or change your name, the macro must be changed. While you could re-record the macro (saving it under the same filename), editing the macro is often easier, particularly if the change is small and the macro is complex.

FIGURE 25.1

Macro terminology

MACRO TERMINOLOGY	
COMMAND	A macro command that tells the program to take a certain action. The command must be typed with the correct spelling, and can be typed in uppercase letters or a combination or upper and lowercase letters. A programming command is often typed in uppercase letters, e.g., PROMPT and a product command is often typed in upper and lowercase letters, e.g., PosCellNext.
PARAMETER	If there are two or more actions that can be directed by one command, the command must have a parameter to specify which action to take. The parameter will be in parentheses after the command, e.g., Display(On!).
ENUMERATED TYPE	Predefined keywords (parameters) that are associated with a numeric value and are typed after a command. For example, the command AttributePosition has three parameters, i.e., Superscript!, Subscript!, and NormalPosition!. If any other word follows the AttributePosition command, an error message will be displayed when the file is compiled and saved.
NUMERIC EQUIVALENT	A number that can be used in place of an enumerated type or the ASCII value of a character. If Macros Help is available on your computer, a command can be selected from the Commands Index list. The numeric equivalent and enumerated type information is displayed for the command under the parameters section. A chart of the ASCII value (numeric) or characters is available in the *WordPerfect 6.0 for Windows Reference Manual* on page 780.
OPERATOR	A symbol or word that performs a function on one or more items in a command statement. For example, the equals sign (=) is used in many statements to compare two items and ask "Are they equal?".
VARIABLE	A variable represents a named place in memory where information is stored. Variables are often used to keep track of words, numbers, and measurements that change while the macro plays.
CHARACTER STRING or CHARACTER EXPRESSION	Any text that is not a command or parameter must be enclosed in quotation marks so that the program will recognize it as text. The words "Character Expression" are synonymous with "Character String."
COMPILE	Compiling is the process that changes the typed or recorded commands and keystrokes into the programming code that the computer uses. The Compiler program also checks for various types of errors.

Start-Up Instructions

- The file named **namehead.wcm**, which will be used in the following steps, is located on the data disk.

Edit a Macro Using the Edit Macro Mode

1. Open the desired macro file.

For example, open the file named **namehead.wcm** located on the data disk.

Note: *The macro displays in the document window and the Macro Edit Feature Bar appears below the Power Bar. Each keystroke that was recorded when the macro was created has been translated into a WordPerfect macro command or a character to be typed. The characters in the name and address are in quotation marks to tell WordPerfect not to interpret them as commands and they are enclosed in parentheses to indicate that they are a "parameter" for the command TYPE. Each line of the macro is numberd to make it easier to edit the macro.*

2. Make the desired changes to the macro.

   For example, replace the name and address shown in lines 2, 4, and 6 with your name and address, being careful not to delete the quotation marks or parentheses.

3. Select the **Save As** button on the Macro Edit Feature Bar. If desired, use a new filename to save the edited macro {Alt and Shift and a}.

   For example, select the **Save As** button and type the location of your file disk followed by your initals and **.wcm** (a:kl.wcm).

   Note: *If a mistake as been made, the macro can be corrected using the Steps to Correct (Debug) Macro Errors on page 593.*

4. Select the **Options** button on the Macro Edit Feature Bar {Alt and Shift and t}.
5. Select **Close Macro** {c}.

Finish-Up Instructions

- Continue with the following Start-Up Instructions in the Correct (Debug) Macros section.

Correct (Debug) Macros

Compiling is the process of converting the commands and recorded or keyed text into codes that the computer can understand. Some errors are identified by the Complier program. For example, if the command TYPE is keyed as TIPE or if the beginning parenthesis is missing after the command TYPE, the compiler will stop and the WordPerfect Macro Facility - Syntax Error dialog box displays containing a description of the error.

When an error is identified, the macro can be corrected. Correcting a macro is often referred to as "debugging." There are some types of errors the compiler cannot recognize, such as the following:

a. Logic errors—forgetting, for instance, to selected a needed menu item.

b. Typographical or grammatical errors in text.

c. Errors that cause the program to do something unintended but perfectly valid from the program's point of view. For example, many options toggle on/off, so a macro that selects the option the first time it is played will deselect it on the second run.

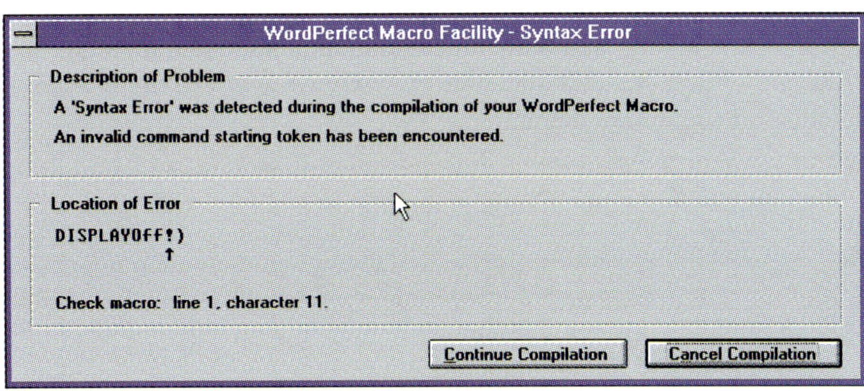

FIGURE 25.2

The WordPerfect Macro Facility - Syntax Error dialog box

Start-Up Instructions

- Open the macro file that is named with your initials.
- To make an error in the macro, delete the left parenthesis to the right of the word "DISPLAY" in line one of the macro.

Correct (Debug) Macro Errors

1. Select the **Save & Compile** button on the Macro Edit Feature Bar {Alt and Shift and s}.

   Note: *The WordPerfect Macro Facility - Syntax Error dialog box displays. The message "A 'Syntax Error' was detected . . ." displays in the Description of Program box (see Figure 25.2).*

2. To correct the error in the macro, select the **Cancel Compilation** button {a}.
3. The insertion point is usually located in the line where the Compiler (macro facility) recognized an error. If necessary, move the insertion point to the position of the actual error. Make any needed correction(s).

   For example, locate the insertion point between DISPLAY and OFF! in line 1 and type a left parenthesis.

4. To compile and save the file, select the **Save & Compile** button {Alt and Shift and s}.

   Note: *The WordPerfect Macro Facility - Syntax Error dialog box should not display because the error was corrected.*

Finish-Up Instructions

- Optional. Replace the "y" in the Type command in line 2 with an "i" so that the command is misspelled. Select the **Save & Compile** button.

  Note: *The WordPerfect Macro Facility - Syntax Error dialog box displays. The message "A 'Syntax Error' was detected . . ." displays in the Description of Program box.*

- Select the **Cancel Compilation** button.
- Correct the error using the general instructions in step 3 in the Steps to Correct (Debug) Macro Errors, then compile and save the file again.
- Close the macro (select the **Options** button on the Macro Edit Feature Bar and choose **Close Macro**).

- Play the macro that was named with your initials (select **Tools**, **Macro**, **Play**; select the List box and choose the disk drive letter where your macro file is located; double-click on the macro filename).
- Select **Play**.

  Note: *In a few moments, your name and address display centered and bold in the document window.*
- Close but do not save the document.

Understanding Macro Commands

Each macro command tells the program to take some action. Some commands, such as *HardReturn*, have only one possible action, while other commands have several possible actions. Therefore, a parameter or several parameters must be included with the macro command to specify which of the possible actions is intended. For example, the command *AttributAppearanceOn* has ten possible enumerated type actions: Bold!, Underline!, SmallCaps!, Italics!, Shadow!, Redline!, DoubleUnderline!, Strikeout!, Outline!, Every!. If the AttributeAppearanceOn command is placed in a macro without any of these parameters, the program has no way of know what it is supposed to do and a compiling error will occur.

The parameters are typed with an exclamation point at the end to distinguish them from variables and operators. Multiple attributes are enclosed in braces and separated by commas. For example, the command AttributeAppearanceOn({Attrib: Italic!, Attrib: Bold!, Attrib: Shadow!}) will turn on the italics, bold, and shadow attributes.

The macro command must be typed in an exact format so that the program recognizes the command. This is called the syntax of the command. Capitalization is usually not important, but may be used to make it easier to sp0t commands when the macro is being created, edited, or corrected. However, spelling and the parentheses around the parameters are very important. The *AttributeAppearanceOn(Bold!)* command must be typed just as it is shown, without spaces separating the words and in that exact order. For example, the program will not recognize *AppearanceAttributeOn(Bold!)*, *Attribute Appearance On(Bold!)*, or *AttributeAppearanceOnBold.*

Start-Up Instructions

- A new document window should be displayed. If necessary, open a new document window.

Find a Command's Purpose, Syntax, and Parameters

Note: *To perform the following steps, the WordPerfect 6.0 for Windows Online Macro Manual must be available on your computer.*

1. Select **Help, Macros** {Alt, h, m}.

   Note: *The WP Online Macros Manual help window displays.*
2. Click on the desired topic {press the Tab key to highlight the desired topic, press Enter}.

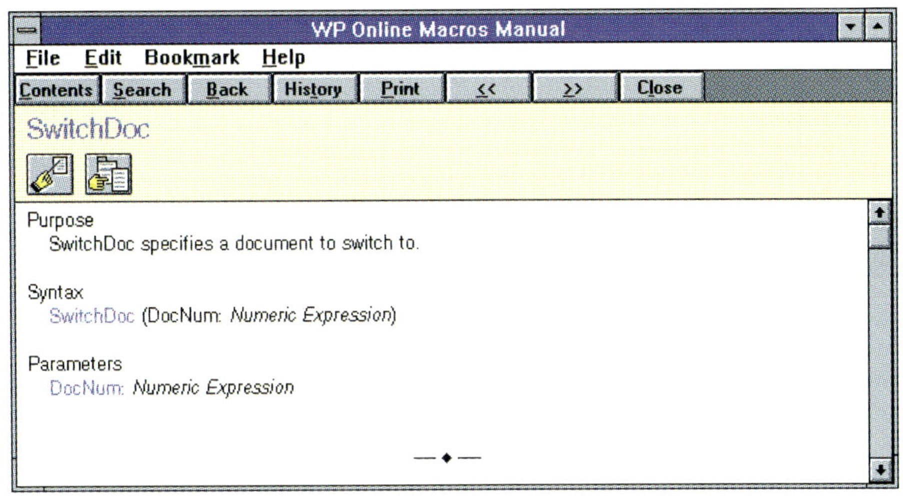

FIGURE 25.3

WP Online Macros Manual help window containing information on the SwitchDoc macro command

For example, click on **Macro Command Index.**

Note: The Macro Commands Index display.

3. Select the **Search** button {s}, type the first few letters of the item to be located, and press Enter.

   For example, click on the **Search** button and type **sw.**

4. Double-click on the desired item {Tab, press the up or down arrow key to highlight the desired topic, Enter}.

   For example, double-click on **SwitchDoc.**

   Note: SwitchDoc displays in the "Select a topic, then choose Go To" area.

5. Select the **Go To** button {Alt and g}.

   Note: The help window displays showing an explanation (the purpose) of the command, the correct syntax, and the possible parameters for the command (see Figure 25.3).

Finish-Up Instructions

- To return to the Macro Commands Index window, select the **Back** button {b}. If desired, other topics can be selected to learn more about WordPerfect macros.
- To exit the WP Online Macros Manual, select the **Close** button {L}.

Additional Editing Techniques for Macros

In addition to changing the characters in a macro, commands may be added, and you can switch between the typing and recording modes to record additional mouse actions and keystrokes. This is very helpful because it is often faster and more accurate to record commands, particularly infrequently used commands, than to type the commands. However, some commands must be typed, such as commands requesting the user to answer a prompt or to enter information.

Start-Up Instructions

- The macro you are creating will add a client's name to an existing data file and provide the option of creating new client letters.
- Copy the file named **client.df** from the data disk to your file disk.
- Display the Macro Tools Button Bar (move the mouse pointer into the Button Bar, click the *right* mouse button, click on **Macro Tools**).
- Before typing macro commands, check that the SmartQuotes feature is not enabled. (Select **Tools**, **QuickCorrect**, check that an X does not display to the left of the Enable SmartQuotes option. If necessary, click on the **Enable SmartQuotes** option to deselect it. Select **Close.**)
- Type the following commands:

```
DISPLAY(On!)
PROMPT("* Please wait *")
WAIT(35)
ENDPROMPT
```

Note: Refer to Figure 25.4 for an explanation of the DISPLAY and PROMPT commands.

Record Keystrokes While Editing a Macro

1. Place the insertion point in the macro at the desired location.

   For example, move the insertion point to the right of the final character on the last line of the macro. Press the **Enter** key once.

2. Select the **Record** button on the Macro Tools Button Bar {Alt, t, m, r, or Ctrl and F10}.

   Note: The Record Macro dialog box displays.

3. Select the **Location** button {Alt and L}.
4. Select the desired "Record to" option.

   For example, select **Current Document** {r}.

5. Select **OK** {Enter}.

   Note: A new document window displays and the Macro Record message displays in the Status bar.

6. Each mouse selection and keystroke will now be recorded.

   For example, an existing data file will be opened, the insertion point will be moved to row 2 of the table, and a new row will be inserted as follows.

   a. Select the **Open** button on the Power Bar.

   b. Type the drive letter where your file disk is located, followed by a colon and the filename **clients.df**. Select **OK**.

   c. Press the down arrow key until the insertion point is in the first cell of row 2.

Note: Use the arrow keys only. The mouse cannot be used to move the insertion point while a macro is being recorded.

d. Select **Table, Insert.**

e. Check that **Rows** is selected, **1** displays in the Rows box, and the **Before** placement option is selected. Choose **OK.**

7. To turn off Macro Record and return the insertion point to the macro file, select the **Record** button on the Macro Tools Button Bar.

Finish-Up Instructions

- Continue with the Steps to Request User Input in a Macro.

Request User Input in a Macro

In many macros, it is convenient to have the user input specific information, for example, typing the name of a file to open or retrieve, providing a Yes or No response to a question, or specifying what action the macro is to take. There are several macro commands that allow user input. We will use two of these macro commands: GETSTRING and Char. Explanations of the GETSTRING, Char, and other commands used in this chapter are shown in Figure 25.4.

Start-Up Instructions

- The keystrokes recorded in the Steps to Record Keystrokes While Editing a Macro on page 596 should be displayed on the screen in the Macro window.
- The insertion point should be located at the end of the macro.
- To insert a blank line, press **Enter.**

Steps to Request User Input in a Macro

1. Type the following information, being sure to enter all parentheses and quotation marks exactly as shown.

   *Note: Press **Enter** only at the end of a command and its associated parameters. WordPerfect automatically wraps any command that extends over multiple lines.*

```
PROMPT("Enter client information. Press Enter after each en-
try.")
WAIT (65)
ENDPROMPT
GETSTRING(title; "Enter title:")
TYPE(title)
PosCellNext()
GETSTRING(first; "Enter first name:")
TYPE(first)
PosCellNext()
GETSTRING(last; "Enter last name:")
TYPE(last)
```

FIGURE 25.4

Explanation of macro commands

Display	The Display command controls whether or not WordPerfect will update the screen display. As a general rule, the screen display should only be updated when it will be useful to the user to see the information, because updating the screen slows down the macro's operation.
PROMPT	PROMPT displays the text shown as a parameter in a Prompt message box. Showing the message "Please wait" for example, lets the user know the macro is functioning even though nothing on the screen is being updated. An ENDPROMPT command often follows a PROMPT command instructing the macro to continue with the next command in the macro.
WAIT	The WAIT command halts the macro for the time specified in the parameter. The time is in tenths of a second. It is often used to give the user time to read the instruction before beginning the data entry.
GETSTRING	This command displays the text string in the parameter in a Prompt message box and places the keystrokes typed by the user in response to the message into the document.
PosCellNext	When the PosCellNext command is used in a macro, the insertion point will move one cell to the right in the current table.
PAUSE	The PAUSE command stops the macro until the user presses the Enter key. This allows the user to review the entries and to make any corrections (as long as they do so without pressing Enter). If PAUSE follows a prompt statement, select OK to continue playing the macro.
FileSave	Saves the current document. If the document has not been saved, the Save As dialog box displays.
Close	Closes the current document.
Char	The command Char can be followed by a variable name (in our sample "CreateVar") and optionally followed by a prompt (shown in quotation marks) to give the user information on what key to press. Instead of storing the actual characters, the Char command converts the character to their numerical equivalents. The list of characters and their numerical equivalents is available on page 780 in the *WordPerfect 6.0 for Windows Reference Manual.*
Quit	The QUIT command ends a macro.

PosCellNext()
GETSTRING(street; "Enter street address, including apartment number:")
TYPE(street)
PosCellNext()
GETSTRING(city; "Enter city")
TYPE(city)
PosCellNext()
GETSTRING(state; "Enter state")
TYPE(state)
PosCellNext()
GETSTRING(zip; "Enter zip code:")

```
TYPE(zip)
PosCellNext()
GETSTRING(phone; "Enter phone number:")
TYPE(phone)
PosCellNext()
GETSTRING(charges; "Enter charges for today's word:")
TYPE(charges)
PosCellNext()
GETSTRING(client; "Is this a new client? Y/N")
TYPE(client)
PROMPT("Check your entry. Make corrections. Select the
Pause button on the Macro Tools Button Bar to continue.")
WAIT(75)
ENDPROMPT
PAUSE
FILESAVE
CLOSE
```

2. Press the **Enter** key once after the last line of the macro. Carefully proofread each line.
3. To save the macro, select the **Save & Compile** button.

   Note: The Macro Save As dialog box displays.
4. Type the disk drive location and macro name.

   For example, type the disk drive letter where your file disk is located followed by a colon and the filename **newclnt** (a:newclnt).
5. Select the **Save** button. The macro will be immediately compiled. If the compiler finds an error, use the Steps to Correct and Debug Macro Errors and correct the error before continuing.

   Note: If the macro is played at this time, the macro will open the data file, ask for the user to input the client information, and find out whether the client is new. The next step is to determine where the user wants to create and print the new client letters and to store the user's response.

Finish-Up Instructions

- Continue with the Steps to Use a Variable on page 600.

Use Variables in a Macro

Storing small pieces of information to be used within the same macro is done through the use of variables. A variable is a small portion of memory that WordPerfect sets aside to hold a piece of information. Once information has been stored in a variable, the variable and the information in it can be used elsewhere in the macro. Think of a variable as a scratch pad that the computer uses to hold information, just as you might jot down a name or phone number to use in a few minutes. A variable is given a name and is then referred to by that name. The name should be something easy to remember and should relate to what is stored in the variable. When variable names are used in a parameter, they are not placed in quotes.

The command used in the following Steps to Use a Variable is the Char command. The variable in the Char command is "CreateVar." (Note: CreateVar is the name we created for the variable.) The same variable, CreateVar, will be used when creating an IF-ELSE statement in the Steps to Create an IF-ELSE Statement in a Macro on page 601.

Start-Up Instructions

- The Macro Tools Button Bar should be displayed.
- The macro named **newclnt** should be displayed in the document window.
- The Macro Edit Feature Bar should be displayed. If necessary, select **Tools**, **Macro**, **Macro Bar**.
- If necessary, locate the insertion point below the last line of the macro.

Use a Variable

1. Type the following command:

   For example, type **Char(Character: CreateVar; Prompt: "Create new client letters now? Y/N")**, then press the **Enter** key to move the insertion point to a new line.

   *Note: The **Enter** key should not be pressed within a character string (i.e., text within quotation marks). For an explanation of the Char command, see Figure 25.4.*

2. To save the macro, select the **Save & Compile** button.

Finish-Up Instruction

- Continue with the Steps to Create an IF-ELSE Statement in a Macro.

Use a Conditional Statement in a Macro

A conditional statement is one that allows the macro to take different actions based on some condition. There are several types of conditional statements, but the most common one is generally referred to as an IF statement, an IF-THEN statement, or an IF-ELSE statement.

An IF statement in a WordPerfect macro will have three parts:

IF
ELSE
ENDIF

The IF portion sets up some condition. In our example, we will compare the information stored in the variable named CreateVar with the numerical equivalents of the possible yes response (Y = 89 and y = 121). The program will evaluate this IF statement, and, if it finds the IF statement to be true, it will continue to read the command(s) under the IF statement.

The ELSE portion of the macro tells the program what to do when it evaluates the IF statement and finds it is false. If, for example, the user presses N or any other key except Y or y, the IF statement will be false because the numbers stored in the variable will not be 89 or 121. When the statement is false, the program skips to the ELSE statement and reads the command(s) under it.

The ENDIF command tells the macro that the IF statement is finished and that it should resume reading the following commands and acting upon them.

Start-Up Instructions

- The Macro Tools Button Bar should be displayed.
- The macro named **newclnt.wcm** should be displayed in the document window.
- If necessary, locate the insertion point below the last line of the macro.

Create an IF-ELSE Statement in a Macro

1. Type the desired IF statement.

   For example, type the following IF statement as shown: **If(CreateVar = 89 OR CreateVar = 121)**. (Do not type the period.) Press **Enter.**

2. Select the **Record** button. Select **Location, Current Document, OK.**

   Note: *A new document window displays.*

3. Record the desired keystrokes and/or mouse selections.

   For example, record the following steps to merge the form and data files, and to print letters ONLY for those clients who have a Y or y in the New? column.

   a. Select **Tools, Merge, Merge** {Alt and t, e, m}.

   b. Select or type the drive letter where your file disk is located followed by a colon and the name of the form file (a:\form1.pf); press **Tab.**

   c. Select or type the drive letter where your file disk is located followed by a colon and the name of the data file (a:\clients.df).

   d. Choose the **Select Records** button {Alt and s}.

   e. Check that **Specify Conditions** is selected {s}.

   f. Click once on the down arrow beside the name "title" in the first Field column {Alt and f, press the down arrow key}.

   Note: *A list of the fields in the data file displays.*

   g. Select the field on which the condition is to be based {press the down arrow key until the field is highlighted}. For example, scroll down and click on the **New?** field.

   Note: *The New? field displays in the first column Field box.*

   h. Click in the **Cond 1** box in the first column {Tab three times}.

   i. Type the condition to be met. If more than one true condition exists, type each with a semicolon between them.

For example, type **Y;y**. (Do not type the period.)

j. Select **OK** twice {press Enter, Tab until the outline displays in the OK button, press Enter}.

Note: The merge operation will take place and create merged letters for the new client. Wait until the merge operation is finished to continue with the next step. The insertion point is located at the end of the last letter.

k. Select the **Save** button; type the filename **macro.if** and select **OK**.

*Note: Selecting the **Save** button and entering a filename place the FileSave() command in the macro. When the macro is played, the Save As dialog box will display so that a filename can be given to the merged letters.*

4. Turn off Macro Record by selecting the **Record** button and return to the document window {Alt, t, m, r}.
5. If necessary, click at the end of the last macro line and press **Enter**.
6. Complete the IF statement by typing the following:

```
PROMPT("New client letters are merged. Select OK.")
WAIT (75)
ENDPROMPT
QUIT
ELSE
PROMPT("Client has been added to data file. Select OK.")
WAIT(75)
ENDPROMPT
ENDIF
CLOSE
QUIT
```

7. Select the **Save & Compile** button {Alt and Shift and s}. If the Compiler finds any errors, use the Steps to Correct (Debug) Macro Errors to find and correct the errors(s).

Finish-Up Instructions

- Close all open document
- Play the **newclnt.wcm** macro (select **Tools**, **Macro**, **Play**, type the drive letter where your file disk is located followed by a colon and the macro name **newclnt**, select **Play**).
- As the macro plays, type the requested information in each Prompt message box. Press **Enter** after each entry.

a. Ms. Dorothy Alarid
503 Oak Creek Dr.
Hayward
CA
94541
555-9903
$75
Y (Press the **Enter** key or select **OK** to save the new client record.)

b. After checking your information in row two, select the **Pause** button on the Macro Tools Button Bar.

c. The message displays "Create new client letters now? Y/N."

d. Press **y** to create new client letters now.

e. In the Save As dialog box, type the filename **25client.ltr**. If necessary, select the drive where your file disk is located. Select **OK**.

Note: *After the merging and saving is completed, a letter for each client that contained a Y in the "New?" field displays. Check that five letters display addressed to Alarid, Morrison, Winters, Mitchell, and Lunn.*

- Optional. Print the merged letters.
- Close the document.
- Display the WordPerfect Button Bar.

Testing the Macro

Although the macro compiles without an error message, errors may still exist in the macro. Always test a macro by running it under all the conditions that you can imagine a user selecting. For example, in the macro just created, you would want to test the following:

Scenario A: A client does not have a phone number. Pressing **Tab** without typing anything else should move the insertion point to the next field (column).

Scenario B: The user responds "Y" to merge and print the new letters.

Scenario C: The user responds "y" to merge and print the new letters.

Scenario D: The user responds "N" to leave the macro without merging the letters.

Scenario E: The user responds "n" to leave the macro without merging the letters.

Scenario F: The user accidentially presses any other key on the keyboard. The macro should respond as though the user pressed N.

As the macro become more complex, testing to make sure it will work under most normal conditions also becomes more complex. The amount of time spent developing and testing a complex macro must be weighed against the time saved or the increased accuracy or efficiency possible once the macro is available.

WordPerfect Supplied Macros

Included with the WordPerfect 6.0 for Windows program are 30+ macros. The *allfonts* macro was used in Chapter 15 and the *dropcap* macro was used in Chapter 18. If the macros help is available on your computer, select **Help**, **Macros**, **Shipping Macros** to obtain a description of each macro. In addition to using these macros, printing and examing them will help you understand more about how WordPerfect macros work and how to create your own macros.

Abbrev.wcm is a supplied (shipping) macro that lets you set up a list of shortcut abbreviations to type in place of longer words or groups of words. For example, the company name *Lake San Antonio Mobile Home Services* might be set up in the macro as *lsa* so that whenever documents contain the company name, you could type *lsa*, then immediately press **Ctrl** and **a**. WordPerfect's abbreviation's macro would then automatically expand the abbreviation into the full company name.

Start-Up Instructions

- A new document window should be displayed.

Create and Use the Abbreviation Macro

1. Type and select the desired text.

   For example, type and select **Lake San Antonio Mobile Home Services**. (Do not type the period.)

2. Select **Insert, Abbreviations** {Alt, i, a}.

   Note: *The Abbreviations dialog box displays.*

3. Select **Create** {r}.

   Note: *The Create Abbreviation dialog box displays.*

4. In the Abbreviation Name box, type the abbreviated form of the word(s).

   For example, type **lsa**. (Do not type the period.)

5. Select **OK** {Enter}.

   Note: *The Abbreviations dialog box displays showing the list of Abbreviations.*

6. Select **Close** {Alt and c}.

Use an Abbreviation

7. Place the insertion point at the desired location in the document.

   For example, locate the insertion point on a blank line.

8. Select **Insert, Abbreviations** {Alt, i, a}.

9. Double-click on the desired abbreviation.

   For example, double-click on the abbreviation **lsa**.

   Note: *The expanded abbreviation displays in the document window.*

Shortcut

1. In the document window, type the abbreviation.

   For example, type the abbreviation **lsa**. (Do not type the period or press the **Spacebar**.)

2. Press **Ctrl** and **a**.

Finish-Up Instructions

- The abbreviation is saved and remembered even when the WordPerfect program is exited. Therefore, the abbreviation should be deleted so that the next student performing the Steps to Create and Use the Abbreviation Macro will be able to create the lsa abbreviation. Ask your instructor or instructional assistant if you are to delete the abbreviation.
- Use the following information to delete the abbreviation:

  a. Select **Insert**, **Abbreviations**.

  b. Select the abbreviation **lsa**.

  c. Select **Delete**.

  d. Select **Yes**.

  e. Select **Close**.

The Next Step

Chapter Review and Activities

Self-Check Quiz

T F 1. The only way to create a macro is to record the keystrokes.

T F 2. When a macro is saved, it is automatically compiled.

T F 3. A macro command instructs the program to perform some type of action.

T F 4. A GETSTRING command can be used to ask the person running the macro for information.

T F 5. The Compiler converts the keystrokes and commands in a macro into codes that the computer can understand.

6. Even though the Compiler finds no errors, a macro should be tested because errors such as _______ may exist.
   a. logic errors
   b. typographical or grammatical errors
   c. errors that cause the program to perform an unintended action
   d. all of these

7. A previously created abbreviation can be retrieved quickly to the screen by typing the abbreviation and pressing _______________.
   a. **Ctrl** and **a**
   b. **Ctrl** and **c**
   c. **Ctrl** and the first letter of the abbreviation
   d. any of these

8. Describe the three parts of a macro IF statement.

9. Where would you begin looking for an error if the WordPerfect Macro Facility - Syntax Error dialog box appeared while you were trying to save the macro?

10. Write a statement that describes the difference between the PROMPT command and the GETSTRING command.

Activities

Activity 25.1—Create a Macro with User Input and an IF-ELSE Statement

1. A macro is need for the following situation: Mr. Juan Beltran, Operations Manager, and Ms. Lucy Bishop, Systems Engineer, share an assistant, James Clark, who is responsible for both of their word processing needs. Create a macro for James to use that will ask him who will sign the letter, then place an appropriate complementary closing, signature line, title, and reference initials in the document.

   Hint: *Make the user input as short as possible (Y/N or one initial for the person's name). Longer input is more likely to be mistyped.*

2. Use the following information to create the macro:

   a. Display the Macro Tools Button Bar and the Macro Edit Feature Bar.

   b. Check that the SmartQuotes feature is not enabled.

   c. If necessary, refer to Figure 25.4 for explanations of the macro commands you will be using.

   d. The macro should start with the following four commands:
   ```
   DISPLAY(ON!)
   PROMPT("*Please Wait*")
   WAIT(35)
   ENDPROMPT
   ```

   e. The Char command is used next in the macro. If necessary, refer to the Steps to Use a Variable on page 600.

f. The IF-ELSE statement is used next. If necessary, refer to the Steps to Create an IF-ELSE Statement in a Macro on page 601.

g. Use the filename **ltrclose.wcm** and save the macro on your file disk.

3. Print one copy of the macro and close the document.
4. Optional. Play the macro.

Challenge Your Skills

Skill 25.1—Create a Macro

1. Use the following information to create a macro that prints and formats the company name using the company format policy.

   a. Your supervisor gives you a document written by several different people. Each person has spelled the company name in a different way. In addition, the company policy is to bold and italicize the name. Moreover, this is going to be a monthly project. Create a macro that will put in the correct company name (Meunneres Villarosa), and format it according to company policy. The document is available on the data disk under the file name **25skill1.mv**.

   b. Open the file named **25skill1.mv**.

   c. Start the macro after selecting the text to be replaced.

   d. Optional. Use the REPLACE and a WHILE/ENDWHILE commands to actually find each occurrence of the company name. The macro commands, syntax, and parameters can be looked up in either the WP Online Macros Manual or the *WordPerfect 6.0 for Windows Macro Manual*, if available.

2. Print one copy of the macro.
3. Play the macro and print one copy of the corrected document.
4. Use the *new* filename **25skill1.rev** and save the file to your file disk.
5. If you have completed your work, exit WordPerfect.

Part 7
Checking Your Step

Production Skill Builder Activities
Chapters 23-25

Production Activity 7.1—Create a Macro with a Table and Formulas

1. Use the following information to create a macro that produces the product report shown on page 610 when played. Remember, before creating a macro, always write down each step *before* selecting **Tools**, **Macro**, **Record**.

   a. Use the macro name **report**.

   Hint: *Remember to type the drive letter where your file disk is located followed by a colon and the macro name.*

   b. Decrease the width of column B so that the column displays in approximately the same size as is shown.

   Hint: *Press* ***Ctrl*** *and the < key to decrease the column width.*

   c. Join the cells in row 1.

   Hint: *To select cells, press the* ***Shift*** *and* ***F8*** *keys to turn on the Select mode. Continue to press the* ***Shift*** *key and use the arrow key to highlight the desired cells.*

   d. Type and format the text shown in row 1 and column A of the product report on page 610. (Do not type any text in column B when creating the macro. Formulas will be created for cells B4 and B5 using the information in step 1f.)

   e. Use decimal align and commas number type with zero digits after the decimal for cells B2-B6.

   f. When creating the table, a formula should be placed in cell B4 that subtracts the actual sales from the projected sales (B3 - B2). Also, a formula that calculates the percentage increase or decrease of actual units sold over the projected unit sales (B4/B2*100) should be placed in cell B5.

   Note: *A WPWin Error Divide by Zero message box may display; select* ***OK****. (When the form is used, numbers will be inserted into cells B4 and B2 and* *the divide by zero error will be eliminated.) A zero displays in cell B4 and two question marks display in cell B5 because the required calculation cannot be performed until data is entered in the cells.*

g. Change the table border to double.

h. Center the table horizontally.

PRODUCT REPORT Product Line:	
Total Projected Unit Sales	
Total Actual Unit Sales	
Total Units Over/Under	.00
% Increase/Decrease of Projected Sales	??
Next Year's Projected Unit Sales	

i. Turn off Macro Record before continuing.

2. After Macro Record is turned off, clear the screen. Do not save this document.
3. Open a new file and change the top and bottom margins to .5".
4. Play the product report macro. Create a product report using the following information:

   Product Line: **Cheese Crackers**
   Projected Sales: **234,680**
   Actual Sales: **238,200**
   Next Year's Projected Sales: **239,100**

5. Place the insertion point below the table and press **Enter** twice. Play the product report macro. Create a product report using the following information:

   Product Line: **Yummy Bars**
   Projected Sales: **219,230**
   Actual Sales: **215,400**
   Next Year's Projected Sales: **220,900**

6. Place the insertion point below the second table and press **Enter** twice. Play the product report macro. Create a product report using the following information:

   Product Line: **Pecan Snacks**
   Projected Sales: **250,600**
   Actual Sales: **253,300**
   Next Year's Projected Sales: **255,500**

7. Place the insertion point below the third table and press **Enter** twice. Play the product report macro. Create a product report using the following information:

   Product Line: **Potato Skin Crunchies**
   Projected Sales: **226,660**

Actual Sales: **224,540**
Next Year's Projected Sales: **226,950**

8. Use the filename **7pact1.rpt** and save the report.
9. Print one copy.
10. Close the document.

Production Activity 7.2—Create a Form Using the Tables Feature

1. Use the Tables feature to create a form similar to the form shown on page 612. Make decisions regarding:

   Margins
   Number of rows and columns
   Font and size for text
   Formulas
   Joining and splitting cells
   Table lines and shading for cells
   Use of graphic images
   Center the table vertically and/or horizontally on the page

2. Use the filename **7pact1.for** and save the form.
3. Print one copy
4. If you have completed your work, exit WordPerfect.

STANLEY SECURITY SYSTEMS
195 SEVER STREET
WORCHESTER, MA 01619
508-774-2400

JOB WORK ORDER

Job Name:		Bill To:	
Address:		Address:	
City/State/Zip:		City/State/Zip:	
Phone:		Phone:	

Description of Work	
	Order Date
	Order Taken By
	Estimated Cost
	Start Date
	Installer
	Date Completed

I hereby acknowledge the satisfactory completion of the above described work.	Labor	
	Materials	
	Tax (8.25%)	0.00
Customer's Signature Date	**Total Price**	$0.00

Appendices

- Appendix A—Customizing WordPerfect
- Appendix B—Summary of Enriching Language Arts
- Appendix C—WordPerfect Graphic Images and ExpressDocs
- Appendix D—Answers to Self-Check Quizzes
- Appendix E—QuickFinder
- Appendix F—Using Other Windows Programs Within WordPerfect
- Appendix G—Sound Boards

APPENDIX

Customizing WordPerfect

WordPerfect Preferences (Setup)

WordPerfect Preferences assist the user in changing options for the WordPerfect program, such as the display, files, keyboard, printer, button bars, and the document summary. WordPerfect creates default options that are suitable for most word processing users. However, by using Preferences, the options are easily changed to accommodate each users' specific needs. Once a Preference is changed, they are in effect each time you load WordPerfect. To obtain specific details for changing any Preference option, use the Help feature.

Preferences is selected from the **File** menu. The different software options that can be changed using Preferences include the Display, Environment, File, Document Summary, Button Bar, Keyboard, Menu Bar, Power Bar, Status Bar, Writing Tools, Print and Import preferences (see Figure A.1).

The *Display* Preference options are used to select choices for displaying various items in the document screen. Following is a list of the Display Preferences Options.

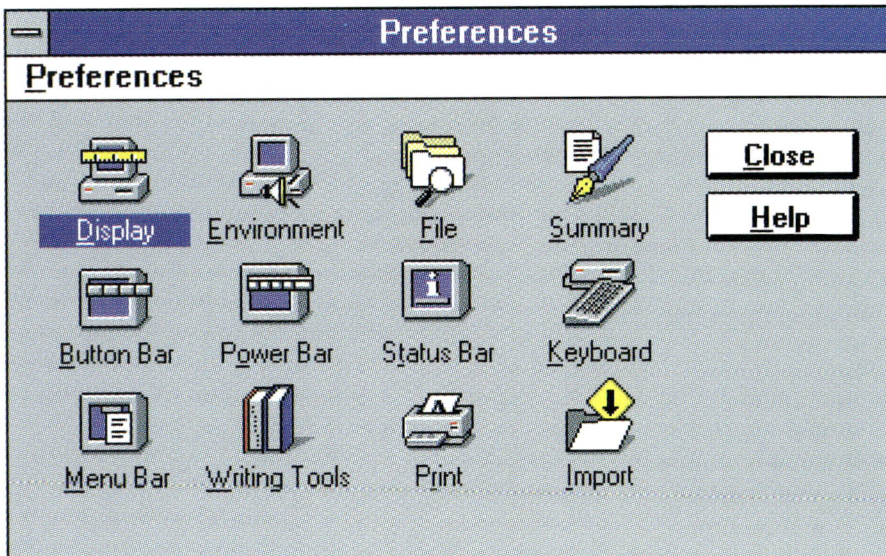

FIGURE A.1

Preferences box

Display Preferences Options	
Document	Show Table Gridlines, Windows System Colors, Comments, Graphics, Hidden Text, Horizontal and Vertical Scroll Bars, Units of Measure (Status and Ruler Bar display) and Sculptured (three-dimensional) dialog boxes
View/Zoom	Default View: Draft, Page or Two Page Default Zoom: standard percentage amounts, Margin Width, Page Width, Full Page or Other
Ruler Bar	Show Ruler Bar on New and Current Document Ruler Bar Options: Tab Snap to Ruler Bar Grid, Show Ruler Bar Guides, Sculptured (three-dimensional) Ruler Bar
Show	Show Symbols on New and Current Document Symbols to display: Space, Hard Return, Tab, Indent, Center, Flush Right, Soft Hyphen, Advance and Center Page
Reveal Codes	Show Reveal Codes on New and Current Document Font and Size options: Wrap Lines at Window, Show Spaces As Bullets, Show Codes In Detail, Show Help Prompts for Codes, Sculptured Codes, and Window Size.
Merge	Merge Codes: Display Merge Codes, Display Merge Codes as Markers, and Hide Merge Codes

The *Environment* Preference options are used to customize settings for various WordPerfect features that are shown in the following table.

Environment Preferences Options	
User Info for Comments and Summary	Name, Initials, User Color
Formatting	Hyphenation Prompt, Confirm Deletion of Codes, Stop Insertion Point at Hidden Codes, Confirm Delete of Table Formulas
Save Workspace	Always, Never, Prompt on Exit
Beep On	Error, Hyphenation, Find Failure
Menu	Display Last Open Filenames, Display Shortcut Keys, Show Help Prompts
Save	Set QuickMark on Save, Reformat Document for Default Printer on Open
Activate Hypertext	

The *Files* Preferences are used to designate the drive and/or directory where files are located for backups, templates, spreadsheets, databases, printers, hyphenation, graphics, and macros. The following table shows each File Preference option.

File Preferences Options	
Documents/Backup	Default Directory, Use Default Extension (wpd) on Open and Save, Backup Directory, Timed Document Backup every (set number of minutes), and Original Document Backup
Templates	Default Directory, Default Template, Additional Directory, Additional Objects Template, and Template File Extension (wpt)
Spreadsheets	Default Directory and Supplemental Directory
Databases	Default Directory and Supplemental Directory
Printers/Labels	Default Directory, Supplemental Directory, Label File, Default Labels to Display: Laser, Tractor Fed or Both
Hyphenation	Default Directory
Graphics	Default Directory and Supplemental Directory
Macros	Default Directory and Supplemental Directory
Update QuickList with Changes	
View All: View File Location Preferences	

The *Document Summary* preferences are used to set Search options for the Default Subject Text and the Descriptive Type. Also, the Use of Descriptive Names and Create Summary on Save/Exit options can be selected.

The *Power Bar* preferences can be changed by adding, moving or deleting items. A list of items, that include attributes such as Superscript and Subscript can be used to select the desired item to be included or deleted from the Power Bar. A separator line can be placed between items to add additional space between desired buttons.

The S*tatus Bar* preferences are similar to the Power Bar preferences. Additionally, boxes on the Status bar can be resized. The Font type and size and appearance can be changed. Also, the Power Bar items can be selected to display evenly spaced and/or to display with a Bold Font.

The *Keyboard* preferences include three choices, i.e., the Equation Editor Keyboard, WPDOS Compatible, and/or WPWin 6.0 keyboard. A new keyboard can be created to assign different functions to the keys. Also, the location for storing the new keyboard can be selected.

The *Menu Bar* preferences include three choices, i.e., Equation Editor Menu, WPWin 6.0 Menu and WPWin 6.0a Menu. Similar to the Keyboard preferences, a new menu can be created and the location for the new menu can be selected.

The *Writing Tools* preferences allow you to specify the tools, i.e., Spelling, Grammatik, that you want to display on the Tools Menu. The chosen item can be moved up or down on the list to display in the order you desire.

The *Print* preferences are used to designate default print settings. The following table shows the Print Preferences options.

Print Preferences Options	
Size Attribute Ratio	Specify percentage amount of text for each size attribute: Fine, Small, Large, Very Large, Extra Large, and Super/Subscript
Copies	Specify Number of Copies Select if Generated by Printer or WordPerfect
Document Settings	Select the Print Quality, Print Color and/or Do Not Print Graphics
Define Color Printing Palette	

The *Import* preferences are used to specify how graphics files, ASCII delimited text files, WP4.2, DCA, and DisplayWrite documents are imported into WordPerfect.

Customizing the Button and Power Bars

The WordPerfect Button and Power Bars can be customized to provide for individual preferences. To create a new Button Bar or to edit an existing Button or Power Bar, select the Preferences option in the File menu and choose the Button Bar or Power Bar icon.

A new Button Bar can be created and/or any of the buttons on a Button Bar can be changed. Also, a Button Bar can be rearranged, relocated, and/or displayed differently in the document window. A Button Bar name can be changed, or an entire Button Bar can be deleted. Buttons on a Button Bar can be used to access menu commands, features, macros, and other Button Bars. Power Bar buttons can be added, moved, or deleted.

WordPerfect provides *fifteen* different Button Bars: Design Tools, Equation Editor, Font, Generate, Graphics, Layout, Legal, Macro Tools, Page, Preferences, Tables, Utilities, WordPerfect, WordPerfect 5.1, and Workgroup. Only one Button Bar can display at one time. The list of Button Bars is displayed by pressing the *right* mouse button.

Add a Button to a Button Bar

1. Point anywhere on the Button Bar and press the *right* mouse button to display the Button Bar list.
2. Select **Edit**.

   Note: The Button Bar Editor dialog box displays.
3. Select the desired **Add a Button to** option.
4. Select the desired Feature Category.
5. Select the desired feature.
6. Select **Add Button**.

*Note: The new button displays at the right of the Button Bar. If a separator (more space) is desired between buttons, point to the **Separator** button, press, hold and drag the line between buttons, release the mouse.*

7. Select **OK**.

Steps to Delete a Button on a Button Bar

1. Point anywhere on the Button Bar and press the *right* mouse button to display the Button Bar list.
2. Select **Edit**.
3. Point to the Button Bar button to be deleted.
4. Press the left mouse button to display a "hand," hold and drag the button off the Button Bar; release the mouse.
5. Select **OK** to exit the Button Bar Editor.

Steps to Move a Button on a Button Bar

Note: A button can be moved to a new location on the same Button Bar.

1. Point to the Button Bar and press the *right* mouse button to display the Button Bar.
2. Select **Edit**.
3. Press the left mouse button to display a "hand," hold and drag the button to the desired location; release the mouse.
4. Select **OK**.

Steps to Relocate a Button Bar in the Document Window

1. Point to the Button Bar and press the *right* mouse button to display the Button Bar.
2. Click on **Preferences**.
3. Select **Options**.
4. Select the desired location.
5. Select **OK**.
6. Select **Close**.

Steps to Change the Text/Picture on a Button Bar Button

1. Point to the Button Bar and press the *right* mouse button to display the Button Bar.
2. Select **Preferences**.
3. Select **Options**.

4. Select the desired Appearance.
5. Select **OK**.
6. Select **Close**.

Create a New Button Bar

1. Point to the Button Bar and press the *right* mouse button to display the Button Bar.
2. Select **Preferences**.
3. Select **Create**.
4. Type a name for the new Button Bar.
5. Select **OK**.
6. Select the desired **Add a Button To** option.
7. Select the desired Feature Category and select the desired Feature.
8. Select **Add Button**.
9. Repeat steps 6 and 7 until all the desired options have been chosen, select **OK** to create the new Button Bar.
10. Select **OK**.
11. Choose **Select**.

Delete a Button Bar

1. Point to the Button Bar and press the *right* mouse button to display the Button Bar.
2. Select **Edit**.
3. Select the name of the Button Bar to be deleted.
4. Select **Delete**.
5. Select **Yes**.
6. Select **Close**.

   Note: To view another Button Bar, select **File, Preferences***; double-click on the* **Button Bar** *icon; highlight the desired Button Bar; choose* **Select, Close**.

Display a Different Button Bar

Note: A mouse is required to select a different Button Bar.

1. Point to any location on the displayed Button Bar, press the *right* mouse button once to display the list of WordPerfect Button Bars.

   Note: If a Button Bar is not displayed below the Menu Bar, select View, Button Bar.
2. Point to the desired Button Bar and click once with the left mouse button.

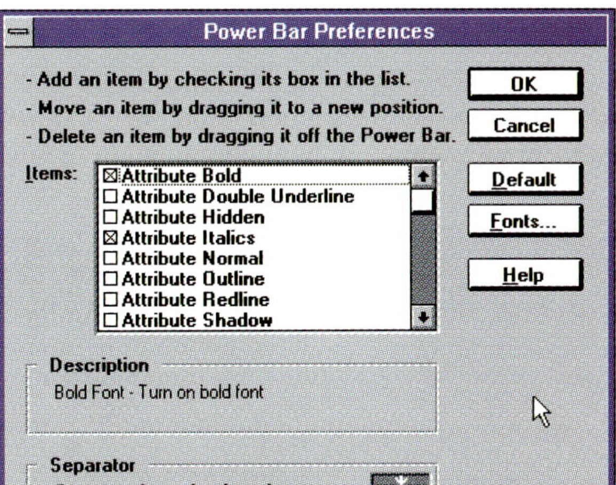

FIGURE A.2

Power Bar Preferences dialog box

Steps to Customize the Power Bar

1. Point to the Power Bar and press the *right* mouse button to display the Quick-Menu list.

   Shortcut: *Point to a button separator on the Power Bar, double-click and skip to step 3.*

2. Select **Preferences**.

   Note: *The Power Bar Preferences dialog box displays (see Figure A.2).*

3. *To add an item*, select the desired item.

   Note: *An X displays in the box beside a selected item.*

4. *To move an item*, point to the item on the Power Bar to be moved, click, hold, and drag the item to the desired location; release the mouse.
5. *To delete an item*, point to the item on the Power Bar, click, hold, and drag the item off the Power Bar; release the mouse.
6. Select **OK**.

Add a Power Bar Item Separator

1. Point to the Power Bar and press the *right* mouse button to display the Quick-Menu list.
2. Select **Preferences**.
3. Point to the **Separator** button to display a hand.
4. Press and hold the mouse button and drag to the line located between the desired Power Bar items; release the mouse button.
5. Select **OK**.

Change the Power Bar Font/Size Lists

1. Point to the Power Bar and press the *right* mouse button to display the Quick-Menu list.

2. Select **Preferences**.
3. Select **Fonts**.
4. Select the desired font and/or size.
5. Select **OK**.

Steps to Add TrueType Font Styles to the Font Item on the Power Bar

1. Point to the Power Bar and press the *right* mouse button to display the QuickMenu list.
2. Select **Preferences**.
3. Select **Fonts**.

   Note: The Power Bar Font/Size Lists dialog box displays.
4. Select the font and/or size to place an X beside the desired choice(s).

   Note: Choose the Select button to select All Fonts and Sizes, No fonts and Sizes, or to select Default Sizes.
5. Select **OK**.

Restore the Default Power Bar

1. Point to the Power Bar and press the *right* mouse button to display the QuickMenu list.
2. Select **Preferences**.
3. Select **Default**.
4. Select **OK**.

Customizing QuickCorrect

The QuickCorrect feature is available starting with the WordPerfect for Windows 6.0a. The QuickCorrect feature corrects errors in the document window as text is typed. For example, if "teh" is typed and the Spacebar is pressed, the correct word "the" displays. A list of commonly misspelled words along with the correctly spelled words display in the QuickCorrect dialog box.

Also, abbreviations can be listed for words or phrases that are frequently typed. When the listed abbreviation is typed followed by a space, WordPerfect automatically displays the word or phrase.

An additional misspelled word(s) and/or abbreviation(s) along with the correctly spelled word(s) and/or word(s) that the abbreviation represents can be included in the QuickCorrect list. The QuickCorrect feature can also correct words that are typed with the first two letters capitalized. For example if "THe" is typed and the space bar is pressed, the correct capitalization "The" displays. The SmartQuotes option can be selected to automatically convert the traditional keyboard quotation marks (") to the correct typography symbols (" ").

Steps to Customizing QuickCorrect

1. Select **Tools, QuickCorrect**.
2. Type the incorrectly spelled word or abbreviation in the Replace box.
3. Click in the With box and type the correctly spelled word or the phrase the abbreviation represents.
4. Select **Add Entry**.
5. *To delete an entry*, select the desired words in the word list, select **Delete Entry**, select Yes.
6. *To replace an entry*, select the desired words in the word list, select **Replace Entry**, type the incorrectly spelled word, select Add Entry.
7. Select **Close**.

WordPerfect Customer Support

If you encounter difficulties installing, changing preferences, or using any WordPerfect feature, WordPerfect's Customer Support is available to assist you at the following numbers (these customer support numbers are for users within the United States, U.S. territories, or Canada).

In April of 1994, a new WordPerfect policy required that all customers obtain a PIN (personal identification number). Customers will receive 180 days of free support after they receive their PIN number. Various plans for payment are available. Call WordPerfect to select the plan that best suits your needs.

Installation	800-228-7610 801-228-9964 (toll)
Equations, Graphics, Sound, Tables	800-228-8720 801-228-9962 (toll)
Macros, Merge	800-228-2021 801-228-9961 (toll)
All other features	800-228-9907 801-228-9960 (toll)
Laser or PostScript printers	800-228-2803 801-228-9965 (toll)
Dot matrix printers and other printers	800-228-6646 801-228-9966 (toll)
Networks	800-228-8807 801-228-9963 (toll)
Customer support fax number	801-222-4377 (toll)

After-hours customer support number	801-228-9908 (toll)
InfoShare Fax Service number	800-228-9960 801-228-9920 (toll)
BBS (1200 or 2400 baud modems)	801-225-4414 (toll)
BBS (9600 baud V.32 modems)	801-22504444 (toll)

APPENDIX

Summary of Enriching Language Arts

Chapter	Vocabulary Words	Grammar/Punctuation Rule
1	acquisition, spiraling, enormous, liquidation	Introductory Adverbs and Phrases—A comma often follows an introductory adverb or phrase, because the word or phrase provides a transition from the previous sentence.
2	commendable, nominated, negotiations	Introductory (Dependent) Clauses—A comma should follow a dependent clause. An introductory dependent clause often begins with *if, in, when, since,* or *as*.
3	telecommunications, tailored, existence, description	Appositives—Appositives are words that immediately follow a noun and further identify the noun but usually are not necessary to the meaning of the sentence.
4	dues, affiliation, outweigh, distinguished	Compound Adjectives and Coordinating Conjunctions—Hyphenate two words that precede and describe a noun and function as a single adjective. A comma is placed before a coordinating conjunction (e.g., *and, or, because*) that joins two independent clauses.
5	initiative, strategic, alliances	Dollar Amounts Formats—Use a comma to separate the number digits into groups of thousands. No space is placed between a number and the dollar sign. If even numbers are used in the body of a document or if a column of numbers has even dollar amounts, the zeros are omitted.
6	adversely, per diem, reimbursement	Single and Double Underlines for Dollar Amounts—Place a single underline between the last column amount and the total amount. In a table without lines or borders, a total amount is usually emphasized by placing double underlines beneath the total amount.

Chapter	Vocabulary Words	Grammar/Punctuation Rule
7	implement, incentive, promotional, wholesalers	Commas Used in a Series—Words and/or ideas listed in a series are separated by commas.
8	prompt, unkempt, offensive, antagonistic, attitude	Using the Abbreviations *e.g.* and *i.e.*—The abbreviation *e.g.* is used in place of "for example" and is often used when one or more of many examples are listed. The abbreviation *i.e.* is used in place of "that is" and is used when all potential conditions are listed.
9	partnership, accrual method, maturity, depreciation, liability, amortized	Speller Hint—The Speller approves words that are correctly spelled; however, a correctly spelled word can be incorrectly used in a sentence.
10	phenomenon, biosphere, analysis, profound, euphoria	Quotation Marks with Punctuation—Always place a comma or period inside a closing quotation mark. Place a question mark or exclamation point inside closing quotation marks if the question or exclamation pertains only to the quoted information. Place a question mark or exclamation point outside the closing quotation marks if the question or exclamation pertains to the entire sentence.
11	confirmation, prime rate, virtually	Nonrestrictive Clause—A nonrestrictive clause is a clause that is not essential to the meaning of the sentence and is, therefore, set off by a comma or commas.
12	warranty, components, reliable	Subject-Verb Agreement—Verbs must agree in number with their subject. If a subject is singular, use a singular verb; if a subject is plural, use a plural verb.
13	extensive, HMO, reputation	Initials Abbreviated—Periods or spaces are not placed after the letters of an acronym such as IRS (Internal Revenue Service) or TWA (Trans World Airlines).
14	derogatory, inclusion, propaganda, rendered, surreptitious	Independent Adjectives—Two adjectives that modify the same noun are separated by a comma.
15	revenue, innovative, integral, acquisition, commingle	Apostrophe Used to Show Possession—If a noun is singular and used to show possession, add an apostrophe (') and an s. If the noun is plural or the final letter in the noun is an s, add only an apostrophe after the s.
16	No vocabulary words	Proofreading Hints—When proofreading a document, read the document twice: once for content and meaning and once to check grammar, spelling, and punctuation.

Chapter	Vocabulary Words	Grammar/Punctuation Rule
17	brochure, paramedic, typography	Parentheses—Parentheses can be used to set off nonessential expressions that might otherwise confuse the reader. The information within the parentheses provides supplemental information that has no direct bearing on the main idea of the sentence or paragraph. Words, phrases, or clauses can be enclosed within parentheses. Unless a comma, colon, or semicolon is necessary to the text within the parentheses, place the punctuation outside the closing parenthesis. If the text within the parentheses is a complete sentence, the final period is placed within the parentheses.
18	compatibility, promulgated, standards	Em and En Dashes—The em dash (—), a typographic symbol about the width of the character m, is often used in place of a comma. Press the hyphen key twice (—) to create a em dash on a typewriter or computer keyboard. Many software programs provide a method to create typographically correct em dashes (see page 440). The en dash (–), a typographic symbol about the width of the character n, is used as a hyphen or as a substitute for the word to, e.g., July–September.
19	coaching, evaluation, feedback	Colons, Capitalization, and Punctuation for Bulleted and Enumerated Lists—Place a colon after an independent clause that introduces a bulleted or enumerated (numbered) list. An introductory clause frequently includes words such as "the following" and "as follows." When creating a bulleted or enumerated list, capitalize the first word and insert a final punctuation mark after each item that is a complete sentence or phrase. Do not capitalize the first word or insert final punctuation when bulleted or enumerated lists are not complete thoughts.
20	demonstrate, mentor, realistic	Contractions—An apostrophe is used to indicate where a letter(s) has been omitted when two words are combined to form a verb contraction. Generally, contractions are not used in formal business writing. Contractions can be used in personal letters or informal business documents.
21	appreciation, dissolution, irrevocable, valid	Percentage Amounts—Use figures for numbers that are followed by the word percent. Spell out the word percent unless the percentage amount is used in a headline/title or in a table that contains statistical information.

Chapter	Vocabulary Words	Grammar/Punctuation Rule
22	cuisine, duty-free, traditional	Basic Rules for Numbers—Generally, in written text numbers one through ten are spelled out as are numbers used in approximations, at the beginning of a sentence, or that are rounded. Related numbers in the same document should be expressed in the same form, i.e., numbers one through ten are written as figures when used with related numbers above ten.
23	quarter, UPC, versus	Abbreviations in Table Column Headings—When creating tables and forms, abbreviations are often used in subtitle and/or column headings because of limited space. However, abbreviations should be used sparingly. If you are unsure of how to abbreviate a word, consult a dictionary.
24	bonus, suitable	Abbreviations for Time—Type a.m. or p.m. with lowercase letters and no spaces. Only one period is used if the abbreviation is the last element of a sentence.

WordPerfect Graphic Images and ExpressDocs

APPROVED

APPROVED

approved.wpg

bord01L.wpg

bord03p.wpg

bord04p.wpg

bord05.wpg

bord08L.wpg

bord10L.wpg

bord11L.wpg

bord12L.wpg

bord13p.wpg

bord16.wpg

bord17.wpg

buck.wpg

buterfly.wpg

centerpc.wpg

cheetah.wpg

cowboy.wpg

crane_j.wpg

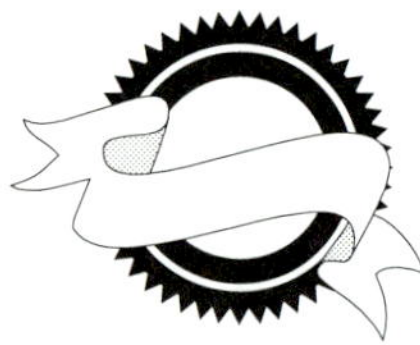
crest.wpg

draft.wpg

dragn.wpg

drtbord.wpg

ender01.wpg

ender03.wpg

ender04.wpg

ender06.wpg

ender11.wpg

ESTIMATE

estimate.wpg

fathrtme.wpg

file_co.wpg

golfswng.wpg

group.wpg

horse_j.wpg

hotair.wpg

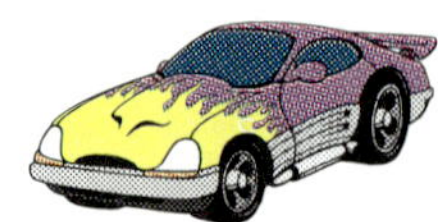
hotrod.wpg

humbird.wpg

IMPORTANT

IMPORTANT

importnt.wpg

inkskier.wpg

marsh.wpg

medical1.wpg

overdue.wpg

padlock.wpg

piano.wpg

racebike.wpg

rose.wpg

silo2.wpg

skipper.wpg

sun_dsg.wpg

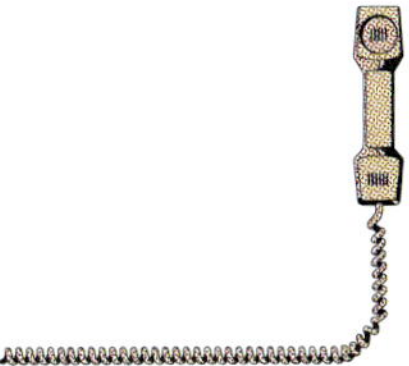

telerec.wpg

thanks.wpg

tiger_j.wpg

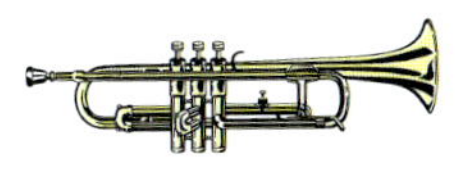

trumpt.wpg

windmill.wpg

winrace.wpg

world.wpg

Sample ExpressDocs

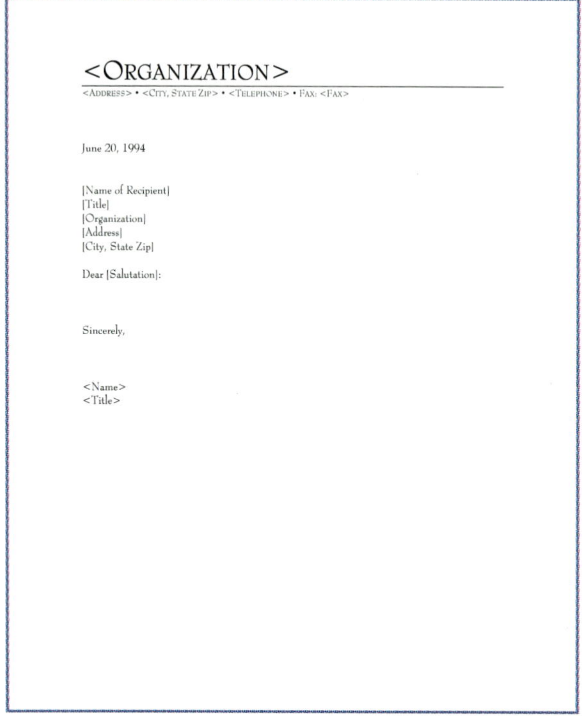

<ORGANIZATION>
<ADDRESS> • <CITY, STATE ZIP> • <TELEPHONE> • FAX: <FAX>

June 20, 1994

[Name of Recipient]
[Title]
[Organization]
[Address]
[City, State Zip]

Dear [Salutation]:

Sincerely,

<Name>
<Title>

letter1.wpt

<Organization>
<Address> • <City, State Zip> • <Telephone> • Fax: <Fax>

December 13, 1994

[Name of Recipient]
[Title]
[Organization]
[Address]
[City, State Zip]

Dear [Salutation]:

Sincerely,

<Name>
<Title>

letter2.wpt

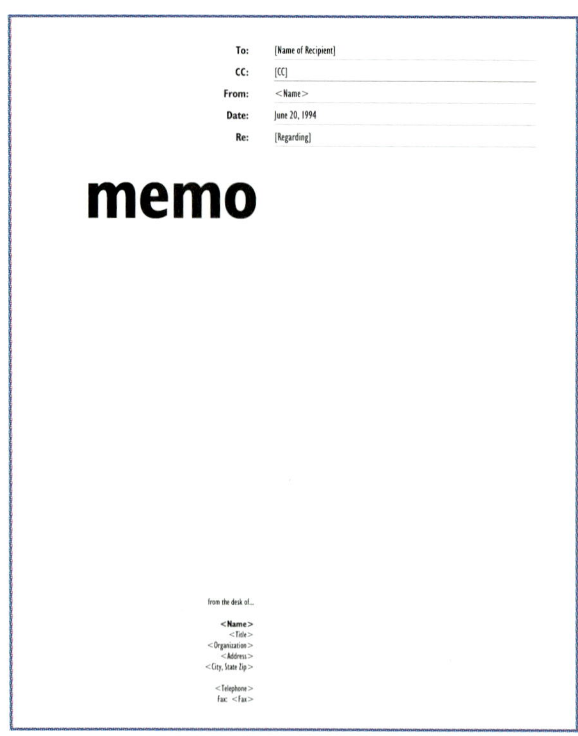

To: [Name of Recipient]
CC: [CC]
From: <Name>
Date: June 20, 1994
Re: [Regarding]

memo

from the desk of...

<Name>
<Title>
<Organization>
<Address>
<City, State Zip>

<Telephone>
Fax: <Fax>

memo1.wpt

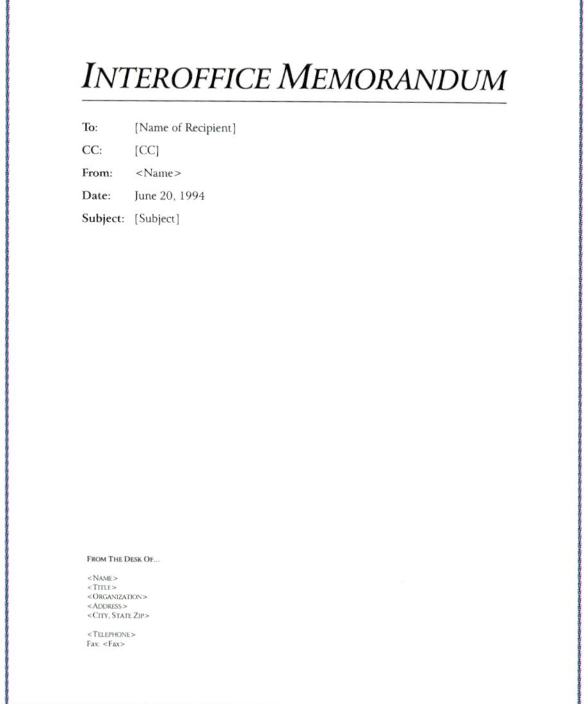

INTEROFFICE MEMORANDUM

To: [Name of Recipient]
CC: [CC]
From: <Name>
Date: June 20, 1994
Subject: [Subject]

FROM THE DESK OF...

<NAME>
<TITLE>
<ORGANIZATION>
<ADDRESS>
<CITY, STATE ZIP>

<TELEPHONE>
Fax: <Fax>

memo5.wpt

To: [Name of Recipient]

Fax: [Fax Number]

From: <Name>

Date: June 20, 1994

Pages: [Pages (including cover sheet)], including cover sheet.

fax

From the desk of...

<Name>
<Title>
<Organization>
<Address>
<City, State Zip>

<Telephone>
Fax: <Fax>

fax1.wpt

<Organization>

<Address>
<City, State Zip>
<Telephone>
Fax: <Fax>

FAX TRANSMISSION COVER SHEET

Date: *June 20, 1994*
To: *[Name of Recipient]*
Fax: *[Fax Number]*
Re: *[Regarding]*
Sender: *<Name>*

YOU SHOULD RECEIVE [Pages (including cover sheet)] PAGE(S), INCLUDING THIS COVER SHEET. IF YOU DO NOT RECEIVE ALL THE PAGES, PLEASE CALL <Telephone>.

fax3.wpt

cal_up.wpt

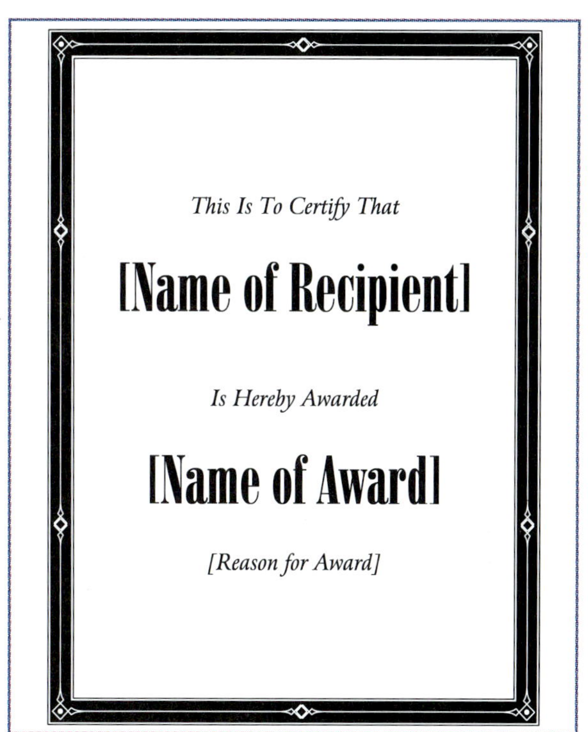

certif1.wpt

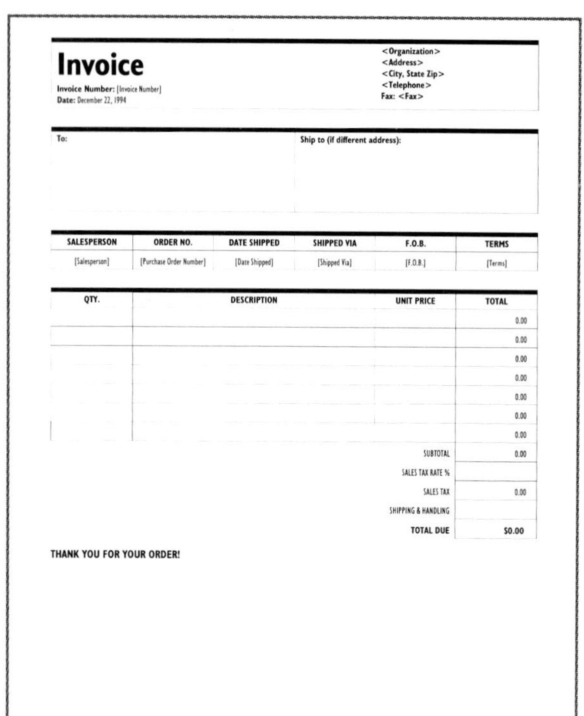

Invoice

Invoice Number: [Invoice Number]
Date: December 22, 1994

<Organization>
<Address>
<City, State Zip>
<Telephone>
Fax: <Fax>

To:

Ship to (if different address):

SALESPERSON	ORDER NO.	DATE SHIPPED	SHIPPED VIA	F.O.B.	TERMS
[Salesperson]	[Purchase Order Number]	[Date Shipped]	[Shipped Via]	[F.O.B.]	[Terms]

QTY.	DESCRIPTION	UNIT PRICE	TOTAL
			0.00
			0.00
			0.00
			0.00
			0.00
			0.00
			0.00
		SUBTOTAL	0.00
		SALES TAX RATE %	
		SALES TAX	0.00
		SHIPPING & HANDLING	
		TOTAL DUE	$0.00

THANK YOU FOR YOUR ORDER!

invoice.wpt

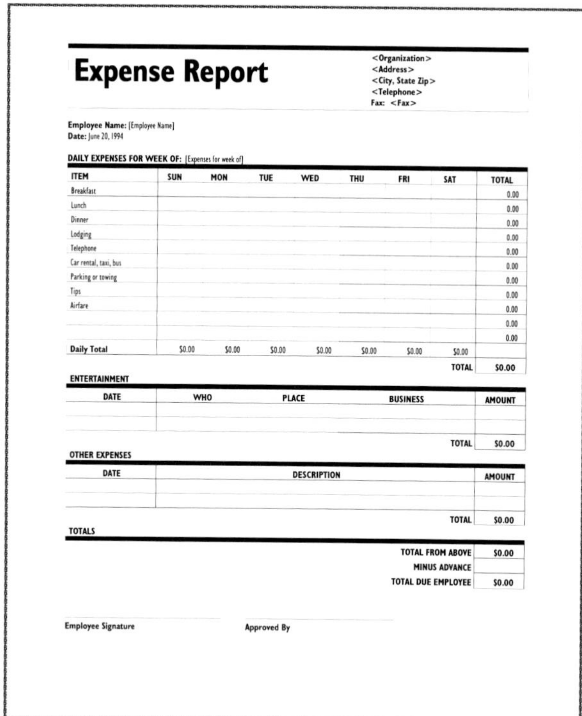

Expense Report

<Organization>
<Address>
<City, State Zip>
<Telephone>
Fax: <Fax>

Employee Name: [Employee Name]
Date: June 20, 1994

DAILY EXPENSES FOR WEEK OF: [Expenses for week of]

ITEM	SUN	MON	TUE	WED	THU	FRI	SAT	TOTAL
Breakfast								0.00
Lunch								0.00
Dinner								0.00
Lodging								0.00
Telephone								0.00
Car rental, taxi, bus								0.00
Parking or towing								0.00
Tips								0.00
Airfare								0.00
								0.00
								0.00
Daily Total	$0.00	$0.00	$0.00	$0.00	$0.00	$0.00	$0.00	
							TOTAL	$0.00

ENTERTAINMENT

DATE	WHO	PLACE	BUSINESS	AMOUNT
			TOTAL	$0.00

OTHER EXPENSES

DATE	DESCRIPTION	AMOUNT
	TOTAL	$0.00

TOTALS

TOTAL FROM ABOVE	$0.00
MINUS ADVANCE	
TOTAL DUE EMPLOYEE	$0.00

Employee Signature

Approved By

expense.wpt

Purchase Order

P. O. Number: [Purchase Order Number]

<Organization>
<Address>
<City, State Zip>
<Telephone>
Fax: <Fax>

To:

Ship to (if different address):

P.O. DATE	PLACED BY	DATE EXPECTED	SHIP VIA	F.O.B.	TERMS
June 20, 1994	[Order Placed By]	[Date Expected]	[Ship Via]	[F.O.B.]	[Terms]

QTY.	DESCRIPTION	UNIT PRICE	TOTAL
			0.00
			0.00
			0.00
			0.00
			0.00
			0.00
			0.00
		SHIPPING & HANDLING	
		SUBTOTAL	0.00
		SALES TAX RATE	
		SALES TAX	0.00
		TOTAL DUE	$0.00

Authorized Signature

purchase.wpt

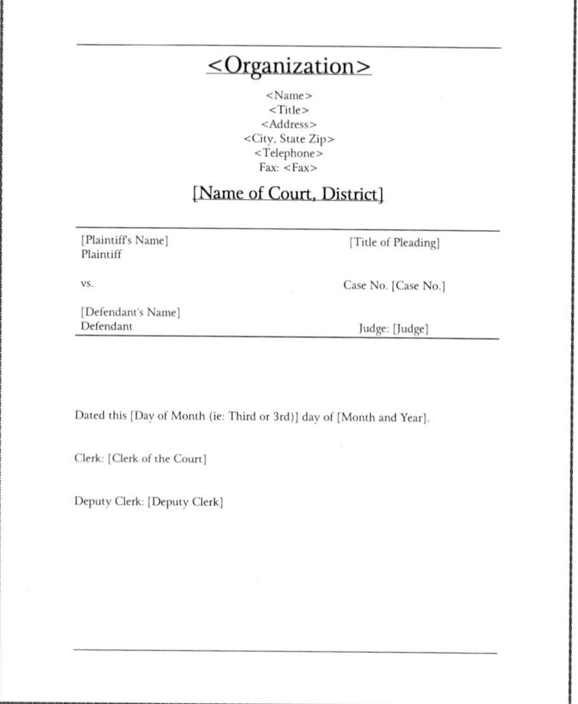

<Organization>

<Name>
<Title>
<Address>
<City, State Zip>
<Telephone>
Fax: <Fax>

[Name of Court, District]

[Plaintiff's Name]
Plaintiff

[Title of Pleading]

vs.

Case No. [Case No.]

[Defendant's Name]
Defendant

Judge: [Judge]

Dated this [Day of Month (ie: Third or 3rd)] day of [Month and Year].

Clerk: [Clerk of the Court]

Deputy Clerk: [Deputy Clerk]

pleadcvr.wpt

APPENDIX

Answers to Self-Check Quizzes

Chapter 1
1. T
2. T
3. T
4. F
5. F
6. a
7. b
8. c

Chapter 2
1. F
2. T
3. T
4. T
5. T
6. d
7. b
8. d

Chapter 3
1. T
2. T
3. F
4. F
5. b
6. c
7. c

Chapter 4
1. T
2. F
3. T
4. T
5. F
6. a
7. d
8. c

Chapter 5
1. T
2. T
3. F
4. T
5. T
6. d
7. c
8. a

Chapter 6
1. T
2. T
3. T
4. T
5. b
6. b
7. d
8. b

Chapter 7
1. F
2. T
3. T
4. F
5. F
6. d
7. d

Chapter 8
1. T
2. F
3. T
4. F
5. T
6. b
7. d

Chapter 9
1. F
2. T
3. F
4. F
5. d
6. a
7. b
8. a

Chapter 10
1. T
2. T
3. F
4. T
5. a
6. d
7. b
8. d

Chapter 11
1. T
2. T
3. F
4. F
5. T
6. b
7. c
8. d

Chapter 12
1. T
2. T
3. F
4. F
5. F
6. b
7. b
8. c

Chapter 13
1. T
2. F
3. F
4. T
5. F
6. b
7. d
8. d

Chapter 14
1. T
2. T
3. T
4. T
5. F
6. a
7. a

Chapter 15
1. T
2. T
3. F
4. F
5. T
6. e
7. b
8. b

Chapter 16
1. T
2. F
3. F
4. T
5. a
6. d
7. b
8. d

Chapter 17
1. T
2. T
3. F
4. F
5. T
6. c
7. d

Chapter 18
1. F
2. T
3. T
4. F
5. T
6. b
7. d

Chapter 19	*Chapter 20*	*Chapter 21*	*Chapter 22*	*Chapter 23*	*Chapter 24*	*Chapter 25*
1. F	1. F	1. F	1. T	1. F	1. T	1. F
2. T	2. T	2. T	2. F	2. T	2. F	2. T
3. F	3. T	3. T	3. F	3. T	3. T	3. T
4. T	4. F	4. T	4. T	4. T	4. T	4. T
5. F	5. F	5. F	5. F	5. T	5. T	5. T
6. T	6. a	6. d	6. d	6. a	6. c	6. d
7. c	7. a	7. a	7. d	7. d	7. d	7. a
8. d	8. d			8. d	8. a	

APPENDIX

QuickFinder

WordPerfect provides a special file indexing program called QuickFinder that is particularly useful if you create many documents and letters and need to find specific files quickly. QuickFinder indexes every word in every document and saves this information in a highly compressed form, which WordPerfect can search quickly. In addition, the documents in multiple directories and drive paths can be indexed so that only one search may be needed to find the document.

One of the drawbacks of a true electronic filing system (a filing system that has no hard copies) is the difficulty of retrieving documents. QuickFinder gives an office a step towards a true electronic filing system by making document retrieval much simpler. For instance, an office could implement an archival system in which all files over six months old are transferred to an optical disk or other storage medium. QuickFinder could then be used to index the archival disk, and documents on the disk could be searched for by name, subject, or by any word in the document. The search would be very fast, and the files that matched the search criteria could then be viewed, opened, or printed.

Create a QuickFinder Index

Before QuickFinder can be used to find documents, the indexes must be created. More than one index can be created using different criteria, such as indexing by drives or directories or by types of files. The QuickFinder File Indexer dialog box is used to define and create the indexes. The default is for WordPerfect to place the index files in the shared directory, under the directory name QFINDEX. (In a standard installation, the path for the shared directory would be C:/WPC20/QFINDEX.) To change the location of the index files, select **Options**, **Preferences** from the QuickFinder File Indexer dialog box. A short version of the Preferences dialog box will appear in which the location of the index files can be changed. To change other defaults, select the **Advanced** button to display the complete Preferences dialog box.

Change the Location of QuickFinder Index Files

1. Select File, QuickFinder {Alt, f, q}.

Note: The QuickFinder dialog box displays.

2. Select the **Indexer** button {Alt and x}.

   Note: The QuickFinder File Indexer dialog box displays.

3. Select the **Options** button, then select **Preferences** {Alt and o, Alt and Shift and down arrow to display the options, p}.

   Note: The short version of the Preferences dialog box will appear. The insertion point will be in the Location of Index Files field at the end of the current path, which will be highlighted.

4. If needed, type the drive letter, a colon, and the path to the directory in which the index files are to be saved.

   Note: If the location of the index files is the only default to be changed, go to step 7.

5. Select the **Advanced** button {Alt and a}.

6. Click in the Exclude Files field, press End, then type **, *.bat** {Alt and x, press End, then type ", *.bat"}.

   Note: The comma separates the new entry from the previous entries. Files with the extension .bat are batch programs used to start programs or to set up paths, and do not need to be included in the document index.

7. Select **OK** to return to the QuickFinder File Indexer dialog box {press Enter}.

Start-Up Instructions

- The QuickFinder File Indexer dialog box should be displayed on the screen.

Steps to Create a New Index

1. Select **Create** {Alt and r}.

2. In the Name field, type a name describing the index (the name may be up to 40 characters).

3. Select **OK** {press Enter}.

   Note: The Create Index dialog box will appear with the insertion point in the Add Directory (and File Pattern) box.

4. Add each directory that is to be included in the index by typing the path to the directory and *.* in the Add Directory (and File Pattern) box, then selecting **Add** {Alt and a}.

   *Note: To view available drives and directories, select the **Browse** button {Alt and w}. Highlight the desired drive and directory, which will then appear in the Add Directory (and File Pattern) box. As each directory is added, it will appear in the Directories to Index list.*

5. Select **Generate** {Alt and g}.

   Note: The Generating Index message box will appear, giving information about the status of the index generation process. When the index has been generated, the Index Complete message box will appear.

6. Select **OK** to return to the QuickFinder File Indexer dialog box {press Enter}.

Note: The index is now ready to be used.

7. Select **Close** twice to return to the document window {press Alt and c twice}.

Use a QuickFinder Index

Once a QuickFinder index has been created, WordPerfect can use the index to locate documents by any word or group of words contained in the desired documents. There are many options to make searches more flexible and to customize QuickFinder indexes. For additional information, see QuickFinder in the *WordPerfect 6.0 for Windows Reference Manual.*

Once the search is completed, any files that match the search will be displayed in the Search Results dialog box. To open or view a file, select it and then select the **Open** or **View** button. The **File Options** button offers the same file management options as in the Open or Save As dialog boxes (see Chapter 16, pages 383–388 for information on File Options).

Use a QuickFinder Index

1. Select **File, QuickFinder** {Alt, f, q}.

   Note: The QuickFinder dialog box will display.

2. The default file pattern is *.*. This will search through all files included in the index. To search only through files with a specific extension, replace the second asterisk with the desired extension.

3. Click once in the **Search For** box, then type the desired word or words for which to search {Alt and s, type the desired word(s)}.

4. Select the desired index by clicking on the down arrow next to the **Search In** box, then move the mouse pointer to the desired index and click once {Alt and i, Tab, Alt and Shift and down arrow, use up or down arrow keys to highlight index}.

5. To limit the search to files edited within a certain date range, click once in the **From** box and enter the earliest date, then click once in the **To** box and enter the latest date. To view and select dates, select the **Calendar** buttons to the right of the From and To boxes.

6. Select **Find** to start the search {Alt and f}.

   *Note: A brief message will appear while WordPerfect is searching the files. If the search is complete, the Search Results dialog box will appear. If no files are found that contain the search criteria, the message "No files found" will display. Select **OK** to return to the QuickFinder dialog box.*

Update the QuickFinder Indexes

As files are added to the directories used in the QuickFinder indexes, the information in them must be added to QuickFinder's compressed data file. This is done by periodically updating the indexes. If many files are added during each working day, the indexes should be updated daily. If the indexes are not updated on a regular schedule, QuickFinder will report inaccurate information during searches.

The indexes can be updated manually, or they can be scheduled automatically using the Kickoff program. For information on using the Kickoff program to update the indexes, see Appendix F, page F-3.

Update QuickFinder Indexes Manually

1. Select **File, QuickFinder** {Alt, f, q}.
2. Select the **Indexer** button {Alt and x}.
3. Select **Generate** {Alt and g}.
4. Highlight the first index to be updated.
5. Select **Update Index With New or Modified Files** {Alt and u}.
6. Select **OK** to start the update process {press Enter}.

   Note: The Generating Index message box will appear briefly, giving the status of the update. When complete, the Index Complete message box will appear.
7. Select **OK** to return to the QuickFinder File Indexer dialog box {press Enter}.
8. Repeat steps 3–7 for each index.
9. When all indexes have been updated, select **Close** twice to return to the document window {press Alt and c twice}.

APPENDIX

Using Other Windows Programs Within WordPerfect

Windows Multitasking

WordPerfect 6.0 for Windows is designed to take full advantage of Windows' ability to run multiple programs (multitasking) by making it easy to create buttons that launch other programs. Sending faxes and electronic mail (e-mail), updating a spreadsheet and inserting it into a document, or scheduling an update of the QuickFinder indexes are just a few of the many possibilities to make your workday more productive.

Launching a Program within WordPerfect

The first step in launching a program within WordPerfect is to add a button for the program to the Button Bar most likely to be in use when the program is needed. After the button is added, click on it to launch the program. To create a button, the filename of the program's executable or initialization file is needed. To find this filename, switch to the Program Manager and click once on the desired program icon. Select **File**, **Properties** to view the Command Line box. If necessary, click once in the Command Line box and press **End** to view the entire path. Write down the path and filename to use in the following Steps to Add a Program Button to the Button Bar.

Steps to **Add a Program Button to the Button Bar**

1. Follow steps 1-2 in Appendix A, Customizing WordPerfect, Steps to Add a Button to a Button Bar on page A-4.
2. At Step 3, select **Launch a Program** as the Add Button To option.

Note: The Button Bar Editor dialog box will change to provide a ***Select File*** *button in the middle of the box.*

3. Click once on the **Select File** button.
4. Double-click on the file that starts the program.

   Note: The program's icon (the same one that appears on the Program Manager for the program) will appear on a new button in the Button Bar.
5. Select **OK**.

Fax Technology

Fax technology allows an exact copy of a document to be transmitted over the telephone system from one fax device to another. Fax, which was originally called facsimile, made its debut in the early 1930s.

The first fax devices sent copies of documents using analog signals, a method that was very slow. In the 1980s, digital signals replaced analog signals for the transmission of faxes. Digital fax transmission is much faster than analog transmission and is one of the fastest-growing communications tools available.

A stand-alone fax machine works by scanning a hard copy of the document being faxed and digitizing it so that it can be transmitted electronically. Many computers now contain fax boards or fax/modem boards. These boards function both as a regular data modem for communicating with other computers and for sending documents as faxes to distant fax machines and other fax/modem boards.

All fax boards require software to control their operation, and such software is usually included with the fax board and installed on the computer when the fax board is installed. In addition, several popular software faxing programs are available, which may offer additional features. To use fax technology within WordPerfect 6.0 for Windows, the fax board or fax machine must be connected to the computer and a Windows fax program must be installed on the computer.

The Fax as a Printer

One way to use the fax within WordPerfect is to install the fax board or fax machine as a printer. If this is possible, the fax reference manual will explain how to do it using the Windows Control Panel or do it automatically as part of the fax software installation program. Once the fax board or machine is listed in the Windows Control Panel as a printer, it can be designated in WordPerfect as the current printer by selecting **File, Select Printer**, highlighting the fax board or machine name, and choosing **Select**. Any document can now be sent to the fax board or machine using the same options that would be used if the document were being sent to a printer. Even a document that is not open in WordPerfect can be sent to the printer by selecting **File, Print, Document on Disk, Print.**

Another way to use the fax within WordPerfect is to create a button to access the fax software. Once a "fax" button is created, click on the button to launch the fax program. Follow the fax reference manual for instructions on how to select the file to be sent and how to start the fax transmission.

E-mail

Electronic mail, or e-mail, has become a popular way to communicate with work colleagues and friends. Many offices provide network hardware and software so that all computers in the company are connected. When e-mail software is added, workers can send messages to one another and can often work together on projects, depending on the features provided in the e-mail package. If your computer is connected to a network, e-mail can be sent to others on your network by selecting **File, WP Mail** (or the name of your mail system). WordPerfect for Windows supports WordPerfect Office 3.0, 3.1, and 4.0 as well as any mail system that uses the VIM or MAPI standards. If desired, a button can be added to a WordPerfect Button Bar to launch an e-mail program.

The Kickoff Program

Kickoff is a software program that is used to start other programs at scheduled times. The Kickoff program ships with WordPerfect 6.0 for Windows and a Kickoff icon automatically displays in the WordPerfect group in Program Manager following a complete installation. One of the Kickoff program's most useful functions is the ability to update QuickFinder indexes at times when the computer is not otherwise in use, such as lunchtime or the middle of the night. The Kickoff program can be added to a Button Bar, or it can be activated from the Program Manager.

Update QuickFinder Indexes using Kickoff

1. Activate the Kickoff program by clicking on the **Kickoff** button in the Button Bar (if it has been added) or by double-clicking on the **Kickoff** icon in the WordPerfect group of the Program Manager window.
2. Select the **Add** button.
3. In the Command Line field, type the path to the program to be started, or select the Browse button and then double-click on the filename.

   For example, to update a QuickFinder index, select the **Browse** button and double-click on the **qfwin20.exe** file. (The QuickFinder index will be located in the shared application files directory, e.g., C:\WPC20 in a standard installation.)

4. Press the **End** key to place the insertion point at the end of the path, press the **Spacebar** once, then type any parameters needed to run the program.

   For example, press **End** to move the insertion point to the end of the path and press the **Spacebar** once. Type **/ra** to rebuild all QuickFinder indexes or type **/ia** to rebuild only those indexes that have new or modified files.

5. Double-click in the **Start Date** box, then type the date on which the program should start. (If the program is to be run every day, skip to the next step, leaving today's date in the Start Date box.)

6. Double-click in the **Start Time** box, then type the time at which the program should start.

7. Select either the **AM** or **PM** option.

8. If the program is to be run periodically, double-click in the **Days** box in the Repeat Intervals section and type the number of days between each time the program is to be started.

   For example, to rebuild the QuickFinder indexes each day, double-click in the **Days** box, then type **1.**

9. Make sure the Disable box is clear (deselected). (When Disable is selected, the program will not run, but can be retained in the Kickoff list for future use.)

10. Select **OK** to return to the Kickoff window.

    Note: *Windows and Kickoff must both be open in order for Kickoff to run the events at their specified times. If Windows is closed or the computer is turned off periodically, add* **Kickoff** *to the Startup Group. It will then be automatically opened when Windows is loaded. For information on how to on add items to the Windows Startup Group, see the Windows reference manual.*

APPENDIX

Sound Boards

A sound board converts the computer's discrete digital signals to continuous analog signals. This process uses circuitry called a Digital Analog Converter (DAC). The quality of the sound depends on the digital input, the design of the board, and the audio amplifiers. Better sound usually means more bytes (megabytes) of digital data (larger files) and more expensive cards and amplifiers.

Sound is converted into digital signals from analog signals through software using circuitry called an Analog Digital Converter (ADC). Not all sound boards can perform this function, although most boards today do so. The choice of which sound board to buy will depend on your current and future uses of the board as well as how much money you want to invest.

Sound boards may interface with a Musical Instrument Digital Interface (MIDI). This is a standard interface that was initially created by Kawai, Korg, Roland, Sequential Circuits, and Yamaha. The MIDI interface allows the computer to generate music in a manner similar to earlier analog synthesizers, but at much less expense. Since MIDI files do not actually store the sound (they store instructions that enable the computer to re-create the sound), they are smaller than other sound files.

Sound clip libraries are available with a wide range of sounds, music, and prerecorded phrases (similar to clip art libraries). Sound clips are commonly available in two formats, MIDI (.mid) and digital audio (.wav). Some boards can only read one type of file, but many boards can handle both. Digital audio files work much like an audio tape. The sounds are digitized and stored on a disk or on the hard drive. The files are usually much larger and require more disk space than MIDI files.

Many sound boards have a joystick port because it was the support of sound in games that provided the market that brought about the proliferation of less expensive, more capable sound boards.

Many sound boards also provide support for CD-ROMs. This allows music and other sound sources to be integrated into programs and attached to data files in the computer. CDs with libraries of sound and sound effects are available.

Install and Configure the Sound Board

The first step in installing a sound board is to follow the instructions from the maker of the board. If two sets of connector fingers are on the bottom of the sound board, the board should be placed into a motherboard slot with two openings (a 16-bit slot). In general, the default values that the manufacturer has set up are used. The IRQ (interrupt request) value is often 5 or 7. The base I/O address is often 220H or 240H. The DMA (direct memory access) is usually 1. Generally, the sound board has accompanying diagnostic software to help set the correct values if conflicts are experienced. If the sound board has a DOS program, try using several of the board capabilities with its own software before trying to access the board through Windows.

Once the sound board is installed, you must configure Windows to work with the sound board. Software drivers (files) are usually provided with the sound board. Follow the manufacturer's instructions to copy the Windows software driver to the hard disk and to identify the sound board in the Windows Control Panel.

Note: The following instructions are generic. If there are differences between these instructions and those in the manufacturer's instruction manual for the sound board, follow the manufacturer's instructions.

Start-Up Instructions

- Place the disk containing the sound board drivers into drive A or B.

Identify the Board for Windows

1. Start Windows by typing **win** at the system prompt.
2. Double-click on the **Control Panel** icon in the Main group.
3. Double-click on the **Drivers** icon in the Control Panel.
4. Select **Add.**

   Note: The Add window appears. The box to the left of the Add window lists all of the current sound device drivers installed in Windows.
5. Highlight the item **Unlisted or Updated Driver**, which should be the first item on the list.
6. Select **OK.**

   Note: The Install Driver window will appear. This window asks you to insert the disk containing the Unlisted or Updated Driver into drive A:\.
7. If you are using drive B, substitute the letter B for the letter A in the field. When the drive letter is correct, select **OK.**

   Note: The name of the sound driver will appear in the Add Unlisted or Updated Driver window.
8. Make sure the name of the driver is highlighted, then select **OK.**
9. Follow the manufacturer's instructions to select the appropriate options for the sound board. These will depend on the individual sound board.

10. When the installation process is complete, select **Close** to return to the Control Panel window, then close the Control Panel by double-clicking on the Control button. Exit Windows, then restart it so that the new driver will be included in the Windows program.

Test the Sound Board in Windows

1. Double-click on the **Control Panel** icon in the Main group.
2. Double-click on the **Sound** icon.
3. To play a sound clip, double-click on any of the **.wav** or **.mid** files in the File List. If sound clip files have been installed but do not appear on the list, select the **Browse** button to access the list of directories and find the directory where the files are installed.
4. When you are satisfied that the sound board is working with Windows, select **OK** to close the Sound window, then close the Control Panel by double-clicking on the Control button.

Record Sounds or Voice in a WordPerfect 6.0 Document File

Plug the microphone into the phone input jack. Check that the on/off switch is in the On position. Because a proper microphone is vital, many manufacturers include a microphone with their sound board. To record sound, WordPerfect for Windows launches the Windows Sound Recorder. It allows the sound to be saved to either a separate sound file or the current document, and it has options and special effects, such as echoing and increasing or decreasing the volume.

Record Sounds or Voice

1. Select **Insert, Sound** {Alt, i, s}.
2. Select **Record** {Alt and r}.

   Note: The Windows Sound Recorder is launched and the Sound Recorder dialog box displays (see Figure G.1). Make sure your microphone is turned on.
3. Select the **Record** button (the button with the microphone on it).

   Note: Sound Recorder will display the amount of available memory and the maximum recording time. Wait until the arrow pointer returns before starting to speak.
4. Speak into the microphone while holding the microphone 6 to 10 inches from your mouth to record your voice.
5. When you are finished, select the **Stop** button.
6. Use the **Rewind, Play,** and **Forward** buttons to evaluate the recording and to make any changes, just as you would when using a standard tape recorder. For

FIGURE G.1

Sound Recorder dialog box

additional options and special effects, refer to the *Windows Reference Manual* for information about using Sound Recorder.

7. When the recording is complete, select **File, Save**, type a name for the sound clip, then select **OK**.
8. Select **File, Exit** to close the Sound Recorder and return to WordPerfect.

Use an Existing Sound File Linked to a WordPerfect 6.0 Document File

After a recording has been made, it can be inserted into a document. Sound clips from other sources can also be used by copying them to the WPWIN60 directory.

A sound clip can either be inserted as a linked file, or the sound clip can be saved within the WordPerfect document. Using a separate sound file linked to the document is an efficient method, because the size of the document file can be minimized. It also allows easy reuse of the sound file in other documents. A directory holding a library of sound clips is similar to the directory of graphics.

The disadvantage of an external sound clip file is that (as with all linked files) moving either the document or sound clip files can break the link because the path information is no longer correct. This can even be a problem on networks if people are allowed to set their own directory to drive letter mappings. When the sound clip file is stored inside the document, the clip is saved and moved with the document. This eliminates the need to remember to move the sound file when the document file is moved or to reset the path information.

When you insert or link a sound file into the document, a sound clip icon, similar to that seen in Figure G.2, will appear in the document.

Link a Sound Clip to a File on Disk

1. Place the insertion point at the location in the document where the sound clip is desired.
2. Select **Insert, Sound, Insert** {Alt, i, s; Alt and i}.
3. Click on the file icon to the right of the File field to display the Select File dialog box. Double-click on the name of the sound clip {Alt and f, Alt and down arrow to display files, use the up or down arrow to highlight name of file, press Enter}.
4. If necessary, select the **Link to File on Disk** option {Alt and L}.

FIGURE G.2

Sound icon in WordPerfect for Windows document

Note: Link to File on Disk is the default and may already be selected. Select the ***Store in Document*** *option to save the sound clip inside the document file.*

5. Select **OK** {Enter}.

Steps to Play the Sound Clip

Method 1

1. Move the mouse pointer to the sound icon in the document and click once.

Method 2

Note: This is the only method that can be accomplished without a mouse.

1. Select **Insert, Sound** {Alt, i, s}.
2. Highlight the sound clip to be played.
3. Select **Transcribe** {Alt and t}.

   Note: The Transcribe Feature Bar will appear. The Transcribe Feature Bar is useful if you want to control the sound clips from the document window rather than access the Sound Clips dialog box.
4. Select the **Play** button to play the sound clip {Alt and Shift and p}.

Method 3

1. Select **Insert, Sound** {Alt, i, s}.
2. Highlight the sound clip to be played.
3. Select the **Play** button.
4. Select **Close** to return to the document window.

Steps to Edit a Sound Clip in a Document

1. Select **Insert, Sound** {Alt, i, s}.
2. To delete the sound clip:
   a. Highlight the sound clip to be deleted.
   b. Select **Delete** {Alt and d}.
   c. Select **Yes**.
3. To edit the descriptive name of the sound clip:
   a. Highlight the sound clip to be edited.
   b. Select **Edit Desc.** {Alt and e}.

c. Type a new descriptive name in the Name field.

d. Select **OK**.

4. When all editing changes have been made, select **Close** to return to the document window.

Sound File Storage Information

Sound files may use much of your storage resources, both memory and disk space. Digital audio files (sound converted to a digital format) are usually stored in the way that the board generated the bytes representing the sound. Two common voice file formats are .wav and .voc, which basically differ in their headers (initial sectors). The headers indicate the characteristics of the recorded data—voice or wave, stereo or mono—for the particular file format.

Sampling sizes (8- or 16-bit) and rates help to determine the quality of the recorded sound as well as the size of the files. Eight-bit cards can produce a 1-byte (8-bit) sample. Sixteen-bit cards store 2-byte samples. An 8-bit card can generate 256 discrete steps. Four bits (a nibble) can represent 16 possibilities; 8 bits can represent two 16-possibility groups (16 x 16 = 256). A 16-bit card can represent 65,536 (256 x 256) possibilities or steps in the sound range. If the sampling rate is 6,000 Hertz (Hz), 6,000 samples are taken per second. This restricts the recording of upper frequency limits. High-quality boards are now sampling at the rate of 44,100 samples per second to provide 22,050 sample rates for each of the two stereo channels. At 6,000 Hz, a 60-second recording uses an entire 360K floppy disk. A 20MB hard disk is filled with 7.7 minutes of stereo at 22,050 Hz.

Sound files can be compressed so that they need less disk space. Generally, compressed files degrade the sound quality. Compressed files cannot be converted to other formats and are not easily edited. Compression techniques, somewhat similar to the methods of data compression used to store larger files or to increase effective disk space, are also used. Although LHARC, PKZIP, STACKER, DOUBLESPACE and other programs can make great reductions in data files, they are not as useful with voice files. The speed needed for sound files requires rapid file decompression, and the complex algorithms of extreme data compression have not been able to provide this speed.

INDEX